Strategic Management Communication

FOR LEADERS

Strategic Management Communication

FOR LEADERS

3e

ROBYN WALKER

Center for Management Communication
Marshall School of Business
University of Southern California

CENGAGE
Learning

Australia • Brazil • Mexico • Singapore • United Kingdom • United States

CENGAGE
Learning

Strategic Management Communication for Leaders, Third Edition
Robyn Walker

Senior Vice President, LRS/Acquisitions & Solutions Planning: Jack W. Calhoun

Editorial Director, Business & Economics: Erin Joyner

Product Director: Mike Schenk

Product Manager: Jason Fremder

Senior Content Developer: Elizabeth Lowry

Product Assistant: Megan Fischer

Senior Brand Manager: Kristen Hurd

Art and Cover Direction, Production Management, and Composition: PreMediaGlobal

Marketing Coordinator: Michael Saver

Senior Media Developer: John Rich

Rights Acquisition Director: Audrey Pettengill

Rights Acquisition Specialist, Text/Image: Amber Hosea

Manufacturing Planner: Ron Montgomery

Cover Image(s): © I Love Images/Corbis

For product information and technology assistance, contact us at
Cengage Learning Customer & Sales Support, 1-800-354-9706

For permission to use material from this text or product, submit all requests online at **www.cengage.com/permissions**
Further permissions questions can be emailed to
permissionrequest@cengage.com

Library of Congress Control Number: 2013935541

ISBN-13: 978-1-133-93375-5

ISBN-10: 1-133-93375-0

Cengage Learning
200 First Stamford Place, 4th Floor
Stamford, CT 06902
USA

Cengage Learning is a leading provider of customized learning solutions with office locations around the globe, including Singapore, the United Kingdom, Australia, Mexico, Brazil and Japan. Locate your local office at **www.cengage.com/global**.

Cengage Learning products are represented in Canada by Nelson Education, Ltd.

To learn more about Cengage Learning Solutions, visit **www.cengage.com**.

Purchase any of our products at your local college store or at our preferred online store **www.cengagebrain.com**.

Printed in the United States of America
3 4 5 6 7 18 17 16

Brief Contents

Table of Contents

Preface

Strategic Management Communication: For Leaders is based upon an alternative theoretical foundation grounded in theory but with connections to communication in the world of business. The text is unique in the business communication discipline in that it shows students how various business courses are related and highlights communication as a practice that is applicable to all business situations regardless of the discipline, department, or organizational level at which it takes place. Unlike many other business communication texts, it also looks at communication not only as the practice of individuals but also has an organizational concern.

Other unique aspects of *Strategic Management Communication: For Leaders* include its spotlight on strategy formulation while making a clear distinction between strategic and tactical elements of communication. Because strategic issues are more difficult to understand and internalize as such, they are treated in an indepth manner before providing the discussion of tactics as they apply to differing contexts and channels of communication. Internalizing the strategic considerations will enable readers to logically make appropriate tactical choices without having to set them all to memory.

Another novel aspect of *Strategic Business Communication: For Leaders* is its focus on leadership, both at the theoretical and practical level. That is, the text integrates discussions of leadership theory and practice aimed at meeting the needs and the abilities of its key audiences—advanced undergraduate and graduate students and the organizations that will employ them. Opportunities for leadership communication practice is provided through the inclusion of two types of case studies in each chapter. The opening case study is intended to look at communication practices at the individual level, while closing cases look at communication from the organizational level. This ability to work at both the micro and macro level of communication within an organization is a necessity for effective leaders and managers.

With all of these unique elements combined, the result is this textbook, which provides comprehensive coverage of the critical elements of business, management, and corporate communications in a compact, highly readable format.

Help students succeed in the business world with the features found in *Strategic Management Communication: For Leaders*!

Comprehensive, yet compact. The text covers all the communication topics that are relevant and critical for successful business, management, and corporate communications—written, oral presentation, interpersonal, and small group communication as well as planning and implementing communication plans for internal and external organizational audiences—in a compact, readable format.

Integrated, comprehensive approach to strategic message formulation. The text provides a comprehensive discussion of the steps of strategy formulation that can be used for any communication context: written, oral presentations, interpersonal, small group, or organizational communications.

These four steps of strategic message formulation are covered in Part 1 the text:

- Chapter 1: Introduction
- Chapter 2: Foundations of Communication
- Chapter 3: Step One: Identify the Purposes of Communication
- Chapter 4: Step Two: Analyze the Audience

- Chapter 5: Steps Three and Four: Consider the Context and Select a Channel of Communication

Comprehensive discussion of tactical elements applied to all communication contexts. Part 2 of the text provides explanation of the tactics that can be applied to achieve strategic goals in all communication contexts—written, oral presentation, interpersonal, group, and internal and external organizational communication situations. These tactical applications are covered in the following chapters of the text:

- Chapter 6: Communicating in Writing
- Chapter 7: Communicating in Oral Presentations and Managing Meetings
- Chapter 8: Preparing Employment Messages
- Chapter 9: Communicating with Employees
- Chapter 10: Communicating in and Leading Teams
- Chapter 11: Strategic Organizational Communication

Boxed features. Each chapter includes boxed features, **Responsible Communication** as well as **Critical Thinking** questions. The Responsible Communication boxed features present an ethical situation or issue that is related to the main focus of each chapter and includes questions to encourage discussion and analysis of each of those issues. Critical Thinking questions can be found throughout each chapter and are intended to encourage more in-depth thought, analysis, and application of the materials presented in each chapter.

End-of-chapter exercises. To further support understanding and information transfer through the application of relevant concepts and principles, the following exercises are included at the end of each chapter: key terms with page number references, discussion questions, applications (or assignments), as well as two case analyses, the first which appears at the beginning of each chapter. One case analysis focuses on "micro" communication skills, developing communication understanding at a personal level, while the second case study found at the end of the chapter focuses on "macro" communication skills or those applied at the organizational level. Each case analysis provides a concise synopsis of real-life business situations as well as discussion questions and assignments, as applicable, intended to aid students in applying strategic and tactical skills.

About the Author

Robyn Walker, Ph.D.
Associate Professor of Clinical
Management Communication
USC Marshall School of Business

Dr. Robyn Walker is a professor of management communication at the Center for Management Communication at the University of Southern California's Marshall School of Business, where she teaches business writing and business communication to undergraduate and graduate students. She earned a master's and a doctoral degree in Communication from the University of Utah, and a master's degree in Professional Writing from the University of Southern California, and holds an MBA. Dr. Walker has held faculty appointments at the University of Arizona and California State University, Fullerton. Before entering academia, Dr. Walker worked as a professional writer and editor with such organizations as United Press International, McGraw-Hill, and Novell. She also has worked as a writing consultant for companies such as Hoffman LaRoche Pharmaceuticals and Franklin-Covey, Inc. She continues to write and conduct research and has delivered dozens of conference papers on intercultural communication, rhetoric, cultural studies, and business communication pedagogy and published articles on intercultural communication in groups, leadership, and place-based identity. She is the editor of the *Journal of Business Communication*, a contributing editor of *BCOM* (Cengage Learning), and co-editor of a volume of research entitled *Discourse Perspectives on Organizational Communication* (Fairleigh Dickinson University Press, 2011). She is a member of the Association of Business Communication, Management Communication Association, National Communication Association, Academy of Management, and the Academy of International Business.

I would like to thank all my colleagues who helped me in the writing of this textbook. First, I thank all those who reviewed a draft of the textbook and who provided me encouragement and support, as well as many valuable suggestions for improvement. Specifically, I would like to thank:

Bill Ackerman
Columbia College

Sue Allesandri
Syracuse University

Jana O'Keefe Bazzoni
Baruch College

Bruce K. Bell
Liberty University

Kim Sydow Campbell
University of Alabama

Joanne M. Crossman
*Johnson & Wales University
Graduate School*

Dr. Joan M. Donnelly
Keene State College

Anna Easton
Indiana University

Tim Flood
University of North Carolina

Ryan Halley
*Mount Vernon Nazarene
University*

Tanya Bender Henderson, Ph.D.
Howard University

Elizabeth Anne Hoger
Western Michigan University

Martha C. Jagel
Rogers State University

Frank Jaster
Tulane University

Kristine Kinard
The University of Alabama

Carl Maugeri
University of Pennsylvania

Evelyn Posey
University of Texas–El Paso

Elizabeth Powell
University of Virginia

Pamela Rooney
Western Michigan University

Carlos Salinas
University of Texas–El Paso

Diza Sauers
University of Arizona

Craig Snow
Cornell University

Lynn Staley
University of Missouri

Strategic Management Communication

FOR LEADERS

Yuri Arcurs/Shutterstock.com

What Is Strategic Communication?

After reading this chapter, you will be able to

▶ Define strategic communication and differentiate between strategy and tactics.

▶ Understand why strategic communication is critically important in today's rapidly changing world and organizational environment.

▶ Use a case study approach to apply textbook concepts and principles, a method that will enhance your learning and hone the critical and analytical skills necessary to become a practiced strategic communicator.

A strategic approach to communication has become of greater importance in recent years for a variety of reasons. Globalization has brought numerous opportunities to organizations while simultaneously increasing the potential for greater instability and heightened competition. Globalization and this intensified competition have increased the need for excellent communication skills as employees deal with diversity and greater responsibility. In addition, communication has become more recognized for its part in the creation of our social realities, including those within organizations. How does the workplace of today differ from that of 50 years ago? Twenty-five years ago? Ten years ago? How have these changes affected communication practices and the responsibilities of employees for effective communication?

What Is Strategic Communication?

Strategy as an element of communication has been around for some time. In fact, one of the earliest attempts at formulating communication strategy dates back to at least the fourth century B.C.E. and Aristotle's *Rhetoric*, a Greek treatise on the art of persuasion. Aristotle's writing on the subject of persuasion is still seen as a foundational text for the discipline; his principles are still used today. Although the concept of strategy as an element of communication has been around for centuries, it is not a coherent system of theory or practice across the widely differentiated discipline of communication; various definitions and aspects of strategy are practiced in rhetoric, composition, and, to some extent, organizational communication, for example.

In this regard, strategy not only is a developing concept and practice in communication, but also has a fairly recent history in the field of business. Strategic management, for example, originated as a discipline in the 1950s and 1960s. Although there were numerous early contributors to the literature, the most influential pioneers were Alfred D. Chandler, Philip Selznick, Igor Ansoff, and Peter Drucker. Management strategy is a future-oriented conception in which the relationship between the industry and the environment is described, and this forms the guiding principles for decision making for people in the industry. In terms of its hierarchical ordering, strategic management is a level of managerial activity below setting goals and above tactics. Broadly speaking, the concept of strategy has been borrowed from the military and adapted for use in business. In business, as in the military, strategy is the bridge between policy or high-order goals on the one hand and tactics or concrete actions on the other.

Strategy is thus a "big picture" look at a problem that focuses on the entire forest and not individual trees. It involves analysis and the synthesis of a coherent plan of action from that analysis. **Tactics** are the concrete actions that are taken to implement a strategy. One major way this textbook differs from others in the field of business communication is that it clearly distinguishes strategic issues from tactical ones. Many business communication textbooks focus on tactics—or skills—with less attention to strategy, but a strategic approach is often what differentiates a manager from a true leader. One of the key purposes of this book is to show you how to differentiate yourself as a leader through your understanding and use of strategic communication. Strategy is primarily a critical-thinking activity, one that is based on analysis, evaluation, and synthesis of information.

Once analysis has taken place, a strategic communicator selects the tactics or the specific behaviors that are needed to enact the strategic goal. This differs from a tactical approach in which instructions or checklists are used to provide methods for dealing with certain tasks. This approach may ignore the differences that come about due to differing audiences and contextual elements (audience analysis and context are strategic elements that will be discussed in more detail in future chapters.) Another way to think about a tactical approach is to consider what Shari Veil (2011) calls "trained mindlessness" as it operates in an organizational setting. "This insensitivity occurs when individuals follow the same routine simply because 'that is the way things have always been done around here.' The goal is to 'get the job done,' even though there are warning signals that require attention and better ways available to complete the task."[1] One of the reasons that trained mindlessness or a tactical approach to problems exists at the organizational level is time pressures, which also negatively affect decision making more generally.

strategy
Plan for obtaining a specific goal or result that involves big-picture analysis.

tactics
Concrete actions taken to implement a strategy.

Communication strategy is part of an effective management strategy or plan, yet most management texts give short shrift to the subject. This is because management as a discipline generally focuses more on logistical issues—products offered, production capability, market needs, method of distribution, size and growth, and so on—rather than on human subjects. When the discipline does deal with human subjects, it is often done from a psychological perspective. This textbook takes a different approach and is based on a different worldview or perspective—a social constructionist view of reality that places communication in a central role in the creation and reproduction of organizations. (The social constructionist view of reality will be explained later in this chapter.)

Strategic communication can be applied at two levels. Just as strategic management is designed to be applied at the organizational level, so can strategic-communication management. But strategic communication as a practice can also be applied at the individual or personal level. This textbook deals with both. The first part of the book provides individual communication strategies, and the second part provides a discussion of the tactics that can be used to implement those strategies in different contexts, connecting these practices to strategic-communication management at the organizational level.

Why Is a Strategic Approach to Communication Important?

A strategic approach to communication has become more important in recent years for several reasons. The first reason involves trends in the workplace, the second is the evolution of our understanding of the communication process, and the third is greater appreciation for the centrality of communication in terms of the creation of our social and organizational realities.

Changes in the Workplace

Globalization has had a dramatic effect on the business environment in which we now operate. Although it has presented numerous opportunities to business organizations, it has also increased the potential for greater instability and greater competition. These two forces have had varied effects, including greater merger activity and the flattening of hierarchies within organizations. To remain competitive in the current business environment, organizations must be flexible; generally speaking, strict rules and procedures are a hindrance in organizations that must be able to move quickly to adapt to the changes in their environment.

These changes in the business world also affect employees, and the primary effect is the increasing importance of communication for the success of individuals and the companies in which they work. The flattening of hierarchies and pressure for companies to improve productivity to remain competitive have made interpersonal relationships and the ability to maintain them more crucial than ever. This change began as early as the 1980s and the work of a manager was particularly affected by these changes in the business environment.[2] Instead of an emphasis on planning, organizing, and coordinating, the focus of the manager moved to communication. This move is an important one to recognize because it also helps to clarify the distinctions between **leadership** and **management**. Managers coordinate and organize activities, but leaders influence people. These differing mind-sets and courses of action often complement each other in the workplace, but it is important to note that anyone can be a leader with the proper way of thinking and skill set.

leadership
Influence of people within an organizational setting through the orchestration of relationships.

management
The coordination and organization of activities within an organization.

Changes such as the flattening of organizational hierarchies mean that "influence must replace the use of formal authority in relationships with subordinates, peers, outside contacts, and others on whom the job makes one dependent."[3] Because positional authority is no longer sufficient to get the job done, a web of influence or a balanced web of relationships must be developed. "Recently managers have begun to view leadership as the orchestration of *relationships* between several different interest groups—superiors, peers, and outsiders, as well as subordinates."[4] The successful development of relationships generally lies in our skills in interpersonal communication, as does our ability to influence others; the result is the increased emphasis on communication, particularly for those in leadership positions or those who are aspiring leaders.

The importance of communication becomes clearer when we consider that leaders potentially differ from managers in regard to the type of power they may yield. Managers are appointed; they have legitimate power that enables them to reward and punish employees. The formal authority given to them by their position gives managers the ability to influence employees. Leaders, on the other hand, may be appointed or may emerge from a group of employees. In the latter case, they have the opportunity to influence others beyond their formal authority in an organization and this influence comes in large part from the ability to communicate well. This can be more clearly seen in the following table that illustrates the six key **power bases** that arise in organizations and groups.[5]

Of the bases of power listed in Table 1-1, the first three are typically conferred on an individual by an institution or organization. They are the types of power that managers often have been given or what have been called *position power*. But, as the table indicates, they are not the only bases of power. Leaders have the opportunity to influence others through the last three types shown in the table: referent, expert, and informational power. In other words, leaders can influence others through their credibility, relationships, knowledge, and expertise. This is called

power bases
The differing sources or bases of power within an organization.

Table 1-1 French and Raven's Six Bases of Power.

BASE	DEFINITION
Reward power	The capability of controlling the distribution of rewards given or offered the target.
Coercive power	The capacity to threaten and punish those who do not comply with requests or demands.
Legitimate power	Authority that derives from the power holder's legitimate right to require and demand obedience.
Referent power	Influence based on the target's identification with, attraction to, or respect for the power holder.
Expert power	Influence based on the target's belief that the power holder possesses superior skills and abilities.
Informational power	Influence based on the potential use of informational resources, including rational argument, persuasion, or factual data.

Source: French and Raven (1959).

personal power, or the influence a leader derives from being seen by others as likable and knowledgeable. As will be discussed later in this book, our communication behaviors help us to establish our credibility with others as well as positive productive relationships. In fact, leadership can be viewed as being a multidirectional influence relationship as compared with management, which is a unidirectional authority relationship.[6] The changes in organizational realities discussed earlier, particularly those that require employees to interact with one other, often unfamiliar individuals, both within and outside of the organization, cope with constant change, and integrate different systems that may mutually affect one another.[7] In this type of setting, leadership may depend less on individual, heroic actions, our common stereotype of a leader, and more on relational behaviors.[8] Such activities include creating team: "activities intended to construct the social reality of team by creating an environment where positive outcomes of relational interactions can be realized."[9] (The concept of social construction of reality is explained next.)

Through communication we also express and demonstrate our knowledge base and expertise, important aspects of leadership influence. Interestingly, studies have shown that power demonstrated through expertise and knowledge have the strongest correlation with performance and satisfaction, whereas the use of coercive power is the least effective reason for compliance and has negative correlations with organizational effectiveness.

CriticalThinking

Identify a situation in which differences in power exist between the communicators. How do these differences affect the rules or expectations regarding how communication occurs in that situation? Have you seen instances where people failed to heed those rules or expectations? What was the outcome?

Leaders also differ from managers in another important way. The overriding function for management is to provide order and consistency in organizations,

Table 1-2 Functions of Management and Leadership.

MANAGEMENT	LEADERSHIP
Produces Order and Consistency	*Produces Change and Movement*
Planning and Budgeting	**Establishing Direction**
■ Establish agendas	■ Create a vision
■ Set timetables	■ Clarify the big picture
■ Allocate resources	■ Set strategies
Organizing and Staffing	**Aligning People**
■ Provide structure	■ Communicate goals
■ Make job placements	■ Seek commitment
■ Establish rules and procedures	■ Build teams and coalitions
Controlling and Problem Solving	**Motivating and Inspiring**
■ Develop incentives	■ Inspire and energize
■ Generate creative solutions	■ Empower subordinates
■ Take corrective action	■ Satisfy unmet needs

Source: Adapted from J. P. Kotter. (1990). *A Force for Change: How Leadership Differs from Management.* (New York, NY: Free Press): 3–8.

whereas the primary function of leaders is to produce change and movement.[10] Leaders change the way people think about what is possible[11] and they do so primarily through by shaping behaviors and by framing change communicatively.[12] Table 1-2 distinguishes the activities of managers and leaders. It is important to note that, according to Kotter, the functions of both managers and leaders are important for the success of an organization.

Two additional effects of globalization that reinforce the importance of communication are the increased diversity of the workforce as well as the increasing interdependency of national, international, and multinational corporations and their employees. Therefore, it is imperative to have an understanding of cultural differences, which may affect communication effectiveness. **Plurality** refers to the fact that people in communication mutually construct the meanings they have for situations and each other. Plurality means that there are always multiple interpretations of any situation and that no one person can control those interpretations, try as he or she might. Recognition of the reality of plurality requires that we be open to or willing to listen to the voices and opinions of others if there is any hope of achieving something approaching shared understanding. In the workplace, attempting to move toward shared understanding is, of course, important if we are to achieve organizational and personal goals. Unfortunately, our common understandings of communication and the notion of reality itself often gets in the way of fully appreciating and accounting for plurality. (The concept of plurality is based in a social constructionist approach, which is discussed later in this chapter.)

plurality
Because people in communication mutually construct the meanings they have for situations and each other, multiple interpretations of any situation always exist, and no one person can control those interpretations.

Evolution of Our Understanding of the Communication Process

Over time, the definition of what constitutes communication and how it occurs has evolved. Our commonsensical views of communication, though, often have not followed suit. If you ask a room full of people to define communication, most will say something like "It is the transfer of information from one person to another." This is an excellent model for communication and was, in fact, one of the first. However, our views of communication have changed with time to give us a more complex view of its process and function. An understanding of communication as an informative process, for example, ignores the effects of distortion on information transfer or the multiple possible interpretations that a receiver might make of a message. Because of the effects of globalization in terms of the increasing diversity of the workforce and the effects and interdependencies of international and multinational corporations, most of us now recognize, to some degree at least, that people of different cultures interpret the world differently. Consequently, this view of communication—as a simple process of transmission of information—is no longer considered useful in thinking about how communication between two or more people occurs. This becomes clearer when one recognizes that the transmission of information model best describes the way that machines communicate, that is, data transmission.

Furthermore, in a business setting, much of the communication that occurs is not merely informative; it is almost always persuasive by its very nature. We are almost always attempting to sell something—if nothing more than ourselves—to someone else. Selling ourselves and influencing others involves yet another important consideration—our credibility, maintaining it and enhancing it—often through our communication practices. And these practices are not relegated to what we write or say. Our communication practices also involve nonverbal cues; in fact, in face-to-face communication situations, more than 90 percent of the available information is transmitted nonverbally. If we ignore nonverbal communication, we may be transmitting information to others that we do not intend to transmit or that does not align with our oral message, creating further confusion. Consequently, much of the communication that takes place in a professional setting has little to do with simply transmitting information but a great deal to do with managing the impressions we make on others.

We also may underestimate the contested nature of meaning in organizational settings. Studies have shown that much organizational communication is characterized by ambiguity, deception, and diversity of viewpoints rather than shared meaning.[13] In fact, some researchers view organizational cultures as contested political domains in which the possibility for genuine dialogue and the arrival at shared meanings is often seriously impaired.[14]

For these reasons, it is imperative to develop a more sophisticated understanding of communication, its purposes, and its processes if we are going to be successful in today's complex and rapidly changing business environment.

The Social Construction of Reality and Its Effects on Conceptualizing Communication

Another development that has placed communication at the center of interest in organizational settings is the development of what is called the *social construction of reality*. Until the late 1960s, it was generally accepted that human beings could easily study and grasp the meaning of objects and processes in our world. In their book *The Social Construction of Reality*, Peter L. Berger and Thomas Luckmann introduced a different view of reality, arguing that all knowledge, including the most basic, taken-for-granted commonsense knowledge of everyday reality, is derived from and maintained by social interactions.[15] When people interact, they do so with the understanding that their respective perceptions of reality are related because they share similar experiences and values. As they act on this understanding over time, their common knowledge of reality becomes reinforced, a process that is largely invisible to the participant because he or she naturalizes the experience. Socially constructed reality is an ongoing, dynamic process; reality is reproduced by people acting on their interpretations and their knowledge of it. A **social construction**, or **social construct**, is any phenomenon "invented" or "constructed" by participants in a particular culture or society, existing because people agree to behave as if it exists or to follow certain conventional rules. One example of a social construct is social status; that is, individual persons do not have greater status than others unless it is socially conferred. Another example of social construction is the use of money, which has worth only because society has agreed to treat it as valuable.

The importance of communication comes at the beginning of the process— actors *interacting* to form mental representations, which become habituated—and continues to the end when these mental representations and roles are institutionalized in practice. This process of creating social reality is one of *meaning making*.

The theory of the social construction of reality might be better understood by comparing it to the natural sciences and their focus of study, the natural world and the universe. For example, it is known that water freezes at 32 degrees Fahrenheit, that light travels at 186,000 miles per second in a vacuum, and the normal body temperature of a human being is 98.6 degrees. These are the laws of nature that we all generally accept as fact. However, when we look at the social sciences, we see that the behaviors and values of human beings vary across the world vary, that is, cultures differ in their values, belief systems, and social practices. A social constructionist perspective understands that these values, beliefs, and cultural practices are created and reinforced through communication thought broadly, as the use of symbols and symbol systems to create meaning, that is, create our cultural and social realities.

The reason that a social constructionist view is significant for leaders or potential leaders because it provides a powerful basis for understanding and marshaling influence within an organization through strategic assessment and planning. In other words, such a perspective provides greater potential empowerment of the individual as compared with traditional leadership theory, which has often viewed leadership as a trait, style, or characteristic that an individual has. This latter view focuses on a particular individual's psychological makeup. A social constructionist view, on the other hand, recognizes that leaders are more involved with the management of meaning, often through the practice of framing events in particular ways; however, meaning making involves the receivers of the message as well because they may or may not accept the message framing that is offered. In other words, leadership is coconstructed, a product of sociohistorical and collective meaning making, and is negotiated on an ongoing basis through complex interplay among leadership actors, be they designated or emergent leaders, managers, or followers. With this understanding, the importance of a strategic approach to communication becomes much clearer. Leadership is achieved—or not—through the processes of communication with others. Through your words and actions, you have the potential to demonstrate leadership by creating new realities for coworkers, customers, clients, and the general public for your organization and its activities. (The rules of reality construction for leaders is provided in Figure 1-1). This textbook will provide you the tools to shape those realities while also

social construction or social construct
Any phenomenon "invented" or "constructed" by participants in a particular culture or society and existing because people agree to behave as if it exists or to follow certain conventional rules.

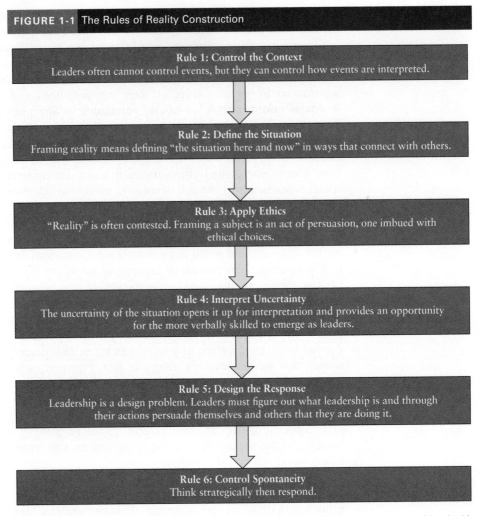

FIGURE 1-1 The Rules of Reality Construction

Rule 1: Control the Context
Leaders often cannot control events, but they can control how events are interpreted.

Rule 2: Define the Situation
Framing reality means defining "the situation here and now" in ways that connect with others.

Rule 3: Apply Ethics
"Reality" is often contested. Framing a subject is an act of persuasion, one imbued with ethical choices.

Rule 4: Interpret Uncertainty
The uncertainty of the situation opens it up for interpretation and provides an opportunity for the more verbally skilled to emerge as leaders.

Rule 5: Design the Response
Leadership is a design problem. Leaders must figure out what leadership is and through their actions persuade themselves and others that they are doing it.

Rule 6: Control Spontaneity
Think strategically then respond.

Source: Adapted from Fairhurst, G. T. (2011). *The Power of Framing: Creating the Language of Leadership.* San Francisco, CA: John Wiley & Sons.

recognizing the contributions to leadership of those who take a more psychological and cognitive approach to the phenomenon.

How to Analyze Case Studies

A business case study is a description of an opportunity or problem faced by an individual, a manager, an executive, or an entire organization that students are asked to read, analyze, and respond to either orally or in writing. Case studies are beneficial because they provide students an opportunity to apply the knowledge they have gained, an activity that leads to and demonstrates a higher level of knowledge acquisition. Application enables students to better understand how the knowledge provided in a text can be used in real-world situations and thus enables them to learn more about issues they may deal with in organizational settings. In addition, case studies enable students to practice critical and analytical thinking,

FIGURE 1-2 The Natural World vs. Social Reality

© Robyn Walker

both higher-order cognitive abilities needed to be a strategic communicator and businessperson.

This text provides both fictional case studies and those based on field and library research. Fictional case studies are often shorter and are useful for introducing concepts to students, whereas field or library case studies are based on actual events and often provide greater detail, depth, and complexity. Because of this, they are useful for higher-order application of text concepts and principles.

Case study analysis first involves reading the case carefully, taking notes, and then analyzing the information to determine the key problems or opportunities involved in the situation, as well as the preferred outcome. All of these aspects are necessary to identify the proper course of action.

Initial Analysis

Analysis involves a simple process of asking the right questions and coming up with the right answers. In order to analyze a case study well, begin by asking and answering the following questions:

1. Who is the decision maker in this case, and what is his or her position and responsibilities?
2. What appears to be the issue(s) of concern (problem, challenge, or opportunity) and its significance for the organization? Ranking the issues in order of their importance can help to identify the best solution.
3. Why or how has the issue arisen? The goal is to identify the cause and effect of the issue identified, which again may help to identify a solution or recommendation.
4. When does the decision maker have to decide, resolve, act, or dispose of the issue? How urgent is the situation?
5. Who is affected most by the issue? It often is helpful to rank stakeholders in order of most affected, since this ranking can help you determine the best solution.
6. What are the constraints regarding the type of decision that might be made? Identifying constraints can often help you determine the best solution as well.

Identification of Solutions and Recommendations

Once you have completed the analysis of the situation and identified the key issues, their causes, and the stakeholders who will be most affected, you are in a position to best identify appropriate solutions and recommendations. But further analysis is needed, since a list of possible solutions must be generated and each assessed for its ability to lead to the desired outcome identified earlier in the analysis. Once this final analysis is completed and the best solution is identified, a plan for implementing and communicating the solution to appropriate stakeholders must be completed—the last step in the process.

How This Book Is Organized

This book is divided into two parts. The first deals with the steps involved in formulating personal communication strategies in the workplace. The second discusses how strategy can be applied at both the personal and the organizational level, with a greater focus on the deployment of tactics or skills.

Another unique feature of this textbook is that it integrates information from various fields of communication research and practice. This approach may be somewhat controversial because these diverse fields have different ontological perspectives and theoretical foundations. However, the purpose for doing so is not to lessen the distinctiveness of these fields or the importance of their contribution to our understanding of communication but rather for pedagogical purposes. In other words, it is intended to provide a more streamlined, coherent method for potential business leaders to apply the findings from these areas without years of study. You will thus find discussions that are drawn from the fields of rhetoric, composition, and interpersonal, group, and organizational communication. The text also integrates personal communication strategies with discussions of topics from the areas of management and corporate communication. Management communication skills are those that are needed to effectively interact with others and to manage and influence groups; corporate communication skills are those abilities that are needed to lead organizations and address a broader community.

Part 1: The Strategic Process

- **Foundations of Communication (Chapter 2):** This chapter discusses foundational principles of communication that are helpful in developing a more nuanced understanding of the process of communication, such as communication models, perception, and self-concept. It also discusses challenges to the practice of strategic yet ethical communication and techniques for overcoming these challenges.
- **Step One: Identify the Purposes of Communication (Chapter 3):** The first step in the strategic-communication process is to identify the purposes of your communication and then devise a communication strategy that effectively achieves those purposes. The four purposes of business communication are to inform, to persuade and influence, to convey goodwill, and to establish credibility. Not only is it important for the communicator to know his or her purpose or purposes, but also it is expected that the purpose will be

apparent to the audience for the message, generally from the beginning of that message. In other words, business audiences generally want to know immediately what your message is about and why they should pay attention to it.

- **Step Two: Analyze the Audience (Chapter 4):** The second step in the strategic-communication process is to conduct an audience analysis. All good communication should be driven by and focused on your audience: its interests, needs, expectations, and concerns. In other words, effective messages should be audience centered.
- **Steps Three and Four: Consider the Context and Select a Channel of Communication (Chapter 5):** The third and fourth steps in the strategic-communication process have to do with considering contextual issues, such as organizational culture, communication climates, and communication flow within an organization and then choosing the appropriate channel and medium for communicating your message.

Business Communication Process Steps and Strategies

Process Steps	Corresponding Strategy
1. Identify the Purposes	Inform
	Persuade
	Convey and Maintain Goodwill
	Establish and Maintain Credibility
2. Analyze the Audience	Achieve audience focus
3. Consider the Context	Make contextual adjustments
4. Select the Channel(s) & Media	Select the appropriate channel(s)/media

Part 2: Communication Tactics for Differing Channels and Contexts

- **Communicating in Writing (Chapter 6):** This chapter discusses the different types of written messages—routine or informative, bad news, and persuasive—and provides tactics for creating them. It also discusses special considerations for electronic messages and provides a discussion of proposals and formal report formats.
- **Communicating in Oral Presentations and Managing Meetings (Chapter 7):** This chapter discusses oral, nonverbal, and visual considerations and tactics for preparing and delivering effective oral presentations, including dealing with question-and-answer sessions. It also includes a discussion of preparing for, managing, and following up on meetings, including the use of video and teleconferencing.
- **Communicating with Employees (Chapter 8):** This chapter opens with a discussion of interpersonal communication issues, such as interpersonal styles, nonverbal communication, and effective listening techniques. It then puts these considerations and tactics to work in discussions of specific employee communication situations, such as providing feedback and conducting performance appraisals.

- **Communicating during the Employment Process (Chapter 9):** This chapter addresses elements of communication as they are applied in the processes of both applying for jobs and screening potential employees and hiring them. The job application process involves researching potential employers, preparing application materials, preparing for and performing interviews, and following up with employers. The hiring process includes writing job descriptions, screening applicants' employment messages, writing or gathering interview questions, interviewing applicants, and communicating a decision to those applicants.
- **Communicating in and Leading Teams (Chapter 10):** This chapter discusses issues involved in group communication, including the team formation process, individual roles within groups, conflict resolution, decision making, and ensuring that process losses do not occur.
- **Creating an Organizational Communication Plan (Chapter 11):** This chapter discusses the importance of creating a strategic plan for communicating with both internal and external audiences. Internal audiences are typically employees whereas external audiences include clients and customers, suppliers, news media, investors, and the public at large.

At the end of the text, you will also find appendices that address common writing problems and provide commonly used templates for business writing.

Summary

The concept of strategy originated with the military and has been adapted to business applications. Formulating strategy involves looking at the overall picture of an organization, including its goals, and formulating a plan to achieve those goals. In terms of communication, strategy may be applied at the personal as well as the organizational level. In other words, individuals may analyze organizational situations and formulate communication strategies for achieving their personal goals; they may also look at organizational situations and formulate communication strategies for achieving organizational goals. Tactics are then selected to enact that strategic plan.

Becoming a strategic communicator has become more important with recent trends in the business world. One trend is the process of globalization, which has created a more competitive business environment as well as the need to work with people and organizations from other cultures. Leadership has become more important because it is through the process of influencing others that many of these tasks are accomplished. In addition, our understanding of the process of communication has become more sophisticated. We now know that communication is not simply the task of transferring information. Because of our differences, we interpret information in different ways, thus messages may become distorted or misunderstood. Communication in the workplace is also multipurpose: We must maintain and often continually enhance our credibility or self-image if we are to successfully influence others. This is accomplished not only through our oral and written messages, but also through our nonverbal practices. Lastly, the power of language to create our social realities is finally getting the recognition it deserves. From a leadership perspective, this understanding provides opportunities to shape others' understanding of organizations and their activities.

Key Terms

strategy, 3
tactics, 3
leadership, 4
management, 4

power bases, 5
plurality, 7
social construction or social construct, 9

Discussion Questions

1. Name and discuss the three reasons why a strategic approach to communication is particularly important today.
2. What is the difference between strategy and tactics?
3. Describe the difference between a manager and a leader. What are the differences in the types of power that they generally hold? Why do these differences make a strategic approach to communication important or useful?
4. In your own words, describe the meaning of the term *social construction of reality*. What are some examples of social constructions that you are commonly exposed to or accept?
5. What is the meaning of *plurality*? What effect does this understanding have on the way that you communicate with others if you wish to be successful in that communication?

Applications

1. Conduct research on the effects of globalization on organizations, focusing on communication issues. Write a report that summarizes your findings and provide recommendations to today's leaders and managers in terms of best communication practices.

2. Conduct research on leadership and communication. Write a report in which you summarize your findings and set goals for yourself in terms of the leadership communication skills you would like to improve or enhance. A well-written goal should be specific, measurable, attainable, and time bound. An example is "I will create a communication strategy to persuade my boss to promote me to manager by the end of 2011 and implement it successfully."

CASE ANALYSIS

WHOLE FOODS MARKET: A CEO'S PUBLIC OPINION AT ODDS WITH A KEY DEMOGRAPHIC

Introduction

On August 12, 2009, the vice president for corporate communications at Whole Foods Market arrived at the Austin, Texas, headquarters amidst uncertainty about reactions to the public opinion of the CEO that had brought national attention to the company the previous day. In the midst of an ideological battle over healthcare, the CEO had publicly taken a position at odds with the store's key customer demography.

The prolific CEO, John Mackey, had written an opinion editorial that was published by the *Wall Street Journal*. Multiple media outlets were picking up on the story of Mackey's op-ed, and they would be followed by customers, bloggers, unions, protestors, and competitors. Many groups saw the seemingly paradoxical position of Whole Foods' CEO as an opportunity to promote their agendas at the expense of Whole Foods.

This was not the first time the outspoken John Mackey had drawn fire for his writings. Some five years earlier it was revealed that he had used a pseudonym to post damaging opinions about a rival organic food market on a financial Web site. When the rival's stock price diminished, Whole Foods acquired them. The SEC finally ruled out any action against Mr. Mackey after an eleven-month probe.[16]

The Whole Foods Market Corporate Communications team would need every ounce of its collective crisis-management experience to weather this coming storm. Whether or not their own political tendencies were aligned with those of the CEO, they agreed that he had a right to state his opinion. It was now up to the rest of the Whole Foods Market Corporate Communications team to respond to the public outcry that followed from John Mackey's decision.

Company History

In 1978, John Mackey started a natural foods store with his then-girlfriend Renee Lawson called SaferWay in Austin, Texas.[17] Two years later, John merged his SaferWay store with Clarksville Natural Grocery to form a new store called Whole Foods Market.[18] The company grew by opening new stores in other cities around the country and by acquiring other natural food chains. Whole Foods now has more than 270 stores in the United States and 4 in the United Kingdom. Sales in 2008 topped $8 billion.

The company is focused on product quality and selecting food ingredients with minimal processing. The company has a list of unacceptable food ingredients, which includes artificial flavors, colors, sweeteners, preservatives, and more. Whole Foods is ranked third in the U.S. Environmental Protection Agency's list of Top 25 Green Power Partners.[19] The company is also consistently ranked among the most socially responsible companies.[20] This focus on the quality of its product, along with its green culture, has won the company many admirers. Whole Foods donates 5 percent of its net profit to charity. Each store also holds 5 percent days four times a year during which the store donates 5 percent of its net sales to a local nonprofit organization. Whole Foods' involvement in social causes has endeared it to its customers and built strong loyalty. A strong customer segment of Whole Foods is comprised of liberals with left-leaning politics, and they like the company's involvement in green and social causes.

Whole Foods has been praised by *Fortune* magazine as one of the "100 best companies to work for" every year since the inception of the list in 1998.[21] The company has approximately 54,000 employees and very limited union influence. All employees who work over thirty hours per week are eligible for the company insurance plan. Almost 89 percent of Whole Foods employees are eligible for its healthcare insurance plan. The plan includes a relatively high deductible of $2,500 for each employee.[22]

John Mackey

John Mackey was born in 1954. In the 1970s, he was a student of philosophy and religion at the University of Texas at Austin, but later dropped out.[23] When he was still a college student, he joined a vegetarian cooperative where he met his girlfriend, Renee Lawson Hardy. She eventually became his business partner. In 1978, at the age of twenty-five, John and Renee opened their first health foods grocery store, named SaferWay Natural Foods, in Austin, a counterculture alternative to the conventional grocery chain Safeway.[24] They borrowed $10,000 and raised $35,000 from family and friends to start the business.[25] The store was the first vegetarian supermarket in Texas.[26]

John Mackey has served as the chairman and CEO of Whole Foods since 1980. According to the BBC, in 2006, he announced that he would reduce his salary to $1 a year, donate his stock portfolio to charity, and set up a $100,000 emergency fund for staff facing personal problems. In a letter sent to his employees on November 2, 2006, he wrote: "I am now 53 years old and I have reached a place in my life where I no longer want to work for money, but simply for the joy of the work itself and to better answer the call to service that I feel so clearly in my own heart." (The letter was reprinted in *Fast Company* magazine, February 1, 2007.)

Mackey's political position as a free-market libertarian is well known.[27] He also is the "driving force" behind significant changes in animal welfare. He started the nonprofit Animal Compassion Foundation. Mackey gives away up to $1 million a year to animal welfare groups and other charities.[28] Whole Foods was the first chain store to set standards for humane animal treatment.[29]

Mackey is a vegetarian, and since late 2003, he has considered himself a vegan. He has two children with former longtime girlfriend Mary Kay Hagen. He married his current wife Deborah Morin in 1992. The couple spends the workweek in Austin and weekends at their 720-acre ranch 40 miles west of Austin. Mackey enjoys reading, and participates in two monthly book clubs.[30]

However, this Healthcare op-ed issue is not the first time Mackey has been in the spotlight for his actions. He is well known for being blunt.[31] On July 20, 2007, the *Wall Street Journal* revealed that Mackey had been using the pseudonym "Rahodeb" (an anagram of his wife's name, Deborah) to post blogs criticizing Whole Foods' competitor, Wild Oats Market, and questioning the value of the company's stock.[32] When Mackey announced his desire to acquire Wild Oats Market for $670 million, the Federal Trade Commission approved a complaint challenging the acquisition.[33] Whole Foods completed the buyout on August 27, 2007. An SEC investigation cleared him in May 2008, and he began to blog again. In a 2,000-word post on his blog, he argued that he made no mistakes in ethics, only in judgment.[34]

The Market for Organic Food

Much like Whole Foods, the organic and natural food industry has experienced rapid growth in the last few years. What originally started in the 1970s as a premium on foods grown without pesticides and synthetic fertilizer is now a major force. Nationwide sales of organic food increased 142 percent, from $2.1 billion in 2003 to $5.2 billion in 2008. These figures do not account for sales of private label organic food, such as Whole Foods' "365" label, which would have increased sales levels markedly. What was once an eccentric and marginal issue has become a common and recognized selling point for consumers, despite its generally higher price. The health benefits of eating organic food, despite its cost, appeals most to two major groups: young adults and high-income consumers.[35]

Forecasts for future sales growth are not as optimistic as the previous six years have been. In year-over-year sales, the market has slowed (starting in 2007). There are many reasons for this, including the same food inflation that affects all food.[36] Other detrimental effects to the industry include the "locavore" movement and a 50 percent increase in farmers' markets from 2001 to 2006. These markets now account for $1 billion in sales. Furthermore, when consumers do shop in stores, they are more likely to seek out private label options that can have significant cost savings.[37] Food, drug, and mass merchandisers (excluding Wal-Mart) account for some 60 percent of organic food sales.

The Current Debate over Healthcare in the United States

Even before President Obama was elected in 2008, he was campaigning for healthcare reform. Upon taking office, revamping healthcare became the president's top legislative priority. In its simplest form, the president's ultimate goal was to extend coverage to the 47 million uninsured Americans and simultaneously slow the growth of healthcare spending.[38]

Support and opposition fell generally along predictable political party lines. Republicans and conservatives portrayed the legislation as a costly government takeover that would ultimately cost the public far more than it saves. Further, Republicans said, it would remove people's fundamental rights to control their own destiny and place too much control in the hands of the federal government. The GOP offered its own healthcare plan that did not include required coverage for the uninsured, but encouraged states to "guarantee access to affordable coverage."[39]

As of early August 2009, the message from the White House was an eight-point list of "Health Insurance Consumer Protections" that the White House Web site promised would "bring you and your family peace of mind."[40] Those basic eight points were expected to remain central to whatever final bill would be presented to Congress:

- No discrimination for preexisting conditions
- No exorbitant out-of-pocket expenses
- No cost sharing for preventive care
- No dropping of coverage for seriously ill
- No gender discrimination
- No annual or lifetime cap on coverage
- Extended coverage for young adults
- Guaranteed insurance renewal

When the first version of this bill was rushed to both houses of Congress, it quickly proceeded out of committee so Congress could vote on it before summer recess. It was during this period that lawmakers attempted to build support for the plan by holding town hall–style meetings and making presentations to the public.

Conservative groups responded by encouraging confrontation at these events, often resulting in disruptive or rowdy tirades widely reported by major news organizations across the country. Conservative media were uniformly opposed to these meetings as well, describing the president's healthcare plan as socialist and threatening to the basic rights of Americans, particularly the elderly.

The primary opposition, according to the White House, came from insurance company procedures that burden physicians, nurses, and patients. At a news conference held July 30, 2009, and also reported by major news organizations, Speaker Nancy Pelosi described the insurance industry's position as "shock and awe, carpet-bombing by the health insurance industry to perpetuate the status quo."

The Op-Ed

John Mackey had alerted the corporate communications group at Whole Foods that he was going to make his opinions known, but he did not indicate that it would be through the nationally distributed *Wall Street Journal*. When the piece was eventually published on August 11, 2009, it came during one of the slowest news weeks of the year, and it surprised even insiders with its impact.

Whether or not the corporate communications team had a hand in working with John Mackey to write and place the editorial, they certainly had their work cut out for them once the piece ran in the *Wall Street Journal* and on its Web site. Certainly, a large demographic among Whole Foods Market shoppers is the progressive, environmental activist—one who is more likely than the average consumer to write, email, or call the company to protest some of John Mackey's messages.

The piece ran the standard length, about 1,300 words. In it, Mackey made some fairly standard conservative arguments about why healthcare should not be controlled by the government. His general argument focused on "less governmental control and more individual empowerment."[41] Mackey offered his own list of eight points, but unlike President Obama's, his list would lower the cost of healthcare for everyone. The list was essentially an explanation of the Whole Foods insurance system in which nearly all employees are given the choice to choose their doctor and a $2,500 annual cash spending account for healthcare. This account would encourage employees to be frugal with their healthcare because they have a significant amount of money to lose.

Mackey examined so-called "universal healthcare" in other countries such as the UK and Canada, and ultimately made the contentious claim that those systems don't recognize any inherent right to healthcare any more than the United States. "A careful reading of the ... Constitution does not reveal any intrinsic right to health care, food, or shelter, because there isn't any."

He finished the piece with a lengthy accusation of the American diet as the real culprit, and extolled the virtues of every American adult taking responsibility for their own health. He specified what a diet ought to be, and showed a recommended diet with a pie chart. It is no coincidence that he recommended "whole foods which are plant-based, nutrient dense, and low fat." He described adoption of this type of diet as exercising "the freedom to make wise lifestyle choices" that will "enrich our personal lives and will help create a vibrant sustainable American society."

In an interview some seven weeks later, Mackey defended his position by saying, "President Obama called for constructive suggestions for health-care reform; I took him at his word." Mackey was unapologetic for his denial of healthcare as a right of all Americans and his support for freedom of choice. As he put it, "I gave my personal opinions. Whole Foods has no official position on the issue."

Public Backlash

In terms of media and public attention, several aspects of the situation created the "perfect storm" for ongoing (and likely unwanted) media coverage: August is a slow news month, Congress was not in session, and in those weeks leading up to the new fall congressional session, the media were eager for any hooks that could expand on the central, controversial topic of healthcare reform. Add a well-known CEO to the mix—one who publicly announces a position on healthcare that most people assume is the opposite of what his famously progressive customer base would agree with—and it becomes delicious fodder for cable news and radio talk shows.

In the meantime, John Mackey left for a lengthy back-country vacation the day after the article was published. This turned out be a blessing in so far as he was not available for interviews. The media feedback was indeed immediate, particularly from news outlets that recognized a fundamental opposition between Mackey's anti-government position, and the typical Whole Foods Market consumer's liberal views on most issues. Fox News and various libertarian sources were the first to carry the story; it was later picked up by news organizations all over the country.

The media attention brought out protesters to a handful of stores, which drove the media coverage into a second week. There were demonstrations in Boston, Chicago, Austin, and the San Francisco Bay area, as well as other cities. Some of them were unobtrusive and typical sign-carrying affairs, but others involved elaborate musical acts and or loud instruments in stores. Still other demonstrations involved people who saw the situation as an opportunity to share their opinions on healthcare, regardless of involvement with Whole Foods. Similarly, the trade unions, which are not a part of Whole Foods, saw it as an opportunity to strike and took the opposite position of whatever Whole Foods was doing.

By week three of the situation, conservative and libertarian groups had been made aware of the boycott and had started a reverse boycott wherein their supporters would go to Whole Foods and shop for groceries in support of Mackey's position.

Social Media Response

Given that the op-ed was available online almost immediately, the response from the online community played a pivotal role in the situation. Whole Foods has a large Twitter presence for a brick-and-mortar store, with more than a million followers. There were thousands of "tweets" going back and forth even though Whole Foods did not take a position.

Whole Foods has always had a "Fan Page" on the social networking site Facebook. It has over 140,000 fans on its official site. Some 152 of its stores have even started their own Facebook sites, clearly showing a company commitment to this new trend. However, following the publishing of the op-ed piece, a "Whole Foods boycott" group sprang up on Facebook and grew to over 27,000 members within two weeks. Whole Foods did respond to this group through its own Facebook page, issuing a response statement through the notes section.

This social networking angle became a news story in its own right, and seemed to encourage more media coverage, which in turn provided more exposure to the social networks. Furthermore, the rise of viral video provided good visuals of protests at stores and material for reports during the slow news period.

John Mackey's own blog on www.wholefoods.com got a great deal of attention, as well, when he tried to further explain his actions a few days after the article was published. He offered a brief explanation of his thoughts and encouraged debate and civil discussion. He clarified that he never included the words "Obamacare" in his title, nor did he ever make mention of the president. He then reprinted his original draft, though it is not appreciably different from the published version.

The posting generated over 4,000 comments on the page, and many other completely unrelated comments on other pages of the Web site. While Whole Foods did delete anything with expletives, or that was posted on a part of the site unrelated to the healthcare debate, the company did not edit those on the Mackey op-ed comment page. A study of these comments found an almost even split between generally negative and generally positive comments, an indication that there is an opportunity for debate. Unfortunately for Whole Foods, many of the negative comments included vows never to shop at the store again. The effects of these boycotts on sales are yet to be determined, but will make an interesting statement about the rights of a CEO to make his opinions known in the context of the company he runs.

Discussion Questions

1. What obligation does a company's leadership have to refrain from taking a public opinion on a potentially contentious topic?

2. Should John Mackey have made himself available in the weeks following the publication of his op-ed?

3. Was Whole Foods' response to the social media attacks appropriate? What would have been an appropriate response?

4. Should a basic understanding of a company's customer base dictate which opinions should be shared and which should not?

5. Should John Mackey be allowed to remain as president, CEO, and chairman of the board at Whole Foods? Are his actions in the best interest of his shareholders and stakeholders?

This case was prepared by Research Assistants Tahir Imtiaz, Jing Ji, and Andrew Mitchell under the direction of James S. O'Rourke, Concurrent Professor of Management, as the basis for class discussion rather than to illustrate either effective or ineffective handling of an administrative situation. Information was gathered from corporate as well as public sources.

Case Study
The Whole Foods Alternative to ObamaCare

The Wall Street Journal

OPINION AUGUST 11, 2009, 7:30 P.M. ET

"Eight things we can do to improve health care without adding to the deficit."

—John Mackey

"The problem with socialism is that eventually you run out of other people's money."

—Margaret Thatcher

With a projected $1.8 trillion deficit for 2009, several trillions more in deficits projected over the next decade, and with both Medicare and Social Security entitlement spending about to ratchet up several notches over the next 15 years as Baby Boomers become eligible for both, we are rapidly running out of other people's money. These deficits are simply not sustainable. They are either going to result in unprecedented new taxes and inflation, or they will bankrupt us.

While we clearly need health-care reform, the last thing our country needs is a massive new health-care entitlement that will create hundreds of billions of dollars of new unfunded deficits and move us much closer to a government takeover of our health-care system. Instead, we should be trying to achieve reforms by moving in the opposite direction—toward less government control and more individual empowerment. Here are eight reforms that would greatly lower the cost of health care for everyone:

- Remove the legal obstacles that slow the creation of high-deductible health insurance plans and health savings accounts (HSAs). The combination of high-deductible health insurance and HSAs is one solution that could solve many of our health-care problems. For example, Whole Foods Market pays 100% of the premiums for all our team members who work 30 hours or more per

week (about 89% of all team members) for our high-deductible health-insurance plan. We also provide up to $1,800 per year in additional health-care dollars through deposits into employees' Personal Wellness Accounts to spend as they choose on their own health and wellness.

Money not spent in one year rolls over to the next and grows over time. Our team members therefore spend their own health-care dollars until the annual deductible is covered (about $2,500) and the insurance plan kicks in. This creates incentives to spend the first $2,500 more carefully. Our plan's costs are much lower than typical health insurance, while providing a very high degree of worker satisfaction.

- Equalize the tax laws so that employer-provided health insurance and individually owned health insurance have the same tax benefits. Now employer health insurance benefits are fully tax deductible, but individual health insurance is not. This is unfair.

- Repeal all state laws which prevent insurance companies from competing across state lines. We should all have the legal right to purchase health insurance from any insurance company in any state and we should be able to use that insurance wherever we live. Health insurance should be portable.

- Repeal government mandates regarding what insurance companies must cover. These mandates have increased the cost of health insurance by billions of dollars. What is insured and what is not insured should be determined by individual customer preferences and not through special-interest lobbying.

- Enact tort reform to end the ruinous lawsuits that force doctors to pay insurance costs of hundreds of thousands of dollars per year. These costs are passed back to us through much higher prices for health care.

- Make costs transparent so that consumers understand what health-care treatments cost. How many people know the total cost of their last doctor's visit and how that total breaks down? What other goods or services do we buy without knowing how much they will cost us?

- Enact Medicare reform. We need to face up to the actuarial fact that Medicare is heading towards bankruptcy and enact reforms that create greater patient empowerment, choice and responsibility.

- Finally, revise tax forms to make it easier for individuals to make a voluntary, tax-deductible donation to help the millions of people who have no insurance and aren't covered by Medicare, Medicaid or the State Children's Health Insurance Program.

Many promoters of health-care reform believe that people have an intrinsic ethical right to health care—to equal access to doctors, medicines and hospitals. While all of us empathize with those who are sick, how can we say that all people have more of an intrinsic right to health care than they have to food or shelter?

Health care is a service that we all need, but just like food and shelter it is best provided through voluntary and mutually beneficial market exchanges. A careful reading of both the Declaration of Independence and the Constitution will not reveal any intrinsic right to health care, food or shelter. That's because there isn't any. This "right" has never existed in America

Even in countries like Canada and the U.K., there is no intrinsic right to health care. Rather, citizens in these countries are told by government bureaucrats what health-care treatments they are eligible to receive and when they can receive them. All countries with socialized medicine ration health care by forcing their citizens to wait in lines to receive scarce treatments.

Although Canada has a population smaller than California, 830,000 Canadians are currently waiting to be admitted to a hospital or to get treatment, according to a report last month in Investor's Business Daily. In England, the waiting list is 1.8 million.

At Whole Foods we allow our team members to vote on what benefits they most want the company to fund. Our Canadian and British employees express their benefit preferences very clearly—they want supplemental health-care dollars that they can control and spend themselves without permission from their governments. Why would they want such additional health-care benefit dollars if they already have an "intrinsic right to health care"? The answer is clear—no such right truly exists in either Canada or the U.K.—or in any other country.

Rather than increase government spending and control, we need to address the root causes of poor health. This begins with the realization that every American adult is responsible for his or her own health.

Unfortunately many of our health-care problems are self-inflicted: two-thirds of Americans are now overweight and one-third are obese. Most of the diseases that kill us and account for about 70% of all health-care spending—heart disease, cancer, stroke, diabetes and obesity—are mostly preventable through proper diet, exercise, not smoking, minimal alcohol consumption and other healthy lifestyle choices.

Whole Food's Facebook Response

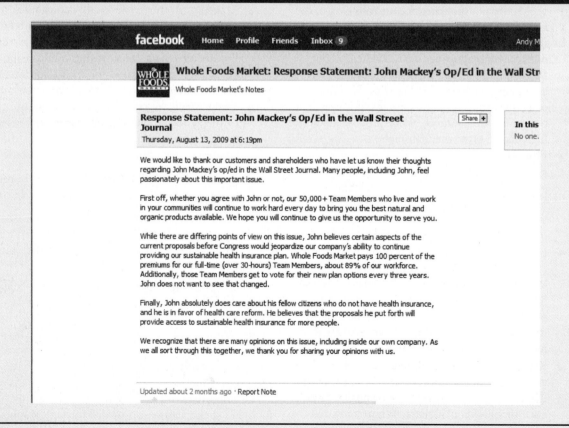

Whole Foods August Stock Price

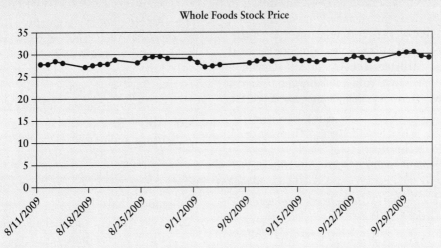

Whole Foods Stock Price

Source: Yahoo! Finance

Recent scientific and medical evidence shows that a diet consisting of foods that are plant-based, nutrient dense and low-fat will help prevent and often reverse most degenerative diseases that kill us and are expensive to treat. We should be able to live largely disease-free lives until we are well into our 90s and even past 100 years of age.

Health-care reform is very important. Whatever reforms are enacted it is essential that they be financially responsible, and that we have the freedom to choose doctors and the health-care services that best suit our own unique set of lifestyle choices. We are all responsible for our own lives and our own health. We should take that responsibility very seriously and use our freedom to make wise lifestyle choices that will protect our health. Doing so will enrich our lives and will help create a vibrant and sustainable American society.

Mr. Mackey is co-founder and CEO of Whole Foods Market Inc.

Endnotes

1. Veil, S. (2011). Mindful learning in crisis management. *Journal of Business Communication*, 48(2), 16–147.

2. Kanter, R. M. (1989). The new managerial work. *Harvard Business Review*, 67, 85–92.

3. Keys, B. & Case, T. (1990). How to become an influential manager. *Academy of Management Executive*, 4, 38–50, p. 38.

4. Keys, B. & Case, T. (1990). How to become an influential manager. *Academy of Management Executive*, 4, 38–50, p. 39.

5. French, J. R. P. & Raven, B. (1959). The bases of social power. In D. Cartwright (Ed.), *Studies in social power*. Ann Arbor, MI: Institute for Social Research.

6. Rost, J. C. (1991). *Leadership for the 21st century*. New York: Praeger.

7. Marion, R. & Ulh-Bien, M. (2001). Leadership in complex organizations. *Leadership Quarterly*, 12(4), 389–418.

8. Carmeli, A., Ben-Hador, B., Waldman, D. A. & Rupp, D. E. (2009). How leaders cultivate social capital and nurture employee vigor: Implications for job performance. *Journal of Applied Psychology*, 94(6), 1553–1561; Fletcher, J. K. (1999). *Disappearing acts: Gender, power and relational practices at work*. Cambridge, MA: The MIT Press; Fletcher, J. K. & Kaeufer, K. (2002). Shared leadership: Paradox and possibility. In C. L. Pearce & J. A. Conger (Eds.), *Shared leadership: Reframing the hows and whys of leadership* (pp. 27–45). Sherman Oaks, CA: Sage Publications; Tsui, A. S.,

Pearce, C. L., Porter, L. W., & Tripoli, A. A. (1997). Alternative approaches to employee-organization relationship: Does investment in employees payoff? *Academy of Management*, 40(5), 1089–1121; and Williams, M. (2007). Building genuine trust through interpersonal emotion management: A threat regulation model of trust and collaboration across borders. *Academy of Management*, 32(2), 595–621.

9. Fletcher, J. K. (1998). Relational practice: A feminist reconstruction of work. *Journal of Management Inquiry*, 7(2), 163–186, p. 169.

10. Kotter, J. P. (1990). *A force for change: How leadership differs from management*. New York: Free Press.

11. Zaleznik, A. (1977). Managers and leaders: Are they different? *Harvard Business Review*, 55, 67–78.

12. Higgs, M. & Rowland, D. (2005). All changes big and small: Exploring approaches to change and its leadership. *Journal of Change Management*, 5(2), 121–152; Rowland, D. & Higgs, M. (2008). *Sustaining change: Leadership that works*. Chichester: Jossey-Bass.

13. Weick, K. (1979). *The social psychology of organizing* (2nd ed.). Reading, MA: Addison-Wesley; Eisenberg, E. M. (1984). Ambiguity as strategy in organizational communication. *Communication Monographs*, 51, 227–242; Conrad, C. (1985). Chrysanthemums and swords: A reading of contemporary organizational communication theory and research. *Southern Speech Communication Journal*, 50, 189–200.

14. Frost, P., Moore, L., Louis, M. Lundberg, C., & Martin, J. (1991). *Reframing organizational culture*. Newbury Park, CA: Sage Publications.

15. Berger, P. L., & Luckmann, T. (1967). *The social construction of reality: A treatise in the sociology of knowledge*. Harpswell, ME: Anchor.

16. McLaughlin, K., & Martin, T. (2009). As sales slip, Whole Foods tries health push. *The Wall Street Journal*, August 5, Eastern Edition: B1, http://online.wsj.com/article /SB124941849645105559.html.

17. Smith, E. (2005). John Mackey. *Texas Monthly*, March, http://www.texasmonthly .com/preview/2005-03-01/talks.

18. Whole Foods company history. Whole Foods Web site, www.wholefoodsmarket /company/history.

19. EPA. (2007). Top 25 partners in the green power partnership. U.S. Environmental Protection Agency, January 8.

20. Alsop, R. (2007). How boss's deeds buff a firm's reputation. *The Wall Street Journal*, January 31, http://online.wsj.com/public /article/SB117019715069692873-92u520ldt 3ZTY_ZFX442W76FnfI_20080131.html? mod=blogs.

21. Two Austin firms make Fortune 100. *Austin Business Journal*, January 8, 2007, http:// austin.bizjournals.com/austin/stories/2007/01 /08/daily7.html?surround=lfn.

22. Mackey, J. (2010). Creating the high trust organization. Whole Foods Web site, March 9, http://www2.wholefoodsmarket .com/blogs/jmackey.

23. Peace, love and profit—meet the world's richest organic grocer. *The Observer*, consulted July 17, 2007, http://www.guardian .co.uk/lifeandstyle/2006/jan/29/foodanddrink .organics.

24. Conversations from the corner office. *Marketplace*, http://marketplace.publicradio.org /segments/corneroffice/corner_mackey_bio.html.

25. Peace, love and profit.

26. Ibid.

27. Rethinking the social responsibility of business. *Reason Magazine*, October 2005, http:// reason.com/archives/2005/10/01/rethinking -the-social-responsi.

28. Peace, love and profit.

29. Little, A. (2004). The Whole Foods shebang. *Grist Magazine*, December 17, http://www .grist.org/article/little-mackey.

30. FLOW: About us. *FLOW*, January 2006, http://www.flowidealism.org/Home/about-us .html.

31. McLaughlin & Martin. As sales slip, Whole Foods tries health push.

32. Kesmodel, D., & Wilke, J. R. (2007). Whole Foods is hot, Wild Oats a dud—so said

"Rahodeb." *The Wall Street Journal*, July 12, http://online.wsj.com/public/article/SB11841 8782959963745-rGivZMgAG2jUzji0DYY7 yEoEaF0_20070719.html?mod=blog.

33. FTC seeks to block Whole Foods Market's acquisition of Wild Oats Markets. Federal Trade Commission Web site, News, June 5, 2007, http://www.ftc.gov/opa/2007/06 /wholefoods.shtm.

34. Mackey, J. (2008). The CEO's blog, back to blogging. Whole Foods Web site, May 21. Accessed September 25, 2009, http://www2. wholefoodsmarket.com/blogs/jmackey/2008 /05/21/back-to-blogging/#more-26.

35. Organic Foods – US – October 2008. Mintel Reports. Accessed September 30, 2009, http://reports.mintel.com/sinatra/reports/display /id=226495.

36. Ibid.

37. Gogoi, P. (2008). The rise of the locavore. *Bloomberg Businessweek*, May 20, http:// www.businessweek.com/bwdaily/dnflash /content/may2008/db20080520_920283.htm.

38. Stolberg, S. G., & Herszenhorn, D. M. (2009). Two sides take health care debate outside Washington. *New York Times*, August 2, http://www.nytimes.com/2009 /08/03/health/policy/03healthcare.html.

39. Ibid.

40. Health insurance consumer protections. The White House Web site, http://www .whitehouse.gov/health-insurance-consumer -protections/.

41. Mackey, J. (2009). The Whole Foods alternative to ObamaCare: Eight things we can do to improve health care without adding to the deficit. *WSJ.com*, August 11, http:// online.wsj.com/articl

dotshock/Shutterstock.com

Foundations of Communication

After reading this chapter, you will be able to

► Approach communication from a more complex and nuanced perspective, one that underscores the importance of a strategic yet ethical approach.

► Understand the process of perception, how it affects the way we interpret information, and its importance in developing a strategic approach.

► Understand the importance of self-awareness as a foundational element of effective communication and its connection to understanding others, a key element of a strategic approach.

► Identify some of the obstacles to strategic and ethical communication, including how perception can affect the way we think and our ability to gather, analyze, and evaluate information (i.e., the critical-thinking process that is imperative for strategic communication).

Case Questions:

1. What unexplored assumptions about the social reality at California Design, Inc. may have contributed to the situation that Lara now faces?

2. How might differing perceptions of the situation by those involved have contributed to the creation of this situation?

3. What are the implicit understandings of those involved in this situation regarding how communication works, that is, their preferred communication model? How might understanding and applying a different, more accurate communication model help to avoid or minimize this situation?

4. What is or should be leadership's or management's role? Who solves, or should solve, these problems and how?

The Case of California Design, Inc.

California Design, Inc. is a small company started in 1990 by Clarence Ross, an interior designer. Throughout the housing boom of the early 2000s, the company grew exponentially, adding designers, a sales consultant group, and a manufacturing facility. The company has survived the recent financial crisis by marketing its services to wealthy clients less affected by the country's economic decline, but it did freeze hiring in the late 2000s and is now short staffed in all of its key departments.

Lara Adams is an interior designer at California Design who joined the firm in 2005. She is frustrated by the frequent communication mix-ups that occur, largely, she believes, due to the increased time pressures on remaining personnel caused by staffing shortages. Today, for instance, she has received an email that informs her the sales department has failed to cancel one of her design consultations with a client. This means that Lara is double booked for her 2 p.m. time slot.

The company's policy is to contact clients to confirm their appointments two days before the scheduled date and time. If the client cannot be contacted or does not respond to calls and messages from the sales department, then the appointment is dropped by the designers' administrative assistant and the time slot is filled with a client who has missed an appointment in the past and has requested a place on a waiting list for last-minute openings.

However, this policy was not followed in the case of client Alfonzo Rio. Sales consultant Louis Freeman writes that Alfonzo contacted him to confirm the appointment and that confirmation was not passed on to Lara or the department's administrative assistant.

Lara is doubly frustrated because she has ordered a custom chaise for another customer through the company's in-house manufacturing facility. The order was submitted two weeks ago, and manufacturing confirmed that the chaise would be completed and delivered this afternoon. She has just gotten off the phone with the angry client who called to loudly complain because she had received an automated email notification that the scheduled delivery of the chaise had been delayed a week. The client had planned a social event at her home this weekend with the understanding that her redesigned living room would be completed. She is now demanding some type of compensation for the company's failure to uphold its contractual obligation.

This isn't the first time that these problems have occurred and been dumped in Lara's lap to resolve. She is so frustrated that she wants to eliminate the waiting list for clients to avoid these sorts of mix-ups and to stop ordering product through the company facility. Both of these moves would involve lost revenues for the company but would make Lara's life easier and would potentially improve customer satisfaction.

Strategic Communicators

To be a strategic communicator requires a number of skills and abilities as well as certain knowledge; some might say it even requires a certain mind-set. This knowledge includes principles and concepts that are considered the foundation of effective communication, including a high level of self-awareness; an ability to understand other people (who often have differing experiences, values, and interests from our own, including cultural differences); a basic knowledge of the complexity of the communication process itself; and the ability to think critically—to analyze and evaluate situations and to use that information to formulate effective communication strategies. The following requirements for strategic communicators closely mirror the competencies for globally literate leaders.[1]

- **Personal literacy.** Understanding and valuing yourself (i.e., self-awareness and self-esteem).
- **Social literacy.** Engaging and challenging other people (which requires an understanding of those others in order to be effective).
- **Business literacy.** Focusing and mobilizing your organization (which requires an understanding of the business environment as well as the organization's culture and processes).
- **Cultural literacy.** Valuing and leveraging cultural differences.

All of these abilities are founded on the ability and willingness to continuously observe and analyze the social realities with which we interact and of which we are a part. Before discussing these issues from the perspective of communication—self-awareness, understanding others, and understanding cultural issues—let's begin with a discussion of how concepts of communication have developed over time so that we may gain a more sophisticated view of how communication operates. (Understanding the business environment and organizational culture and communication processes will be discussed in Chapter 5.)

Models of Communication

How would you define communication? Without looking ahead, take a moment and write down a short definition or say it aloud.

Odds are that you came up with something like "conveying information to other people," perhaps with a bit more elaboration. Pat yourself on the back if you did use this definition because you exemplify a theorist of communication, identifying one of the first models to describe the process. However, as was mentioned in Chapter 1, the definition of what constitutes communication and how it occurs has evolved over time. This section will provide a basic overview of the development of the different ways of thinking about communication, ending with the dialogic model, which is the foundation for this textbook. The purpose of this discussion is also intended to show that how we think about communication has also become more nuanced and complex as we have studied its processes and as our world has become more complex. To be an effective strategic communicator, the way we think about communication should reflect this understanding. Understanding the models of communication also help us better understand our own personal model of communication and whether and how it may need to be adjusted to improve our communication competence. The models of communication that will be discussed are (1) information transfer, (2) transactional process, (3) strategic control, and (4) dialogic process.

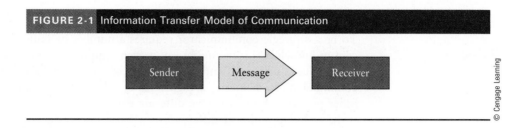

FIGURE 2-1 Information Transfer Model of Communication

© Cengage Learning

Communication as Information Transfer

Communication as information transfer, as was discussed in Chapter 1, assumes that one person can transmit the information in his or her head to another without distortion or personal interpretation (see Figure 2-1). We now know that this approach to communication ignores the effects of distortion on information transfer or the multiple possible interpretations that a receiver might apply to a message. Because of the effects of globalization in terms of the increasing diversity of the workforce and the influence and interactions of international and multinational corporations, most of us know that people of different cultures interpret the world differently. Even people from the same culture may have multiple interpretations of the same event, depending on their worldview, value system, and life experiences. This model also does not adequately account for the power of nonverbal communication. Consequently, this model of communication is no longer considered useful in thinking about how communication occurs; it more accurately describes communication between machines in the form of electric impulses.

That is, human beings communicate to do more than simply transfer information. As Chapter 3 will discuss in more detail, there are several purposes for communicating in a business environment—to create relationships, to convey our credibility, and to persuade and influence others—and these are all the more important because of the political nature of many organizations. Because of these potential challenges—differing perspectives and a variety of purposes—it is often beneficial to analyze important or new communication situations so as to better adapt to those situations before proceeding with critical communication tasks.

Communication as Transactional Process

Model 2, communication as transactional process, acknowledges that both senders and receivers are active and simultaneous interpreters of messages (see Figure 2-2). One advantage of this model over the information-transfer approach is that it acknowledges the importance of feedback, particularly the nonverbal type, in meaning making. However, this model of communication also has received criticism for

FIGURE 2-2 Transactional Process Model of Communication

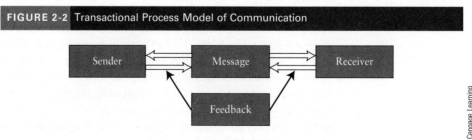

© Cengage Learning

its emphasis on shared meaning. Therefore, it is most usefully applied in interpersonal relationships in which shared meaning is the goal, those involving friends, families, and intimate partners.

This goal is often not the case in organizations, however, studies have shown that much organizational communication is characterized by ambiguity, deception, and diversity of viewpoints rather than shared meaning.[2] In fact, some researchers view organizational cultures as contested political domains in which the possibility for genuine dialogue is often seriously impaired.[3] Consequently, this model is generally not the best to apply because it doesn't recognize the political nature of many organizations. In fact, management professor Kathleen Reardon (2005) goes so far as to claim that it's all politics in organizations. "In any job, when you reach a certain level of technical competence, politics is what makes all the difference with regard to success. At that point, it is indeed all politics. Everyday brilliant people take a backseat to politically adept colleagues by failing to win crucial support for their ideas."[4] What does Reardon mean by politics? Basically, it's the ability to be a strategic communicator, which entails understanding the workings of power within an organization—who has it and who doesn't; listening to others; fostering and managing important relationships; and analyzing different organizational contexts so as to better adapt to political landscapes. Doing so, according to Reardon, also involves the ability to be persuasive and influential, the basic mark of a leader, as you may recall from the discussion of leadership in Chapter 1.

Communication as Strategic Control

Model 3, communication as strategic control, assumes that communication is a tool that individuals use to control their environment and thus it recognizes the play of power and politics within an organizational setting. From this perspective, a competent communicator chooses strategies appropriate to the situation and accomplishes multiple goals. The major criticism of this approach is its recognition that people should not be expected to communicate in any objectively rational way. Instead, communication choices are personally, socially, politically, and ethically motivated. In extreme cases, this model could lead to communicative practices that ignore the goals of clarity and honesty when it is in the communicator's best individual interest to do so.[5] In other words, an "ends justifies the means" approach might take hold in which concern about damage to others (and oftentimes one's own credibility) takes a back seat to short-term personal goals. In addition to these potentially ethical issues, an overly self-interested approach may lead us to ignore the larger "political" elements at work in many organizations, sometimes at our own peril. An example would be an individual who believed he or she was right and focused on proving it, but in the process, alienated his or her colleagues and caused so much trouble for management that the person was ultimately let go. Because of the limitations of the strategic control approach, there is a need for a model of communication that recognizes the interdependency of human beings in most organizational situations to help balance the pursuit of short-term personal gain.

Communication as Dialogic Process

Model 4, the dialogic model, mitigates against many of the problems associated with the previously discussed approaches. It goes beyond the information-transfer model to focus on the contribution of the "receiver's" perspective to an interpretation and course of action jointly decided upon. In other words, the sender and

dialogic model of communication
This model of communication takes other people's points of view into account, acknowledging that the speaker and the listener may have different perspectives.

dialogue
A conversation among two or more persons. From the dialogic perspective, that dialogue would be characterized by such attributes as trust, lack of pretense, sincerity, humility, respect, directness, open-mindedness, honesty, concern for others, empathy, non-manipulative intent, equality, and acceptance of others as individuals with intrinsic worth, regardless of differences of opinion or belief.

monologue
Talking to oneself. From a dialogic perspective, a monologue is characterized by such qualities as deception, superiority, exploitation, dogmatism, domination, insincerity, pretense, personal self-display, self-aggrandizement, judgmentalism that stifles free expression, coercion, possessiveness, condescension, self-defensiveness, and viewing others as objects to be manipulated.

receiver are jointly creating social reality. This perspective is critically important to the strategic communicator because the focus of a good strategic communicator is not on himself or herself but rather on the audience and the context within which communication takes place. Audience analysis, combined with an examination of the communication context, should generally drive strategy and message formulation.

The **dialogic model of communication** also attempts to deal with the contested nature of communication that is ignored by the transactional model by acknowledging that differences of perspective may exist between communicators. In other words, it doesn't assume that meaning or even the goal of communication is shared but instead recognizes the interplay between the difference and similarity of those involved in the communication process. Finally, it also attempts to moderate the ethical problem of the strategic model by acknowledging that we are not isolated individuals; rather, we live in groups and communities and our actions affect others. According to Dean C. Barnlund (1986), communication is inherently ethical. Privately, human beings are "free to invent whatever meaning they can. But when [people] encounter each other, a moral issue invades every exchange because the manipulation of symbols always involves a purpose that is external to, and in some degree manipulative of, the interpreter of the message."[6] Barnlund's statement recognizes the socially constructed nature of reality—human beings create meaning through communication—and the possibility that a strategic approach to communication may go awry in an ethical sense through manipulation, deception, or the withholding of information.

According to the dialogic model, the strategies that we use to communicate must consider how our messages affect others' perception of us as well as the effect of our communication on others. This model implicitly recognizes the growing importance of interpersonal relationships on our own success and happiness in the workplace, as well as our personal lives, as the boundaries between these two have become blurred with the proliferation of technology—cell phones, laptops, email, the Internet, and so on.

Communication understood as **dialogue** is characterized by such attributes as trust, lack of pretense, sincerity, humility, respect, directness, open-mindedness, honesty, concern for others, empathy, nonmanipulative intent, equality, and acceptance of others as individuals with intrinsic worth, regardless of differences of opinion or belief.[7] This attitude contrasts with the understanding and practice of communication as **monologue**, which is characterized by such qualities as deception, superiority, exploitation, dogmatism, domination, insincerity, pretense, personal self-display, self-aggrandizement, judgmentalism that stifles free expression, coercion, possessiveness, condescension, self-defensiveness, and viewing others as objects to be manipulated.[8] Communication as monologue means that the communicator is essentially talking to himself or herself, ignoring the effects that communication has on others. Communication as monologue is an **egocentric** process in which little or no concern or empathy is shown for the needs or feelings of others.

To better demonstrate the differences between a monologue and a dialogue, Barnlund (1986) offers three types of communication. The first type comprises messages whose intent is to coerce others. Meaning is controlled by choosing symbols that so threaten the interpreter of the message that he or she becomes incapable of, and blind to, alternative meanings.[9] Second, there are messages of an exploitative sort in which words are arranged to filter the information, narrow the choices, and obscure the consequences so that only one meaning becomes attractive or appropriate.[10] The third type involves what Barnlund calls "facilitative" communication in which words are used to inform, enlarge perspective, deepen sensitivity, remove external threat, and encourage independence of meaning.[11] "The values of the listener are, in the first case, ignored, in the second, subverted, in the third, respected."[12] As will be discussed in the next chapter, facilitative communication can be beneficial in achieving two important purposes of communication in organizations: establishing and maintaining relationships (i.e., conveying goodwill), and establishing and maintaining credibility as a person respectful of others.

The dialogic model differs from the earlier models of communication in which other people are sometimes viewed as beings to be acted upon, communicated to, ordered, and controlled.[13] In contrast, the dialogic model perceives others as *interdependent* partners capable and deserving of their own voice to influence the organizational dialogue. The dialogic model thus is considered an index of the ethical level of communication to the degree that participants in communication display the preceding attributes.[14]

Even though this recognition of our interdependence with others may seem like commonsense in terms of our understanding, it may not as easily be practiced. That's because people in the United States tend to have an individualistic perspective in which the focus is on looking out for and valorizing the self rather than the group.

Another reason that the dialogic model is potentially most useful has to do with the changes in the business environment due to the process of globalization. As was discussed in Chapter 1, organizations have increasingly diverse workforces and are increasingly involved in international business dealings. Thus, **plurality** often exists within these organizations. Plurality means that there are always multiple interpretations of any situation and that no one person can control those interpretations, try as he or she might. Recognition of the reality of plurality requires that we be open or willing to listen to the voices and opinions of others if there is any hope of achieving something approaching shared understanding. In the workplace, attempting to move toward shared understanding is, of course, important if we are to achieve organizational and personal goals and demonstrate our full leadership potential.

Therefore, the dialogic model of communication is compatible with many of the concerns and goals of intercultural communication. **Intercultural communication** is the exchange of information between individuals who are unalike culturally.[15] The most effective way to deal with the challenges posed by conducting business across cultures is to be open to what may be learned about another culture and how that knowledge can be applied to communicate more effectively with its members. In this regard, plurality and its requirement of openness to the opinions of others help us to practice more effective intercultural communication. (Cultural differences are discussed in more detail in Chapter 4.)

The characteristics of dialogue overlap with much of the research on intercultural sensitivity. For example, several studies have identified empathy, understanding of others, valuing of difference, adaptability, and being nonjudgmental and open-minded as elements of intercultural competence.[16]

Perception

Hopefully, with the discussion of social reality in the previous chapter, you are more aware of the possibility that your perceptions of reality may differ from

egocentric
Concerned with the self rather than others or society.

plurality
The recognition that there are multiple different interpretations of any situation and that no one communicator can control all these interpretations.

intercultural communication
The exchange of information among people of different cultural backgrounds.

ResponsibleCommunication

One ethical problem that is exposed by the dialogic model of communication is what is termed *moral exclusion.* According to Susan Opotow (1990), moral exclusion occurs when the application of moral values, rules, and fairness is not considered necessary for particular individuals or groups. The practice of moral exclusion results in individuals being perceived as nonentities, expendable, or undeserving. The result is that harming such individuals becomes acceptable, appropriate, or just.

Persons who are morally excluded are thus denied their rights, dignity, and autonomy. In her analysis, Opotow identifies several dozen ways in which moral exclusion is manifested; of those, many involve communication and language use. For example, showing your belief in your superiority or the superiority of your group by making unflattering comparisons to other individuals or groups is one manifestation of moral exclusion. Another example of language use to morally exclude others is by characterizing them as lower life forms or as inferior beings. Other examples of moral exclusion include

- placing the blame for any harm on the victim;
- justifying harmful acts by claiming that the morally condemnable acts

committed by "the enemy" are worse;
- misrepresenting harmful behaviors by masking or conferring respectability on them through the use of neutral, positive, technical, or euphemistic terms to describe them; and
- justifying harmful behavior by claiming that everyone is doing it or that it is an isolated case.

Question for Thought

- Can you think of recent examples in the news of the use of moral exclusion? In these examples, how has moral exclusion been used to manipulate meaning for others?

those around you? For example, if you have had an argument with a friend or family member, chances are it was based on different perceptions of a particular situation. **Perception** is closely linked to the notion of the social constructionist nature of reality, which was discussed in Chapter 1. Some would say that because of our experiences, beliefs, and values, it is impossible to comprehend what is really "out there" because everything is interpreted or filtered through those experiences or beliefs. Because we all have different life experiences, value systems, worldviews, and beliefs, we may perceive reality differently. Even common barriers such as our mood and distractions such as noise, stress, and tiredness can affect what we perceive. These differences in perception can be enormous obstacles to effective communication, especially if we are not aware of them. These differences become even more important with the increased diversity of the workplace and the increased internationalization of business activities—that is, globalization.

The perceptual process reveals how differences in judgments of reality may occur. The first step in the process of perception is the receipt of information through our senses (see Figure 2-3). This sensory data is then selected and organized into a pattern from which we infer meaning. Selection is the way that we pay attention to sensory cues. It is often not a conscious process, and it is *selective*, which means that we generally pay attention only to some cues, not all of them. Obviously, then, selection can lead to misunderstanding if we are communicating with someone who is paying attention to different cues than we are. You have probably had myriad conversations in which you asked your companion, "Did you see that?", and the response was, "No, I was paying -attention to X." This is the process of selection at work.

perception
Awareness of the elements of the environment made possible through our senses.

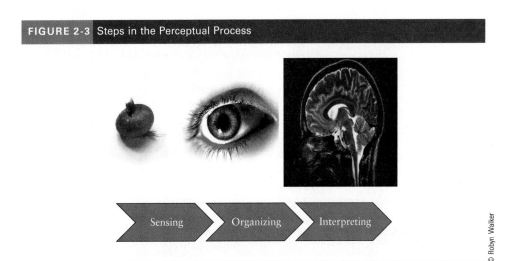

FIGURE 2-3 Steps in the Perceptual Process

Sensing   Organizing   Interpreting

© Robyn Walker

stereotyping
A standardized mental picture that is held in common by members of a group and that represents an oversimplified opinion, prejudiced attitude, or uncritical judgment.

projected cognitive similarity
The tendency to assume others have the same norms and values as your own cultural group.

Misunderstanding can also arise at the organization level of the perceptual process because we may fit the information into patterns that differ from the way that others see things. You have probably done exercises in class or elsewhere where you have been shown a diagram similar to the one in which some people see the face of a beautiful woman while others see the face of a crone.

During the perceptual process, misunderstanding may occur based on the inferences we draw from the previously mentioned patterns. You have certainly had the unwinnable argument: "I think the movie was excellent because [fill in the blank here]," while your companion replied something like, "You've got to be kidding! That was the biggest disappointment of the century!" Because of differing values, experiences, and tastes, the inferences that we draw from stimuli may be unlike those of others and, if these inferences are not questioned, can create many misunderstandings. These sorts of inferential errors are more likely in a world that is characterized by diversity of cultural backgrounds and demographic differences.

Because our opinions may often differ from others, it is not useful to try to ascertain who is right or wrong because it may simply depend on a matter of taste, values, beliefs, or personal preferences. We have all had experiences where our perceptions differ from others, a recognition that creates a problem for our more commonsense understanding of the process of communication—the basic assumption that just because we communicated information, it was successfully received as we intended it and that meaning was shared.

Perceptual differences may lead to additional problems, such as those having to do with stereotyping, attribution, impression formation, and culture. **Stereotyping** is not necessarily a bad thing. On the one hand, it can be a label for a process of making sense out of what we perceive by categorizing or generalizing about it. On the other hand, it can be an oversimplified way of labeling people with the intention of denigrating them in some way. This can be particularly problematic when dealing with people of other cultures. One type of stereotype that can be formed when interacting with people of other cultures is **projected cognitive similarity**, which is the tendency to assume others have the same norms and values as your own cultural group.[17] Research has shown that when an aggressive style of communication is exhibited in intercultural team decision making, people of East Asian cultures are less participatory, since this style contrasts with their own norms of politeness and modesty.[18] A second stereotype common to intercultural interactions is the **outgroup homogeneity effect**, which is the tendency to think members of other groups are all the same.[19] Although there are cultural tendencies, this belief denies the variation among individuals of any cultural group and can detract from the development of positive working relationships.

A second type of perceptual inference is called an **attribution**. When we form an attribution, we develop a "theory" for another's behavior. Attribution can also apply to how others see us. For example, if we are late to arrive at work, our boss may think we have a poor work ethic, when we simply had a flat tire that delayed us that day. If we are not aware of these perceptual problems, then we can find ourselves in serious problems at work by discriminating against others, damaging relationships, and doing things that damage our own credibility or image.

CriticalThinking

What are some of the common stereotypes that you hold? Can you identify persons or situations in which those stereotypes do not hold? How might you gain more accurate knowledge about those persons you tend to stereotype?

outgroup homogeneity effect
The tendency to think members of other groups are all the same.

attribution
The assignment of meaning to other people's behavior.

impression formation
The process of integrating a variety of observations about a person into a coherent impression of that person.

A similar concept is **impression formation**. Basically, impression formation is the process of integrating a variety of observations about a person into a coherent impression of that person. Again, understanding this principle is important for the strategic communicator because we also attempt to manage the impression that others form of us. Today, for example, did you worry about your choice of clothing and how it might affect how others saw you? Did you worry about the state of your hair or whether you might have bad breath? Our ability to manage the impressions we make on others depends on our ability to see ourselves as others might see us.

Perceptions also may differ by culture. (More on culture can be found in Chapter 4.) The increased interdependence of people around the world and diversity in the workplace requires recognition of the contested perceptual nature of reality and our interpretation of it. It thus requires openness to others' views and opinions if we are to communicate effectively to reach anything approaching shared meaning.

Understanding the role of perception in communication is critical for strategic communicators. Without this recognition, we may assume that others are perceiving reality just as we are, and if this assumption is in error, miscommunication is likely. Misunderstanding may be introduced during each of the steps in the perceptual process, and thus we may need to adjust our communication to lessen the occurrence of these problems. This adjustment relies on our ability to observe situations, analyze what is happening, and then make intentional choices about how best to manage the communication process. Finally, it is important to recognize that people make judgments about us based on our communication practices; this understanding gives us power to actively shape those perceptions.

CriticalThinking

Have you experienced a situation in which people perceived a situation in different ways? What could have contributed to these differences in perception?

wavebreakmedia/Shutterstock.com

Self-Awareness and Communication

A discussion of perception naturally leads to a look at self-concept and self-awareness. This is because how we perceive ourselves plays a critical role in communication. Our self-concept and awareness of it are important for effective strategic communicators for several reasons. First, to be effective, we must know ourselves, our strengths and our weaknesses, so that we can leverage our strengths to better achieve our career goals and work on eliminating our weaknesses so that they don't become a stumbling block to that achievement. Second, our self-concept affects how we interact with others. These two reasons are interconnected: In the political climate of many business organizations, other people will be making observations and judgments about us regarding our strengths and weaknesses, and our ability to talk about both intelligently can help to enhance our credibility. Leveraging our strengths and minimizing our weaknesses can also help to create productive work relationships that enable us to influence others and successfully navigate political terrains.

Self-Concept

Self-concept is how we think about ourselves and describe ourselves to others. It is often the product of our experiences and, to some degree, the result of our interpretation of the messages that others send us. In other words, communication is foundational in the forming our self-concept; people are the products of how others treat them and of the messages others send them. Dean Barnlund (1970) introduced the idea that individuals "construct" themselves—or their identities—through the relationships they have, wish to have, or perceive themselves as having. Barnlund developed the idea that "six persons" are involved in every two-person communication. These six persons emerge from the following:

- How you view yourself
- How you view the other person

self-concept
How we think about ourselves and describe ourselves to others.

- How you believe the other person views you
- How the other person views himself or herself
- How the other person views you
- How the other person believes you view him or her

Barnlund's model emphasizes the relational nature of communication and the centrality of the self and our perception of the self in communication. It also implicitly recognizes not only the socially constructed nature of reality, but also our social identities. Perception is key in this process. From Barnlund's model comes the notion of the **self-fulfilling prophecy**, or the idea that you behave and see yourself in ways that are consistent with how others see you.[20] With this understanding, it should be obvious that, depending on our relationship and the situation, some people have differing expectations of us and will see us in ways that are different from how others see us. For example, friends and family may have an emotional attachment to us that makes us feel special, accomplished, and well loved. This emotional attachment is important for the development of self-esteem. However, those who do not have that strong emotional attachment—teachers, employers, new acquaintances, and strangers, among others—may see us in a different light, one in which they see our positive attributes as well as those areas that might be improved; in fact, they may focus on the negative, creating a perception that is very different from who we believe we are.

Depending on our experiences and relationships, our self-concept thus may be positive or negative, accurate or inaccurate. And how you view yourself can make a big difference in your ability to communicate and achieve your purposes.

Self-Awareness and Emotional Intelligence

For this reason, it is important to develop high levels of **self-awareness** or an understanding of the self, including your attitudes, values, beliefs, strengths, and weaknesses. Self-awareness is developed in two ways: by communicating with oneself and by communicating with others. Communication with ourselves is called **intrapersonal communication**, which includes "our perceptions, memories, experiences, feelings, interpretations, inferences, evaluations, attitudes, opinions, ideas, strategies, images, and states of consciousness."[21] According to Gardner and Krechevsky (1993), **intrapersonal intelligence** is the capacity to form an accurate model of oneself and to be able to use that model to operate effectively in life. Intrapersonal intelligence is developed by reflecting on our thoughts and actions to understand what motivates those thoughts and actions. Another word for this process is **reflexivity**.

Intrapersonal intelligence is a correlative ability to **interpersonal intelligence.**[22] Interpersonal intelligence is the ability to understand other people: what motivates them, how they work, and how to work cooperatively with them. Essentially, Gardner and Krechevsky claims that we must have self-awareness in order to understand others. For example, if our self-concept does not match the perception that others have of us, then we may misinterpret their responses to our messages. We may also misinterpret the way that our communication is interpreted by others. For instance, we may believe that we are highly reliable; however, others may believe the opposite about us. This commonly happens in student teams in which a member is commonly late for meetings and with assignments but doesn't see a problem with his or her behavior, whereas others begin to mistrust the person's reliability. Such contradictions in perception held by others can obviously negatively impact our ability to work with others. Furthermore, if we are unaware of these contradictions, then

self-fulfilling prophecy
The idea that we see ourselves in ways that are consistent with how others see us.

self-awareness
An understanding of the self, including one's attitudes, values, beliefs, strengths, and weaknesses.

intrapersonal communication
One's communication with oneself, including memories, experiences, feelings, ideas, and attitudes.

intrapersonal intelligence
The ability to form an accurate model of oneself and to use this model effectively.

reflexivity
The capacity for reflection.

interpersonal intelligence
The ability to understand others.

we are unable to change our communicative behaviors, both verbal and nonverbal, to better correspond with the message we want to send about ourselves. In addition, it is important that the messages we send through our actions correspond to those we send orally and in writing because people are more likely to believe the nonverbal communication cues. A third problem that may occur due to a lack of self-awareness is that we may not recognize differences in others; we may project our self-understanding onto them. This latter issue is a particular problem in diverse cultural settings and can negatively affect our ability to communicate as well as to demonstrate recognized leadership behaviors.

The second part of self-concept is **self-esteem**, or how we feel about ourselves and how well we like and value ourselves. Perception and communication are both affected by self-esteem. In the contemporary business world, high levels of self-awareness and self-esteem may help us be more open to the opinions and perspectives of others—the basis of dialogic communication.

Without high levels of self-awareness and self-esteem, we may feel threatened when we meet others who are different from us, and that feeling may get in the way of our ability to be open to listening to and considering others' perspectives and opinions. A high level of self-esteem also is important because we must be willing to admit that perhaps we don't know everything; we always have opportunities to learn. According to Evered and Tannenbaum (1992), in order to engage in dialogue we must be able to take "the stance that there is something that I don't already know." We must be able to engage with others "with a mutual *openness* to learn," rather than becoming defensive or closed to other opinions.[23]

A related concept and outgrowth of Gardner's and others' work in the area of intrapersonal and interpersonal intelligence is that of **emotional intelligence**. Emotional intelligence refers to an assortment of noncognitive skills, capabilities, and competencies that influence a person's ability to successfully cope with environmental demands and pressures. Studies indicate that high levels of emotional intelligence are better indicators of job performance than academic IQ.[24]

Emotional intelligence consists of five dimensions:

- **Self-awareness,** or the ability to be aware of what you are feeling
- **Self-management,** or the ability to manage your emotions and impulses
- **Self-motivation,** or the ability to persist in the face of setbacks and failures
- **Empathy,** or the ability to sense how others are feeling
- **Social skills,** or the ability to handle the emotions of others

In addition to self-awareness, empathy, and social skills, emotional intelligence involves emotional control, or the ability to delay gratification and resist impulses, which can greatly affect our career success and our ability to communicate with others. Studies have shown that those who were able to resist temptation as small children are more socially competent as adolescents.[25] They were more personally effective, self-assertive, and better able to cope with life's frustrations. They were less likely to be negatively affected by stress or to become disorganized when pressured; they embraced challenges, were self-reliant and confident, trustworthy and dependable, and took initiative. More than a decade later, they were still able to delay gratification. Those who were less able to delay gratification were more likely to shy away from social contacts, to be stubborn and indecisive, to be easily upset by frustrations, to think of themselves as unworthy, to become immobilized by stress, to be mistrustful and resentful about not getting enough, to be prone to jealousy and envy, and to overreact to irritations with a sharp temper, thus provoking arguments.

self-esteem
How we like and value ourselves and how we feel about ourselves.

emotional intelligence
The assortment of noncognitive skills that influence our ability to cope with the pressures and demands of the environment.

The role of emotional intelligence is still debated among researchers, but it is generally acknowledged to be an important construct when thinking about leadership abilities. The underlying premise of the construct is that those who are more sensitive to their own emotions and the impact of their emotions on others will be more effective leaders.

Cultural Intelligence

A similar construct, cultural intelligence, is particularly relevant in today's diverse business world and for global leaders. There are three elements of cultural intelligence:

- **Cognitive knowledge:** The possession of a wide-ranging information base about a variety of people and their cultural customs.
- **Motivation:** Healthy self-efficacy, persistence, goals, value-questioning, and integration.
- **Behavioral adaptability:** The capacity to interact in a wide range of situations, environments, and diverse groups.[26]

The Global Literacy Competence (GLC) Model offers a road map to begin to conceptualize the stages of cultural intelligence development (see Figure 2-4).[27] The competencies that are described in Figure 2-5 are consistent with emotional intelligence work. The GLC assumes that ascending to a higher level of global leadership function is not only possible but also is required for excellence in a cross-cultural environment.

The developers of the GLC model challenge the application of Western cultural idiosyncrasies, such as American individualism, which they believe are counterproductive in many cultural settings, particularly Asia.[28] They are supported by the

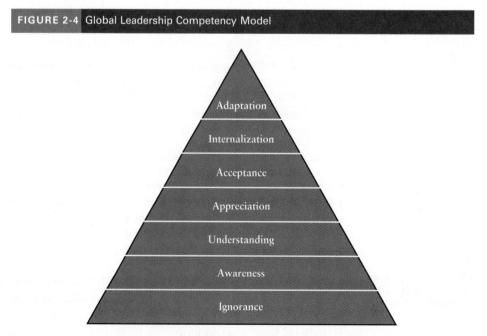

FIGURE 2-4 Global Leadership Competency Model

Adaptation

Internalization

Acceptance

Appreciation

Understanding

Awareness

Ignorance

Source: Chin, C. O., Gu, J. & Tubbs, S. (2001). Developing global leadership competencies. *Journal of Leadership Studies*, 7(4), 20–35.

FIGURE 2-5 Levels of Global Communication Competence.

Level	Description
Awareness	This is the novice stage; with exposure come vague impressions. They are brief sensations of which people are barely conscious. At this level, there is little or no sense-making, but a dawning awareness of something different and possibly interesting, strange, frightening or annoying.
Understanding	At this stage individuals begin to exhibit some conscious effort to learn why people are the way they are and why people do what they do. They display interest in those who are different from themselves. Sanchez et. al. (2000) refers to this as the "transition stage." This is a stage whereby the individual collects information through reading, observation and real experiences as well as by asking questions to learn more about the new cultural phenomenon.
Appreciation	Individuals begin to take a "leap of faith" and experience a genuine tolerance of different points of view. Through understanding the basic differences as well as areas where one thinks, acts, and react similarly, a positive feeling toward the "new" cultural phenomenon begins to form. Individuals not only put up with the "new" culture but also display a genuine appreciation of and, in some cases, preference for certain aspects of the "new" culture.
Acceptance	In this stage, the possibility of interaction between cultures increases appreciably. People are more sophisticated both in terms of recognizing commonalities and in terms of effectively dealing with differences. At this stage, there is the willingness to acquire new patterns of behavior and attitudes. This is a departure from the ethnocentric notion that "my way is the best way and the only way."
Internalization	At this stage, the individual goes beyond making sense of information and actually embarks on a deliberate internalization process with profound positive feelings for the once unknown cultural phenomenon. At this stage, there is a clear sense of self-understanding leading to readiness to act and interact with the locals/nationals in a natural, appropriate and culturally effective manner.
Adaptation	Cultural competence becomes a way of life. It is internalized, to the degree that it is out of one's consciousness, thus becomes effortless, and second nature. Individuals at this level display and possess the (1) capacity for gathering knowledge about different cultures, (2) drive or motivation, and (3) behavioral adaptability—the capacity to act effectively based upon their knowledge and motivation.

Source: Chin, C. O., Gu, J. & Tubbs, S. (2001). Developing global leadership competencies. *Journal of Leadership Studies*, 7(4), 20–35.

findings of the GLOBE researchers, which are discussed more in Chapter 4. The model is also consistent with contingency theory, which assumes that as context changes, so must the behaviors of leaders.[29] That is, for leaders working abroad, the context is very different from their home country's cultural context. (Context is discussed in more detail in Chapter 5.)

CriticalThinking

Using an Internet search engine, search for Web sites that offer free self-assessments of emotional intelligence, and cultural intelligence. After completing the self-assessments, consider the steps you might take to improve your competence in these areas.

Needed Skills for Strategic and Ethical Communication

We have already explored how a lack of understanding about the potential complexity of communication processes in different situations can lead to strategy errors and even unethical practices. Another practical challenge is posed by the sheer amount of information with which we are bombarded each day. More information has been produced in the last 30 years than in the previous 5,000. A single edition of the *New York Times* contains more information than the average person was likely to be exposed to in an entire lifetime in seventeenth-century England.[30] In fact, more information is generated worldwide in a twenty-four-hour period than you could process and absorb in all your years on Earth. With the increasing use of the Internet, we are approaching a point at which more information will be generated in one hour than could be processed and absorbed in your lifetime.[31]

The corresponding overload affects our ability to gather, analyze, and identify information on which to base sound decisions and communication strategies. It thus requires that we become aware of the subconscious processes we use to process information that may lead us to faulty decisions.

It also requires that we spend some time developing our critical-thinking abilities because analysis is the basis of strategic thinking, or the ability to formulate communication strategy. In his book *Academically Adrift: Limited Learning on College Campuses*, Richard Arum reveals the results of a study that followed 2,322 traditional-age students from the fall of 2005 to the spring of 2009 and examined testing data and student surveys at a broad range of twenty-four U.S. colleges and universities, from the highly selective to the less selective. The study found that 45 percent of students made no significant improvement in their critical thinking, reasoning, or writing skills during the first two years of college. After four years, 36 percent showed no significant gains in these so-called higher order thinking skills.[32] Students majoring in business, education, social work, and communications showed the least gains in learning.

Higher-order thinking skills needed for strategic thinking go beyond rote learning or memorization of concepts. Rote learning or memory of learned materials is needed for understanding, but higher-order learning also includes the ability to comprehend, apply, analyze, synthesize and evaluate information, the latter three abilities being part of critical thinking (see Figure 2-6).[33]

The ability to learn and think well is also needed for living in our more complex and rapidly changing world, in which "the work of the future is the work of the mind, intellectual work, work that involves reasoning and intellectual discipline."[34] Because of the rapidly changing world we now live in, well-regarded management writer Peter Senge has called for a need to develop "learning organizations."[35] In these types of organizations, leadership is decentralized so as to enhance the capacity of people to work productively toward common goals. Senge's basic rationale for such organizations is that in situations of rapid change, only those that are flexible, productive, and adaptive will excel. To create such an organization, people must have the capacity to learn, and to learn, they must have a structure and culture that is conducive to reflection and engagement.

There are several obstacles to thinking well and good decision making, including perceptual mindsets and certain thinking styles.

FIGURE 2-6 Categories in the Cognitive Domain of Bloom's Taxonomy

| Analyze | Evaluate | Create |

Apply

Understand

Remember

Source: Krathwohl, D. R. (2002). A revision of Bloom's taxonomy: An overview. *Theory into Practice*, 212–218.

Perceptual Mind-sets

As discussed earlier, the process of perception is often overlooked in the course of human meaning making, and the unique ways that individuals organize and interpret information is shaped by their values and experiences. These psychological and cognitive predispositions are called **perceptual mind-sets**, which can pose another challenge to evaluating information well. These biases, preconceptions, and assumptions can get in the way of our ability to make effective decisions and to solve problems. Because of our mind-sets, we are prepared to receive only certain messages and to ignore others. To put it bluntly, we are conditioned to view the world narrowly. One example might be our choice to affiliate with a political party. We may so closely identify with the party's platform that we are unable to listen to others with different political affiliations and to be open to ideas that may provide viable solutions. One outcome is the polarization that currently characterizes American political discourse and paralyzes decision making at the highest levels of government.

Our mind-sets are affected by several practices that limit our ability to consider information thoroughly and objectively. These include confirmation bias, false dichotomies, and inferential errors.

Confirmation Bias

Confirmation bias is a tendency to distort information that contradicts our currently held beliefs and attitudes.[36] Confirmation bias exhibits itself in group communication situations and also affects our individual decision making.

In groups, research indicates a strong tendency among members to "show - interest in facts and opinions that support their initially preferred policy and take up time in their meetings to discuss them, but they tend to ignore facts and opinions that do not support their initially preferred policy."[37]

For individuals, confirmation bias can also distort evidence that disconfirms our viewpoints and perceptions. This process is called *self-confirmation*.[38] Women, for

perceptual mind-set
Our cognitive and psychological predispositions to see the world in a certain way.

confirmation bias
A tendency to distort information that contradicts the beliefs and attitudes we currently hold.

example, often have to deal with self-confirming beliefs of supervisors and colleagues.[39] In other words, women may believe they must conform to stereotypes by acting in accommodating, unassertive ways; they may have more difficulty being taken seriously by others and thus receive fewer promotions and raises. However, refusing to accept these stereotypes may also have negative consequences. In some cases, assertive women may be judged as too aggressive and uncooperative, and thus they may be deemed undeserving of promotion or advancement. Women leaders must thus find a way to negotiate what is called this "double bind." Research shows that adopting an androgynous communication style can often help resolve this problem.

To combat confirmation bias, Rothwell suggests the following:

1. Actively seek out disconfirming information and evidence.
2. Vigorously present and argue disconfirming evidence to others or the group.
3. Play devil's advocate.
4. Gather allies to challenge confirmation bias.[40]

False Dichotomies

Dichotomous, either–or thinking is the tendency to see the world in terms of black and white or opposites. Either–or thinking often leads us to describe situations in the language of extremes. Such thinking is typically false because there are almost always more than two possibilities in our complex world. In these cases, we have created a **false dichotomy**, which blinds us to other possibilities.

The bell-shaped curve is an example of an alternate view—one in which there are numerous possibilities along a certain range. In a bell curve, if specific information is gathered from a random group of individuals, the data tend to bunch up in the middle. However, someone who applies either–or thinking would focus on the few individuals or situations that lie at the extreme ends of the spectrum and ignore the more numerous cases in the middle.[41] Such thinking can lead to poor decisions because it may ignore the bulk of the most valid information available on the subject.

To avoid the pitfalls of false dichotomies, you should

1. Be suspicious of absolutes. Look for alternatives to the one or two suggestions recommended.
2. Employ the language of qualification. Speak in terms of degrees by using such terms as *sometimes, rarely, occasionally, mostly, usually,* and *moderately.*[42]

Inferential Errors

Inferences are conclusions about the unknown based on the known. We draw inferences from previous experiences, factual data, and predispositions. Because of this tendency, inferences are guesses varying from the educated to the uneducated.

Making inferences is not necessarily a negative practice, as was discussed in the previous section on perception. We could not function on a daily basis without making inferences. However, the principal problem with inferences is that we are often unaware that we are making them and thus rarely question their accuracy.

The two general sources of inferential errors are (1) a faulty information base or misinformation and (2) a seriously limited information base.[43] However, more specific sources of inferential errors exist. These are vividness, unrepresentativeness, and correlation.

false dichotomy
A dichotomy that is not jointly exhaustive (i.e., there are other alternatives) or that is not mutually exclusive (i.e., the alternatives overlap). A false dichotomy may be the product of either–or thinking.

inference
A conclusion about the unknown based upon the known.

Vividness   Graphic, outrageous, shocking, controversial, and dramatic events draw our attention and tend to stick in our minds. We tend to overvalue vivid, concrete information and undervalue abstract, statistical information. Statistical information tends to be dry and lifeless in because it leaves out of the equation representations of people and the real consequences of decisions on their lives. This is important to remember when it comes to communicating information to others: We remember vivid images much better than abstractions. If we are not aware of this, it can skew our ability to make good decisions.

Unrepresentativeness   When we make a judgment, we tend to assess its accuracy based on our knowledge of information in a general category. However, if the information is not representative or does not agree with that general information, our inference will be incorrect. It is thus a good idea to ask whether information was derived from a representative sample or whether the sample size was too small or not inclusive enough to be considered representative. Unrepresentative samples can lead to overgeneralizing.

Correlation   A **correlation** is a consistent relationship between two or more variables. An example of a positive correlation is that as you grow older, your ears grow larger. In this case, a correlation exists between age and ear size. However, a correlation is not necessarily a cause—that is, old age does not cause larger ears, but growth processes do. Another common correlation is that the death penalty decreases the instance of crime. However, no significant evidence exists that this is the case. In fact, Stephen Jay Gould finds that "the vast majority of correlations in our world are, without a doubt, noncausal."[44]

To avoid the problems associated with inferential errors, ask the following questions:

1. Is the evidence sufficient to draw the inference?
2. Is the evidence the best available?
3. Is the evidence recent?
4. Is the evidence relevant to the inference? Does it really prove the claim?
5. Is the evidence one-sided? Is there contradictory information?
6. Can you verify the facts? How do you know that what is said is actually true?
7. Are the sources of the information reliable?
8. Are the sources of the information authorities for the subject? Are the authorities trustworthy or biased?
9. Is the statistical sample representative of the whole? Is the sample size adequate?
10. Is the example typical or is it an exception?
11. Is the relationship only a correlation or is it causal?[45]

Other Perceptual Errors

In additional to perceptual mind-sets, other common barriers exist that can contribute to inaccurate perceptions. Beware of the following:

- **Oversimplifying.** People tend to prefer simplicity over complexity because it takes less effort.
- **Imposing consistency.** Because we look for patterns, we may impose consistency where it doesn't exist.
- **Focusing on the negative.** People tend to focus more on the negative than the positive. Experiments have shown that if just one negative characteristic is included in a list of personal attributes, people will rank the person being

correlation
A consistent relationship between two or more variables.

described significantly lower than if the negative characteristic wasn't included.

- **Making a fundamental attribution error.** When other people fail, we assume it was their fault—but when they succeed, we assume it was the situation that determined their success.
- **Exhibiting a self-serving bias.** Similar to the fundamental attribution error, we assume that our successes result from our personal qualities but that our failures result from circumstances beyond our control.

Thinking Styles

In addition to perceptual challenges, the way we process information can affect our ability to think well and make good decisions. For example, we can process information in one of two ways: We can absorb it like a sponge, or we can filter it. Perhaps the more common way of processing information is by absorbing it. This process is passive and requires little thinking. Although the advantage of this process is that it enables you to absorb a lot of information, the disadvantage is that it provides you with no method to decide whether information is valid or useful.

In contrast, the filter method provides you a way of processing information more actively, effectively giving you a choice in what you absorb and what you ignore. Using the filter model requires that you ask questions about the material being presented. Your mission is to critically evaluate the material and formulate personal conclusions based on that evaluation. In other words, critical thinking should be applied. **Critical thinking**, as defined by the National Council for Excellence in Critical Thinking, is as follows:

> *The intellectually disciplined process of actively and skillfully conceptualizing, applying, analyzing, synthesizing, and/or evaluating information gathered from, or generated by, observation, experience, reflection, reasoning, or communication, as a guide to belief and action. In its exemplary form, it is based on universal intellectual values that transcend subject matter divisions: clarity, accuracy, precision, consistency, relevance, sound evidence, good reasons, depth, breadth, and fairness. It entails the examination of those structures or elements of thought implicit in all reasoning: purpose, problem, or question-at-issue, assumptions, concepts, empirical grounding; reasoning leading to conclusions, implications and consequences, objections from alternative viewpoints, and frame of reference.*[46] *(www.criticalthinking .org, 2009)*

critical thinking
The intellectually disciplined process of actively and skillfully conceptualizing, applying, analyzing, synthesizing, and/or evaluating information gathered from, or generated by, observation, experience, reflection, reasoning, or communication as a guide to belief and action.

Critical thinkers actively seek alternative hypotheses, explanations, conclusions, and sources and are open to them. They endorse a position only to the extent that the information justifies it. They are well-informed and consider seriously points of view other than their own.[47]

There is also an ethical component to critical thinking. In other words, critical thinkers communicate a position honestly and clearly: theirs as well as that of others. This means that they are reflectively aware of their own basic beliefs and care about the dignity and worth of every person. It requires that they discover and listen to others' views and reasons, avoid intimidating or confusing others with their critical-thinking prowess, and take into account others' feelings and level of understanding. You should notice by now that this ethical component mirrors some of the concerns of the dialogic model.

In addition, to be a critical thinker requires that we are able to deal with ambiguity. When evaluating information, it is helpful to recognize that no single correct answer exists for many contemporary issues. Because our world is a complex place, many points of views and perspectives have valid points. Depending on the broader goal or a person's value system, choosing the best solution can be a difficult process.

Emotions can also get in the way of our ability to evaluate information fairly and accurately. Emotions can get in the way of our ability to be open to all the relevant information and to weigh that information as objectively and thoroughly as it deserves, especially if the information doesn't correspond with our core values and beliefs. In other words, our self-concept or identities can get in the way of our ability to think critically.

Finally, it is important to ask, "Who cares?" Because we are human beings, we often have personal interests at stake in the arguments that we make. Therefore, it is useful to ask yourself the following: Who will benefit from certain perspectives or proposals? Is the information that is presented colored by that perspective? Is this a one-sided argument? If so, what is the other side of the issue, and does it offer information potentially valuable for good decision making?

Learning how to evaluate information critically can help us to better gather information on which to base decisions that may affect our career and life choices. Such skill is critical to being a strategic communicator. It can also help us to achieve a critical goal of business communication: establishing our credibility by highlighting our cognitive abilities, a common characteristic of those recognized as leaders.

Summary

Three models have historically been used to explain the communication process. They are communication as information transfer, communication as transactional process, and communication as strategic control. A fourth model, the dialogic model of communication, better meets the needs of today's organizations because it recognizes the growing importance of interpersonal relationships on our own success and happiness in the workplace as well as in our personal lives. According to the dialogic model, the strategies that we use to communicate must take into account how our messages affect others' perception of us as well as the effect of our communication on others. The dialogic model also highlights the inherently ethical nature of communication and helps address the challenges of communicating with others from different cultures.

Perception involves the use of our senses to interpret our surroundings. Because the perceptual process is based on interpretation, it introduces opportunities for misunderstanding as we communicate with others. It is thus foundational to an understanding of the communication process. It is also important to understand that others may perceive us in ways that we do not intend; for this reason, it is important to be sensitive to those interpretations and to use our strategic-communication skills to ensure that we are being perceived as we intend or hope. The way that we think about ourselves and an awareness of the self in terms of understanding are also important to our communication abilities. It is through self-understanding that we begin to understand others, a critical part of the dialogic model that is the foundation of this text.

However, perceptual mind-sets and our thinking style can get in the way of our ability to be strategic yet ethical communicators. Our perceptual mind-sets are affected by several practices that limit our ability to consider information thoroughly and objectively. These include confirmation bias, false dichotomies, and inferential errors. In addition to perceptual challenges, the way that we process information can affect our ability to think well and make good decisions. We can process information in one of two ways: We can absorb it like a sponge, or we can filter it. The filter method provides you a way of processing information more actively, effectively giving you a choice in what you absorb and what you ignore. Using the filter model requires that you ask questions about the material being presented. Your mission is to critically evaluate the material and formulate personal conclusions based on that evaluation. In other words, critical thinking should be applied.

Key Terms

dialogic model of communication, 30

dialogue, 30

monologue, 30

egocentric, 31

plurality, 31

intercultural communication, 31

perception, 32

stereotyping, 33

projected cognitive similarity, 33

outgroup homogeneity effect, 34

attribution, 34

impression formation, 34

self-concept, 35

self-fulfilling prophecy, 36

self-awareness, 36

intrapersonal communication, 36

intrapersonal intelligence, 36

reflexivity, 36

interpersonal intelligence, 36

self-esteem, 37

emotional intelligence, 37

perceptual mind-sets, 41

confirmation bias, 41

false dichotomy, 42

inference, 42

correlation, 43

critical thinking, 44

Discussion Questions

1. Explain each of the four models of communication and what distinguishes them, including their strengths and weaknesses. Why might the dialogic model better meet the needs of today's workplace?
2. Identify examples of moral exclusion and describe the intent and effect of their use. Based on this analysis, discuss whether such practices are ethical. Support your response with evidence.
3. How have differing perceptions affected your communication with others? What steps might you take to avoid misunderstandings created by perceptual differences?
4. What are three different errors that may occur due to our perceptual mind-sets? How might these be avoided?
5. What are some examples of black-and-white, or dichotomous, thinking from recent news reports or opinion columns you have seen or read? What other possibilities might exist to broaden the views or options presented in these reports?
6. What are the benefits of thinking critically?

Applications

1. Use a SWOT (strengths, weaknesses, opportunities, threats) analysis to determine your career goals. This is an exercise in analysis, evaluation, and, ultimately, strategic thinking. First, identify the opportunities available to you and their corresponding possible risks; second, identify your strengths and weaknesses; third, identify the resources available to you to attain these opportunities; and fourth, match the opportunities available to you with those that are attainable. From this analysis should emerge an attainable career goal. It should also help you to identify personal characteristics that you might leverage in a career search as well as those liabilities for which you might set goals to eliminate or reduce.
2. Using the Internet, search for free online self-assessments of emotional intelligence, locus of control, leadership traits, and self-monitoring. One place to start is at www.queendom.com. After completing the assessments and reading the results, summarize them and then write three goals for self-improvement for each personality measure, including your plan for achieving each of them.
3. Using YouTube, identify examples of persons who you think exemplify a leader. Make a list of your observations: What does the person do that exemplifies leadership? You might look at the way he or she speaks, looks, or behaves. From this list, what traits of a leader did you infer from your observation? What did you notice about the way this person communicated? Set some personal goals for yourself to help you to begin to incorporate the traits you identified in your own communication practices.
4. Choose a culture that differs from your own and then describe your beliefs and attitudes about and perceptions of this culture. Now conduct research to find out as much about the culture and its values, beliefs, and practices as you can. You may also wish to interview someone from this culture, if the opportunity is available. After learning more about the culture, what misperceptions did you hold about it? Has your researched changed your attitudes and beliefs about the culture?

Case Study
Kaplan University: The Business of Education

When Donald Graham, CEO of the Washington Post Company, learned that Bennie Wilcox had filed a whistle-blower lawsuit accusing Kaplan University of myriad unethical and illegal practices, he may not have initially believed he had much reason to worry. After all, Wilcox, Kaplan's former dean of

Law and Legal Studies, was currently being indicted for six felony counts of hacking and e-mail harassment against the *Washington Post* subsidiary.[48] His credibility seemed questionable at best, and Kaplan's legal department was well equipped to handle the charges. However, it quickly became apparent that the accusations leveled by Wilcox and others had set off a chain of events leading to a serious reputational crisis.

By early 2011, Kaplan University was facing an array of allegations regarding fraudulent admissions practices, new federal regulations that could undermine its business, and intense media scrutiny about the value of its courses and the amount of debt carried by its students.

This criticism was fueled by the notion that for-profit schools put their shareholders'[49] interests ahead of students' through an overemphasis on increasing enrollment at all costs. The for-profit sector of the education industry had faced these criticisms for years, and the pressure on Kaplan was intensifying.

False Claims Act Lawsuits

In 2007, several former employees, beginning with Bennie Wilcox, began approaching the Justice Department to sue the company under the False Claims Act. The suits alleged a range of violations by company employees and admissions officers. Charges included:[50]

- Targeting unqualified students
- Exaggerating job prospects for graduates
- Falsifying grades to maintain financial aid
- Signing up "phantom" students to improve enrollment numbers

The False Claims Act creates an avenue for whistle-blowers to bring charges against companies that engage in wrongdoing. When suits are filed, whistle-blowers are protected from scrutiny as the documents are kept confidential until the Justice Department determines whether to move forward with charges.[51] When cases prove fraudulent collection of federal funds, companies are required to repay the government and whistle-blowers are entitled to a portion of recovered funds.[52]

Kaplan, Inc.

Stanley Kaplan founded Kaplan, Inc. from his basement in 1938 when he began tutoring students for standardized admissions tests that were beginning to gain popularity with American colleges and universities. At the time, some colleges viewed standardized testing as a means of limiting the number of immigrants and ethnic minorities admitted to their schools, with the assumption that applicants from supposedly less intelligent races would not excel on an exam to test critical reasoning skills and that they would not be able to study for an exam that did not rely on outside knowledge. Kaplan believed that standardized tests were, in fact, coachable and proved it as his test preparation business expanded to more than 150 nationwide testing centers over the next forty years. Throughout this growth, Kaplan continued to be passionate about his company's mission to open educational opportunities to people who would not otherwise have access to them.[53]

In 1994, Jonathan Grayer became the CEO of Kaplan, Inc. at the age of 29. Within a year, he made a series of aggressive moves to transform Kaplan from a small test prep company that was losing money into a major part of the Washington Post portfolio. In a move to consolidate control of the Kaplan brand and products, he ended the franchise contracts for over 150 independent test preparation centers and hired the center staff members as Kaplan employees,[54] increasing the Kaplan payroll from 500 to 5,000 virtually overnight. Grayer was succeeded by his COO Andrew Rosen in 2008.

Kaplan University

In 1998, Grayer and Rosen brought Kaplan into the for-profit higher education industry with the establishment of Concord Law School.[55] Two years later, Kaplan purchased Quest College and renamed it as Kaplan College. The re-branded school continued to expand through the development of online degree programs and the continued acquisitions of brick-and-mortar campuses and facilities. Between 2000 and 2004, Kaplan grew at a rate of about 40 percent per year. The acquisition of for-profit education institutions accounted for approximately two-thirds of this growth. In August 2004, Andrew Rosen was named president of Kaplan College. The following month, Kaplan began offering graduate degree programs and renamed itself as Kaplan University.[56]

Kaplan University provides flexible class scheduling and nontraditional course structures and uses technology such as online classes for degree and certificate programs. Its students tend to be

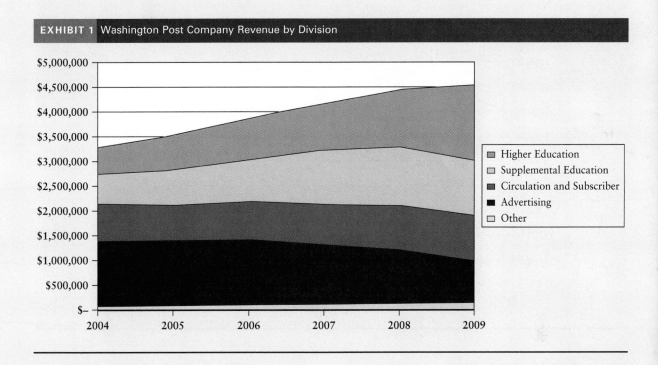

EXHIBIT 1 Washington Post Company Revenue by Division

low-income and nontraditional students for whom traditional higher education institutions are not a realistic option.

Today, Kaplan Higher Education is the second largest education company in the world.[57] It represents almost 60 percent of Kaplan's total revenue and about one-third of the Washington Post Company's total revenue (see Exhibits 1 & 2). In addition to its online degree programs, Kaplan has sixteen brick-and-mortar locations in eight different states.[58]

The Washington Post Company

Eugene Myer purchased the *Washington Post* newspaper out of bankruptcy in 1933 and published the paper until he was succeeded by his son-in-law Philip Graham in 1946. Although the Washington Post Company became a publicly traded firm in 1971, the Graham family still owns the majority of the company's shares and continues to play an important role in the company's leadership.

In 1984, Richard D. Simmons at the *Washington Post* approached Katharine Graham with the proposal to purchase Kaplan, Inc. as a means of diversifying the portfolio of the Washington Post Company. She was initially lukewarm about the

idea, but responded, "If you think it will be profitable, let's do it."[59] With the purchase, Kaplan became a fully owned subsidiary of the Washington Post Company, although it was a fairly minor part of the company's holdings for the next decade until Jonathan Grayer came from the *Washington Post* to take leadership of Kaplan in 1994.

As Kaplan became an increasingly important part of the Washington Post Company's revenue stream, the Post re-branded itself as a media and education company in 2004, and further recognized Kaplan's importance in 2007 when it re-branded itself as an education and media company with the tagline, "Informing People through Education and Media."

The For-Profit Education Industry

The for-profit sector of the education industry consists of companies that operate postsecondary colleges and universities and are also publicly traded companies. Major for-profit education providers include Apollo Group (the company that operates University of Phoenix), Washington Post Company, Career Education Corporation, and Corinthian.

For-profit colleges are criticized for their students' dire job prospects,[60] disproportionate

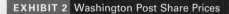

EXHIBIT 2 Washington Post Share Prices

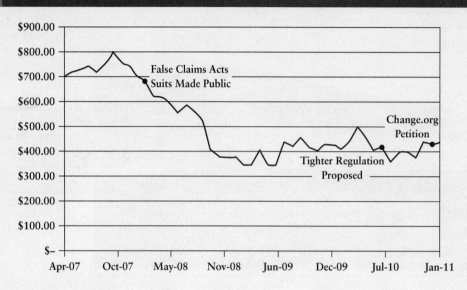

reliance on financial aid,[61] and high default rates on student loans. Critics also point out that for-profit schools devote the vast majority of their resources to marketing and recruiting as opposed to conducting research and training teachers. This implies that the schools put shareholder interests ahead of student interests.[62] These criticisms were supported when the Government Accountability Office conducted an undercover investigation of the admissions departments of fifteen for-profit colleges and found each school guilty of some fraudulent practice. Findings included schools exaggerating post-graduation salaries and school graduation rates.[63]

Senator Dick Durbin held a Congressional hearing in August 2010 to discuss marketing practices employed by schools as well as the high debt levels carried by students. Intense criticism has hurt shareholder value. On the day of the hearing, the *Wall Street Journal* reported that for-profit education stocks were down double-digits in 2010 when the rest of the market had rallied coming out of the recession.[64]

In addition to the cost of education and the resulting debt levels of students, the quality of the education itself has also come under fire. Since for-profit institutions tend to brand themselves as career-focused, they typically do not offer a broad general education. Several studies by the Government Accountability Office have found that occupation-specific training without a general education component puts graduates at a severe disadvantage for employment.[65]

Defenders of the for-profit model point out that the industry provides opportunities for an underserved segment of the population and that for-profit institutions have led innovation in technology practices used in colleges. They point to the role for-profit institutions play in providing access to education through aggressive outreach and flexibility.[66] Jeff Leshay, former SVP of Public Relations & Corporate Communications for Career Education Corporation (a top competitor of Kaplan), feels that for-profit educators need to do a better job of communicating their success stories. "When an industry is under fire, the most important thing is to be transparent. But to do that, you need good data, and this sector has not traditionally had a lot of data to track all its graduates. I think the sector has to continue to do a better job building relationships with graduates to track success 5–10 years down road and see how meaningful was education in terms of sustaining a meaningful career. Frankly the sector has a ways to go."

Proposed Regulation

Title IV of the Higher Education Act of 1965, as amended, establishes the Office of Federal Student Aid within the Department of Education. Under Title IV, the Office of Federal Student Aid administers federal grants, loans, and work study programs for students pursuing postsecondary education. The secretary of education has broad authority to set standards and regulations for schools that receive Title IV funds on behalf of their students.

On July 26, 2010, the Department of Education proposed a new federal rulemaking on Gainful Employment in response to the increased degree of public and governmental concern about the effectiveness of for-profit education institutions. Under the new rules, all postsecondary education institutions using Title IV programs would be evaluated based on their graduates' debt-to-income ratios and student loan repayment rates. Schools whose graduates did not meet minimum standards based on these metrics would no longer be eligible for Title IV funds.[67] For companies such as Kaplan who receive approximately 90 percent of their revenue from Title IV programs, these tighter regulations would represent significant threat to their continuing profitability.

Donald Graham responded to this threat by actively lobbying for the for-profit education industry on Capitol Hill. To make his case, he personally visited legislators, including Tom Harkin, chairman of the Senate Health, Education, Labor and Pensions Committee.[68]

Media Response

In the weeks following the release of the proposed rulemaking, the *New York Times*[69] and the *Los Angeles Times*[70] both ran editorials in support of the proposed rulemaking.

On August 22, 2010, the *Washington Post* published an editorial entitled, "How to Discourage College Students," decrying the new legislation as anti-student. The editorial argued, "… it's difficult to imagine achieving Mr. Obama's goal of 8 million more college graduates by 2020 if the for-profit sector is severely constricted" and that effect of the new rules would be to "deprive many working students of their best option for higher education—and to worsen the national problem that Mr. Obama has dedicated himself to solving."[71] Donald Graham also wrote an op-ed column for the *Wall Street Journal* in support of the for-profit education industry.[72]

Change.org Petition

As Kaplan's reputational crisis continued to slowly unfold in the legal system and the op-ed pages of major print newspapers, online social media outlets began to take interest, accelerating the spread of information.

On December 22, 2010, the *Huffington Post* posted an article highlighting some of the more serious accusations against Kaplan.[73] The same day, Change.org, a social networking site devoted to connecting users who care about the same social causes, published an article referencing the *Huffington Post* article and urging members to sign a petition entitled "Tell Kaplan and the *Washington Post*: Don't Steal From Students."[74] The article ended with a call for former Kaplan students and staffers to contact Change.org and share their story.

About one month later, after the initial petition had garnered fewer than 150 signatures, former Kaplan student Shannon Croteau posted a new petition aimed at Kaplan called, "Tell Kaplan & the *Washington Post*: Stop Cashing In On Low-Income Students." This petition included Shannon's personal story of accumulating $30,000 of debt in pursuit of a Kaplan degree that she later learned would not be valid in her home state of New Hampshire. This new petition went so far as to demand that the Washington Post Company make significant changes to Kaplan University's recruiting and enrollment practices, or shut down the higher education side of its business. Within two days of the petition's posting, over 7,000 people had signed. Over the next two months, the number grew to more than 40,000.[75] With each online signature, Change.org sends an automated email to Donald Graham and other members of the Kaplan leadership team.[76]

Unlike the editorials in major newspapers and blogs, or the debates on Capitol Hill, the Change.org petition ostensibly represented the voice of thousands of past, current, and potential customers. The need for decisive action had never been more critical.

Discussion Questions

1. Moving forward, how should the Washington Post Company communicate

   ■ To the public?
   ■ To investors?
   ■ To students?

2. Does the perception of conflict of interest damage the *Washington Post*'s credibility?
3. Should Kaplan University change its business model?
4. What can Kaplan University do to build more credibility for its academic programs?
5. What should be done by the Washington Post Company or Kaplan, Inc. in response to the online petition to close Kaplan University?
6. What steps can the Washington Post Company and Kaplan University take to prepare for future communications challenges?
7. Who are the key stakeholders?

Endnotes

1. Rosen, R., Digh, P., Singer, M., & Phillips, C. (2000). *Global literacies: Lessons on business leadership and national cultures.* New York: Simon & Schuster.
2. Conrad, C. (1985). Chrysanthemums and swords: A reading of contemporary organizational communication theory and research. *Southern Speech Communication Journal, 50,* 189–200; Eisenberg, E. M. (1984). Ambiguity as strategy in organizational communication. *Communication Monographs, 51,* 227–242; Weick, K. (1979). *The social psychology of organizing* (2nd ed.). Reading, MA: Addison-Wesley.
3. Frost, P., Moore, L., Louis, M., Lundberg, C., & Martin, J. (1991). *Reframing organizational culture.* Newbury Park, CA: Sage Publications.
4. Reardon, K. K. (2005). *It's all politics: Winning in a world where hard work and talent aren't enough.* New York: Doubleday.
5. Conrad, C. (1985). Chrysanthemums and swords: A reading of contemporary organizational communication theory and research. *Southern Speech Communication Journal, 50,* 189–200; Okabe, R. (1983). Cultural assumptions of east and west: Japan and the United States. In B. Gudykunst (Ed.), *International communication theory* (pp. 212–244). Newbury Park, CA: Sage Publications.
6. Barnlund, D. C. (1986). Toward a meaning-centered philosophy of communication. In J. Stewart (Ed.), *Bridges not walls: A book about interpersonal communication* (pp. 36–42). New York: Newbury Award Records.
7. Larson, C. U. (2004). *Persuasion: Reception and responsibility* (10th ed.). Belmont, CA: Wadsworth/Thomson Learning, p. 36.
8. Ibid., p. 36.
9. Barnlund, 1986, p. 41.
10. Ibid.
11. Ibid.
12. Ibid.
13. Eisenberg, E. M., & Goodall, Jr., H. L. (1993). *Organizational communication: Balancing creativity and constraint.* New York: St. Martin's Press.
14. Larson, 2004, p. 36.
15. Rogers, E. M., & Steinfatt, T. M. (1999). *Intercultural communication.* Prospects Height, IL: Waveland Press.
16. London, M., & Sessa, V. I. (1999). *Selecting international executives: A suggested framework and annotated bibliography.* Greensboro, NC: Center for Creative Leadership; Kuhleman & Stahl, 1996, 1998, reported in Stahl, G. K. (2001). Using assessment centers as tools for global leadership development: An exploratory study. In M. E. Mendenhall,

T. M. Kuhlmann, & G. K. Stahl (Eds.), *Developing global business leaders: Policies, processes and innovations* (pp. 197–210). Westport, CT: Quorum.

17. Varner, I. & Beamer, L. (2009). *Intercultural communication in the global workplace.* Thousand Oaks, CA: Sage.

18. Aritz, J. & Walker, R. (2012). The effects of leadership style on intercultural group communication in decision-making meetings. In P. Heynderickx, S. Dieltjens, G. Jacobs, P. Gillaerts, & E. D. Groot (Eds)., *The language factor in international business: New perspectives on research, teaching and practice. Linguistic insights series.* Bern: Peter Lang.

19. Varner, I. & Beamer, 2009.

20. Wood, J. T. (1997). *Communication theories in action.* Belmont, CA: Wadsworth.

21. Shedletsky, L. J. (1989). The mind at work. In L. J. Shedletsky (Ed.), *Meaning and mind: An intrapersonal approach to human communication.* Bloomington, IN: ERIC and the Speech Communication Association.

22. Gardner, H., & Krechevsky, M. (1993). *Multiple intelligences: The theory in practice.* New York: Basic Books.

23. Evered, R., & Tannebaum, R. (1992). A dialog on dialog. *Journal of Management Inquiry, 1,* 43–55, p. 45.

24. Robbins, S. P. (2001). *Organizational behavior* (9th ed.). Upper Saddle River, NJ: Prentice Hall.

25. Schoda, Y., Mischel, W. & Peake, P. K. (1990). Predicting adolescent cognitive and self-regulatory competencies from preschool delay of gratification. *Developmental Psychology, 26,* 978–986.

26. Earley. P. C., & Ang, S. (2003) *Cultural Intelligence.* Stanford University Press: Stanford, CA.

27. Chin, C. O., Gu, J. & Tubbs, S. (2001). Developing global leadership competencies. *Journal of Leadership Studies, 7(4),* 20–35.

28. Ibid.

29. Ibid.

30. Wurman, R. (1989). *Information anxiety.* New York: Doubleday, 1989.

31. Davidson, J. (1996). The shortcomings of the information age. *Vital Speeches, 62,* 495–503.

32. Rimer, S. (2011). Study: Many college students not learning to think critically. *The Hechinger Report.* Retrieved Feb. 1, 2013, from http://www.mcclatchydc.com/2011/01 /18/106949/study-many-college-students-not .html#storylink=cpy

33. Krathwohl, D. R. (2002). A revision of Bloom's taxonomy: An overview. *Theory into Practice, 41(4),* 212–218.

34. Paul. R. (1993). *Critical thinking: What every person needs to survive in a rapidly changing world, An anthology on critical thinking and educational reform* (3rd ed.). Tomales, CA: Foundation of Critical Thinking Press, p. 13.

35. Senge, P. (1990). *The fifth discipline.* New York: Doubleday Business.

36. Hunt, M. (1982). *The universe within: A new science explores the human mind.* New York: Simon and Schuster.

37. Janus, I. (1983). *Groupthink: Psychological studies of policy decisions and fiascos.* Boston MA: Houghton Mifflin, p. 10.

38. Postman, N. (1976). *Crazy talk, stupid talk.* New York: Dell.

39. Haslett, B., Geis, F. L., & Carter, M. R. (1992). *The organizational woman: Power and paradox.* Norwood, NJ: Ablex Publishing.

40. Rothwell, J. D. (1998). *In mixed company: Small group communication* (3rd ed.). Fort Worth, TX: Harcourt Brace College Publishers. p. 186.

41. DeVito, J. (1989). *The interpersonal communication book.* New York: Harper and Row.

42. Rothwell, 1998, p. 188.

43. Ibid.

44. Gould, S. J. (1981). *The mismeasure of man.* New York: W.W. Norton, p. 241.

45. Rothwell, 1998, p. 202.

46. Scriven, M., & Paul, R. (1987). Critical thinking defined. Presented at the 8th Annual International Conference on Critical Thinking and Education Reform, Summer 1987.

Retrieved Feb. 1, 2013, from http://www
.criticalthinking.org/pages/defining-critical
-thinking/766

47. Ennis, R. H. (2002). A super-streamlined conception of critical thinking. Retrieved June 29,
2009, from www.criticalthinking.net/.

48. Harris, A. M., & Deprez, E. E. (2010). Ex-
Kaplan legal dean convicted of e-mail, web
threats. *Bloomberg Businessweek*, December
10, 2010, http://www.businessweek.com/news
/2010-12-10/ex-kaplan-legal-dean-convicted-of
-e-mail-web-threats.html.

49. Gonzalez, J. (2010). Advocate for for-profit
colleges mounts a strong defense before Senate
hearing. *The Chronicle of Higher Education*,
June 23, 2010, http://chronicle.com/article
/For-Profit-Colleges-Mount-a/66027.

50. Lewin, T. (2010). Scrutiny takes toll on for-
profit college company. *The New York
Times*, November 9, 2010, http://www
.nytimes.com/2010/11/10/education/10kaplan
.html?_r=1&pagewanted=2.

51. Blumenstyk, G. (2008). 3 former employees
accuse Kaplan U. of bilking government out
of billions. *The Chronicle of Higher Education*, March 21, 2008, http://chronicle.com
/article/3-Former-Employees-Accuse/10495.

52. Andrews, E. L. (2006). Suits say U.S. impeded
audits for oil lease. *The New York Times*,
September 21, 2006, http://www.nytimes
.com/2006/09/21/business/21royalty.html.

53. Gladwell, M. (2001). Examined life: What
Stanley H. Kaplan taught us about the S.A.T.
The New Yorker, December 17, 2001.
Accessed through http://www.gladwell.com
/2001/2001_12_17_a_kaplan.htm.

54. Machan, D. (2000). Dr. Cram. *Forbes Magazine*, January 24, 2000. Accessed through
http://www.dyanmachan.com/grayer.html.

55. Concord Law School. "Law School History."
Accessed February 26, 2011, at http://info
.concordlawschool.edu/Pages/School_History
.aspx.

56. Kaplan University. "Fact Sheet." Accessed
February 26, 2011, at http://talent.kaplan
.edu/Assets/PDF/kaplanhistory.pdf.

57. Grayer, J. (2007). The Washington Post Company Shareholders Meeting. Fair Disclosure

Wire. September 20, 2007. Available through
http://goliath.ecnext.com/coms2/gi_0199
-9746899/The-Washington-Post-Company
-Shareholders.html.

58. Kaplan University. "Campus Learning at
Kaplan University." Accessed through http://
portal.kaplanuniversity.edu/Pages/MicroPortal
Home.aspx.

59. Adams, R., & M. Korn. (2010). For-profit
Kaplan U. hears its fight song. *The Wall Street
Journal*, August 30, 2010, http://www
.nytimes.com/2010/03/14/business/14schools
.html.

60. Goodman, P. S. (2010). In hard times, lured
into trade school and debt. *The New York
Times*, March 13, 2010, http://www.nytimes
.com/2010/03/14/business/14schools.html.

61. Lewin, T. (2010). Scrutiny takes toll on for-
profit college company. *The New York
Times*, November 9, 2010, http://www
.nytimes.com/2010/11/10/education/10kaplan
.html?_r=1.

62. New York Times Editorial Board. (2010).
Who profits? Who learns? *The New York
Times*, July 28, 2010, http://www.nytimes
.com/2010/07/29/opinion/29thu2.html.

63. Los Angeles Times Editorial Board. (2010).
New restrictions on for-profit colleges don't
seem strict enough. *Los Angeles Times*,
August 9, 2010, http://articles.latimes.com
/2010/aug/09/opinion/la-ed-college-20100809.

64. Zuckerman, G., & J. Strasburg. (2010). Not
all are true to schools—Investors differ over
prospects of for-profit education; hearing this
morning. *The Wall Street Journal*, August 31,
2010, http://online.wsj.com/article/SB100014
24052748704323704575462091376655542
.html.

65. Federal Register: July 26, 2010 (Volume 75,
Number 142) Proposed Rules, http://www2
.ed.gov/legislation/FedRegister/proprule/2010-3
/072610a.html.

66. Telephone conversation with Jeff Leshay, the
former SVP, Public Relations & Corporate
Communications for Career Education
Corporation, February 24, 2011.

67. Federal Register: July 26, 2010 (Volume 75,
Number 142) Proposed Rules, http://www2

.ed.gov/legislation/FedRegister/proprule/2010-3/072610a.html.

68. Watching a watchdog. *Inside Higher Ed*, August 24, 2010, http://www.insidehighered.com/news/2010/08/24/post.

69. New York Times Editorial Board. (2010). Who profits? Who learns?

70. Los Angeles Times Editorial Board. (2010). New restrictions on for-profit colleges don't seem strict enough.

71. The Washington Post Editorial Board. (2010). How to discourage college students. *The Washington Post*, August 22, 2010, http://www.washingtonpost.com/wp-dyn/content/article/2010/08/21/AR2010082102468.html.

72. Graham, D. E. (2011). Avoiding disaster for low-income students. *The Wall Street Journal*, January 14, 2011, http://online.wsj.com/article/SB10001424052748703583404576079781835777552.html.

73. Kirkham, C. (2010). At Kaplan University, 'guerilla registration' leaves students deep in debt. *The Huffington Post*, http://www.huffingtonpost.com/2010/12/22/kaplan-university-guerilla-registration_n_799741.html.

74. Scott, C. (2010). How the Washington Post helps rip off college students. Change.org at http://news.change.org/stories/how-the-washington-post-helps-kaplan-rip-off-students.

75. Change.org. (2011). Tell Kaplan & the Washington Post: Stop cashing in on low-income students. Change.org at http://www.change.org/petitions/tell-kaplan-the-washington-post-stop-cashing-in-on-low-income-students.

76. Quiznon, D. (2011). Disgruntled students petition Washington Post company to close Kaplan U. *The Chronicle of Higher Education*, January 27, 2011, http://www.change.org/petitions/tell-kaplan-the-washington-post-stop-cashingin-on-low-income-students.

michaeljung/Shutterstock.com

Step One: Identify the Purposes of Communication

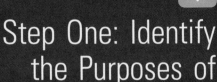

After reading this chapter, you will be able to

▶ Identify the four purposes of business communication: to inform, to convey goodwill, to establish credibility, and to persuade and influence.

▶ Begin to apply the four purposes of business communication in your communication practices.

Case Questions:

1. What is the role of communication in establishing the credibility of an employee? How does this credibility contribute to the overall reputation of the employer?

2. What is the role of communication in establishing long-term relationships with clients and customers? How does this take place in practice?

3. What is the role of credibility and trusted relationships in a firm's ability to influence its customers, clients, and other stakeholders?

The Case of Barnaby Consulting Corp.

Lincoln Frazer, director of recruiting for Barnaby Consulting Corp., has just come from a meeting with the directors of marketing and human resources. Marketing Director Martha Reynolds called the meeting to report that several clients have recently complained about the interpersonal skills of Barnaby's consultants. To help eliminate this problem, Martha has asked the human resources and recruiting directors to review their practices to make sure that Barnaby is hiring consultants with the needed skills to communicate with clients well and make sure that current consultants have sufficient training in building and maintaining excellent customer relations.

Barnaby Consulting Corp., a "boutique" firm, provides consulting services in the area of virtual management. Virtual management, brought about by the rise of the Internet, globalization, outsourcing, telecommuting, and virtual teams, is the management of widely dispersed groups and individuals, perhaps without ever meeting them face to face. Because of this, team leaders face challenges of coordinating work across different time zones and physical distance, of establishing effective working relationships in the absence of face-to-face communication, and of dealing with choices of appropriate technology and its use. In global virtual teams, the added dimension of cultural differences impacts a team's functioning. Barnaby's consultants' role is to provide solutions to clients to address these multifaceted challenges.

The challenge of identifying consultants with excellent communication skills is no news to Frazer. Because of young people's reliance on technology as a primary means of communication, Frazer has noticed a decline in their skills at and comfort with communicating face to face. This lack can impede their ability to maintain the reputation of Barnaby in their interactions with clients and to build the long-lasting relationships upon which many organizations depend for future business.

Four Purposes of Communication

This chapter deals with the first step in strategy formulation: identifying the purpose(s) of your communication so that you can more effectively plan and formulate your messages. Note that being an effective strategic communicator requires knowledge and specific skills: (1) self-awareness, (2) the willingness and ability to understand others, and (3) the ability to think critically. These were discussed in Chapter 2.

More than 2,000 years ago, Greek philosopher and writer Aristotle (384–322 B.C.E.) identified three purposes of communication: to inform, to persuade, and to entertain. Although entertainment is the purpose of much of the communication that occurs in American culture today, it is not emphasized in communication for business purposes. In fact, communication intended to entertain can have a negative effect on the relationship you have with others, or it can damage your credibility. For example, if you use humor in oral presentations or email messages at work, you take the risk of offending others who might not share your sense of humor or of creating an image of yourself as unprofessional. Some attempts at humor may even violate the law if they are considered racist, sexist, ageist, or otherwise discriminatory of others.

For these reasons, entertainment will not be considered one of the foundational purposes of communication in organizational settings. However, four purposes of communication still exist in the professional workplace:

- To inform
- To convey goodwill
- To establish credibility
- To persuade and influence

Many authors group the purpose of credibility and goodwill into a single category, but these have been separated in this text to emphasize the importance of both to communication and to help you better understand their nuances.

Communicating to Inform

When asked the purpose of communication, most of us respond with one simple answer: to inform. Our common sense tells us that we communicate to tell someone about something. To inform is to pass on information. In the world of work, you are informing when you explain something to your colleagues, your employees, or your customers and clients. If you tell an employee how to write a report, you are informing; if you tell a customer how to fill out a form, you are informing. You also inform when you tell another person what happened. Perhaps you received a phone call from a customer who is angry about his or her service, and you need to describe the call to your supervisor to learn what to do next. This situation is another example of communicating to inform.

Because most of us have been using the model of communication as information transfer for much of our lives, we assume we are experts at informing. Therefore, little space will be devoted to the purpose of communicating information in this text, although all the steps of strategy formulation can be applied to informative messages. For example, you should analyze your audience to make sure that you are delivering the information that it needs and wants, consider the context of the communication, and use the channel or medium of communication that is best suited for your purpose and your audience's preferences. These strategic issues will be discussed more in the chapters that follow.

Communicating to Convey Goodwill

According to *Merriam-Webster's Collegiate Dictionary*, **goodwill** has three definitions: "1. friendly disposition; kindly regard; benevolence. 2. cheerful acquiescence or consent. 3. an intangible, salable asset arising from the reputation of a business and its relations with its customers." For those of you who have taken accounting courses, you are probably familiar with the third definition of goodwill; in business contexts, goodwill is considered an asset. As a purpose of business communication, goodwill can be thought of as the ability to create and maintain positive, productive relationships with others and can be viewed as an intangible asset as well.

CriticalThinking

Think about a time that you were unsuccessful at persuasion. Why were you unsuccessful? In retrospect, in terms of your communication approach what could you have done differently to have improved your chances of succeeding?

As discussed earlier, Conger (1998) has studied how individuals use language to motivate people. His research indicates that people with high credibility on the relationship side, that is, goodwill, have demonstrated that they can be trusted to listen and to work in the best interests of others. Recognition of the value of conveying and maintaining goodwill in organizational settings is one important way of compensating for one of the weaknesses of the strategic control model: narrowly pursuing your own interests without regard to others.

If you have work experience, you understand the practical value of relationships in organizational settings. Establishing and maintaining relationships with others, or **networking**, is one of the most successful forms of job hunting, for example. Likewise, the best form of advertisement is word of mouth, not only because it is inexpensive, but also because people are more likely to trust the judgment of those they already know. When working with others or in groups, people are more likely to cooperate with those they know, like, and trust.

Having a positive relationship with another person or being an expert in a relevant field often enables us to be more successful at persuasion. As long ago as the middle of the fourth century B.C.E., Aristotle made this assertion in *On Rhetoric*. For Aristotle, the problem of communication essentially boiled down to seeing the available means of persuasion in each particular case. According to Aristotle, to persuade successfully, communicators must know the extent to which they enjoy the trust, respect, and affection of the people with whom they are communicating. Aristotle recognized that the importance of the character of the speaker (or writer) is a legitimate concern in effective communication.

From an organizational perspective, relationships can play an important role in producing effective supervision, promoting social support among employees, building personal influence, and ensuring productivity through smooth work flow. The need for good interpersonal relationships in organizations is particularly important from both the standpoint of the individual, who requires social support in an

goodwill
In the business communication context, the ability to create and maintain positive, productive relationships with others.

networking
Establishing and maintaining relationships with others.

increasingly turbulent world, and the standpoint of the organization, which must maintain high levels of cooperation among employees to meet customer demands and remain competitive.

Trust

As discussed in Chapter 1, the recent flattening of organizational hierarchies and resulting interdependence of work tasks among employees, as well as the increasing diversity of the workplace, requires corporate cultures of trust built on respect for differences and mutual cooperation. Informal interpersonal relationships and communication networks are the most dynamic sources of power in organizations today.[1] (Communication networks are discussed in more detail in Chapter 5, "Steps Three and Four: Consider the Context and Select Channels of Communication.") In contrast, more formal relationships are slower and less trustworthy sources of information. Most decision makers rely heavily on verbal information from people they trust.

Interpersonal skills and the ability to work well in a team are frequently cited as the top characteristics that recruiters find most attractive in prospective employees. These skills and abilities are founded on trust. **Trust** can be understood as the confidence that our peers' intentions are good.[2] In other words, we must believe that those with whom we work will not act opportunistically or take advantage of us and others to narrowly pursue their own self-interest.

Studies indicate that trust is a complex concept consisting of five components: integrity, competence, consistency, loyalty, and openness (see Figure 3-1).[3] *Integrity* refers to a person's ethical character and basic honesty. To feel that our

trust
The confidence that others' intentions are good.

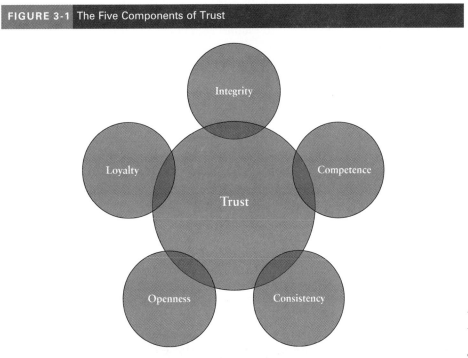

FIGURE 3-1 The Five Components of Trust

© Cengage Learning

peers are *competent*, we must be convinced that they have the technical knowledge and interpersonal skills required to perform their jobs. If you don't believe a coworker is competent, then you are unlikely to depend on that person or respect his or her opinion on work-related matters. We are more able to trust those who appear *consistent* in their behavior or who are reliable, predictable, and demonstrate good judgment. We tend to trust others who are *loyal* and willing to protect and help others to save face. Finally, we tend to trust those who are *open*; conversely, we find it difficult to trust those who appear evasive, deceptive, or secretive.

Interpersonal Communication Styles

Additional factors affect our ability to forge the relationships businesspeople depend on: valuing relationships, assertiveness, and active listening.[4] The first step in building interpersonal relationships at work is learning to *recognize the importance of relationships* in business, if you haven't already done so. For many individuals, interpersonal communication *is* the work, particularly among managers and leaders.

The importance of *assertiveness* becomes obvious when you consider alternative communication styles. On one hand, the avoiding, passive-aggressive individual whines, complains, and frets about problems at work but says nothing when asked directly what is wrong.[5] This strategy, known as **avoidance**, is defined as a conscious attempt to avoid engaging with people in the dominant group.[6] Avoidance is also considered *passive*, an attempt to separate by having as little to do with the dominant group as possible. The result of an avoiding, passive approach is a consistent inability to raise and resolve problems, needs, issues, and concerns.

At the other extreme, aggressive individuals sabotage their ability to meet their needs and to establish supportive relationships by creating defensiveness and alienating others.[7]

Aggressiveness is a series of behaviors and characteristics that include hurtful expressiveness, self-promotion, attempts to control others, and argumentativeness.[8] Aggressive individuals, also described as argumentative, are not only more aggressive but also more insecure and less likely to be well regarded or happy at work.[9]

In contrast to avoidance and aggression, **assertiveness** is defined as "self-enhancing, expressive communication that takes into account both the communicator's and others' needs."[10] Assertiveness clearly involves articulating what you want from others in terms of behavior while remaining sensitive to the effect of your words and actions on others. It is direct but not attacking or blaming. Assertiveness is associated with positive impressions and overall good quality of work experience.

Like assertiveness, *listening* is a learned skill and one that very few individuals ever master. Talking to someone who really knows how to listen actively makes you feel valued, important, and free to speak your mind.[11] (Active listening is discussed in more detail in Chapter 8, "Communicating with Employees.") In an ideal communication situation, assertiveness and active listening go hand in hand as people are able to express their own perceptions and desires and at the same time attend to those of others. As you may recognize, these two skills

avoidance
The strategy of knowingly avoiding engagement with those in the dominant group.

aggressiveness
Asserting one's rights and needs at the expense of others through hurtful expression, self-promotion, attempts to control others, and argumentativeness.

assertiveness
Self-enhancing, expressive communication that takes into account one's own needs as well as those of others.

Michael Blann/Digital Vision/Getty Images

are the foundation of the dialogic model of communication introduced in Chapter 2. They are also important if we are to influence others or to demonstrate leadership.

Communicating to Establish Credibility

Aristotle recognized that the importance of the character of the speaker—or writer—is a legitimate concern in effective communication. In our time, when the facts are often complex and hard to determine for ourselves—and when television, cell phones, video, the Internet, and other technologies bring speakers "up close and personal" for our inspection—the importance of credibility has been magnified several times beyond that of ancient Greece.

Credible people demonstrate that they have strong emotional character and integrity; they are known to be honest, steady, and reliable. Credibility is akin to reputation at the organizational level. Sophisticated customers do not make financial decisions based solely on an organization's competitive advantage in the marketplace.[12] Instead, customers are increasingly sensitive to a company's reputation. In fact, public relations developed as a functional area to manage the reputations of companies.

Just as an organization understands that its reputation and image can affect its successful continuation, savvy employees are aware that these same concepts can be applied in their own careers. One study indicates that 92 percent of more than 2,300 executives said that if a person loses credibility with them, it would be very difficult to gain it back.[13]

To make matters worse, most managers overestimate their own credibility considerably.[14] In the worst-case scenario, they may revert to the old command-and-control style of leadership, which studies have shown damages productivity and morale in skilled, well-educated workers and creates frustrated, silenced employees who steal all the pencils and sabotage the company's computer system. Not understanding or ignoring the importance of credibility may ultimately lead to a Machiavellian game of terror and threats in which strong tactics of domination and control are used to gain influence rather than softer, less-destructive methods.

Factors that help to build credibility include the following (Figure 3-2):

- Expertise and competence
- Personal ethics and integrity, or trustworthiness
- Control of emotions
- Development and maintenance of a professional image

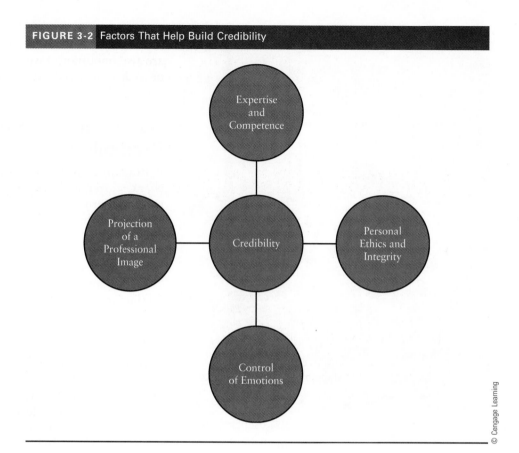

FIGURE 3-2 Factors That Help Build Credibility

© Cengage Learning

Expertise and Competence

Clearly, your relevant job knowledge and ability to perform your job well affect your credibility. Skill levels and competency are also important for the effective functioning and performance of small groups and teams. Attitude and personality characteristics can also improve your reputation as a competent, conscientious employee. For example, those who complain without offering solutions to the problem are perceived more negatively than those who discuss problems in terms of their solutions. The former may be seen as whiners, whereas the latter become known as problem solvers. These perceptions contribute to your overall image within a company and may help or detract from your ability to establish yourself as a leader.

Competence also extends to communication skills. Speaking correctly and being articulate generally enhance our credibility by indicating to others that we are well educated and intelligent. The same goes for our written communication. If our written messages are full of errors, then we may be perceived as undereducated, lazy, or not detail oriented. All of these negative judgments can affect our credibility. For example, a résumé or letter with a grammatical error eliminates a job applicant from further consideration. Likewise, consistent problems producing correct writing or speaking articulately may eliminate an employee from a position working with external audiences, where his or her communication skills may negatively affect the reputation of the organization.

This recognition provides an opportunity for those who can communicate well in today's competitive business environment. In other words, one way you can positively distinguish yourself from others is by demonstrating excellent communication skills. Employees who can write clearly and speak articulately can create a better impression of a firm with customers, suppliers, and outsiders than can any public relations program ever devised.

CriticalThinking

What competencies and areas of expertise do you possess that can help you build your feelings of confidence as well as your credibility with professional audiences? What skills in communication can help you do the same?

Effective communication skills have become crucial for both personal performance and organizational productivity. With the proliferation of personal computing, more and more employees at all levels in the company are producing written messages that represent an organization, and the quality of this material can have a significant effect on both perceptions and performance. Technology has also created a problem of exposure. Voice mail, email, text messaging, blogs, social media, audio/video conferencing, and other technologies expose businesses to an ever-growing array of diverse audiences.

Email is a particular problem because of its wide use. "Your company's voice is often judged by what pops into your client's inbox. That first impression better be a good one," says Adam Chandler, national account director for Yahoo![15] Jonathan Herschberg, a communications developer based in New York, says, "If I get an e-mail that's full of errors and I know nothing else about you, there's no reason for me not to think you'll handle my business in the same way you handled that writing."[16]

CriticalThinking

Discuss your greatest challenges in achieving grammatical correctness and precise word choice in your written and oral communication. Have these affected your confidence or your credibility with your communication audiences? Have you taken steps to become more correct and thus more confident in your written and oral communication? If not, what steps might you take?

Personal Ethics and Integrity

In addition to interpersonal skills and the ability to work in teams, personal ethics and integrity are among the top five characteristics sought by recruiters. The attractiveness of ethical employees may be a result of the continuing problems of unethical and illegal practices by U.S. businesses. This renewed concern with ethics began in the 1990s and early 2000s due to the illegal accounting practices of such companies as Enron, WorldCom, and Tyco, and has continued today with the recent concerns about the legality and ethics of the practices of the world's largest financial institutions, practices that have resulted in the most severe recession since the Great Depression of the 1920s.

The causes of such unethical behavior have been widely studied. For example, Lehman and DuFrene (2008) claim unethical behavior stems from a number of causes, including the following:

- Excessive emphasis on profits by managers. According to former Federal Reserve Chairman Alan Greenspan, "infectious greed" ultimately pushed companies such as Enron, Global Crossing, and WorldCom into bankruptcy. Greed has also been blamed for the recent debacle in the financial sector.
- A misplaced sense of corporate loyalty may cause an employee to do what seems in the best interest of the corporation, even if it is illegal or unethical.
- An obsession by employees to gain personal advancement.
- An expectation that illegal or unethical actions will not be caught.
- An unethical tone set by top management.
- Uncertainty about whether an action is wrong.
- Unwillingness to take a stand for what is right.

Eisenberg and Goodall (1993) claim that another possible related reason for unethical communication behavior may be the increased pressure to compete. The increasing complexity of organizations may also lead to lies or distortion, turf building, and cover-up.[17]

Terence Mitchell and William Scott (1990) attribute unethical behavior to the United States' "ethic of personal advantage." This ethic has three themes:

1. A present versus future orientation
2. An instrumental as opposed to a substantive focus
3. An emphasis on individualism contrasted with community

Other scholars agree with this assessment. For example, Eisenberg and Goodall (1993) state that the "greatest weakness of businesspeople in the past two decades has been short-term thinking, or the willingness to trade off long-term value for immediate gain."[18]

Likewise, in his study of the Los Angeles riots, Michael Lerner (1992) contends that the looters were merely "living out the cynical American ethos." Lerner claims that we live in a culture of looting in which the highest goal is to "look out for number one" and to "get what you can when you can."[19] This assessment echoes that of Mitchell and Scott, who advance the case that unethical behavior is caused in part by an emphasis on individualism and instrumentalism.

> *Any cost to others is acceptable as long as you don't get caught or don't hurt your own future chances…. Within this ethos, concern for the future—of the planet, of one's own country or even of one's own children—seems naive and silly, something to be left to "do-gooders." The ethos of looting is the "common sense" of the society.*[20]

The unethical practices of corporations and their employees can have far-reaching consequences. Those affected by the decisions, the *stakeholders*, can include people inside and outside the organization. Financial markets can suffer from an erosion of public confidence. With globalization, this erosion has negative repercussions for the entire world, as evidenced by the recent world financial crisis.

Leaders may unintentionally make unethical decisions because they lack the necessary knowledge, skills, and experience. Not understanding how to go about making ethical decisions can be an issue, as can ignorance of ethical perspectives that

Table 3-1 Milestones for Assessing Ethical Competence.

Greater self-awareness	Greater self-understanding should help you develop a clearer grasp of your values and moral blind spots.
Greater self-confidence	Greater self-confidence should help you shoulder the heavier ethical burdens that come with increased responsibility.
Stronger character	Character consists of displaying admirable qualities in a variety of settings.
Healthy moral imagination	Expanding ethical capacity will make you aware of a wider array of ethical problems and help you develop creative solutions grounded in moral principles.
Sounder moral reasoning	Rejecting faulty assumptions, gathering information, building arguments, and taking a systematic approach to problem solving are part of reasoned ethical decision making.
Greater resistance to outside pressure	Resisting group, organizational, and cultural pressures to set aside moral principles is an integral part of a moral bearing.
Better follow-through	Holding good values and making choices based on those values leads to more ethical decision making.
Healthier ethical climate	Expanding ethical capacity means working to change the climate of your small group, organization, and community for the better.

Source: Adapted from Johnson, C., & Hackman, M. Z. (2002). "Assessing Ethical Competence." Paper presented at the meeting of the National Communication Association, Atlanta (November).

can be applied to ethical dilemmas. Table 3-1 provides a list of milestones for developing ethical competence.

As the information in the table implies, integrity is the ability to adhere to a strong set of moral or ethical principles regardless of the situation or the pressures that come to bear. Leaders with integrity inspire confidence that they can be trusted to do what they say they are going to do. They are loyal, dependable, and not deceptive.

Making and implementing ethical decisions takes both critical thinking and communication skills. (Chapter 2 explained steps in the critical thinking process.) In addition to displaying integrity, you can do something to ensure that your communication is ethical. Putting ethical practices first will not only benefit your employer, colleagues, clients, and customers but also enable you to maintain your credibility and create a reputation of fairness and good judgment that can enhance your ability to communicate and succeed in your career goals.

In Table 3-2, you will find the "Nine Commandments" of the National Communication Association that help to ensure ethical communication practices.

As was discussed previously, communication is inherently ethical. This is because whenever people interact with one another, ethics invades every exchange because the manipulation of symbols involved in language use also involves a purpose that is external to, and in some degree manipulative of, the audience for or interpreter of the message.[21] Communication thus can be intended to prevent, restrict, or stimulate the cultivation of meaning. In the first case, messages can be intended to coerce others by choosing symbols that are threatening to the audience or interpreter of the message. The values of the listener are ignored in this type of

Table 3-2 The National Communication Association Credo for Communication Ethics.

Questions of right and wrong arise whenever people communicate. Ethical communication is fundamental to responsible thinking, decision making, and the development of relationships and communities within and across contexts, cultures, channels, and media. Moreover, ethical communication enhances human worth and dignity by fostering truthfulness, fairness, responsibility, personal integrity, and respect for self and others. We believe that unethical communication threatens the quality of all communication and consequently the well-being of individuals and the society in which we live. Therefore, we, the members of the National Communication Association, endorse and are committed to practicing the following principles of ethical communication:

- We advocate truthfulness, accuracy, honesty, and reason as essential to the integrity of communication.
- We endorse freedom of expression, diversity of perspective, and tolerance of dissent to achieve the informed and responsible decision making fundamental to a civil society.
- We strive to understand and respect other communicators before evaluating and responding to their messages.
- We promote access to communication resources and opportunities as necessary to fulfill human potential and contribute to well-being of families, communities, and society.
- We promote communication climates of caring and mutual understanding that respect the unique needs and characteristics of individual communicators.
- We condemn communication that degrades individuals and humanity through distortion, intimidation, coercion, and violence, and through the expression of intolerance and hatred.
- We are committed to the courageous expression of personal convictions in pursuit of fairness and justice.
- We advocate sharing information, opinions, and feelings when facing significant choices while also respecting privacy and confidentiality.
- We accept responsibility for the short- and long-term consequences of our own communication and expect the same of others.

© Cengage Learning

communication. In the second, messages can be intended to exploit by arranging words to filter information, narrow the choices, or obscure the consequences so that only one meaning becomes attractive or appropriate. The values of the listener are subverted in this type of message. Finally, messages can be facilitative. In such communication, words are used to inform, enlarge perspective, deepen sensitivity, remove external threat, or encourage independence of meaning.[22] The values of the listener are respected in this type of interaction.

Just as certain communicative behaviors are considered ethical, it is easy to identify those that are considered unethical. W. Charles Redding (1991) has developed the typology of unethical messages in organizations shown in Table 3-3.

Because of the potential for unethical communication practices, both senders and receivers of messages hold responsibilities. Responsible communicators carefully analyze claims, assess probable consequences, and weigh relevant values.[23] In addition, responsible communicators exercise the ability to respond and are responsive to the needs and communication of others in sensitive, thoughtful, and fitting ways.[24] More specifically, both parties in an interaction bear mutual responsibility for active participation, which occurs through two steps: reasoned skepticism and appropriate feedback.

Table 3-3 Typology of Unethical Messages.

TYPE	EXAMPLES
Coercive	An employee criticizes the boss's "pet" development program in a meeting and is fired on the spot for her remarks.
Destructive	A supervisor makes a sexist joke at the expense of an employee.
Deceptive	Federal Aviation Administration employees falsify employee work records to justify the firing of air-traffic controllers during their 1981 strike.
Intrusive	Electronic surveillance of employees is conducted through hidden video cameras.
Secretive	Some investment firms suppressed information about the value of commercial mortgage-backed securities.
Manipulative or Exploitative	Management threatens union members with a plant closing if they don't ratify a contract.

Source: Adapted from Redding, W. C. (1991). "Unethical Messages in the Organizational Context." Paper presented at the Annenberg Convention of the ICA, Chicago.

ResponsibleCommunication

Have you been on the receiving end of the types of unethical messages listed in Table 3-3? How did you feel? What might be appropriate responses to such unethical communication practices?

Messages can be used to harm or mislead others.

In particular, persuasive messages always contain the potential for unethical practices. This is because persuasion involves the following:

- a person or group attempting to influence others by altering their beliefs, attitudes, values, and overt actions;
- conscious choices among ends sought and means used to achieve those ends; and
- a potential judge (any and all receivers of the message).

Reasoned skepticism involves actively searching for meaning, analyzing and synthesizing information, and judging its soundness and worth. **Appropriate feedback** requires that you are honest and reflect your true understanding and judgments. However, such feedback should also be appropriate for the subject, audience, and occasion or context—primary elements of business communication strategy.

reasoned skepticism
The process of actively searching for meaning, analyzing and synthesizing information, and judging the worth of that information.

Emotional Control

Employees are expected to maintain a professional demeanor while in the office or when they represent their office in the field. Part of our ability to accomplish that goal often has to do with our ability to control our emotions. According to a study done by the University of Missouri–Columbia, "many employees do not want their coworkers to express any type of strong emotion—positive or negative."[25] In this study, the employees were asked to describe situations in which they believed their coworkers acted appropriately and inappropriately. The consensus of the employees was that negative emotion should never be expressed, and positive emotion should be shown in moderation.

Expressions of negative emotions, such as fear, anxiety, and anger, tend to be unacceptable except under fairly specific conditions. For example, verbalized anger is direct, aggressive, and intentional. When people allow anger to control their communication, the results are generally unproductive. Outbursts of anger tend to make others uncomfortable, especially when irrational forms of anger are exhibited. If construed as harassment in the workplace, excessive displays of anger can lead to disciplinary measures. Outbursts of anger may also be interpreted by others as a sign of a lack of self-control, which might negatively affect our credibility. Not only can negative emotions be conveyed verbally, but they can also be communicated in writing. As will be discussed in Chapter 6, tone is particularly important to consider when writing because of the prevalence of email for communication in many organizations. Just as tone of voice can convey emotions, so can tone in writing.

Developing a Professional Image

All the aspects of credibility discussed thus far help us cultivate a professional image: our expertise and competence in a variety of job skills, our integrity, and our ability to control our emotions. Our communication skills, both written and oral, can enhance our image as professionals. Personality traits can also contribute to a more credible and professional image. If we show ourselves to be dependable, reliable, careful, thorough, able to plan, organized, hardworking, persistent, and achievement oriented, we are more likely to be perceived as professional and competent.

Our appearance—dress, body type, and posture—also communicates to others. Every time you walk into a room, your appearance communicates who you are even before you speak.[26] For example, in most organizational cultures, it would not be appropriate for the company president to walk into a business meeting wearing flip flops and shorts. On the other hand, a fishing guide would not show up for work in a three-piece suit. Dressing appropriately for a particular situation or context can affect whether others perceive us as professional and credible. It also sends the message that we are a part of the group, because we understand and respect its norms for behavior. This message can help you in the relationship area of communication goodwill, as well.

Some people are better able to consciously cultivate a professional image. **Impression management** is the control of communication information through a performance. In impression management, people try to present an "idealized" version of themselves to reach desired ends. The idea that self-presentation is a kind of performance comes from the work of Erving Goffman, who described everyday interactions using a theatrical lens. In other words, he viewed individuals as "actors" and interaction as a "performance" shaped by the context and situation and constructed to provide others with "impressions" consistent with the actor's desired goals.

We all attempt to manage the impressions we make to varying degrees in various situations. For example, when you are with your friends, you probably try to dress and act like them so as to be seen as part of the group. When you go on a

appropriate feedback
Feedback that is honest, reflects the communicator's true understanding and judgment, and is appropriate for the subject, audience, and occasion or context.

impression management
The attempt to control the impression of ourselves that we present to others in any communication situation.

date, you are likely to be on your best behavior to reduce the risk of doing or saying something that may not be viewed as attractive by the other person. In small-group situations, you often hold back during the forming stage of the group process for the same reason—so as not to leave a lasting, potentially negative first impression.

Three essential types of communication are used to manage impressions: manner, appearance, and setting.[27] Manner includes both verbal and nonverbal communication. Manner, for example, might be seen as indifferent, silly, businesslike, intelligent, immature, friendly, warm, or gracious. Manner might be considered an indication of attitude. Our appearance may suggest a role we play, a value we hold, our personality, or how important we view the communication setting. Setting includes your immediate environment as well as public displays of who you are (your car, your clothes, your jewelry).

In addition to manner, appearance, and setting, those who aspire to leadership positions or greater influence might give some thought to the traits they display. The trait approach to leadership was one of the first systematic attempts to study leadership. Trait theory has ebbed in its popularity over the years, but more recent studies have shown that personality traits are strongly associated with individuals' perception of leadership.[28] The traits associated with leadership that have been most commonly identified by these studies are the following:

- **Intelligence**. Zaccaro, Kemp, and Baker (2004) found support for the finding that leaders tend to have higher intelligence than nonleaders. Having strong verbal ability, perceptual ability, and reasoning appears to make one a better leader.
- **Self-confidence**. Self-confidence can help us establish our credibility and have the assurance needed to influence others.
- **Determination**. Determination is the desire to get the job done and includes such characteristics as initiative, persistence, dominance, and drive. People with determination are willing to assert themselves, are proactive, and have the capacity to persevere when faced with obstacles.
- **Integrity**. As already discussed in a previous section of this chapter, integrity is the quality of honesty and trustworthiness.
- **Sociability**. Sociability includes such characteristics as being friendly, outgoing, courteous, tactful, and diplomatic. Social leaders have good interpersonal skills and create cooperative relationships with others.

Knowledge of leadership traits can help us assess our strengths and weaknesses in these areas and provide us the opportunity to make changes that increase the potential impact of these traits or better manage the impressions that we make through our communication practices.

Effectively managing the impression we make requires us to be participants in our communication with others as well as an observer of that process. In other words, we must be able to assume a detached view of ourselves so that we can effectively perceive how others are responding to us and adjust our communicative behavior if necessary to improve our ability to communicate with them. As discussed in Chapter 2, self-awareness and perception are important parts of communication because they affect the way we understand ourselves, events, and others, and how others do the same.

The activity of observing ourselves in communicative situations is called *self-monitoring*. **High self-monitors** are those individuals who are highly aware of

high self-monitors
People who are highly aware of their impression-management behavior and efforts.

their impression-management behavior.[29] On the other hand, **low self-monitors** communicate with others with little attention to how others respond to their messages. They have little idea about how others perceive them and know even less about how to interact appropriately with others.

Impression management, or managing how others perceive us, can help us achieve our goals through our communication practices, particularly in the image-conscious business world. When we use language that is appropriate for the occasion or situation; when we use nonverbal communication to demonstrate understanding or empathy, self-confidence, and other leadership traits; and when we wear clothing that is within appropriate guidelines for the situation, we increase the likelihood that we will be viewed as credible and professional, which can better enable us to achieve our goals.

Impression management is one aspect of a natural and productive process called **anticipatory socialization** through which most of us develop a set of expectations and beliefs concerning how people communicate in particular occupations and in formal and informal work settings.[30] The communication course you are now enrolled in—as well as some of the other university courses you are now taking—is part of that process. Any internships or other job-related activities you may have also contribute to that process. In fact, learning how to work in a position probably begins in early childhood.

Because anticipatory socialization process probably begins in childhood, it is also a part of our self-concept. Most discussions of anticipatory socialization recognize that, as people mature, they use the information they gather about jobs from their environment to compare against their self-concept. This comparison helps them make judgments about choosing occupations and specific jobs.[31] This process may be likened to an informal and ongoing self-inventory to determine career opportunities that best match an individual's skills and attitudes. It might also be compared with the social construction of our identities as we use outside information to define and determine who we are.

Some people believe that impression management is unethical or deceptive. Another view is that impression management is necessary for successful communication in specific situations. It relies on the ability to develop an awareness of the appropriate behavior, communication practices, and self-presentation for a particular occasion or situation and adjust to meet those expectations to better ensure successful communication outcomes.

Impression management can help others and ourselves save face or avoid embarrassment. When we act in ways that are appropriate to the situation, we are respecting the expectations of others. In these cases, impression management is a matter of politeness.

Like many matters of communication, the ethics of impression management come down to intent. Behaviors and presentation style that attempt to deceive or mislead others can be judged as unethical. That is another reason why the dialogic model can be helpful: Our actions must be guided by consideration of others and their effects on them. Even in their least offensive form, actions to manage the impression we make may be seen as superficial, pretentious, lacking integrity, or as "sucking up" by others. Having a strong sense of personal integrity and conviction in our beliefs can help offset these types of judgments. As discussed earlier, attempting to judge our actions from the viewpoint of others can be a helpful guide in determining their effectiveness and appropriateness to a situation.

low self-monitors
People who have little awareness about how others perceive them and little knowledge about how to interact appropriately with others.

anticipatory socialization
The process we use to develop a set of expectations and beliefs about how people communicate in various formal and informal work settings.

Discuss your own application of the four purposes of business communication. Do you agree that you generally should consider and apply all four in business contexts? Why or why not?

Communicating to Persuade and to Influence

Although we may believe that most of our communication is intended to inform others, in the business world almost all communication is persuasive. In other words, you are trying to get another person to do or believe something. In business, you are almost always selling: selling your ideas, yourself, your products, your services, or your organization and its mission. Selling and persuading are nearly synonymous in the business world. You may be trying to persuade your supervisor to give you a raise, you may be attempting to persuade a colleague to change a portion of a project on which you are both working, or you may be trying to sell a customer your company's service or product. All of these are examples of persuasion at work. Persuasion is known by a number of terms, including *motivation, influence,* and *leadership,* depending on the context of the communication. (*Influence* is an interpersonal communication term and will be discussed in more detail later in this section.)

To succeed at persuasion, you must generally give the person you are communicating with good reason to do or believe what you want them to. That is one reason why it is important to identify your purposes before you communicate in the workplace. If you believe you are only informing, then you may fail to provide the good reasons or evidence necessary to persuade, if that is indeed your primary purpose.

Evidence consists of a variety of types of information, such as facts, anecdotes, examples, and statistics. These types of evidence and their usage are discussed in more detail in Chapter 6.

As will be discussed in more detail below, achieving the purposes of conveying goodwill, or establishing positive relationships, as well as establishing our credibility, helps to make our goal of persuasion much easier.

Conger's Multistep Model of Persuasion

According to Conger (1998), persuasion is a difficult and time-consuming activity, but it is a necessary skill in today's business environment because the old "command-and-control" managerial model now often results in poor or unwanted outcomes.

> *As AlliedSignal's CEO Lawrence Bossidy said recently, "The day when you could yell and scream and beat people into good performance is over. Today you have to appeal to them by helping them to see how they can get from here to there by establishing some credibility and by giving them some reasons and help to get there. Do all those things, and they'll knock down doors."*[32]

According to Conger (1998), there are four essential steps to effective persuasion: establish credibility, provide a frame for common ground, provide evidence, and connect emotionally.

1. **Establish credibility.** For Conger, credibility has two aspects: expertise and relationships. People are considered to have high levels of expertise if they have a history of sound judgment or have proven themselves knowledgeable and well informed about their proposals.[33] As for relationship, or what is called *goodwill* in this text, people with high credibility have demonstrated *over time* that they can be trusted to listen and to work in the best interest of others.[34]

2. **Provide a frame for common ground.** To strengthen the appeal of your proposal to others, you must first identify its tangible benefits to the people you are trying to persuade. To do this, you must thoroughly understand your audience and its needs and concerns.

3. **Provide evidence.** According to Conger (1998), effective persuaders should use a variety of types of evidence—numerical data, examples, stories, metaphors, and analogies—to make their positions come alive[35] and to support their claims.

4. **Connect emotionally (convey goodwill).** In our culture, we may like to believe that people make decisions based on reason, but emotions are always at play.[36] In fact, Conger claims that emotions play a primary role in persuasion. To connect emotionally with an audience, Conger suggests that the communicators

   (a) show their own emotional commitment to the proposal being made— they must show conviction and even passion—and

   (b) adjust their arguments to their audience's emotional state. However, in showing their own emotional commitment to their proposal, communicators must use some restraint to maintain credibility.

Conger attempts to reconceptualize our understanding of persuasion from that of simply convincing and selling, which might veer off into a monologue involving manipulation and even coercion, to that of learning and negotiating. According to Conger's approach, persuasion is generally not easily accomplished in a single moment in time, but rather it involves the stages of discovery of information, preparation, and dialogue. Dialogue must happen before and during the persuasive process. "A persuader should make a concerted effort to meet one-on-one with all the key people he or she plans to persuade."[37] In some cases, through this dialogue, effective persuaders may find that they need to adjust their positions to better achieve their goals. This approach supports and underscores the importance of using the dialogic model, discussed in Chapter 2, to achieve our communication purposes. Conger's model also emphasizes the interdependence of the purposes for communication to successful persuasion: To be successful, one must also establish his or her credibility, convey goodwill, and establish a relationship built on trust. He or she must know his or her audience and focus on its concerns and interests.

Conger's model recognizes the complexity of communication and, more specifically, persuasion, particularly in political environments in which participants have varying interests and resources are often limited, thereby, revealing the value of a strategic, yet ethical approach.

Interpersonal Communication and the Role of Influence

In Conger's model, interpersonal communication is critical to effective persuasion. Here we can see the usefulness of applying concepts from differing communication perspectives to actual practice. In interpersonal and small-group communication situations, persuasion is often referred to using another term: **influence**. The definition of *influence* is very similar to that of persuasion: It is the power that a person has to affect other people's thinking or actions.[38]

In the area of interpersonal influence, one area of research focuses on **compliance-gaining** and **compliance-resisting** behaviors. Compliance-gaining is defined as those attempts made by a communicator to influence another to "perform some desired behavior that the [other person] otherwise might not perform."[39] Compliance-gaining occurs whenever we ask someone to do something for us. For example, we may ask our supervisor to give us a raise or promotion or a coworker to switch days off with us. Like Conger's view that effective persuasion takes time and may consist of several stages, research into compliance-gaining shows that its success also often involves a series of attempts. In other words, think of persuasion or influence as a process best approached with thought and planning rather than as a one-time event.

Research on compliance-gaining indicates that people generally prefer socially acceptable, reward-oriented strategies.[40] In other words, people are more apt to be persuaded or influenced if they are offered some kind of reward or benefit for doing so. Conversely, people do not respond well to negative, threatening, or punishing strategies used to gain compliance. This is where some scholars draw the line for the similarities between persuasion and influence: specifically, actions aimed at compliance-gaining. Compliance-gaining behaviors that rely on coercion and threats can be seen as abuses of power rather than the ethical pursuit of persuasion or influence. Studies indicate that as more resistance is encountered, compliance-gaining efforts generally move from positive tactics to more negative ones. At this point, compliance-gaining efforts may move from ethical attempts to influence to coercion.

Compliance-resisting is defined as the refusal to comply with influence attempts.[41] When resisting requests, people tend to offer reasons or evidence to support their refusal.[42] People who are more sensitive to others and who are more adaptive are more likely to engage in further attempts to influence.[43] They may address some of the obstacles they expect when they initiate their request and adapt later attempts to influence by offering counterarguments.

For example, if you are preparing to ask your supervisor for a raise, you might consider some of the reasons he or she might refuse. Your supervisor might respond by saying money isn't available, you don't deserve a raise compared to your peers' contributions, or you have not performed in such a manner as to deserve a raise. In such a case, a person who is adaptive and sensitive to his or her audience's needs and concerns will respond with information or evidence intended to counter these claims.

Another term that is closely related to compliance-gaining is **interpersonal dominance**, which is defined as "a relational, behavioral, and interactional state that reflects the actual achievement of influence or control over another via communicative actions."[44] The term *dominance* often carries a negative connotation, especially when the objective is to control others, but Burgoon argues that dominance may comprise positive qualities, as well, including aspects of social competence.

Interpersonal dominance is better understood by examining its four dimensions. *Persuasiveness and poise* refer to a person's ability to act influentially and to behave with dignity. *Conversational control and panache* refer to the individual's presence and expressiveness. *Task focus* refers to an individual's ability to remain focused on the task at hand. *Self-assurance* refers to a person's level of confidence and ability to avoid either arrogance or timidity. These dimensions also coincide with the traits

influence
The power to affect the thoughts or actions of others.

compliance-gaining
Attempts made by a communicator to influence another person to do something that the person otherwise might not do.

compliance-resisting
The refusal to comply with another person's attempts at influence.

interpersonal dominance
The relational, behavioral, and interactional state that reflects the actual achievement—by means of communication—of influence or control over another person.

that we associate with leaders and can be applied in interpersonal, group, and public-speaking situations.

CriticalThinking

The construct of interpersonal dominance can be a useful one in thinking about yourself as a leader as it is similar to some of the elements identified by trait approaches to leadership. Identify someone who projects all of the characteristics of interpersonal dominance. Can you imagine what it would sound like, look like, and feel like to be that person? Can you incorporate some of these elements into your own communication practices?

As discussed in Chapter 2, the recent flattening of organizational hierarchies and the resulting interdependence of work tasks among employees have resulted in a greater need for excellent interpersonal skills. Because of these changes, Bernard Keys and Thomas Case (1990) claim that "influence must replace the use of formal authority in relationships with subordinates, peers, outside contacts, and others on whom the job makes one dependent."[45] This means that because positional authority is no longer sufficient to get the job done, a web of influence or a balanced web of relationships must be developed. "Recently managers have begun to view leadership as the orchestration of *relationships* among [*sic*] several different interest groups—superiors, peers, and outsiders, as well as subordinates."[46]

Just as managers must learn how to foster and orchestrate relationships between people, often through the process of influence, so must subordinates. According to Keys and Case (1990), of the types of influence that subordinates use on superiors, **rational explanation**, which includes some sort of formal presentation, analysis, or proposal, is the most frequently used. It usually involves the presentation of evidence. A host of other tactics—such as arguing without support and using persistence and repetition, threatening and manipulation—were not found to be effective. In fact, Keys and Case (1990) found that subordinates who used these tactics usually failed miserably. Nevertheless, no one influence tactic will be best in all situations; instead, subordinates must learn to tailor their approaches to the audiences they are attempting to influence and the objectives being sought.[47]

Similarly, Riley and Eisenberg (1992) claim that the primary skill individuals must cultivate in managing their bosses is advocacy—the process of championing ideas, proposals, actions, or people to those above them in the organization. Advocacy requires learning how to read your superior's needs and preferences and designing persuasive arguments that are most likely to accomplish your goals. (Analyzing audiences is discussed in Chapter 4, "Step Two: Analyze the Audience.") Successful advocacy involves the following considerations:

1. **Plan (strategize).** Think through a communication strategy that will work.
2. **Determine why your boss should care or analyze your audience.** Connect your argument to something that matters to your boss such as a key objective or personal value.
3. **Tailor your argument to the boss's style and characteristics.** Adapt your evidence and appeal to those things that are persuasive to your boss, not those things that are persuasive to you.
4. **Assess your audience's prior technical knowledge.** Do not assume too much about your boss's level of knowledge and vocabulary or jargon.

rational explanation
Explanation that includes some sort of formal presentation, analysis, or proposal and usually involves the presentation of evidence.

5. **Build coalitions.** Your arguments need the support of others in the organization.
6. **Hone your communication skills.** An articulate, well-prepared message is critical to building your credibility with your boss.

Building coalitions is one way to influence others if you do not have a position of power. Building coalitions involves identifying like-minded individuals in your organization and developing trusted relationships with them. The value and importance of establishing a positive relationship with your audience and others involves the third purpose of business communication—goodwill.

Summary

The purposes of business communication are to inform, persuade and influence, convey goodwill, and establish credibility. These purposes should be considered whether you are planning to communicate in writing, in person, using the phone, or via email or other electronic media. It is also important to recognize that most business communication is generally not intended solely to achieve one purpose. Because most business communication includes some aspect of sales or persuasion and successful persuasion also often depends on your relationship with your audience—that is, goodwill and your credibility—you should pay attention to achieving all four purposes in many, if not all, of your messages.

Your ability to establish credibility and create and maintain relationships with others depends a great deal on how others perceive you. Consequently, to be an effective communicator, you must have a large measure of self-awareness as well as insight into how others perceive and respond to you. If you become aware of weaknesses in certain areas that may negatively affect your abilities to communicate with others and ultimately your attainment of career goals, then you have an opportunity to change for the better.

Key Terms

goodwill, 58
networking, 58
trust, 59
avoidance, 60
aggressiveness, 60
assertiveness, 60
reasoned skepticism, 67
appropriate feedback, 68
impression management, 68

high self-monitors, 69
low self-monitors, 70
anticipatory socialization, 70
influence, 73
compliance-gaining, 73
compliance-resisting, 73
interpersonal dominance, 73
rational explanation, 74

Discussion Questions

1. What characteristics do you look for to determine the credibility of your coworkers, classmates, or other speakers? What strategies can speakers use to establish credibility?

2. Instructors use a variety of compliance-gaining tactics in the classroom. What are some of these tactics? What are some strategies that students use to resist instructors' compliance-gaining efforts? Have you seen examples of these tactics used in the workplace or in other organizations of which you are a part? Were they effective? If so, why?

3. What are the five components of trust? What role do these components play in your relationships with family members? Friends? Coworkers?

4. What are the elements of credibility? How have you seen each one applied in your organization (this might also be a student organization to which you belong)? How might they be applied better?

5. Are you aware of your own impression-management practices? How do you manage the impressions you make in differing contexts or situations?

Applications

1. Observe a live or recorded speech or oral presentation in which the speaker is attempting to persuade. How credible was the speaker?

What did he or she say or do that enhanced or detracted from his or her credibility? How effective was the speaker in conveying goodwill or establishing a relationship with his or her audience? What did the speaker say or do that helped to build or detracted from his or her goodwill? Finally, how persuasive was the speaker? What did he or she say or do that supported or detracted from the talk's persuasiveness? How did the speaker's credibility or ability to convey goodwill affect his or her persuasiveness?

2. Find a persuasive business message at least one page long. Do the content and appearance of the document enhance or detract from the writer's credibility? Did the writer use language or style to establish or maintain a relationship with the reader? If so, how? Were there words or phrases that detracted from the writer's goodwill? How successful was the writer in his or her attempts to be persuasive? What contributed to that success or detracted from it?

3. Observe a group or watch an episode of a television show, such as *Survivor*, that focuses on group dynamics. Identify group members and then analyze their behaviors, looking for clues to their level of emotional intelligence and their ability to self-monitor. How do these behaviors affect their membership in and relationship to others in the group?

4. Find a reality television show or a video posted on YouTube in which a participant in a group situation exhibited a low ability to self-monitor. In other words, the person failed to successfully manage the impression he or she was making on others. What was the effect on others? If decision making was involved, what was the effect on the quality of the decision-making process?

5. Begin to visualize yourself as a leader or as a more effective leader. Create a list of the communication behaviors—written, oral, and nonverbal—that are involved in the successful creation of this role for yourself. For each item in the list, write an affirmative statement that details how you will enact that behavior in future interactions when leadership is appropriately enacted or applied.

Case Study
Taco Bell Corporation: Where's the Beef?

"We are asking that they stop saying that they are selling beef."[48]

"Thank you for suing us." On January 28, 2011, Taco Bell placed full-page advertisements with this phrase in big bold letters in local and national newspapers, including the *New York Times, USA Today*, and *Wall Street Journal*. Taco Bell was striking back against a lawsuit that challenged the beef content in the chain's beef tacos.

Days earlier, on January 19, Taco Bell was served with a lawsuit, filed by a disgruntled customer, alleging that the chain's taco mixture consists of more filler than meat.[49] News of this claim became widespread on the Internet. Soon after the lawsuit, the situation was parodied by Stephen Colbert on his Comedy Central show, *The Colbert Report*. Taco Bell's reputation was being threatened and the company would be forced to react swiftly and decisively.

The Lawsuit

Amanda Obney, a resident of California, alleged that Taco Bell's advertising and labeling led her to believe that the taco meat filling was seasoned beef. Based on this assumption, she purchased food items labeled as "beef," and in doing so suffered injury and lost money as a result of the alleged misrepresentations.[50]

The consumer rights class-action suit filed by Alabama law firm Beasley Allen challenges Taco Bell's practice of representing to consumers that the filling in many of its "beef" food products is "seasoned ground beef" or "seasoned beef," claiming that a substantial amount of the filling contains substances other than beef. The lawsuit states that the "seasoned beef" does not meet the minimum standards set by the United States Department of Agriculture (USDA) and should be labeled as "taco meat filling." This action seeks to require Taco Bell to properly advertise and label these food items and to engage in a corrective advertising campaign to educate the public about the true content of its food items. The lawsuit values the damages as exceeding $5,000,000.

The lawsuit pertains only to those items referred to as "seasoned beef" and not to Taco Bell's items containing chicken or *carne asada* (roasted beef) steak. Those items are acknowledged as actually being chicken or *carne asada* steak.

Specifically, the lawsuit alleges that Taco Bell misrepresents certain ingredients as "seasonings" when, in fact, they are not added for flavor, but rather to increase the volume of the product. The lawsuit refers to these ingredients as "binders" and "extenders" (e.g., "isolated oat product"). Given the belief of the plaintiff that there are binders and extenders, the labeling of the products should be "taco meat filling." To further support this change in labeling, the lawsuit notes that internally, Taco Bell refers to its "seasoned ground beef" and "seasoned beef" as "taco meat filling," as evidenced by the labels on the containers shipped to its restaurants.

Beef Defined

Merriam-Webster defines "beef" as "the flesh of an adult domestic bovine (a steer or cow) used as food."[51] The USDA defines "beef" as "flesh of cattle,"[52] and states that "ground beef" "shall consist of chopped flesh and/or frozen beef with or without seasoning and without the addition of beef fat as such, shall not contain more than 30 percent fat, and shall not contain added water, phosphates, binders, or extenders."[53]

The USDA developed the *Food Standards and Labeling Policy Book* (the "Policy Book"). The Policy Book provides guidance to help manufacturers prepare product labels that are truthful and not misleading. In regard to food labeled as "taco filling," such food items must contain at least 40 percent fresh meat and the label must show the true product name, such as "Taco Filling with Meat," "Beef Taco Filling," or "Taco Meat Filling."[54]

Taco Bell Corporation

Taco Bell Corporation, which is based in Irvine, California, is the nation's leading Mexican-style quick-service restaurant (QSR) chain serving tacos, burritos, signature quesadillas, Border Bowls,

nachos, and other specialty items. As of 2011, Taco Bell serves more than 35 million consumers each week in approximately 5,600 restaurants in the United States. The company is credited with reforming the nature of the QSR industry, including revolutionizing new kitchen preparation systems and supply chain management processes.[55]

Taco Bell was founded in 1962 by Glen Bell, a former U.S. Marine, in Downey, California, serving what his customers called "Tay-Kohs."[56] Before Glen Bell created Taco Bell, he started Bell's Drive-In and Taco Tia in the San Bernadino area in 1954. Taco Bell's growth continued and in 1964 retired L.A. policeman, Kermit Becky, became Taco Bell's first franchisee, opening a restaurant in Torrance, California. In 1967, Taco Bell's hundredth restaurant opened in Anaheim, California. In 1970 Taco Bell went public with a total of 325 restaurants. Glen Bell sold 868 Taco Bell restaurants to PepsiCo Inc. in 1978 and became a PepsiCo shareholder.

Of Taco Bell's operating units, approximately 75 percent are franchised. The top three states with the largest number of operating units are California, Florida, and Ohio. Franchisee requirements are stringent, with a minimum net worth requirement of $1 million, and an average total investment of $1.45 million.[57]

Taco Bell is well known for its innovative advertising and marketing strategies. In 1989, Taco Bell pioneered the concept of linking fast-food marketing promotions with major movie blockbusters. Its "Batman" promotion placed Taco Bell in the spotlight and was a huge success.

In 1991, Taco Bell opened the first Taco Bell Express in San Francisco. This restaurant concept incorporates a reduced-size restaurant with a limited menu, meant to emphasize volume.[58] Typically, the menu consists of items priced under $1. Locations where Taco Bell Express stores operate include shopping malls, airports, rest stops, and inside convenience stores.

PepsiCo, seeking to boost its stock value by narrowing its business focus to soft drinks and packaged snacks, divested their ownership of Taco Bell in 1997.[59] A new company, called Tricon Global Restaurants Inc., was formed.[60] Under this structure, Taco Bell's president reported directly to the president and CEO of Tricon.

Tricon announced in 2002 that it received shareholders' approval to change its corporate name to

Yum! Brands, Inc. (NYSE: YUM). According to David Novak, Yum! Brands chairman and chief executive officer, this name change, "better reflects the company's expanding portfolio of brands and the unique fun and recognition culture" that is driven across the global company.[61] Yum! Brands is head-quartered in Louisville, Kentucky. The company's brands include A&W Restaurants, KFC, Long John Silver's, Pizza Hut, and Wing Street. KFC, Pizza Hut, and Taco Bell are the global leaders of the chicken, pizza, and Mexican-style food categories.

Beasley Allen Law Firm

Founded in 1979, Beasley, Allen, Crow, Methvin, Portis & Miles, P.C., represents plaintiffs and claimants in civil litigation ("Beasley Allen"). The firm is a leader in civil litigation on behalf of claimants and holds state and national records for the largest jury verdicts in various categories:

- Largest verdict against an oil company: $11.9 billion – ExxonMobil Corp.
- Largest pharmaceutical drug settlement: $4.85 billion – Merck & Co.; Vioxx-related claims
- Largest private environmental settlement: $700 million – PCB damage claims; 20,000 current and former residents of Calhoun County, Alabama (toxic tort damages)
- Largest predatory lending verdict – $581 million: family in Hale County, Alabama

Lawyers within the firm have been profiled in national publications such as *Forbes, Businessweek,* the *Wall Street Journal,* and the *New York Times* as well as on television shows such as *60 Minutes* and *Good Morning America*. The firm has a national reputation for being at the forefront of consumer litigation and publishes a monthly consumer news report, *The Jere Beasley Report.*

The firm's areas of expertise include personal injury, products liability, consumer fraud, business litigation, environmental litigation, and pharmaceutical litigation.[62]

Negative Publicity

Taco Bell has experienced negative publicity in the past and has demonstrated the ability to overcome negative headlines and attacks on their brand. Particularly, Taco Bell has dealt with a StarLink corn issue (i.e., genetically modified food), an *E. coli* contamination, rat infestation, and Salmonella poisoning.

StarLink Corn

In 1996, Taco Bell entered into a licensing agreement with Kraft Foods to distribute Taco Bell-branded taco shells in grocery stores. An NGO (nongovernmental organization) known as "Friends of the Earth" identified the fact that these taco shells contained a genetically modified corn ingredient unapproved for human consumption.[63] Although a Kraft supplier was ultimately responsible for the product, Taco Bell took the brunt of the criticism as the packages were branded primarily with Taco Bell's logo. Kraft initiated a recall of the corn shells, and Taco Bell subsequently filed a class-action lawsuit against those producers of corn flour and tortillas containing StarLink corn.[64]

E. Coli *Outbreak*

Several years later, in December 2006, Taco Bell voluntarily closed stores in three states after lettuce, consumed in certain Taco Bell restaurants and contaminated with *E. coli*, sent several dozen people to the hospital. Preliminary testing by an independent lab found that green onions may have been the cause of contamination, and Taco Bell subsequently removed green onions from every store in the country. Taco Bell usually purchases onions from California, but in winter months the onions are often imported from Mexico, which was considered to be the root of the problem.[65] However, health officials later identified lettuce as the health concern, and Taco Bell responded by replacing one of its lettuce suppliers.[66]

Rat Infestation

In February 2007, a joint KFC/Taco Bell restaurant in New York City closed after rats were discovered inside the building. Taco Bell said they would work with the local franchisee to correct the problem.[67]

Salmonella Outbreak

Most recently, in August 2010, a multistate Salmonella class-action lawsuit was filed against Taco Bell. Approximately 155 people across twenty-one states were confirmed with salmonellosis.[68] Taco

Bell's only comment stated how seriously they take food safety, and that their food is perfectly safe to eat.[69]

Unique Approaches to Marketing

The company has a reputation of going to extreme measures to portray themselves as a clever, light-hearted organization intent on providing value to their consumers.

Taco Liberty Bell

One of the publicity efforts that made national headlines took place on April Fools' Day in 1996, when Taco Bell placed an advertisement in seven leading newspapers announcing that they had purchased the Liberty Bell and renamed it the Taco Liberty Bell. Taco Bell also urged other companies to do their part to help reduce the national debt.[70]

Mir Space Station

In March 2001 during the reentry of the Mir space station, Taco Bell announced they had placed a large target in the middle of the Pacific Ocean. If a piece of debris struck the target, they stated that all Americans would be rewarded with a free taco courtesy of Taco Bell. As is customary with these types of promotions, Taco Bell purchased an insurance policy in the rare instance that the target was hit by a piece of the space station.[71]

World Series

The 2002 World Series provided a similar opportunity. A batter simply had to hit a target placed in San Francisco Bay in order to win tacos for the entire country.[72] When no batters accomplished this feat, Taco Bell put a target in the home run area left of center field at Busch Stadium in St. Louis, in game three of the 2004 World Series with the same promise of free tacos.[73] Failure to hit this target prompted Taco Bell to make it even easier for the batters in the 2006 World Series by just requiring a home run in the entire area left of center field.[74] Again, this failed to occur. As such, in 2007, Taco Bell lowered the bar with its "Steal a base, steal a taco" campaign, in which a base runner simply had to steal a base in order to win a taco. Taco lovers across the country were not disappointed, and Taco Bell subsequently made a $20,000 donation to the Boys & Girls Clubs of America.[75]

Next Steps

Taco Bell President Greg Creed understands the urgency of the situation and the fragile ground his company stands on when it comes to food quality. Is this an issue that Taco Bell should quietly address to avoid any future negative publicity? Or, should Taco Bell respond to the lawsuit head-on in an attempt to improve Taco Bell's damaged reputation? These questions and more will weigh on his mind as he and his team work to compile a response to help their brand weather the oncoming storm.

Discussion Questions

Retrospective Questions

1. How effective were Taco Bell's responses prior to the "Thank You for Suing Us" ad?
2. What is Taco Bell hoping to accomplish with the ad, and are they likely to reach that goal?
3. What obligations did Taco Bell have to its consumers in terms of product ingredients and advertisements?
4. Should Taco Bell have avoided the added publicity and instead pursued a quick settlement?
5. What other alternative strategies should Taco Bell have implemented in place of the "Thank You" ad?

Prospective Questions

1. What other public relations strategies should Taco Bell pursue moving forward?
2. What are some other ways that Taco Bell can communicate the quality of its products?
3. Should Taco Bell follow industry suit and use the quality of its ingredients as an advertising theme in the future?
4. How can Taco Bell avoid this type of scrutiny in the future? Or are they truly grateful for the opportunity to utilize paid-media?

This case was prepared by Research Assistants Christopher Roper and David Samikkanu under the direction of James S. O'Rourke, Teaching Professor of Management, as the basis for class discussion rather than to illustrate either effective or ineffective handling of an administrative situation. Information was gathered from corporate as well as public sources.

Endnotes

1. Kanter, R. M. (1989). The new managerial work. *Harvard Business Review, 67*, 85–92.

2. Lencioni, P. M. (2002). *The five dysfunctions of a team.* San Francisco: Jossey-Bass.

3. Robbins, S. P. (2001). *Organizational behavior* (9th ed.). Upper Saddle River, NJ: Prentice Hall.

4. Eisenberg, E. M., & Goodall, Jr., H. L. (1993). *Organizational communication: Balancing creativity and constraint.* New York: St. Martin's Press, p. 252.

5. Ibid.

6. Pearson, J. C., Nelson, P. E., Titsworth, S., & Harter, L. (2003). *Human communication.* New York: McGraw-Hill, p. 214.

7. Eisenberg, E. M. & Goodall, Jr., H. L. 1993, p. 252.

8. Orbe, M. P. (1996). Laying the foundation for co-cultural communication theory: An inductive approach to studying "nondominant" communication strategies and the factors that influence them. *Communication Studies, 47*, 157–176, p. 170.

9. Infante, D., Trebling, J., Sheperd, P., & Seeds, D. (1984). The relationship of argumentativeness to verbal aggression. *Southern Speech Communication Journal, 50*, 67–77.

10. Orbe, 1996, p. 170.

11. Eisenberg & Goodall, 1993, p. 252.

12. Eisenberg & Goodall, 1993.

13. Pagano, B., Pagano, E., & Lundin, S. (2003). *The transparency edge: How credibility can make you or break you in business.* New York, NY: McGraw-Hill.

14. Conger, J. (1998). The necessary art of persuasion. *Harvard Business Review, 76*, 84–95.

15. Moerke, A. (2004). Business writing brush-up. *Sales and Marketing Management, 156*(5), 63.

16. Ibid.

17. Eisenberg & Goodall, 1993, p. 333.

18. Ibid.

19. Lerner, M. (1992, May 14). Looters living out the cynical American ethos. *Los Angeles Times,* B7.

20. Ibid.

21. Barnlund, D. C. (1986). Toward a meaning-centered philosophy of communication. In J. Stewart (Ed.), *Bridges not walls: A book about interpersonal communication* (pp. 36–42). New York: Newbury Award Records, p. 40.

22. Barnlund, 1986, p. 41.

23. Larson, C. U. (2004). *Persuasion: Reception and responsibility* (10th ed.). Belmont, CA: Wadsworth/Thomson Learning, p. 29.

24. Ibid.

25. Dealing with emotions in the workplace (2002, November). *USA Today Magazine Online.* Retrieved December 13, 2003, from http://www.findarticles.com/cf_dls/m1272/2690_131/94384310/p1/article.jhtml, p. 1.

26. Buhler, P. (1991). Managing in the 90's. *Supervision, 52*, 18.

27. Wiggins, J. A., Wiggins, B. B., & Vander Zanden, J. (1993). *Social psychology.* (4th ed.). New York: McGraw-Hill.

28. Bass, B. M. (1990). *Bass and Stogdill's handbook of leadership: A survey of theory and research.* New York: Free Press; Bennis, W. G., & Nanus, B. (1985). *Leaders: The strategies for taking charge.* New York: Harper & Row; Kirkpatrick, S. A., & Locke, E. A. (1991). Leadership: Do traits matter? *The Executive, 5*, 48–60; Lord, R. G., DeVader, C. L., & Alliger, G. M. (1986). A meta-analysis of the relation between personality traits and leadership perceptions: An application of validity generalization procedures. *Journal of Applied Psychology, 71*, 402–410; Nadler, D. A., & Tushman, M. L. (1989). What makes for magic leadership? In W. E. Rosenbach & R. L. Taylor (Eds.), *Contemporary issues in leadership* (pp. 135–139). Boulder, CO: Westview; and Zaleznik, A. (1977). Managers and leaders: Are they different? *Harvard Business Review, 55*, 67–78.

29. Snyder, M. (1979). Self-monitoring processes. In L. Berkowitz (Ed.), *Advances in experimental social psychology.* New York: Academic Press.

30. Jablin, F. M. (2001). Organizational entry, assimilation, and disengagement/exit. *The new handbook of organizational communication* (pp. 732–818). Thousand Oaks, CA: Sage Publications.

31. Ibid.

32. Conger, 1998, p. 86.

33. Ibid., p. 88.

34. Ibid.

35. Ibid., p. 92.

36. Ibid., p. 93.

37. Ibid., p. 89.

38. Pearson, J. C., Nelson, P. E., Titsworth, S., & Harter, L. (2003). *Human communication.* New York: McGraw-Hill.

39. Wilson, S. R. (1998). Introduction to the special issue on seeking and resisting compliance: The vitality of compliance-gaining research. *Communication Studies, 49,* 273–275, p. 273.

40. Miller, G. R., Boster, F. J., Roloff, M. E., & Seibold, D. (1977). Compliance-gaining message strategies: A typology and some findings concerning effects of situational differences. *Communication Monographs, 44,* 37–51.

41. Pearson et al., 2003.

42. Saeki, M., & O'Keefe, B. (1994). Refusals and rejections: Designing messages to serve multiple goals. *Human Communication Research, 21,* 67–102.

43. Ifert, D. E., & Roloff, M. E. (1997). Overcoming expressed obstacles to compliance: The role of sensitivity to the expressions of others and ability to modify self-presentation. *Communication Quarterly, 45,* 55–67.

44. Burgoon, J. K., Johnson, M. L., & Koch, P. T. (1998). The nature and measurement of interpersonal dominance. *Communication Monographs, 65,* 308–335, p. 315.

45. Keys, B., & Case, T. (1990). How to become an influential manager. *Academy of Management Executive, 4,* 38–50, p. 38.

46. Ibid., p. 39.

47. Keys & Case, 1990.

48. Caulfield, P. (2011). Taco Bell is using false advertising when it calls its food "beef" according to lawsuit. NYDailyNews.com, January 25, 2011, http://articles.nydailynews.com/2011-01-25/news/27096673_1_anti-dusting-amanda-obney-ground-beef.

49. Jargon, J., Steel, E., & Lublin, J. S. (2011). Taco Bell makes spicy retort to suit. *Wall Street Journal,* January 31, 2011, http://online.wsj.com/article/SB10001424052748704832704576114280629161632.html.

50. Amanda Obney, On Behalf of Herself, All Others Similarly Situated and the General Public, Plaintiff, v. Taco Bell Corporation, Defendant. Accessed through Scribd, http://www.scribd.com/doc/48740872/Taco-Bell-Lawsuit.

51. *Merriam-Webster Dictionary,* http://www.merriam-webster.com/dictionary/beef.

52. *Justia.com.* Definitions, Beef. http://law.justia.com/cfr/title07/7-10.1.1.1.16.1.257.19.html.

53. *Vllex.* Miscellaneous beef products. Text 319.15, http://cfr.vlex.com/vid/319-15-miscellaneous-beef-products19611343.

54. *Food Standards and Labeling Policy Book,* United States Department of Agriculture, August 2005, Page 183, http://www.fsis.usda.gov/OPPDE/larc/Policies/Labeling_Policy_Book_082005.pdf.

55. Our brands. Yum! Brands Web site, http://www.yum.com/company/ourbrands.asp.

56. Company information, 1950s, 1960s and 1970s. Taco Bell Web site, http://www.tacobell.com/company.

57. The definitive guide to the world of franchising. World Franchising, http://worldfranchising.com/franchises/Taco-Bell.html.

58. Trager, L. (1991). Taco Bell Express offers fast food at a frantic pace; typical transaction takes 20 seconds. *San Francisco Examiner,* November 10, 1991, available through westlaw@westlaw.com.

59. Martin, R. (1997). PepsiCo to divest all chain holdings; spin-off would create mega corporation. *Nation's Restaurant News,* February 3, 1997.

60. 1990s. Taco Bell Web site, http://www.tacobell.com/company.

61. Tricon Global Restaurants shareholders approve company name change to Yum! Brands, Inc. *QSR Magazine,* May 16, 2002,

http://www.qsrmagazine.com/news/tricon
-global-restaurants-shareholders-approve
-company-name-change-yum-brands-inc.

62. About us. BA Law Firm, http://www
.beasleyallen.com/about.

63. Taylor, M. R., & Tick, J. S.. The StarLink
case: Issues for the future, page 17, http://
www.pewtrusts.org/uploadedFiles/wwwpew
trustsorg/Reports/Food_and_Biotechnology
/hhs_biotech_star_case.pdf.

64. Associated Press. (2001). Taco Bell sues over
StarLink corn fiasco. Accessed through
Organic Consumers Association, September
19, 2001, http://www.organicconsumers
.org/gefood/tacobellsues092501.cfm.

65. Taco Bell acts after *E. coli* outbreak.
MSNBC, updated December 6, 2006,
http://www.msnbc.msn.com/id/16035176/ns
/health-infectious_diseases/.

66. Lettuce suspected in Taco Bell *E. coli*.
WebMD Health News, December 4, 2006,
http://www.webmd.com/diet/news/20061214
/e-coli-at-taco-bell-lettuce-suspected.

67. Scurrying rats take over NYC-Taco Bell restaurant. Fox News, February 23, 2007,
http://www.foxnews.com/story/0,2933,2540
26,00.html.

68. Schreck, S. (2010). Mexican fast food linked
to 2 salmonella outbreaks. *Food Safety News*,
August 5, 2010, http://www.foodsafetynews
.com/2010/08/mexican-fast-food-linked-to-2
-salmonella-outbreaks.

69. Best, J. (2010). Taco Bell mum about salmonella outbreak, Wendy's/Arby's set to launch
in Russia. *Slash/Food*, August 11, 2010,
http://www.slashfood.com/2010/08/11/taco
-bell-mum-about-salmonella-outbreak-wendy
-s-arby-s-set-to-l.

70. Leroux, C. (2006). Fool's paradise: Some of
the greatest April pranks in history. *Chicago
Tribune*, March 31, 2006, http://web.archive
.org/web/20080309174128/ http://www
.accessmylibrary.com/coms2/summary_028631
371252_ITM.

71. Free tacos for U.S. if Mir hits floating Taco Bell
ocean target-Taco Bell sets 40 by 40 foot target
in South Pacific for Mir's re-entry. Spaceref,
March 19, 2001, http://www.spaceref.com
/news/viewpr.html?pid=4152.

72. PR Newswire Association. (2002). America
eats free tacos if World Series home run hits
Taco Bell® target; Taco Bell thinks outside
the park with 15-foot floating target in
San Francisco Bay. Accessed through the
Free Library by Farlex, http://www.thefree
library.com/America+Eats+Free+Tacos+If+
World+Series+Home+Run+Hits+Taco+Bell
%28R %29...-a093114935.

73. Will the World Series feed America? *CNN
Money.com*, October 25, 2004, http://
money.cnn.com/2004/10/25/news/fortune500
/tacobell_baseball.

74. Taco Bell ties free tacos to World Series.
PROMO, October 24, 2006, http://promo
magazine.com/incentives/tacobell_worldseries
_102406.

75. Taco Bell's 2007 World Series promotion.
Fast Food News, October 22, 2007, http://
www.foodfacts.info/blog/2007/10/taco-bells
-2007-world-series-promotion.html.

Michael DeLeon/iStockphoto.com

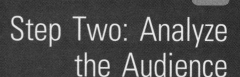

Step Two: Analyze the Audience

After reading this chapter, you will be able to

▶ Use a variety of frameworks to analyze business audiences to identify their values, preferences, interests, attitudes, and concerns.

▶ Discuss general types of business audiences and their needs.

▶ Describe the differences between messages that focus on the audience's needs and expectations and those that are conveyed from the writer's or speaker's perspective.

Case Questions:

1. What are the interests of Sheila's audience, Speedy's management team? What are its concerns? What objections might it have to Sheila's proposal?

2. How might Sheila best address her audience's concerns and objections? To what shared interests might she appeal in her message?

3. Would the way the message is structured make a difference in terms of its success? If so, what issue(s) should Sheila address first? Second? Third? Why?

4. What sales message might Sheila provide in terms of identifying the benefits of a new marketing strategy?

The Case of Speedy Travel Inc.

Sheila Markham let out a long sigh as she sat looking at her computer screen. She had been hired four months ago by Speedy Travel, whose key target market was college students, to increase its sales. Her investigation of the company and its competitors led her to the conclusion that the small full-service firm needed to update its distribution methods and change its product offerings to better suit the desires of its customers. Although most of Speedy Travel's traditional market had been students from the local college, it had failed to transition to a solid Internet presence, where most young people made their travel arrangements. Its "product line" consisted primarily of package tours, whereas young people tend to prefer making their own travel arrangements. Worse yet, it seemed that the company had adopted a "bad" business model since it relied almost solely on new customers, a new student population, rather than building repeat business. This made the challenge of marketing and sales even more difficult. Another market that was being missed was the growing diversity of the student population attending the nearby university, which had the highest international student population of any in the country.

Speedy Travel was family-owned and had been since its start thirty-five years ago. At that time, the company's business model had made it a success, but with little change since then, the agency was struggling. Sheila had spent enough time with management to know that its members believed the problem wasn't the business but was with the customer.

Somehow, though, she needed to find a way to persuade management to adopt her suggested changes, regardless of the anticipated resistance she believed her message would receive.

Analyze the Audience

On its face, audience analysis may appear to be a simple task. But think about it: To truly see the world from another's perspective would require that one have the ability to leave one's own body and mind behind for a time and occupy those of another. Does that seem like a practical exercise? If not, then what tools are available for us to understand another person and how he or she sees and experiences the world?

Understanding how others both differ from and are similar to us are necessary skills for effective communication. To be persuasive, for example, we often need to know the common goals that we and our audience share in order to positively frame or begin a discussion. But differences are also important; recognition of differences may be the first step in "getting out of our bodies" so that we might imagine what it might be like to be another person. This can be a challenging activity if we have limited life experience or lack the ability to empathize with others. It can be potentially even more challenging in an individualist culture such as the United States, where we tend to privilege self-interest and are thus primarily focused on ourselves and our own needs, particularly in a competitive workplace.

Some people have an advantage in their ability to see the world through others' eyes. Those who are not in a privileged position in society often are provided the perspective of those with power through media, schools, and other institutions. They also must operate in the world of those who have more power and privilege, so they have a greater opportunity to understand how that world works. "Border" persons, or those who must navigate two or more cultures, may have more insight into others' differences because they must be able to live in and navigate differing realities or worldviews. On the other hand, those who have privilege may have a greater challenge in recognizing how others differ because that privilege—and potential difference—is often invisible to them and taken for granted.

Learning how to see through another's eyes—to *empathize*—can be a difficult yet important skill in communicating successfully with others in the workplace as well as in our personal lives. Without the ability to empathize with others and understand their views and feelings, we are unable to successfully enact a dialogic model of communication.

When you are crafting important business messages or those to new audiences, you should analyze your audience or audiences. Such an analysis is the basis for deciding the appropriate channel or medium for communication to use, the content of the message, the organization, and the tone and style. Such an analysis might also help to determine whether a message should even be sent or, if so, when to do so. Such an analysis is therefore critical for successful communication. However, analyzing audiences can be particularly challenging, so this chapter provides a variety of lenses to apply to identify your audience's interests and concerns.

There are other ways to expand our ability to see and understand differences. We can go out of our way to have conversations with those who are different from ourselves and to ask such simple questions as "What do you care about?" and perhaps, more tellingly, "What are your fears?" We can also spend time in other cultures—even those that exist in our own country, state, and city—proactively learning how they differ from our own.

This chapter discusses the following lenses through which you might gain a better understanding of your audience:

- The audience's demographics, including age, ethnicity, socioeconomic status, and education level. Special attention is given to generational differences, culture, and personality types.
- Its knowledge of your company, product, service, or the situation; its interests in and attitudes about the topic of your message; and its concerns, reservations, or questions about the topic of your message.
- Types of business audiences.

Your audience's preferences and interests should always guide the decisions you make as a strategic communicator. The most successful messages construct win–win situations for both you and your audience. That's because such messages generally ensure quicker agreement and better relationships. Therefore, it is of critical importance to spend time analyzing your audience in order to achieve this goal.

Audience Demographics

If you have taken marketing courses, then the term **demographics** is probably a familiar one. Demographics are the statistical data about a particular population, including its age, income, education level, and so on. Marketing and business communication have a great deal in common because both fields are generally concerned with sales or persuasion. Just as you should consider a potential market's characteristics before you can go about creating a successful marketing plan or campaign, you should also consider a potential audience's characteristics before creating a message that has the best chance of success.

For example, if you are marketing home-health products to seniors, then you would consider the preferences of older people regarding advertising media, product distribution, and pricing. In the selection of an advertising medium, for instance, you would be more likely to select the local newspaper for a senior market than for a product aimed at young adults. Older people are more likely to read the local newspaper than teenagers and college students.

When crafting messages intended for an older audience, you would probably create messages with a more formal tone and avoid the use of slang words that may not be familiar to its members. When considering visual presentation of a written message intended for older people, you might select larger font sizes to make the message more readable and include illustrations of older people so they can more easily identify with the message you are sending.

We should also consider our audience's ability to identify with the content of our messages. As mentioned above, it is easier for people to identify with messages that contain images of people like themselves. Likewise, using examples and anecdotes that are easier for your specific audience to identify with or relate to can help make your communication more effective. If you are writing messages aimed at persuading a female audience to purchase your company's automobile, for example, you would probably focus on the vehicle's reliability and safety. In contrast, if your audience is male, then you might instead focus on the vehicle's performance as an attractive feature. Rural audiences or persons employed in the construction trades might simply prefer a different model—a pickup truck—as compared with the sedan or the sports utility vehicle that is marketed to suburbanites.

demographics
The statistical data about a particular population, including its age, income, education level, and so on.

Your ability to provide the appropriate amount of information for your particular audience can affect your ability to fulfill your intended communication purposes, the first element of communication strategy discussed in Chapter 3, "Step One: Identify the Purposes of Communication." If you don't provide sufficient or relevant information aimed at meeting your audience's specific needs, then you will be less able to fulfill your purposes of informing, persuading, conveying goodwill, and establishing your credibility. For these reasons, the elements of communication strategy are interdependent; they depend on each other for the success of your messages.

CriticalThinking

Identify an audience, an individual or group with whom you find it difficult to communicate. Describe the audience. What are its demographic features? What are its needs in the particular context in which you communicate with it? Concerns? Expectations? How might taking these elements into consideration help you to communicate with this audience more successfully?

Generational Differences

Generational differences fall under the category of *demographics*, but because they have been the focus of much research and writing recently, a separate discussion has been devoted to them here. Generational differences have become of particular interest to organizations because it has been shown that problems formerly associated with employee loyalty and work ethics can be ascribed to generational differences. Sixty-five percent of respondents say that generational gaps make it difficult to get things done in an organization; problems include lack of communication, differences in values, and tension between change and stability.[1] Thus, understanding generational differences can be particularly helpful to those already in or aspiring to be in leadership positions.

There are four generations that may be found in today's workplace: traditionalists, or those born before 1946; baby boomers, or those born between 1946 and 1964; Gen Xers, those born between 1965 and 1981; and millennials, those born after 1982.

- **Traditionalists.** Forged by war and depression, this generation honors hard work, respects leaders, and maintains loyalty to institutions. In return, its members expect to receive a job for life. Weaned on deprivation and duty, they prefer to save their money and defer gratification and rewards until retirement.
- **Baby boomers.** Boomers have had to compete with their generational colleagues for limited openings all the way up the hierarchy. They have learned political skills and how to read their bosses. And yet they have been called the "me" generation because their parents spoiled them and, from the beginning of the television age, advertisers have catered to them. Basically optimists, they have taken to heart a message from their parents and from various cultural icons of the 1960s: Make the world a better place.

- **Generation Xers (or nexters).** These are the so-called latchkey kids, fending for themselves after school and the first to experience—in great numbers—divorcing parents and one-parent families. They have learned to be resourceful and independent. Most have created surrogate "families" through networks of close, reliable friends. Having seen mergers and downsizing devastate people they care about over the years, they tend not to trust companies or the individuals who manage them.
- **Millennials (or Generation Y).** The front end of this cohort has just recently started entering the full-time workforce. "Techno-savvy"—they have always known computers—they arrive at the workplace fully expecting to have input in all decisions affecting their work because they were often the center of attention in their families. Millennials grew up immersed in diversity at school, on TV, and via the World Wide Web, so they accept working with many cultures, races, and lifestyles. Because of the structure in their families, they also expect structure in the workplace.

Understanding these generational differences can help the strategic communicator identify the values and expectations of a particular audience and formulate messages that take those values into account.

Culture

If we assume that others have the same experiences, beliefs, and values as ourselves, then we suffer from what is called **ethnocentrism**. Ethnocentrism is the belief that our own cultural background, including ways of analyzing problems, values, beliefs, language, and verbal and nonverbal communication, is correct. This belief can lead to an ignorance about and insensitivity to others that, as has been discussed, can negatively affect our ability to communicate with others.

Culture has an important effect on communication. **Culture** is defined as the learned beliefs, values, rules, norms, symbols, and traditions that are common to a group of people. It is a way of life, customs, and script for a group of people.[2]

In the United States, the study of culture began in earnest in the 1960s with research on ethnic and racial identities and has since expanded to look at differences among people of different countries, societies, and regional groups. In the past few decades, many studies have focused on identifying and classifying the basic values of different cultures. Each has produced greater understanding of cultural differences, but each also has its limitations and critics. However, understanding these concepts can provide us some insight into cultural differences and how they may affect our communication effectiveness.

The GLOBE Studies

The GLOBE (Global Leadership and Organizational Behavior Effectiveness) research program has involved more than 160 investigators who have used quantitative methods to study the responses of 17,000 managers in more than 950 organizations representing 62 different cultures. The researchers divided the data from the sixty-two countries into ten regional clusters and identified nine cultural dimensions: uncertainty avoidance, power distance, institutional collectivism, in-group collectivism, gender egalitarianism, assertiveness, future orientation, performance orientation, and humane orientation.[3]

ethnocentrism
The belief that your own cultural background—including its ways of analyzing problems, values, beliefs, language, and verbal and nonverbal communication—is correct and that other cultures are somehow inferior.

culture
The learned beliefs, values, rules, norms, symbols, and traditions that are common to a group of people.

- **Uncertainty avoidance.** This dimension refers to the extent to which a cultural group relies on established social norms, rituals, and procedures to avoid uncertainty.
- **Power distance.** This dimension refers to the degree to which members of a cultural group expect and agree that power should be shared unequally.
- **Institutional collectivism.** This dimension describes the degree to which a cultural group encourages institutional or societal collective action. It is concerned with whether cultures identify with broader societal interests rather than with individual goals.
- **In-group collectivism.** This dimension refers to the degree to which people express pride, loyalty, and cohesiveness in their groups or families.
- **Gender egalitarianism.** This dimension measures the degree to which a cultural group minimizes gender role differences and promotes gender equality.
- **Assertiveness.** This dimension refers to the degree to which people in a culture are determined, assertive, confrontational, and aggressive in their social relationships.
- **Future orientation.** This concept refers to the extent to which people engage in future-oriented behaviors such as planning, investing, and delaying gratification.
- **Performance orientation.** This dimension describes the extent to which a cultural group encourages and rewards its members for improved performance and excellence.
- **Humane orientation.** This dimension refers to the degree to which a culture encourages and rewards people for being fair, altruistic, generous, and caring to others.

The United States falls into the Anglo cluster, which also includes Canada, Australia, Ireland, England, South African whites, and New Zealand. These countries are high in performance orientation and low in in-group collectivism. This means that people in these countries tend to be competitive, results-oriented, and less attached to their families and other groups as those in other countries. The other nine regional clusters identified by the GLOBE studies are Confucian Asia, Eastern Europe, Germanic Europe, Latin America, Latin Europe, Middle East, Nordic Europe, Southern Asia, and Sub-Saharan Africa. Table 4-1 provides a classification of the cultural clusters with regard to how they scored on each cultural dimension.

Although the GLOBE study has generated a great deal of data from many sources, it has some criticisms. It does not provide a clear set of assumptions or propositions that form a single theory about the way that culture relates to leadership. It also measures a broad variety of characteristics that are difficult to identify as a set of universal attributes in isolation from the context in which they occur.

Hofstede's Cultural Dimensions

Perhaps the most referenced study of culture is the research of Geert Hofstede. Hofstede analyzed questionnaires obtained from more than 100,000 respondents in more than 50 countries and identified five major dimensions on which cultures differ: power distance, uncertainty avoidance, individualism–collectivism,

Table 4-1 Cultural Clusters Classified on Cultural Dimensions.

CULTURAL DIMENSION	HIGH-SCORE CLUSTERS	LOW-SCORE CLUSTERS
Assertiveness Orientation	Eastern Europe Germanic Europe	Nordic Europe
Future Orientation	Germanic Europe Nordic Europe	Eastern Europe Latin America Middle East
Gender Egalitarianism	Eastern Europe Nordic Europe	Middle East
Humane Orientation	Southern Asia Sub-Saharan Africa	Germanic Europe Latin Europe
In-group Collectivism	Confucian Asia Eastern Europe Latin America Middle East Southern Asia	Anglo Germanic Europe Nordic Europe
Institutional Collectivism	Nordic Europe Confucian Asia Latin Europe	Germanic Europe Latin America
Performance Orientation	Anglo Confucian Asia Germanic Europe	Eastern Europe Latin America
Power Distance	No clusters	Nordic Europe
Uncertainty Avoidance	Germanic Europe Nordic Europe	Eastern Europe Latin America Middle East

Source: Adapted from House, R. J., Hanges, P. J., Javidan, M., Dorfman, P. W., & Gupta, V. (Eds.). 2004. *Culture, Leadership, and Organizations: The GLOBE Study of 62 Societies* (Newbury Park, CA: Sage Publications).

individualistic culture
A culture with an "I" focus in which competition, not cooperation, is encouraged and individual initiative and achievement are highly valued.

collectivist culture
A culture in which cooperation rather than competition is encouraged and in which individual goals are sacrificed for the good of the group.

masculinity–femininity, and long-term versus short-term orientation.[4] (The more recent GLOBE study identified similar dimensions but developed additional cultural categories.)

- **Power distance.** The extent to which less powerful people expect and accept the fact that power is unequal. People in Malaysia, Panama, Guatemala, the Philippines, and Mexico are most accepting of power distance, while Austrians, Israelis, Danes, New Zealanders, and the Irish are the least accepting. The United States also was shown to have greater equality among different societal levels.
- **Individualism versus collectivism.** In **individualistic culture,** the autonomy of the individual is of paramount importance, whereas commitment to the group is most important in **collectivist culture.** The individualism–collectivism continuum is thought by some scholars to be the most important dimension that distinguishes one culture from another.[5]

The United States ranks number one in individualism. Venezuela is the most collectivist of countries, with Mexico, Thailand, Singapore, and

Table 4-2 Characteristics of Individualist versus Collectivist Cultures.

INDIVIDUALISTIC CULTURES	COLLECTIVIST CULTURES
Value individual freedom; place "I" before "we."	Value the group over the individual; place "we" before "I."
Value independence.	Value commitment to family, tribe, and clan.
Value competition over cooperation.	Value cooperation over competition.
Value telling the truth over sparing feelings.	Value "saving face" by not causing embarrassment.
Examples: United States, Australia, Great Britain, Canada, Netherlands	Examples: Venezuela, Pakistan, Peru, Taiwan, Thailand

© Cengage Learning

Japan also ranking on the collectivist side of the continuum.[6] Approximately 70 percent of the world's population lives in collectivist cultures.[7] Table 4-2 summarizes the characteristics of individualistic and collectivist cultures.

- **Masculinity versus femininity.** In this dimension, masculinity indicates distinct gender-based roles in the culture, whereas a feminine culture implies blurring between the roles of men and women. Consequently, Middle Eastern cultures are masculine while Scandinavian countries are feminine. The United States also ranks fairly high in masculinity.
- **Avoidance of uncertainty.** This dimension has to do with a cultural group's tolerance for uncertainty and ambiguity. The United States has a relatively low avoidance of uncertainty.
- **Long-term versus short-term orientation.** Values associated with long-term orientation are thrift and perseverance; values associated with short-term orientation are respect for tradition, fulfilling social obligations, and protecting one's "face." The United States falls within the long-term orientation.

Because of the saliency of the individualist–collectivist distinction, two additional concepts related to this distinction have been developed. These are low-versus high-context cultures and face negotiation theory.

Low-versus High-Context Cultures Anthropologist Edward T. Hall gave us another way to look at cultural difference in terms of high and low context. Individualist and collectivist cultures emphasize different kinds of communication. People in collectivist cultures pay a great deal of attention to the context of the communication rather than the explicit, transmitted code or words. For example, in Japan, Korea, China, and Arab and Latin American countries, a good deal of time is spent in relationship building—formal communication and getting acquainted—before business takes place and intentions are stated. Table 4-3 shows examples of low- versus high-context cultural characteristics.

In contrast, low-context cultures pay more attention to the explicit code or words than to the context. In the United States, Switzerland, Germany, and Scandinavian countries, people get to the point and clearly state what they want.

These cultural differences also can affect how people perceive verbal and nonverbal cues. Those in low-context, individualistic cultures tend to pay more

Table 4-3 Characteristics of Low- and High-Context Cultures.

LOW-CONTEXT	HIGH-CONTEXT
Northern Europe, North America	Japan, Saudi Arabia, Mediterranean Europe, Latin America
<ul><li>Less formality</li><li>Direct, explicit communication</li><li>Getting right to business</li><li>Needing larger personal space</li></ul>	<ul><li>Very formal</li><li>Indirect, implicit communication</li><li>Building a relationship and trust before conducting business</li><li>Being comfortable with little personal space (Latin America, Saudi Arabia)</li></ul>

© Cengage Learning 2015

attention to verbal skills, whereas those from high-context, collectivist cultures tend to pay more attention to nonverbal skills.

Regional cultures within the United States also display these differences. For example, African-American cultures tend to be more collectivist and high context than do those of whites of European descent, and working-class people tend to be more collectivist and high context than white-collar professionals.

A strategic communicator isn't limited by his or her cultural predilections, however. Instead, he or she learns to pay attention to both verbal and nonverbal skills, as well as the context in which communication takes place, because these all provide vital information about differing situations and the people involved in them.

Face Negotiation Theory Face negotiation theory is a theory first postulated by Stella Ting-Toomey in 1985 to explain how different cultures manage conflict and communicate. The theory has gone through multiple iterations since that time and was updated most recently in 2005. In essence, the theory explains that the root of conflict is based on identity management on an individual and cultural level. The various facets of individual and cultural identities are described as *faces*. **Faces** are the public images of an individual or group that the society sees and evaluates based on cultural norms and values. Conflict occurs when a group or individual's face is threatened. This can occur in two directions: embarrassing another can make individuals of certain cultures uncomfortable since this entails a potential act of impoliteness. Conversely, saving one's own face, or avoiding embarrassing one's self, can also be a concern.

Many different strategies and factors affect how cultures manage identity. Ting-Toomey argues that the face of the group in collectivist cultures is more important than the face of any individual in that group. In individualist cultures, the face of the individual is more important than the face of the group. Furthermore, there are small and large power distances associated with each culture. A small-power-distance culture believes that authority is earned, power is distributed equally, and everyone's opinion matters. The individual is highly valued, as in the United States, for example. In large-power-distance cultures, authority is inherited, power is from top to bottom, and the boss is infallible. The good of the group is valued.

faces
The public image of individuals, or groups, that their society sees and evaluates based on cultural norms and values.

CriticalThinking

Identify an audience from a different culture than your own. What cultural differences might affect the content of or your approach to a message intended for that audience?

ResponsibleCommunication

Language can be used to exclude, denigrate, and discriminate against others. Language can also be used in more subtle ways that ignore or minimize the contributions of one sex in society. Such language use can be considered sexist and should be avoided in the professional workplace.

The following are specific guidelines for avoiding sexist language use:

1. Replace *man* or *men* as words or in expressions. For example, instead of *man* use *human being*, *person*, or *individual*.

2. Use gender-neutral terms when possible to designate occupations, positions, and roles. For example, instead of *businessman* use *business owner*, *manager*, *executive*, *retailer*, and so on.

3. Refer to members of both sexes by parallel terms, names, or titles. For example, instead of *man and wife*, use *husband and wife*. Rather than using *men and ladies*, use *men and women*.

4. Avoid the third-person singular masculine when referring to an individual who could be of either sex. Instead of saying, "When a manager holds a meeting, he ... ," use the plural form of the pronoun when speaking generally, or the name of the person and the appropriate pronoun when communicating specifically. For example, "When managers hold meetings, they ..." or "When our manager, Ms. Johns, holds a meeting, she ..."

5. Avoid language that disparages, stereotypes, or patronizes either sex. Avoid referring to adult females as *girls* or unmarried women as *spinsters* or *old maids*, for example. In addition, you should avoid terms such as *womanly*, *manly*, *feminine*, or *masculine* in ways that stereotypically associate certain traits with one sex or another.

Audience Knowledge, Interests, Attitudes, and Concerns

A macrolevel analysis of an audience's demographic features can provide valuable insights into its values and beliefs. This knowledge may help us decide the best way for communication to occur as well as determine message content, organization, tone, and style. A microlevel audience analysis can be helpful in providing us even more specific guidance regarding the content of our messages. Such microlevel analysis includes a questioning of our audience's knowledge about our topic, as well as its interests, attitudes, and concerns.

Knowledge

Your audience's knowledge about the topic of your message should be considered before crafting it. For example, if you are communicating to your coworkers about a product on which all of you have been working for the past six months, it is probably safe to use acronyms related to the product and your company because you can assume that your audience is knowledgeable about the meanings of those abbreviations. However, if you are crafting messages for new customers, then you should avoid the use of acronyms because they are probably not familiar with their meaning. If you ignore this fact, your message will probably not be as successful in clearly communicating the information you intended.

Likewise, when communicating with audiences who lack knowledge of a product, service, or situation, you should provide more explanation or information. One common characteristic of inexperienced business communicators is that they are often unable to recognize the difference between their knowledge of a particular topic and that of their audience.

As stated earlier, your ability to provide the appropriate amount of information for your particular audience can affect your ability to fulfill your intended communication purposes. Without adequate or relevant information aimed at meeting your audience's needs and expectations, you are less likely to fulfill your purposes of informing, persuading, conveying goodwill, and establishing credibility.

Interests and Attitudes

As discussed in the earlier section "Audience Demographics," providing information that your audience is interested in and can relate to is one of the strategies of successful business communication. In an oral presentation, for instance, if you focus on information that does not address your audience's interests, then you are likely to lose its attention and fail at your communication purpose. The examples and content you provide in an oral presentation aimed at college students should differ significantly from those you might use in a presentation delivered to college administrators, even if the purposes are similar (for example, to persuade, inform, establish credibility, or convey goodwill).

Likewise, it is important to consider the attitudes of your audience toward the topic of your message in formulating a successful communication strategy. If your audience is reluctant to agree with the content of your message or the position you present, then give some thought to how to present your message in a way that might overcome this reluctance.

One tactic is to think about the beliefs, values, or goals that you and your audience have in common. If you can begin your message by establishing agreement that you and your audience share the same interests or goals, then you are showing that you and your audience share some commonalities of belief that should reduce resistance to the content and purpose of the remainder of your message. This tactic, which is referred to as establishing **common ground**, is generally effective in situations where your purposes include persuading and conveying goodwill. Another useful tactic is to focus your message on the benefits to your audience. Doing so will likely ensure a positive reception for your message. Again, this tactic is often used when your purposes are to persuade and convey goodwill.

common ground
The interests, goals, and commonalities of belief that the communicator shares with the audience.

Concerns and Questions

You are unlikely to be successful in attempts to persuade and convey goodwill if you do not effectively address your audience's concerns and questions. What is more frustrating than receiving a message that leaves you with many of your questions unanswered or your concerns completely ignored? Such lapses in communication can negatively affect the relationship the communicator has with his or her audience, as well as his or her credibility. Such lapses can also negatively affect morale and productivity, both of which may affect a company's bottom line.

In oral presentations, this situation can create problems for the presenter, particularly if he or she is attempting to persuade or influence. In an ideal situation, the presentation would accomplish that goal. However, if presenters are not attentive to the questions, concerns, and objections their audiences might have, then they may find themselves back at square one when the question-and-answer session begins. Ideally, in these situations, a presenter would have anticipated all of the audience's questions, concerns, and objections and answered or eliminated them during the presentation. This is true of written messages as well.

Types of Business Audiences

Another way to identify an audience's concerns is to think about its role within the organization. Business audiences are often quite different from those you may be familiar with in your academic experience. For example, most writing in school is intended for a teacher, who knows a great deal about the subject and who is required to read or listen to your message. However, this situation may not be true in the workplace. You may communicate with audiences who have little understanding of your topic, and it is very likely that you will write or speak to people who are not obliged to spend time reading or listening to your messages, such as potential customers. For these reasons, it is important to consider their interests and concerns if we are to achieve a greater likelihood of success in our communication attempts.

Another difference between communication in an academic setting and in the workplace is that you may be communicating with a variety of people rather than

Golden Pixels LLC/Shutterstock.com

a single person. If you are communicating with several or many people, they may have varying knowledge and needs. They may also differ in the strategies they use and skills they have for listening, reading, and processing information.

According to a typology devised by Olsen and Huckin (1991), in the workplace you will generally be communicating with five types of audiences: (1) managerial, (2) nonexperts, (3) expert, (4) international or multicultural, and (5) mixed.

Managerial Audiences

Managers are often the most important audiences you will communicate with because they have decision-making ability and power over your future. According to Henry Mintzberg (1975), managers fulfill three types of roles that affect the way they communicate: *interpersonal*, *informational*, and *decisional*. The primary managerial role is interpersonal. Managers must lead and motivate a group of employees and often communicate with external audiences such as suppliers, clients, and other departments. In this role, managers are also expected to disseminate information to these various audiences. Finally, managers must use information to make decisions that affect the various audiences with which they interact.

Because of the demands of these various roles, managers often have to deal with enormous time pressures. They have little time to listen or read carefully. Mintzberg's study found that 50 percent of the activities that executives engaged in lasted less than nine minutes. Many also treat message processing as a burden to be dispensed with as quickly as possible.

To ensure that your messages are received by managers, you can use a few tactics. You can, for example, put key information up front where it is easily accessible. James Souther (1985) studied how managers read reports and found that all of them read the executive summary and most read the introduction, background, and conclusions sections. Only 15 percent read the body of the report. In general, managers look for the "big picture" and tend to ignore details.

Nonexpert Audiences

Nonexpert audiences may be the most difficult to address because they know little about a subject and will need more details. (Managers are also often nonexperts, but they often ignore details unless they are micromanagers or specialists.) If you are communicating with a customer or client or perhaps a fellow employee from another department, then you are probably communicating with a nonexpert audience.

The problem with communicating with a nonexpert audience is that you probably think like a specialist. In other words, you may think about your topic differently than a nonexpert and use different terminology than he or she might when discussing that topic. In addition, you may have difficulty identifying exactly what a nonexpert audience doesn't know because you are so familiar with the topic.

As with managers, there are strategies you can use to communicate with nonexpert audiences. These include the following:

1. Use a conventional mode of presentation.
2. Refer to common knowledge as much as possible without distorting the meaning of your message.

3. Provide an overview at the beginning of the message that explains what it is about and what it will cover.
4. Provide appropriate background information.
5. Include lots of definitions and explanations. For more complex concepts, you can incorporate examples, illustrations, and analogies to aid in clarifying their meaning.

Expert Audiences

Expert audiences are those who know as much about the topic as you do. Generally, expert audiences, who may be your peers, speak the same language as you do—that is, they understand the jargon associated with your profession. They also understand the same concepts, so you don't need to provide as much explanation and examples. In other words, they can fill in the gaps by making inferences about material that is common knowledge to both of you.

Strategies for communicating with expert audiences include the following:

1. Use standard technical terms.
2. Use a conventional format.
3. Emphasize data and display it in standard ways using graphs, tables, equations, and so on.
4. Make your points clear and easy to find.
5. Do not overstate your claims, because doing so may undercut your credibility.

International or Multicultural Audiences

The global economy and the growing diversity of the workplace mean that we will likely communicate with audiences whose first language may not be English and who have differing cultural interpretations of symbols and behaviors. When communicating with people whose first language may not be English, you should

1. Avoid long or complicated sentences, because this may be more difficult for them to follow and comprehend.
2. Avoid slang, colloquial, or other idiomatic vocabulary uses. Such sayings as "in the ballpark," "under the weather," and "do an end run" may be interpreted literally by nonnative speakers of English, which will obviously cause confusion in terms of meaning.

Mixed Audiences

Even more difficult to communicate with are audiences who are composed of a variety of people: managers, nonexperts, experts, and nonnative speakers, or some combination of these. For example, you may be writing marketing literature that will be read by experts, nonexperts, and nonnative speakers or speaking to a group composed of the same individuals. There are two strategies for dealing with mixed audiences:

1. "Layer" a written message so that different sections are aimed at different audiences.
2. "Democratize" your message so that all audiences can understand all parts of it.

An example of the layered approach is a formal report. Such a report might include an executive summary, background information, and recommendation sections aimed at managers, while the body and appendices contain the details needed by specialists who are charged with implementing the report.

However, if you are speaking to a mixed audience, you may wish to use the democratic strategy. In this case, you aim your message primarily at the most important audience, but you add information in appropriate places that is needed for understanding by the other audiences. Although this approach is similar to the layered one, it differs in that you add examples, definitions, and explanations throughout the message that are needed for understanding by all audiences.

Audience-Centered Messages

One of the most common manifestations of communication that does not consider the needs, concerns, and interests of its audience is **self-centered communication**. Although some of the reasons for self-centered communication might be cultural as well as developmental—that is, the psychological maturity of the writer or level of self-awareness—another cause is our lack of awareness about our own message-formulation process.

In the first draft of a written message, for example, many of us write to ourselves in an attempt to figure out what we want to say. Such documents may begin without identifying a purpose or topic; in this process, we are often writing to identify the purpose or topic of our message for ourselves. This process may also be applied to oral presentations if we tend to work from a written script.

In this stage of the process, beginning ideas may be general, abstract, or somewhat unrelated to the topic at which we eventually arrive. In addition, such writing is generally not well organized. Paragraphs may cover several topics; they may lack topic sentences, or the topic may not be clearly stated. But as we continue to write, we usually narrow our topic and then *voila!* We discover our purpose for writing. It is at this point that we may stop the process. But we have only discovered the topic of our communication for ourselves; it has been a writing exercise that was intended to clarify our own thinking. The next step—and the step that is often missed or skipped—is to transform that information into a message that is intended for an audience.

Much writing for school assignments, particularly essay exams, follows this process and can be described as *self-centered* writing. The writer begins to write about a general topic, perhaps making some detours along the way into related topics. In essay exams, the goal is often to get down on paper as many relevant ideas as possible—often in no particular order—to demonstrate to the teacher that you remember all the topics he or she discussed in class.

In this case, the teacher is required to read this jumble of thoughts as part of his or her job and interpret whether the jumble is adequate coverage of the topic. However, businesspeople are not required to interpret such jumbles—they often don't have the time—and this is when it is important to recognize the difference between self-centered and audience-centered message formulation.

As indicated earlier, a self-centered message is generally the first draft of a message. The writer is writing to discover what he or she wants to say. But in doing so, several problems may emerge. One problem that often characterizes self-centered

self-centered communication Communication that fails to consider the needs, concerns, or interests of its audience.

messages is that the main topic comes at the end. The message may also skip important information or provide it in an illogical order.

The following steps should be applied to change self-centered messages to **audience-centered communication**:

1. Check whether the message should be turned upside down: Is the main topic or point at the end? If so, put it at the beginning of the second draft.
2. Eliminate any information that is not relevant to the main topic or its subpoints.
3. Organize what remains into a logical order.
4. Elaborate on any points that need additional explanation.
5. Proofread for correctness.

A self-centered process for message formulation and delivery can also occur when creating oral presentations, so it also is important to adjust planning and preparation to achieve greater audience focus.

Application of Audience-Centered Communication

Résumés and application letters are excellent examples of the importance of audience-centered content and organization. Your planning for job-application messages should always begin with an analysis of your audience's needs, interests, questions, and concerns. Prospective employers want to know whether you can do the job they have to offer. To put it bluntly, they want to know what you can do for them. Employers are not offering jobs with the main objective of fulfilling your needs. Therefore, résumés and cover or application letters need to be focused on showing that you have the skills and experience for which they are looking. Employers want to know that you are the best-qualified applicant for the job.

In terms of purposes, then, employment messages are persuasive. But it is important to remember that successful persuasion also often relies on our ability to establish credibility and a trusting relationship with our audience, so it is important to provide evidence to support the claims that we make about ourselves in order to be persuasive and establish credibility. Fortunately, it is often fairly easy to discover what an audience's needs are when creating employment messages. These are generally found in the job description or job posting. We then just need to identify those skills or characteristics that the employer is looking for, match them with our own, and make this match apparent and persuasive to our audience, the prospective employer.

The application letter in Figure 4-1 is a response to a job advertisement that asks for applicants who have a bachelor's degree in marketing and proven sales experience, as well as evidence of the ability to self-motivate. Ask yourself whether the letter focuses on providing the information an employer would need to make a decision about whether the writer is qualified for the position of customer service representative. How might the letter be improved?

In your analysis, you should have noticed that it is not apparent that the applicant knows what the job qualifications are, nor does the letter clearly state that the applicant has those qualifications. More specifically, it does not provide evidence that shows that the applicant has the qualifications for which the employer is looking. Rather than focusing on discussing the issues in which the reader is

audience-centered communication Communication that considers the needs, concerns, and expectations of the audience.

FIGURE 4-1	Self-Centered Employment Letter

Leon Freund
4234 Meadowlark Lane
Nashville, TN 78000

January 15, 2013

Juan Ruiz, Sales Manager
Westside Digital Products, Inc.
1237 34th Street East
Nashville, TN 78001

Dear Mr. Ruiz:

I am applying for the entry-level sales position you advertised on the JOBS Web site. I believe the position will suit my personality and provide me the opportunities for which I am looking.

I am a fun-loving person who enjoys interacting with others. I believe the sales position you are offering would enable me to meet a lot of new people. As the social chair of my fraternity, I excelled at creating fun ways for others to meet and interact.

I am looking for a position that will take advantage of my people skills and provide me opportunities for rapid promotion and pay raises. For those reasons, I believe your company will find me a good match for its needs.

Sincerely,

Leon Freund

© Cengage Learning 2015

interested, it addresses only what the writer enjoys and wants. This letter is an extreme case of a message that is self-centered rather than audience-centered. The letter in Figure 4-2 is a better example of an audience-centered message.

In the second letter, the writer does the following:

1. He addresses the specific skills that will help him perform the job of customer service representative.
2. He states how his skills will contribute to the company's goals. This tactic, which focuses on the benefits that the writer provides, is a common one in persuasive messages.
3. He has organized his information into short, concise paragraphs devoted to a single subpoint, which makes it easy for the reader to skim. The document's organization also attends to the reader's needs.
4. He provides the most important information first to emphasize it. Typically, relevant work experience is the most persuasive evidence a job applicant can present to employers.
5. He ends with a proactive statement that indicates high interest in the job, as well as initiative.

FIGURE 4-2 Example of an Audience-Centered Employment Letter

Leon Freund
4234 Meadowlark Lane
Nashville, TN 78000

January 15, 2013

Juan Ruiz
Westside Digital Products, Inc.
1237 34th Street East
Nashville, TN 78001

Dear Mr. Ruiz:

I am applying for the entry-level sales position you advertised on the JOBS Web site. I am well qualified for the position, since I have the experience, education, and personal characteristics you are seeking.

My experience working for Mayfield Electronics as a salesperson will enable me to quickly become a productive member of your team. At Mayfield I used my interpersonal skills successfully to become the top salesperson in the store twice in my first six months there.

I will complete my bachelor's degree in marketing this May. My education has provided me much useful knowledge that I can apply as a sales representative for your company. My courses in marketing, customer service, and business communication have provided me an excellent understanding of sales techniques, and practice in the communication skills necessary to satisfy your business clients.

I am hard-working and have excellent time-management skills. While taking a full load of courses, I worked part time or interned during my entire college career. I was still able to participate in the Student Marketing Organization, eventually being elected president, and to maintain a 3.5 cumulative grade point average.

I will call you in a week to make an appointment to talk to you in more detail about how I might contribute to the continuing success of Westside Digital.

Sincerely,

Leon Freund

CriticalThinking

Do you write to yourself to discover what it is you want to write? If so, have you recognized that this is just the first draft and that you may now need to edit the document heavily for others to read? Have you read writing that was clearly written from the writer's perspective and did not consider the reader? What were your reactions?

Summary

A second critical component of communication strategy formulation is the analysis of your audience or audiences. If your message is not tailored to take into account your audience's perspective as well as its knowledge, interest, needs, and expectations, then it will likely not succeed in fulfilling its purposes. As simple as audience analysis appears, though, it can be difficult to perform effectively because we often have difficulty understanding that others differ from us in many important and perhaps subtle ways. Because of the strong emphasis on the individual in American culture, we may be egocentric and ethnocentric, which means we have difficulty empathizing with or understanding others and their cultural differences. To overcome this tendency, a systematic method for analyzing audiences should be applied. When analyzing an audience, you should consider the following characteristics:

- Its demographics, including age and generational differences, ethnicity, socioeconomic status, education level, and culture (including regional differences), if appropriate
- Its knowledge of your company, product, service, or the situation—the topics—you address in your message
- Its interests in and attitudes about the topic of your message

- Its concerns, reservations, or questions about the topic of your message

Writing to business audiences differs dramatically from writing to an academic audience or teacher. Teachers are obliged to read your writing; they often are knowledgeable about the topic of your messages. However, this is not always true in a business setting, where people often face enormous time pressures. Because of these differences, you can use strategies to communicate more effectively with the various types of business audiences: managerial, nonexpert, expert, international or multicultural, and mixed.

It is important to recognize the difference between communication that is aimed at meeting your audience's needs and that formulated from the perspective of the writer or the speaker. In the process of developing a message, we often create messages that help us to solve a problem or decide what we want to communicate. It is important to remember that this message probably is not structured in such a way as to best meet our audience's needs; it may also fail to contain the information for which the audience is looking. It is important to understand our own process for formulating messages so that we can take the necessary steps to create audience-centered communication.

Key Terms

demographics, 86
ethnocentrism, 88
culture, 88
individualistic culture, 90
collectivist culture, 90

faces, 92
common ground, 94
self-centered communication, 98
audience-centered communication, 99

Discussion Questions

1. When you are communicating with friends, what demographic issues might affect the way that you deliver your message and its content? What are their expectations regarding the content and delivery of messages that you convey to them, and how do you meet those expectations? How might you better meet their expectations?

2. When communicating with your instructors, what demographic issues might affect the way that you deliver your message and its content? What are their expectations regarding the content and delivery of messages that you convey to them, and how do you meet those expectations? How might you better meet their expectations?

3. If you work as a supervisor or manager, what demographic issues might affect the way that you deliver your message and its content? What have been the expectations of your team or employees regarding the content and delivery of the messages that you convey to them? How did you meet those expectations? How might you better meet them?

4. If you work or have worked part time, what demographic issues might affect the way that you deliver your message and its content? What have been the expectations of your supervisor regarding the content and delivery of the messages that you convey to him or her? How did you meet those expectations? How might you better meet them?

5. When you are applying for an internship or job, what are employers' expectations regarding the content and delivery of your employment messages? How can you meet these expectations?

Applications

1. Using an Internet search engine, identify an organization that was faced with a problem and needed to communicate to various audiences who held different interests that might affect the way the organization deals with the problem.
   a. Identify each audience that held an interest in the decision.
   b. Identify each audience's interests, expectations, beliefs, and concerns.
   c. Assess the effectiveness of the organization's messages in meeting each audience's concerns and addressing them in a satisfactory manner.
   d. In those cases in which the organization might have done a better job in addressing the audience's interests, explain how it might have better accomplished this task.

2. Your company is planning to announce a series of layoffs that will affect 10 percent of your employee population. Write an analysis that addresses the following issues:
   a. What audience concerns and questions would you need to address to attain the maximal communication outcome?
   b. To which purposes of communication would you need to attend?
   c. At what type of audience would the message be aimed?
   d. What would be the focus and content of your strategy to effectively communicate this decision to employees?

3. Using an Internet job search Web site, identify potential positions for which you might apply on graduation. Review the job advertisements to identify the types of applicant qualifications and experience for which the organizations are looking. Choose one advertisement for which your skills best meet the organization's needs. Write an application letter that demonstrates that you understand the organization's needs and are qualified to fulfill them.

4. Identify a culture different from your own and use an Internet database to research the beliefs, values, attitudes, and practices of its people. Write an essay in which you discuss these characteristics and compare them to those of your own culture. How might these differences affect your communication with people of this culture? What similarities do you hold that might provide opportunities for establishing common ground?

5. Interview a working professional in your intended field to discover how businesspeople's concerns, expectations, and communication practices differ from those of college students. Write an essay that discusses the results of your interview and concludes with a list of goals you intend to pursue to adjust your communication practices—written, oral, and nonverbal as well as those involving the use of technology—to better meet the expectations of the professional workplace.

CASE ANALYSIS

CARNIVAL CRUISE LINES: FIRE ABOARD A STRANDED CRUISE SHIP

"During the next 10 minutes I kept talking to the guests reminding them to stay in their cabins and did my best to keep them calm. I also spoke to the crew, telling them to remember their training and to also stay calm. And they did, both the guests and the crew did exactly what I asked of them and meanwhile I waited for the captain to tell me what was next. And what was next was that the smoke was so intense and so thick that, even with breathing apparatus on, the teams could not get close to the source."[8]

These were the words of Cruise Director John Heald as he reflected on the events that transpired during the early hours of Monday, November 8, 2010. Thick smoke was billowing from the aft engine room of Carnival *Splendor*, one of the largest vessels owned and operated by Carnival Cruise Lines, and none of the ship's fire squads could stay in the engine room long enough to determine the cause of the smoke.

As cruise director, Heald was responsible for keeping the guests informed of any emergencies during the cruise, and to do so calmly, reassuringly, truthfully, and as often as possible. Thus, with limited information and a sense of urgency, Heald began making frequent updates to guests regarding the "smoke" situation. Little did he know that the thick smoke was the product of a debilitating fire that would leave Carnival *Splendor* without electrical power 200 miles off the coast of California. The next three days would prove to be among the most trying experiences in the company's history as John Heald and Tim Gallagher, Carnival Cruise Lines' vice president of corporate communications, attempted to control the situation and ensure the safety and well-being of all passengers onboard the stranded cruise ship.

Carnival Cruise Lines

Carnival Cruise Lines was founded in 1972 by entrepreneur Ted Arison with the vision of making cruising, a vacation experience once reserved for the rich, available to the average. Carrying more passengers than any other cruise line, Carnival has become the largest cruise line in the world, and in 1987, earned the distinction, "The Most Popular Cruise Line in the World." Carnival operates 1,400 voyages per year with a fleet of twenty-two ships, and serves approximately 4 million passengers per year.[9]

Carnival has 3,800 shoreside employees and 33,500 shipside employees. It operates voyages ranging from three to sixteen days in length to some of the most popular vacation destinations in the world, including the Bahamas, Caribbean, Mexican Riviera, Alaska, Hawaii, Canada, Europe, the Panama Canal, and Bermuda.[10] The company prides itself on providing an entertaining and relaxing experience for all guests onboard its "Fun Ships." Carnival builds all its ships with one goal in mind: "to make sure that every time you walk up the gangway, you get the sense that you're crossing over into a whole new world of fun."[11]

Carnival Cruise Lines is the flagship brand in a portfolio operated by its parent company, Carnival Corporation & plc. Carnival Corporation has headquarters in Miami, Florida, and London, England, and is publicly traded under the ticker symbol CCL on the New York and London Stock Exchanges. Carnival Corporation & plc is the only group in the world to be included in both the S&P 500 and the FTSE 100 indices.[12]

Operating many of the world's best-known cruise brands including Carnival, Princess, Holland America, Seabourn, Cunard, and P&O, Carnival Corporation & plc is a global cruise company. As one of the largest vacation companies in the world, the corporation's mission is to deliver exceptional vacation experiences that cater to a variety of different geographic regions and lifestyles, while delivering outstanding value.[13] The corporation maintains its top position in the industry by leveraging its cruise lines to penetrate a variety of markets. For instance, Carnival Cruise Lines and Princess both target families, retirees, and other upper-middle-class customers with competitively priced cruise packages whereas the Seabourn brand provides its upscale travelers with luxury cruises to exotic destinations.[14] Carnival Corporation has a decentralized operating structure and each of its brands has its own headquarters and operating team. The company believes this system helps create the ownership culture it believes to be an important driver of performance.[15]

The company maintains a strong balance sheet with the goal of investing in new and innovative ships, a strategy the company feels is critical in strengthening the leadership position of its brands. Across all brands, Carnival Corporation operates ninety-eight ships and plans to add two to three ships annually in 2012 and beyond. Carnival Cruise Lines operates approximately 18 percent of Carnival Corporation's total passenger capacity of 191,464 cabins, while serving approximately 4 million of Carnival Corporation's 8.5 million guests annually.[16]

To fuel its future growth and fill its expanding inventory of cruise ships, Carnival Corporation has expanded its number of home ports to move its cruises closer to its customers. In addition, it has invested heavily in marketing, especially targeting those consumers who have never before sailed. Since 2009, the firm has been moving away from print media and expanding its efforts in social media, such as Facebook, YouTube, Twitter, Flickr, and Podcasts. For instance, Carnival Cruise Lines manages its own "Funville" blog through its Web site, with the goal of engaging in two-way conversations with potential customers about the experience of cruising. Through such tools, Carnival hopes to attract new guests and create brand fans to continue its reign as the world's largest cruise operator.[17]

During the fiscal year ending November 30, 2010, Carnival Corporation reported earnings of $2.47 per share diluted on nearly $14.5 billion in total revenue.[18] Following the engine fire aboard *Splendor*, in a press release dated November 16, 2010, the company estimated that the total impact from voyage disruptions for Carnival *Splendor* and related repair costs will result in an approximate $0.07 reduction in the company's 2010 fourth quarter earnings per share. The company stated that impact of voyage disruptions in the first quarter of 2011 is not expected to be material to the company's 2011 earnings.[19]

The Cruise Line Industry

According to the Carnival Corporation's 2010 Annual Report, "The multi-night cruise industry has grown significantly [over the past decade], but still remains relatively small compared to the wider global vacation market, which includes a variety of land-based travel destinations around the world. For example, there were only about 215,000 cabins in the global cruise industry on November 30, 2010, which is less than the 265,000 rooms in just two North American vacation destinations: Orlando, Florida, and Las Vegas, Nevada. Within the wider global vacation market, cruise companies compete for the discretionary income spent by vacationers. Within that context, a recent Nielsen Global Confidence Survey found that after providing for savings and living expenses, the number one global spending priority is for vacations."[20]

As a result of these factors and other favorable cruise industry characteristics, Carnival Corporation believes that the cruise industry exhibits opportunities for growth. The industry's customers have increased at a compound annual growth rate of 5.7 percent from 2005 to 2010. In 2010, the global cruise industry marketed capacity of 423,000, with Carnival Corporation & plc representing 44 percent of this capacity. The cruise industry points to exceptional value proposition, wide appeal, low market penetration, positive guest demographics, and high guest satisfaction rates as positive growth dynamics that demonstrate the high potential within the industry.[21]

Trouble at Sea

The cruise industry has experienced its fair share of crises at sea. Facing issues that range from pirates to virus outbreaks to fires, cruise ships must develop and practice extensive contingency plans and drills that meet the International Maritime Organization (IMO) and U.S. Coast Guard standards. The Cruise Lines International Association (CLIA) states that these standards are internationally mandated and govern the design, construction, and operation of cruise vessels. To ensure compliance with both international and U.S. regulations, the U.S. Coast Guard examines all new cruise vessels and, thereafter, inspects each quarterly. If any deficiencies are discovered, the U.S. Coast Guard may require correction before allowing any passengers aboard the ship.[22]

Despite comprehensive precautionary measures, crises aboard cruise ships still occur regularly. One of the more notable occurred on August 4, 1991, when the cruise ship *Oceanos* sank off the coast of South Africa. The disaster could have been avoided had the ship not been in a "state of neglect," with loose hull plates, missing valves, and a hole in what was supposed to be a watertight bulkhead.[23] Although all 571 guests and crew survived, the captain and crew were widely ridiculed as cowardly and irresponsible for being among the first to leave the sinking vessel.[24]

Unlike the *Oceanos* incident, which was attributed to human neglect, many cruising hazards originate outside of the cruise line's direct control. Cruise ships are subject to a dangerous movement known as roll, which is a nautical term for rotation about the ship's longitudinal (front to back) axis, when encountering rogue waves or making sharp turns. On April 21, 2010, sixty passengers were injured aboard Carnival *Ecstasy* when the ship rolled twelve degrees after suddenly turning to avoid a drifting buoy that could have caused a hole in the ship's hull upon impact.[25] In 2008, a P&O cruise ship operated by Carnival Corporation caught in severe storms off the coast of New Zealand sent passengers and furniture flying as waves lashed up as high as the fifth deck, injuring forty-two people.[26] More recently, on March 3, 2010, two guests were killed and six others injured when three abnormally high waves up to 26 feet high smashed glass windows in a public lounge in the forward section of *Louis Majesty*, sailing near the French Mediterranean port of Marseilles.[27] Such an incident could have been avoided if only the crew had instructed passengers to remain in their cabins during the storm.[28]

A cruising vacation may also be ruined by an outbreak of norovirus, a one- to two-day infection often transmitted through food that causes diarrhea, vomiting, nausea, and stomach cramping. The Centers for Disease Control and Prevention (CDC) warns that the norovirus can spread rapidly from person to person in crowded, closed areas such as cruise ships.[29] Since neither a vaccine nor a treatment exists for the norovirus, many cruise ships have found themselves helpless in the face of an outbreak once the ship has already left port. If presence of the norovirus is discovered early enough in the trip, the crew may altogether cancel or cut short the cruise, as in the case of the Holland America cruise liner MS *Oosterdam* operated by Carnival Corporation in March of 2009.[30]

Depending on the geographic area of cruising, pirate attacks may pose a significant threat. In November of 2005, *Seabourn Spirit*, a ship operated by the Carnival Corporation subsidiary Seabourn Cruise Line, was chased and attacked by Somali pirates. The cruise ship was able to repel the two speedboats carrying the pirates without returning fire by using an onboard loud acoustic bang to create the illusion of gunfire. None of the 151 terrified passengers were injured, and the cruise line spokesmen were pleased that their safety measures worked.[31] According to the International Maritime Bureau (IMB) Annual Report 2010, a total of 445 actual and attempted pirate attacks occurred around the world, with a strong concentration of the attacks around Africa.[32] The IMB, a nonprofit division of the International Chamber of Commerce created to fight against maritime crime and malpractice, advises all mariners to exercise caution and take all necessary precautionary measures when operating in certain areas.[33]

Finally, fires pose a serious concern for anyone sailing hundreds of miles from land. In 2006, *Star Princess*, another ship owned by Carnival Corporation, was set ablaze as she sailed toward Jamaica. Believed to be caused by a cigarette left on a passenger balcony, the fire killed one guest, injured eleven others, and damaged 150 cabins before the crews could douse the flames.[34] As a result, additional sprinklers were installed on balconies and the ship had fewer designated smoking areas.[35]

Carnival *Splendor* Sets Sail

Carnival *Splendor*, a 113,300 ton, 952 foot long behemoth, is one of the largest vessels owned by Carnival Cruise Lines. With thirteen passenger decks, *Splendor*'s 1,503 guest staterooms can accommodate over 3,000 guests per voyage.[36] A ship the size of *Splendor* requires six diesel engines, three of which are housed in the aft engine room and the other three in the forward engine room. Two electric switchboards are connected to each engine's generator by electric cables.[37]

Cruise ships are governed by the laws of the country under which each ship is registered. Since *Splendor* is registered in Panama, any issues that arise at sea would be under the scrutiny of the Panamanian government. However, small countries such as Panama are usually reluctant to conduct strenuous investigation into any mishaps at sea because that could result in the ship operator being required to make costly improvements, which would hurt Panama's flag of convenience business.[38]

Carnival *Splendor* departed Long Beach, California, on Sunday, November 7, 2010, for a weeklong cruise of the Mexican Riviera. The ship's normal itinerary included stops in Puerto Vallarta, Mazatlan, and Cabo San Lucas, Mexico. The seven-day, six-night cruise was scheduled to arrive back in Long Beach with its 3,299 guests and 1,167 crew on Saturday, November 13, until a crisis struck during the first leg of its journey.[39]

Fire!

By early morning on Monday, November 8, 2010, the ship was sailing in calm seas 200 miles south of San Diego, California. At 6:00 a.m., a fire started in the aft engine room and passengers reported smelling smoke and seeing it billow out of the rear of the ship. The blaze was extinguished within a few hours by crew members with the aid of the built-in fire-suppression system. No passengers or crew members were injured as a result of the engine fire.[40]

Engineers were unable to restore ship power, and auxiliary generators had to be used. Though the ship was designed by reputable Italian shipbuilders to ensure that damage to a single generator and switchboard wouldn't inhibit the rest of the ship's engines, the fire unexpectedly disabled all power generation onboard *Splendor*. The intense heat of the fire severely damaged the power lines housed in the ceiling of the aft engine room, which consequently made the forward engine room also inoperable. As a result, the destruction caused by the fire was much more widespread.[41] The ship had previously been regularly inspected by the Coast Guard and other maritime regulators and found in regulatory compliance.[42]

Initial speculation about the cause of the fire was that one of the generators for an aft engine ignited and damaged its accompanying switchboard. The damage to the switchboard and overhead power lines prevented electrical transmission to propulsion, communication, and other operating systems, leaving the ship dead in the water.[43] Gerry Cahill, CEO of Carnival Cruise Lines, later confirmed that the fire was a result of a catastrophic failure in one of six diesel generators. Cahill said he doubted that any of the other ships in the company's fleet were at risk.[44]

Because the ship was registered in Panama, the Panamanian government would be responsible for probing into the official cause of the fire. However, because most of the passengers traveling aboard *Splendor* were U.S. citizens, Panama agreed to allow the U.S. Coast Guard and the National Transportation Safety Board, an independent U.S. federal agency charged with determining the probable cause of transportation accidents and promoting transportation safety, to join the investigation. The three parties would conduct a full examination into the causes of the fire after first ensuring the safety of the passengers and the crew.[45]

At 6:30 a.m. on Monday, passengers were awakened by a message transmitted over the ship's public address system from *Splendor* Cruise Director John Heald. Guests were initially instructed to remain in their cabins but were soon evacuated to the ship's upper deck.[46] Although passengers were later allowed to return to their cabins, many spent the majority of the remainder of the voyage on the upper levels of the ship. By the afternoon, the U.S. Coast Guard had dispatched three cutters and an airplane to provide aid and medical assistance to *Splendor*. The Mexican navy also responded with aircraft and relief boats.[47] Ongoing announcements from Heald about the fire, decisions, and progress kept passengers informed about the situation.

The "Circus" Aboard Carnival

In one of his first public statements about the incident, CEO Gerry Cahill acknowledged that the passengers endured "an extremely trying" situation aboard the Carnival *Splendor*. He publicly apologized for the distress and inconvenience of the passengers. Guests endured challenging circumstances including no electrical power, no Internet service, no refrigerated food, very long lines to obtain food, sanitation problems, and boredom. Air conditioning and hot food service were also unavailable, and the disabled elevators due to the lack of electrical power meant that passengers would have to climb as many as thirteen floors to get to the food. Some passengers reported that plumbing was almost to capacity and that the odor in sections of the ship smelled of vomit.[48]

Cahill admitted that in thirty-five years of business, nothing like the *Splendor* situation had happened before.[49] Cruise Director John Heald tried to keep passengers' spirits up with frequent announcements from the bridge using the ship's PA system. Heald, an avid blogger of johnhealdsblog.com, a blog featured on Carnival Corporation's Web site, told his 8 million readers in a post on Wednesday, November 10, that he didn't know how his attempts to add humor in his announcements were being received by the guests. Heald praised the passengers, saying, "... the guests have been magnificent and have risen to the obvious challenges and difficult conditions onboard."[50]

After the fire, Carnival *Splendor* was about 200 miles south of San Diego and dead in the water. Originally scheduled as a seven-day cruise from Long Beach to Puerto Vallarta, the new objective was to safely transport the passengers to a port as soon as possible. Within two hours of the fire, Gallagher had opened and fully staffed the crisis command center at the Carnival corporate office and worked collectively to aid the *Splendor* crew and passengers.[51] Their initial plan was to tow *Splendor* to the Mexican port of Ensenada;[52] however, the crisis response team soon decided to change the destination to San Diego.[53] The rationale was that passengers would be more comfortable onboard the ship and that the new plan would not require the customers to go through the difficult customs process in Mexico.[54]

The Mexican navy sent multiple tugboats to the aid of *Splendor*, one of which had to turn back because it wasn't powerful enough. Tugboats reached the cruise ship at midday on Tuesday, November 9, 2010.[55] In addition, to the good fortune of Carnival Cruise Lines, the U.S. Navy was doing regularly scheduled training in the area. At the request of the Coast Guard, the U.S. Navy resupplied the ship on Tuesday with 70,000 pounds of bread, canned milk, and other food including Pop Tarts and Spam, and supplies that had been flown from North Island Naval Station in Coronado. The supplies were then ferried by helicopter from the USS *Ronald Reagan* (CVN-76), an aircraft carrier diverted from maneuvers nearby.[56] According to Navy officials, maritime tradition, customs, and treaties demand that ships in the area must respond to other vessels in distress whenever possible.[57]

Toilet service to all public bathrooms and most cabin rooms as well as cold running water was restored late Monday night much to the relief of uncomfortable passengers.[58] One passenger considered the voyage a "diet cruise" because of the lack of hot food. Instead of the fine dining expected aboard any cruise line, passengers were served salads, fruit, small sandwiches, and canned crabmeat. First-time Carnival guest Peg Fisher said, "This could be the only cruise ever where people lost weight instead of gaining weight."[59] With no power, swimming pools were closed due to lack of filtration and casinos were also closed. Interior staterooms were pitch black and stuffy due to the lack of electricity and air flow. Passengers passed the time with live music, scavenger hunts, trivia contests, and card games. However, bars were open and offered free drinks.[60]

Less than one day after the engine fire, Carnival Cruise Lines announced that they would offer all passengers a full refund for the cruise and a credit equal to the price they paid for a future Carnival cruise. In addition, Carnival arranged and paid for all necessary hotels and flights for passengers arriving in San Diego.[61] The ship was expected to arrive in San Diego the morning of Thursday, November 11, more than sixty-two hours after the fire disabled *Splendor*. Initially, it was unknown how long the ship would be out of service until the necessary repairs could be made.

News & Social Media Response

The events on Monday and Tuesday happened outside of cellular phone service range. In addition, Internet service was knocked out due to the loss of power. Passengers were unable to personally update friends and family of their safety until the ship drew closer to the coast on Wednesday, November 10, 2010.[62] On Wednesday, individuals could finally assure loved ones of their safety and share their experiences on the cruise. Passengers called home and sent text messages to communicate with family about arrival in San Diego.[63] Witnesses tweeted pictures and messages about the ship's arrival.[64] In addition, national news outlets began interviewing passengers aboard the ship via cell phones, and their reports covered the evening news.

Carnival used Twitter, Facebook, and its Funville blog primarily as push mechanisms to provide factual updates about the cruise.[65] John Heald also used his personal blog to provide a brief update to readers about the cruise ship on Wednesday, November 10. Passengers had been taking pictures and videos throughout the cruise and many videos were uploaded to YouTube following arrival.[66] The increasing volume of social media that mentioned Carnival *Splendor* created significant buzz on the Internet.

After learning about the delivery of Spam to *Splendor*, some media outlets used "Spam Cruise" as a tagline for articles about the event. Carnival attempted to use Twitter to address the incorrect view that Spam was served to its passengers: "Despite media reports to the contrary, Carnival *Splendor* guests were never served Spam!"[67] However, news and social media outlets continued to embrace the Spam angle, and a new phrase, "Spamcation," emerged online. As passengers departed the ship on Thursday, November 11, they were eager to buy $20 T-shirts emblazoned with the phrase: "I survived the 2010 Carnival Cruise Spamcation."[68]

Decision Point

As Carnival *Splendor* approached the San Diego port at 8:30 a.m. on the morning of Thursday, November 11, Gerry Cahill and Tim Gallagher knew that their work was just beginning. Carnival Cruise Lines had already announced that all guests would receive reimbursement for the trip and travel costs. Cahill and Gallagher had been working around the clock to coordinate the arrival of the ship by arranging transportation and hotels for all guests. But unless Gallagher and his team could quickly address the other issues, Carnival Cruise Lines was at risk of losing a lot more than simply one week of cruise revenues.

Discussion Questions

1. Should the company have done anything differently in their communication efforts while the ship was being brought back to port?
2. Who are the key stakeholders? Who, in your opinion, is (are) the most important stakeholder(s)?
3. What channels of communication should Carnival Cruise Lines use and what should the message be? What audiences do they need to address?
4. How does Carnival Cruise Lines manage its brand reputation in the aftermath of this event? What damage, if any, has been caused? How can it be mitigated? What measures of reputation should the company use?
5. What should Carnival Cruise Lines do to prepare for similar situations in the future? What, if any, performance issues does Carnival Cruise Lines need to address?
6. How may this situation impact future business for Carnival Cruise Lines and the entire cruising industry?

Writing Assignment

Please respond in writing to the issues presented in this case by preparing two documents: a communication strategy memo and a professional business letter.

In preparing these documents, you may assume one of two roles: You may identify yourself as a Carnival Corporation senior manager who has been asked to provide advice to Mr. Gerry Cahill regarding the issues he and his company are facing. Or, you may identify yourself as an external management consultant who has been asked by the company to provide advice to Mr. Cahill.

Either way, you must prepare a strategy memo addressed to Gerry Cahill, president and CEO, Carnival Cruise Lines, that summarizes the details of the case, rank orders the critical issues, discusses their implications (what they mean and why they matter), offers specific recommendations for action (assigning ownership and suspense dates for each), and shows how to communicate the solution to all who are affected by the recommendations.

You must also prepare a professional business letter for Mr. Cahill's signature. That document should be addressed to all Carnival *Splendor* cruisers who have been inconvenienced or disappointed by the events described in the case.

This case was prepared by Research Assistants Russ Cramer, Sam De Lemos, and Laura Divel under the direction of James S. O'Rourke, Teaching Professor of Management, as the basis for class discussion rather than to illustrate either effective or ineffective handling of an administrative situation. Information was gathered from corporate as well as public sources.

Endnotes

1. Lancaster, L. C., & Stillman, D. (2002). *When generations collide: Who they are. Why they clash. How to solve the generational puzzle at work.* New York: HarperBusiness.

2. Gudykunst, W. B., & Ting-Toomey, S. (1988). *Culture and interpersonal communication.* Thousand Oaks, CA: Sage Publications.

3. House, R. J., Hanges, P. J., Javidan, M., Dorfman, P. W., & Gupta, V. (Eds.). (2004). *Culture, leadership, and organizations: The GLOBE study of 62 societies.* Thousand Oaks, CA: Sage Publications.

4. Hofstede, G. (1980). *Culture's consequences: International differences in work-related values.* Beverly Hills, CA: Sage.

5. Hui, C. H., & Triandis, H. C. (1986). Individualism-collectivism: A study of cross-cultural research. *Journal of Cross-cultural Psychology, 17,* 225–48.

6. Hofstede, G. 1980.

7. Triandis, H. (1990). Cross-cultural studies of individualism and collectivism. In J. Berman (Ed.), *Cross-cultural perspectives,* (pp. 41–133). Lincoln, NE: University of Nebraska Press.

8. Heald, J. (2010). Smoke on the water: Part 1. John Heald's Blog, November 12. Accessed February 28, 2011, http://johnhealdsblog.com/2010/11/12/smoke-on-the-water-part-1.

9. McWhirter, C. (2010). U.S. news: Aided by tugs, stranded cruise ship heads to San Diego. *Wall Street Journal,* November 11: A.7.

10. Carnival Cruise Lines fact sheet. (2009). Carnival Cruise Lines, July 8. Accessed February 12, 2011, http://carnivalpressroom.wordpress.com/2009/07/08/carnival-cruise-lines-fact-sheet.

11. Carnival Fun Ships. Carnival Cruise Lines. Accessed February 26, 2011, http://www.carnival.com/FunShips.aspx.

12. Investor relations. Carnival Corporation & plc. Accessed February 12, 2011, http://phx.corporateir.net/phoenix.zhtml?c=140690&p=irol-irhome.

13. 10-K. (2010). Carnival Corporation & plc, January 31. Accessed February 12, 2011, page 4, http://phx.corporate-ir.net/phoenix.zhtml?c=140690&p=irol-sec.

14. Carnival Corporation: Overview. Hoovers, delivered via ProQuest, February 12, 2011, http://cobrands.hoovers.com/global/cobrands/proquest/overview,xhtml?ID=11803.

15. 10-K. Carnival Corporation & plc, page 4.

16. Ibid, page 3.

17. Carnival Corporation: Overview.

18. 10-K. Carnival Corporation & plc, Exhibit 13, page F-1.

19. Carnival Corporation & plc reports financial impact of voyage disruptions in the 4th quarter. (2010). Carnival Corporation & plc, November 16. Accessed February 12, 2011, http://phx.corporate-ir.net/phoenix.zhtml?c=200767&p=irolnewsArticle&ID=1497049&highlight.

20. 10-K. Carnival Corporation & plc, page 5.

21. 10-K. Carnival Corporation & plc, page 6.

22. Safety standards. (2011). Cruise Lines International Association, February 20, http://www2.cruising.org/industry/safety.cfm.

23. Walker, J. (2011). Top five worst cruise ship disaster videos. *Cruise Law News*, January 23. Accessed February 20, 2011, http://www.cruiselawnews.com/2011/01/articles/rough-weather-1/top-five-worst-cruise-ship-disaster-videos.

24. Chua-Eoan, H. G. (2001). Disaster: Going, going … *Time.com*, June 24. Accessed February 20, 2011, http://205.188.238.109/time/magazine/article/0,9171,157677,00.html.

25. Gavazzi, D. (2010). Carnival *Ecstasy* cruise ship tilts and injures passengers. Associated Content from Yahoo!, April 23. Accessed February 20, 2011, http://www.associated content.com/article/2927054/carnival_ecstasy_cruise_ship_tilts.html?cat=16.

26. Pickup, O. (2010). P&O cruise ship horror: CCTV footage captures moment when severe storm sends passengers and furniture flying. Mail Online, September 8. Accessed February 20, 2011, http://www.dailymail.co.uk/travel/article1310056/P-O-Pacific-Sun-cruise-ship-caught-storm-New-Zealand-coast.html.

27. Garrison, L. (2010). Two killed when rogue wave hits *Louis Majesty* cruise ship in the Mediterranean. About.com, March 3. Accessed February 20, 2011, http://cruises.about.com/b/2010/03/03/rogue-wave-mediterranean.htm.

28. Walker. Top five worst cruise ship disaster videos.

29. Prevent the spread of norovirus. Centers for Disease Control and Prevention. Accessed February 20, 2011, http://www.cdc.gov/Features/Norovirus/.

30. Virus hits cruise ship on first day at sea. (2009). ConsumerAffairs.com, March 2. Accessed February 20, 2011, http://www.consumeraffairs.com/news04/2009/03/cruise_illness.html.

31. Cruise ship repels Somali pirates. (2005). *BBC News*, November 5. Accessed February 20, 2011, http://news.bbc.co.uk/2/hi/4409662.stm.

32. Piracy and Armed Robbery Against Ships Annual Report 2010. ICC International Maritime Bureau. Accessed February 20, 2011, page 6, http://www.simsl.com/Downloads/Piracy/IMBPiracyReport2010.pdf.

33. Piracy prone areas and warnings. ICC International Maritime Bureau. Accessed February 20, 2011, http://www.icc-ccs.org/piracy-reporting-centre/prone-areas-and-warnings.

34. Nguyen, D., & J. Rogers. (2010). Troubled cruise shows unpredictability of the sea. Associated Press, *ABC News*, November 13. Accessed February 12, 2011, http://abcnews.go.com/Business/wireStory?id=12135725.

35. Martin, T. (2010). U.S. news: Thousands stranded on disabled cruise liner—navy delivers food to 4,500 passengers, crew off Mexican coast after fire cripples ship; Carnival offers refund, free trip. *Wall Street Journal,* November 10: A.6.

36. Carnival *Splendor*. Carnival Cruise Lines. Accessed February 5, 2011, http://www.carnival.com/cms/fun/ships/carnival_splendor/default.aspx.

37. Stroller, G. (2010). Carnival *Splendor* stranding baffles marine experts. *USA Today*, November 12. Accessed February 12, 2011, http://www.usatoday.com/travel/cruises/2010-11-12-cruise-inside_N.htm?loc=interstitialskip.

38. Nguyen & Rogers. Troubled cruise shows unpredictability of the sea.

39. Ruiz, M. (2010). Updates Carnival *Splendor*. Carnival Cruise Lines, November 8. Accessed February 12, 2011, http://www

.carnival.com/Funville/forums/p/140814 /730198.aspx.

40. Vercammen, P., Martinez, M., & Gast, P. (2010). Crippled cruise ship expected in San Diego Thursday. *CNN*, November 11. Accessed February 12, 2011, http://edition .cnn.com/2010/TRAVEL/11/10/cruise.ship/? hpt=T2.

41. Telephone interview with Tim Gallagher, Carnival Cruise Lines' vice president of corporate communications, March 1, 2011.

42. Stroller. Carnival *Splendor* stranding baffles marine experts.

43. Ibid.

44. Spagat, E. (2010). Travelers disembark "nightmare" cruise amid cheers. Associated Press, *ABC News*, November 11. Accessed February 12, 2011, http://abcnews.go.com /Business/wireStory?id=12122689.

45. McWhirter. U.S. news: Aided by tugs, stranded cruise ship heads to San Diego.

46. La Ganga, M. L., & Perry, T. (2010). Stranded cruise ship offers lesson in huge vessels' vulnerabilities. *Los Angeles Times*, November 10. Accessed February 12, 2011, http://articles.latimes.com/print/2010/nov/10 /local/la-me-cruise-ship20101110.

47. La Ganga & Perry. Stranded cruise ship offers lesson in huge vessels' vulnerabilities.

48. Vercammen, Martinez, & Gast. Crippled cruise ship expected in San Diego Thursday.

49. Ibid.

50. Heald, J. (2010). Here I am. John Heald's Blog, November 10. Accessed February 12, 2011, http://johnhealdsblog.com/2010/11 /10/here-i-am-2.

51. Telephone interview with Tim Gallagher.

52. Heald, J. (2010). Update on the Carnival *Splendor*. John Heald's Blog, November 8. Accessed February 12, 2011, http://john healdsblog.com/2010/11/08/update-on-the -carnival-splendor.

53. Heald, J. (2010). Latest Carnival *Splendor* update. John Heald's Blog, November 9.

Accessed February 12, 2011, http://john healdsblog.com/2010/11/09/latest-carnival -splendor-update.

54. Watson, J., et al. (2010). Carnival CEO apologizes to stranded cruisers. *MSNBC Travel News*, November 11. Accessed February 12, 2011, http://www.msnbc.msn .com/id/40084109/ns/travel-news.

55. Ibid.

56. Perry, T. (2010). Tugboats, Navy copters head for cruise ship damaged by fire off Mexico. *Los Angeles Times*, November 9. Accessed February 12, 2011, http://latimesblogs.latimes .com/lanow/2010/11/tugboats-navy-copters -head-for-cruiseship-damaged-by-fire-off -mexico.html.

57. McWhirter, C. (2010). Disabled cruise ship reaches San Diego Harbor. *Wall Street Journal* (Online), November 11, http://online.wsj.com /article/SB100014240527487038482045756083 81063993198.html.

58. Heald. Latest Carnival *Splendor* update.

59. Spagat. Travelers disembark "nightmare" cruise amid cheers.

60. Watson et al. Carnival CEO apologizes to stranded cruisers.

61. Martin. U.S. news: Thousands stranded on disabled cruise liner.

62. Vercammen, Martinez, & Gast. Crippled cruise ship expected in San Diego Thursday.

63. Sloan, G. (2010). Carnival *Splendor* passengers disembark in San Diego. *USA Today*, November 11. Accessed February 12, 2011, http://www.usatoday.com/travel/cruises/2010 -11-11-1Acruise11_CV_N.htm.

64. Benabia, J. (2010). Carnival *Splendor* cruise ship being towed back home (from my balcony). Twitter, November 11. Accessed February 12, 2011, http://twitter.com/dermdoc /status/2751684606431234.

65. Schaal, D. (2010). Carnival *Splendor* and 1-way social media response from Carnival. *tnooz*, November 10. Accessed February 12, 2011, http://www.tnooz.com/2010/11/10

/news/carnival-splendor-and-1-way-social-media-response-fromcarnival.

66. Hoffer, S. (2010). Footage gives peek into cruise ship ordeal. *AOL News*, November 12. Accessed February 12, 2011, http://www.aolnews.com/2010/11/12/passenger-footage-gives-inside-look-at-carnival-splendor-cruise.

67. Sloan, G. (2010). Carnival: No spam was served on Carnival *Splendor* during crisis. *USA Today*, November 11. Accessed February 12, 2011, http://travel.usatoday.com/cruises/post/2010/11/carnival-splendor-cruise-ship-fire-spam-/130847/1.

68. Spagat. Travelers disembark "nightmare" cruise amid cheers.

Javier Larrea/age fotostock/Getty Images

Steps Three and Four: Consider the Context and Select a Channel of Communication

After reading this chapter, you will be able to

▶ Recognize the importance of considering context as part of the strategic-communication process.

▶ Analyze the context of a communication situation to identify factors that need to be taken into account when formulating a message.

▶ Learn about the elements that affect the quality of communication that occurs within an organization, including corporate culture and structure, as well as formal and informal communication networks.

▶ Select a channel and medium that will best help you fulfill your purpose(s) for communicating and properly engage your audience(s).

Case Questions:

1. Why is working virtually potentially more problematic than working in an organizational environment in which members can occasionally meet face to face?

2. If you were leader of this virtual team, what would you do to build a culture of trust among its members?

3. What additional concerns might need to be addressed when attempting to create a communication strategy that accounted for cultural differences and that would make all feel included and appreciated?

The Case of the Virtual Team

Jennifer was frustrated. She had submitted her contribution to the software project on which she was working electronically to her team four days ago and had heard nothing from anyone since. Enough was enough. She keyed in the message: "Are you not in the … assignment anymore?" and pressed the Send key.

In fact, in the past three months, Jennifer estimated that she accounted for more than 50 percent of the communications for the team. This lack of responsiveness was one of the challenges of working in a virtual team, with members scattered across the globe. Jennifer was part of a project management team responsible for creating SmartPhone apps that would be compatible with phone technologies used around the world. Team members were located in East Asia, Europe, and South America. Although they worked for the same company, TekTron, their native languages were different as well as their cultural values. The latter created challenges in regard to team members' expectations about communication, time, and relationships.

These differences and their effect on the team had not been well addressed by company management. It had also led Jennifer to believe that she couldn't rely on her team members; it had damaged her ability to trust.

Contextual issues—particularly those dealing with organizational context—and channel-choice considerations are both elements of the strategic-communication process that can be applied at both the individual (or personal) and corporate levels. You should consider these issues when strategizing personal messages; the consideration of these issues should also be done at the corporate level to create an effective communication plan for an organization. Potential leaders and managers will thus read the following information with both goals in mind.

Organizational Context

"Communication is the lifeblood of any organization, big or small," says Ronald Gross, head of Censeo Corporation, a Maitland, Florida, human resources consulting firm.[1] However, a company's policies, programs, and structures can support or interfere with good communication. The context within which communication occurs can also affect how, what, when, and whether we should communicate. The corporate culture of an organization also can affect the quality of communication that occurs within it. This section discusses these issues in addition to the types of communication networks that exist in organizations, formal and informal.

Context Defined

Context is the situation or setting in which communication occurs. Context can influence the content, the quality, and the effectiveness of a communication event.

There are several ways to think about context in terms of communication. For example, the discipline of communication itself arranges its areas of research and study by context: intrapersonal communication, interpersonal communication, small-group communication, public speaking, organizational communication, and mass communication. The differences among these communication situations will affect your choices of the most appropriate oral, nonverbal, or written codes. This textbook draws on all of these differing contexts and situates them within a broader one—that of the organization. Organizational context is the situation (e.g., the corporation, the accounting firm, the manufacturing plant, the not-for-profit) in which communication takes place. Social rules, modes of behavior, type of dress, language style, nonverbal communication, communication media choice, and topics of discussion are all affected by where and under what circumstances they occur within an organization.

Context as a Strategic Issue

Context is developed within an organization through the process of individuals interacting. What that means is that context is not something "out there"; it is something that is being created and re-created all the time in organizations (and other settings) primarily through communication practices as thought broadly. That means that communication includes oral, written, and nonverbal elements, such as symbols, artifacts, behaviors, and so on. Creating a common context in the minds of communicators is a product of repetitive exposure to people in certain roles under similar circumstances and in comparable settings. (This understanding is

context
The situation or setting in which communication occurs.

based on the social construction of reality theory that was discussed in Chapter 1.) Through repeated experience, a series of probable interpretations of symbols, messages, behaviors, artifacts, and so on become the norm while other interpretations are ignored or given less credence. Context is important for helping us understand the meaning of communication behaviors within a particular situation, but it also is often overlooked because of this process of context creation: It is so much a part of our reality that we often have difficulty seeing it and thus analyzing it. In other words, we cannot get outside our "box."

Trained mindlessness describes this condition, which also might be termed a lack of strategic focus. Trained mindlessness might even be part of the organization's culture. Individuals who follow the same routine every day without change become "mindless experts" who concentrate on the end result and pay little attention to the process. The problem is that such individuals are not attentive to the task environment or the context and thus do not notice things out of the ordinary.[2] Such indifference to the environment or the context of a situation may affect not only the organization at a strategic level but also our ability as individuals to act strategically in terms of our communication.

The importance of developing a sensitivity to context has become a requirement for leaders, too. In *In Their Time: The Greatest Business Leaders of the Twentieth Century*, Tony Mayo notes that business opportunities emerge when environmental factors and individual action come together. Environmental factors create specific and sometimes unique contexts for business. Within this contextual framework, some individuals envision new enterprises or new products and services, while others see opportunities for maximizing or optimizing existing businesses, and still others find opportunities through reinvention or recreation of companies or technologies that were considered stagnant or declining.

This awareness of and ability to adapt to the context is called **contextual intelligence**. This ability to "seize the zeitgeist" of the time moves to the fore the study of situational context and places a secondary focus on developing individual characteristics of leadership.[3]

The ability to succeed in multiple contexts is based on what Warren Bennis and Robert Thomas in *Geeks & Geezers* called **adaptive capacity**—the ability to change one's style and approach to fit the culture, context, or condition of an organization.[4] Success in the twenty-first century will require leaders to pay attention to the evolving context.

Dimensions of Context

contextual intelligence
The awareness of and ability to adapt to the context.

adaptive capacity
The ability to change one's style and approach to fit the culture, context, or condition of an organization.

As discussed, all communication occurs within a particular context or situation. For this reason, it is important to spend some time analyzing the context, situation, or environment in which communication takes place to formulate an effective strategy for that particular set of circumstances.

There are several dimensions to context, including the physical, social, chronological, and cultural. The *physical* context or setting can influence the content and quality of interaction. For example, if you were to ask your boss for a raise, the effect of the setting might dramatically affect your chances for success. How might the following settings affect the success of such an interaction, how it might take place, or whether it should take place: In the boss's office? At a company picnic? Over lunch at a restaurant? In your work area with others observing?

The *social context* refers to the nature of the relationship between the communicators as well as who is present. In the same situation mentioned above, imagine how the relationship between your manager and yourself might affect your request for a raise if

- You and the manager have been friends for several years, as opposed to a situation in which you and your manager have no personal relationship.
- You are the same age as your manager, *or* she or he is fifteen years older (or younger) than you.
- You and the manager have gotten along well in the past, compared to a situation in which you and the manager have been involved in an ongoing personal conflict.

The *chronological context* refers to the ways time influences interactions. For example, how might the time of day affect the quality of an interaction? How might the communicator's personal preferences regarding time affect communication and its success? Is it a busy time of year for employees and managers? Has there just been a major layoff, downsizing, or profit loss? In this last case, you might want to put off your request for a raise until conditions improve.

The *cultural context* includes both the organizational culture as well as the cultural backgrounds of the people with whom you may be communicating. **Organizational culture** refers to a system of shared meanings and practices held by members that distinguish the organization from other organizations. Organizational culture can affect the means and style of communication that takes place in an organization. (Organizational culture is discussed more fully in the following section.)

A person's cultural influences also can affect the kind and quality of communication that takes place, and they can help determine approaches that will be more effective. For example, young people have different expectations than seniors, Hispanics have different expectations than Asians, Californians have different expectations than people from the Midwest or East Coast, and men may communicate differently than women. (Several approaches to cultural values were discussed in Chapter 4, "Step Two: Analyze the Audience.")

Environmental factors may also affect what should be communicated and how. For example, if the economy is doing poorly, then some messages may be inappropriate or may have little chance for success. If you work in a highly litigious environment or one that is strongly regulated, then constraints may exist for what you can communicate and how. Larger social, political, or historical events may affect whether certain messages are appropriate or have a chance of success.

Organizational Structure and Culture

organizational culture
The system of shared meanings and practices within an organization that distinguish it from other organizations.

Organizational culture "provides an immediate, familiar outline of what you should pay attention to and the constraints within which you should steer your actions."[5] *Organizational culture* is "a pattern of shared basic assumptions that the group learned as it solved its problems of external adaptation and internal integration and which has worked well enough to be taught to new members as the correct way to perceive, think, and feel in relation to these problems."[6] Boreham and Morgan note that "Schein makes the crucial claim that an organization's culture determines what it can and cannot do, and that the extent of individual members' socialization into that culture determines what they can and cannot do."[7] This is true of actions and behaviors as well as communicative practices and behaviors.

In other words, organizational structure and policies that affect organizational culture affect the quality of communication within an organization. The culture of a business provides part of the *context* (explained in the previous section) for interpreting the meaning of everyday organizational life as well as determining what are considered appropriate messages and the proper or expected ways to convey them.

For example, Zappos, an online retailer, has created a good deal of its reputation through its message about its unique corporate culture: Its number one core value is to "deliver WOW through service" to its customers. The use of "WOW" is just one clue to Zappos's unique culture. Other values include "create fun and a little weirdness," "do more with less," "build open and honest relationships," and "be humble." Compare these values with the type of culture that you might find in an investment banking firm in which competition, individualism, and the drive for profits and bonuses would likely be key elements and it should be easy to see how culture might affect how communication occurs and what is expected and accepted within an organization in terms of behaviors.

Research suggests that there are seven primary characteristics that, when taken as a whole, capture the essence of an organization's culture.[8] These are

1. **Innovation and risk taking,** or the degree to which employees are encouraged to innovate and take risks.
2. **Attention to detail,** or the degree to which employees are expected to exhibit precision, analytical skills, and attention to detail.
3. **Outcome orientation,** or the degree to which management focuses on results or outcomes rather than on the techniques and processes used to achieve these outcomes.
4. **People orientation,** or the degree to which management decisions consider the effect of outcomes on people within the organization.
5. **Team orientation,** or the degree to which work activities are organized around teams rather than individuals.
6. **Aggressiveness,** or the degree to which people are aggressive and competitive rather than easygoing.
7. **Stability,** or the degree to which organizational activities emphasize maintaining the status quo rather than focusing on change.

Each characteristic is listed in Table 5-1 and exists on a continuum from low to high. Appraising the organization on each of these characteristics can provide a picture of the organization's culture.

More generally speaking, the culture of business can be characterized as typically having a bias toward action, a demand for confidence, and a results orientation.[9] The culture of business can be seen in everyday office interactions. Being knowledgeable about an organization's culture can help you gauge the type and quality of communication that takes place as well as whether you are a good match with an organization. For example, do people wear T-shirts and shorts or suits to work every day? Does the organization have an "open door" policy or are you expected to obey the hierarchical ordering of management when communicating concerns? Does the office have an open floor plan or do employees have private offices? The first situation in each of these cases probably signals that the culture is less formal in terms of its expectations and communication patterns while the second situation may indicate a culture that is more formal in terms of its expectations regarding punctuality and communication choices and behaviors.

Although what constitutes a healthy organizational culture can be debated, one description of a good organization that includes communication behaviors and

Table 5-1 Primary Characteristics of Organizational Culture.
1. The degree to which employees are encouraged to be innovative and take risks.
2. The degree to which employees are expected to exhibit precision, analysis, and attention to detail.
3. The degree to which management focuses on results or outcomes rather than on the techniques and processes used to achieve those outcomes.
4. The degree to which management decisions consider the effect of outcomes on people within the organization.
5. The degree to which work activities are organized around teams or groups rather than individuals.
6. The degree to which people are aggressive and competitive rather than easygoing and cooperative.
7. The degree to which organizational activities emphasize maintaining the status quo compared to promoting change.

Source: O'Reilly, III, C. A., Chatman, J., & Caldwell, D. F. (1991). "People and Organizational Culture: A Profile Comparison Approach to Assessing Person–Organization Fit," *Academy of Management Journal*, September: 487–516.

KIMBERLY WHITE/Reuters/Landov

Applied Materials Inc. President and Chief Executive Michael Splinter speaks during a panel discussion at the Fortune Brainstorm Tech conference in Half Moon Bay, California, July 22, 2008.

supportive communication climate
An organizational climate in which individuals do not feel threatened.

attitudes that contribute to positive communication is provided in the following list.[10] Good organizations are places where authentic (as opposed to pretentious) people

- Listen well.
- Respect the validity of others' experience.
- Feel free to be assertive.
- Have a clear sense of direction and control.
- Get good feedback about their performance.
- Feel valued as intelligent human beings.[11]

In addition, good organizations provide opportunities for employees to voice their opinions and concerns, encourage conversations that are simultaneously supportive and critical, promote a positive experience of work, and are able to remain profitable in a competitive marketplace. Many of the characteristics of good organizations are elements of communication, including the ability to listen well, provide good feedback, and communicate assertively yet respectfully with others.

Such organizations have also been described as having a **supportive communication climate**.[12] An organization that exhibits a supportive communication climate is one in which you feel free from threat. You perceive that although the content of your communication may be evaluated and even rejected, no one is passing judgment on your personal worth. In the absence of threat, and perceiving that others are open and honest, you freely express your opinions and feelings, trust others, and are open to them.

In contrast, unhealthy work conditions include

- Authoritarian and detailed supervision.
- Tasks characterized by restrictions on employees' abilities to use resources.
- Work-production systems that do not provide opportunities to contribute initiative, responsibility, or personal knowledge to the job.

Table 5-2 Characteristics of Defensive and Supportive Organizational Climates.

DEFENSIVE	SUPPORTIVE
1. Evaluation. To pass judgment on another.	1. Description. Nonjudgmental. To ask questions, present feelings, refrain from asking the other to change his or her behavior.
2. Control. To try to do something to another; to try to change behavior or attitudes of others.	2. Problem orientation. To convey a desire to collaborate in solving a mutual problem or defining it; to allow the other to set his or her goals.
3. Strategy. To manipulate another, to engage in multiple or ambiguous motivations.	3. Spontaneity. To express naturalness, free of deception; straightforwardness; uncomplicated motives.
4. Neutrality. To express a lack of concern for the other; the clinical, person-as-object-of-study attitude.	4. Empathy. To respect the other person and show it; to identify with his or her problems; to share his or her feelings.
5. Superiority. To communicate that you are superior in position, wealth, intelligence, and so on, to arouse feelings of inadequacy in others.	5. Equality. To be willing to enter into participative planning with mutual trust and respect; to attach little importance to differences of worth, status, and so on.
6. Certainty. To seem to know the answers and be dogmatic, wanting to win an argument rather than solve a problem; seeing one's ideas as truths to be defended.	6. Provisionalism. To be willing to experiment with your own behavior; to investigate issues rather than taking sides; to solve problems, not debate.

Source: Gibb, J. (1961). "Defensive Communication," *Journal of Communication, 11*, 141–148.

- Limited opportunities for employees to exercise influence in the planning and organizing of tasks.
- Tasks that deprive the individual of the self-determination of work rate and methods for carrying out the work.
- Tasks that limit human contacts during work.[13]

Such an organization can be characterized as one that does not value its employees as intelligent human beings and does not trust them to make responsible, knowledgeable decisions. Although these characteristics have little to do with communication, they do concern a characteristic that is necessary for effective communication: trust.

Just as healthy organizations are characterized as having supportive climates, unhealthy ones are characterized as having **defensive communication climates**. A defensive communication climate is one in which you feel threatened. You perceive that your communication can be used against you, carefully edit your comments to protect yourself from real or anticipated threat, and mistrust others and thus are closed to them. Table 5-2 distinguishes those behaviors that characterize defensive and supportive organizational climates.

Most organizations are a combination of these characteristics. Therefore, the ability to be strategic in our communication practices is helpful, at least in the United States where competition is common in many organizations, if only in performance appraisal and compensation policies.

defensive communication climate
An organizational climate in which individuals feel threatened.

CriticalThinking

Identify a group or an organization in which you have been involved. Was its communication climate defensive or supportive? What aspects of the group or organization characterized its communication climate as such? If you are a leader, what can you do to improve the communication climate where you work?

Formal Communication Networks

An organization's formal communication network is typically reflected in its structure or organizational chart. Such charts summarize the lines of authority; each position in the hierarchy represents a link in the chain of command, and each line represents a formal channel for the transmission of official messages. Information may travel three ways in an organization: down, up, and horizontally.

- **Downward flow.** Organizational decisions are usually made at the top and then flow down to the people who will carry them out. Most of what flows downward is intended to maintain the formal organizational culture and the company's overall profitability.
- **Upward flow.** Because the employees who perform the work of the organization often have the most information, managers should have access to their feedback to improve processes, productivity, morale, decision making, and, ultimately, organizational profitability or sustainability. Because upward communication may be less formalized than downward flow, it "has to be constantly fostered and reinforced, so that people see it's something that's valued."[14]
- **Horizontal flow.** Communication also flows within and between departments. This information helps departments and employees share and coordinate their activities to improve productivity and the quality of decision making.

Network communication flow can be an indicator of corporate culture. For example, if most communication is downward, the organization is generally more hierarchical and formal in its culture. In contrast, an organization that provides formal mechanisms for upward horizontal flow and acts on the information provided is likely to be less formal and more egalitarian.

In addition, effective leaders and managers should assess the formal communication network to see where there are gaps in communication that might negatively affect the overall health of the organization. (The steps in organizational communication strategy formulation are discussed more in Chapter 11). On an individual level, assessing and understanding the flow of communication within an organization can help you better strategize your own communication practices.

Informal Communication Networks

Every organization also has an informal communication network—the grapevine—that supplements formal channels. Most of this information is conveyed through casual conversations between employees. Although these conversations may also deal with personal matters, 80 percent of the information that travels through the grapevine deals with business.

Savvy managers will pay a great deal of attention to the informal communication network within an organization and will use it to disseminate accurate information to employees. If ignored, the informal communication network is another means by which managers can lose control of the flow of information within an organization, causing other problems such as poor morale or distrust.

However, awareness of the informal communication network should be tempered with recognition of the need for flexibility. Organizations must be flexible to remain competitive. Strict rules and procedures can be a hindrance to this needed flexibility in the current business climate, which is characterized by the constant of change. Without the time to formalize some relationships, their effectiveness often depends on the trust that can develop over time among employees.[15]

One way to provide more control over the informal communication network is to constantly update employees on changes in company policies, practices, earnings perspectives, and product and service lines and to encourage an open flow of communication upward. Good formal communication can help to minimize the potential negative effects of the grapevine.

Choosing a Communication Channel and Medium

Broadly speaking, four channels of communication exist: written, oral, nonverbal, and visual. However, these broad categories can be broken down further. For example, written communication can be disseminated using a variety of media or forms, including memos, letters, emails, instant or text messaging, faxes, press releases, company Web sites, blogs, blog applications, and reports. Oral communication can also use various media or forms such as face-to-face or interpersonal, telephone, voice messages, teleconferences and videoconferences, speeches, meetings, and podcasts. Typically, nonverbal communication supplements oral forms, but it shouldn't be underestimated because most communication in face-to-face situations is nonverbal. Similarly, visual communication supplements both written and oral forms of communication in the form of diagrams, photographs, charts, tables, video, and artwork.

Channel choice might be influenced or informed by earlier steps in the strategic process. For instance, purpose of communication might affect channel choice; in a situation in which the purpose is primarily to establish relationship or convey goodwill, a face-to-face meeting might be the best choice to achieve this goal. Audience analysis might yield information that indicates it prefers a particular medium of communication such as email or phone discussions. Similarly, an examination of organizational context issues might indicate that written memos are still the conventional medium for communicating with staff in a particular organization, whereas text messaging is the preferred mode in others.

Figure 5-1 lists additional issues that might be considered when selecting the channel and medium that best suits a particular communication situation.

These considerations are discussed in more detail in the following sections.

Richness versus Leanness

Some channels of communication provide more information than others. Generally, the richest channels of communication provide nonverbal information in addition to that provided in written or oral form. For this reason, the richest channel of

---

FIGURE 5-1 Channel Selection Considerations

Richness versus leanness

Need for interpretation (ambiguity)

Speed of establishing contact

Time required for feedback

Cost

Amount of information conveyed

Permanent record

Control over the message

© Cengage Learning

---

communication is face-to-face, or what is often called *interpersonal communication*. Face-to-face communication provides participants a rich source of information, including vocal cues, facial expressions, bodily movement, bodily appearance, the use of space, the use of time, touching, and clothing and other artifacts.

In addition, face-to-face communication provides opportunities to facilitate feedback and establish a personal focus. These aspects also contribute to the richness of interpersonal communication as a channel of communication.

Face-to-face communication is thus particularly useful for job interviews in which the prospective employer is presumably interested in gathering as much information as possible from applicants. Similarly, personnel issues involving an individual may best be explored in a face-to-face communication situation because this mode might provide more information about the person's feelings, attitudes, or nonverbal clues to issues that are preventing him or her from functioning at the highest possible level.

Other channels of communication that provide access to nonverbal information are oral presentations, meetings, and group work. This is true regardless of whether this communication is mediated or not. In other words, presentations might take place using Skype, podcasts, or other technology that allows audiences to view speakers who are not in the same place. Similarly, presentations might be recorded and viewed at a later time. Opportunities for checking the accuracy of interpretation of information may be more limited in these situations, though, because one person may more easily exercise control over the exchange of information.

Voice communication also provides some nonverbal information—much less than communication that enables us to view another's facial expressions, body language, clothing, and other artifacts, but potentially more than is provided by written communication. However, even some nonverbal information such as some emotions can be communicated via email and text messaging. Even in more formal types of written communication, such as paper memos and letters, tone can be communicated and can be an indicator of the writer's attitude or mood, and emoticons can be used in less formal types of writing, such as text and email messages.

Perhaps the leanest medium of communication is a text or instant message. Lean media are useful for sending routine simple messages, such as short responses to queries or meeting times. However, they should not be used for persuasive purposes, more complex messages, or when establishing credibility or goodwill is the focus. They can maintain credibility and goodwill, however, to some degree, after these have been established. Similarly, they can damage credibility and goodwill, so even when using this lean medium some care should be taken.

Need for Interpretation

Some channels of communication are more ambiguous or leave more room for interpretation of the message being sent than others. Nonverbal communication may be the most ambiguous channel of communication because it requires the audience to interpret almost the entirety of the message. Nonverbal communication is difficult to interpret for a variety of reasons, mainly because it is not generally considered a coded language. Because of this, one nonverbal code may communicate a variety of meanings. For example, you may stand close to someone because you are in a crowded room, are having difficulty hearing him or her, or are attracted to the person. Studies indicate that receivers of nonverbal cues can often only guess about the meaning of those cues.[16]

Similarly, nonverbal communication can be difficult to interpret because a variety of codes may communicate the same meaning. This problem is particularly apparent when cultural differences come into play in a communication situation. In a public-speaking situation, for example, you might show respect for the speaker by looking directly at him or her, whereas in some cultures listeners show respect when they avert their eyes from the speaker.

A third issue that may affect a person's ability to interpret nonverbal codes accurately is intentionality. Some nonverbal codes are sent intentionally, and others unintentionally. If you smile at a friend, you are intentionally showing him or her that you are glad to see that person. However, the same nonverbal cue may be sent unintentionally yet interpreted as intentional. You might be thinking about a pleasant experience you had the night before and unintentionally smile. But if this occurs while you are walking down the street, the stranger approaching you may interpret this unintentional signal as an intentional cue of interest in him or her.

For this reason, face-to-face communication may be more ambiguous than other channels of communication. Furthermore, depending on our sensitivity to nonverbal communication codes, we may overreact to certain nonverbal messages; conversely, we may be only somewhat aware or completely unaware of such information. Culture may play a role as well. The United States tends to be what is termed a "low-context" culture, which means that we tend to pay less attention to the contextual features of a situation and focus more on the verbal aspects, or what is said.

Written communication has the potential to be the least ambiguous channel of communication, particularly if it is prepared by a highly skilled writer who is able to precisely encode such a message. Such a writer must understand his or her purposes and audiences and have an excellent command of the language and its correct usage. For this reason, many official or legal messages such as contracts are delivered in the form of written documents. Similarly, instructions are often provided in written form, which also serves as a record that can be skimmed to quickly provide the needed information.

However, written communication can also become ambiguous when sending text messages, instant messaging, or using such social media as Twitter. That's because the abbreviations used for words or phrases may be unknown to some readers. Therefore, the audience's knowledge of such jargon should be considered when using these media.

Speed of Establishing Contact

Another important consideration, particularly in the business world, is the time it will take for a message to be delivered. As the old saying goes, time is often money. For this reason, electronic forms of communication have become popular. Using the telephone, writing an email or text message, using blogs and blog applications (such as Twitter) or other social media such as Facebook or LinkedIn, posting to wikis, Skyping, using virtual team applications, or sending a fax are nearly instantaneous channels of communication. In contrast, sending a written message or package by mail may take days. If you wish to communicate with someone who lives or works in another state or nation, then it may take days or even weeks to arrange a face-to-face meeting. For these reasons, electronic channels of communication have become extremely useful in the modern workplace. More and more companies are creating shared digital spaces or virtual teams where employees who are located in different areas of the country and even the world collaborate electronically to get their work done. Even communication within the same building is often conducted electronically through email—the preferred method in most organizations—or text messaging.

Time Required for Feedback

Just as we may need to contact someone immediately, we may also need a response from that person just as rapidly. The most rapid forms of communication, as explained above, are generally electronic. However, depending on the person with whom you are communicating, his or her personality, and your relationship, communicating with a person via an electronic channel does not guarantee prompt feedback. In other words, corporate cultures and individuals may have preferences for specific communication channels or mediums and differing communication practices. As mentioned earlier, much communication now occurs in organizations using email, while some individuals may prefer face-to-face communication and thus may be more responsive to messages delivered using this medium. Others may prefer the telephone or electronic means. It is important to consider corporate and industry practices as well as the preferences of individuals to ensure the most prompt response to your messages. For example, if you are attempting to communicate with individuals working in a large shipping facility, they may not have access to computers or smartphones. Instead, they may communicate using radios or even interpersonally.

Cost

Many channels of communication are relatively inexpensive for business users. Mail, email, text messages, telephones, faxes, wikis, blogs and blog applications, social media, videoconferencing and teleconferencing tools, and Skype are generally considered inexpensive forms of communication. These tools have made it much less expensive for stakeholders both inside and outside organizations to communicate with each other, regardless of their location. Still, there are times when it may be appropriate to choose the greater expense of arranging a face-to-face meeting. Such cases might include introducing members of a virtual team who will be working on an important project for some time, interviewing job applicants for key positions, or meeting with important clients or accounts. The benefits of establishing rapport in these instances are expected to offset the increased costs of such arrangements.

Amount of Information Conveyed

The best channel for conveying large amounts of information is generally a written one. One reason is that most of us are generally poor listeners. Studies indicate that we retain only 10 percent or so of what we hear. Therefore, if you want people to have the opportunity to process and remember the information you have to deliver, particularly if the message is long or complex, then it is generally best delivered using a written channel.

You can see this channel-choice consideration practiced in everyday news delivery. If you want more information about what is happening in your community, state, country, or the world, you will probably read a print or electronic version of a newspaper or newsmagazine or visit an Internet news site. If you want less information about these issues or have less time, then you might watch or listen to a television newscast or listen to a radio news program on your way to work. Typically, less information is delivered by these electronic, oral channels, because they appeal to people who do not have much time or do not wish to invest much time in such information, who have shortened attention spans, or who do not like to read. These media generally deliver less information about the topics they address, although the Internet is making these distinctions less important as more news is delivered online in a variety of formats.

Regardless of whether the information is delivered electronically or on paper, though, if you have a fairly large quantity of complex or detailed information to deliver, a written communication channel is generally the best because it provides readers the opportunity to take the time necessary to process that information, often at their own convenience.

There are times, though, when a written channel may not be sufficient for delivering complex information; one example is training. Although more and more training programs are being delivered online, some situations may require a two-channel delivery system to provide trainees written materials as well as face-to-face instruction to ensure that information is understood and to answer participants' questions. The two-channel approach might also be used for important or persuasive messages. An email, memo, report, or proposal might be provided and then followed up with a meeting or oral presentation, for example, or vice versa, depending on the communication goals. In addition, performance appraisals and reprimands are typically delivered both face-to-face and in writing. In this instance, the face-to-face meeting is intended to maintain rapport while the written message serves as a record of the exchange.

Need for a Permanent Record

Businesspeople are often involved in situations where they must keep records of what occurred during various work activities throughout the day or week. These situations include the need to record what occurred at a department meeting, an employee's work history, the findings of an audit of a client's financial records, and an employee's travel expenses. Most legal documents, including contracts, use the written channel of communication for this reason: the need to maintain a record. Email messages and other electronic forums such as Web sites, social networking sites, and blogs, if stored and backed up properly, can also serve as a record. This ability is not only a benefit, though; it can have very negative consequences for those who take advantage of the spontaneity of these electronic communication tools without taking the time to consider the strategic issues mentioned in this text. In other words, it is important to consider the impact of the message on the audience as well as to consider whether it might negatively affect our own credibility or relationship with the receiver. In the worst case, it may have much more negative consequences, such as losing our job if we anger a client, present a negative image of the company to the public, or reveal company information that is intended to remain internal to the organization.

Control over the Message

Written channels of communication also are often the best choice when you wish to maintain greater control of the message that you send. The reason? If information is presented orally and interpersonally, you have a greater chance of persons who disagree with you speaking out and potentially derailing or confusing the message. That is why many negative messages are sent using a written channel of communication.

For example, if you must tell a job applicant that he was not selected for the position for which he recently interviewed, you can maintain control over the act of delivering that information by doing so in the form of a letter or even a well-written email message. Although calling the person to deliver the message might exhibit greater goodwill on your part because you have taken the time to interact using a channel that enables you to send nonverbal codes (vocal cues), you also risk a situation that might spin out of control if the person does not take the news well or wishes to take more of your time to find out why he or she was not selected. In this case, you also may be put in a position to explain the decision more fully. However, by sending a polite letter or email, you are able to convey the same basic message without the risk of losing control of the situation or your time. But even this selection matters. If you send an email rather than a letter, you are more likely to be contacted by the receiver, so you should consider whether you want to encourage further interaction on the matter. If not, a letter might be a better choice.

Similarly, in crisis situations, some companies refuse to speak to the news media for fear of losing control of the message or releasing information that may be damaging. These situations may be handled by using the written communication channel to send a press release to the media or post a message to the public on the company Web site. The press release delivers information but does not provide an opportunity for the receiver to question the communicator and for the communicator to potentially lose control of the message that the company intends to convey. Oral channels of communication are often riskier because they expose the speaker to differences of opinion, conflict, and personalities that may be difficult to control. On the other side, conflict situations demand greater control of the nonverbal elements of communication and thus expose the communicator to risk in terms of unintentionally sending a negative message. One common example occurs in legal situations in which the defendant may not "appear" to be sorry for his or her actions and this lack of remorse may affect sentencing.

However, if one of the primary purposes of the message is to convey or maintain goodwill, then it is generally better to deliver the bad news face-to-face. Table 5-3 provides a summary of the proper use of differing media within an organizational context.

New Media and the Organization

Rapid technology changes have made communication cheaper and faster for organizations, providing more avenues for connecting with employees, suppliers, and current and potential customers. People who use the Internet to share relevant

Table 5-3 Use of Communication Media.

MEDIUM	BEST USES
Memo	■ Simple, routine messages ■ Confirming policies ■ Distributing to a large, internal audience ■ Providing information when a response isn't required ■ Communicating with an external audience
Letter	■ Conveying formality ■ Providing a written record ■ Writing a complaint ■ Communicating condolences or thanks ■ Sending brief, impersonal, or routine messages
Email	■ Providing a hard copy ■ Sending a visual display of information
Fax	■ Communicating general information about a company and its products or services
Web page	■ Sharing information with large audiences in an economical fashion ■ Inspiring and motivating others ■ Demonstrating products or training
Oral presentation	■ Introducing a persuasive message or following up on one when goodwill and credibility are especially important ■ Delivering bad news to a large audience when goodwill and credibility are especially important
Face-to-face	■ Communicating confidential information ■ Negotiating ■ Promoting or firing an employee ■ Communicating personal warmth or care ■ Reading nonverbal communication cues
Telephone	■ Providing quick feedback or response ■ Sending confidential information ■ Discussing bad news ■ Confirming
Voice mail	■ Informing when feedback isn't needed ■ Confirming ■ Sending a simple message
Videoconferencing	■ Making a personal connection with a large audience ■ Training

© Cengage Learning

video contribute to the capture of a marketing advantage for their companies.[17] On a macro level, "the use of social networking sites or even Internet-based virtual worlds such as Second Life may become important for organizations to establish their brands, especially among young people."[18] The business networking and blogging application Twitter and others like it are growing in popularity and usefulness in the business realm. Likewise, Facebook has become an important marketing tool for many organizations. A number of authors indicate that Web-based training and education, once seen only in the most progressive organizations, should be expected by nearly everyone entering the workforce or hoping to advance.[19]

Although the benefits of new media should be considered by organizations, it is also important to be aware of the potential risks, such as the damage that hurtful or misunderstood words sent via mediated channels can cause in organizational environments.[20] Other research emphasizes the pitfalls of overreliance on technology and the importance of developing communication management skills to avoid burnout. Such skills include the ability to prioritize mediated communication tasks, learning to disconnect from work by turning off cell phones during nonbusiness hours, and only checking email at several designated times during the work day.[21]

The sections that follow discuss both the benefits and the potential risks involved in the use of new technologies, specifically the most used media in organizations today—email—as well as the burgeoning world of social media.

Email

More information is probably available on email use than any other technology because it has been around for some time and is relied on by many organizations as a primary medium of communication among employees, customers and clients, and the public. In fact, 98 percent of business-to-business communications employed email.[22] Email provides several advantages to organizations, but its extensive use also exposes organizations to several potential challenges.

Benefits of Email

Email is a highly effective communication medium that is central to the way that organizations function, enabling virtual teams, working at home, and collaboration in many forms.

- **Knowledge sharing and communication networks.** Email is a core communication technology for the creation, distribution, and application of knowledge in organizations. In a survey of email users, respondents commented that email had improved teamwork and information flow and allowed information to be shared with multiple coworkers. The researchers also found that the majority of respondents reported that the net effect of email is improved organizational communication.[23]
- **External communications and image.** Prompt response to external emails and professional language are as important for maintaining external relationships as they are for communication between employees.

Challenges of Email

However, the growing dependence on email also invites problems. The average corporate user receives 126 email messages a day, a 55 percent increase since 2003.[24] Twenty percent of an employee's eight-hour day is spent working with email,[25] and knowledge workers spend one to two hours a day managing email.[26]

This trend poses a number of challenges to organizations and individuals alike. The literature on email use in organizations reveals four major concerns:

1. **Individual email efficiency**—the time spent handling email and time recovering from email interruptions to work flow.
2. **Individual email pressure**—anxiety caused by email volumes and the perceived need to respond to emails quickly.
3. **Organizational email effectiveness**—using email to support effective decision making and knowledge sharing, as well as improving business processes that depend on email.

Table 5-4 Email Characteristics.

EMAIL CHARACTERISTICS	ANTICIPATED EFFECT	NEGATIVE PERSONAL OR ORGANIZATIONAL CONSEQUENCES
Speed and convenience	Increased number of messages and increased expectation of response speed	Work overload, errors
Recordability	Increased potential for control	Resentment, reduced autonomy
Multiple addressability, processing, and routing	Communication manipulation	Potential harassment, possible litigation
Lack of social cues	Weakened interpersonal bonds; lowered commitment	More misunderstanding, lower decision quality, context, escalation of disputes
Lack of conversational cues	Focus of attention on internal (negative) states	Greater susceptibility to negative affect (mood) and negative evaluations

Source: Taylor, J. R., Flanagin, A. J., Cheney, G., & Seibold, D. R. (2001). "Organizational Communication Research: Key Moments, Central Concerns, and Future Challenges." In W. Gudykunst (Ed.), *Communication Yearbook 24* (pp. 99–138). Newbury Park, CA: Sage.

4. **Organizational risk**—the risk of litigation resulting from unguarded comments made by an employee in an email and regulatory action resulting from the deletion of email.

Email may cause stress because of its speed, recordability, use of multiple addresses, processing, routing, and lack of social and conversational cues[27] (see Table 5-4). Email may encourage an inhospitable working environment, isolation, and inconsiderate behavior. Close supervision and rigid performance monitoring contributes significantly to job pressure, and email may be an instrument of harassment and bullying and has been shown to escalate disputes. Even those who do not receive a specific email may be affected because others within the organization are affected by that email and are themselves affected by other emails that, in aggregate, can create a climate of stress within an organization.

In fact, according to one report, more than one-third of workers suffer from "e-mail stress."[28] Self-reported email checking suggests more than one-third of workers check their email inbox every fifteen minutes, but monitoring software reveals that workers actually check email more regularly, some as often as forty times an hour. Email is a problem for employees, who are overwhelmed by the volume, lose important items, and feel pressured to respond quickly, often within seconds.[29] However, the sources of email pressure extend beyond overload and include email interruptions to work, unclear priorities, lost email, unclear timescales, inappropriate language, and inappropriate use of the medium.

The proliferation of email use has also created problems for organizations. Although unwanted emails or spam is undoubtedly a problem, it is intra-organizational email that consumes employees' time and intellectual bandwidth. At 3M

- 16 percent of emails received were copied unnecessarily.
- 13 percent of emails received were irrelevant or untargeted.
- 41 percent of emails received were for information purposes.
- Only 46 percent of actionable emails received stated what action was expected.

- 56 percent of employees agreed email is used too often instead of phone or face-to-face communication.
- Only 45 percent of employees said their emails were easy to read.[30]

In fact, it is estimated that email overload cost the U.S. economy nearly $1 trillion in 2010.[31]

In addition, emails create a permanent written record that can be obtained and used in a lawsuit against individuals or their company. What might seem like a private communication can be obtained and interpreted by lawyers suing a company as key evidence of admissions, breach of contract, tortious wrongdoing, or improper motive. Seemingly innocuous comments can come back to haunt an organization, possibly many years later. Deleting an email is not equivalent to shredding: Email is semipermanent. Deleting or tampering with email can come under "spoliation" and is also illegal.[32]

To address these issues, companies should take two steps:

1. Assess email usage, develop policies and procedures, and communicate them clearly to employees. Surveys of business partner relationships, such as customers and supplier satisfaction, should include a section on communications effectiveness and address email competence in particular.
2. Develop training programs to ensure that email is used properly and messages are well written. Such programs should also provide methods for employees to better manage email and reduce stress.

Email can increase speed of communication among organizational stakeholders, but organizations need to take steps to ensure that they have policies in place to maintain productivity levels and protect themselves against legal threats.

ZUMA Wire Service/Alamy

social media—student looking at a social media page

Social Media

Over the last two years alone, social media have dramatically transformed the pace at which information is shared—and the information being shared isn't just social. Millions of employees use Facebook, Twitter, blogs, wikis, and other applications to communicate with one another and the world. Many companies—79 percent of the Fortune Global 100 alone—use social media to communicate with customers and allow customers to in turn generate their own content through product reviews, blog entries, and other messages about the organization. Corporate blogs, applications like Yammer, and intranet discussion boards have accelerated the flow of information inside companies as well.

Four common types of social media used by organizations are described below:

- **Social networking:** Social network sites are for groups of people who share common interests or activities. Facebook and MySpace are social networking sites with which most of us are familiar, while LinkedIn is a professional networking site. Organizations are now taking advantage of these sites to market their products and services and communicate with customers.
- **Wikis:** Like social networking sites, wikis are developed collaboratively by a community of users with one additional feature: Users can add and edit content. You are probably familiar with Wikipedia, which is a free, Web-based, collaborative, multilingual encyclopedia project supported by the nonprofit Wikimedia Foundation. Organizations can create their own wikis that enable workgroups to communicate online, write collaboratively, and manage schedules.
- **Blogs:** A blog is a Web site on which an individual or group of users can record opinions and information on a regular basis. Companies commonly use blogs either internally to communicate with employees or externally to communicate with customers. Successful blogs provide an avenue for customers to engage interactively with thought leaders in an organization with the goal of developing relationships. One downside of blogs, however, is that this interactive element does not always result in positive comments.
- **Microblogs:** A microblog is used for short messages where quick delivery is important. For example, Twitter, a popular microblogging tool, allows for only 140 characters per message. To take advantage of Twitter, many organizations have designated official "tweeters" to communicate with customers: Ford Motors, General Motors, Honda, Jet Blue, Southwest Airlines, Marriott International Hotels, the list goes on. The official "tweeter" at Ford Motors, Scott Monty, head of social media, said the use of Twitter is "part of a larger social media strategy to humanize the Ford brand and put consumers in touch with Ford employees."[33] As this statement demonstrates, microblogging has become another important communication tool in organizations.

According to *BusinessWeek*'s Corporate Executive Board, 71 percent of companies plan to increase their investments in social media—but only a third have guidelines for how it should be used. This development points to a series of internal and external risks that companies should move fast to manage as employees' use of social media accelerates.

Risks from Internal Communications

Even purely internal use of social media can present real risks to companies. Information simply flows faster through this medium—it's faster than the grapevine—and may have more credibility and impact. The question that organizations need to address is, when can that fast flow of information cause problems?

- **Secrets are harder to protect.** Know that material information about company plans and strategies will flow down through the organization faster. Be sure that key employees know just how slippery this slope is.
- **Compensation isn't confidential any more.** Assume that information about employee compensation will no longer stay with the employee. Disparities in pay, benefits, and work arrangements will be rapidly exposed and compared among employees.
- **Strategic actions may be signaled in advance.** If employees are asked to implement strategic actions, those strategies will be almost impossible to conceal from those outside the organization. Organizations will need to anticipate leaks and be prepared for quick action if and when they occur.
- **Inconsistencies within an organization may be exposed.** Different departments within organizations inevitably take different positions regarding customers, employees, and regulators. The blogosphere will quickly reveal these inconsistencies for all to see. When information is flowing more freely than ever before, managers will need to take steps to ensure that all company positions are in harmony.

Risks from External Communications

When employees use external social media—blogs, Twitter, Facebook, and so on—they can easily harm the company, sometimes without even knowing it. A few examples include the following:

- **Premature release of new product information.** Employees commonly leak pictures or descriptions of a new product before its official release. Even a casual tweet revealing the location of a key employee can signal new product or business development activity before it is ready for public release.
- **Exposure of company problems.** Employee "venting" is ubiquitous on Facebook and Twitter. In some cases, that frustration is an indictment of the company's own products, services, or, perhaps most commonly, management culture.
- **Harassment.** Social media almost immediately gave rise to claims of workplace harassment—a superior using Facebook or another medium to make unwanted advances.

Companies need a plan to manage fast-evolving social media risks. Because so few companies have taken even initial steps in this area, the best approach is to start with a basic checklist:

- Develop a policy on the use of social media, both internally and externally.
- Work with the legal department to create records-retention policies for social media.
- Partner with the corporate communications department to monitor the organization's brand in social media.
- Work with the information systems department to incorporate secure social media in the organization's information technology (IT) road map.
- Understand employees' workflows to build awareness about proper use of social media and effective information protection.

Employees also need to be aware of the risks of social media. Employees should not broadcast confidential company information on social network sites and should be careful about expressing their opinions about the company, their manager, or their colleagues on the Internet if they don't want to risk reprimands or dismissal.

Summary

- The context of communication should be considered when formulating a message. Context includes various internal and external environmental factors. The culture of the corporation as well as the communication climate can affect whether messages are communicated and how they are conveyed. For those interested in organization-wide planning, it is helpful to understand the flow of communication in an organization, both formal and informal networks.

- After considering the context for communicating and the organizational culture in which you will communicate, you are in a better position to select the appropriate channel and media to convey your message. Broadly, the four channels of communication are written, oral, nonverbal, and visual. There are a number of media from which to choose to communicate using written and oral channels.

- The choice of medium can be influenced by knowledge gained during earlier steps in the strategic-communication process. In other words, the purpose of communication, the audience, and the context might inform media choices. Other factors to consider include the amount of complex information you wish to convey. Or you might select a written channel because this also serves as a record to which the receiver can refer back and because the information is less costly to deliver using your company mail service. Likewise, you might select an oral channel to communicate with your colleague in the next office because you want the additional information it provides ("richness" in the form of nonverbal communication), and you also desire immediate contact and feedback.

- The proliferation of new media has presented new opportunities and benefits to organizations as well as led to new challenges and threats. In recent years, email in particular has proliferated in organizations and has led to increases in productivity as well as greater costs to organizations and stress to employees. Social media presents the next challenge to organizations in terms of creating effective programs to monitor and manage its use. Training employees in effectively and appropriately using new media and implementing company policies can greatly alleviate some of the potential challenges they create.

Key Terms

context, 115
contextual intelligence, 116
adaptive capacity, 116

organizational culture, 117
supportive communication climate, 119
defensive communication climate, 120

Discussion Questions

1. As a current or future leader, what can you do to create supportive communication climates in your department and organization?

2. You want to ask your supervisor for a raise. How might context effect your decision about when and how to deliver this message? What channel and medium of communication would you use and why?

3. You are the salesperson for a company and have unknowingly sold faulty product to a dozen customers. Are there contextual or environmental factors that might affect the delivery of this message? What is the best channel and medium of communication for dealing with this problem and why? Would you use more than one channel? If so, in what order?

4. You are the owner of a midsized company, and one of your managers has been arrested for fraud. Are there contextual and environmental factors that might potentially affect the delivery of this message? With what audiences would you wish to communicate? What is the best channel and medium of communication for each audience and why?

5. How do you feel about email monitoring practices? Are there ethical concerns involved in such a decision? If so, what are they?

Applications

1. Identify an organization of which you are a part. This organization can be your workplace or a church, sports, or university organization in which you participate. Identify the formal communication network the organization uses and consider the following questions:

   - Does it primarily use upward, downward, or horizontal flow or some combination of these?
   - Does it use its formal communication network as effectively as it might?
   - What role does the grapevine play in this organization?
   - What are its favored channels or media of communication? Are these effective or not, and why?

   Based on your analysis, write an informal report summarizing the use of formal and informal network channels in the organization and provide recommendations for improving their use.

2. Identify an organization of which you are a part. This organization can be your workplace or a church, sports, or university organization in which you participate. Identify and analyze the media that are typically used to communication in the organization. If possible, try to identify the audiences who typically use each medium and for what purpose. Then write an informal report that summarizes your findings and provides recommendations for improving the use of media in your organization. Explain why your recommendations will improve communication based on channel choice considerations.

3. Conduct research on organizational policies regarding email use in the workplace. Write a report to your supervisor that summarizes your findings and presents recommendations for implementing an email use policy in your organization.

4. You are the marketing manager of your organization. Conduct research on the uses of social media by organizations for marketing aims and write an informal proposal to the president of the company in which you report your findings and recommend actions for the use of social media for marketing purposes based on those findings.

5. Conduct research on email monitoring policies in organizations. Use the information you have found to write a report to your manager, either recommending that an email monitoring practice be instituted by the firm or avoided. Use your research to support your recommendation.

CASE ANALYSIS

BP AND THE GULF OIL SPILL (A)

The Event

On the morning of April 20, 2010, crew members of the giant oil rig *Deepwater Horizon* were completing their work on an exploratory well known as the Macondo prospect, in the Gulf of Mexico. The crew was made up of British Petroleum workers, Transocean oil rig workers, Halliburton cementers, Schlumberger mud specialists, and various other specialized engineers. Halliburton engineers had started cementing the bottom of the oil well four days earlier.[34]

As part of the completion work, mud specialists were to conduct a host of inspections on the cementing job. Because all parties involved were initially satisfied with the mud operations, the BP well team leader, John Guide, decided to postpone the inspection until production drilling started. This would save the BP team a fee of $128,000 and significant amounts of time.[35]

Further testing that day, however, revealed some pressure problems. One engineer, Wyman Wheeler, was convinced that "something wasn't right."[36] His shift was ending, leaving the matter to other testers. Like Wheeler, subsequent testers were not able to reach an acceptable pressures level from the main line. However, they reached zero pressure on a separate pipe, known as the "kill line," and concluded that all operations were safe. Workers then started pumping seawater into the main pipeline to remove mud from the pipeline at 9:20 p.m.[37]

That night, a series of vibrations and hisses alerted the crew that there was a serious problem. Soon after, mud started spewing on the oil rig. A large explosion occurred and all power went out. The crew was alerted over a public address system that there was a fire on board. Chaos reigned. Many people were injured. Lifeboats were dropped, and individuals were jumping into the ocean. The mud propelled equipment 50 feet into the air, posing another major threat. A supply vessel, the *Bankston*, maneuvered to rescue fallen workers.

Steve Bertone, the oil rig's chief engineer, told a subsea engineer to use the emergency disconnect switch (EDS) to activate the blowout preventer. Control panel lights indicated the blowout preventer was activated. But upon further inspection, the generator would not start.

Coast Guard helicopters arrived at 11:22 p.m. By 11:30 p.m., final muster was taken with a result of eleven men missing. By April 22, the rig was turned 180 degrees and far away from the well.

Offshore Drilling Challenges

In September of 2009, BP discovered 4 to 6 billion gallons worth of oil reservoirs in the Gulf of Mexico. The reservoirs were 35,000 feet (10,668 meters) beneath the earth's surface. At this depth, water pressure totals 10,000 pounds per square inch, well temperatures can exceed 350 degrees Fahrenheit (176 degrees Celsius), and blowout preventers could only be installed by remote-operating vehicles. Drilling foundations were unstable due to pockets of methane in the sea floor.[38]

The purpose of offshore oil drilling is to find hydrocarbons that are trapped in the rock bed of the earth. The deeper the well, the greater the pressure of the rock bed above the hydrocarbons. Thus, drillers must ensure pressure is in equilibrium so that hydrocarbons do not shoot out of control to the surface. They do this by pumping mud into the wellbore to act as a counter balance. If the pressure is too great, the rock bed will break. If it's too low, fluids and gas will enter the well and produce a "kick" or jolt.[39]

To ensure situations would not get out of control, blowout preventers could seal the well by squeezing the drill pipe shut. The blowout preventer had five sets of rams to cut the drill pipe. It would be initiated by an automated system known as the "deadman" system.

Cementing operations are necessary to bind the casing string to the hydrocarbon rock bed. The casing string is the apparatus used to draw the hydrocarbons from the rock bed. Cement is pumped through the casing string, and mud will force the cement out and around the string to the surrounding annular for a tight seal. This would ensure that the equipment is tightly sealed to the ocean floor so no pressure can escape.[40]

BP and Halliburton made a number of compromises in the planning phase, such as limiting the amount and rate that Halliburton could pump down the annulars, to ensure that the process would produce maximum gains while reducing risk. Engineers feared that a larger amount of cement would cause a structural problem within the well.[41] Thus, a less than conventional amount of cement was used to seal the annular.

Key Entities
British Petroleum

British Petroleum was tottering on the brink of bankruptcy in the early 1990s. It was exiled by Nigeria and the Middle East. Sir John Browne was the force that turned the company around and ventured into the Gulf of Mexico for new oil well explorations.[42] In August 2002, BP pumped $15 billion into the Gulf of Mexico drilling. In March 2008, BP paid more than $34 million to the Minerals Management Service for an exclusive lease to drill in Mississippi Canyon Block 252, a nine square mile plot in the Gulf of Mexico.[43] By 2010, it was the world's fourth largest corporation and produced over 4 million barrels of oil day from thirty countries. In 2010, 10 percent of BP's output was drilled from the Gulf of Mexico.[44]

Transocean

Transocean is the largest drilling contractor in the industry. A series of mergers throughout the 1990s and early 2000s led to the company known as Transocean. In 2000, it acquired R&B Falcon, whose assets included the *Deepwater Horizon*, a semi-submersible under construction.[45]

Transocean also owned the oil rig *Marianas*, which had initiated work on the Macondo well before the *Deepwater Horizon* took over. (The *Marianas* was badly damaged on November 9, 2009, by Hurricane Ida and had to be towed in for repair. The *Deepwater Horizon* took over the exploratory drilling in January 2010). Transocean produced revenues of $11.6 billion in 2009, and made more than $1 million per day by leasing out the giant rig to BP.

Halliburton

Halliburton engineers were responsible for cement operations on the rig.[46] Cementing was necessary to close the bottom of the oil well from which the *Deepwater Horizon* was attempting to extract oil.

Federal Government

The U.S. government wrestles with two responsibilities that it must meet concurrently. First, the government operates the National Environmental Policy Act (NEPA), to monitor activities that could pollute public lands, including offshore drilling. Normally, the secretary of the interior would approve offshore drilling, and the approval processes would delay initial production for about six years. At the same time, the federal government also pushes to reduce the country's dependence on foreign oil. That pressure stems, in part, from an oil embargo in 1973 and creation of the Department of Energy in 1977 by the Carter administration when laws were passed to promote development of domestic energy supplies.[47]

In order to compromise between these competing priorities, the Gulf of Mexico was given an exception to the NEPA Act because it was deemed that the oil and gas industry was already mature in the Gulf of Mexico.[48]

Minerals Management Services

At the time of the Gulf oil spill crisis, the chief federal agency responsible for overseeing drilling and operations was the Mineral Management Services, or MMS. The MMS was charged with the mandate for environmental protection but also to drive the United States to energy independence. In the Gulf, safety and environmental oversight was rendered ineffective because of these conflicting priorities. The agency lacked resources, technical training, and experience in the complicated world of offshore drilling.[49] In other words, "The result was that the same agency became responsible for regulatory oversight of offshore drilling—and for collecting revenue from that drilling."[50]

Furthermore, the MMS was, "...in one entity, authority of regulatory oversight with responsibility for collecting for the U.S. Treasury the billions of dollars of revenues obtained from lease sales and royalty payments from producing wells."[51]

A Brief History of British Petroleum

In 1901, William Knox D'Arcy, a wealthy British miner, secured a concession from the grand vizier of Persia to search for petroleum throughout most of the Persian Empire. Persia was devoid of infrastructure and politically unstable at the time, making D'Arcy's search physically challenging and more expensive than he anticipated. By 1905, D'Arcy was in critical need of additional capital in order to continue his search. With help from the British Admiralty, the Burmah Oil Company joined D'Arcy in a Concessionary Oil Syndicate in 1905 and supplied further funds in return for operational control. In May 1908 oil was discovered in the southwest of Persia at Masjid-i-Suleiman, the first oil discovery in the Middle East. The following April the Anglo-Persian Oil Company was formed, with the Burmah Oil Company holding most of the shares.[52]

Shortly after the discovery, the British government bought up a majority of the Anglo-Persian Oil shares, an effort due in no small part to Winston Churchill. Churchill, who was then the chief of the

British Navy, believed that the oil supplied from the Middle East would fuel the British fleet through World War I and far into the future. The Anglo-Iranian Oil Company (AIOC) (as it was named in 1935) made handsome profits throughout the 1920s and 1930s as Western societies became more and more dependent on automobiles and petroleum-burning manufacturing plants.[53] In an effort to keep up with the rapidly growing demand from the West, the AIOC constructed the largest refinery in the world near the Iranian city of Abadan. This behemoth of a refinery employed over 200,000 Iranian workers in brutally harsh conditions. "Observers recounted the inequities between the Iranian workers housed in a rickety slum known as Kaghazabad, or 'Paper City,' and the British officials who supervised from air-conditioned offices and lawn-fringed villas. Water fountains were marked 'Not for Iranians.'"[54]

The refinery became the biggest supplier of oil to the Allied Powers during World War II, despite shortages of food and outbreaks of diseases throughout the workers and the region. Conditions became especially grim during the winter season, as the director of the Iranian Petroleum Institute wrote in 1949, "In winter the earth flooded and became a flat, perspiring lake. The mud in town was knee-deep and canoes ran alongside the roadways for transport. When the rains subsided, clouds of nipping, small-winged flies rose from the stagnant waters to fill the nostrils, collecting in black mounds along the rims of cooking pots and jamming the fans at the refinery with an unctuous glue."[55]

Horrific working conditions, unequal distribution of revenues, and small dividends began to fuel Iranian discontent with the AIOC. Additionally, the Iranian government became increasingly upset when the AIOC signed 50/50 revenue-sharing agreements with other oil-producing countries such as Venezuela and Saudi Arabia in 1948 and 1950, respectively. Discontent reached a tipping point in 1951 when the democratically elected prime minister of Iran, Mohammed Mossadegh, formally nationalized Iran's oil industry, effectively pushing the AIOC out of the country.

A few years of failed negotiations followed, and finally in 1953 the CIA and British intelligence staged a coup in a joint effort, which was successful in the overthrow of Mossadegh. With Mossadegh removed, the newly installed shah of Iran allowed the return of the AIOC, which was renamed as the British Petroleum (BP) Company. However, BP's terms of returning to the country were less favorable than before, as BP held a 40 percent interest in a newly created consortium of Western oil companies, formed to undertake oil exploration, production, and refining in Iran.[56]

Tensions between BP and Iran never cooled as generations of Iranians believed that the company's intention was always to take advantage of cheap Iranian labor and exploit the country's natural resources. These tensions played a large part in the growing anti-Western attitudes that developed throughout Iran and eventually helped pave way to the 1979 Iranian Revolution. Amidst growing anti-Western sentiment throughout the entire Middle Eastern region, BP began to look in different regions to expand its production, including the British North Sea and the Alaskan wilderness. In 1977, BP began pumping oil near Prudhoe Bay in northern Alaska through a 1,200 km-long pipeline that ran all the way to refineries in the southern part of the state. According to Ishaan Tharoor of *Time* magazine, "The project became one of the largest infrastructure projects ever attempted in North America and BP prided itself on the environmental sensitivity of its planning, which included raised platforms in certain stretches so as to not impede the natural migrations of caribou."[57] Despite having great success beyond the Middle East, BP's public image has been damaged by flagrant safety violations, a misleading green marketing campaign, and, most recently, the *Deepwater Horizon* offshore drilling rig explosion.

BP and the Green Marketing Campaign

BP began a massive $200 million marketing campaign in 2000 to re-brand itself as "Beyond Petroleum." BP's shield logo, which had been in use for over seventy years, was redesigned into the BP "helios," a graphic that was intended to promote warm, green, and clean energy sentiments about the company and its environmental-friendly attitude. BP's CEO at the time, Lord John Browne, speaking at Stanford University in 2002, stated, "I believe the American people expect a company like BP ... to offer answers and not excuses." Additionally, Lord Browne proclaimed that, "Climate change is an issue which raises fundamental questions about the relationship between companies and society as a whole, and between one generation and the next." He even said, "Companies composed of highly skilled and trained people can't live in denial of mounting evidence gathered by hundreds of the most reputable scientists in the world."[58] With an advertising campaign focused on BP's apparent efforts to invest in solar, wind, natural gas, and hydrogen sources of energy, BP seemed heavily invested in a eco-friendly culture and moving away from fossil fuels. Behind the popular tag line "It's a start," BP successfully branded itself as a new leader in alternative-energy research and production.

BP's Recent Safety Record

BP's recent string of mishaps, excluding the Gulf of Mexico disaster, seems to strongly contradict its environmental and safety-friendly marketing effort. In 2005, a major explosion occurred at the BP Texas City Refinery, in which 15 workers died and 170 were seriously injured.

The ensuing investigations by the federal government strongly suggested that BP leadership was heavily focused on reducing maintenance and capital costs at the expense of a proper safety environment.[59] The U.S. Chemical Safety and Hazard Investigation Board organized an independent investigation, which was headed by former Secretary of State James Baker. The findings of the commission suggested that BP promoted a culture in which "occupational safety" and "process safety" could not be differentiated. Since the accident, there have been four subsequent safety violations in which workers have been injured at the same Texas City refinery, further suggesting that BP's culture has not changed.

In August of 2006, an estimated 5,000 barrels of crude oil began leaking from one of BP's pipelines in Prudhoe Bay, Alaska. Investigators determined that corrosion in a number of pipelines caused the leak. The public began to doubt that BP's self-proclaimed environmentally friendly culture was sufficient enough to prevent future disasters. Finally, in a three-year time span prior to the Gulf of Mexico disaster, the U.S. Occupational Safety and Health Administration stated that BP racked up 760 "willful and egregious" safety violations, which constituted 97 percent of all industry safety violations during the period.

Tony Hayward's Ascent

Tony Hayward received a PhD from the University of Edinburgh and began his career with BP in 1982.[60] He excelled in his initial assignments and was given positions of greater responsibility throughout Europe and Asia in the first decade of his career. While attending a leadership conference in the United States in the early nineties, Hayward caught the eye of (then) BP CEO Lord Browne. After serving as an executive assistant to Browne for a couple of years, Hayward began to rise quickly through the ranks.[61] He served as president of BP's operations in Venezuela, as a director of BP exploration, a group vice president, and eventually as group treasurer, where he was responsible for a variety of key financial decisions that affected the entire company. Hayward replaced Lord Browne as CEO in May of 2007 after the Texas City Refinery explosion killed 15 people and wounded nearly 200 others.

Prior to assuming the role of CEO, Hayward made it clear that he intended to integrate all levels of leadership in the decision-making process. He believed, as he said in 2006, that "the top of the organization doesn't listen hard enough to what the bottom of the organization is saying."[62] Taking charge of the company, Hayward vowed to intensify BP's safety efforts, improve its financial performance, and adhere to core BP values.[63] With such considerable experience throughout the company, it seemed as though Hayward was poised to follow through with his ambitious vision.

Initial Communications

Word got back to BP headquarters soon after the April 20 explosion. After a tumultuous evening, Tony Hayward released a brief statement on BP's Web site. In his statement he offered condolences to the families of the eleven men who were killed, and offered "support" to Transocean as it tried to make sense of the disaster.[64] The statement conveyed BP's genuine sincerity, but it also indicated that BP initially intended to play a supporting role in the recovery and cleanup effort. BP released its quarterly earnings report on April 27 and briefly mentioned the spill after a thorough discussion about robust earnings.[65] On April 30, in a surprising change of tone, Hayward was quoted as saying that BP assumes "full responsibility for the spill."[66]

Then, on May 2, Tony Hayward appeared on the *Today Show* remarking: "It's not our accident."[67] He then went on to say that although BP was not responsible for the incident, it would play a direct role in containing the oil spill. The first few days following the incident were certainly marred by confusion and contradiction on BP's part.

In the same two-week period following the explosion, the federal government took a much more active role in finding fault and placing blame. In a special televised address on May 2, President Obama said "BP is responsible for this; BP will be paying the bill."[68] Two days earlier, President Obama appointed Admiral Thad Allen as national incident commander and gave him the authority to engage the public regarding current recovery efforts. Admiral Allen, highly regarded as an expert in disaster recovery, carried the full weight of the federal government when he spoke about the deepwater crisis. BP would often have to work closely with Admiral Allen or even under his guidance during certain parts of the recovery.

BP's Communications Strategy

In addition to daily press conferences and remarks from senior leadership, BP used three key communications methods to engage local, national, and global audiences.

Social Media

Prior to April 20, 2010, BP posted very few items and updates to its Twitter and Facebook accounts. In the week following the explosion, BP was silent on the social media scene. On April 27 at 8:26 p.m., BP posted a message on its Twitter account, simply saying "BP PLEDGES FULL SUPPORT FOR DEEPWATER HORIZON PROBES."[69] After the initial post on Twitter, BP gave daily Twitter updates to interested followers. BP used Twitter to list important contact information for each of its emergency response teams as well as to provide key updates on the search, rescue, and recovery processes.

BP used Facebook in a similar way. On May 2, BP America entered its first Facebook post, announcing that BP officials had established a hotline for those who would like to support the cleanup and recovery efforts in the Gulf.[70] BP's Facebook page provided those who "liked" BP's page with a

detailed account of how much oil had been recovered that day and since the beginning of the spill. It also provided a variety of information regarding the compensation claims process, key Coast Guard updates, and commerce in the Gulf area. BP officials would update Facebook followers several times a day (even on weekends and holidays) in order to make their efforts and intentions as transparent as possible.

On May 5, BP began releasing official Gulf of Mexico oil spill updates on its Web site.[71] Each update was linked to the Twitter and Facebook pages so that all users could funnel towards the official www.bp.com Web site to receive their information. The updates were robust and offered a detailed account of the day's recovery efforts as well as a wealth of pictures, maps, graphics, diagrams, comments, and assessments. All of this information would eventually lead to the creation of the "Gulf of Mexico Response" tab on the BP Web site. Anyone who wanted an update on the Gulf spill could easily and quickly get one from the BP Web site or through its social media outlets.

Paid Media: "We Will Make This Right"

BP invested in a massive print and television campaign in order to make its case as a responsible company that was willing to do the right thing at all costs and against all odds. The campaign began on June 3 with a television advertisement featuring Tony Hayward. In the advertisement, which aired in markets all over the United States, Hayward outlines BP's immense recovery effort and pledges to stay in the Gulf as long as it takes to fix the problem.[72] In addition to the national television campaign, BP also ran print advertisements in high-visibility newspapers, including the *New York Times*, *USA Today*, the *Wall Street Journal*, and the *Washington Post*.[73] This comprehensive advertisement strategy, designed to appeal to a national audience, carried with it a $50 million price tag.[74] According to a spokesman with BP, Tony Hayward justified the cost of the campaign by alluding to his obligation to keep the public informed about ongoing recovery efforts.

Not everyone was pleased with the information Hayward communicated, at least not at a cost of $50 million. President Obama, upon hearing an estimated cost of the campaign, said, "What I don't wanna hear is when they're ... spending that kind of money on TV advertising and they're nickel and diming fishermen."[75] Mr. Obama was referring to the way that BP had been handling compensation claims for fishermen who were out of work as a result of the spill. He felt that the money may have been better spent supporting the people directly affected by the disaster, as opposed to financing a campaign to appeal to seemingly unaffected people.

Spillcam

Congressman Ed Markey, the representative from Massachusetts's 7th District, began criticizing BP for not giving the public access to its twenty-four-hour camera feed of the oil spill. He believed that the public should have full disclosure to each camera angle in order to get a better idea of just how severe the spill really was.[76] On May 18, BP made such footage available via its Web site. "Spillcam," as the live feed eventually became known, drew immense fascination across the country. In the days following Spillcam's release, more than 300,000 people visited BP's Web site to view the feed. "BP oil spill live feed" and "top kill video" were both among the most popular Google searches after Spillcam's release.[77] BP disclosed the footage in an effort to prove its willingness to disclose vital information to the public and to highlight its cooperation with federal agencies. While Spillcam certainly represented transparency, it also gave the public a clear picture of the staggering oil flow that plagued the Gulf.

Missteps along the Way
Downplaying the Effects

A week after the *Deepwater Horizon* disaster, BP released noticeably upbeat quarterly earnings. In the notes section following the impressive earnings report, the Gulf oil spill was casually mentioned in a mere three sentences.[78] The oil spill acknowledgment was sandwiched in between detailed descriptions of lucrative acquisitions and operating results. On the same day that BP went public with Spillcam, Tony Hayward did an interview with SkyNews. In the interview, he contended that the overall effects of the spill will be "very, very modest"[79] and that the spill would be relatively small compared to the entire ocean.[80] In early June, months before the leak was sealed, Doug Suttles, BP's chief operating officer,

remarked that the oil flow "will be down to a relative trickle" within a few days.[81] A week later, oil was still flowing from the leak at a rate of 10,000 to 35,000 barrels per day. Suttles then went on to say, "I would eat fish from these waters."[82] He made the comment about a month before the well was sealed and while many fishermen were still out of business. The comment, though likely true, continued to aggravate people whose lives had been greatly disrupted by the disaster.

Self-Inflicted Wounds

BP's extensive communications and advertisement effort would likely have been much more successful had it not been for a few avoidable mistakes. Tony Hayward, in an attempt to apologize to Gulf residents, said, "There's no one who wants this thing to be over more than me. I'd like my life back."[83] He made the statement just three days before releasing the "We will make this right" advertisement. Many Gulf residents felt the comment was unbelievably insensitive, especially considering the fact that eleven men *actually* lost their lives in the incident. Two weeks before that statement, Tony Hayward was spotted at an exclusive yacht race off the coast of England, apparently on vacation with his son. The jet-setting lifestyle complete with luxurious yacht races was countered by the hardships and struggles Gulf residents were enduring every day. Many people affected by the spill were appalled by Hayward's seemingly flippant and arrogant behavior. Hayward was not the only one to make a serious gaffe after the spill. Carl Henric Svanberg, BP's chairman of the board, told President Obama that BP cares about "America's small people."[84] The comment was not received well by Gulf residents, who detected a hint of superiority and arrogance in the comment.

On July 20, in the midst of another attempt to plug the oil flow, BP digitally altered a photo of employees viewing data screens in a command and control center. The photo was prominently displayed on the company Web site and was intended to show how closely BP was monitoring the situation. An online blogger noticed that the image had been "Photoshopped" to make it appear as though the employees were monitoring more screens than they actually were.[85] BP had to admit to the embarrassing mistake and apologize to the public once again.

Moving Forward

Bob Dudley replaced Tony Hayward on October 1 as BP's CEO. After enduring the company's most devastating accident and a number of public relations gaffes, Dudley has to rebuild BP's image and regain credibility with customers and investors. In the aftermath of such a disaster, he must find a way to convince the public that BP is still a valuable energy company that will help solve global energy problems in the future.

Discussion Questions

1. Do you think BP's turbulent history contributed to its present-day culture and general attitude towards safety and operational procedures?
2. How would you assess the effectiveness of BP's green campaign?
3. What should BP have communicated to the world immediately following the explosion?

4. Who should BP have used as the public relations "point man" during the cap effort?
5. Will America ever forgive BP?
6. Will BP be able to repair its image and convey a new attitude of safety consciousness?
7. How does BP ensure a similar crisis does not occur in the future?
8. What is Bob Dudley's greatest challenge as he tries to improve BP's public image and grow profitability?

This case was prepared by Research Assistants Dan Marques, Jonathan Kim, and John Mikols under the direction of James S. O'Rourke, Teaching Professor of Management, as the basis for class discussion rather than to illustrate either effective or ineffective handling of an administrative situation. Information was gathered from corporate as well as public sources.

BP AND THE GULF OIL SPILL (B)

On May 22, 2010, President Obama established the BP Oil Commission to find the causes of the Gulf of Mexico oil spill. By January 2011, the commission's investigation concluded, and they published their report entitled *Deep Water: The Gulf Oil Disaster and Future of Offshore Drilling*. This 400-page report established the key players, the history of oil drilling, how the industry works, and, most importantly, the causes of the disaster.

The report concluded that "the well blew out because a number of separate risk factors, oversights, and outright mistakes combined to overwhelm the safeguards meant to prevent just such an event from happening." The report noted, however, that "most of the mistakes and oversights at Macondo (the well itself, apart from the *Deepwater Horizon* rig) can be traced back to a single overarching failure—a failure of management."

Had there been better management on behalf of BP, Halliburton, and Transocean, the blowout would have been prevented by improving "the ability of individuals involved to identify the risks they faced, and to properly evaluate, communicate and address them."

Special caution needed to be taken "before relying on the primary cement as a barrier to the hydrocarbon flow," and failure to do so was a fundamental mistake. The commission's report states that "there is nothing to suggest that BP's engineering team conducted a formal, disciplined analysis of the combined impact of risk factors on the prospects for a successful cement job. There is nothing to suggest that BP communicated a need for elevated vigilance after the job."

Furthermore, government regulators were unable to react as they "lacked the authority, the necessary resources, and the technical expertise" to prevent the disaster from occurring. Therefore, "the Macondo blowout was the product of several individual missteps and oversights by BP, Halliburton, and Transocean" and the commission reported the "immediate cause of the Macondo blowout was a failure to contain hydrocarbon pressures in the well."

The report highlighted several key points:

1. BP's management process did not adequately identify or address risks created by late changes to well design and procedures.
2. Halliburton and BP's management processes did not ensure that cement was adequately tested.
3. BP, Transocean, and Halliburton failed to communicate adequately.

The federal government implemented swift action to improve the Minerals Management Services (MMS). By June 19, 2010, the MMS was broken into three distinct entities: the Bureau of Ocean Energy Management, the Bureau of Safety and Environmental Enforcement, and the Office of Natural Resources Revenue. This breakup was implemented in order to prevent the conflicts of interest associated with the MMS in generating offshore drilling revenue while maintaining oversight of industry regulations.

In conclusion, the commission found that all three stakeholders, BP, Transocean, and Halliburton, shared the responsibility for the disaster. Public perception, however, focused the majority of the blame on BP, which quickly became the focus of smear campaigns by environmentalists and other special interest groups.

From a corporate communications standpoint, BP CEO Bob Dudley has had an uphill battle. Since taking over, BP has written off $40 billion for the *Deepwater Horizon* disaster. This led to its first annual loss in twenty years and caused BP to sell off about $30 billion of oil and gas production assets and half of its U.S. refining capacity to cover the cost.[86] Mr. Dudley has attempted to move forward with prosperous new ventures in Russia and highlight the possibility of large future earnings. He has attempted, by charting a new direction for the company, to distance BP from the deepwater spill. It also seems as though he has made painstaking efforts to avoid the pitfalls of his predecessor. His public remarks and stances concerning ongoing recovery efforts in the Gulf are well calculated and thoughtful. As he tries to establish better relationships with Gulf residents (and American officials), he is also helping to improve the image of BP, slowly but surely.

This case was prepared by Research Assistants Dan Marques, Jonathan Kim, and John Mikols under the direction of James S. O'Rourke, Teaching Professor of Management, as the basis for class discussion rather than to illustrate either effective or ineffective handling of an administrative situation. Information was gathered from corporate as well as public sources.

Endnotes

1. Wessel, H. (2003, Februrary 12). Speaking their piece: Feedback from workers plays a major role in the vitality of a company. *Orlando Sentinel*, G1.

2. Veil, S. (2011). Mindful learning in crisis management. *Journal of Business Communication*, 48(2), 116–147.

3. Mayo, T. (1980). *In their time: The greatest business leaders of the twentieth century.* Boston: Harvard Business School Press.

4. Bennis, W., & Thomas, R. J. (2002). *Geeks and geezers.* Boston: Harvard Business Review Press.

5. Weick, K. E., & Sutcliffe, K. M. (2001). *Managing the unexpected: Assuring high performance in an age of complexity.* New York: Jossey-Bass, p. 146.

6. Schein, E. H. (1992). *Educational culture and leadership.* New York: Jossey-Bass, p. 12.

7. Boreham, N., & Morgan, C. (2004). A sociocultural analysis of organisational learning. *Oxford Review of Education*, 30 (3), 307–326, p. 309.

8. Chatman, J. A., & Jehn, K. A. (1994). Assessing the relationship between industry characteristics and organizational culture: How different can you be? *Academy of Management Journal*, 37, 522–553; O'Reilly, C. A., III, Chatman, J., & Caldwell, D. F. (1993). People and organizational culture: A profile comparison approach to assessing person-organization fit. *Academy of Management Journal*, 34, 487–516.

9. Peters, T., & Waterman, R. (1982). *In search of excellence.* New York: Harper and Row.

10. Spencer, D. (1986). Employee voice and employee retention. *Academy of Management Journal*, 29, 488–502.

11. Ibid.

12. Gibb, J. (1961). Defensive communication. *Journal of Communication*, 11, 141–148.

13. Eisenberg, E. M., & Goodall, Jr., H. L. (1993). *Organizational communication: Balancing creativity and constraint*. New York: St. Martin's Press.

14. Wessell, 2003.

15. Eisenberg & Goodall, 1993, p. 235.

16. Motley, M. T., & Camden, C. T. (1988). Facial expression of emotion: A comparison of posed expressions versus spontaneous expressions in an interpersonal communication setting. *Western Journal of Communication*, 52(1), 1–22.

17. Moran, G. (2007, July). Now see this: Online video can breathe new life into your business. *Entrepreneur*, 35(7), 30.

18. Schramm, J. (2007, September). Internet connections. *HRMagazine*, 52(9), 176.

19. Education. (2005, November). *Inc.*, 27(11), 147–148.

20. Lyons, D. (2005, November 14). Attack of the blogs. *Forbes*, 176(10), 128–138.

21. *HR Magazine*. (2006). Technology spurring stress, decreasing productivity. *HR Magazine*, 51(1), 14.

22. Taylor, J. R., Flanagin, A. J., Cheney, G., & Seibold, D. R. (2001). Organizational communication research: Key moments, central concerns, and future challenges. In W. Gudykunst (Ed.), *Communication Yearbook 24* (pp. 99–138). Thousand Oaks, CA: Sage.

23. Tassabehji, R., & Vakola, M. (2005). Business email: The killer impact. *Communications of the ACM*, 48(11), 64–70.

24. Radicati Group. (2007). Addressing information overload in corporate e-mail: The economics of user attention. White paper (April). Retrieved October 5, 2007 from www.radicati.com.

25. Davenport, T. (2005). *Thinking for a living*. Harvard Business School Press.

26. Cain, M. (2006). Who needs training on e-mail? Gartner Research, July 2006, ID no. G00141290.

27. Taylor et al., 2001.

28. N. A. (2007). One in three workers suffers from 'e-mail stress.' *Daily Telegraph*, (13 August), Retrieved August 14, 2007, from http://www.telegraph.co.uk/news/main.jhtml?xml=/news/2007/08/13/ne-mail113.xml.

29. Jackson, T., Burgess, A., & Edwards, J. (2006). Simple approach to improving e-mail communication. *Communications of the ACM*, (June 2006), 49(6), 107–109.

30. Jackson et al., 2006.

31. Spira, J. (2011). Information overload: None are immune. *Information Management*, 21(5), 32.

32. Sinrod, E. (2004). Where's my e-mail? The legal implications of disappearing e-mail. *Journal of Internet Law*, (September) 8(3), 23–24.

33. Ford Media. (2009). Allure of social media helps Ford reach new customers. Retrieved March 28, 2013 from http://media.ford.com/article_display.cfm?article_id=30634

34. Internal Halliburton document (HAL-0011208); Testimony of Nathaniel Chaisson, Hearing before the Deepwater Horizon Joint Investigation Team, August 24, 2010, as cited in Graham, B., et al., *Deepwater: The Gulf oil disaster and the future of offshore drilling*, National Commission on the BP Deepwater Horizon Oil Spill and Offshore Drilling, January 2010: page 2, http://www.oilspillcommission.gov/sites/default/files/documents/DEEPWATER_ReporttothePresident_FINAL.pdf

35. Internal BP document (BP, presentation to Commission, August 9, 2010, slides 5 & 12 as cited in *Deepwater: The Gulf oil disaster and the future of offshore drilling*, p. 4.

36. Brian Morel, email message to Richard Miller and Mark Hafle, April 14, 2010, 13:31 as cited in *Deepwater: The Gulf oil disaster and the future of offshore drilling*, p. 6.

37. BP, Deepwater Horizon Accident Investigation Report, Testimony of Chris Pleasant, pp. 118–119, as cited in *Deepwater: The Gulf oil disaster and the future of offshore drilling*, p. 7.

38. Bureau of Ocean Energy, Management, Regulation, and Enforcement (BOEMRE), "Gulf of Mexico Oil and Gas Leasing Offering," http://www.gomr.boemre.gov /homepg/Isesale/swiler/swiler.html as cited in *Deepwater: The gulf oil disaster and the future of offshore drilling*, pp. 51–52. Also, Priest, T., *The offshore imperative: Shell Oil's search for petroleum in postwar America* (College Station: Texas A&M Press, 2007, pp. 81–91 as cited in *Deepwater: The Gulf oil disaster and the future of offshore drilling*, pp. 51–52.

39. *Deepwater: The Gulf oil disaster and the future of offshore drilling*, p. 91.

40. Ibid, pp. 94–99.

41. Testimony of John Guide, Hearing before the Deepwater Horizon Joint Investigation Team, July 22, 2010, p. 87 and John Gisclair, Sperry Sun data, April 20, 2010 (annotations, Sept. 20, 2010). Commission calculation based on internal Halliburton document (HAL 10994) as cited in *Deepwater: The Gulf oil disaster and the future of offshore drilling*, pp. 99–100.

42. Salpukas, A. (1999). BP Amoco's leader remakes an oil giant, again. *New York Times*, April 1, as cited in *Deepwater: The Gulf oil disaster and the future of offshore drilling*, p. 45.

43. John Guide (BP), interview with Commission staff, Sept. 17, 2010 as cited in *Deepwater: The Gulf oil disaster and the future of offshore drilling*, p. 89.

44. Global 500. *CNNMoney.com*, July 26, 2010, http://money.cnn.com/magazines /fortunre/global500/2010/full_list/index.html, as cited in *Deepwater: The Gulf oil disaster and the future of offshore drilling*, p. 2.

45. Colton, T., & L. Huntziner. (2002). *A brief history of shipbuilding in recent times*. Alexandria, VA: CNA Corporation; Hunt, M., & L. Gary. (2000). Gulf of Mexico fabrication yards built 5,500 platforms over 50 years. *Offshore* (January) as cited in *Deepwater: The Gulf oil disaster and the future of offshore drilling*, p. 44.

46. Testimony of Nathaniel Chaisson, 411: U.S. Department of Energy as cited in *Deepwater: The Gulf oil disaster and the future of offshore drilling*, pp. 1–2.

47. *Deepwater: The Gulf oil disaster and the future of offshore drilling*, p. 59.

48. Ibid, p. 80.

49. Ibid, p. 67.

50. Ibid, p. 65.

51. U.S. Department of the Interior, "Statement by Secretary of the Interior James Watt Instituting Changes in the Mineral Royalty Management Program - July 21, 1982," Commission on Fiscal Accountability of the Nation's Energy Resources: Subject Files, 1981–1982, RG 48, Entry 994, Box 1 (National Archives and Records Administration, Washington, DC) as cited in *Deepwater: The Gulf oil disaster and the future of offshore drilling*, p. 56.

52. The British Petroleum Company plc. Funding Universe, http://www.fundinguniverse.com /companyhistories/The-British-Petroleum -Company-plc-Company-History.html.

53. Tharoor, I. (2010). A brief history of BP. *Time* magazine, June 2, http://www.time.com/time /business/article/0,8599,1993361,00.html.

54. Ibid.

55. Ibid.

56. The British Petroleum Company plc. FundingUniverse.

57. Tharoor. A brief history of BP.

58. Frey, D. (2002). How green is BP? *The New York Times*, December 8, http://www.nytimes .com/2002/12/08/magazine/how-green-is-bp .html.

59. Goodwyn, W. (2010). Previous BP accidents blamed on safety lapses. *NPR*, May 6, http:// www.npr.org/templates/story/story.php?story Id=126564739.

60. Cronin, J. (2009). Tony Hayward – BP's new boss. *BBC News*, January 12, http:// news.bbc.co.uk/2/hi/business/6257149.stm.

61. Tony Hayward biography. BP Web site, http://www.bp.com; Tony Hayward biography. Bio.True Story, http://www.biography.com/articles/Tony-Hayward-586098.

62. Hayward shares candid views on 2006. *The Telegraph*, December 18, 2006, http://www.telegraph.co.uk/finance/2952547/Hayward-shares-candid-views-on-2006.html.

63. Ibid.

64. BP offers full support to Transocean after drilling rig fire. BP Web site, April 21, 2010, http://www.bp.com/genericarticle.do?categoryId=2012968&contentId=7061458.

65. BP p.l.c. Group Results, First Quarter 2010, page 4, http://www.bp.com/liveassets/bp_internet/globalbp/STAGING/global_assets/downloads/B/bp_first_quarter_2010_results.pdf.

66. Bergin, T. (2010). Exclusive: BP CEO says will pay oil spill claims. *Reuters*, April 30, http://www.reuters.com/article/2010/04/30/us-bp-oilspill-idUSTRE63T2VR20100430.

67. Interview with Tony Hayward. *The Today Show*, May 2, 2010; *TPM Muckraker*, May 4, 2010, http://tpmmuckraker.talkingpointsmemo.com/2010/05/bp_chief_claims_oil_spill_wasnt_our_accident.p hp.

68. Obama, B. (2010). Presidential remarks on the oil spill. The White House, May 2, Louisiana, USA, http://www.whitehouse.gov/the-press-office/remarks-president-oil-spill.

69. BP Twitter account, April 27, 2010, http://twitter.com/BP_America/status/12984677193.

70. BP America Facebook page, May 2, 2010, http://www.facebook.com/topic.php?uid=121928837818541&topic=133.

71. Update on Gulf of Mexico oil spill response. BP Web site, May 5, 2010, www.bp.com.

72. A message from Tony Hayward. YouTube, June 3, 2010, http://www.youtube.com/watch?v=KKcrDaiGE2s.

73. Smith, A. (2010). BP's television ad blitz. *CNN Money*, June 4, http://money.cnn.com/2010/06/03/news/companies/bp_hayward_ad/index.htm.

74. Ibid.

75. Reid, C. (2010). Obama lashes out at BP's PR spin. *CBS News*, June 4, http://www.cbsnews.com/stories/2010/06/04/eveningnews/main6549303.shtml.

76. Wheaton, S. (2010). Gulf reality show draws a big web audience. *The New York Times*, May 26, http://www.nytimes.com/2010/05/27/us/27spillcam.html.

77. Ibid.

78. BP p.l.c. Group Results, First Quarter 2010, Page 4, http://www.bp.com/liveassets/bp_internet/globalbp/STAGING/global_assets/downloads/B/bp_first_quarter_2010_results.pdf.

79. Milam, G. (2010). BP chief: Oil spill impact 'very modest.' *SkyNews*, May 18, http://news.sky.com/skynews/Home/World-News/BP-Oil-Spill-In-Gulf-Of-Mexico-Will-Have-Very-Modest-Environmental-Impact-Says-Firms-CEO/Article/201005315633987.

80. Webb, T. (2010). BP boss admits job on the line over Gulf oil spill. *The Guardian*, May 14, http://www.guardian.co.uk/business/2010/may/13/bp-boss-admits-mistakes-gulf-oil-spill.

81. Interview with Doug Suttles. *The Today Show*, June 9, 2010. Video available on *The Huffington Post*, http://www.huffingtonpost.com/2010/06/09/underwater-plumes-doug-su_n_605613.html.

82. Weber, H. R. (2010). BP executive says he would eat fish from Gulf of Mexico. *Associated Press*, August 1, http://blog.al.com/live/2010/08/bp_executive_says_he_would_eat.html.

83. BP CEO Tony Hayward: "I'd like my life back." *The Today Show*, May 30, 2010. Available from YouTube, http://www.youtube.com/watch?v=MTdKa9eWNFw&feature=player_embedded.

84. Bazinet, K. R. (2010). BP boss Svanberg says "we care about the small people" after oil spill faceoff with President Obama. *NYDailyNews.com*, June 17, http://articles

.nydailynews.com/2010-06-17/news/270673
79_1_small-people-oil-spill-toby-odone.

85. Mufson, S. (2010). Altered BP photo comes into question. *The Washington Post*, July 20, http://www.washingtonpost.com/wp-dyn /content/article/2010/07/19/AR2010071905256 .html.

86. Herron, J. (2011). Go steady with Shell or get a buzz with BP? *Wall Street Journal*, February 3, 2011. Available from http://blogs .wsj.com/source/2011/02/03/go-steady-with -shell-or-get-a-buzz-from-bp.

Andre Blais/Shutterstock.com

Communicating in Writing

After reading this chapter, you will be able to

▶ Plan and develop content for informative and persuasive messages as well as longer documents: reports and proposals.

▶ Consider and incorporate the elements of visual impression into a written message, as appropriate.

▶ Revise written messages for coherence and logical flow.

▶ Revise written messages for style and tone.

▶ Proofread for mechanical correctness.

Case Questions:

1. What was wrong with the email message sent by Alex?
2. What are the specific changes that should be made to improve it? How will each change improve the message?
3. What is the appropriate response that Kevin should make to Alex's request? Why?
4. What tips can you provide to writers to avoid creating messages such as the one sent by Alex?

The Case of the Consultants

"Hey, Josh." At the sound of his name, Joshua Suchin turned to identify the caller. Kevin Lee stood motioning him to come into his office.

"What's up?" Josh asked upon entering.

"Look at this email message. Can you believe this?" Kevin said, as he stared at the computer screen in front of him.

Josh moved to Kevin's side to read the message, but his colleague couldn't wait. "I was very put off by your comments during our meeting this morning," Kevin read out loud. "You said that employees who do not report at least twenty billable hours spent with clients a week will be penalized with lower quarterly bonuses. That is patently unfair and ridiculous! How can you expect me to put in twenty hours with clients when I have been on workers' comp because of my back injury for the past six months? I just get back in the office and you think I will immediately go back to my prior level of productivity? You need to rethink this policy change. I await your response. Alex."

"Wow! It sounds like Alex is all fired up," Josh said.

"Do ya think?" Kevin replied, then laughed. "I think I'll print this message out and hang it by the water cooler. It's a prime example of how 'not to make friends and influence people.'"

Josh chuckled. "That's what he probably deserves, but how are you really going to deal with this?" he asked.

Good writing skills are critical to your success in the workplace. According to a survey of human resource directors, "people who cannot write and communicate clearly will not be hired and are unlikely to last long enough to be considered for promotion."[1] Unfortunately, the *Wall Street Journal* reports that 80 percent of businesses surveyed believed that their employees' biggest weakness was written communication.[2] This finding presents an opportunity, however, for those who can communicate well in writing. They can positively distinguish themselves from their peers through their written communication skills.

When writing, as with all messages, you should first identify your purposes for communicating; analyze your audience to identify its values, beliefs, interests, concerns, and objections; consider the context of the communication; and choose a medium. After considering these strategic issues, you should then select the appropriate tactics to help you achieve your broader communication goals.

This chapter addresses the tactical elements that can be deployed for messages using the written channel of communication. These tactical elements can be broadly categorized as follows:

1. Planning and developing the message: routine, persuasive, and more formal types such as reports and proposals
2. Selecting and incorporating visual elements
3. Revising for coherence and flow
4. Revising for style and tone

Depending on the audience, purpose, and context of the message, some of these steps may be eliminated. For example, if you are sending a text or instant message response to a query you received ten seconds ago from a colleague using the same medium, no planning, little development, no visual aids, and little concern for coherence and flow may be needed. In contrast, an important response to a request for proposal from a government agency may require all of the steps in the writing process be followed to the letter. As with most communication situations, once you are accustomed to following the steps in the strategic process—identifying the purpose, analyzing the audience, considering the context, and selecting the channel—you will find it much easier to determine when all the steps in the tactical portion of the writing task are necessary. Figure 6-1 provides an illustration of applicability of the steps in the writing process for different formats.

Planning and Developing Informative Messages

Like much of workplace communication, business writing has changed significantly with the increased use of technology. Paradoxically, while workplace writing may have diminished significantly in terms of average message length and time spent composing, the use of writing as a key tool for communication has increased, primarily because of the predominance of email use.

FIGURE 6-1 Applicability of the Steps in the Writing Process for Different Formats

Steps in the Writing Process	Message Format			
	Text Message	Email	Memo or Letter	Report or Proposal
STRATEGIC ELEMENTS Planning: Identify the Purposes Analyze the Audience Consider the Context Select the Channel and Media	Generally, no; the context may drive the process as might the medium if you are responding in kind	Depends. An immediate response to a query may require little planning, while a longer message would likely require planning	Yes	Yes
TACTICAL ELEMENTS Develop the Content and Organization	No	Depends on length and importance.	Yes	Yes
Consider and Develop Visual Elements	No	Depends on length and importance.	Yes	Yes
Revise for Coherence and Flow	No	Depends on length and importance.	Yes	Yes
Revise for Style and Tone	No	Depends on length and importance.	Yes	Yes
Proofread for Mechanical Correctness	Depends. If the audience uses text abbreviations, you can, too.	Yes	Yes	Yes

© Cengage Learning 2015

While many email messages are often short responses to inquiries, some are more lengthy, providing instructions, changes in procedures or policies, and other types of information. Similarly, in some organizations, these types of messages may be delivered on paper in the form of a memo, although this is occurring less and less today. External messages to customers, clients, and suppliers also may be printed in the form of a letter. Other types of informative messages include good and bad news messages.

Regardless of the media or format of delivery, however, some rules of business writing apply to all of these informative messages, as shown in Figure 6-1. These are covered in the following sections.

Parts of a Message

Good organization helps you achieve two objectives: (1) It helps your reader understand your message and (2) it demonstrates the quality of your thinking. From a strategic perspective, the first objective is also aimed at meeting your audience's needs, which may help you achieve one of the purposes of communication—conveying goodwill. The second objective performs a second purpose: It reflects on your credibility or image as a professional.

For these reasons, it is important to plan the development of both longer, complex messages and those to important or unfamiliar audiences. Even for the most routine of messages, though, a little thought to organization, structure, and content can go a long way to ensure that a message is clear, considers audience knowledge and needs, maintains your credibility, and potentially enhances your relationship with your audience. These considerations may be even more important with the advent of email and instant and text messaging because of their spontaneous nature.

All informal business messages—emails, memos, letters, informal reports—typically contain three parts, however brief: the introduction, the body, and the close. The only exception to this rule might be text messages and brief, routine emails. More and more, electronic communications are like a conversation, particularly those that are immediate responses to a query such as instant or text messages. For these, the response may be the only content, particularly if it is part of an immediate conversation where contextual or background information isn't necessary for the reader's understanding.

The Introduction

There are two types of message approaches, depending on the purpose of a message. These are the *direct* and *indirect approaches*. The direct approach is used for most messages in the United States, while the indirect approach is used for bad news messages and some persuasive messages when you expect the audience may be resistant to your proposal.

Direct Approach In longer routine messages and those where a more formal approach is appropriate, depending on the audience, you should develop a brief introduction that states the purpose of the message and provides an overview of those subtopics. In a good news message, the "good news" or purpose would also be stated immediately. For example, an introduction to a good news message written to a colleague who recently has been promoted might read: "Congratulations, Amy, on your promotion to director of communications. All of your excellent work on the recent corporate responsibility campaign appears to have paid off in a well-deserved promotion."

Stating the purpose of the message and providing a road map of its contents is important in professional messages because businesspeople are typically pressed for time and bombarded with information, as was discussed in Chapter 4. Given these pressures, they often try to find ways to process information more rapidly or to cull messages that are not of high importance. In fact, you have only one to seven seconds to convince a reader that the information is relevant and only 90 seconds to confirm and keep the reader's interest.[3]

An introduction should indicate to your audience why it is important for it to read your message. It should also provide your audience with a road map of what the message contains to either help it skim a written document or better follow the logic or contents of your message.

In addition, the beginning and the end of a message are considered its most important parts because they are the most read and therefore often the most remembered. For that reason, you should make it clear in the introduction why your message is important to your audience.

Examples of a direct introduction to an informative message include the following:

You will find the agenda for next Monday's meeting below. As the agenda shows, we will discuss new product lines, product manager assignments, and initiate beginning discussions on scheduling.

Congratulations on selecting Lifelong as your insurance carrier! We would like to introduce you to all the benefits you will receive, provide you information on additional products you may wish to learn more about, and give you information about contacting customer service if you have any questions or wish to change or upgrade your insurance package.

Indirect Approach The *indirect approach* is sometimes used for bad news messages as well as some persuasive messages. In the case of a bad news message, you might need to tell a client that you cannot grant a request, you may need to inform a job applicant that he or she was not selected for a position, or you may need to tell employees that they will not be receiving raises this year.

With the indirect approach, the purpose of a bad news message is not stated immediately. Instead, the message opens with what is called a *neutral buffer*, which is intended to maintain goodwill with the recipient. In addition, the buffer should logically lead the reader to the bad news, which is delivered and explained in the body of the message.

Thank you for choosing Primo, Ltd. for your credit needs. Primo specializes in services to small businesses just like yours who need ready access to credit for day-to-day operations and rapidly changing financial situations.

In this example, the bad news is cushioned by expressing gratitude to the reader for considering the company to do business with as well as recognizing the reader's specific needs. The "bad news" of the credit rejection is not delivered until the second paragraph, as shown in Figure 6-2.

CriticalThinking

Do you always immediately state the purpose of longer messages in such a way that it is clear to your readers or listeners why your message is important to them? Do you also provide a brief yet clear overview of the topics your message will address?

The Body

The body of an informative message may differ in content depending on the approach.

Direct Approach The body of a message that uses the direct approach provides the necessary supporting details for the purpose of the message. These might include the reason for the decision, procedures for the reader to follow, background information, a description of the situation, or evidence to support the claims that are made in the case of a persuasive message.

Indirect Approach For bad news messages using the indirect approach, the body of the message might provide the details that led to the bad news being communicated. After the reason for the bad news has been conveyed, the bad news would be delivered tactfully. Alternatively, the body might discuss ways to avoid similar bad news or explain what is being done to avoid such situations in the future. An example of a bad news message is provided in Figure 6-2.

FIGURE 6-2 Example of a Bad News Message Refusing a Credit Card Application

Primo, Ltd.
1800 Olney Avenue
Philadelphia, PA 19140
215-555-7800

April 8, 2013

Holly Leonard
2407 Kearney St.
San Francisco, CA 98807

Dear Ms. Leonard:

Thank you for choosing Primo Ltd. for your credit needs. Primo specializes in services to small businesses just like yours who need ready access to credit for day-to-day operations and rapidly changing financial situations.

After checking your credit rating with the three national credit-reporting firms, we are unable to fulfill your request for a Primo Select Credit Card at this time.

We are eager to fulfill your credit needs and encourage you to obtain your credit report so that you can discover whether errors regarding your credit history are affecting your credit status. You can obtain your credit report via the Internet at creditrating.com.

Once your credit rating has improved, please reapply for your Primo Select Credit Card. Primo Ltd. provides many benefits to its clients, including a competitive interest rate and signature loans for quick access to needed operational funds.

Sincerely,

Lucy Wang
Customer Service Manager

© Cengage Learning

The Close

As stated earlier, the conclusion is one of the most important parts of a message because your audience will be more likely to remember it because of the *recency effect*, or the principle that the most recently presented items or experiences will most likely be remembered best. Consequently, you should take care to ensure that the conclusion is, in fact, memorable and focuses on the final message that you want your audience to take away.

There are three basic types of conclusions: goodwill, summary, and sales. Goodwill conclusions are used for short, routine messages in which another type of conclusion might be inappropriate or for messages sent simply for goodwill purposes. They are also used for bad news messages. Summary conclusions are typically used for more complex, informative messages, and sales conclusions are used for persuasive messages. Each type is discussed below.

Goodwill Conclusions   If you are sending a goodwill message or even if you are conveying a short routine message such as an email, then you will probably want to close with a few simple sentences or statements aimed at maintaining your relationship with your reader. This type of conclusion is called a *goodwill close* and might sound something like this: "I look forward to meeting you Tuesday to further discuss the proposed flex-time plan." A goodwill close should avoid sounding generic because your purpose is to maintain your relationship with your audience. Therefore, your close should be as specific as possible to the situation and the person with whom you are communicating, as in the example above. A goodwill close provides you an opportunity to distinguish yourself as a person who truly recognizes and appreciates others. Because we often feel like little more than numbers in our busy, impersonal society, the ability to make others feel like special individuals can be a welcome, appreciated talent.

A goodwill close is also appropriate for bad news messages. A goodwill close in this situation might suggest an alternative course for the reader or point to a brighter future or a continued relationship. (See Figure 6-2 for an example.)

Summary Conclusions   If you are conveying a longer, more complex, informative message, such as procedural or policy changes or an informal report, you should create a summary conclusion in which you restate the subtopics of your message in a slightly different manner. You have probably heard the old saw: "Tell 'em what you're going to tell 'em, then tell 'em, then tell 'em what you just told 'em." This is the organizational formula for an informative message and is intended to ensure that readers who skim or who are not listening well get your message through repetition. Repetition is not the same as redundancy, however; when you repeat information, you should do so in a slightly different manner. Sometimes stating information differently can also help your reader or listener with comprehension. The first time we hear or read something, its meaning may not be completely clear. But if additional explanation is provided or if the message is stated again in a slightly different way, then the chances improve that the meaning will be understood.

Sales Conclusions   If you are conveying a persuasive message, your conclusion should focus on restating the benefits your reader will receive from adopting your proposal. This type of conclusion is considered a sales conclusion. In some persuasive situations, it may also be appropriate to conclude with a **call to action**. You use a call to action when you want your audience to take the next step in your proposal. A call to action might be "Let's meet later this week to discuss the details of my proposal. I will call you tomorrow to discuss a day and time that is convenient for you." In this example, you are attempting to get the reader to fully consider your proposal and, ideally, to commit to a decision.

Calls to action are generally not as effective, however, if you as the communicator are not the person charged with following through. For instance, in the example above, you might write, "Let's meet later this week to discuss the details of my proposal. Please call me to let me know a convenient time for you." In this case, you have provided the reader an opportunity to "drop the ball" or not follow up. If he or she does not call to set up an appointment, then your proposal is dead unless, after a week passes without a call, you follow up instead to schedule the meeting.

Planning and Developing Persuasive Messages

In business situations, we are almost always persuading or attempting to influence others. We are almost always attempting to sell ourselves, our ideas, our company's products or services, or our company and its reputation to others. Included in these

call to action
A conclusion to a persuasive message that is intended to convince the reader to fully consider the writer's or speaker's proposal and, ideally, commit to a decision or take the next step.

types of messages are sales messages, job-application letters and résumés, persuasive requests, proposals, and so on. Even if we believe that we simply are informing our audience, it is important to recognize that there may be some elements of persuasion to which we should attend, that is, we may also be attempting to persuade our audience that we are credible and knowledgeable and that we value our relationship with it. As this latter sentence implies, to be more successful at persuasion, you should pay attention to the third and fourth purposes of communication: establishing and maintaining goodwill and credibility. If we do not have a credible, likable persona or image, then it will be more difficult for us to persuade an audience to accept our ideas.

The information you provide in persuasive situations is almost totally dependent on your audience's perspective or view of your proposal. For example, if you believe that your audience is very receptive to your idea, you might simply ask it to accept your proposal with minimal information provided. This approach is sometimes called a *direct request*. However, the less receptive your audience is to your proposal, the more time you may need to take to formulate a strategy for its presentation and the more information you may need to provide to be persuasive. To determine the strategy and information you will need to provide in a persuasive message, you should ask and answer the following questions:

1. **How will my audience initially react to my proposal?**

A second question that may help to clarify the issues involved in the first is "What feelings or fears might my proposal elicit in my audience?" The answers to this question may help you to determine whether using the direct or indirect approach, as discussed earlier, would be most effective. If your audience might have a negative reaction to your proposal, you might be more indirect. For example, you would likely not open a sales message with the statement: "You are going to need a funeral sooner or later, so please consider Thompson's Funeral Services." Instead, a better approach might be: "No one likes to think of their own passing, but doing the necessary planning can make a difficult time much easier for one's family and friends." The key message in both examples is the same, but in the latter case, it would come later in the message.

2. **How does my audience feel about me, my company, or my product or service?**

You or other representatives of your organization may have had past encounters with your audience that did not go well. These events may have left your audience feeling reluctant to communicate with you or your organization's representatives. If this is the case, it would be helpful to consider what you might say to help overcome or eliminate this reluctance. One way might be to approach the situation directly with some recognition of what you have learned. In this case, an indirect introduction to the situation might be used:

Although our last meeting did not result in a contract between our companies, the information that you provided us has helped us to develop a product that is much more effective in addressing the needs of small businesses like yours. Our new product, AccountAble, can be scaled to meet the specific needs of small companies like yours, and as they grow, affordable add-ons can be easily installed with no downtime.

3. **What are your audience's needs? In what ways does your idea or proposal fulfill those needs?**

If you can identify your audience's needs, you then can tailor the content of your message to explain how your proposed idea—or, in the case of customers, your product or service—meets those needs. In other words, answering Question 3 might provide most of the content you need for the entire message This step can thus make the message much easier to draft and organize. A second advantage is that your audience will likely be more interested in the information you present if it is narrowly focused on explaining how your proposal meets its needs or will benefit it. Thirdly, this strategy shows that you are interested in your audience, which helps you to convey goodwill.

4. **What benefits does your proposal provide to your audience?**

The answer to this question may be similar to that of the previous one. However, you may find in asking this question that you may be placed in the role of educating your audience about your proposal. For example, your audience may have voiced its needs, but it may not have identified all the potential benefits your idea will provide. By giving some thought to all the benefits that your proposal might deliver to your audience, you have the potential to make your idea more persuasive. In fact, as mentioned earlier, the bulk of the content of your message might focus almost solely on the benefits your audience will derive from your proposal.

Generally, the type of benefit that is most persuasive to a business audience has to do with money: making it or saving it in some way. That does not mean that you ignore the other types of benefits that might accrue, such as the satisfaction one might feel from a job well done. Such a benefit is called an *intrinsic motivation*. However, this type of benefit is generally less persuasive than more *extrinsic motivations* such as those that save or make money in some way. Typically, you would use intrinsic motivators such as satisfaction, pleasure, and so on as additional information to make your proposal more persuasive. As always, let your audience be the guide. For example, a nonprofit organization may be more influenced by calling on intrinsic motivations that fall within their mission than extrinsic motivations such as making money.

5. **What obstacles or objections must you overcome?**

Answering this question might help you to determine whether the direct or the indirect approach would be most effective. It may also help you to identify what information you need to provide in your message as well as how much. For example, if your audience is resistant to your proposal, then you will probably need to provide more information in the form of benefits or good reasons to persuade it than you might for an audience to which you know you can simply make a direct request and it will be acted upon. If your audience holds another position, you may need to provide information that shows that view is not the best and explain why. How you accomplish this goal has to do with the tone as well as the content of your message. That is, a tactful approach would be required to show that a desired solution is not the best. (Tone is discussed later in this chapter.)

Often you must eliminate your audience's objections in order to set the stage for it to be open to hearing your proposal. If you do not eliminate your audience's objections or weaken the strength of its position through the quality of the information you provide in a tactful manner, then you will probably be faced with addressing those objections once you deliver your proposal, and you may ultimately find yourself back at step one in the process of persuasion.

If your audience is resistant, another tactic that may make your message more persuasive might be to supply information that shows that your proposal is easy to accept. For example, if you are attempting to persuade your department manager to change a procedure, you should also explain how to implement that procedure and may even volunteer to do so. Doing so makes the change easier for your manager to accept and implement and thus makes your message potentially more persuasive. A secondary benefit is that such an approach may lend you credibility as a person with initiative and good problem-solving skills. However, in some politically charged environments, be wary of such proposals. An insecure boss may read such a proposal as a threat and your credibility will instead be damaged. Again, let the context, in the form of the corporate culture and your audience, be your guide.

6. **Is this a sales proposal or competitive message? If so, what do my competitors offer? How might I distinguish myself or my ideas favorably from my competitors?**

Whenever you are competing with others for scarce resources—a job, a contract, a raise, a promotion, or a sale—you must consider how you compare to your competitors for those resources and how you can favorably distinguish yourself from them. You must therefore have some idea of what your competitors offer. This entails an additional step in the strategic process in which you not only must analyze your audience to identify its needs, concerns, and expectations but also your competitors to identify what they offer and how they differ from your or your organization's offerings, not only in terms of additional benefits but in terms of weaknesses. This knowledge should enable you to showcase the advantages of going with you or your organization and help you to anticipate how to respond to questions about your or your organization's shortcomings, if these exist.

When you apply for a job, for example, you are competing with dozens, perhaps hundreds, of others. You should give some thought to the qualifications those competitors might bring to the situation and then attempt to show that you are at least as well qualified as they are and ideally, more so. Reaching this objective depends on the quality of the content or information about yourself that you are able to provide and whether that information speaks to your audience's needs as well or better than your competitor—other job applicants—might.

Once you have answered these questions, you should have a good idea about the amount and type of information you need to provide to successfully persuade your audience to accept your proposal. These questions may also help you determine the most effective organizational approach to your message.

CriticalThinking

Identify a time that you were unsuccessful at persuasion. Why were you unsuccessful? In retrospect, what could you have done to have improved your chances of success?

Basic Components of a Persuasive Message

Entire courses are devoted to the teaching and learning of persuasion. In fact, persuasion, or *argumentation* as it is called in the academy, is its own field of study. Subsequently, the study of persuasion involves a detailed history, content, and discussion that will not be reproduced here. However, it is helpful to know the basic components of a persuasive message. At the most foundational level, persuasion consists of two parts: a **claim** and the information or **evidence** that supports it. Another way to think about these two components is that a claim is often general or more abstract, while evidence is more specific. This way of thinking about evidence also helps us understand why evidence is often necessary for the clarity of our message in addition to persuasiveness. Below are examples of claims and supporting evidence.

Claim: Effective writing will save your business money.

Evidence: Studies indicate that employees waste one hour a day attempting to interpret or follow up on poorly written messages. This means that a company loses one hour of pay a day for each employee because of poorly written messages. This hour could be used more productively for other activities, or the money that goes to pay that wasted wage could be invested in other resources.

Claim: You should buy our hybrid automobile, the Solare, because it will provide you with several benefits.

Evidence: The largest benefit you will receive from purchasing our hybrid automobile, the Solare, is the savings you will receive from lower gasoline use and its purchase. The Solare is primarily fueled by hydrogen and requires gasoline only for sudden acceleration or unusual engine loads such as driving up steep inclines. If most of your vehicle use is confined to city streets and you avoid rapid acceleration, then you may rarely, if ever, require a stop at the gas station!

Types of evidence include facts, statistics, examples, analogies, and expert testimony, and almost all of these help us to show our logic and reasoning abilities (the quality of our thinking) as well as our knowledge of the topic (our credibility). Other types of evidence such as anecdotes and stories may help us to pique our audience's emotional interest. These three types of classic appeals are discussed in the next section.

claim
Often a general or abstract idea presented as fact.

evidence
More specific statement of fact that supports a statement.

Types of Persuasive Appeals

More than 2,000 years ago, Greek philosopher Aristotle (384–322 B.C.E.) proposed that evidence or the information provided in a persuasive message could be divided into three broad categories: logical, ethical, and emotional. Although this schema is centuries old, it is still useful to us today.

A logical appeal, or **logos**, consists of such information as facts and statistics. It is a fact, for example, that mammals breathe oxygen. A fact is any information that is broadly accepted as true. Business audiences tend to be persuaded by logical evidence, particularly numbers, dollar or other currency amounts, and statistics. They also often prefer that this information be presented in the form of graphs. (Choosing and integrating graphs into text is discussed later in this chapter.) Both of the examples of claims and evidence previously provided largely rely on logical appeal for their persuasiveness.

An ethical appeal, or **ethos**, does not refer to ethics as we normally think of the concept but rather to information that provides credibility for ourselves or to our position. One of the easiest ways to make an ethical argument is to cite authorities in the subject of discussion. Most of us have used this method when we have been asked to write a research paper in school. In the first example of a claim and its evidence in the previous section, the reference to "studies" is an ethical appeal because it implies that experts were involved in the gathering of this information. This appeal might be stronger if the names of the experts involved in the studies were known to the audience. In this case, this information might carry greater weight or persuasiveness.

Another way to build credibility is to consider both sides of an issue. If you discuss both the pros and the cons, you will probably be considered fair-minded and thus more credible (i.e., you are not biased and therefore one-sided in your argument). You can also establish your credibility by showing that you are experienced and knowledgeable in a particular relevant area. For example, if you are selling photocopiers, you might tell your audience that you have been in the photocopier business for ten years. Such a statement indicates that you are knowledgeable about that industry, your product line, and most likely your competition.

The final type of evidence is the emotional appeal, or **pathos**. An emotional appeal does not work by simply writing or stating emotional words. An emotional appeal often depends on telling a story or evoking a picture or experience that your audience can identify with or feel empathy toward. For example, commercials that show pictures of starving children are intended to make us empathize with them so that we will contribute money to help lessen their plight. Similarly, advertisements that show young people at the beach in an SUV are intended to make us identify with them. Advertisers want us to identify with the youthful fun we see and then associate that fun with the SUV. These feelings are expected to make us want to buy the SUV so that we can have the same experience. Most of this emotional work goes on at the subconscious level, making it very effective at influencing our feelings and behaviors.

An emotional appeal might be used in a professional setting to motivate employees or colleagues. For example, if you want your staff to increase its quarterly sales, then you might hold a meeting at a lush resort that also involves group activities aimed at increasing camaraderie and overall good feelings toward the company and among sales staff members. Such an event might include an awards ceremony and closing speech intended to motivate employees to feel valued and to do their best to reach company goals. Such an event is intended to play on the emotions and identities of the participants in such a way as to make them feel special, recognized for their efforts, and part of a team—all effective at the emotive level in persuading them indirectly to put in the necessary effort to achieve the company's objectives.

---

logos
Consists of information such as facts or statistics; also known as *logical appeal*.

ethos
An ethical appeal that refers to information that provides credibility to ourselves or our position.

pathos
An emotional appeal; an attempt to win over the audience by appealing to its emotions, often by telling a story or evoking a picture with which the audience can empathize.

Different types of audiences are convinced by different types of evidence and by varying amounts. Generally, the more resistant an audience is to your idea, the more evidence you will need to present. More resistant audiences may also require the use of all three types of evidence in varying amounts. Sometimes the situation dictates, to some degree, the type of evidence required. For example, when we are at home in front of the television or computer, we may want to relax and be entertained. That's why so many commercials rely on the emotional appeal; they work subtly on our feelings rather than requiring a lot of mental work. After a long day at work, we may be less receptive to a half-hour-long, fact-filled discussion of the benefits and disadvantages of buying a particular product, although that sort of discussion is generally expected in the workplace.

CriticalThinking

What are the key elements of persuasion as a strategy? Should you state the opposing view when you write a persuasive message?

Quality of Evidence

Not all evidence is relevant or of high quality. Evidence can be used to mislead an audience intentionally or unintentionally. However, evidence can also be tested for its validity. The three primary tests of evidence and its quality are provided in Box 6-1.

The misuse of statistics is common when one instance is used to represent all cases. For example, the statement "Intel saved $10 million by outsourcing the production of its microprocessors to India" would be misused if it were used to support the claim "All companies will save millions of dollars by outsourcing their

---

Box 6-1   Tests of Evidence

- **Statistics.** Tests for quality of statistical evidence include the following:
  1. Is the sample from which the statistics are drawn a representative one?
  2. Is a single instance used as an example of all instances?
- **Testimony.** Tests for quality of testimonial evidence include these:
  1. Is the person an authority on the subject? If so, how reliable is he or she?
  2. Was the person giving the testimonial close enough to witness the event?
  3. Is it possible that the person giving the testimony is biased?
- **Comparison and analogies (the fallacy of faulty comparison or faulty analogy).** Tests for the quality of a comparison or analogy include the following:
  1. Do both items or activities have the same resources or authority?
  2. Are both items or activities governed by the same rules?
  3. Do both activities occur during the same time period?
  4. Are both items or activities measured in the same way?

manufacturing and services to foreign countries." One company's experience does not represent the experiences of all companies, because organizations have varying resources, produce different products with differing requirements, provide various services, have differing resources and needs, and so on.

Similarly, testimonial evidence can be used to present a biased opinion. For example, if the testimony of a U.S. Department of Commerce official is used to support outsourcing, then the testimony might be considered biased because such a person would presumably lean toward supporting probusiness interests and positions and would thus ignore or downplay social or ethical considerations.

Finally, analogies can be faulty. For example, the analogy "Outsourcing is like farming because most farm labor in the United States is now provided by migrant workers from Mexico" is faulty. Not all outsourced jobs can be performed by relatively unskilled workers, for example, so there may be other costs of outsourcing that do not occur in the farm-labor situation. Furthermore, the pay scales of U.S. farmworkers may not match those of workers in another country in relation to the costs of living of both countries. Finally, it might be argued that many migrant workers from Mexico provide U.S. farm labor because U.S. citizens are unwilling to do that work. However, U.S. jobs might be outsourced even though a workforce exists that is willing to perform those particular jobs. In summary, the conditions and details of the two situations may not match in ways that then make the comparison dissimilar.

Organizing Persuasive Messages

Various models are available for organizing persuasive messages, because persuasion can be a more difficult communication purpose to achieve and thus may require more preparation, strategy formulation, and time.

Broadly speaking, two persuasive situations exist: one in which you believe your audience is more or less receptive to your ideas or proposal and one in which you believe your audience is resistant or even hostile to you, your organization, or your ideas. In the former case, your audience may be so receptive that you simply need to request its agreement and you will receive it, as mentioned earlier in the case of a direct request. In other cases, it might be useful to consider the use of one of the models for persuasive messages.

One popular model for organizing persuasive messages is called the **AIDA approach**. AIDA is an acronym that stands for *attention*, *interest*, *desire*, and *action*. The AIDA approach can be adjusted to meet the needs of both types of audiences in persuasive situations: those who are more or less receptive and those who are resistant or even hostile. However, it is more difficult to use for resistant or hostile audiences if you are a less experienced persuader. For that reason, a more detailed discussion of an indirect organizational strategy for dealing with resistant and hostile audiences is also provided in this section.

AIDA approach
A popular model for organizing persuasive messages; AIDA is the acronym for *attention, interest, desire,* and *action*.

Using the AIDA Approach

Each step in the AIDA approach is discussed below. An example of a persuasive message created using the AIDA approach can be found in Figure 6-3.

1. **Attention.** The first step is to gain the audience's attention and interest, so you should begin every persuasive message with a brief statement that is personalized, audience-centered, and relevant to the situation and the

FIGURE 6-3	Example of a Persuasive Message Using the AIDA Approach

To: Juan Garcia <jgarcia@hotmail.com>

From: Peggy Newman <pnewman@motorsports.com>

Hi, Juan,

Renowned racing legend Mike Nichols is coming to town! Jackson Motorsports is happy to host the twenty-time winner at its May 20 event to recognize its gratitude to loyal customers like you on our annual Customer Appreciation Day.

Nichols will be representing CustomRods, Inc., which will be rolling out its new line of chrome accessories designed especially for "rods" like yours. Car enthusiasts have voted CustomRods' line of classic car accessories "Best in the Business" for the past five years in *HotRod* magazine.

This year's Customer Appreciation Day promises to be the best yet. Nichols will be signing autographs, the rock band *Haywire* will play, free tacos will be served, and special sales will occur every half hour during the day.

We hope to see you at this year's event. Please accept the included special 40 percent off coupon sent only to our most loyal customers. The coupon can be used toward any purchase on your special day!

Best regards,

Peggy Newman
Marketing Manager

© Cengage Learning

audience. Your audience probably wants to know "What's in this message for me?" so you might call attention to the benefits it will receive.

2. **Interest.** In the second step, you should attempt to heighten the audience's interest in your topic or proposal. You can do this by explaining in more detail why your message is relevant to your audience. In this section, you might explain why current practices are not the best, if appropriate. In other situations, you might provide examples, data, testimony, or other kinds of evidence to show your audience what life would be like if it adopts your proposal.

3. **Desire.** In the third step, you should provide evidence to prove the claims made earlier in your message. In product-related persuasion, you might provide evidence of the benefits your audience will receive.

4. **Action.** In the fourth step, you should suggest a specific step the audience can take and make that action easy. You might also restate how the audience will benefit by acting as you wish. This last stage is similar to the issues discussed earlier in the section "Sales Conclusions."

Using the Indirect Approach for Resistant Audiences

As discussed earlier in this chapter, attempting to persuade a resistant or hostile audience requires a somewhat less direct approach. This is because such an audience may have already made up its mind about you, your organization, or your ideas. Even though you, your organization, and your ideas are separate from one another, they are associated, and some audiences will make this association. In this situation, you need to use a communication that will best help to ensure that your audience is open to hear or read and consider your persuasive message. For this reason, you may not want to announce your specific solution or proposal at the beginning of the message because your audience already has an opinion about it and will stop listening to your message. That is why the ordering of a message delivered to a resistant or hostile audience is important if you are to get the opportunity to persuade it.

The steps in persuading a resistant or hostile audience are explained below.

1. You should open your message with a statement of common ground to defuse any differences that may exist between you and your audience. This statement should be followed with an indirect statement of purpose that generally explains your idea. You should also provide an overview of the contents of the body of your message but generally should not include your specific recommendation.

2. The body of your message should begin by explaining the need for your proposed idea. Your goal is to show in a persuasive manner that there is a need for change of the type you are proposing.

3. After demonstrating the need for change, you must eliminate your audience's objections to your proposal. Your audience's objections might focus on several issues. In fact, you may have already addressed one objection: your belief in the need for change. Another objection your audience might have is that it favors another approach or solution. In this case, you must consider all the alternatives, discussing their benefits and disadvantages. In this section of your argument, you are working toward showing that your proposed solution is clearly best of all the alternatives. You must do so in an objective, tactful way, however, to reduce the potential for judgments of bias. Your intent is to show that you are a reasonable, knowledgeable, and objective person who is systematically yet thoroughly exploring the various options and the relevant issues.

4. After you tactfully eliminate your audience's objections through your careful analysis, you announce your specific solution or recommendation and emphasize why it is the best of all possible choices. The strategy in this situation is to eliminate your audience's objections before announcing your idea; announcing it earlier might affect the audience's receptivity to your idea. In other words, you are attempting to keep the audience open to your message so that you have an opportunity to be persuasive.

5. If appropriate, an additional step might include a plan for implementing your proposed solution. The easier the change is to make, the more attractive it may be to your audience.

When using this approach to persuasion, however, it is important to avoid deception or misleading statements.

Planning and Developing Reports and Proposals

Depending on your position and the industry in which you work, you might be called on to write longer messages, reports, or proposals. Common types of reports include feasibility reports, research reports, progress reports, incident reports, and proposals. This section discusses not only how to prepare to write a report but also how to select the appropriate report type. It also explains the different sections that are commonly included in reports and proposals.

Preparing to Write the Report

The report-writing process is much like that for any message that requires some thought and preparation. For most reports, this process includes the following steps.

1. Define the problem that will be addressed in the report.
2. Gather information and data. Before developing recommendations, it is a good idea to gather information about the problem. Generally, research for reports consists of primary evidence, which is gathered by conducting interviews, surveys, experiments, and observation. Secondary research—that which has already been published—might also be helpful in determining appropriate recommendations to solve the problem that is the focus of the report.
3. Develop recommendations. Data and evidence gathered during step two should be selected to support the report recommendations.

Selecting the Report Type

Reports and proposals can be either informal or formal in design, style, and content. Informal reports and proposals typically use memo formats. A formal report format should be used when the preparation time is longer, the findings and recommendations are more significant, a formal report format has been used in the past, and the importance of the audience demands it.

Report Format

An informal report contains the same parts as a typical memo: an introduction, a body, and a close. As with a regular memo, the body of an informal report may be divided into a number of sections set off by headings. These sections may correspond to the contents of the body of a formal report (see the following).

The format of a formal report is more complex than an informal report in that it generally includes front and back matter in addition to the body. The front matter of a formal report may include the following:

- **Title page.** This page tells the reader the name of the report, the names of the writers and company submitting the report, and the date it was completed.
- **Transmittal document or cover letter.** The cover letter tells the reader the subject of the report, what is of most importance in it, the action that should be taken, and what follow-up will occur or is needed.
- **Table of contents.** The table of contents should be a complete listing of the major and minor topics addressed in the report. Typically, it is a listing of the headings contained in the report along with the number of the page on which each section begins.
- **List of illustrations.** If the report contains tables or figures, they should be listed on this page.
- **Executive summary.** The executive summary summarizes the major topics covered in the report. These topics include a purpose statement for the report,

an overview of the key ideas, identification of key problems that will affect the outcome of the report, solutions to the problems, and a recommended course of action.

The report proper or body of the report typically includes the following sections:

- **Introduction.** An introduction should include the purpose of the report, an overview of the report, and background information if appropriate, or an identification of the problem addressed in the report.
- **Discussion or body.** This section consists of the analysis of relevant information or a discussion of the details relevant to the problem solution.
- **Conclusions.** This section is typically a summary of the discussion that focuses on the important implications of the analysis provided in the body or discussion, and it provides the solutions and their benefits.
- **Recommendations.** This section provides the suggested course of action.

The back matter may include references, a bibliography, or appendixes. An appendix typically includes additional related information that is not of primary importance such as letters, tables, figures, survey results, or previous report findings. An example of an informal report can be found in Appendix A, "Model Documents."

Proposal Format

Proposals are sales documents that are intended to recommend changes or purchases within a company—or show how your organization can meet the needs of another if the proposal is intended for an external audience. Some external proposals are responses to a request for proposal (RFP) that is submitted by outside entities, such as government agencies and other contracting entities. Like reports, proposals may be informal or formal. Like informal reports, informal proposals typically use a memo format. A formal proposal may include the following components:

- Proposed idea and purpose, or what is often called the "project description"
- Scope, or what you propose to do
- Methods or procedures to be used
- Materials and equipment needed
- Qualifications of personnel who will be working on the project
- Follow-up or evaluation of the project
- Budget or costs of the project
- Summary of proposal
- Appendixes, if appropriate

An example of an informal proposal can be found in Appendix A, "Model Documents."

Visual Impression in Written Messages

More and more messages these days are sent electronically. With this development, the need to understand the various formatting conventions for business messages has declined. However, it is useful to understand when the use of conventional business formats is appropriate. Memos are typically used for more formal occasions to send messages to internal audiences. Likewise, letters are also used for more formal occasions but for external audiences. Templates for creating different types of written business messages and examples of different types of business messages are provided in Appendix A, "Model Documents." Most word processors also provide templates for common business documents, making formatting of these more formal documents much easier.

One important formatting feature for email messages is the subject line. As with any message, because of time pressures and the deluge of information that most businesspeople must deal with every day, it is important to get your audience's attention by providing an informative subject line. The best way to do this is to signal that this message is relevant and needed by the reader. For example, the subject line "Meeting Dates for Project Development Team" is much more informative than a single-word subject line such as "Meeting." "Please Call Me Regarding Insurance Report" is better than "Call me."

In addition to format, a number of other visual elements can be incorporated into written business messages. These include white space, headings, lists, and graphics.

White Space

One difference in academic writing and business writing is a concern with *white space*. The inclusion of sufficient white space is also of concern when writing content for Web messages, since as with other business writing, most readers skim to find the information they are looking for.

Because of time pressures felt by most business professionals, it is important for writers to ensure that their writing looks easy to read and accessible or what is called "skimmable." This goal is partially accomplished by *chunking* information in short, well-focused paragraphs. Paragraphs should be kept short—no more than eight or nine lines in length—to provide more white space between paragraphs. Chunking makes a message appear easier to read because it divides it into easily digestible chunks. The increased white space also makes the message look less dense.

To enhance "skimmability," paragraphs would also begin with a clear, concise topic sentence. Developing coherent paragraphs is discussed later in "Revising for Coherence and Flow."

In addition to chunking, writers should ensure that sufficient white space is provided for margins. Additional white space can be provided through the use of visual aids as well (also discussed later in this chapter).

Use of Headings

The use of design features such as *headings* and lists is both a graphic technique and a tactical issue because you, as the writer, decide whether and how to use them and what form they will take. The use of headings is considered a graphic technique; it is one way to incorporate additional white space into a document and thus add visual interest. Headings also are cueing devices that let your audience know what to expect in terms of content and organization. They are therefore very useful as a skimming device. Headings should not, however, take the place of accurate topic sentences, because people read differently: Some people read headings, and some people skip them and read the first sentence of each paragraph.

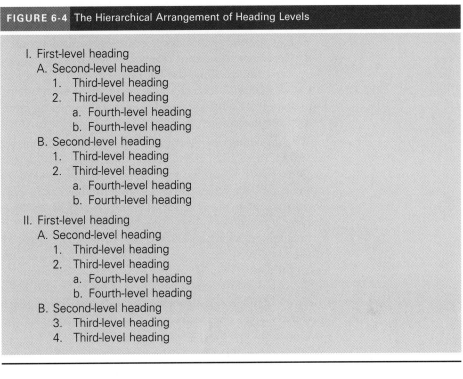

FIGURE 6-4 The Hierarchical Arrangement of Heading Levels

I. First-level heading
   A. Second-level heading
      1. Third-level heading
      2. Third-level heading
         a. Fourth-level heading
         b. Fourth-level heading
   B. Second-level heading
      1. Third-level heading
      2. Third-level heading
         a. Fourth-level heading
         b. Fourth-level heading

II. First-level heading
   A. Second-level heading
      1. Third-level heading
      2. Third-level heading
         a. Fourth-level heading
         b. Fourth-level heading
   B. Second-level heading
      3. Third-level heading
      4. Third-level heading

© Cengage Learning

Headings also indicate the relationship between ideas. For less complex documents such as memos and longer emails, most headings indicate an equal or parallel relationship between ideas. However, for more complex documents such as reports and proposals, information can be arranged in a hierarchy. In other words, some elements of the information provided in the document are more important than others, encompass others, and come before or after others. An outline is an example of a hierarchy of information. Figure 6-4 illustrates the hierarchical arrangement of heading levels.

What this means in terms of heading use is that more complex documents need headings that show your reader the hierarchical ordering of information. Typically, ideas of a higher order in the hierarchy are indicated by a heading that is of larger size than headings that indicate information lower in order.

The most important considerations for headings are that you use a consistent style and format and that you place them strategically to position your points to their best advantage and for your audience's benefit. When choosing a heading design, you can consider the use of three characteristics: font appearance, font size, and placement.

- **Font appearance.** Font appearance refers to whether the font is italicized, bolded, underlined, or capitalized. As with font type, the appearance of the font you choose to use can affect the impression of your document. For example, the use of italicized or all-capital-letter headings tends to make a document feel more traditional or conservative, whereas the use of upper- and lowercase letters makes a document appear more modern.

- **Font size.** A common way to distinguish heading levels is to use a different font size. As explained earlier, higher-order headings typically use a larger font size; those of a lower order use a smaller font.
- **Placement.** Placement refers to where the heading is placed on the page. Typically, headings are left justified, centered, or indented, depending on the feel you wish to create and the order of the heading. Centered headings, like the use of serif type, tend to give a document a more conservative feel than those that are left justified.

When deciding on a heading design, you should limit the number of devices you use to no more than three. More than three may detract from the professional image you wish to convey by making your design look amateurish and chaotic. A common practice for creating business headings is to use the same font type and placement and to distinguish different heading levels by size only. This creates a simpler, more contemporary look to a message.

In addition, headings should be informative: They should contain sufficient information to be meaningful. One-word headings are called *labels* and tend to be less informative than short phrases used as headings. On the other hand, you should avoid overly long headings that begin to read like a topic sentence. In that case, you may have inadvertently provided two topic sentences for the section you are referencing—one your actual topic sentence and the other your heading—creating a redundancy problem.

Use of Lists

Lists are useful devices for providing more white space in a document and making it easier to skim. Two types of lists exist—numbered and bulleted—and they have differing purposes. *Number lists* are used for information that is to be used sequentially, as in a series of steps for instructions. *Bullet lists* are used to identify separate items that are equal and related or parallel in importance. Bullet lists are often useful devices for forecasting the contents of a message, as in the case below.

Example of a bullet list for forecasting:

> *This memo will show you the advantages of adopting a flex-time policy for employees. More specifically, it will explain*
>
> - *Why a policy change is needed.*
> - *How the policy change will benefit employees and the company.*
> - *How to implement the policy change.*

You should resist the temptation to overuse or misuse bullet lists. Inexperienced business writers often make the mistake of believing that they can use bullet lists to provide all the information in a message. This belief arises from an understanding that business messages should be concise; however, it ignores the corresponding importance of clarity. If your entire message is made up of bulleted phrases, for example, those phrases may not convey complete meaning but merely fragments of information that your reader must attempt to interpret, elaborate on, and connect. Such messages often take on the appearance and content of an outline rather than a well-written and well-reasoned message. The overuse of bullet lists is particularly problematic in persuasive messages that generally require solid reasoning and quality evidence to support major claims.

Whenever you place the burden of interpretation on your reader, you risk two outcomes: (1) Your reader will not wish to take on that burden, so he or she will stop reading in frustration and (2) your reader will interpret your meaning incorrectly. Furthermore, if you are attempting to persuade, a list format typically will not help you achieve that goal because it will probably not contain the necessary evidence.

To reiterate, lists are typically used as forecasting devices, not to deliver the main content of your message.

Lists should be grammatically parallel in structure, which means that each item in the list should begin with the same kind of word. For example, in the sample list just presented, each list item begins with an adverb. In business writing, it is useful to consider using a verb as the beginning word of a list because it implies action.

Use of Graphics

Using graphics appropriately provides three main benefits:

1. Information is more easily understood than the use of words alone.
2. Visuals help to make the information conveyed more memorable.
3. Visuals enhance your professionalism and credibility.

However, as with all forms of information, graphic information can be misused. When using graphics to convey information, be sure your data is valid, reliable, and drawn from a representative sample if appropriate.

The most common forms of visual aids used in both written and oral presentations are the graph, table, and diagram or drawing. Many of these elements can easily be developed with the use of word processing, spreadsheet and presentation programs, and other graphic tools.

Graphs

Graphs, sometimes called *charts*, are used to compare the value of several items: the amount of advertising money spent on different media, the annual profit of a company over time, and so on. Two common types of graphs are the bar graph and the pie graph. Examples of each are provided in Figure 6-5 and Figure 6-6.

The bar graph is typically used to emphasize comparisons or contrasts between two or more items. A pie graph is often used to indicate the distribution of something or the relative size of the parts of a whole.

Tables

Tables are useful for emphasizing key facts and figures. They are especially effective for listing steps, highlighting features, or comparing related facts. A **table** presents data in words, numbers, or both in columns and rows. An example of a table comparing the benefits of large and small companies is shown in Figure 6-7.

Tables easily convey large amounts of numerical data and often are the only way to show several variables for a number of items.

Diagrams and Drawings

Diagrams are two-dimensional drawings that show the important parts of objects. They are useful for conveying information about size, shape, and structure.

graph
A visual element used to compare the values of several items.

table
A visual element used to present data in words, numbers, or both, in columns and rows.

diagram
A two-dimensional drawing that shows the important parts of objects.

FIGURE 6-5 Example of a Bar Graph

Month	Value
December	65,000
November	72,000
October	45,000
September	29,000
August	32,000
July	21,000
June	13,000
May	25,000
April	20,000
March	35,000
February	60,000
January	82,000

0   16,400   32,800   49,200   65,600   82,000

© Cengage Learning

FIGURE 6-6 Example of a Pie Graph

Favorite Type of Movie

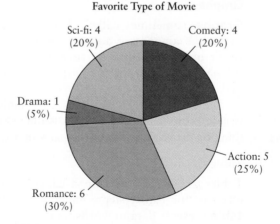

Sci-fi: 4 (20%)
Comedy: 4 (20%)
Drama: 1 (5%)
Action: 5 (25%)
Romance: 6 (30%)

Source: U.S. Department of Labor.

Types of diagrams include drawings, maps, and floor plans. An example of a diagram is shown in Figure 6-8.

An organizational chart is a form of block diagram that indicates lines of authority and responsibility in an organization.

Box 6-2 offers a guide for selecting appropriate graphics.

ResponsibleCommunication

Statistics can be misused in a myriad of ways. Some misuses are intentional, but others are not. Even some scientists have been known to fool themselves accidentally with statistics because of a lack of knowledge of probability and a lack of standardization in their tests. Common methods of misusing statistics follow.

Misuse of Statistics by Being Selective or Discarding Data

In marketing terms, all you have to do to promote a product is to find one study with a certainty level of 95 percent that is favorable to the product. There may be nineteen other studies with unfavorable results, but these studies are simply ignored. Similarly, a study might indicate that a product is inferior in all aspects except for one very narrow range in which it is considered superior. When the statistics are used from the narrow range and the rest is not used, this is known as *discarding data* and is lying by omission.

Choosing the Question to Get a Certain Answer

You can easily influence the answer to a survey question by asking it in a different way. You can also precede the question by ten others that make the respondent aware of ten issues that seem unfavorable to your cause or candidate. Or you can omit the third-party view from the questionnaire; this will make many would-be third-position supporters take the side you favor.

Biased Samples

If you conduct a survey of homelessness by calling participants' home phone numbers, you will find a homeless rate near zero. That's because homeless people don't have home phones! For samples to be unbiased, they must be representative of the general population. For that reason, studies that are conducted using college students are not representative of the general population; they are only representative of college students.

The Truncated Graph or One-Dimensional Drawing

Sometimes graphs can be misleading. This can occur when the bottom portion of a graph is cut off, which can make a trend look more significant than it is because of the change in proportion. Likewise, you might use a drawing to indicate double the proportion of a comparable object; however, the drawing might be twice as tall but four times as large in total volume. Therefore, the drawing looks twice as large as you intended.

The Well-Chosen Average

Most measures follow a normal bell-curve distribution. However, not all things follow this distribution, one of them being income. For example, most incomes may fall below $35,000, but if you add in the comparatively small number of people with incomes above $1 million, the average will raise disproportionately. Therefore, when an income average is given in the form of a mean, nearly everybody makes less than that.[4]

Statistical Error

Many measures are useful within a certain range of statistical error. For example, the revised Stanford-Binet IQ test has a statistical error range of 3 percent. What that means is that a child who measures 97 may not be less intelligent than one who measures 100 on the test because the precision of the test may vary by as much as 3 percent. Ignoring this range of reliability can significantly affect the intelligibility of the results of some surveys with outcomes of little variability.

False Causality

The interrelation of cause and effect can also be obscured by statistics. Throughout the ages, many erroneous assumptions of cause and effect have occurred. For example, leeches were believed to cure sick people when it was often unknown what actually caused the recovery. Similarly, the people of the Hebrides once believed that body lice produced good health. It didn't occur to them that the inverse might be true: Body lice preferred healthy people.[5]

Questions for Discussion

1. Have you heard of incidents in which statistics were misused to make a false or misleading argument? Can you identify advertisements that misuse statistics?
2. What are some steps you might take to avoid the misuse of statistical information?

FIGURE 6-7 Example of a Table

Comparison of Company Benefits by Size

Type of Benefit	Companies with Fewer than 100 Employees	Companies with 100 or More Employees
Paid vacation	88%	96%
Paid holidays	82	92
Medical insurance	71	83
Life insurance	64	94
Paid sick leave	53	67
Dental care	33	60

Source: U.S. Bureau of Labor Statistics.

FIGURE 6-8 Example of a Diagram: Organizational Chart

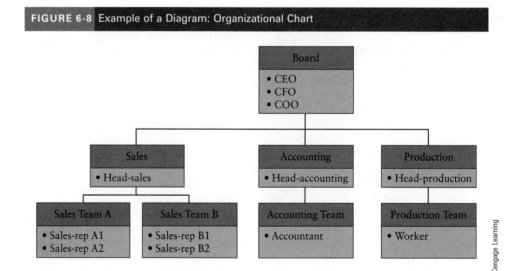

© Cengage Learning

Box 6-2 Selecting the Right Graphic

- To present detailed, exact values, use a table.
- To illustrate trends over time, use a line graph or a bar graph.
- To show frequency or distribution, use a pie graph or segmented bar graph.
- To compare one item with another, use a bar graph.
- To compare one part with the whole, use a pie graph.
- To show correlations, use a bar graph, a line graph, or a scatter graph.
- To show geographic relationships, use a map.
- To illustrate a process or a procedure, use a flowchart or a diagram.

© Cengage Learning

CriticalThinking

What type of information would best be illustrated through the use of a bar graph? A pie graph? A table? A diagram or drawing? Why?

Integrating Graphics into Text

Once you have identified the need for a graphic and then selected the appropriate type and created it, you need to consider how best to integrate it into your text if you are using a written message. Those considerations include the following:

- **Place the graphic in an appropriate location.** For ease of use by your reader, a graphic should be placed directly after the related point in the text.
- **Label the graphic.** Every graphic should have a brief, clear, and informative label.
- **Introduce the graphic in the text.** You should refer to the graphic in the text before it appears.
- **Explain the graphic in the text.** You should explain in the text what your readers should learn from the graphic.

Revising for Coherence and Flow

Writing is a reflection of the quality of our thinking—or at least it should be. Some readers will certainly read it as such. Therefore, it is important to take the time after drafting the message to revise for logical flow and coherence. There are three steps to this process:

1. Check for accurate topic sentences.
2. Check for paragraph coherence.
3. Include transitions and forecasting where appropriate.

Check Topic Sentences

A crucial element in making written messages easy to skim is the inclusion of an accurate topic sentence for each and every paragraph. Ideally, in business messages, each paragraph should *begin* with an accurate topic sentence or transitional phrase that mentions one of the subtopics referred to in the introduction if the direct approach was used. This strategy makes your messages more coherent because you are providing the connections between your ideas, announcing the progression of your ideas, and reminding your audience of your topic and its subtopics. This strategy also makes written messages easier to skim. If you have announced the subtopics in your introduction, your reader may decide that he or she only wants to read information about one of them. In that case, your reader will attempt to skim the paragraphs of your message to locate that information.

In written messages that your reader may skim, you should focus the content of each paragraph narrowly on the subtopic announced in the topic sentence. Otherwise, if paragraphs cover more than one topic, your reader may be unable to quickly locate the information that he or she is looking for—or your reader may become confused about the relationship of the ideas covered in a paragraph. In either case, you have created a written message that is not audience-centered and that may not reflect well on the quality of your thinking.

Ensure Paragraph Coherence

Another issue to consider at the paragraph level is **coherence**, or the logical flow of ideas throughout and within a paragraph. In other words, each sentence should clearly lead to the next, and clear connections should be provided between each point or each sentence. An easy way to establish coherence is to consistently end each sentence with the topic that will be discussed in the sentence that will follow. The example below indicates how sentences can be constructed to provide coherence within a paragraph.

> *John is an avid golfer. He loves golf so much that he has purchased a miniature golf game that he has set up in his office. As I entered his office last week, he almost put my eye out with a wild, flying golf ball!*

In the example, the first sentence ends and the second begins with a reference to golfing, while the second sentence ends and the third begins with a reference to "office." The final sentence also ends with the topic stated in the first and second sentences, golf. This repetition provides coherence between each sentence, carrying the topic over from one sentence to the next and clearly focusing the entire passage on a single, primary topic—golf. In contrast, writing that is not coherent is often described as "choppy" or as lacking "flow."

Provide Transitions and Forecasting

Transitions assist your audience in moving from one topic to another through words and phrases that link the ideas you are developing. It is important to recognize that a little repetition is not a bad thing in business messages. Again, because businesspeople are often faced with time pressures and we are poor listeners in oral situations, it is often necessary to restate information briefly yet in a slightly different manner to ensure that our audience receives our message successfully. Repetition is also helpful because it is aids retention for many types of information. In other words, to move information from our short-term memory to long-term recall, it may need to be repeated. Repetition is not the same as redundancy, however. Redundancy is saying the same thing in the same way without adding anything new or moving the message forward through the progression of its ideas or toward its intent.

Forecasting, like transitions, tells your audience what you will cover next. Bulleted lists, summaries, and preview statements or overviews are also effective forecasting devices.

Revising for Style and Tone

A communicator selects the style and tone, or verbal expression of a message, depending on the purposes of that message, the audience's needs and expectations, the communicator's relationship with the audience, and an organization's culture.

Style is the level of formality of your written communication. Business communication typically should use business style, which is less formal than traditional academic writing but more formal than a conversation. Business style is friendly

---

coherence
The logical flow of ideas throughout a paragraph.

transitions
Elements that assist the audience in moving from one topic to another through words and phrases that link the ideas being developed by the writer or speaker.

forecasting
Elements that tell the audience what the writer or speaker will cover next.

style
The level of formality in written communications.

and personal (you may refer to your audience by name and to its specific circumstances) yet correct.

This means that written business messages should use the following:

- Short, simple, precise words, and yet avoid slang
- Short yet complete sentences and short paragraphs
- Standard English
- First- and second-person pronouns

Using first- and second-person pronouns such as *I*, *we*, and *you* helps you achieve a friendly and personal style that can help you convey goodwill. Using *you* as the predominant pronoun in your writing also subtly sends the message that you are interested in your audience and in meeting its needs, concerns, and interests. Some examples of the *you* focus follow.

Examples of you focus:

The benefits you will receive from the Solare hybrid-fuel vehicle include lower fuel bills, a quieter ride, and the satisfaction that you are doing your part to protect the environment.

In this package, you will find the information you requested to put you on the path to a more secure financial future.

However, there are instances when you should not use *you* as the predominant pronoun in your writing: in cases where it might sound as if you are blaming your audience. In these cases, you should communicate as impersonally as possible, focusing on the solution rather than the problem and its cause. Not only does this approach avoid blame and the subsequent potential for alienating your audience and blocking effective communication, but it also sends the positive message that you are a solution-oriented person. Examples of the improper use of the *you* focus follow.

Examples of improper use of you focus:

How can you justify these departmental expenditures?

You improperly filled out the form for supplies, and now our department will have no copier paper for another week.

If these statements were aimed at you, how would you feel? You might become defensive. That is because the problem has become personal; in effect, you are the problem, and the intent of such a message is to find fault rather than solutions.

Tone is the implied attitude of the communicator toward his or her audience. Just as tone of voice can convey the speaker's attitude about his or her audience or a situation, attitude can also be conveyed in writing. When considering tone, you should think about language choices, level of formality or familiarity, the power relationship between you and your audience, and your use of humor or sarcasm. In other words, appropriate tone depends on who you are, who your audience is, your relationship, and the situation. Consideration of the corporate culture and the context of the situation may also be helpful in determining the appropriate tone of a message.

tone
The implied attitude of the communicator toward his or her audience.

This assessment leads to another general principle of business communication: Focus on the positive whenever possible. In the preceding examples of the improper use of *you*, how might you rephrase or reframe the statements to have a more positive tone, one that avoids blaming?

Phil McCarten/Landov

PIMCO CEO and Co-Chief Investment Officer Mohamed el-Erian learned early on the value of different points of view in business.

Generally, such statements can be rephrased by removing the personal pronouns, writing the sentence in passive voice, or taking responsibility for the situation yourself. Sometimes the situation can be reframed as an opportunity to implement better procedures to avoid such problems in the future, or what might be considered a "problem-solving orientation." The following two examples have rephrased the preceding examples to create a more positive communication situation.

Examples of neutral tone and problem-solving orientation:

I am concerned that some of the money that was spent in the department might have gone to more productive uses. We need to review the department expenditures, identify ways to better spend our funds, and perhaps implement policies to ensure that this objective is consistently reached in the future.

Because of a mistake that was made in the ordering of supplies last week, we will not have copier paper for another five days. To ensure that this situation does not recur, I have attached instructions for properly ordering supplies to this email message.

As mentioned above, effective business communication should be positive in tone whenever possible. In the worst-case scenario, it should be neutral. Business messages should *never* be negative in tone because that will likely have adverse effects on your relationship with your audience—and potentially your credibility.

Some people confuse a negative tone, however, with the ability to analyze and identify problems and to promote positive change. What this means is that being able to identify areas for improvement in an organization and to communicate steps to achieve that improvement—being a critical thinker and problem solver—is not the same as being negative. However, some people are extremely sensitive to any communication that might be considered critical—this is because we often have a tendency to take such criticism personally—so it is generally useful to phrase such suggestions as positively as possible and to downplay any critical aspects. In some cases, depending on your audience and its attitude and personality, you may want to avoid any mention of the problems that are being experienced and focus your message solely on your ideas for improvement and their benefits. However, you may run the risk that some individuals will still interpret such messages as personal criticism, even though the intended message is not about them at all. In such cases, working to establishing a trusting relationship with these individuals may lessen their defensiveness.

More generally, it is critically important to avoid communicating negative emotions in a business situation. In other words, you should not send messages that sound angry, frustrated, or hostile, because they have the potential to diminish your credibility as well as negatively affect your relationship with your audience.

This is because businesspeople are generally expected to be reasonable persons who make objective decisions based on good information. Consequently, expressing excess negative emotion can make you appear irrational, unreasonable, and lacking in judgment and self-control.

Anger can also be communicated in our written communication. We should never write a message when we are feeling a negative emotion. Instead we should wait until we have calmed down to express ourselves. Although it can feel good to vent negative feelings, we should immediately delete or erase messages written in anger. Unfortunately, with the popularity and proliferation of email, it is easy to pound out our frustrations in an electronic message. "Then we click 'send.' In a frenzied span of 15 minutes we have managed to do some real psychological damage, usually more to ourselves than to anyone else."[6] That damage may come in the form of a loss of credibility and damaged relationships.

CriticalThinking

Have you read email or other written messages that conveyed a negative tone? What was your reaction? Did the tone of the message affect the writer's credibility? Did the tone affect your relationship with the writer?

Proofreading for Mechanical Correctness

The last step in the message-formulation process is to proofread for mechanical correctness. Mechanical correctness includes the use of proper formatting conventions as well as correct spelling, grammar, sentence structure, and word choice. Most word processors provide templates for most common business messages, which makes formatting much easier. (Examples of common business formats can be found in Appendix A.)

Proofreading for mechanical correctness has become a bit simpler as well through the use of spelling and grammar checkers provided in most word processing applications. Many email applications also provide spell checking tools. These resources should be turned on at all times to help eliminate spelling errors in messages that may negatively affect your credibility as a professional.

If you have trouble with grammar and punctuation, you might consider drafting email messages using a word processor that provides a grammar checking tool and then copying and pasting the revised message to your email program for sending.

Not all errors in writing are created equal, however. Unlike academic writing in which a great deal of focus is aimed at correct grammar, sentence structure, and punctuation—"word smithing" as it is sometimes referred to—business readers are often more interested in clarity and conciseness because of time pressures. In Box 6-3, writing errors are categorized from the most severe to the least in terms of their effects on message clarity and writer credibility. As you will notice, those that affect the clarity of the message such as wrong word choice or unintelligible sentences are much more damaging, while errors that are commonly seen in the writing of some nonnative English speakers, what are called *accent errors*, are much less disruptive. These include missing articles and pronouns.

For more on common mechanical errors and instructions on how to fix them, please see Appendix B, "Punctuation, Sentence Structure, and Usage."

Box 6-3 The Varying Severity of Mechanical Errors in Communication

Mechanics and Error Interference

Assess whether errors interfere with a writer's clarity and credibility. A writer's communication may be judged partly on how closely the language follows conventions in sentence structure, grammar, usage, mechanics, spelling, and so on. Severe and frequent errors (and, in some circumstances, even milder forms and degrees of error) can negatively affect both clarity and credibility. All errors are not equally intrusive or offensive to all readers, however. Below, errors are categorized by severity, beginning with the most severe and ending with the least.

Disruptive errors may interfere with communication, preventing the reader from comprehending what the writer means. These include unintelligible sentences, unclear pronoun references, incorrect verbs, run-on sentences, fragments, and the use of wrong words.

Credibility errors don't usually disrupt communication, but they do tend to reflect negatively on the writer's credibility, reducing the reader's confidence in what a writer has to say. These include faulty subject–verb agreement, passive voice, and punctuation and spelling errors.

Etiquette errors are errors that many readers—but not all—hardly notice, especially if reading quickly for meaning. However, etiquette errors can reduce a writer's credibility, especially with those readers who are concerned about professional image or those who believe that critical thinking is reflected in the observance of grammar rules. These include pronoun usage, false subjects, and misplaced apostrophes.

Accent errors commonly characterize the writing of nonnative speakers or the use of local idioms and dialects. Accent errors, which are nearly impossible for nonnative speakers to correct in the short term, may be ignored by readers. These errors rarely interfere with communication and usually do not damage the writer's credibility. These generally entail missing or wrong articles or prepositions.

Source: Adapted from Rogers, P. S., & Rymer, J. (1996). *Analytical Writing Assessment Diagnostic Program* (McLean, VA: Graduate Management Admission Council): 41.

Submitting the Message

Now that all of the needed steps in the writing process have been completed, the message or document is ready to be sent to its audience. In the past this last step was fairly minimal, involving only the application of proper postage or routing to the proper audience through the mailroom. But with the use of email and other technological tools, this step has gained increased importance. The final considerations below can help to reduce some of the problems associated with email use in organizations discussed in Chapter 5.

- Consider the formality of the salutation. Typically, "Hi," or "Hello," are used for those in your organization. But a greater level of formality may be appropriate for those outside your organization or circle, particularly if they are not known by you. When requesting a favor of someone you don't know, it may be more appropriate to use the more formal "Dear Mr. Johns" on the first contact. A response will typically provide a clue as to the level of formality the person prefers in the signature line.

- Only send copies to those who *need* the information. If you do copy the message, make the appropriate adjustments to the content for these audiences.
- Avoid the use of "BCC" (blind carbon copy). Using BCC may be perceived as sneaky and may involve ethical concerns or result in more serious consequences. It is better to be open about information in a healthy organizational culture.
- Include a signature line. Email programs provide the option of creating a signature line that includes your full name, title, company, and possibly your phone number. Once created, your signature line will appear automatically in every email that is sent and create a greater air of professionalism.

Summary

- Plan and develop content for routine messages. Identify the type of message. These correspond to the purposes of communication: informative, persuasive, and goodwill messages. Informative messages also include good news and bad news messages. After identifying the type of message, the parts of the message—the introduction, body, and close—should be planned and drafted. Two organizational approaches—direct and indirect—may be used. The direct approach in which the purpose of the message is immediately stated is most commonly used. However, the indirect approach may be chosen for some bad news messages and for some persuasive messages. When using the indirect approach, the message begins with a neutral buffer that enables the writer to introduce the topic broadly before stating the bad news—or, in the case of a persuasive message, presenting good reasons why the proposed idea should be accepted before announcing that recommendation.

- Persuasive messages often consist of two basic components: a claim and evidence to support that claim. Common types of evidence include facts, statistics, examples, and analogies. In addition to considering the claims and evidence to be used in a persuasive message, writers should also consider the types of persuasive appeal that might be most appropriate for the audience. *Logos*, or the logical appeal, depends on facts; *ethos*, or the ethical appeal, is a call to the credibility of the writer or to other experts. *Pathos*, or an emotional appeal, often uses images to evoke an emotional response in the reader. When selecting evidence, it is important to test for quality. Tests of quality of evidence focus on the quality of statistics, testimony, and comparisons and analogies.

- In addition to routine and persuasive messages, longer documents such as reports and proposals are commonly written in professional environments. Both reports and proposals may be informal or formal, depending on their length, the intended audience, and the significance of the information they contain. Informal reports and proposals typically use a memo format, whereas formal reports and proposals may include front and back matter in addition to the body of the message.

- In addition to selecting the proper format for a message, most messages regardless of format may use a number of visual elements to make them easier to read and to convey information more quickly. These visual elements include the use of headings, bullet and step lists, and graphic elements such as charts, tables, diagrams, and drawings.

- After drafting the contents of a message, the writer should revise for coherence and logical flow. To improve the logical flow and readability of a message, accurate topic sentences should be provided at the beginning of each paragraph, and the writer should ensure that the content of the paragraph is narrowly focused on that topic. Writers can also use forecasting and transitions to improve the logical flow and coherence of a message.

- Business writing should also be professional yet friendly in style and tone. This can often be accomplished by using a "you attitude," although this device should be avoided in bad news messages because it can create a negative, blaming tone. Written messages should never be negative in tone; at worst, they should be neutral. This can be accomplished by using passive voice when constructing sentences.

- The last step in the writing process is to proofread for mechanical correctness, which includes checking that formatting follows conventions and that spelling, grammar, word choice, and sentence structure are correct.

Key Terms

call to action, 154
claim, 158
evidence, 158

logos, 159
ethos, 159
pathos, 159

Discussion Questions

1. How do the reading practices of academic audiences, such as instructors, differ from those of businesspeople? What are the factors that lead to these differences?
2. What tactics have you used to ensure that your messages are logically organized? What new tactics might you incorporate into your message-creation process to ensure well-organized messages?
3. Do you think that using the indirect approach to organizing a message is manipulative or unethical?
4. What are some of the challenges you have encountered while attempting to persuade? How might the AIDA approach be used to better deal with these situations?
5. Which types of evidence would be most persuasive to a business audience? Give examples.

Applications

1. Revise the following message so that it is more logically ordered. You may also discover that some of the content is irrelevant and thus can be eliminated and that the message also is missing some critical information needed to fulfill the customer's request. Be sure to check the subject line of the message for clarity.

   To: Martha Reeves
   <mreeves@prooffice.com>
   From: Stan Liu
   Subject: Accounting Software

   Dear Ms. Reeves:
   I recently purchased your new accounting software at Professional Office Products. When I got the product home, I was unable to install the product on my Apple brand computer. I am a small business owner and think that your product will be very helpful to me in improving my productivity and potentially my company's profits.
   I returned the product to your store to receive a refund or to exchange the product for one that might work on my computer. The manager told me that he could not make the exchange but that I should contact you, the maker, with my request.

   Can you help me? I have overnighted the product to your office.

   Regards,
   Stan Liu
   902 Oak Street
   Portland, OR 90042

2. You are a customer service representative for RichRUs, a company that organizes and holds seminars across the United States. These seminars are intended to help educate "regular" people on how to become financially independent through the purchase, resale, and rental of foreclosed properties. In addition to the seminars, the company sells DVD recordings of its founder, Leonard Samson, espousing his sales methods and techniques. Leonard's seminars and DVDs have become so popular that your production has not kept up with demand. To make matters worse, you advertise "same-day" shipping in your promotional materials. You have just received approximately 50 orders for the two-volume DVD set that sells for $95. Write a bad news letter that you can send to these customers in which you explain the situation.

3. Using the AIDA approach, create a message to persuade your boss to approve your plan to hire two new people. You must show that the benefits will outweigh the costs of hiring and additional salaries and benefits.

4. Using the steps to formulate a message to a reluctant or hostile audience, create a message to persuade a customer to consider the purchase of a new service or product your company is offering. Assume that the customer has previously had a bad experience with your company that involved the late delivery of your product or service, which resulted in a small financial loss for the customer. Also assume that the customer is currently pleased with the services he or she is receiving from one of your competitors.

5. You work in the information services department of SynSystems, Inc., a maker of computer connectivity products. Your job, along with the other members of your department, is to provide computer support to the employees of SynSystems. Several years ago, SynSystems was purchased by computer products giant World Connectivity Solutions (WCS). Because your company had an excellent reputation for its customer service and extensive and positive brand recognition, WCS chose to leave your division with its well-respected name.

Coincidentally, perhaps, SynSystems uses the same product—GroupPRO—as its parent company for electronic collaboration among project development teams. GroupPRO was created by another company that WCS now owns, but it is not the only product of its kind on the market. Because of lingering bitter feelings about the company takeover, there is a move among the employees of your department to switch to a newer collaboration product, TeamMAX. Write a persuasive letter to your supervisor, Jonathan Reeves, to persuade him to stay with the GroupPRO product. Include a visual element to compare the values of several items.

CASE ANALYSIS

DHL: CLOSING OPERATIONS IN THE UNITED STATES

Manfred Harnischfeger, executive vice president for corporate communications at DHL, sat at a table in the press room of Deutsche Post World Net (DPWN) as he introduced Frank Appel (CEO DPWN), John Mullen (CEO DHL Express), and John Allen (CFO DPWN). The date was November 10, 2008, and from the mood in the room and the looks on the faces of the company's top executives, there was some big news to be announced. Without hesitation, Mr. Appel stepped up to the podium and shared with the world the decisions made at the directors' meeting earlier that day.

After running though a quick background of the scope of the decisions about to be announced, Mr. Appel spoke of the fate of DHL: "Our activities in the United States will now be limited to our cross-border business. We will hence withdraw from all domestic activities in the air and on the ground."[7] With this statement, the CEO disrupted the lives of some 13,000 DHL employees in the United States. As of January 30, 2009, all domestic ground and air shipping in the United States would cease to exist.[8] This could mean layoffs of a massive proportion and yet another heavy blow to the struggling U.S. economy.

From 3 to 300

In 1969, Adrian Dalsey, Larry Hillblom, and Robert Lynn combined their last names to form the document shipping company called DHL, serving as the company's sole employees. The company's first big achievement was personally shipping papers by airplane from San Francisco to Honolulu.[9] After gaining quick success in the local market, DHL began expanding operations worldwide.

In its first five years of existence, DHL provided service throughout the United States and the Far East (including Japan, Hong Kong, Singapore, and Australia). By this time, DHL had also set up an office in London. By 1974, the company had expanded from one office with 3 employees to a multi-office company with 314 employees serving 3,052 customers.[10]

The expansion of DHL's services did not stop there. By the end of the decade, DHL was present in all six of the inhabited continents. While the expansion of the service area was going on, DHL also expanded the scope of its services. For the first ten years, DHL was only shipping documents, but in 1979, the company began delivering packages to its service areas around the world.[11]

Expanded Business through Global Partnerships

In order to become a successful business, a company needs to stay ahead of the game and maintain its competitive advantage. The first ten years of the company's life were so successful that in the years to follow DHL was able to become the world leader in international shipping. In the early 1980s, distribution hubs were established in Cincinnati, Ohio, and Brussels, Belgium. These hubs allowed for a faster flow of packages throughout the world. More than 160,000 packages were handled per night in the Brussels hub alone.

In keeping ahead of the competition, DHL formed a joint venture with the People's Republic of China in 1986, becoming the first express shipping company active in China. Along with this joint venture, DHL also began partnering with global airlines in order to speed the shipping process for its customers. Along with its own airline system, partnerships with Lufthansa and Japan Airlines expanded reach and speed throughout the DHL system.[12]

German Takeover

DHL's success attracted the attention of many investors. In 1998, the German company Deutsche Post (Bonn, Germany) became a shareholder in DHL. Deutsche Post had its origins with Deutsche Reichspost, an independent mail service that dates back to 1924. Through the German postal reforms of 1989 and 1995, Deutsche Post became its own entity[13] and in 2002, became the major shareholder in DHL. By the end of the year, a 100 percent shareholding was complete.[14]

Scope of Services

Today DHL is split into four managing divisions, two of which have subdivisions: Express; Global Forwarding, Freight; Supply Chain, Corporate Information Solutions; and Global Mail.

DHL Express

DHL Express is the leading global provider of international road-, air-, and rail-based courier and express services for business and private customers. The division works with the world's most expansive network, covering more than 220 countries and territories in Europe, the Americas, Asia-Pacific, and emerging markets.[15]

DHL Global Forwarding, Freight

This division comprises international air and ocean freight as well as European overland transportation services. DHL Global Forwarding is the international market leader in the air and ocean freight business. DHL Freight is one of the largest freight forwarders in the European overland transportation business. This business unit stands for flexible, individualized solutions: national and international full-container-load and less-than-container-load services via road, rail, or intermodal transportation. In addition, the comprehensive customs brokerage services ensure smooth cross-border shipments.[16]

DHL Supply Chain, Corporate Information Solutions

This division comprises contract logistics services and Corporate Information Solutions (Williams Lea). Both business units focus on tailor-made customer solutions. The business unit Supply Chain provides warehousing and warehouse transportation services as well as solutions along the entire supply chain for customers from various sectors of industry, including the key automotive, life sciences, technology, fast-moving consumer goods, retail, and fashion sectors. The subsidiary Williams Lea is the heart of the business unit Corporate Information Solutions, which gathers, digitalizes, prints, stores, sorts, addresses, packages, dispatches, and archives documents of all types. Williams Lea is also handles electronic invoicing and marketing services.[17]

DHL Global Mail

DHL Global Mail provides mail and communication services with direct connections to more than 200 countries around the world as well as offering integrated solutions for corporate communications.[18]

Employees

As of 2007 DHL Express Worldwide had more than 124,000 employees in more than 220 countries and territories. DHL Logistics Worldwide, which includes DHL Global Forwarding, DHL Exel Supply Chain, and DHL Freight, had more than 162,500 employees.

DHL Global Forwarding operated in the most countries in the DHL Logistics Worldwide group (150 countries).[19]

Operating Assets

As of 2007 DHL Express Worldwide operated 36 hubs, 4,700 bases, 72,000 vehicles, and 350 aircraft worldwide. It is also utilized 900 Packstations, all of which were located in Germany.[20]

Express and Logistics Financials

In 2007, the Express segment of Deutsche Post World Net posted €13,874 million of revenue with a loss of €174 million of earnings before interest and taxes (EBIT) for the year. Revenue was up from 2006 (€13,463 of revenue), but EBIT was down from the 2006 total of €288 million.[21] The Logistics segment reported €25,739 million of revenue in 2007, which was up 5.5 percent from €24,405 million in 2006. Additionally, EBIT increased from €751 million in 2006 to €957 in 2007, which was a 27.5 percent increase.[22]

Impact on United States

Since the November 10, 2008, announcement of DHL Express domestic-only services closing operations on January 30, 2009, DHL U.S. Express has closed all eighteen of its U.S. ground hubs. Its number of U.S. stations has been reduced from 412 to 103. In conjunction, 9,500 DHL Express jobs have been cut, in addition to the 5,400 jobs that had been eliminated since January 2008. DHL U.S. Express plans to retain between 3,000 and 4,000 employees

to serve their international express customers. These business changes will reduce DHL U.S. Express's operating costs by over 80 percent, from $5.4 billion to under $1 billion.[23] DHL's U.S Express air network pre-closure capacity was 1.2 million shipments per day. By shifting to an international-only focus, DHL's U.S. Express air network will process less than 100,000 shipments per day.[24] Post-closure, DHL Express's cross-border customers will be able to ship their packages through three different logistical systems. Packages can either be shipped through dropboxes and drop-off facilities or they can be shipped through DHL Authorized Shipping Centers, which are partnerships DHL has made with other shipping companies such as Mail Boxes, Etc. Lastly, a limited number of DHL staffed facilities will remain open to be used for cross-border shipment drop off.

The operations at the DHL U.S. Express distribution hub in Wilmington, Ohio, its main U.S. hub, have been greatly reduced. In May 2008, ABX Air, which operates the Wilmington hub for DHL, had 10,000 employees globally, including 7,000 in Wilmington. ABX now employs 4,200 globally, including 3,500 in Wilmington. John Graber, president of ABX Air Inc., said on January 26, 2009, that he anticipated more layoffs in the next thirty days as DHL changed the scope of its international operation.[25] Additionally, hubs in Riverside, California, and Allentown, Pennsylvania, and eighteen sorting centers across the United States are expected to close.[26] All other DHL business units will continue operations in the United States. These business units include DHL Global Forwarding, DHL Exel Supply Chain, and DHL Global Mail. These business units employ more than 25,000 people in the United States.[27]

Local Impact

"This is a catastrophic event for the entire region," said David L. Raizk, the mayor of Wilmington, Ohio, a city of about 12,000 citizens located in Clinton County. Since 1980 Airborne Express has been a major employer for citizens of Wilmington and the surrounding area. Airborne Express established Wilmington as a hub in 1980 by moving into the abandoned Air Force base and providing thousands of jobs to the area. Locals refer to the hub as the "air park." And, the mayor of Wilmington has stated that one in three households have a family member who was employed there. Many of the laid-off workers have been working for the air park for years and look back at their time there with fond memories.[28]

In order to grow its U.S. presence and compete in the United States with UPS and FedEx, DHL bought Airborne Express in 2003. This merger was a less than smooth transition and DHL was never able to get the U.S. presence they anticipated and hoped for. In conjunction with the economic downturn and resulting general decline in the shipping business, DHL was losing $6 million a day in the United States, or over $1 billion for the year in 2008.[29, 30]

Clinton County officials expect an approximate loss of $423 million in tax revenue from the air park closure. Additionally, U.S. Senator Sherrod Brown of Ohio believes that Wilmington and the surrounding area could lose three or four indirect jobs per every direct job lost at the air park.[31] Mayor Raizk has said that 20 percent of the region's business is dependent upon the hub.[32]

Federal assistance has come to Wilmington and the surrounding communities in the form of a federal grant in the amount of $3.87 billion. This grant is to help with job training for those who have lost their jobs at the DHL facility in Wilmington.[33] DHL has also been assisting those who have been laid off, spending $260 million on severance pay and health insurance for laid-off employees.[34]

Stories abound of families in Wilmington, Ohio, and the surrounding area who are struggling to cope financially from the layoffs. A telling example is Angela and John Pica, who both worked at the air park. Angela started working at the air park when she was 19 and as a supervisor had, on multiple occasions over the final few months of operations at the air park, to escort her laid-off employees off the premises. John, on the other hand, may have the possibility for another DHL job in another city, but the Picas can't sell their house in the current real estate market. Angela was busy looking for new jobs in anticipation of being laid off and applied to approximately forty jobs to no avail. When Angela was finally laid off it was especially emotional for her because she, like so many others, had worked at the air park for so long. At age 37, she had spent nearly half of her life working there.[35]

Corporate Communication at DHL

As one segment of a large, multinational, multisegment company, DHL has multiple levels of corporate communication to utilize and manage. DHL America's director of corporate communication Jonathan Baker and vice president of corporate communication and public affairs Michele Nadeem are the most local to the issue at hand. Others within the corporation who manage corporate communication are Christina Koh, senior vice president of communication and sustainability for DHL Global Express, and Professor Manfred Harnischfeger, executive vice president for corporate communication for Deutsche Post AG.

Discussion Questions
Retrospective Questions

1. What are the critical issues in this case? What issues are most critical?

2. Who are the stakeholders? Which stakeholders have been most affected and have the potential to be the most affected? What are the critical issues to the different stakeholders? What do the different stakeholders have at stake?

3. Was the sequence of events and time span that DHL utilized to announce the end of domestic-only operations in the United States and the subsequent shutdown appropriate? Should DHL have made the announcement earlier? Should they have waited longer after the announcement to shut down all operations?

4. Is there any way that DHL could have postponed or avoided a shutdown of U.S. Express operations? Should a company leave the market during poor economic times?

Prospective Questions

1. What does DHL need to communicate to its non-U.S. customers in order assure them of the viability of its new business model?

2. How does the closure affect DHL's image in the United States? What does DHL need to do in order to convince American customers to continue using DHL for international shipping needs?

3. Is there a need for DHL to take further action in the United States in general and in Wilmington, Ohio, in particular? If so, what actions should DHL take?

4. Is there a need for Deutsche Post to send a message to its stakeholders? If so, what message should Deutsche Post send?

5. How should Deutsche Post or DHL's corporate communications department deliver its message, who should deliver the message, and to whom should it be sent?

6. What responsibility does DHL have to its employees and the communities in which it is a significant source of employment and revenue?

7. Should DHL be concerned about its future prospects in the United States? Should they be concerned about the effect this will have on its international operations? Should they be concerned about the possibility of reentry into the U.S. domestic shipping market?

This case was prepared by Research Assistants Rebecca J. Herrman and Jason B. Nowak under the direction of James S. O'Rourke, Concurrent Professor of Management, as the basis for class discussion rather than to illustrate either effective or ineffective handling of an administrative situation. Information was gathered from corporate as well as public sources.

Endnotes

1. Casner-Lotto, J., Rosenblum, E., & Wright, M. (2009). *The ill-prepared U.S. workforce: Exploring the challenges of employer-provided workforce readiness training.* New York: The Conference Training Board, Inc. Retrieved from http://www.conference-board.org/publications/publicationdetail.cfm?publicationid=1676.

2. Price, H. T. (2004). Writing well in business. *Business & Economic Review, 50*(3), 13.

3. Watson, J. (n.d.). Writing: Expanding your sphere of influence through better business communications. Retrieved April 27, 2004, from http://jwatsonassociates.com/Articles, p. 2.

4. Huff, D. (2005). How to lie with statistics. In K. J. Harty (Ed.), *Strategies for business and technical writing* (pp. 347–354.) New York: Pearson Education.

5. Huff, D. 2005.

6. Manley, W. (2001). Mightier than the pen, *American Libraries, 32*(9), 124.

7. 9M 2008 press conference. DPWN.de. Accessed February 23, 2009, http://www.dpwn.de/dpwn?tab=1&skin=hi&check=yes&lang=de_EN&xmlFile=2010489.

8. Press Release: DHL Express to focus its U.S. business on its core international services. DHL-USA.com. Accessed February 23, 2009, http://www.dhl-usa.com/restructuring/index.asp.

9. Our history. DHL.com. Accessed February 23, 2009, http://www.dhl.com/publish/g0/en/about/history.high.html.

10. Steps to success. DHL.com. Accessed February 23, 2009, http://www.dhl.com/publish/g0/en/about/history/history2.high.html.

11. Steps to success. DHL.com.

12. Fact sheet. DHL.com. Accessed February 23, 2009, http://www.dhl-usa.com/restructuring/resources/FactSheetWebsiteNov10.pdf.

13. History. DPWN.com. Accessed February 23, 2009, http://www.dpwn.de/dpwn?lang=de_EN&xmlFile=2001321.

14. Our history. DHL.com.

15. DHL divisions. DHL.com. Accessed February 23, 2009, http://www.dhl.com/publish/g0/en/about/divisions.high.html.

16. DHL divisions. DHL.com.

17. Ibid.

18. Ibid.

19. About DHL: DHL network. DHL.com. Accessed February 23, 2009, http://www.dhl.com/publish/g0/en/about/network.high.html.

20. About DHL: DHL network. DHL.com.

21. Annual Report 2007: Corporate divisions. Investors.DPWN.com. Accessed February 23, 2009, http://investors.dpwn.com/reports/2007/ar/subjects/corporatedivisions.html?subjects=03.

22. Annual Report 2007: Corporate divisions. Investors.DPWN.com.

23. Press Release: DHL Express to focus its U.S. business on its core international services.

24. Restructuring of DHL U.S. Express – group 9-month results. DPWN.de. Accessed February 23, 2009, http://www.dpwn.de//mlm.nf /dpwnew/presse/news_ab_10_2008/nov_10_ presentation_en.pdf.

25. Nolan, J. (2009). No end in sight for DHL-UPS talks. *Dayton Daily News*, January 27.

26. Driehaus, B. (2008). DHL cuts 9,500 jobs in U.S., and an Ohio town takes the brunt. *The New York Times*, November 11.

27. Restructuring of DHL U.S. Express – group 9-month results.

28. Economic storm batters Ohio town. *Cbsnews.com*, January 25, 2009, http://www .cbsnews.com/stories/2009/01/22/60minutes /main4747832.shtml.

29. Economic storm batters Ohio town. *Cbsnews.com*.

30. Restructuring of DHL U.S. Express – group 9-month results.

31. Sen. Brown asks for disaster aid after DHL restructuring. *ChillicotheGazette.com*, January 14, 2009, http://www.chillicothegazette .com/article/20090114/NEWS01/901140313.

32. Driehaus. DHL cuts 9,500 jobs in U.S., and an Ohio town takes the brunt.

33. Grant will retrain workers at DHL. *Columbusdispatch.com*, November 21, 2008, http://www.columbusdispatch.com/live/content /business/stories/2008/11/21/DHL_jobs_grant .ART_ART_11-21-08_C13_TOBV4HU.html? sid=101.

34. DHL to pay $260 mln for worker severance. *Reuters.com*, September 9, 2008, http://www .reuters.com/article/rbssAirFreightCourier Services/idUSWNAB025820080909.

35. Economic storm batters Ohio town. *Cbsnews.com*.

Adam Gregor/Shutterstock.com

Communicating in Oral Presentations and Managing Meetings

After reading this chapter, you will be able to

▶ Understand when and how to use the oral channel for presentations.

▶ Plan the message and select a proper organizational structure for a presentation.

▶ Develop the presentation.

▶ Design visual aids to support an oral presentation.

▶ Achieve the appropriate vocal delivery and become more aware of your nonverbal communication to better align it with the oral message you wish to express.

▶ Prepare for an oral presentation and reduce speech apprehension.

▶ Handle question-and-answer sessions.

▶ Plan and execute effective meetings, which often involve presentations in a more interactive form.

Case Questions:

1. From a strategic perspective, how would you rate Ben's presentation thus far? Has he clearly identified the communication purpose(s) of his presentation during the planning stage and executed them well? What are they? How well has he focused on addressing his audience's needs, interests, and concerns?

2. If his presentation could be improved from a strategic perspective, what changes would you make? Why?

3. What nonverbal communication messages has he been implicitly sending? How might these be interpreted by his audience in terms of his ability to meet his strategic goals? How should these nonverbal communication messages be changed? Why?

The Case of the Novice Presenter

"Good morning, everyone," Lara Bright, head of marketing, announced with a smile from the front of the conference room. "I am excited to welcome Georgia Egans, president of Interactive Learning, and Tom Hayes, her marketing director, to LearningFun. We are eager to show you our new line of interactive computer learning programs aimed at elementary school children. We believe they are the best programs available in terms of the graphic elements and game-based learning tools. Now let me turn the time over to our marketing person for this product line, Ben Williams, and he will walk you through the Play&Learn series. Ben?"

Ben rose abruptly from his chair, bumping the table and spilling everyone's coffee. "Oops, sorry, everyone. Let me get some more napkins. He quickly turned to the side table and grabbed a stack that he then placed randomly around the table as he made his way to the computer located at the front of the room.

"Well, that was a bad start," he said, followed by an awkward laugh. "I wish I was better at making jokes—this would be a prime place to insert one." Another awkward chuckle bubbled out as he turned his attention to the computer screen.

Clearing his voice loudly then taking a few audible breaths, he clicked to the next presentation slide. He began, looking up at his audience. "This morning, we will begin by discussing the company background of LearningFun. Then we will move on to a brief overview of our complete product line, then I will get to the stuff you are probably here to learn more about, the new Play&Learn system."

He jammed his pointer finger down loudly on the Enter key once again as if to punctuate that segment of the presentation, then went on, "As you probably know, LearningFun was created ten years ago by Georgia Egans..."

As with all messages, when planning an oral presentation, you should first identify your purposes for communicating; analyze your audience to identify its values, beliefs, interests, concerns, and objections; consider the context of the communication; and choose a channel—in this case, an oral one.

This chapter explores tactics that can be deployed in oral presentations and meetings to more effectively reach your strategic-communication goals. The tactical elements to be applied in oral presentations can be broadly categorized as follows:

1. Planning and organizing
2. Developing the content
3. Designing the visual aids
4. Practicing the delivery, including the reduction of presentation anxiety
5. Giving the presentation, including handling the question-and-answer session

But before moving on to a discussion of the steps in the tactical process, let's review how and when presentations should be used as a communication medium.

Channel Considerations

Probably one of the most misused media of communication is the oral presentation. For this reason, it is important to emphasize when to choose an oral presentation as the method of message delivery. Presentations are good for the following situations:

- **Inspiring and motivating others.** If the presenter is able to bring enthusiasm and energy and an inspirational message to the situation, then oral message delivery is highly appropriate.
- **Demonstrations of products or for training purposes.** Oral presentations work well when audience members are able to view how a product works and better understand its functions. They are also useful for training purposes, particularly if the audience is able to apply the presented material through practice or use as part of the presentation.
- **To introduce a complex persuasive written message (generally a report or a proposal).** This helps increase audience interest by emphasizing the key benefits of the proposal in an engaging manner and allows the presenter to answer audience questions.
- **As a follow-up to a complex persuasive written message (generally a report or a proposal).** The personal presence of an advocate can help establish goodwill and credibility and move the persuasive process forward. In these cases, the oral message should generally emphasize the benefits of the proposal and answer audience questions.
- **To deliver bad news to a large audience.** In some circumstances, the personal presence of an organizational representative helps to establish or maintain goodwill and credibility and, by extension, the image and reputation of the firm.

Presentations are often not good for delivering a large amount of complex information, simply because (1) audience members won't remember it all and (2) they will likely become bored and tune out. This last occurrence can also damage the presenter's credibility because a boring presentation often reflects poorly on the reputation of the presenter as a communicator.

The biggest mistake that presenters make is not clearly understanding that oral presentations as a medium of communication are quite different from written messages in terms of the kind of information they are useful for conveying. In other words, the biggest mistake that presenters make is treating a presentation as if it were a written document or formal report. The written channel and the oral channel are generally good for communicating different kinds of information and for achieving quite different goals. Even if a presentation is based on written material, the presenter should start planning as if he or she was developing an entirely new message because of this fact. If this isn't understood from the beginning, an oral presentation is likely to fall flat—and the presenter with it.

Planning and Developing the Presentation

As stated in the previous section, the oral channel of communication should be used differently from the written channel. The main reason for giving a presentation is to benefit from the nonverbal cues that a person brings to the message and to illustrate information that is best conveyed visually. To put it another way, the skill of the presenter should be the primary consideration when choosing an oral presentation as the mode of communication. Steve Jobs of Apple Computer was often noted for his skill at presenting. One reason his presentations were so successful is that he understood the channel and treated a presentation as an event. In other words, a good presentation should engage the audience as only a skilled presenter can. If you cannot engage the audience, then it might be worth considering another medium of communication for message delivery.

Planning the Presentation

To make presentations more engaging, some time should be spent identifying the key message or theme and considering other aspects of a strong oral message. These are simplicity, interest, stories, and vividness.

- **Simplicity.** In presentations, you should aim to achieve or communicate one idea. The first question to ask is, What is the idea or theme of my presentation? This step can be the most time-consuming and may require some creative thinking. An example of the use of an excellent theme is the presentation by epidemiologist Elisabeth Pisani entitled "Sex, Drugs and HIV—Let's Get Rational" found on TED Talks (www.ted.com).

    The purpose of that presentation is to ask the audience to support HIV and AIDS programs. However, the presenter apparently knows that HIV is not a burning issue for much of the audience, which is largely made up of well-educated, upper-middle-class people, most of whom don't have to cope with the challenges of the disease. Therefore, Pisani is faced with the challenge of engaging the audience with this topic, and she does so by making it real to them. She begins her talk with the statement, "People do stupid things—that's what spreads HIV," and follows with the explanation, "Yes, people do stupid things for perfectly rational reasons." In this way, she introduces her theme of "rationality." She then proceeds to tell the story of AIDS from the perspective of those most likely to have the disease by explaining what "rationality" means from each one's perspective. By the end of her story, she has succeeded in educating her audience about the predicament of HIV and AIDS sufferers, making the audience more likely to care about it and them.

- **Interest.** As indicated in the previous example, you need to engage your audience and keep them engaged. One way is to raise questions that your audience wants answered and then answer them as you proceed through the presentation. What are the questions that your audience may have? How might you use these to organize your message? Can you tie them to your theme? Another way to raise interest is to tell a story that your audience may find engaging.

- **Stories.** As the previous example illustrates, the use of stories is a way to humanize your message and draw in your audience through the use of emotional appeal or *pathos*. Stories help engage your audience if its members can relate to them. Stories also make your presentation easier to follow and your message often more concrete and vivid.

- **Vividness.** Generalities are boring and, in some cases, unclear. To avoid this problem, use concrete and vivid language and descriptions that bring your presentation to life and make them memorable.

Above all else, when planning a presentation, keep the message simple. Most experts say that a presentation can only cover one topic effectively. Using a theme can help you to accomplish this goal by hanging all of your points on that theme.

In addition, in the workplace, you generally present information about which you are a recognized expert. When planning a presentation, it is important to recognize this fact because it can make you much more confident in your ability to deliver your message and eliminate any presentation anxiety. If you find yourself in a situation, though, in which you are presenting material about which you do not feel like an expert, then you should consider how you might frame your topic in such a way so as to connect it to a relevant issue about which you are an expert. This step may be the key to unlocking the theme of your presentation, in fact.

For example, you may be asked to present a motivational speech to a group of inner-city youth. If you came from a different socioeconomic background, are of a different race or ethnic group, have a different educational level, and are in a different age group, you may feel as if you have little in common with your audience or it with you. In this case, rather than pretending to be of this group, you might call upon your own youthful experiences to create a story that links with some of their concerns. In this way, you will likely sound, feel, and appear more confident and sound, feel, and appear more authentic while at the same time, hopefully, telling an engaging story that addresses some of their own concerns in an enlightening way. This approach should then help you to establish your credibility and convey goodwill, while at the same time appealing to your audience's interests and concerns. It can heighten your credibility as well because you will likely feel and look more confident.

As this discussion implies, some messages require considerable time spent in the planning stage. In addition to identifying the topics you will cover and the theme, you may need to spend time creating a logical structure through the process of outlining and gathering additional information, perhaps by conducting research, to enhance your presentation's informative and persuasive appeal. Doing research to provide relevant, concrete details can make the presentation more interesting because details such as examples and anecdotes make points more vivid and clear than generalizations and abstractions. This time spent in planning, though, can make the remainder of the process much easier and much quicker to complete and the final product much more successful.

Selecting the Appropriate Structure

Depending on the purposes, the audience, the situation, or the information you are providing, the ordering of your message may affect its success. Several strategies are available to make your messages more logical and understandable for your audience. You can choose to put information in different types of order, including these:

- Old information before new
- By chronology
- Spatially
- From general to particular
- By problem and solution
- By cause and effect
- By comparison and contrast

These common organizing patterns are illustrated in Figure 7-1.

Present old information before new. One organizational strategy is to present information that is known to your reader or listener before you present new information. This strategy makes the new information easier to understand because your reader or listener has a basis of understanding—the old information—on which to draw to comprehend the less familiar material.

FIGURE 7-1 Common Organizing Patterns for Presentations

Old Information Before New	Present information that is known to your reader or listener before you present new information.
Organize Information Chronologically	Presents ideas in the order of their occurrence.
Geographical/Spatial	Organizes ideas conceptually, according to an actual spatial arrangement or a physical metaphor or analogy.
General to Particular	Arrange ideas from the general to the particular.
Problem/Solution	Explain the problem then present the solution.
Cause/Effect	Explain the cause then present its effect(s).
Comparison/Contrast	Compare and contrast one topic with another.

© Cengage Learning

Organize information chronologically. Chronological ordering presents ideas in the order of their occurrence. Such a pattern might also be used to explain the steps for a procedure. In this case, each step must be performed in a particular order to achieve the desired result. Chronological ordering is easy to achieve, easy to recognize, and easy to follow, partly because it is similar to the narrative pattern used in storytelling of all kinds—movies, novels, and television sitcoms. Because of our exposure to such media, we are all familiar with chronological ordering.

Use a geographic or spatial pattern. The spatial pattern organizes ideas conceptually, according to an actual spatial arrangement or a physical metaphor or analogy. For example, you might give a presentation about your company's worldwide distribution network and how that provides a competitive advantage. The talk would then discuss each of the distribution centers located in different areas of the globe.

This pattern can also be used to arrange topics in a spatial pattern such as a pyramid or concentric circles. The pyramid, for example, might be used to represent the five platforms of your product that distinguish it from others.

Use a general-to-particular pattern. Another common organizational strategy is to arrange ideas from the general to the particular. General to particular is a common organizational arrangement in persuasive messages. The general statement is considered your claim. For example, you might state, "Our company has made a number of changes to benefit our employees." The particular information would then include the specifics of those changes as well as the benefits. Another way to think about the general-to-particular strategy is in terms of levels of abstraction. In other words, the general statement is more abstract than the particular information, which is more concrete.

Use a problem–solution pattern. The problem–solution pattern is common in business because it is highly persuasive and can include other patterns of reasoning such as question and answer. When using this pattern, the communicator begins with a shared, recognizable problem, situation, or question and progressively moves to a solution supported by information or evidence. Such a pattern typically begins with a definition of the problem that proceeds to an analysis of the problem or an evaluation of the solutions, and then concludes with a redefinition of the problem or a suggestion for action. In business, this pattern might also be tweaked to discuss issues and actions, which are quite similar to problems and solutions, or to propose opportunities and discuss how your organization is best suited to leverage those opportunities.

Use a cause-and-effect pattern. The key to using the cause-and-effect pattern successfully is to build a case that supports your claim of cause and effect. In other words, this pattern forces you to make and support an inference that one event caused or will cause another. The fact that one event followed another (the chronological ordering discussed earlier) does not prove that one event caused the other.

Use a comparison-and-contrast pattern. In a business presentation, this type of pattern might be used to compare an organization with its competitors to illustrate where it stands in the industry. This pattern should be used strategically to show that your company clearly is the best in all regards to the competition. If the pattern is not used wisely, however, it might backfire.

Developing the Presentation

Once the theme of the message has been determined, thought has been given to how to engage the audience related to the theme, and an appropriate structure has been

---

Presentation Planner

Introduction:

Attention-getting material:

Purpose statement:

    Subpoint:

    Subpoint:

    Subpoint

    Transition to body of presenttion:

Body

Main Point 1:

    Transition to main point 2:

Main Point 2:

    Transition to main point 3:

Main Point 3:

    Transition to conclusion:

Conclusion

Summary:

Concluding remarks:

© Cengage Learning

---

determined, it is time to develop the presentation in more detail. This generally involves developing the three parts of the presentation: the beginning or introduction, the middle or body of the message, and the end or conclusion. See the template for planning oral presentations.

Each of the main parts included in the presentation planner is discussed in more detail in the sections that follow.

The Beginning

After identifying the main topic of your message and its subtopics, you should develop an introduction that provides an attention-getting statement, gives the purpose of the message, and provides an overview of those subtopics.

An introduction should get the audience's attention and indicate why it is important to listen to your message. It should also provide your audience with a road map of what the message contains to help it better follow the logic or contents of your message.

In oral presentations, many techniques exist for gaining your audience's attention at the start. (Examples of attention getters are provided in Figure 7-2.) These include

FIGURE 7-2 Attention Getters in Business Situations

Highlighting the Benefits	I am here today to tell you about a product that will lessen your costs for employee healthcare, simplify the process of administering the program, and provide better, more comprehensive benefits to employees.
Asking a Question	What if I told you that your problem of escalating healthcare costs for employees could be addressed by a single, simple-to-administer product?
Telling a Relevant Story	My mother used to tell me to keep my mouth shut unless I had something good to say. I don't know what prompted her to make such a remark. It might have been a product of her philosophy on life. It might also have been recognition of the fact that I tend to see both sides of an issue, both the good and the bad, and to make that known. Today, I'm here.....
Stating a Striking Fact	"The average American drinks more carbonated soft drinks—56 gallons per year—than citizens of any other country in the world."
Delivering a Relevant Quotation	As baseball player Yogi Berra once said, "You've got to be very careful if you don't know where you're going, because you might not get there."

© Cengage Learning

- **Showing the product or the object.** If you are going to be speaking about a product, show it and perhaps demonstrate its use.
- **Highlighting the benefits.** Briefly state the benefits your audience will receive from your proposal.
- **Asking a question.** Invite your audience to participate by asking relevant questions about the audience itself or your topic. Be careful about the use of rhetorical questions, though, because they can sound unplanned from a strategic perspective and they open up the possibility that your audience might respond negatively (at least in their head) to the query.
- **Opening with a relevant video or sound clip.** These might include slides containing pictures or other images, a short film or video, and music or a sound clip. This technique should be used with care; you don't want the film or video to become your presentation, only to introduce and highlight your message.
- **Telling a relevant story or personal anecdote.** Arouse audience curiosity by telling an engaging yet related story, perhaps about the history of the company or an experience you had recently that illustrates the theme of the presentation.
- **Stating a striking fact or statistic.** A startling fact or statistic can be used to alert your audience to a problem or opportunity that needs to be addressed.
- **Delivering a relevant quotation.** A well-known or apt quotation can often sum up the theme of a presentation and set the stage for its elaboration.

As stated earlier, identifying the theme of your presentation and its key message can help you determine the appropriate attention getter for an oral presentation.

One last note: Some speakers think that every presentation should begin with a joke, but if a joke is inappropriate or irrelevant, or you are poor at telling jokes, then it's much better to skip it. Only tell a joke if it is relevant to the topic of your presentation and you know that your audience will appreciate it.

The Middle

As stated in Chapter 6, a skilled business communicator will not place the burden of interpreting a message on the receiver. Therefore, you should make sure that you use all available means to "connect the dots" or provide a road map for your audience. Two of those elements that can be used in an oral presentation are forecasting and transitions.

Forecasting tells your audience what you will cover next. Summaries and preview statements or overviews are effective forecasting devices.

Transitions assist your audience in moving from one topic to another through your use of words and phrases that link the ideas you are developing. In oral presentations, a transition should clearly and thoroughly link the topic you are moving from to the one you are moving to. An example of a complete transition is the following: "Now that I have explained why we should adopt a policy allowing flex-time scheduling, I will tell you about some of the benefits such a change would provide to the company and its employees." This type of transition can begin to sound mechanical, though, so it can be worthwhile to spend some time creating transitions that show the logical connections between the topics. An example might be "Not only would a flex-time policy address some current challenges we face, it will provide the company additional benefits. Let me illustrate a few of them for you."

In oral presentations, it is particularly important to fully link the topic you have just discussed to the one you are about to discuss. Remember, we tend to be poor listeners. Your intention in restating the topic you have just covered is to remind those listeners who may tune out for a moment what you are covering and to indicate where you are in the overall structure of your presentation. Generally, the transitions commonly used in written messages—"first," "second," "third," "next," and so on—are not sufficient for a presentation. None makes the connection between the previous point and the one that follows, and they can pass so quickly that the listener's ear may not catch them.

As stated in Chapter 6, it is important to recognize that a little repetition is not a bad thing in business messagesbecause of time pressures and poor listening habits In addition to providing a clear road map of your message, it is important to determine the types of information and evidence that would best enable you to achieve your communicative goals. Please refer to "Planning and Developing Persuasive Messages" (page 154) in Chapter 6 for more on the content of a persuasive message. Figure 7-3 illustrates these concerns in abbreviated form.

The End

As stated in Chapter 6, the conclusion is one of the most important parts of a message. Your audience will be more likely to remember it because of the *recency effect* (the principle that the most recently presented items or experiences will most

---

forecasting
Elements of a text or oral presentation that tell the audience what the reader or speaker will cover next.

transitions
Elements that assist the audience in moving from one topic to another through words and phrases that link the ideas the writer or speaker is developing.

FIGURE 7-3 Elements of a Persuasive Message

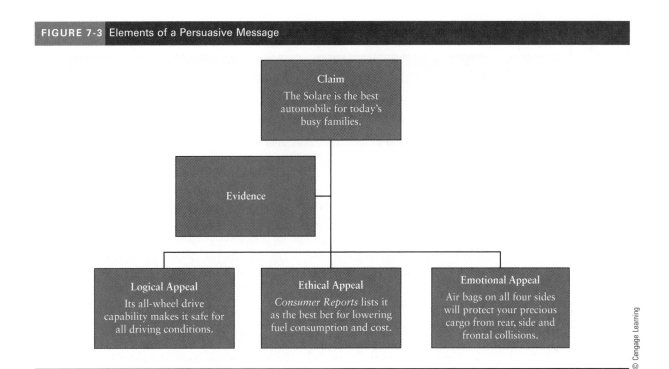

© Cengage Learning

likely be remembered best). Consequently, make sure that the conclusion is, in fact, memorable and focuses on the final message that you want your audience to take away.

As discussed in Chapter 6, there are three basic types of conclusions: goodwill, summary, and sales. Goodwill conclusions are generally not appropriate for a presentation, so they will not be discussed here. Summary conclusions are typically used for informative messages, and sales conclusions are used for persuasive messages.

Summary Conclusions for Informative Messages. If you are conveying an informative message, you should create a summary conclusion in which you restate the subtopics of your message in a slightly different manner. Sometimes stating information differently can also help your listener with comprehension. The first time people hear something, its meaning may not be completely clear. But if additional explanation is provided or if the message is stated again in a slightly different way, then the chances improve that the meaning will be understood.

Sales Conclusions for Persuasive Messages. If you are conveying a persuasive message, your conclusion should focus on restating the benefits your listeners will receive from adopting your proposal. In some persuasive situations, it may also be appropriate to conclude with a **call to action**. Use a call to action such as "Visit our Web site today to sign up for a 10 percent discount on our call-package rates" when you want your audience to take the next step in your proposal. In this way you can encourage your audience to commit to your proposal.

call to action
A conclusion to a persuasive message that is intended to convince the reader to fully consider the writer's or speaker's proposal and, ideally, commit to a decision or take the next step.

CriticalThinking

Do you generally provide clear beginnings, middles, and ends in your messages? If so, what are the results? If not, what strategies might you use to produce these three parts of a message consistently?

Designing Visual Aids

The power of conveying information visually has been recognized for hundreds of years. In 1801, William Playfair, the father of modern graphics, claimed, "As much information may be obtained in five minutes [from a graph] as would require whole days to imprint on the memory" if it were communicated in a series of figures. Playfair's quotation clearly communicates the purpose of a visual aid. Using graphics appropriately provides three main benefits:

- Information is more easily understood than with the use of words alone.
- The use of visuals helps make the information conveyed more memorable.
- The use of visuals enhances your professionalism and credibility.

These are the *only* reasons to incorporate or use visual elements. Delivering the content of your message in text form is not an appropriate use of visual aids. The content of the message should be delivered orally by the presenter. Visual aids are intended to be just that—an aid to the presentation—not a way to deliver content. In other words, the script of your presentation should not be provided on presentation slides. If you believe this is the best way to deliver the information to your audience, you might consider email, memo, or informal report instead. You don't want your audience to respond to a text-based presentation aid that asks it to read along while you recite the script of the presentation. Some audience members may react with frustration by questioning why they were asked to waste their time in a presentation when they could have read the message from their own computer screen at their convenience.

Other types of visual aids exist, including whiteboards, transparencies, flip charts, and handouts, but the most commonly used in the workplace is slide presentation software such as Microsoft PowerPoint. It is not the only slide presentation software used, however. Some Apple users prefer Keynote, while Prezi, a Web-based program, provides a more interactive approach to transitioning between topic illustrations and visual elements. Much has been written about the uses and misuses of slide-presentation software. As stated above, the biggest mistake that presenters make is believing that all of their information should be delivered in text form on their slides. Instead, presentation software, like other visual aids, should be used for two primary purposes: (1) to indicate the main ideas you will cover or the structure of your presentation and (2) to convey information that is more easily understood visually.

Designing PowerPoint Presentations

When designing presentation aids, make sure all their elements are *visible* from anywhere in the room. Presentation aids should *emphasize* the main points of your speech. Visuals should therefore be simple, and each one should make only one point.

The basic rules for creating PowerPoint slide presentations follow:

- The colors for the slide background and the text should have high contrast: light on dark or dark on light.
- The type size should be large enough to be read from the back of the room (generally 28 points or larger).
- Consider altering the background colors on PowerPoint design templates to create a fresher look or create your own master slides. Potentially, the best design element you might use on your PowerPoint master slide is your company logo and colors to add name recognition and a more custom look.
- Use the "SmartArt" feature in PowerPoint to incorporate more graphic elements onto your slides. Even a simple bullet list can become a graphic element through the use of the SmartArt features.
- If you must use text, limit it to informative phrases presented using a bullet-list format. Avoid presenting text in sentence or paragraph form.
- As a rule of thumb, try to limit text-based slides to "Agenda" or "Overview" and "Conclusion" slides, if possible. Remember, the SmartArt feature can help you to convert text-based slides to visual aids.
- If used, bullet lists should be grammatically parallel in structure and, whenever possible, begin with or contain a verb so that list items are more informative. In other words, you should avoid list items that contain only one word, because one word often does not convey much information and is more like a placeholder.
- Each slide should contain no more than five to six bullet points.
- Consider the use of clip art. Make sure that it clearly relates to your topic, and avoid pictures that might appear too cartoonish for the occasion.

Remember that a PowerPoint presentation should not deliver all of the details of your oral presentation. It is a *visual aid*. Therefore, it is best used to remind your audience of the main points you will cover (like a map) and illustrate information best conveyed in visual form such as charts, tables, and diagrams. These are discussed more below.

CriticalThinking

Whether you are a traditional student or a workplace professional, you have probably viewed many Power-Point presentations. What is the most common mistake you observe in the presentations you've seen? Do you believe that PowerPoint is often misused or overused? Why?

Organizing PowerPoint Presentations

Just as in a written message, your PowerPoint presentation should include slides for each of the three main parts of a message: introduction, body, and conclusion.

The Introduction

The introduction should include two slides:

- **Opening title slide.** This slide contains the title of your presentation, the name of the presenter, and the organization he or she represents.
- **Overview slide.** This slide lists the main topics covered in the presentation.

Examples of a title and overview slide are provided in Figures 7-4 and 7-5.

The Body

For the body of your presentation, you should include at least one slide for each of the main points of your presentation. In addition, you should include slides that convey the information that is best communicated visually in the form of tables, charts, graphs, and diagrams (see also Chapter 6) or use the SmartArt feature included in PowerPoint to add visual interest to text-based slides.

FIGURE 7-4 Example of a Title Slide

**Dexus Computer Systems:
Solutions for Business**

Presented by Joseph Williams
Sales Manager

© Cengage Learning

FIGURE 7-5 Example of an Overview or Agenda Slide

Today's Agenda

- Features of the Dexus Computer System

- Ease of use of the Dexus Computer System

- Financial benefits of using the Dexus Computer System

© Cengage Learning

The most common forms of visual aids used in both written and oral presentations are the graph, table, and diagram or drawing. All of these elements are easily created using the tools provided in most presentation programs, including PowerPoint.

Graphs Sometimes called charts, **graphs** are used to compare the value of several items: the amount of advertising money spent on different media, the annual profit of a company over time, and so on. The bar graph is typically used to emphasize comparisons or contrasts between two or more items. A pie graph is often used to indicate the distribution of something or the relative size of the parts of a whole. Examples of bar and pie graphs as used in PowerPoint slides are provided in Figures 7-6 and 7-7.

FIGURE 7-6 Example of a Bar Graph Presented on a PowerPoint Slide

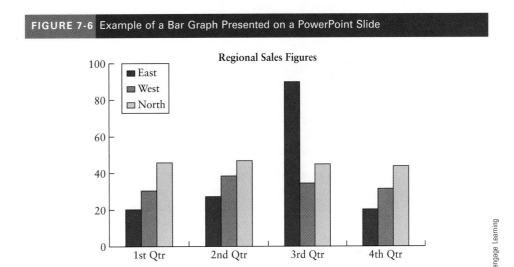

© Cengage Learning

FIGURE 7-7 Example of a Pie Graph Presented on a PowerPoint Slide

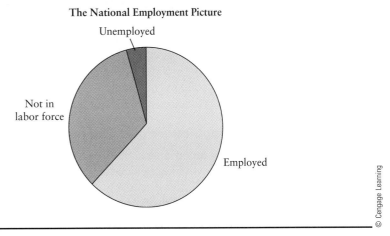

© Cengage Learning

graphs
A visual element used to compare the values of several items; sometimes called *charts*.

FIGURE 7-8 Example of a Table Presented on a PowerPoint Slide

Comparison of Company Benefits by Size

Type of Benefit	Companies with Fewer than 100 Employees	100 or More Employees
Paid vacation	88%	96%
Paid holidays	82	92
Medical insurance	71	83
Life insurance	64	94
Paid sick leave	53	67
Dental care	33	60

Source: U.S. Bureau of Labour Satatistics.

Tables Tables are useful for emphasizing key facts and figures. They are especially effective for listing steps, highlighting features, or comparing related facts. A **table** presents data in words, numbers, or both, in columns and rows. An example of a PowerPoint slide containing a table is shown in Figure 7-8.

Tables easily convey large amounts of numerical data and often are the only way to show several variables for a number of items.

Diagrams and Drawings **Diagrams** are two-dimensional drawings that show the important parts of objects. They are useful for conveying information about size, shape, and structure. Types of diagrams include drawings, maps, and floor plans. An organizational chart is a form of block diagram that indicates lines of authority and responsibility in an organization. Figure 7-9 provides an example of a diagram presented on a PowerPoint slide.

The Conclusion

The conclusion of your presentation should include two slides.

- **The conclusion slide.** This slide should summarize your main points or, in the case of a persuasive presentation, highlight the benefits of your proposal to your audience.
- **Ending title slide.** Ending with the slide you began with provides closure for your audience because it indicates you have come full circle. In addition, this slide acts as a subtle sales message, much like giving your audience your business card, which contains your name and the name of your company. It is a better backdrop for a question-and-answer session than a slide that contains the single word "Questions" or the phrase "Thank you" because it enhances name recognition.

Using PowerPoint Slides

Presentation aids should be skillfully *integrated* into the presentation. That means that a visual should not be displayed until you are ready for it and it should be removed after discussing it. The use of visual aids should be *practiced* so that their use does not distract from your presentation or adversely affect your credibility by making you look unprepared.

table
A visual element used to present data in words, numbers, or both, in columns and rows.

diagram
A two-dimensional drawing that shows the important parts of objects.

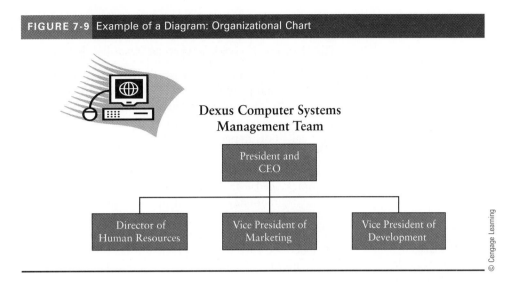

FIGURE 7-9 Example of a Diagram: Organizational Chart

Dexus Computer Systems
Management Team

President and CEO

Director of Human Resources

Vice President of Marketing

Vice President of Development

© Cengage Learning

Remember, your presentation slides are intended to engage and guide your audience. Although many presenters often use them as note cards, you should avoid reading from them or using them in such a way that your attention is drawn away from your audience.

Delivery in Oral Presentations

Nonverbal communication is critically important in oral presentations. It is the primary reason to give a presentation over other channels or media of communication, because nonverbal communication enables us to make that personal connection and establish our credibility by demonstrating confidence and composure. Nonverbal communication includes the qualities of the voice and spoken patterns as well as body language, dress, and general appearance.

Vocal Delivery

Your voice plays an important role in the meanings listeners find in your words. By varying the volume, rate of delivery, pitch, or inflection of your voice and message delivery, you can easily change the meaning of your message. In oral presentations, your vocal delivery can also enhance your message by making it more lively, interesting, and convincing to your audience. Vocal delivery can also affect your relationship with the audience and your credibility. As discussed in Chapter 3, you are better able to establish a relationship with your audience if you are considered likable. Your vocal delivery, as well as the content of your speech, will help you achieve this goal. It is also important to appear confident; if you lack this characteristic, your credibility may also be undermined. We are less likely to believe people who lack confidence in themselves and their ideas.

Norms of vocal delivery differ by culture. For example, Arabs speak loudly because they believe doing so is a sign of strength. In contrast, people from the Philippines tend to speak softly, believing this is a sign of good breeding and education. Rate of delivery also differs among cultures: Arabs and Italians speak faster than do most people in the United States.

The elements of vocal delivery are described below.

- **Volume.** The **volume** of your speech must be loud enough to be heard but not so loud as to be overwhelming. When speaking before a group, you generally need to speak louder than you do in general conversation.
- **Rate of delivery.** The **rate of delivery** refers to the speed at which you speak. For a speech to be effective, vary the rate of delivery to reflect changes in the content of the material being presented or its desired effect. Serious material calls for a slower, more deliberate rate, while lighter topics need a faster pace. Beginning speakers, because of their anxiety, have a tendency to speed up their presentations and run their words together, making it difficult to understand their message. An audience will thus interpret rapid delivery as a sign of anxiousness or lack of confidence. Be sure to focus your efforts on slowing your delivery so that your credibility is not undermined, even if you are struggling with speech apprehension.
- **Pitch.** **Pitch** ranges from low and deep to high and squeaky. Optimal pitch is the level at which you can produce your strongest voice with minimal effort and also allow variation up and down the scale. Pitch is an issue that deserves some attention; those with high, squeaky voices or breathy ones may be judged as being less competent, serious, and credible. Through practice and training, you can lower the pitch of your voice.
- **Vocal variety.** **Vocal variety** refers to the varying use of the vocal aspects of volume, rate, and pitch. Speaking in a monotone without such variations sends the message that the speaker is not interested in his or her topic, is nervous, or lacks confidence. Making any of these impressions can undermine your credibility as well as make your message less engaging.
- **Articulation.** Speakers should **articulate** words clearly. Clear articulation is important for two reasons: (1) so you are easy to understand and (2) to avoid negatively affecting your credibility with your audience.
- **Pauses.** **Pauses** should be used to emphasize important points and enhance the meanings of words and phrases. Beginning speakers often do not use pauses effectively because they feel uncomfortable with silence. This lack of comfort with silence also can lead to the problem discussed below: vocal distractions or disfluencies.
- **Fluency.** Avoid **vocal distractions or disfluencies**. These include stammers, stutters, double starts, and the excessive use of empty filler words such as *uh* and *um*. Too many vocal distractions make a speaker sound disorganized, nervous, and uncertain, leading to a potential loss in credibility. You can reduce vocal distractions in your delivery by focusing on them and practicing to eliminate them during day-to-day conversations.

Many of these aspects of vocal delivery can positively or negatively affect your credibility, so it is important to sensitize yourself to each one and to identify those that you might work to improve. Mastering these aspects of vocal delivery can also help make your speaking more engaging and even charismatic. However, vocal delivery is just one aspect of successful oral presentations. The next section discusses another element—nonverbal expression or body movement.

volume
The relative sound level of speech; it must be loud enough to be heard, but not so loud as to be overwhelming.

rate of delivery
The speed at which one speaks.

pitch
The sound quality of the speaker's voice, ranging from low and deep to high and squeaky.

vocal variety
The varying use of the vocal aspects of volume, rate, and pitch.

articulate
To pronounce all words clearly and fluently.

pauses
Temporary breaks in speech used to emphasize important points and enhance the meanings of words and phrases.

vocal distractions or disfluencies
Speaking "errors" such as stammers, stutters, double starts, and excessive use of filler words such as *um* and *uh*.

CriticalThinking

How important is the quality of vocal delivery in a presentation? Have you witnessed presenters whose vocal delivery was lacking in one of the elements mentioned above? What was your reaction? Do you struggle with any of the elements of vocal delivery in your oral presentations?

Body Movement

Nonverbal communication is critical in making an oral presentation effective. Your nonverbal communication in an oral presentation situation can help you engage your audience and convey goodwill. It can also help reinforce your message.

For beginning speakers, it is important to pay attention to and identify the types of nonverbal signals you give your audience, because they can have an immediate and immense impact on your credibility and perceived professionalism. To develop a professional, credible persona, you must identify the particular nonverbal signals you may be sending that indicate you lack confidence or are anxious. (See "Reducing Presentation Anxiety" later in this chapter.)

Nonverbal Signals That Indicate Anxiety. Common indicators of a lack of confidence include these:

- Poor eye contact
- Rigidity or stiffness of the body and its movements
- Crossed arms or hands jammed into pockets
- Unintentional body movements

Some nervous speakers look at the floor, for example. Another common cause of poor eye contact is the overuse or inappropriate use of notes. You should *not* use notes if you have a tendency to read them once you become nervous.

Standing stiffly with your arms locked (behind your back, for example) also is often interpreted as a sign of fear by audiences. Ideally, you should stand with your hands hanging loosely at your sides so that you can more easily, naturally, and spontaneously gesture. Letting your hands hang loosely at your sides sends a second message to the audience: You are open to it and its ideas. Placing your hands or arms across the front of the body may be interpreted as a sign of defensiveness or anxiety or as cue that you are not open to your audience and its perspectives.

Unintentional body movements include playing with or tossing your hair or an article of clothing, twisting your body, swaying, pacing, and fidgeting with your feet. All these actions may be signs of anxiety. Ideally, speakers stand solidly on the floor with their feet apart and only move their body to lean forward or to gesture naturally to emphasize their message. Moving intentionally around the room can help you engage your audience, but beginning speakers should first master the ability to stand in one place without displaying other unintentional body movements before they move on to this step. If you begin moving around the room before you have learned to control your anxiety, then your nervousness may be exhibited through pacing.

Each person typically displays anxiety in a way unique to him- or herself. It is helpful if you can enlist the help of others to observe you presenting and to provide you feedback on the body movements you might be making that indicate your nervousness. Once you identify how you display your anxiety, you can focus your attention on eliminating that behavior.

Nonverbal Signals That Indicate Confidence. An important goal of a business presentation is to make an immediate, positive, and confident impression of yourself with your audience. (This objective is true for all business communication situations.) To do so, smile confidently at your audience when your presentation begins and greet it warmly and sincerely, if appropriate for the message you are about to deliver. As the presentation continues, be sure your body language is not telling your audience that you are unduly fearful, anxious, or nervous, because this knowledge can undermine your credibility. In professional presentation situations, you never want to "let them see you sweat."

A list of the specific nonverbal behaviors that generally enhance a professional presentation follows:

- A speaker should establish and maintain *direct eye contact* with the audience. Talking directly to the audience is seen as more sincere and more engaging with the audience.
- An effective speaker should *stand up straight and use good posture* without becoming stiff. Good posture projects a confident yet relaxed image. For smaller people, good posture can also help you to take up more space. For those in a leadership position or who aspire to be perceived as leaders, this is important because studies show that confident, charismatic leaders generally take up more space; they don't make themselves small by slouching or crossing their arms or legs.
- Speakers should use *natural gestures* to animate the presentation. Gestures should grow out of a response to your material and appear natural and spontaneous, prompted by your feelings. If you are speaking to a large group that may have trouble seeing your gestures, then make the gestures larger than in normal conversation.
- Speakers should *move* around the presentation area or room to engage the audience and keep its attention. Again, for smaller persons, moving around the room with intention can help you to take up more space and appear more like our stereotype of a confident leader. Moving around a room, though, always should be purposeful. Nervous pacing distracts the audience from your message and makes you appear less confident.
- Speakers should use *facial expressions* to communicate and build rapport with the audience. Your face should reflect and reinforce the meanings of your words. An expressionless face suggests that the speaker is afraid or indifferent.

Establishing a relationship with your audience, maintaining its interest in your topic, and developing your credibility are important objectives for a successful professional presentation. To accomplish these goals, you must be well prepared and control your anxiety about speaking. Hopefully, preparation can help you reduce speech apprehension. These two issues are discussed later in this section.

CriticalThinking

What nonverbal behaviors do you exhibit during oral presentations that may indicate to your audience that you are nervous? What can you do to eliminate or control these behaviors?

Mika Brzezinski, Co-Host of Msnbc's Morning Joe, advocates being "yourself" as a speaker.

Dress and Appearance

Clothing, jewelry, hairstyle, and general appearance create an immediate impression of who you are. These aspects can also affect your credibility, your image as a professional, and whether you belong to the group. For these reasons, it is important to select clothing and other aspects of appearance that are appropriate for each presentation situation. If you are uncertain about what is appropriate for a particular situation, such as an employment interview, err on the side of formality and conservatism.

Preparing for Your Presentation

Preparing for your presentation involves three basic steps: (1) planning your presentation, (2) gathering and organizing your material, and (3) practicing your delivery.

As stated earlier, planning the presentation can help make preparation easier by focusing the message on a single theme or key point. Many presentations are too ambitious in terms of the amount of information intended for delivery. A better approach is to simplify the message to one key point that is illustrated in various ways to increase impact. Simplifying the message in this way also makes preparation easier because complexity is reduced.

A second way to reduce anxiety and enhance your credibility is to increase your confidence by being or becoming an expert in the subject you will be discussing. Consequently, it is very important that you thoroughly research your topic and look at it from all angles. This latter point is important because your audience may detect that you have a one-sided or superficial understanding of the topic, which would undermine your credibility. Another way to confront this issue is to find a way to approach the topic by attaching it or relating it to something you already know or care about. This can help you to connect more personally with the topic, potentially increasing your passion or conviction.

You may also be faced with questions from your audience, some of which may be objections to your idea, and you must be able to answer these questions with reasonable, quality information in order to maintain your credibility and persuasiveness, so it is important to plan for those questions and be prepared to answer with confidence All of these steps can help you to actually feel confident when it comes time for your presentation.

After you have simplified the message and gathered needed information, practice delivering your presentation. Typically, business presentations are expected to be delivered **extemporaneously**. That means that you should be well prepared for your presentation but be able to deliver your material spontaneously. In other words, you should not read your material or memorize it, although you may want to memorize important parts of your speech such as quotations, figures, or examples. If you read your presentation, you will lose your audience's interest because you will probably have difficulty maintaining eye contact with people, and your voice will tend to be monotone in delivery.

In addition, if you memorize your speech, you increase the risk of heightening your anxiety and losing credibility; if you forget a passage, you probably will need to stop and repeat your presentation quietly to yourself to find the place in your memorized script at which you can resume speaking. These long pauses can be distracting to your audience and increase your own discomfort, affecting the overall quality and credibility of your speech. Memorized speeches also tend to lack spontaneity, which decreases audience interest. Your goal should be to appear and sound like an expert in your subject, one who can speak about it in an informative, well-organized yet spontaneous manner. To eliminate these problems, it is helpful to avoid writing a script for the presentation. Instead, identify the key points and parts of the presentation, develop examples to illustrate these points, and then design the needed visual aids. This process will help you to refine and internalize your message. Practice delivering this information from memory until you feel confident that you can remember and deliver it in a spontaneous way.

To enhance the spontaneity of your presentation, use notes sparingly and judiciously. If you can deliver your presentation without notes, your credibility and ability to relate to the audience will be enhanced. However, if you need to use notes, the following guidelines will help you use them properly.

- **Use only 3″ × 5″ note cards.** Small note cards are less obtrusive and distracting for your audience. If you use 8½″ × 11″ sheets of paper, you may become nervous and unintentionally wave them as you gesture. You don't want to look like a sailor on a flight deck, guiding a plane through its landing, signal flags waving.
- **Put only an outline or keywords on your notes.** If you write out your entire presentation on the cards, you are more likely to read from them.
- **When you look at your notes, stop speaking.** The proper way to reference your notes is to stop speaking, glance down at your cards, and then look up and resume speaking. In most cases, you should not speak unless you are looking at your audience.

extemporaneous speaking
Public speaking that is delivered spontaneously rather than being read or memorized in advance.

You might find it helpful to practice your presentation in front of a mirror or before a small audience of family members or friends. Either way, you can receive feedback about how you look and sound, and you can adjust your delivery and nonverbal communication to better support the message you wish to send. Practice can also help you reduce your anxiety about speaking because it may help you feel more confident. Techniques to reduce speech apprehension are discussed in the following section.

Lastly, as part of preparation, it is also advisable to consider the setting in which the presentation will take place. How large is the room? How many people will be in attendance? What type of equipment is available? Are there distractions that you need to consider or try to eliminate? How should you transport your presentation software? Is the software that is available compatible with what you are using? These considerations can help eliminate problems and ensure that you will be confident and well prepared for the event.

Reducing Presentation Anxiety

As mentioned earlier, preparing properly for a presentation can go a long way in eliminating presentation anxiety. Simplifying the message, selecting a topic about which you feel confident, and practicing sufficiently should enable you to feel more confident about the material.

However, feeling some anxiety when faced with an oral presentation situation is not unusual or necessarily bad. Generally, we perform better if we feel a small amount of anxiety. However, it is best to keep your anxiety at a manageable level, one that does not affect your ability to perform.

If you still feel some anxiety after following the appropriate planning and preparation steps, it may be reduced through visualization and breathing techniques. Visualizing yourself giving a successful presentation can sometimes help you achieve those results. Taking deep, slow, regular breaths—during which you visualize yourself drawing your breath down into and expanding your stomach rather than your chest—can also help calm you. This technique triggers a natural relaxation response. You might try both these techniques to find which one works better for you.

Another technique is to ask yourself whether your fears are reasonable. For example, we may believe that if we make one mistake, our audience will judge us harshly. But this is typically not the case; most audiences want us to succeed. By realizing that your audience is probably on your side, you may be able to reduce some of your fears and perform more confidently. It can be helpful to ask yourself whether some irrational belief is fueling your anxiety. If so, identify it and eliminate it by changing it to a more realistic, positive belief.

Handling Question-and-Answer Sessions

Question-and-answer (Q&A) sessions are a common part of business presentations and typically take place at the end of a presentation. How you handle Q&A sessions can affect your ability to maintain credibility and goodwill as well as achieve your larger communication purposes. Because of their importance in achieving your communication goals, these sessions also deserve adequate preparation and strategy formulation. These issues are addressed in the following sections.

Preparing for Q&A

The steps for preparing for an important question-and-answer session follow. Prepare for questions by listing every fact or opinion you can think of that challenges your position.

1. Divide potential questions into three categories: the known, the knowable, and the notable.
   - The known list contains questions to which you know the answers. Depending on how well you know the particulars, you may want to write down the answers and practice them out loud.

- The knowable list contains questions to which you may not know the answers. Do the research, find the answers, and practice them.
- The notable list contains the questions that require a strategy. These are the broad questions that do not have simple answers or which may jeopardize the success of the presentation without planning. Your strategy for answering these questions should validate the overall purpose and message of your presentation.

2. Treat each objection seriously and try to think of a way to deal with it.
3. If you are talking about a controversial issue, then you may want to save one point for the question period rather than make it during the presentation.
4. Speakers who have visuals prepared to answer questions seem especially well prepared and thus enhance their credibility and professionalism.

During the Q&A

During the Q&A session, follow some basic rules. Remember, you are in control of the Q&A period, so you should state the rules for the process, if appropriate. For example, near the beginning of your presentation, you might ask the audience to hold its questions until the end of the presentation. At the beginning of the Q&A session, you might state a time limit, limit the number of questions per person, and identify who will answer the audience's questions (if this has been a team presentation).

During the Q&A, keep the discussion focused on the topic or issue at hand. Most important, you do not want to lose your temper, appear confused, or become emotional. Your objective is to appear well prepared, confident, objective, reasonable, and calm. If you become agitated or confused, or if the session becomes a free-for-all, then you have lost control of the situation and probably damaged your credibility and perhaps jeopardized your ability to achieve your other communication purposes. The basic rules for question-and-answer sessions follow:

- Don't nod your head to indicate that you understand a question as it is being asked; it may be misinterpreted as a sign of agreement.
- Look directly at the questioner.
- When you answer the question, expand your focus to take in the entire group.
- If the entire audience may not have heard the question or if you want more time to think, repeat the question before you answer it.
- Ask for clarification if you don't understand the question.
- If a question starts to take your talk into a new direction, offer to discuss that issue at a later date.
- Link your answers to the points you made in your presentation.
- Keep the purpose of your presentation in mind and select information that advances your goals.
- Sometimes someone will ask a question that is designed to state his or her opinion. Respond to the question if you want or say, "I'm not sure what you are asking" or "That's a clear statement of your position. Any other questions?"
- If someone asks a question that you have explained in your presentation, answer it rather than embarrass him or her.
- Look for a point of agreement in your answers. An example is provided below.

Audience member: Your ideas about this new business proposal sound far-fetched to me. I think that we need to solidify our regional market before we try to expand abroad.

Speaker: You have a good point—our regional sales have traditionally been the backbone of this company. But we need to expand so that we can avoid slumps if the regional economy takes a downturn.

If you don't know the answer to a question, say so. You can tell the questioner that you will get back to him or her with the answer. You might also ask if someone else in the room knows the answer; if they don't, then your "ignorance" is vindicated. This strategy can also present a risk: Don't do it if you think you will lose control of the questioning period. You can also ask your group members if one of them knows the answer and you are presenting as a team.

At the end of the Q&A, take the opportunity to summarize your position one more time. Take advantage of having the floor to repeat your message briefly and forcefully.

Dealing with Hostile Questions

On some occasions, you may be faced with audience members who do not like you, your company, your product or service, or your proposed idea. Sometimes, these audience members may have such strong feelings that they are unable or unwilling to control them. Do not stoop to their level. Your goal in these situations is to enhance yourself and your position by remaining confident, objective, reasonable, and calm. In these cases, the hostile audience members may undermine their own credibility without your help or comment. However, if you are faced with hostile questions, the following are strategies for dealing with them.

- If a question is hostile or biased, rephrase it before you answer it. "You're asking whether…," or suggest an alternative question: "I think there are problems with both positions you describe. It seems to me that a third solution …" By rephrasing or reframing the question, you are attempting to remove the hostile or biased perspective from the situation.
- Be fair to a hostile questioner, perhaps by indicating the need to disagree, and then agree on a statement of that disagreement.
- Most important, if someone asks a hostile question, do not respond in kind. You might even try to respond with a compliment as long as it isn't insincere. "That's a very important question. Thank you for asking it."

To handle Q&A sessions effectively, you must anticipate your audience's questions and prepare answers that advance the overall purposes of your message. You must strategize ways to maintain control of the session and to remain calm, confident, and reasonable.

Meeting Management

Managing meetings is an important part of facilitating effective group or departmental communication. Meetings are a common means of communication within organizations because they provide the potential for employees to ask and answer questions in an efficient manner. Probably the most effective use of meetings, however, is for problem solving and decision making. Meetings also provide communicators access to nonverbal cues, which enable those who have good observation skills to check and respond to messages that are not verbalized. Just as with most communication media, though, meetings present challenges, the primary one being the cost in time. There are 11 million meetings in the United States every day, according to the National Statistics Council. Furthermore, professionals attend an average of 61.8 meetings a month and say that fully half of that time is wasted.[1] With such numbers, it is imperative to consider whether a meeting is the best media of communication. One rule of thumb to apply is that if the communication goal can be reached via any other medium—an informational email, an informal report, or a departmental wiki, for example—then use that medium rather than plan a meeting.

However, if a meeting is the best way to convey the information and achieve your purpose for communicating, there are ways to make it productive and efficient. This section discusses the common types of meetings and the steps for ensuring a successful and efficient meeting. Special considerations for electronic meetings—videoconferencing, teleconferencing, and Web conferencing—are also discussed.

Types of Meetings

Defining the purpose of a meeting can help you prepare for it. There are three key reasons to hold a meeting: to inform, to discuss or evaluate decisions, and to discuss performance.

- Informative meetings focus on giving or receiving information. They may incorporate discussions, demonstrations, or lectures to aid in the exchange of information. The group size for these types of meetings can vary from as few as two people to as many as a hundred individuals.
- Discussions are held to form decisions or agree on a plan of action. These meetings are successful if participants actively brainstorm, discuss, and evaluate ideas. These meetings work best with small groups of three to nine participants.
- Performance meetings are held to accomplish a specific task or to plan an event. The key to making these meetings successful is to make sure everyone understands their particular responsibilities. Performance meetings are more effective when limited to six or fewer participants.

Steps in Meeting Management

After you have identified the primary purpose of your meeting, spend time on the three phases of meeting management to ensure that the discussion is productive and efficient. These three steps are (1) planning the meeting, (2) conducting the meeting, and (3) following up after the meeting has been held.

Planning the Meeting

When considering a meeting, you must recognize that you have an obligation to show respect for all participants and the time they spend attending this meeting. This is why planning is the most critical step in conducting a meeting. Before you send out notifications to initiate any type of meeting, answer the following questions:

- Which participants are essential to achieve the purpose of the meeting? What are the key roles each participant will have in the meeting? Will the setting be formal or informal? Meetings are productive only when attended by the right people. It may not be to the best advantage to invite those who are simply interested. Your team should comprise individuals who have direct experience with the issues to be discussed or decided and who have a stake in the outcome of such discussions.

- What agenda will be most effective and efficient for the purpose of the meeting? You will need to decide how to bring the participants together in terms of when and where you will meet. Will the meeting be by teleconferencing, videoconferencing, email, on site of the business location, or away from its premises?
- What information, equipment, and tools are required to conduct the meeting?
- How much time will be needed for decision making or to obtain the information needed to achieve the results of your objectives? Allow enough time to have questions answered and clarity established for the meeting.

Although the arrangements may be complex and the nature of your meeting will vary, the following suggested guidelines apply in most cases in conducting a successful meeting:

- Give advance notice to all participants.
- Provide information such as the date, time (both starting and predicted ending), and location (include travel arrangements, if needed), and include the names of participants, their key roles, titles, and business affiliations.
- Design a structured agenda with the stated objectives, a list of the main topics of interest, and time allotted for each topic of discussion. Group related topics together to avoid having to backtrack on a subject in order to keep the meeting flowing in an orderly fashion. Limit the agenda to one page in length. (A generic format for an agenda is provided in Figure 7-10.)
- Provide the agenda in advance to all participants so they can be prepared. Inform all attendees what is expected from each one in preparing for the meeting. Confirm that all participants have received the notice of the meeting agenda.

Conducting the Meeting

Meetings have four major stages: (1) the introduction and vision statement, (2) the meeting kickoff, (3) the summary of accomplishments and the management presentation, and (4) an evaluation exercise and closing remarks.[2] The facilitator is responsible for making sure these steps are followed and completed. The success of the meeting largely depends on the facilitator's communication skills.

The facilitator's first goal is to set a positive, professional tone from the very beginning that is intended to make attendees say, "I'm glad to be here." Creating a welcoming atmosphere can be accomplished by encouraging open communication. Effective facilitators promote individual participation to gain the benefit of diverse points of view. To gain the most information, facilitators should ask open-ended questions to avoid getting simple "Yes" or "No" responses. Facilitators are responsible for getting attendees to participate. They can do so by asking such questions as "What do you think about the topic?" "Can you tell me what we can do to make this better?" or "What other suggestions do you have?" The best solutions are always the result of input from many people.

The facilitator needs to be aware of the time and, with that in mind, keep the conversation on topic. It has been estimated that executives spend an average of 7.8 hours a week in meetings that are unnecessary.[3] Many inefficient or unnecessary

FIGURE 7-10 Formal Generic Agenda for Meetings

**Agenda for [name of group] Meeting Prepared on
[date agenda created] by [name of author of agenda]**

Attendees: [those invited to attend, often in alphabetical order]
Date and time of meeting:
Location of meeting:
Subject: [major issues to be discussed or purpose of meeting]
Agenda items:

1. Call to order
2. Routine business [procedural or administrative matters]   (10–15 mins.)
   a. Approval of agenda for this meeting
   b. Reading and approval of minutes of last meeting
   c. Committee report
3. Old business [unfinished matters from previous meeting]   (15–20 mins.)
   a. Discussion of issue(s) carried over from previous meeting
   b. Isssue(s) arising from decision(s) made at previous meeting
4. New business   (20–25 mins.)
   a. Most important issue
   b. Next most important issue
   c. Other issues in decreasing order of importance
   d. Business from the floor not included on the agenda [only as time permits;
      otherwise, these issues should be addressed in the next meeting]
5. Adjournment

© Cengage Learning

meetings can be directly tied to a late start time, poor facilitation, or a late ending time. Good facilitators keep a meeting on schedule and on topic. Everyone's time is valuable. It's very important to respect others' time; it shows that you value the presence and schedules of those who were prompt. Keeping a meeting on schedule not only establishes goodwill and your credibility as a facilitator but also has a positive effect on future meetings.

Facilitators and presenters should avoid lecturing. According to a study by the MPI Foundation, meeting attendees do not care for "speakers who have poor presentation skills."[4] Speakers who wish to catch the attention of listeners should try to involve the participants emotionally in the meeting. Speakers should be spontaneous, but that does not mean that such discussions should not be planned. Just as with other types of presentations, speakers should plan what they have to say but deliver their message as extemporaneously as possible.

Holding a difference of opinion about the same subject is typical in meeting discussions. But proving a point or being right is secondary to your team's objectives. By following the suggestions below, facilitators can demonstrate leadership and, most importantly, focus everyone's energy on a solution that will progress the group.

- Try to see things from each participant's point of view.
- When someone is speaking, never say, "You're wrong."
- Avoid right or wrongs; treat different opinions as different ways of looking at the same issue.
- Remember that you and others are all working toward the same goal.

Meeting conflicts can be harder to solve than some of the toughest mathematical problems. One way to handle conflict is to turn the point of conflict into a question and get other opinions on the topic. Another strategy is to try to lighten the situation with humor. Facilitators can also show concern by asking the person who seems to have the biggest issues what is wrong. If the person is standing, then the facilitator can ask him or her to sit down. It is harder to be mad when sitting. More generally, facilitators should try to make it a win–win situation for everyone involved in the conflict. They can do so by staying neutral and avoiding taking sides. As the meeting draws to a close, facilitators should summarize the main discussion points and any decisions that are made during the meeting. This information can help pull all information together for attendees.

After the Meeting

After the meeting has concluded, minutes should be posted as soon as possible—within two days at the latest. The meeting minutes should include key topics covered, any decisions or conclusions that were drawn, any projects due and their deadlines, and specific information on future meetings. More specifically, the meeting minutes should include the following:

- Time, date, and location
- Names of attendees
- Agenda items and any other items discussed
- Decisions made
- Assignments and the persons responsible
- Length of meeting
- Time, date, and location of the next meeting

It may also be appropriate to communicate to participants any progress being made on the implementation of decisions or plans of action arrived at during the meeting.

Additional Considerations for Electronic Meetings

As discussed in Chapter 5, the rapid development of technology has provided a number of means for holding meetings with those who are not in the immediate proximity. These include videoconferencing, teleconferencing, and Web conferencing. Even though these technologies are convenient and comparatively less expensive than air travel, they do have such potential disadvantages as lost connections or other technical problems.

To avoid some of these problems, it is important to train participants in the use of the technology and to test it for proper performance before the meeting. As with face-to-face meetings, participants should be informed of the time, date, time zone, and length of the meeting and provided any necessary written materials before the meeting.

In addition, at the beginning of the meeting, all participants should introduce themselves. All questions and comments should then be directed to specific individuals. It is also important to reduce outside noise and distractions, so cell phones and pagers should be turned off and side conversations should be limited.

For videoconferences, it is also important to remember that you are on camera, so avoid distracting behaviors (such as playing with your hair or a pencil) or those that might not be perceived as professional. Because you are on camera, it is important to look at the camera as you speak and thus maintain eye contact.

Summary

- Oral presentations are probably the most misused of all communication media. They are best used to excite and motivate an audience or to deliver a simple message. Unless you are training personnel, detailed and complex information should be left to the written channel because it is too difficult to remember when presented orally and will likely bore the audience.

- When planning a presentation, try to simplify the message and identify a theme or central idea that will interest your audience. Stories and vivid language that will evoke an emotional response should be used to make your presentation more interesting and memorable.

- A variety of patterns are available for organizing a presentation. Select the one that best fits the purpose of your message or that would best enable you to communicate the key aspects of your message. Just as in written messages, presentations should include an introduction, a body, and a close. Introductions of presentations include an additional element, the attention getter, to gain audience interest in your presentation. Design the remainder of the presentation to keep the audience's attention and achieve your strategic purposes.

- Visual aids can make information easier to understand than words alone. Using visuals also helps make the conveyed information more memorable and can enhance your professionalism and credibility. PowerPoint is commonly used as a visual aid in business presentations. The design of a PowerPoint slide show should ensure that the information can be clearly seen by the audience and readily grasped.

- Vocal delivery and other aspects of nonverbal communication are important for achieving goodwill and demonstrating credibility. Presenters should ensure that they maintain eye contact, speak loudly enough to be heard, and convey enthusiasm about their topic. They should use purposeful movement to convey a confident demeanor and consider dress and other aspects of appearance to suit the occasion and demonstrate belongingness to the group.

- Preparation is one of the most important aspects of delivery in a presentation. Adequate preparation can do much to enhance our credibility as well as reduce our speech apprehension. Other methods of reducing speech anxiety are to use visualization and breathing techniques.

- Not enough time is generally spent anticipating and preparing for question-and-answer sessions after presentations. A well-planned and rehearsed presentation can easily be derailed by a bumpy session, so presenters should try to anticipate their audience's questions and prepare answers and perhaps visual aids to respond to them. They should also be prepared for hostile or quirky audience members who might try to derail the presentation, and should have tactics available to maintain control of the session.

- Probably nothing damages a manager's credibility more than a poorly conceived or planned meeting. Meetings, like presentations, are a medium that should be used to leverage nonverbal communication. They should also be carefully planned so as not to be perceived as a waste of time, which will certainly damage the meeting caller's credibility. Meetings should also be followed up to ensure that attendees have a record of the actions that were taken.

Key Terms

forecasting, 196
transitions, 196
call to action, 197

graph, 201
table, 202
diagram, 202

Discussion Questions

1. When should a presentation be used to communicate a business message? For what types of information are other media of communication better choices?
2. What are the critical elements that should be incorporated into an oral presentation to better ensure that an audience understands and can follow the logical progression of the message?
3. What is the purpose of visual aids that accompany an oral presentation? What sorts of information should not be provided on visual aids such as PowerPoint slides?
4. What is the worst possible thing that could happen to you during a speech? What strategies might you use to reduce this fear?
5. What are some pitfalls to avoid when planning and conducting a meeting? How might these be avoided?

Applications

1. Using the presentation planner on page 194, create an outline for a presentation to your class that communicates the trends that will affect your industry in the next five to ten years. Make sure to create a complete, relevant, and effective attention getter; include complete transitions between the main points; and wrap up with a memorable conclusion.
2. Find and observe a speaker. Analyze his or her vocal delivery and nonverbal communication. How did these elements contribute to or detract from the speaker's credibility and goodwill? Use this information to create a list of concrete actions you might take to improve your own presentation skills.
3. You work in the information services department of SynSystems, Inc., a maker of computer connectivity products. Your job, along with the other members of your department, is to provide computer support to the employees of SynSystems. Several years ago, SynSystems was purchased by computer products giant World Connectivity Solutions (WCS). Because your company had an excellent reputation for its customer service and extensive and positive brand

recognition, WCS chose to leave your division with its well-respected name.

Coincidentally, perhaps, SynSystems uses the same product as its parent company—GroupPRO—for electronic collaboration among project development teams. GroupPRO was created by another company that WCS now owns, but it is not the only product of its kind on the market. Because of lingering bitter feelings about the company takeover, there is a move among the employees of your department to switch to a newer collaboration product, TeamMAX.

Create a persuasive presentation for your boss and the management team of SynSystems. In selecting the content of your presentation, focus on the benefits that you must communicate to the management team and how you can convey those benefits in a clear, vivid, and memorable way.

4. Your team should prepare an agenda for an actual meeting it plans to hold. Your agenda for this meeting should include the following introductory items:

   ■ The primary purpose of your meeting (to generate ideas, narrow a field of options, or to make a decision?)

- The time, date, and place of your meeting
- The names of those attending
  Following this information, you should provide a list of *specific* topics you intend to discuss during your meeting that are organized in the order of their importance (the most important first). You may wish to include a time limit for the discussion of each item.

5. After your team holds a planned meeting, you may wish to analyze its effectiveness by discussing what you observed, including the communication behaviors and roles that each team member tended to play. In providing this assessment, you might consider the following:

- What did we do in this meeting that worked well?
- What happened that we would not want to repeat? Are there bad habits into which we keep falling?
- What roles did different team members take on? Were these helpful in achieving group goals? Why or why not?

- What type of communication behaviors did team members display? Were these helpful in achieving group goals? Why or why not?
- Other issues to consider include how well your group was able to attend to both the task and social functions of a team. More specifically, you might wish to consider the following:
- Were you able to keep the discussion of a particular topic within a reasonable amount of time?
- Were you able to keep the discussion focused on the agenda topics?
- Did participants feel valued and respected because others listened to them and responded to what they said in a way that fostered participation?
- Were you able to deal with conflict and individualistic behaviors effectively and productively?
- Were you able to reach your goals for the meeting?

CASE ANALYSIS

OLD DOMINION TRUST COMPANY

"It was a quarter to four on Friday afternoon," said Rob Leonard. "I was just closing out my accounts and trying to clear up a few more issues before the end of the business day. Then along came my division vice president. Since my desk is in the center of the mortgage banking division, I could tell long before he got to me that I was the one he was looking for. And, frankly, the folder he dropped on my desk was the last thing in the world I expected to see."

Rob Leonard is a 26-year-old assistant broker in the mortgage banking division of Old Dominion Trust, a relatively small interstate bank located in the mid-Atlantic region. Rob's branch has regional responsibility for home mortgages in Northern Virginia and the Washington, D.C., area. Although he had joined Old Dominion Trust following graduation four years earlier, he was still among the more junior people in his branch.

The boss went directly to Leonard's desk and asked if he had a minute. "Of course, I have a

minute," said Leonard, "Who hasn't got a minute for the branch V.P.?" Brian Lorigan was senior vice president, mortgage banking for Old Dominion and executive vice president for the Annandale branch office. He was not only Leonard's supervisor but his mentor and partner in several important projects.

Leonard and Lorigan and had been working on a new, federally funded mortgage program that would permit low-to-middle-income, first-time home buyers to obtain financing at very low rates. It was an important project that would require both thorough explanation to the community and careful screening of each of the applicants. The program had been in development for more than six months and would require the cooperation of state and local officials if it were to work. It was an impressive attempt, Leonard thought, on the bank's part to provide mortgage financing to people who would otherwise never qualify for a home loan.

"I thought he would want to review the screening procedures we'd been working on or perhaps talk about the software I planned to use to help set up the program," said Leonard. What he had in mind frightened Leonard a lot more. Lorigan said that Dick Gidley, his principal assistant, had been scheduled to speak to a Capitol Hill neighborhood group about the federally assisted home loan program. Unfortunately, Gidley was in Philadelphia and had just been "bumped" from his return flight to Washington.

Lorigan asked if Leonard would fill in for Gidley at the neighborhood group meeting that evening and speak about the new loan program. "The details are all in this package," he said. He got a phone number, a set of street directions to a renovated fire station on Rhode Island Avenue, and the name of the woman who would introduce him. The rest of the information would have to come from documents he had prepared for the bank and for the Select Committee that had drafted the legislation.

Leonard was philosophical about the request. "It wasn't that I minded canceling dinner plans I had for that evening. It was just that I wasn't sure I was ready to stand up in public and explain a bank loan program that I wasn't in charge of. After Mr. Lorigan shook my hand and said thanks, I looked at my watch. It was five minutes to four, and this thing in Washington was scheduled for seven o'clock."

Discussion Questions

1. Assuming you're in Rob Leonard's position, what would you do? Would it be a good idea to tell Mr. Lorigan you're just not ready (or willing) to give that speech?
2. What would you want to know about the audience that you don't already know? Where could you find that information?
3. What would you want to know about the occasion and speaking situation that you don't already know?
4. Is there anything you think you should know about the physical layout of the room or the arrangements in the fire station that you'll be speaking in?
5. How would you go about preparing your notes for this speech?
6. What else would you bring with you for this event? Do you have time to get visual aids or flip charts made? Is that a good idea?
7. How should you dress for this occasion?
8. What do you think your principal message should be for these people?

This case was prepared from field interviews by James S. O'Rourke, Concurrent Professor of Management, as the basis for class discussion rather than to illustrate either effective or ineffective handling of an administrative situation. Personal and corporate identities have been disguised.

Endnotes

1. Ethridge, M. (2004, January 12). Workplace expert offers advice on conducting meetings. *Akron Beacon Journal, via Ohio Knight Ridder/Tribune Business News*, NA.
2. Friedman, M. (1996). Facilitating productive meetings. *Training & Development, 50*(10), 11.
3. Messmer, M. (2002). Conducting effective meetings. *National Public Accountant, 47*(6), 15.
4. Clark, R. (1998). Meetings: Valuable but misunderstood. *Cornell Hotel & Restaurant Administration Quarterly, 39*(4), 12.

Lisa S/Shutterstock.com

Preparing Employment Messages

After reading this chapter, you will be able to

▶ Perform research needed to conduct a job search and complete the application process.

▶ Write employment messages, including résumés, application letters, and thank-you notes.

▶ Understand the steps in the job interview process and be more confident in both performing and conducting them.

▶ Implement an effective performance appraisal process and become more confident in both receiving and giving performance feedback.

Case Questions:

1. How important is it for employers to create a working environment that is attractive to potential employees? What would be the characteristics of such an environment?

2. From an employee perspective, how important is it to target positions in which one would be a good fit? What are the advantages to the employee and the employer?

3. What steps are needed to identify organizations in which an applicant will potentially fit well with the culture? Does taking these steps provide a potential persuasive opportunity for the applicant? If so, how?

The Case of the Gen-Y Workforce

"I have called today's meeting to discuss our recent numbers on job turn-over rates here at DataTel," Jennifer Fielding announced from the head of the table. Jennifer, head of human resources, scanned the twelve first-line supervisors and managers attending the meeting to see if she had gotten their attention before going on. "In the past twelve months, 19 percent of our employees in the Gen-Y age group have left the com-pany. That may sound surprising given today's sluggish job market, but it is in line with industry forecasts. I would like to get your ideas about how we might better keep these employees, since hiring costs continue to increase while our budget for hiring remains static.

"Before we get into the discussion phase of the meeting, however, I would like to provide you with some information about this age group. Because they have grown up with technology and understand the flexibility it can bring to the workplace, they expect companies to capitalize on that flexibility. Gen-Yers don't mind long hours as long as they have the flexibility to choose when and where they work.

"Some companies have moved in this direction, but they are the excep-tion. For example, Google designated 20 percent of employees' paid time as time to work on creative personal projects. The company also offers unlimited fruit, Luna Bars, and Vitamin Water, a gym, and a playroom to keep people energized and let them take breaks when needed.

"We don't need to copy Google's program, but I would like us to take this opportunity to consider what we could do regarding our HR policies to be more attractive to Gen-Yers, who are expected to make up 77 percent of the workplace within the next ten to twelve years," Fielding said. "So what is your response? What can we do to become a company that will attract and hold the Millennial generation?"

As was discussed in Chapter 6, employment messages are persuasive messages. Furthermore, they are persuasive messages that require that two additional business communication purposes also are achieved: credibility by demonstrating that the applicant is knowledgeable and experienced, and goodwill by showing that he or she is a likeable, responsive person to work with. Therefore, the same steps provided in Chapter 6 for analyzing the audience and the competitors should be followed when preparing résumés, application letters, and thank-you notes as well as for interviews.

In less competitive job markets, the goal of establishing credibility and goodwill also is important for the employer who is hiring. The employer also may be competing with others for the best job applicants and thus should consider how knowledgeable, well prepared, and pleasant to work with he or she appears. This concern should expand to include the type of workplace environment and culture that the employer offers.

In addition to these strategic issues, this chapter will explore the tactical elements involved in applying for jobs as well as hiring. The final section will discuss another important element related to employment: Conducting performance appraisals and receiving performance feedback.

Steps in the Application Process

If you have not been involved in the hiring process, it can be challenging to take on the perspective of your audience, the employer. The employer will likely receive many applications for one position, depending on the economic climate and the available job pool. The employer will likely have many applicants to choose from. His or her job may thus involve several steps to winnow down the pool to a number that could reasonably be interviewed. These steps might involve

- Quickly eliminating candidates who on the surface do not appear to be qualified. This task might be done by a computer program that is searching for keywords found in the job advertisement or description. It might also be done by an assistant who has little knowledge of the job but, like the computer program, has been asked to look for particular keywords or skills. Additional considerations in this process might include eliminating applications that are
  - Improperly submitted
  - Improperly formatted
  - Incomplete
  - Poorly written and that include grammatical, punctuation, or spelling errors.

  In this step, most of the applications are generally eliminated for one of these reasons.
- Reviewing the remaining application packages more carefully. This step involves comparing the remaining applicants' materials to identify who appears to be the best qualified. It is this step that many first-time job applicants may miss. In other words, if you have followed all of the instructions provided in most classes on creating job application messages, you still may not get an interview if you don't recognize that you are competing with

others for a scarce resource, that is, a job. Therefore, in addition to addressing the qualifications listed in the job description and creating a well-written and professionally formatted employment package, you should also attend to how you might distinguish yourself positively from other applicants.

This step can be a bit daunting not only for first-time applicants but for more seasoned professionals as well. But it might be easier than it appears on the surface by following the steps discussed in this section.

1. Perform a self-inventory: List your skills, abilities, and experiences.
2. Identify your purposes: To inform, persuade, establish your credibility, and convey goodwill.
3. Analyze your audience by conducting research to learn more about its needs, concerns, and objectives.
4. Match the audience's expectations with your abilities and skills.
5. Consider your competition and how you might distinguish yourself from it.
6. Prepare the employment messages that are requested or required.
7. Review and revise your social media content.

Performing the Self-Inventory

In order to be persuasive and to increase self-confidence in the job application process, it is generally necessary to do a thorough self-inventory. A self-inventory involves listing all of the skills, experiences, and abilities you have that may be transferable or applicable in a workplace situation. For those who have held relevant jobs, this process can be relatively simple, since they should have many of the skills that are needed if they are applying for a similar position. However, for those entering the professional workplace or changing jobs, this task can be more challenging. It is not uncommon for first-time applicants to believe they have little to offer beyond some attractive personal characteristics and the proper college degree. However, performing a thoughtful self-inventory can often illuminate other needed skills and abilities.

To get started, it is generally helpful to identify the skills and abilities that employers are looking for. Start by finding job descriptions for positions to which you would like to apply. Read them carefully, and list all of the skills, abilities, and personal characteristics for which they are looking. Then match those skills and abilities with your own personal experiences. These do not have to be demonstrated on the job but can also be skills and abilities that you have demonstrated in classes, college organizations, volunteer organizations, and your personal life.

Below is a list of questions to help get you started on a self-inventory:

1. What jobs have you held?
2. What organizations have you belonged to?
3. What training or education do you have?
4. In all of the above categories, what skills have you used or exhibited?
5. What have been your concrete achievements in all of these categories?
6. Based on this analysis, what personal characteristics, abilities, and skills might you address during the job application process?

For example, if you are a student, it is likely that you have been involved in a number of group projects during your academic career. Many organizations nowadays expect employees to have excellent group communication skills. If this is the case, what experiences have you had in your group work that would highlight and communicate your skills in this area? These examples can be used when writing a résumé or application letter or during job interviews.

Analyze Your Audience, the Industry, and the Overall Job Climate

The next step in the process is to do a careful analysis of your potential audience, the industry in which you hope to work, and the overall job climate. It is important to understand the overall job climate for a variety of reasons. If the job market is tight, it is likely that the applicant will have much less leverage in negotiating salary, work location, and benefits. However, this depends on the industry. For example, you may be looking for work in a tight job market generally speaking, but there may be industries or fields that are begging for applicants. This is why it is helpful to get a sense of the broader context of the job market, so that you will have a better understanding of your overall value in that market.

It is also important to determine the specific skills for which your audience is looking, so that you can show that you are well qualified for a particular position. This is the first goal of any job applicant: to demonstrate that he or she is qualified for the job, so that his or her application will not be eliminated from further consideration. Figure 8-1 provides an example of a typical job description, this one for an office manager. It is important to recognize that most job descriptions contain two parts: a description of the overall job and a list of requirements. When analyzing job descriptions, be sure to carefully read the entire job description and list all of the skills that are listed. For example in the job description shown in Figure 8-1, interaction with other departments, customers, and management is required. Carefully reading this job description would provide the applicant with an opportunity

---

FIGURE 8-1 Job Description for an Office Manager Position

Regional environmental laboratory is seeking a motivated individual for Office Manager. Responsible for 3 departments central to the operations of Energy Laboratories:

Sample Receiving and Sample Preparation/Login

Report Preparation/Customer Service

Shipping and Receiving

Requires professional interaction with all aspects of the laboratory, including all analytical departments, upper management, project management, accounting, sales, and customer service.

Office Manager is responsible for database management and related problem solving. Must have ability to gather necessary information and resources to make effective decisions that impact laboratory operations.

Requirements:

- Proven and demonstrated leadership experience
- Goal-oriented management style
- Independent problem solver
- Decision making
- Microsoft Office suite programs
- Customer service focus
- Experience in the environmental services industry or laboratory setting

© Cengage Learning 2015

to highlight his or her communication skills and experience interacting with varied audiences successfully.

The final consideration is the competition. If it is a tight job market, the employment process may be extremely competitive. If so, the question is, "What can you provide an employer that will make you as attractive or even more so than your competition?" A thorough self-analysis as well as an analysis of the industry, job market, and competition should provide you some ideas about how to answer this question. Sometimes the answer to this question may be a collection of small actions, such as better addressing the employer's needs in your application package, writing a follow-up thank-you note after the interview, and conveying the right attitude during the job interview.

Drafting and Developing a Résumé

When applying for a position, there are two common documents that the employer might request: the application letter and a résumé. With most positions now applied for online, you will find that some only request a résumé. There are two key differences between a résumé and an application letter: (1) the format and (2) the content. A résumé is little more than a bullet list, while a letter is a persuasive message. A résumé can be a bit more general in terms of its content because it is aimed at a position. For example, if you are applying for an entry-level accounting position at a number of organizations, the content may need little change, since most entry-level accounting positions are similar in the types of skills that are required. The content of a letter, on the other hand, should be more focused on a particular employer and its needs. Therefore, the content of a letter might change more depending on the particular employer to whom it is aimed.

The steps in drafting and developing a résumé are listed below:

1. Choose or create a template.

Most résumés are one page in length in the United States, particularly for those just entering the workforce, and most other countries, such as Canada and France. There are exceptions, though, such as in Germany, where a complete dossier of perhaps twenty pages is not unusual. In the United States, if you have been working in a profession for several years, your résumé may be longer than a page.

The simplest way to develop a résumé is to start with the templates that are provided in Microsoft Word or another program and then customize the template. A typical résumé format is provided in Figure 8-2.

2. Generally, provide three categories of information with an eye toward audience expectations and interests. These categories are typically

   - Education
   - Work experience
   - Organizations, awards, and leadership

However, there are additional categories you may want to include, such as "Career Objective," which would appear at the top of the résumé before "Education." Categories included in a résumé also may differ depending on the country. For example, in China personal information is included while in Germany and Spain information about one's family may also be included.

Depending on your career situation, there are other résumé formats that may be used. For example, if you have worked in several different professional positions

FIGURE 8-2 Sample Résumé

Jennifer Isaacs
141 Rowman Street, Apartment 1, Torrance, CA 90081, (213) 556-2323, jisaacs@gmail.com

Education
California State University, Los Angeles, CA

- Bachelor's Degree in Business Administration, 3.7 GPA, Expected Graduation 2014
- Dean's List All Semesters
- Coursework: Business Communication, Introduction to Marketing, Micro and Macro Economics, Fundamentals of Accounting, Fundamentals of Management, Introduction to Public Relations, Sales.

Employment
Kaiser Public Relations, Los Angeles, CA

Public Relations Intern, 2012–Present
- Met with clients to determine their public relations needs
- Wrote public relations materials, such as press releases, company backgrounders, brochure content, and information sheets
- Contacted media outlets to inform them about newsworthy events involving clients

Torrance Parks Department, Torrance, CA

Lifeguard, Torrance City Beach, 2009–2012
- Responsible for safeguarding the lives of swimmers at Torrance City Beach
- Interacted with the public, coworkers, and supervisors to ensure the safety and well-being of the public
- Received the Torrance City Beach "Best Lifeguard" Award in 2011 and 2012

Organizations and Leadership
- Vice President, Alpha Kappa Psi Sorority, 2012–Present
- Volunteer, Habitat for Humanity, 2010–2012
- Member, CSU Marketing Association, 2010–Present

© Cengage Learning 2015

and are wishing to change careers, a functional résumé may be more suitable than the chronological résumé described earlier. A functional résumé organizes information by skills or accomplishments that best address future career goals.

The organization of the main headings in a chronological résumé may also change depending on the place you are at in your career. For example, if your most recent and most notable accomplishment is attaining a bachelor's degree in your desired field, the category "Education" will likely appear first on your résumé. However, if you have been working in your chosen field for several years, the category "Work Experience" may appear first and "Education" may drop to the bottom. This is because work experience is generally more desirable to employers than a college degree without relevant work experience.

When deciding which information to provide, remember to consider your audience. Are there certain phrases or words that are commonly used in your desired profession to describe certain skills or abilities? If you don't know, you can find out by reading job descriptions and other information related to your chosen profession. Then use these words and phrases as appropriate to describe the skills and abilities you offer.

In addition, avoid "padding" your résumé with unnecessary information. Based on your previous research, you should have a very clear understanding of the types of skills and abilities for which employers are looking. Provide only information that relates to these skills and abilities. Finally, if you are in college, you should avoid listing accomplishments from high school unless they are relevant to the job because it may make you look as if you have not achieved much in college if you need to rely on past honors.

3. Use a bullet list format.
   a. Begin with an action word
   b. Use parallel structure
   c. Ideally, include concrete achievements

A list of common action words used at the beginning of lists in résumés is provided in Box 8-1.

When creating bullet lists of skills and abilities, refer back to your self-inventory for evidence of accomplishments. Including these in your résumé is another way that you can distinguish yourself from the competition.

Examples of a bulleted item without specific evidence or a relevant accomplishment:

■ Managed the budget of the Kappa Kappa Pi Fraternity
■ Won the "Best Salesperson of the Year" Award

Box 8-1 List of Action Words for Use in Résumés and Lists

accomplished	demonstrated	handled	performed	repaired
achieved	determined	hired	planned	reported
administered	developed	improved	predicted	researched
advised	devised	increased	prepared	retrieved
aided	diagnosed	initiated	presented	reviewed
allocated	directed	interviewed	prioritized	revised
analyzed	distributed	inventoried	processed	scheduled
balanced	earned	led	produced	screened
budgeted	enlisted	maintained	programmed	selected
calculated	established	managed	promoted	served
coached	estimated	mediated	provided	sold
communicated	expedited	monitored	purchased	started
compared	facilitated	motivated	recommended	supervised
compiled	formed	negotiated	recorded	taught
coordinated	formulated	operated	recruited	trained
created	generated	organized	reduced	verified
decided	guided	oversaw	reorganized	

Examples of a bulleted item with specific evidence or a relevant accomplishment:

- Managed the $250,000 annual budget of the Kappa Kapa Pi Fraternity
- Won the "Best Salesperson of the Year" Award for sales of more than $300,000 in clothing and accessories

Hopefully, as these latter examples show, a few additional words that provide specific evidence and results is more vivid, clear, and impressive than the general information provided in the first examples.

4. Ensure that you have included keywords from the job description.

Since most job applications are done electronically, it is important to check that you have included important words from the job description in your résumé. That's because most companies use software programs called application tracking systems to scan electronically submitted résumés and search for such keywords to identify applicants who are potentially qualified for a position. These systems typically look for nouns that are related to the industry, so your earlier research should serve you well in accomplishing this step. Place the keywords in the proper context within your listing of accomplishments.

Drafting and Developing the Application Letter

The first objective of an application letter is to show you are well qualified for the position for which you are applying. Reaching this objective depends on the quality of the content or information about yourself that you are able to provide and whether that information speaks to your audience's needs as well or better than your competitors—other job applicants—might. In other words, much of your ability to accomplish this goal depends on your knowledge of the audience and your ability to write in such a way to show that you have that knowledge. Earlier steps in the job application process should have prepared you well to draft and develop the application letter. The steps in drafting the application letter are

Step 1: Analysis of your strengths, abilities, knowledge, experience, and weaknesses.

Step 2: Research the organization and its needs beginning with the job description and other resources about the company.

Step 3: Analysis of the organization's needs and culture. Analyze each job description carefully. Identify the abilities and skills for which the organization is looking. Don't limit your analysis to the listed qualifications. Also analyze the job description portion to identify more specific descriptions of those qualifications written in the context of the organizational or job task.

Step 4: Match the most valued or important needs of the organization with your abilities and experience.

Step 5: Draft a statement for each that

1. Clearly identifies the skill or ability.
2. Provides a concrete example of a time you have demonstrated that ability or skill.
3. Ideally, mentions an achievement or concrete outcome of that skill or ability demonstration.
4. Ends with a statement of how that skill or ability might contribute to the organization's specific needs or goals.

Sample body paragraph:

I HAVE HAD SEVERAL PUBLIC RELATIONS INTERNSHIPS, WHERE I HAD THE OPPORTUNITY TO PRACTICE MANY OF THE SKILLS FOR WHICH YOU ARE LOOKING. I HAVE WRITTEN PRESS RELEASES, COMPILED PRESS KITS, PITCHED STORIES TO THE MEDIA, TAGGED EDITORIAL COVERAGE, AND WORKED WITH EDITORS TO PROVIDE CONTACTS AND OTHER INFORMATION. WHILE INTERNING AT MICRON, INC., I ACTED AS HEAD PR PERSON FOR THE RELEASE OF ITS X10 PROCESSOR AND SUCCESSFULLY OBTAINED COVERAGE IN MAJOR TRADE MAGAZINES, INCLUDING *LAN TIMES, COMPUTER WORLD,* AND *SOFTWARE NEWS.*

Step 6: Write an introduction that

1. States the position you are looking for and where you learned about the opening.
2. Provides a confident statement that introduces the skills and abilities you will address in your application letter.

FIGURE 8-3 Sample Job Application Letter

Clara Robards
1312 Apple Avenue, Boise, ID 87402, (208) 324-6779, crobards@gmail.com
January 4, 2013

Linda Edwards, Public Relations Manager
Idaho Forestry Products, Inc.
2330 Fairview Avenue
Boise, ID 87421

Dear Ms. Edwards:

I am writing to apply for the Public Relations position that was posted on your Web site. I believe I am well qualified for this position because I have a degree in communication with a public relations emphasis, experience working in the public relations field, and am self-motivated and hard working.

While a student at Boise State University, I had several public relations internships, where I had the opportunity to practice many of the skills for which you are looking. I have written press releases, compiled press kits, pitched stories to the media, tagged editorial coverage, and worked with editors to provide contacts and other information. While interning at Micron, Inc., I acted as head PR person for the release of its X10 processor and successfully obtained coverage in major trade magazines, including LAN Times, Computer World, and Software News.

I am able to multitask, manage time well, and maintain a high level of performance. At BSU, I maintained a 3.8 GPA, while working part time, interning, and serving as scholarship chair for my sorority.

I would like to schedule an interview with you to discuss my qualifications further. I will call next week to set up an appointment with you at your earliest convenience.

Sincerely,

Clara Robards

Sample introduction:

I am writing to apply for the Public Relations position that was posted on your Web site. I believe I am well qualified for this position because I have a degree in communication with a public relations emphasis, experience working in the public relations field, and am self-motivated and hard working.

Step 7: Write a conclusion that
1. Confidently restates how you might contribute to the organization's needs or goals.
2. Closes with a positive forward-looking statement.

Sample conclusion:

I would like to schedule an interview with you to discuss my qualifications further. I will call next week to set up an appointment with you at your earliest convenience.

Reviewing Your Social Media Content

If you have a Facebook page or Twitter feed, remember that your résumé isn't the only thing job recruiters will have an eye on. They'll be looking at your social media sites as well to determine whether you are the type of person they want to hire. What this means is that before starting the job application process, you should review the content of the social media in which you are involved. Here are a few tips:

Know the red flags. Certain issues are likely to create a question in an employer's mind about you as an employee. These include provocative photographs, inappropriate remarks, illegal activities, discriminatory or insensitive language, and negative comments. Remember to dig deep: With Facebook's recent switch to timeline profiles, users can quickly search a few years back with the click of a button.

Change your settings. If your accounts aren't set up to be private, now's the time to make that switch.

Use Facebook as a mini résumé. Consider using your Facebook as a way to highlight your skills and abilities, particularly those that are attractive to potential employers. Likewise, eliminate anything that reflects poorly on you—even complaints about homework.

Get rid of "text speak." Consider eliminating the use of numbers instead of words and extra letters and check for proper punctuation. Employers may use your posts as an indicator of your writing ability or the care that is taken when writing and doing other tasks.

Job Interviews

A successful interview depends on the quality of research you have done on the employer and the industry or field, your preparation, and good interpersonal skills. During an employment interview, the interviewer is typically attempting to discover whether the interviewee is a good match with the company culture in terms of attitude, values, and motivation as well as attempting to ensure that the interviewee has the skills, knowledge, and experience needed for the position. Like the initial steps in the application process, an interview is a competitive situation in which the interviewee must show that he or she is a better match and has the best skills compared to other applicants. During this process, both parties—the interviewee and the interviewer—can learn much about the other participant by demonstrating good listening skills and paying close attention to nonverbal cues. Because of this, both parties should ensure that their nonverbal cues are in alignment with the verbal message that they are attempting to send.

This section will discuss interviews from both perspectives: what an applicant should do to prepare for, perform, and follow up on an employment interview and what the interviewer should do to prepare and perform an effective interview.

Preparing for an Employment Interview from the Applicant's Perspective

Many of the issues of concern for effectively handling presentations and question-and-answer periods—as well as the techniques for preparing for and handling both those situations—are similar to those for employment interviews. In both, you have a communication purpose or purposes to achieve; often these are to persuade, to convey goodwill, and to establish your credibility. In the case of an employment interview, the purpose is to persuade your audience that you are the best person for the job by informing the interviewer that you have the skills, experience, knowledge, and personal characteristics for which the organization is looking. You are also attempting to convey goodwill by establishing the beginnings of a relationship with the interviewer and to show that you are a professional, honest, likeable, competent, motivated, and responsible person and potential employee.

In addition, in both presentations and question-and-answer sessions, as well as in job interviews, you must prepare by conducting research, strategizing, and practicing your message or answers to help ensure your ability to achieve your communication purposes and to meet your audience's needs. To prepare for a job interview, you should follow the same steps as those for writing a résumé and application letter. These are

1. Research the organization. The most important information you must gather is related to the job for which you are applying. What skills, experience, and knowledge is the organization looking for? What personal characteristics does the job require or does the company seek in applicants? This information is critical because it will help you to identify the key messages you must successfully convey to the interviewer. The best resource for this information can often be the advertisement for the job itself. Typically, the job posting includes all the qualifications and skills for which the company is looking.

   Of course, you should also gather other information about the company, such as the industry in which the organization is involved, the company's history, its products and services, its financial situation, its future directions and growth potential, and its corporate culture. You will need this information to show how your skills, experience, knowledge, and personal characteristics are useful to the organization. Your secondary purpose is to show the interviewer that you want the job enough to spend time learning more about the organization. Showing that you are knowledgeable about the company can also indicate that you possess other personal characteristics, such as thoroughness, preparedness, initiative, and professionalism. Demonstrating these characteristics can help set you apart from other applicants who may be less well prepared.

Gathering this information can also help you to determine whether you are a good fit for the organization and its culture. The theory of person–organization fit essentially says that people leave jobs that are not compatible with their personalities.[1] So it is important to know yourself and your preferences regarding the kind of environment in which you will work, and to find out whether prospective employers offer that type of environment.

In addition to the organizational culture, you should also ask questions about your direct supervisor and perhaps the company's general management philosophy. According to employment consultant Gary Moore, "It's easy to underestimate the influence individuals you'll interact with on a daily basis will have on your accomplishment or failure".[2] Moore recommends that you ask the following questions to determine the organizational culture and management philosophy of a company:

- How does the manager deal with problems in the workplace?
- Does the employee group work well together as a team?
- Are there internal candidates for the position? (If not, it may be indicative that the job, or the boss, really isn't a desirable one, according to Moore.)
- Why do the employees like to work for the company?
- What is the average length of employment for employees? (If the average is less than one year or more than five years, this may be a clue to the attractiveness of working at this organization.)

2. Identify your skills, experience, knowledge, and personal characteristics that match those for which the company is looking. For example, if you are applying for a position that has a lot of customer contact, the hiring organization is probably interested in your people skills. These might include patience, desire to help others, and the ability to put others at ease. If you are applying for a job in which you produce data that others use, the organization might be interested in your analytical skills. In this case, you might talk about your accuracy, attention to detail, and systematic or organized approach to completing tasks.

3. Obtain lists of the various types of questions an interviewer might ask you. (Refer to Table 8-1 for a list of behavioral interview questions.)

4. Practice answering the interview questions you have gathered. Your answers should, whenever possible, highlight the skills, experience, knowledge, and/or personal characteristics that you know the company is seeking (see the previous step 2). Your goal is to show that you are a perfect fit for the job and the organization.

Because hiring can be a costly undertaking for organizations, some have begun to practice interview techniques designed to better identify how an individual will actually perform on the job. One such technique is called a *behavioral interview*, which is intended to identify an individual's attitude toward and abilities in planning, communicating, problem solving, leadership, teamwork, goal setting, and decision making, among others. (See Table 8-1 for a list of sample behavioral interview questions.) One technique for formulating responses to behavioral interview questions is called the STAR, an acronym for situation, task, action, and result. To use the STAR approach, briefly describe the situation you want to use as an example, the task you or your team were to complete, the action you took to complete the task, and the result of your actions.

Table 8-1 Behavioral Interview Questions by Skill.

To answer behavioral interview questions effectively, you should first identify the skill the interviewer is asking you about; provide a brief yet relevant example in which you exercised that skill; describe your actions in the situation; and end by stating the results of that action. The following are some typical behavioral interview questions by skill.

ADAPTABILITY

- Tell me about a situation when you had to be tolerant of an opinion that was different from your own.
- Tell me about a time when you had to adjust to changes over which you had no control.

COMMUNICATION

- Tell me about a time when you were able to use persuasion to convince someone to see things your way.
- Tell me about a time when you dealt with an irate customer.

GOAL SETTING

- Describe a goal you set for yourself and how you reached it.
- Tell me about a goal that you set and did not reach.

PROBLEM SOLVING

- Tell me about a situation where you had to solve a difficult problem.
- Tell me about a time when you had to analyze information and provide a recommendation.

TEAMWORK

- Tell me about a time when you worked on a team and a member was not doing his or her share.
- Tell me about a time when you were working in a team in which the members did not get along.

TIME MANAGEMENT

- Describe a situation in which you had to do a number of things at the same time.
- Tell me about a time when you were unable to complete a project on time.

© Cengage Learning

Example:

Question: Tell me about a time when a team member was not doing his or her share.

Response: I was working in a team for a marketing class project and one of our team members came to meetings unprepared. I decided that I would call this person every day to see whether he needed help and to see where he was on the project. I think my daily contact with him made it more difficult for him to blow off our meetings, and he realized that I valued him as a team member. The result was that he no longer came to meetings unprepared.

5. Prepare questions to ask the interviewer about the job and the company. (Some of these questions were addressed in step 2, but Table 8-2 provides additional questions to ask interviewers.)

- What challenges might I anticipate in this position?
- What are the expectations for the person who will fill this position?

Table 8-2 Questions to Ask Interviewers.

1. Why is this position open? *(The response to this question may provide the interviewee insight into why the previous job holder left.)*
2. What challenges might I anticipate in this position?
3. What are the expectations for the person who will fill this position?
4. How would you describe the culture around the office?
5. What do you like about your job?
6. What do you like about the company?
7. What don't you like about your job?
8. If given the opportunity, what suggestions would you provide if asked the following question: How might this organization be improved?
9. What is the average length of employment for most of the organization's employees?
10. *(Question to ask immediate supervisor)* How would you describe your management style?
11. Can you provide me some feedback based upon our interview and my employment materials regarding my fit for this position?

© Cengage Learning

- How would you describe the culture around the office?
- What do you like about your job?
- What do you like about working for this organization?
- What don't you like about your job?
- If given the opportunity, what suggestions would you provide if asked the question: how might this organization be improved?
- What is the average length of employment for most of the organization's employees?
- (Question to immediate prospective supervisor) How would you describe your management style?
- Can you provide me some feedback based upon our interview and my employment materials on my fit for this position?
- What is a typical day like in this job?
- What types of people would I be working with, both peers and supervisors?
- Would you describe the initial training program for this position?
- When do you expect to make a decision about this position?
- What initial advice do you wish you had been given when starting this career?

Performing the Employment Interview

As in other business communication situations, your primary purposes in a job interview are to (1) convey goodwill by showing your enthusiasm and general likeability; (2) establish credibility as a professional; and (3) persuade the interviewer that you are the best person for the job by providing quality evidence of your skills, experience, knowledge, and personal characteristics.

In other words, you must immediately make a good impression on the interviewer and then show that you are a doer—an action-oriented individual—who knows how to be a valuable contributor to the organization. Making a good first impression is critical, because research shows that most interviewers make up their minds about an applicant in the initial thirty seconds of an interview.

prodakszyn/Shutterstock.com

To achieve these purposes, you should do the following during the interview:

1. Dress professionally to help you establish your credibility. This means that, in most cases, you should dress conservatively: Wear a suit; avoid excessive jewelry, makeup, perfume, or cologne; and wear conservative shoes and a conservative hairstyle.
2. Arrive on time; be friendly to the receptionist; and bring a notepad, pen, and extra copies of your résumé.
3. Greet the interviewer with a smile and a firm handshake.
4. Sit forward in your chair to indicate interest, show enthusiasm for the interview and job, maintain eye contact, and be clear and specific in your answers and questions.
5. At the close of the interview, you should bring up any positive points about yourself that you may not have been able to address during the interview. Depending upon the situation, you might ask for feedback from the interviewer regarding your suitability for the position. If the interviewer has not provided this information, you should ask what the next steps in the hiring process are, when you might receive a response, or what you need to do to follow up. If you are really interested in the job, you might ask for it.

After the interview, if you are interested in the position, you should write the interviewer a thank-you note, reiterating your interest in the position and covering any points you were unable to make in the interview. This is one last opportunity for you to distinguish yourself from other applicants, who often do not follow through with this last step. Handwritten notes often make the best impression, because they are personal. However, if you have been communicating with the interviewee via email, this channel has become more acceptable as a means of expressing appreciation.

CriticalThinking

Based on your past interviewing experiences, with which steps in the interviewing process do you feel most confident? Which steps might you improve? What can you do immediately to improve your interviewing skills?

ResponsibleCommunication

Those little lies on people's résumés tend to grow during important job interviews, say researchers at the University of Massachusetts at Amherst. "Basically, the more stringent the job requirements, the more candidates lie about their qualifications," says Brent Weiss, a psychology graduate student and coauthor of a study presented at a meeting of the Society for Personality and Social Psychology.[3]

Weiss's study examined how often people lied in job interviews and how personality influences the propensity to fib. Thirty-eight college students applied for and were granted interviews for tutorial jobs that didn't exist.[4] The interview

focused on their math or verbal skills. After researchers came clean about the study, they asked students to review their videotaped interviews and identify what they had lied about. Overall, 84 percent admitted to lying at some point. People told straight-out lies, such as, "I'm very good at math," when they had no facility with arithmetic whatsoever.[5]

Other studies indicate the rate of lying on résumés or in job interviews at 20 to 44 percent.[6] That includes lies about degrees, past jobs, and responsibilities.

"A lot of HR managers are recognizing that lying is pervasive," said Westaff vice president and director of human

resources Joe Coute. "For too many candidates, the desire to get ahead at all costs is more important than honesty. Because of that, interviewers can find themselves focusing on what might be wrong with what someone's saying rather than what might be right. They figure that if a candidate will lie during the interview, then they are going to lie once they're in the door."[7]

Questions for Discussion

1. What are the dangers of lying during a job interview?
2. Is omitting information during an interview a form of lying?

Writing the Thank-You or Follow-Up Message

Another simple way to distinguish yourself from the competition is to write a thank-you email immediately after the interview. According to a study by Accountemps, only half of job applicants send thank-you messages, while 88 percent of executives say that a thank-you note influences their hiring decisions. A thank-you message should

1. Sincerely state the main idea of appreciation for the interview and the information gained
2. Include unique points discussed during the interview and relate them to the position, which ideally increases goodwill
3. Assure the employer of continued interest in the position

FIGURE 8-4 Sample Thank-You Email

To: Daniel Rosko

From: Terri Edwards

Subject: Thank You for the Interview

Dear Mr. Rosko:

Thank you for the opportunity to visit Global Aerospace for an on-site interview yesterday. I enjoyed meeting you and appreciated the tour of your operation and the opportunity to learn about the exciting technological developments being made at Global Aerospace.

I was impressed with the many friendly and knowledgeable employees and their willingness to speak with me about their work and loyalty to Global Aerospace.

My visit reinforced my interest and assured me that my internship with Stark Technologies would enable me to contribute immediately to your design efforts. My work at Shelland University on the drone project is particularly applicable to some of the projects being developed in your labs.

Mr. Rosko, I am eager to receive an offer from Global Aerospace for the entry-level engineering position. If you need additional information in the meantime, please contact me.

Thanks again,

Terri Edwards

© Cengage Learning 2015

---

4. Close on a confident, forward-looking note

Figure 8-4 provides a sample thank-you email.

Conducting Employment Interviews

Conducting employment interviews is a critical task because of the potential costs to the organization. One survey shows that the direct cost to fill a $60,000 position ranges from $9,777 to $49,000: costs of advertising, interviewing, testing and conducting background and reference checks, relocation fees, and training costs.[8] However, indirect costs can be even higher. These include opportunity costs or lost revenue; ramp-up time, which is about three months in length; and consulting fees, among other things. If an appropriate candidate isn't selected, then costs go even higher as a replacement must be sought.

The Pre-Interview Process

A number of steps are involved in the pre-interview process. Depending upon the company's policies and procedures, managers may be involved in different aspects of this process.

The interview process typically begins by communicating that an employee is being sought. A variety of media is used to advertise open positions, including word of mouth, electronic job boards, company Web sites, and print media, such as magazines and newspapers. These postings should identify the qualifications that are being sought for the position; these can help to weed out applicants who are not qualified.

Applications can be received in a variety of ways as well. More and more, applications are being received via electronic methods, although some organizations still solicit and accept paper submissions.

Once the application packages start rolling in, the interviewer's work generally begins. The first step might be to screen the application packages to identify potentially well-qualified applicants. If the job posting contained a list of qualifications, skills, and experiences for the position, this list can be used to identify the potentially well-qualified candidates as well as those who may not be qualified or not as well qualified. The appearance and completeness of the application package might also be used as an indicator of applicants' care and attention to detail.

Once potentially qualified candidates are identified, a telephone interview might be considered as a low-cost, efficient way of determining whether a candidate's qualifications, experience, workplace preferences, and salary needs are congruent with the position and organization.

Once the best candidates have been identified, the interviewer must develop a list of questions for the interview itself. An interviewee's list of qualities, skills, knowledge, and experience developed for the résumé-screening process should be used to create or select the questions. Because hiring can be such a costly undertaking, you might consider using behavioral interviewing to determine how an individual will actually perform on the job. As discussed previously, behavioral interviewing is intended to identify an individual's attitude toward and abilities in planning, communicating, problem solving, leadership, teamwork, goal setting, and decision making, among others. (See lists of sample behavioral interviewing questions in Table 8-1.)

When developing the list of interview questions, it is important to avoid those that might make your company the target of a lawsuit from the U.S. Equal Employment Opportunity Commission (EEOC). Avoid questions that have to do with a person's marital status, age, weight, race, sexual orientation, religion, or ethnicity, and whether they have children, a disability, or an arrest record.

The following are examples of questions to avoid in interviews because they may be alleged to show illegal bias:

- Are you a U.S. citizen? (national origin)
- Do you have a visual, speech, or hearing disability?
- Are you planning to have a family? When?
- Have you ever filed a workers' compensation claim?
- How many days of work did you miss last year due to illness?
- What off-the-job activities do you participate in?
- Would you have a problem working with a female partner?
- Where did you grow up?
- Do you have children? How old are they?
- What year did you graduate from high school? (age)

In addition to preparing a list of questions, the interviewer should consider how to open the interview, the order of the questions, and how to close the interview. The opening for an interview establishes the climate of the exchange. Nonverbal communication plays a critical role. A friendly greeting, firm handshake, and smile should help to put interviewees at ease. Some time might also be spent on small talk to help establish rapport and a friendly, positive climate for the exchange.

This climate can be extended into the interview itself by positioning more general, less pointed questions at the beginning and then working toward more specific questions or those that are more difficult or pointed.

The close of the interview should reinforce the initial climate of the interview. The interviewer might summarize the next steps in the process, offer to answer questions, and provide a statement of appreciation and a handshake. Any promises of employment should be avoided.

Holding the Interview

One of the challenges of an employment interview is the fact that the interviewer and the interviewee have differing interests. That is, the interviewer wants to know what the prospective employee's strengths *and* weaknesses are, whereas the interviewee generally wishes to focus on strengths. There are also the problems associated with inaccurate perceptional inferences, such as stereotyping, attribution, and impression formation, which were discussed in Chapter 2.

During the job interview, the interviewer should be aware of these challenges and try to compensate for them. The interviewer should try to make the candidate feel comfortable so as to better enable him or her to demonstrate knowledge, skills, and experience.

As an interviewer, you might consider taking brief notes during the conversation so that you can provide a more complete report at the end. However, note-taking should not detract from your ability to listen to the candidate or to maintain eye contact and provide other nonverbal behaviors that signal interest. Remember, you are there to gather information, so let the interviewee do the bulk of the talking.

After the interview, you should immediately flesh out your notes, because we don't retain much of what we hear. You might consider creating a form to streamline the evaluation and note-taking process.

Performance Appraisals

Second only to firing an employee, managers cite performance appraisal as the task they dislike the most.[9] This is understandable given that the process of performance appraisal, as traditionally practiced, is often not well planned or carried out. **Performance appraisal** may be defined as a structured formal interaction between a subordinate and supervisor that usually takes the form of a periodic interview in which the work performance of the subordinate is examined and discussed, with a view to identifying weaknesses and strengths as well as opportunities for improvement and skills development.

Performance appraisal systems began as a simple method to determine whether the salary or wage of an individual employee was justified. Little consideration, if any, was given to the developmental possibilities of appraisal. It was felt that a cut or rise in pay should provide the only required impetus for an employee to either improve or continue to perform well. However, studies found that extrinsic motivators were not the only issues that mattered to employees. In addition to pay rates, it was found that other issues, such as morale and self-esteem, could also have a major influence on performance.

In many—but not all—organizations, appraisal results are used, either directly or indirectly, to help determine reward outcomes. That is, the appraisal results are used to identify the better-performing employees who should get the majority of available merit pay increases, bonuses, and promotions.

performance appraisal
A structured formal interaction between a subordinate and supervisor that usually takes the form of a periodic interview in which the work performance of the subordinate is examined and discussed, with a view to identifying weaknesses and strengths as well as opportunities for improvement and skills development.

Appraisal results are also used to identify the poorer performers who may require some form of counseling or, in extreme cases, demotion, dismissal, or decreases in pay. (Organizations need to be aware of laws in their country that might restrict their capacity to dismiss employees or decrease pay.) Whether the assignment and justification of rewards and penalties are an appropriate use of performance appraisal is a very uncertain and contentious matter.

Many reputable sources have expressed doubts about the validity and reliability of the performance appraisal process. Some have even suggested that the process is so inherently flawed that it may be impossible to perfect it.[10]

At the other extreme, there are many strong advocates of performance appraisal. Some view it as potentially "… the most crucial aspect of organizational life."[11]

Clearly, there are many different opinions on how and when to apply the performance appraisal process. For instance, some believe that performance appraisal has many important employee development uses, but scorn any attempt to link the process to reward outcomes, such as pay raises and promotions.

This group believes that the linkage to reward outcomes reduces or eliminates the developmental value of appraisals. Rather than an opportunity for constructive review and encouragement, the reward-linked process is perceived as judgmental, punitive, and uncomfortable. In addition, employees under review may feel compelled to distort or deny the truth. They may become defensive. Whenever the employee's performance is rated as less than the best, or less than the level at which he or she perceives, the appraiser may be viewed as punitive. This can affect the manager's credibility and negatively impact the relationship with the employee. Even worse, the result can be resentment and serious morale damage, leading to workplace disruption and productivity declines.

Many appraisers feel uncomfortable with the combined role of judge and jury. The task also requires good record-keeping and interpersonal skills. The manager should justify the evaluation with specific examples. No one likes receiving criticism, so the manager must be skilled at avoiding a defensive response from the employee and dealing with conflict productively if it occurs. Because of a lack of comfort with these potential outcomes, managers may avoid giving honest feedback.

It is important, however, that when appraisals are conducted, the results are clearly linked to the rewards. This can help avoid situations in which employees perceive that merit raises and bonuses are decided arbitrarily and sometimes in secret by managers and supervisors.

Most of these problems can be avoided with the proper process in place and effective communication skills. Creating an effective performance management system starts with how a position is defined and ends when it has been determined why an excellent employee left the organization for another opportunity.

Within such a system, feedback to employees occurs regularly. Individual performance objectives are measurable and based on prioritized goals that support the accomplishment of the overall goals of the total organization. The vibrancy and performance of the organization can better be ensured because the focus is on development and providing appropriate opportunities for each employee.

Providing Performance Feedback

In a performance management system, feedback remains integral to successful practice. Ideally, however, the feedback is a discussion. Both the staff member and the manager have an equivalent opportunity to bring information to the dialogue.

Feedback is often obtained from peers, direct-reporting staff, and customers to enhance mutual understanding of an individual's contribution and developmental needs. (This is commonly known as 360-degree feedback.) The developmental plan establishes the organization's commitment to help each person continue to expand his or her knowledge and skills. This is the foundation upon which a continuously improving organization builds.

When providing performance feedback, consider the following:

- **Encourage discussion.** Research studies show that employees are likely to feel more satisfied with their appraisal result if they have the chance to talk freely and discuss their performance. It is also more likely that such employees will be better able to meet future performance goals.[12]

  Employees are also more likely to feel that the appraisal process is fair if they are given a chance to talk about their performance. This is especially so when employees are permitted to challenge and appeal their evaluation.[13]

- **Be constructive.** It is very important that employees recognize that negative appraisal feedback is provided with a constructive intention, that is, to help them overcome present difficulties and to improve their future performance. Employees will be less anxious about criticism and more likely to find it useful when they believe that the appraiser's intentions are helpful and constructive.[14]

  In contrast, other studies have reported that "destructive criticism"— which is vague, ill-informed, unfair, or harshly presented—will lead to such problems as anger, resentment, tension, and workplace conflict, as well as increased resistance to improvement, denial of problems, and poorer performance.[15]

- **Set performance goals.** It has been shown in numerous studies that setting goals is an important element in employee motivation. Goals can stimulate employee effort, focus attention, increase persistence, and encourage employees to find new and better ways to work.[16]

  The usefulness of goals as a stimulus to human motivation is one of the best-supported theories in management. It is also quite clear that goals that are "... specific, difficult and accepted by employees will lead to higher levels of performance than easy, vague goals (such as do your best) or no goals at all."[17]

- **Maintain credibility.** It is important that the appraiser be well informed and credible. Appraisers should feel comfortable with the techniques of appraisal and should be knowledgeable about the employee's job and performance. When these conditions exist, employees are more likely to view the appraisal process as accurate and fair. They also express more acceptance of the appraiser's feedback and a greater willingness to change.[18]

Dealing with Conflict

Invariably, when conducting performance appraisals, the need arises to provide an employee with less than flattering feedback. The skill and sensitivity used to handle these often difficult sessions is critical. If the appraisee accepts the negative feedback and resolves to improve, all is well. However, if the result is an angry or hurt employee, then the process of correction has failed. The performance of an employee in such cases is unlikely to improve and may deteriorate even further.

When providing criticism to an employee, consider the following techniques:

- **Self-auditing.** Appraisers should not confront employees directly with criticism. Rather, they should aim to let the evidence of poor performance emerge "naturally" during the course of the appraisal interview. This is done by way of open-ended questioning techniques that encourage employees to identify their own performance problems.[19]

  Instead of blunt statements or accusations, an appraiser should encourage an employee to talk freely about impressions of his or her performance. For example, consider the case of an employee who has had too many absent days. The appraiser, in accusatory mode, might say:

  "Your attendance record is unacceptable. You'll have to improve it."

  A better way to handle this might be to say:

  "Your attendance record shows that you had seven days off work in six months. What can you tell me about this?"

  Using this technique allows an appraiser to calmly present the evidence (resisting the temptation to label it as good or bad) and then invite the employee to comment. In many cases, an employee with problems will admit that weaknesses do exist. This is more likely to occur when an employee does not feel accused of anything, nor forced to make admissions that he or she does not wish to make. This technique described by Krein is a type of self-auditing, because it encourages underperforming employees to confront themselves with their own work and performance issues.

- **Ownership of problems.** Perhaps the most powerful aspect of the self-auditing process is that employees are generally more willing to accept personal "ownership" of problems that have been self-identified. This sense of ownership provides an effective basis for stimulating change and development.

  Nevertheless, some individuals will not admit to anything that appears to reflect poorly on them. With ego defenses on full alert, they will resist the process of self-auditing very strongly. In such cases, appraisers may have no choice but to confront the poor performer directly and firmly with the evidence they have.

  Sometimes the shock of direct confrontation will result in the employee admitting that he or she does need to make improvements. Sometimes it will just make his or her denial of the problem worse.

  In providing any feedback—especially negative feedback—appraisers should be willing and able to support their opinions with specific and clear examples. Vague generalizations should be avoided. The focus should be on job-related behaviors and attitudes. If a specific observation cannot be supported by clear evidence, or touches on issues that are not job-related, it may be best to exclude all mention of it.

Receiving Performance Feedback

As uncomfortable as giving performance feedback might be without the proper skills and preparation, receiving feedback might be worse, particularly if we aren't prepared. Probably the biggest danger of receiving feedback is becoming defensive. It is natural to want to defend ourselves if we feel we are being attacked. However, becoming defensive isn't helpful because it might damage our credibility and it inhibits our ability to listen. It can be helpful to remember that the comments from a trusted supervisor or manager are not meant to hurt you but to help you to perform better. Therefore, your purpose is to listen and to gather important information during the feedback process.

If you do have a tendency to become anxious or defensive in performance appraisal situations, you might find the tactics for dealing with presentation anxiety that were described in Chapter 7 to be helpful. Tactics for receiving feedback include the following:

- Listen carefully and avoid interrupting the appraiser.
- Ask questions for clarification.
- Acknowledge the feedback. Use the active listening techniques described in Chapter 9, such as paraphrasing, to let the appraiser know you understood what was said.
- Agree with what is true and possible, and acknowledge the appraiser's point of view (for example, "I can see how you got that impression."). Agreeing with what's true or possible does not mean that you agree to change your behavior or that you agree with a value judgment about you.
- Try to understand the appraiser's perspective. Doing so may enable you to gain a greater understanding of the issues.
- Ask for time to reflect, if needed. It is reasonable to ask for time to think about what was said, but don't use this time to avoid the issue. Make an appointment to get back to the appraiser.

Summary

When preparing for the job application process, researching potential employers, your chosen field or industry, and the overall job market will provide you the information you need to develop most of the content of your employment message. The other information you will need are the skills, abilities, experience, and personal characteristics that might appeal to a potential employer. With this information, you are prepared to draft and develop a résumé and an application letter as well as prepare for the job interview process.

A résumé is a list of the skills, abilities, and experience that you bring to an employer and is aimed at getting you a job interview. Templates for creating résumés are available in Microsoft Word and other software programs. A résumé must show that you are qualified for the position for which you are applying and should be carefully prepared to eliminate any errors.

An application letter is generally targeted to a specific employer and is a persuasive message that is intended to highlight your accomplishments and relate them to the specific contributions you can make to an organization. Your research should provide the information you need to identify the organization's needs and match your own abilities and skills to those needs.

During the job interview process, the interviewer and the interviewee are attempting to convey and obtain information verbally, a process that requires good listening skills on both their parts. Much information that is passed may also be in the form of nonverbal communication. As with many communication situations, proper preparation and planning can help ensure a successful interview, both on the part of the interviewee as well as the interviewer. After each interview, it is important to immediately send a thank-you email to help distinguish yourself from the competition.

During the performance appraisal process, preparation on the part of the appraiser as well as the appraisee can help to ensure that the appraisal is useful to both parties. To ensure success, an effective performance appraisal process needs to be in place, one that ensures that both parties know the specific requirements of the job so that specific issues related to its performance can be addressed clearly.

Key Term

performance appraisal, 238

Discussion Questions

1. What is the purpose of researching employers, your chosen field or industry, and the job market before beginning the application process? How can doing so benefit the applicant?
2. What are the differences between a résumé and an application letter?
3. What is behavioral interviewing? Describe the STAR approach for formulating responses to behavioral interview questions.
4. Why is it important to send a thank-you email after an interview?
5. What is the appropriate stance to take during a performance appraisal? What are some of the phrases or statements that might be used to help create this stance?

Applications

1. Find and print a job description for a position for which you might apply. Working alone, write down the skills and abilities that are described in the job description.

   - Identify situations in which you have demonstrated these skills.
   - Write down an example of a time you exhibited that skill.

- Consider whether you can add a specific result.
- Pair up with another student and share your list.
  - Could the wording be improved?
  - Brainstorm additional skills you might address and their wording.

  How would this exercise change the content or approach to your résumé? Application letter? Job interview?

2. Review your Facebook page, Twitter feed, or other social networking site. Identify the changes that need to be made and write a plan for revising your content so that it showcases the abilities and skills that employers may find attractive.

3. Prepare written answers to all the behavioral interview questions listed in Table 8-1, which can be found on page 232 of this chapter.

4. Identify a job for which you might be interviewing applicants in the future. Prepare a list of questions that you might use to conduct an employment interview for the position.

5. Prepare for a performance appraisal by listing your accomplishments over the past year and your goals for improvement and growth for the coming year. Be sure to provide specific evidence of your accomplishments and identify the concrete ways that your goals will benefit your employer and you as an employee in terms of your contribution.

CASE ANALYSIS

THE NEW YORK STOCK EXCHANGE: AN IDENTITY IN JEOPARDY

Robert Zito, executive vice president of communications for the New York Stock Exchange (NYSE), could predict the outcome of the late-day board meeting currently in progress. Recent events had proven particularly damaging for the NYSE and its executive team. Now, several influential stakeholders were upset and calling for NYSE Chairman and CEO Richard Grasso to step down. The chief executive and his board of directors were meeting to discuss this issue.

Zito thought back over the media relations nightmare that began with the August 27 announcement of a $139.5 million payout of the CEO's deferred compensation package. Initially, the head of corporate communications felt this story played fairly well in the press. There was plenty of criticism about the size of the package, but he thought his team had been effective in delivering the message of why Grasso deserved the money.[20] But, instead of fading away, new developments kept making the story worse.

The phone rang at Zito's desk. The communications director picked it up to see if his prediction was true.

New York Stock Exchange

The New York Stock Exchange has had a long and illustrious history rooted in the very foundation of America's financial markets. In the mid-1700s,

stockbrokers, merchants, and auctioneers bought and sold equities in offices and coffeehouses both on and around Wall Street.

In the absence of both a set location to trade and a time to meet, potential buyers and sellers had to search for one another, making trading difficult. On May 17, 1792, two dozen Wall Street brokers met and signed an agreement to trade strictly with one another. Signed at an informal location underneath a buttonwood tree at 68 Wall Street, this two-sentence document became known as the "Buttonwood Agreement" and would evolve the group into today's New York Stock Exchange.[21]

In 1934, the exchange registered as a national securities exchange with the Securities and Exchange Commission (SEC), hired its first paid president in 1938 and established a thirty-three-member board of governors. This board, consisting of exchange members, nonmember partners, and public representatives, was converted into a board of directors in 1972, a year after the Big Board incorporated as a not-for-profit corporation. The board consists of twelve directors from the securities industry and twelve public directors, and includes the chairman and CEO, two presidents, co-COOs, and executive vice chairmen.[22]

In 1817, thirty stocks traded on the "New York Stock and Exchange Board." By 1863, the name was changed to New York Stock Exchange, still listing thirty stocks. In an open auction, brokers would call out their bids to buy or sell stock from their assigned chairs. This is why members are said to have a "seat" on the exchange. This membership gives the right to trade stocks and can be bought directly from owners of the 1,366 seats. Large financial firms and specialist firms own the majority of seats in the modern NYSE. Seats first were sold for $25; today the price exceeds $2 million.

Chairman and CEO Richard Grasso

Richard Grasso grew up in the Jackson Heights section of Queens in New York City and aspired to be a policeman. After two years at Pace University, he dropped out and joined the army, earning a good conduct medal and a badge as a sharpshooter. His first job after the army was in 1968 as a clerk in the NYSE's stock-listing department, paying $80 a week. Rising swiftly through the ranks, Grasso became a vice president in nine years, an NYSE president ten years later, and then chairman and chief executive in his twenty-sixth year with the Big Board.[23]

The last seven years were strong for the NYSE. Under Dick Grasso's leadership, the exchange remained competitive and relevant despite the growth of the NASDAQ, a slew of corporate scandals, and a major terrorism attack. In fact, the events of September 11, 2001, could have been devastating to the NYSE and the American economy. Instead, under his leadership, the NYSE was up and running within one week of the falling of the Twin Towers. The opening bell rang on Monday, September 17, 2001, delivering to the world a message that the U.S. economy had not been beaten and firmly establishing Chairman and CEO Grasso as an exceptional and renowned leader.

NYSE Trading Model and Electronic Exchanges

Trading on the NYSE continues to use the original model. Buy and sell orders arrive at the exchange via brokers and are handled at the trading post by a specialist. Each specialist handles a very small number of stocks (or just one). It is the specialist who handles the "book" listing all *limit orders* (see glossary) awaiting execution. Specialists are required to trade from their own portfolios in the

situation where there is an imbalance in the number of buyers and sellers, thereby improving liquidity.

The American Stock Exchange (AMEX) founded its roots in the early days of the NYSE, when individuals traded stocks that did not meet NYSE listing requirements on the street at the steps of the NYSE. (Currently, these requirements include $40.0 million market capitalization, $40.0 million in assets, and $2.0 million in earnings each of the past two years, among other requirements.) Despite developing into a major exchange, the AMEX now handles mostly small stocks as a result of a recent merger with the NASDAQ.

In 1961, the SEC commissioned a study to examine the fragmentation of the *over-the-counter market* (OTC: see glossary). As a result, the National Association of Securities Dealers (NASD) was commissioned in 1971 by the SEC to implement a solution. The NASD created the NASDAQ (National Association of Securities Dealers Automated Quotation), an electronic "exchange," or a place where buyers and sellers could electronically meet and agree on prices for securities not listed on the NYSE or any other formal exchange. Over the next thirty years, the NASDAQ has surpassed the NYSE in trading volume (both number of shares traded and the value of those shares).[24]

The NASDAQ differs from the NYSE in that there is no trading floor; all trades occur electronically, providing faster trades, potentially superior *spreads* (see glossary), and lower transaction costs. In this electronic marketplace, millions of participants compete for orders, improving prices. The addition of *market makers* (see glossary) improve liquidity, as they trade from their own portfolios (as do NYSE specialists).

The advent of electronic communication networks (ECNs) has further improved the competitive advantages of the non-NYSE markets. ECNs are networks that allow investors to trade *directly* with one another, routing and matching orders through bypassing an "exchange" altogether. Advocates of ECNs claim fair, neutral, and efficient trading, better anonymity, lower-cost trading, and the ability to trade after-hours.

The NYSE remains the premier exchange despite the strong competition from the NASDAQ and ECNs. Some industry pundits claim the NASDAQ model offers lower trading costs under the guise of faster trades and therefore better prices; many others see the NYSE delivering the better deal for investors by actually delivering a more competitive price as well as lower volatility.[25] However, the prestige, selectivity, and brand recognition associated with the Big Board drives the biggest firms to continue to list with the NYSE.[26]

Corporate Governance on the Hot Seat

Throughout the late 1990s and into early 2002, several major issues arose that questioned corporate governance measures in corporate America. Among these are Enron's off-balance-sheet financing leading to the demise of auditor Arthur Anderson, accounting scandals at WorldCom and Global Crossing, and arrests of senior executives at Tyco International accused of looting hundreds of millions of dollars from corporate coffers. In February 2002, then-SEC chairman Harvey Pitt appealed to the NYSE to review corporate governance policies of firms listed on the NYSE. As a result, the NYSE Board approved a list of changes in August 2002 and submitted them as a request for rules changes to the SEC. By April of the following year, the SEC issued a document soliciting comments from "interested persons."[27] Comments received were supportive of the primary changes, focusing on board composition (sufficient outside directors) and audit procedures. Throughout the summer of 2003, the general tone in the business press was extremely supportive of the proposed governance improvements.

A Time of Turmoil

At the end of 2002, the NYSE wielded perhaps the strongest brand equity to date. But a series of events in 2003 would become a dangerous weight on the Big Board's name. It all began in February 2003, when Dick Grasso was appointed to the board of Home Depot Inc. Along with his board membership of Computer Associates Inc., the move is criticized as a potential conflict of interest as both companies are listed on the NYSE.[28]

On March 23, 2003, the NYSE announced its intention of naming Citigroup chairman and chief executive Sanford Weill to the board as a public director.[29] The exchange was publicly criticized for naming a CEO whose brokerage firm (Salomon Smith Barney) was part of a Wall Street research analyst scandal.[30] Two days later, the nomination was withdrawn.

On March 26, 2003, SEC chairman William Donaldson sent a letter to all self-regulating organizations (SROs) regarding corporate governance issues. In the letter, the chairman requested a review of the corporate governance of the NYSE, in a reply due May 15, 2003.

On April 17, 2003, the *Wall Street Journal* broke a story stating the NYSE was investigating front-running on its trading floor, which is a federal offense. In response, the NYSE released a statement indicating that the investigation was regarding treading "ahead" of investors, not front-running.[31] Although the front-running part of the story was inaccurate, the *Wall Street Journal*'s attention to the issue forced the NYSE to reveal information regarding its investigation of possible specialist violations.[32] This announcement triggered criticism of the NYSE trading model.

On May 7, 2003, the *Wall Street Journal* broke a story announcing Grasso's $10 million 2002 pay package. This article put the NYSE on the defensive and angered its floor traders, who were not aware of the large executive pay. The news also began a very public debate about the NYSE and its role as a regulator. The exchange itself establishes stiff regulations and rules regarding corporate governance, yet the exchange was paying its chairman a salary on par with some of the highest-paid CEOs in the country.

To meet the SEC requirement mandated in the March 26 letter, the NYSE Board of Directors formed a special Governance Committee. Chairman Grasso forwarded a copy of the draft report (an ongoing process) in his May 15, 2003, response.

U.S. Securities and Exchange Commission

Founded in 1934 by Congress, the U.S. Securities and Exchange Commission was created to monitor the securities industry. The SEC exists to protect investors and maintain the integrity of the securities markets. To achieve this goal, the SEC regulates the information public companies must disclose, including key financial data and other information necessary to make an informed investing decision. Additionally, the SEC oversees other members of the securities world including stock exchanges like the NYSE, broker-dealers, investment advisors, mutual funds, and public utility holding companies. The SEC also has enforcement authority and every year brings civil enforcement actions against individuals and institutions that break securities laws.[33]

The current chairman, William H. Donaldson, was appointed February 18, 2003, by the president of the United States. Donaldson served as chairman of the NYSE from 1990 to 1995 and brings an extensive business background to the chairman seat.

An Unusual Pay Package

On August 27, the NYSE promulgated a press release announcing a contract extension for Chairman and CEO Dick Grasso from 2005 to 2007. His pay would be maintained at $1.7 million with a bonus of $1.0 million, and would include a payout from his deferred compensation, retirement, and savings plan. According to the press release, this includes his "savings account balance of $40.0mm, his previously accrued retirement benefit of $51.6mm and his previously earned account balance of $47.9mm relating to prior incentive awards."[34]

The business press, fund managers, government, and regulators immediately released a flurry of press releases, articles, and letters criticizing the $139.5 million package as far too large for an executive whose primary role is to be a regulator. Members of the compensation committee defended the contract provisions, saying Grasso deserved to be paid commensurate with the level of other financial services industry executives because he both runs a competitive business and serves as a regulator.

Dissent arose from within the ranks; traders on the NYSE floor were particularly upset because the NYSE had been raising fees required of them to support technological advances to thwart the rising competition from the NASDAQ, totaling nearly $80 million over only a few years. As well, decimalization[35] further squeezed profits from the specialists and brokers by narrowing the quoted prices from 12.5 cents to one penny.

Corporate governance questions were now the key issue and the criticisms were directed at the core of the Big Board itself. The key governance issues at the NYSE were the perceived conflicts of interest of the owners, management, and customers of the Big Board. Brokers and specialists handle the orders of individual investors, and at the same time own the NYSE itself. These same seat owners choose the board of directors of the exchange who sit on the audit and compensation committees and set the pay of the CEO. This same CEO and board oversee the regulatory arm of the NYSE, responsible for policing the very brokers and specialists who own the exchange.

The SEC Steps In

On September 2, 2003, Donaldson sent a letter to H. Carl McCall, NYSE compensation committee chairman. In the letter, Donaldson expressed great concern about Grasso's pay package, stating, "In my view, the approval of Mr. Grasso's pay package raises serious questions regarding the effectiveness of the NYSE's current governance structure."[36] Also included in the letter was a list of nine requests regarding the terms of the pay package and related information due to the SEC by September 9, 2003. As Zito read the letter, it was clear the amount and type of information Donaldson was requesting was going to be an enormous task given the short time allotted for a response. In addition, Donaldson's letter was public information, which meant Zito had to address the deluge of media calls, coming in by the dozens.

Complications, Complications

A complex communication challenge became significantly more difficult when, on September 9, the NYSE responded to SEC chairman Donaldson's letter of a week earlier. In this communiqué, the NYSE revealed that Grasso was owed an *additional* $48.0 million previously undisclosed payout. While the NYSE's position was that this information was not significant (because it was *future* compensation), the public outcry was enormous. Appearing on CNBC and in newspaper interviews, the CEO publicly announced that he would forgo the additional monies to end the time when the exchange was "preoccupied talking about the compensation of its leader."[37]

The Rest of the Story

By September 16, 2003, Grasso was clearly under fire and the fervor was only increasing. Several strong stakeholders, including major fund managers, were calling for his resignation, and floor traders were visibly upset with the giant pay package. One NYSE seat-holder stated, "People have problems down here on the floor with how much [Mr. Grasso] has made, especially considering the slowdown in business, [and] the increase in technology costs."[38]

Late in the day on September 17, Grasso called an emergency board meeting to discuss the situation. In the meeting, he offered to resign as chairman and CEO only if the board requested it. The board voted for his resignation, 13 to 7. High-profile directors, including the Goldman Sachs CEO, former secretary of state Madeline Albright, and the CEO of J.P. Morgan, all voted for Grasso to leave.[39]

What Now?

Zito has several problems on his hands. The NYSE has no senior leadership and reaction from the SEC and other stakeholders demonstrates the NYSE has a larger problem than an overpaid executive. How should he proceed from here? Who are his key audiences at this point, and how does he go about reestablishing the NYSE brand in the face of harsh criticism by the SEC?

Discussion Questions

1. Which stakeholders are most important to Zito and the NYSE?
2. What are the critical issues in this case? Can you rank order them?
3. What are the NYSE's business problems? Which ones need to be addressed first?
4. How can Zito begin to rebuild the NYSE brand?
5. Do you think the NYSE has a place in the future of securities markets?

This case was prepared by Research Assistants Stephen A. Abdalla and Stephanie J. Sanderson under the direction of James S. O'Rourke, Concurrent Professor of Management, as the basis for class discussion rather than to illustrate either effective or ineffective handling of an administrative situation.

Endnotes

1. Robbins, S. P. (2001). *Organizational behavior* (9th ed.). Upper Saddle River, NJ: Prentice Hall, p. 103.
2. Moore, G. (2004, August 29). Investigation during job search allows you to select wisely. *The Daily Breeze*, E1.
3. Pirisi, A. (2003). Lying in job interviews. *Psychology Today* (May–June). Retrieved March 25, 2005, from http://www.psychologytoday.com/articles/pto-20030711-000001.html.
4. Ibid.
5. Ibid.
6. Lying: How can you protect your company? (n.d.) *Your Workplace, Monthly Newsletter of Westaff* XXXVI. Retrieved March 25, 2005, from http://www.westaff.com/yourworkplace/ywissue37_full.html.
7. Lying: How can you protect your company? (n.d.) *Your Workplace, Monthly Newsletter of Westaff* XXXVI. Retrieved March 25, 2005, from http://www.westaff.com/yourworkplace/ywissue37_full.html.
8. Del Monte, J. (2009). IT employer information—Cost of hiring/turnover. JDA Professional Services, Inc. Retrieved October 16, 2009, from http://www.jdapsi.com/Client/articles/Default.php?Article=coh.
9. Heathfield, S. M. (2009). Performance appraisals don't work: The traditional performance appraisal process. Retrieved October 16, 2009, from http://humanresources.about.com/od/performanceevals/a/perf_appraisal.htm.
10. Derven, M. G. (1990). The paradox of performance appraisals. *Personnel Journal*, 69 (February), 107–111.
11. Lawrie, J. (1990). Prepare for a performance appraisal. *Personnel Journal*, 69 (April), 132–136.
12. Nemoroff, W. F., & Wexley, K. N. (1979). An exploration of the relationships between the performance feedback interview characteristics and interview outcomes as perceived by managers and subordinates. *Journal of Occupational Psychology*, 52, 25–34.
13. Greenberg, J. (1986). Determinants of perceived fairness of performance evaluation. *Journal of Applied Psychology*, 71, 340–342.

14. Fedor, D. B., Eder, R. W., & Buckley, M. R. (1989). The contributory effects of supervisor intentions on subordinate feedback responses. *Organizational Behavior and Human Decision Processes, 44,* 396–414.

15. Baron, R. A. (1988). Negative effects of destructive criticism: Impact on conflict, self-efficacy, and task performance. *Journal of Applied Psychology, 73,* 199–207.

16. Locke, E. A., Shaw, K. N., Saari, L. M., & Latham, G. P. (1981). Goal setting and task performance: 1969–1980. *Psychological Bulletin, 90,* 125–152.

17. Harris, D. M., & DeSimone, R. L. (1994). *Human resource development.* Fort Worth, TX: Dryden Press.

18. Bannister, B. D. (1986). Performance outcome feedback and attributional feedback: Interactive effects on recipient responses. *Journal of Applied Psychology, 71,* 203–210.

19. Krein, T. J. (1990). Performance reviews that rate an "A." *Personnel Journal, 67* (May), 38–40.

20. Telephone Interview with Robert Zito, executive vice president – communications, New York Stock Exchange, October 24, 2003.

21. New York Stock Exchange. (2002). Guide to the world's leading securities market. http://www.nyse.com (PDF document).

22. http://www.nyse.com.

23. Kelly, K., & Craig, S. (2003). NYSE's Grasso quits at a critical moment for financial markets. *Wall Street Journal Europe,* September 18.

24. http://www.nasdaq.com/about/index.html.

25. Non, S. G., & Kary, T. (2001). NYSE, NASDAQ joust for tech companies. *CNET.com,* May 28, http://news.com.com/2100-1017-258270.html?legacy=cnet.

26. Telephone Interview with Wendy Wilson, executive vice president – investor relations, Hillenbrand Industries, October 28, 2003.

27. U. S. Securities and Exchange Commission. (2003). NYSE rulemaking: Self-regulatory organizations; notice of filing of proposed rule change and amendment no. 1 thereto by the New York Stock Exchange, in relating to corporate governance. April 11.

28. NYSE's Grasso remains under the gun. *Reuters,* September 16, 2003, http://www.forbes.com/newswire/2003/09/16/rtr1083379.html.

29. NYSE Statement, "Investigation of specialist trading practices," April 22, 2003, www.nyse.com.

30. White. (2003). SEC chairman assails NYSE on Grasso pay. *Washington Post,* September 3, E0.

31. *Front-running* is when a specialist purposefully uses information regarding trades to make additional profits (equivalent to "insider trading"). Trading "ahead" of investors is less severe, and occurs when a specialist executes his/her portfolio trading prior to that of a valid order from an investor.

32. Berkowitz. (2003). NYSE's Grasso is greener. *Newsday,* August 28.

33. About us, www.sec.gov/about/whatwedo.html.

34. New York Stock Exchange. (2003). NYSE announces new contract for Dick Grasso through May 2007. August 27.

35. In early 2001, the NYSE shifted from quoting prices in 1/8 dollar (12.5 cent) increments to decimals.

36. Statement by SEC chairman: Letter to NYSE regarding NYSE executive compensation, September 2, 2003, www.sec.gov/news/speech/spch090203whd.htm.

37. Harrigan, S. NYSE says it owes Grasso $48M more: But chairman decides to tear up IOU. *Newsday,* http://www.newsday.com.

38. Kelly. (2003). NYSE member calls for change in management. *Wall Street Journal,* September 9.

39. Costello, C., & Lee, C. (2003). Big Board resignation: Richard Grasso quits as NYSE chairman. *The America's Intelligence Wire,* September 18.

Communicating with Employees

Grady Reese/iStockphoto.com

After reading this chapter, you will be able to

▸ Identify different interpersonal styles of communication and recognize the importance of being assertive and creating a genuine dialogue in the workplace.

▸ Understand the different elements of nonverbal communication.

▸ Identify whether you are an effective listener and put into practice the steps to become a more effective listener.

▸ Understand how to motivate employees through communication practices.

▸ Communicate change to employees.

Case Questions:

1. As a newcomer to the organization, what does Lucy need to do to successfully make change within her team? What obstacles must she overcome and how might she do so?

2. Did Lucy's supervisor make the right call in appointing Lucy team leader? Are there advantages to her being a newcomer to the organization? What might her supervisor have done, if anything, to make Lucy's transition to team leader easier?

3. How difficult is it to make change within an organization? What factors may affect the success of organizational change efforts?

The Case of Resisted Change Efforts

"What's wrong?" Rita asked her friend Lucy as the waiter placed their coffee on the table. Both women said "thanks" simultaneously to the young man and then Rita resumed. "You sounded so demoralized on the phone. I hope it isn't your new job."

"Well, unfortunately, it is," Lucy replied, taking a sip of coffee. "I feel like I've been bushwhacked."

"How so?" Rita asked.

"You know that I've been appointed team leader for the COMPLEXion line. My supervisor told me that she was appointing me because she wanted to see some changes. When I got hired, I heard so many positive things about my colleagues, but now I'm wondering if any of them are true." Lucy paused and picked up a menu. "You know, I haven't had any lunch. Do you want to get something to nibble on?"

"Unfortunately, I've had my lunch and I'm afraid I overate," Rita giggled, then added, "As usual. But please, go ahead and get something. I don't mind if you eat. Just don't order anything too yummy. I may be tempted to eat more."

Lucy signaled to the waiter.

"So what's going on?" Rita prodded. "What's the deal with your colleagues?"

"Well, to sum it up, they don't want to change. They have been working on this product line, some for ten years or more, and they don't see any need for it. You know the old saw, 'If it ain't broke, why fix it?' And, of course, they wonder who am I—a newcomer—to tell them any different. You would have thought that my supervisor would have expected this and would have warned me. After all, she's worked there a decade, too." Lucy stopped and took another drink from her cup, then added, "Maybe I'm not the right person for the job."

She turned to the waiter who had approached the table. "Yes, Miss," he said. "What can I get you?"

Interpersonal Communication in the Workplace

From an organizational perspective, relationships can play an important role in producing effective supervision, promoting social support among employees, building personal influence, and ensuring productivity through smooth work flow. **Interpersonal communication** involves mutual influence, usually for the purpose of managing relationships.[1]

The recent flattening of organizational hierarchies and resulting interdependency of work tasks among employees, as well as the increasing diversity of the workplace, creates a need for corporate cultures of trust built on respect for differences and mutual cooperation. Informal interpersonal relationships and communication networks are the most dynamic sources of power in organizations today. (Communication networks were discussed in Chapter 5.) This change provides an opportunity for leaders and aspiring leaders whose task is to motivate and inspire others through their communication skills and knowledge. Compared to these dynamic sources of power, more formal relationships are slower and less trustworthy sources of information. Knowing this, most decision makers rely heavily on verbal information from people they trust.

The need for excellent interpersonal skills is echoed in a *Wall Street Journal* survey, in which recruiters said that such skills and the ability to work well in a team were the top two characteristics they found most attractive in prospective employees. Interpersonal skills and the ability to work well in a team are founded upon trust. **Trust** can be understood as the confidence that our peers' intentions are good.[2] In other words, we must believe that those with whom we work will not act opportunistically or take advantage of us and others to narrowly pursue their own self-interests.

Recent studies indicate that trust has five components: integrity, competence, consistency, loyalty, and openness.[3] *Integrity* refers to a person's ethical character and basic honesty. To feel that our peers are *competent*, we must be convinced that they have the technical knowledge and interpersonal skills to perform their jobs. If we don't believe coworkers are competent, we are unlikely to depend upon them or respect their opinions on work-related matters. We are more able to trust those who appear *consistent* in their behavior or who are reliable, predictable, and demonstrate good judgment. We tend to trust others who are *loyal* and willing to protect and help others to save face. Finally, we tend to trust those who are *open* and, conversely, find it difficult to trust those who appear evasive, deceptive, or secretive.

Additional factors affect our ability to forge the relationships businesspeople depend upon so much: valuing relationships, assertiveness, and active listening.[4] The first step in building interpersonal relationships at work is learning to *recognize the importance of relationships* in business—if you haven't already. This issue was discussed in much detail in Chapter 3 in the examination of the purposes of communication, in which establishing goodwill was seen as critical in the workplace. For many individuals, interpersonal communication is the work, particularly for managers.

interpersonal communication
Communication involving mutual influence, usually for the purpose of managing relationships.

trust
The confidence that our peers' intentions are good.

CriticalThinking

Of the five elements of trust, which do you most consistently demonstrate in your relationships? To which element might you devote more attention to develop more trusting relationships, not only with friends but also with colleagues and peers?

Interpersonal Style

In addition to valuing relationships in the workplace, it is also important to develop an effective interpersonal style of communicating. Broadly, there are three interpersonal styles: assertiveness, avoidance, and aggressiveness. Of these, assertiveness is generally considered the most effective. This becomes clearer when you consider the alternatives.

Avoiding, passive-aggressive individuals tend to whine, complain, and fret about problems at work, but when asked directly what is wrong, they say nothing.[5] This strategy, known as **avoidance**, is defined as a conscious attempt to avoid engaging with people in the dominant group.[6] Avoidance, which is an attempt to separate by having as little to do as possible with the dominant group, is also considered *passive*. The result of an avoiding, passive approach is a consistent inability to raise and resolve problems, needs, issues, and concerns.

At the other extreme, **aggressiveness** in individuals sabotages their ability to meet their needs and to establish supportive relationships by creating defensiveness and alienating others.[7] Aggressive behaviors include those perceived as hurtfully expressive, self-promoting, and assuming control over the choices of others.[8] Aggressive individuals are also described as argumentative. Not only are such individuals more aggressive, they are more insecure and less likely to be well regarded or happy at work.[9]

In contrast to avoidance and aggression, **assertiveness** is defined as "self-enhancing, expressive communication that takes into account both the communicator's and others' needs."[10] Assertiveness involves clearly articulating what you want from others in terms of behavior. It is direct, yet not attacking or blaming. Assertiveness is associated with positive impressions and overall quality of work experience.

It is common to withdraw in conflict situations, but you can be more assertive by following these four steps:

1. Describe how you view the situation.
   Example: *I noticed that you didn't clock in on time three days this week.*

2. Disclose your feelings.
   Example: *I'm concerned that this may become a pattern.*

3. Identify the effects.
   Example: *When you are late, it disrupts the work flow in assembly.*

4. Be silent and wait for a response. Make sure that your nonverbal cues are in alignment with your message.

Assertiveness, however, should not be confused with aggression, because it not only involves stating our own needs clearly but also being sensitive to the needs of others. The goal of conversations should be to establish a genuine dialogue rather than to debate or win an argument.[11] As was discussed in Chapter 2, dialogue involves establishing a climate of equality, listening with empathy, and trying to bring assumptions out into the open. Table 9-1 illustrates the difference between an argumentative style of communication and a dialogue.

As was discussed in Chapter 5, organizations may have supportive or defensive climates of communication. As a leader, you can do much to create a supportive communication climate by adhering to the following steps:

1. **Describe your own feelings rather than evaluate the behavior of others.** One way to avoid evaluating others is to use a passive sentence structure and eliminate the use of the word *you*. Instead, use the word *I* to describe your own thoughts or feelings about the situation.

avoidance
A conscious attempt to avoid engaging with people in the dominant group.

aggressiveness
Behavior in which individuals sabotage their ability to meet their needs and to establish supportive relationships by creating defensiveness and alienating others.

assertiveness
Self-enhancing, expressive communication that takes into account both the communicator's and others' needs.

DEBATE	**DIALOGUE**
There is one right answer and you assume that you have it.	Many people may have part of the answer; together we can find the best solution.
The goal is to win.	The goal is to seek common ground and agreement.
The focus is on winning; to do so, you must prove the other person wrong.	You search for the strengths in what others say and value those aspects.
You defend your views.	You use the contributions of others to improve your own thinking.

Table 9-1 Comparison of Debate versus Dialogic Style of Communication.

Source: Adapted from Yankelovich, D. (1999). *The Magic of Dialogue: Transforming Conflict into Cooperation* (New York: Simon & Schuster).

Example: *I am concerned that we won't meet the deadline if we all aren't here every day performing our part of the project.*

2. **Solve problems rather than try to control others.** In reality, we have little control over others. Consequently, it is generally better to get people involved in providing solutions to problems that exist.
Example: *What are your thoughts on dealing with this issue?*

3. **Empathize with others.** Empathy is the ability to understand the feelings of others and to predict the emotional responses they may have to situations. (Recall the discussion of emotional intelligence in Chapter 2.)
Example: *I can see that you are very frustrated by this situation.*

4. **Be genuine rather than manipulative.** A manipulative person has hidden agendas. A genuine person discusses issues and problems openly and honestly.

5. **Be flexible rather than rigid.** A "you're wrong, I'm right" attitude creates a defensive climate. Instead of making rigid pronouncements, you can qualify your statements.
Example: *I may be wrong, but it seems to me that ...*

6. **Present yourself as equal rather than superior to others.** Although you may have authority over others, "pulling rank" does not create a cooperative communication climate.
Example: *Let's work on this together.*

Like assertiveness and dialogue, *listening* is a learned skill and one that very few individuals ever master. Talking to someone who really knows how to listen actively makes you feel valued, important, and free to speak your mind.[12] (Active listening is discussed in more detail later in this chapter.) In an ideal communication situation, assertiveness and active listening go hand in hand as people are able to express their own perceptions and desires and simultaneously attend to the perceptions and desires of others. As you may recognize, these two skills are the foundation of the dialogic model of communication introduced in Chapter 2.

Nonverbal Communication

Developing an awareness of nonverbal communication is important, because during face-to-face communication, most of the information that is provided comes in the form of nonverbal cues. In fact, some say that nonverbal cues provide 93 percent of the meaning exchanged in face-to-face communication situations, including oral presentations and meetings. Of that percentage, 35 percent of the meaning comes from tone of voice, whereas 58 percent comes from gestures, facial expressions, and other physical cues.

These statistics mean that the way business communicators think and talk about themselves and others must be consistent with the way they act in that regard to be believable and credible. This notion is reflected in the adage "actions speak louder than words." Because of this belief, it is important to ensure **strategic alignment** between your oral messages and your nonverbal ones.

Nonverbal communication is defined as the "attributes or actions of humans, other than the use of words themselves, which have socially shared meaning, are intentionally sent or interpreted as intentional, are consciously sent or consciously received, and have the potential for feedback from the receiver."[13]

In nonverbal communication, communication signals are multiple and simultaneous. These signals include information that we receive from another person's facial expressions and eyes; body posture, movement, and appearance; the use of space; the use of time; touching; vocal cues; and clothing and other artifacts.

Paralanguage

Paralanguage refers to the rate, pitch, and volume qualities of the voice that interrupt or temporarily take the place of speech and affect the meaning of a message.[14] Paralanguage includes such vocal qualifiers as pitch (high or low); intensity (loud or soft); extent (drawls and accents); emotional characterizers, such as laughing or crying; and segregates, such as saying, "uh," "um," or "uh-huh." In the United States, some vocal qualifiers may communicate emotion; increased volume or rate may indicate anger, for example.

Cultural differences also exist. Arabs speak loudly to indicate strength and sincerity, while Filipinos speak softly to indicate good breeding and education. Italians and Arabs speak more rapidly than Americans.

The lack of vocalization, or silence, also communicates differing meanings depending on culture. People in the United States, Germany, France, and Southern Europe are uncomfortable with silence. People in East Asia consider silence an important part of business and social discourse and not a failure to communicate. Silence in Finland and East Asia is associated with listening and learning; silence protects privacy and individualism and shows respect for the privacy and individualism of others.[15]

Bodily Movement and Facial Expression

The study of posture, movement, gestures, and facial expression is called **kinesics**. Like many aspects of communication, the meaning of body movements and facial expressions can differ by culture. Although many people in the United States may sprawl when they are seated and slouch when they stand, such postures would be considered rude in Germany. Crossing the legs or feet is common in the United States, but doing so in the Middle East is inappropriate, because showing the sole of your shoe or bottom of your foot to someone is considered rude.

Gestures have different meanings depending on the culture, too. In the United States, people generally gesture moderately, whereas Italians, Greeks, and some Latin Americans use more dramatic gestures when speaking. The Chinese and

strategic alignment
The degree to which your nonverbal messages match your oral ones.

nonverbal communication
The attributes or actions of humans, other than the use of words themselves, which have socially shared meaning, are intentionally sent or interpreted as intentional, are consciously sent or consciously received, and have the potential for feedback from the receiver.

kinesics
The study of posture, movement, gestures, and facial expression as channels of communication.

Japanese, in contrast, tend to keep their hands and arms close to their bodies when speaking.

Even the use of facial expressions differs by culture. In China, people rarely express emotion, whereas the Japanese may smile to show a variety of emotions, such as happiness, sadness, or even anger.

Gaze and eye contact also differ by culture. People of the United States, Canada, Great Britain, and Eastern Europe favor direct eye contact. In these cultures, eye contact is considered a sign of respect and attentiveness. People who avoid contact may be considered untrustworthy, unfriendly, insecure, or inattentive.[16] People from Germany and the Middle East favor direct eye contact but the gaze is so intense it may make people otherwise accustomed to direct eye contact uncomfortable. In other countries, respect is shown by avoiding direct eye contact. These places include Japan, China, Indonesia, Latin America, the Caribbean, and parts of Africa. In Egypt, there is no eye contact between men and women who do not know each other and in India, eye contact is avoided between people of different socioeconomic levels.[17]

In the United States, Albert Mehrabian studied nonverbal communication by examining the concepts of liking, status, and responsiveness of people in communication situations. He found the following:

- Liking was often expressed by leaning forward, standing face-to-face and in close proximity, increased touching, relaxed posture, open arms and body, positive facial expression, and eye contact.
- High status or power is communicated nonverbally by taking up more space through bigger gestures and a relaxed posture, including when sitting, and less eye contact. This is an important issue for women and some people from cultures other than the United States to consider since they may have been socialized to appear small by taking up less space.
- Responsiveness is exhibited nonverbally by moving toward the other person, using spontaneous gestures, shifting posture and position, and facial expressiveness. The face and body should provide positive feedback to those with whom you are communicating.

In other words, body language is a strong indicator of the extent to which communicators like one another and are interested in each other's views. In addition, it indicates the perceived status, or power relationship, between the communicators. Understanding the use and meaning of body language is helpful in all types of face-to-face communication situations, including job interviews. During a job interview, you can indicate your interest in the position by leaning forward in your chair, maintaining eye contact with the interviewer, using animated facial expressions, and varying the volume, rate, and pitch of your voice.

All these nonverbal communication behaviors can be used when appropriate to increase your ability to establish credibility and a positive relationship with your audience in speaking situations.

Bodily Appearance

somatotype
Body type, which is a combination of height, weight, and muscularity.

Our body type and physical attractiveness also affect our ability to communicate with others because of their perceptions about these issues.

Body type, or **somatotype**, is comprised of a combination of height, weight, and muscularity. Tall people are generally more successful and are viewed more positively by others. Taller people are more likely to be hired in employment interviews, and they tend to have higher incomes.[18] Regarding attractiveness, women generally find tall men more attractive than short ones; however, they view men of medium height as the most attractive and likeable. Those who are short, soft, and round are often judged negatively in terms of their personalities and their concern about self-presentation.

Particular physical characteristics are considered as universal aspects of attractiveness: bright eyes, symmetrical facial features, and a thin or medium build.[19] Physical attractiveness generally leads to more social success in adulthood; attractive people receive higher initial credibility ratings than do those who are viewed as unattractive.[20] Physically attractive people are more likely to be hired and to receive higher salaries.[21] However, these views may not hold for gender. Studies have shown that attractive females are sometimes judged as less competent than less attractive females.[22]

Even though there is little that we can do to change our height, we can control to some degree our body type and our attractiveness, the latter through attention to good grooming and by conveying a positive attitude.

Space

The study of human space, or **proxemics**, revolves around two concepts: territoriality and personal space. **Territoriality** refers to your need to establish and maintain certain spaces as your own. In a workplace environment, the walls of your cubicle or office often establish your territory. **Personal space** is the distance between you and others with which you feel comfortable. When someone invades your personal space, you often automatically move away from that person. However, personal space preferences can differ among people. For example, large people also usually prefer more space, as do men.

Similarly, personal space preferences differ by culture. People of the United States tend to need more space than those from Greece, Latin America, or the Middle East. The Japanese tend to prefer a greater distance in social situations than do people of the United States.

Anthropologist Edward T. Hall defined four distances people use when they communicate. **Intimate distance** is used more in private than in public and extends to about 18 inches. This distance is used to communicate affection, give comfort, and to protect. **Personal distance** ranges from 18 inches to 4 feet and is the distance used by those in the United States for conversation and nonintimate exchanges. **Social distance** ranges from 4 to 8 feet and is used for professional communication. The higher the status of the person, generally the greater the social distance he or she maintains. **Public distance** exceeds 12 feet and is used most often for public speaking.

Your relationship to other people is related to your use of space. You stand closer to friends and farther from enemies, strangers, authority figures, high-status people, physically challenged people, and people from different racial groups than your own. The effectiveness of communication, or the way you respond to others, can be affected by personal space violations.

What this knowledge means for those who are leaders or who aspire to be leaders is that they need to become attentive to their use of space. As mentioned earlier, this is particularly true for women since studies have shown that they tend to take up less space than men and thus may sabotage their efforts to be seen as a person of power. Even though many women may be of smaller stature than some men,

---

proxemics
The study of human space, which revolves around two concepts: territoriality and personal space.

territoriality
Our need to establish and maintain certain spaces as our own.

personal space
The physical distance between yourself and others with which you feel comfortable.

intimate distance
This distance is used to communicate affection, give comfort, and to protect. It is used in private rather than public situations and extends to about 18 inches.

personal distance
The distance, ranging from 18 inches to 4 feet, that is used by those in the United States for conversation and nonintimate exchanges.

social distance
This distance ranges from 4 to 8 feet and is used for professional communication.

public distance
This distance exceeds 12 feet and is used most often for public speaking.

they can better claim their space by squaring their shoulders, pulling themselves up to their full height, using larger gestures, and when appropriate, such as in presentation situations, using the entire room. They can also work to create an authoritative voice that commands respect. This is also true culturally, since some cultures socialize people to take up less bodily space.

Cultural differences also extend to how people communicate through space in seating arrangements and the layout of offices. People in the United States, for example, prefer to converse face-to-face, while people in China prefer to sit side by side. This preference may allow them to avoid direct eye contact, which is the custom in that culture. In terms of the office environment, private offices have more status in the United States, while in Japan, only executives of the highest rank may have a private office, although it is just as likely that they have desks in large work areas.[23] In the United States and Germany, the top floor of office buildings is generally occupied by top-level executives, while in France, high-ranking executives occupy the middle of an office area with subordinates located around them.[24]

Time

Chronemics, or values related to time, refers to the way that people organize and use time and the messages that are created because of our organization and use of time. Our use of time communicates several messages. Our urgency or casualness with the starting time of an event could be an indication of our personality, our status, or our culture. Highly structured, task-oriented people may arrive and leave on time, whereas relaxed, relation-oriented people may arrive and leave late. People with low status are expected to be on time, whereas those with higher status are granted more leeway in their arrival time. Being on time is more important in some cultures than others; for example, being on time is more important in North America than in South America, whereas people of Germany and Switzerland are even more time-conscious than people from the United States.

Another cultural issue to recognize is whether a country follows **polychronic time (P-time)** or **monochronic time (M-time)**. Countries that follow polychronic time work on several activities simultaneously. In these cultures people are more important than schedules so they don't mind interruptions and are accustomed to doing several things at once. People in polychronic cultures borrow and lend things and tend to build lifelong relationships. People from high-context cultures tend to be polychronic, including Latin America, the Middle East, and Southern Europe.[25]

Countries that are monochronic in their time orientation include the United States, Germany, Switzerland, and England. In monochronic cultures, time is considered as something tangible, as is reflected in such sayings as "wasting time" and "time is money." Time is seen as linear and manageable in such cultures. It is considered rude to do two things at once, such as answering the phone while someone is in your office or stopping to text someone while in a conversation. However, with the prevalence of cell phones, this consideration is rapidly changing. Monochronic people tend to respect private property and rarely borrow or lend and are accustomed to short-term relationships.[26]

Touching

Haptics, or touch, communicates a great deal. What is appropriate and people's tendency to touch differs by gender and culture. Studies indicate that women in the United States value touch more than men, women are touched more than men,

---

chronemics
Values related to time, which refer to the way that people organize and use time and the messages that are created because of our organization and use of time.

polychronic time (P-time)
A cultural orientation to time in which people are well adapted to doing several things at once and do not mind interruptions.

monochronic time (M-time)
A cultural orientation to time in which people do one thing at a time and are more task-oriented than relationship-oriented.

haptics
Communicating through the use of bodily contact or touch.

men touch others more than women do, and men may use touch to indicate power or dominance.[27]

People from different countries also handle touch differently. Sidney Jourard determined the rates of touch per hour among adults of various cultures. Adults in Puerto Rico touched 180 times per hour; those in Paris touched about 110 times an hour; those in Gainesville, Florida, touched 2 times per hour; and those in London touched once per hour.

In touch-oriented cultures, such as those of Italy, Spain, Portugal, and Greece, both males and females may walk arm in arm or hold hands. In Mexico, Eastern Europe, and the Arab world, embracing and kissing is common. However, in Hong Kong, initiating any physical contact should be avoided.[28]

Some cultures also restrict where touching may occur on the body. In India and Thailand, it is offensive to touch the head because it is considered sacred. In Korea, young people do not touch the shoulders of elders.[29]

Clothing and Other Artifacts

Your clothing and other adornments, such as jewelry, hairstyle, cosmetics, shoes, glasses, tattoos, and body piercings, communicate to others your age, gender, status, role, socioeconomic class, group memberships, personality, and relation to the opposite sex. Such cues also indicate the historical period, the time of day, and the climate. Clothing and other artifacts also communicate your self-concept or the type of person you believe you are.[30] Conforming to current styles has been correlated to a person's desire to be accepted and liked by others.[31]

Individuals believe that clothing is important in forming first impressions.[32] Clothing has been shown to affect others' impressions of our status and personality traits.[33] For this reason, most advise that you should pay attention to dressing professionally in business situations because it can affect your credibility, attractiveness, and perceived ability to fit within a professional culture. This rule can be particularly important when dealing with international audiences because they tend to make assumptions about another person's education level, status, and income based upon dress alone.[34] Therefore, those who are interested in careers in international business should follow Molloy's rules for business dress: Clothing should be conservative, upper class, and traditional.[35]

CriticalThinking

How important is another person's dress to you? Does it affect your response to that person or your judgment about him or her? Do you clearly understand the expectations regarding professional dress in the workplace?

Effective Listening

Although you may be asked to communicate orally in a professional workplace setting, you will more likely be on the receiving end of such messages. In fact, in the business world, people, both those with and without management responsibilities, spend most of their time listening. Businesspeople, in general, spend nearly

33 percent of their time listening, about 26 percent of their time speaking, and nearly 19 percent of their time reading.[36] Executives may spend more time listening—as much as 80 percent of their day.[37]

Although we spend most of our time in communication situations involved in listening, the skill often receives little attention. A survey conducted by a corporate training and development firm indicated that 80 percent of the corporate executives who responded rated listening as the most important skill in the workforce. However, nearly 30 percent of those same executives said that listening was the communication skill most lacking in their employees.[38] Only 35 percent of us are efficient listeners.[39] The lack of effective listening can often lead to missed opportunities, misunderstanding, conflict, or poor decision making.

Conversely, the ability to listen effectively can have a big impact on our ability to communicate well with others. Effective listening can help us build relationships, be more productive, and determine whether others are being deceptive.

Listening does not mean the same thing as hearing. Hearing is the sensory ability to receive sound. Hearing takes no effort or energy on your part. You receive and hear sounds constantly. However, listening is a more active, engaged process. According to the International Listening Association, listening is "the active process of receiving, constructing meaning from, and responding to spoken and/or nonverbal messages. It involves the ability to retain information, as well as to react empathically and/or appreciatively to spoken and/or nonverbal messages." Listening requires energy and effort, whereas hearing is automatic and passive.

We tend to be poor listeners for a number of reasons. We may be distracted by the external environment or by internal factors: We may be ill or tired, or we may have other tasks that need our attention. A speaker may say something that triggers a negative emotion in us and we may tune out or turn our attention to formulating our rebuttal. Another big problem is that we think much faster than a person can speak. Because of these distractions or barriers, listeners need training to slow down the mental processes and focus on what others are saying.

Listening Styles

There are three levels of listening, and it is beneficial to distinguish between them and identify which type of listener you are.

Level one is referred to as a good listener. A level-one listener exhibits all the qualities of being involved in conversations, including taking the other person's interests into consideration and staying focused on the speaker.[40] A level-one listener keeps an open mind and is always eager to hear what the other person has to say. A level-one listener is respectful of the other person's feelings and is not quick to pass judgment.

Level-two listeners hear the words being spoken but do not have full understanding of what the words mean.[41] Many times, listening involves recognizing nonverbal forms of communication. Level-two listeners focus on the words being said, but might not pay attention to the facial expressions, hand gestures, or tone of voice. They do not give much effort to understanding the speaker's intent, and this oversight can lead to conflicts and misunderstandings.

Level-three listeners do not acknowledge the speaker at all. While another person is speaking level-three listeners spend time thinking about something else.[42]

Level-three listeners' thoughts are centered on themselves, and they may only appear to be listening. The problem that arises with this level of listening is the amount of confusion it can create. While the speaker is talking, these listeners are daydreaming about something else and may have possibly missed an important piece of information. This can lead to making unhealthy life decisions and to poor judgment, and can create barriers to effective communication.

Only about 20 percent of people in the workforce listen at level one. The rest (80 percent) go back and forth between levels two and three, and only sometimes are at level one.[43]

Listening Types

Listening is classified into four main types: active, empathic, critical, and listening for enjoyment. Listening for enjoyment is typically not an activity in which we engage in the workplace, so it will not be discussed here.

However, the other three types of listening are relevant to and useful in the workplace. **Active listening** is "listening with a purpose."[44] Active listening is a key part of successful interpersonal or face-to-face communication. It involves the following four steps:

1. Listen carefully by using all available senses, including observation.
2. Paraphrase what is heard both mentally and verbally. This step is intended to help you remember the information and to accomplish step 3. Paraphrasing involves such statements as "If I hear you correctly, you are saying. . ."
3. Check your understanding to ensure accuracy. To check understanding, you might follow your paraphrased statement by asking, "Is that right?"
4. Provide feedback.

Table 9-2 provides a short quiz you can take to get some insight into your listening skill level.

Table 9-2 Are You a Good Listener?

Take this short quiz, using the following rating scale: A "3" means you are very strong in this area; a "2" means you try to perform the stated behavior; and a "1" means you are not sure how often you perform the behavior.

1. I am aware that I must listen with a purpose to listen effectively.
2. I have trained myself to listen at least twice as much as I speak.
3. I listen for understanding rather than evaluation.
4. I recognize the importance of my nonverbal signals to the speaker.
5. I am aware of the words, phrases, or behaviors that are likely to make me defensive.
6. I wait until the speaker has finished before responding.
7. I have often heard a person say to me, "Thank you for listening."
8. I concentrate on what the speaker is saying, even though other things could distract me.
9. I am able to exercise emotional control when listening, even if I disagree with the message.
10. I realize that listening powerfully may be the key to my success.

If you scored 12 or less, you probably need a listening program. If you scored 13 to 20, you are an average listener. If you rated higher than 20, you are an excellent listener.

Source: Adapted from "Effective Listening Skills." (1994). *Women in Business, 46*(2), 28–32, March/April.

---

active listening
Listening with a purpose, which involves paraphrasing, asking questions for clarification, and providing feedback.

Feedback consists of the listener's verbal and nonverbal responses to the speaker and his or her message. Feedback can be either positive or negative. Positive feedback consists of the listener's verbal and nonverbal responses that are intended to affirm the speaker and his or her message. Negative feedback consists of a listener's verbal and nonverbal responses that are intended to disaffirm the speaker and his or her message. In productive communication situations, negative feedback should not be used to disaffirm the speaker or typically to discredit the message, because this may negatively affect your relationship and your ability to communicate effectively in the future. However, you should feel free to say "no" to the speaker or to disagree with the message. Disagreement is generally more effective if you can provide good reasons for doing so.

Empathic listening is a form of active listening with the goal of understanding the other person. To listen empathetically, you must be fully engaged in the conversation at the moment and empathize with the person who is speaking. Empathic listening is useful in the workplace if you find yourself in a situation in which it is appropriate to be supportive of colleagues and team members or if you are a supervisor dealing with an employee with a problem. Empathic listening is useful in establishing and maintaining relationships with others by showing that you care about them and their concerns. Empathetic messages include such statements as "I understand why you feel that way" and "I can see how you might interpret my actions as you did."

Critical listening is used to evaluate the accuracy, meaningfulness, and usefulness of a message. In the workplace, critical listening is particularly important in any decision-making process. Critical listening can help you to determine whether information is sound, relevant to the issue, and adequate. It can also help you to determine whether the speaker is pursuing a hidden or personal agenda or the objectives of the group, and whether the person is objective and forthright. All this information is necessary and may affect your ability to reach a sound business decision.

Your skills as a critical listener are dependent upon your abilities as a critical thinker. *Critical thinking* is necessary to analyze a communication situation—your purposes, your audiences, and the situational factors that affect the way you communicate—and based upon that analysis, to create an effective communication strategy for that situation. Conversely, critical thinking is also used to analyze a speaker, the situation, and the speaker's ideas to make critical judgments about the message being presented. This last issue, message analysis, requires two steps: (1) evaluating the process by which information or knowledge was discovered and (2) evaluating specific elements of message content. In other words, you should evaluate whether the information contained in the message is accurate and unbiased to ensure that the speaker has drawn logical conclusions from the information.

feedback
The listener's verbal and nonverbal responses to the speaker and his or her message.

empathic listening
A form of active listening with the goal of understanding the other person.

critical listening
Listening used to evaluate the accuracy, meaningfulness, and usefulness of a message.

CriticalThinking

Are you skilled at practicing active listening? Empathic listening? Critical listening? If not, what steps might you take to become a more effective listener? How might improving your listening skills provide you opportunities in the workplace?

Verbal Tactics for Effective Listening

One way to indicate to the person with whom you are communicating that you are actively engaged in the listening process is to use effective verbal communication techniques, such as the following:

- **Ask questions.** Asking questions shows that you are interested in what the speaker has to say and enables you to gather more information, which is necessary for clear understanding.
- **Show interest and support.** You can do this by encouraging the speaker to continue or by encouraging him or her to share ideas.
- **Use descriptive, nonevaluative responses when paraphrasing or responding.** An example of such a statement would be: "Your information comes from a think tank that has openly expressed its partisan affinities. I am not sure that the data gives us a complete picture of the situation." Compare that to the following response: "You give us biased and therefore one-sided information, because its source clearly has a political agenda." The second response contains language that has negative connotations—"biased," "one-sided," "political"—which can put the speaker on the defensive or make him or her feel attacked. Use of such language can also be interpreted as a subtle form of name-calling because it implies that the speaker is biased, one-sided, and political in his or her intentions.
- **Identify areas of agreement or common interests.** An example of such a statement is: "I believe we both are interested in pursuing decisions that will enable the department to meet its objectives." Such statements are intended to reduce the perception that you and the speaker are far apart in your bigger concerns or experiences.
- **Respond with affirming statements.** Making such statements as "I understand," "I know," and "yes," indicates support for the speaker and his or her ideas or feelings, as well as empathy.
- **Avoid silence.** Silence can be interpreted in a variety of negative ways, such as a sign of a lack of interest, inattentiveness, or disapproval. However, the use of silence has cultural dimensions. Some cultures have a greater tolerance and appreciation for silence, so in cases in which you are dealing with persons from such cultures, silence might be appropriate.
- **Don't dominate a conversation or cut off the other person.** If you wish to indicate that you are interested in a speaker's ideas or feelings, you should allow that person to express himself or herself fully. If you are perceived as someone who dominates a conversation or cuts off people, others will typically begin to avoid conversing with you.
- **Restate and paraphrase the speaker's message as well as the intent.** This activity shows that you are listening and are concerned about interpreting the speaker's message accurately. It may be appropriate in certain situations to openly express your interpretation of the speaker's intentions. An example might be, "As I understand it, you are telling me this information so that it can be used to make a decision about the pending policy change. Is that correct?"

In Table 9-3, active listening responses are compared to those that block communication.

Table 9-3 Active Listening versus Blocking Responses.

- **Active response: Paraphrasing content**
  "You're saying that you don't have time to finish the report by Friday."
  Blocking response: Ordering, threatening
  "I don't care how you do it. Just get the report on my desk by Friday."
- **Active response: Mirroring feelings**
  "It sounds like the department's problems really bother you."
  Blocking response: Preaching, criticizing
  "You should know better than to air the department's problems in a general meeting."
- **Active response: Stating one's feelings**
  "I'm frustrated that the job isn't completed yet, and I'm worried about getting it done on time."
  Blocking response: Interrogating
  "Why didn't you tell me that you didn't understand the instructions?"
- **Active response: Asking for information or clarification**
  "What parts of the problem seem most difficult to solve?"
  Blocking response: Minimizing the problem
  "You think that's bad? You should see what I have to do this week."
- **Active response: Offering to help solve the problem together**
  "Is there anything I could do that would help?"
  Blocking response: Advising
  "Why don't you try listing everything you have to do and seeing which items are most important?"

Source: The five responses that block communication are based on a list of twelve in Thomas Gordon's and Judith Gordon Sands's *P.E.T. in Action* (New York: Wyden): 117–118.

Nonverbal Tactics for Effective Listening

As has been expressed earlier, your nonverbal communication is as important, if not more so, than your oral statements in interpersonal communication situations. Therefore, providing appropriate nonverbal communication is also useful in indicating that you are actively listening to others. The following are nonverbal communication behaviors that indicate active listening:

- **Use movements and gestures to show understanding and responsiveness.** You can nod your head to show approval or understanding or shake your head in disbelief.
- **Lean forward.** Leaning toward a speaker shows interest. This technique is also useful in job interview situations, because it expresses your interest in the speaker and the position for which you have applied.
- **Establish an open body position.** Crossing your arms or legs sends a subtle message that you are not completely comfortable with the speaker or that you are not receptive to the ideas. This principle is also true in oral presentations. You should maintain an open body position while delivering speeches or presentations to indicate your confidence and receptiveness to the audience.
- **Use an alert but relaxed posture.** In other words, do not look too relaxed or too stiff. Being too relaxed may indicate that you don't take the speaker or situation seriously. Being too stiff may show that you are uncomfortable or rigid in your thinking.

- **Use direct body orientation.** You should face the speaker or your audience directly rather than from an angle. An angled position may be interpreted as a sign that you are attempting to move away from the speaker. It may also inhibit your ability to observe the nonverbal communication of the speaker.
- **Use facial expressions that indicate involvement.** You can raise your eyebrows to express interest and smile to show encouragement.
- **Maintain direct eye contact.** Failing to maintain direct eye contact may be interpreted as showing deceptiveness, a lack of interest, or a lack of confidence in some cultures, particularly in the United States.

Motivating Employees

This textbook opened with a discussion of the importance of leadership in today's organizations. In that discussion, the leader's task was distinguished from that of the manager. "What leaders really do is prepare organizations for change and help them cope as they struggle through it. It's the manager's job to promote stability, and only organizations that embrace both sides of the equation can succeed in tough times."[45]

Kotter maintains that many U.S. companies today are overmanaged and underled. Organizations need to recognize that leaders are responsible for setting direction, whereas managers plan and budget. Setting a direction requires developing a vision as well as strategies to achieve that vision.

A second task for leaders is to identify those who can help spread the vision and are committed to its achievement. This task is largely a communication issue. It requires active involvement, credibility, and empowering people. Empowerment promotes buy-in and communication.

To achieve the vision, leaders must motivate and inspire those in the organization. Successful motivation ensures employees will have the energy to overcome obstacles. It is useful to repeat that leaders are not necessarily given organizational power but can influence others through their strategic abilities, knowledge, and communication skills. What this means is that the information provided in this chapter not only applies to those with formal power but to those who also wish to practice the leadership skill of motivating others.

Motivation Defined

need
A lack or imbalance that creates dissatisfaction in an individual.

drive
The state of an individual associated with the need, such as hunger or thirst.

goal
The outcome that the person perceives will eliminate a need.

motive
The learned state that affects behavior by moving an individual toward a perceived goal.

Motivation consists of three interrelated elements: needs, drives, and goals. A lack or imbalance that creates dissatisfaction in an individual is a **need**. Needs may vary in type and intensity among people and may change over time, but they significantly influence behavior. A **drive** is the state of an individual associated with a need, such as hunger or thirst. The **goal** is the outcome that the person perceives will eliminate the need. For someone who is hungry, the goal might be a meal. Although the drive arouses activity, a **motive** is the learned state that affects behavior by moving an individual toward a perceived goal. Motivation is the reason behind the behavior or action.

Within an organization, symptoms of low motivation among employees may be low morale, high waste costs, absenteeism, high turnover, high training costs, and high health insurance costs. Individual symptoms of low motivation include boredom, inattention, lack of concentration, resistance, apathy, sabotage, errors, and resistance to change.

Many theories of leadership have been developed to deal with the problem of motivating employees. Some of the early work on motivation and control of employees was driven by traditional human relations values and beliefs in the linkage between communication and effective supervision. One important study in the area of organizational communication that examined supervisors' communication dispositions and drew the following five major conclusions:

- The best supervisors tend to be more "communication-minded." They enjoy talking and speaking in meetings, they are able to explain instructions and policies, and they enjoy conversing with employees.
- The best supervisors tend to be willing, empathic listeners. They respond to silly questions from employees with understanding, they are approachable, and they will listen to suggestions and complaints with an attitude of fairness and openness to take action.
- The best supervisors tend to be sensitive to the feelings of others. For example, they reprimand in private rather than in public.
- The best supervisors tend to "ask" or "persuade" rather than to "tell" or "demand."
- The best supervisors tend to more readily pass along information. They give notice of impending changes and provide reasons for the change.[46]

The conclusions of this study bear a strong resemblance to many of the prescriptions of traditional human relations theorists who claimed that management gained compliance by promoting employee morale and satisfaction. The study indicates that employee morale and satisfaction depend on effective interpersonal communication skills, namely, empathy, sensitivity, and receptivity.

It is important to recognize that employee morale and satisfaction are not entirely dependent upon the behavior of leaders and managers. For example, employee satisfaction was negatively related to role ambiguity and positively related to fatigue. As role ambiguity increased, satisfaction went down, whereas fatigue, to some extent, led to greater satisfaction.[47] In other words, good management practices at the organizational level are also important for better ensuring a motivated workforce.

In fact, some early motivational theories have also pointed to the limits of quality leader-member relationships to influence motivation. For example, Herzberg's motivator-hygiene theory found that satisfaction and dissatisfaction are not opposite conditions. That is, the opposite of satisfaction is simply the absence of satisfaction. Herzberg found that factors leading to job satisfaction and to motivation are different from those that lead to job dissatisfaction.[48]

Herzberg called the factors that lead to job satisfaction *motivators*. These include achievement, recognition, advancement, the work itself, responsibility, and potential for growth. The factors that led to dissatisfaction were identified as *hygiene factors*. These were policy and administration, technical supervision, relationship with supervisor, relationships with peers, relationships with subordinates, salary, job security, personal life, work conditions, and status. Failure to provide for employees' hygiene needs will lead to job dissatisfaction and poor performance, but merely meeting these needs does not provide motivation to improve performance.

Developing Communication Networks

Many senior managers and leaders use their personal contacts to have things done or to get information. As discussed earlier in this text, one of the more recent changes in the business world is the rise in the power of interpersonal communication and use of technology for communication purposes. These changes have

---

FIGURE 9-1 Example of an Informal Network Analysis Map

Finding Central Connectors and Peripheral Specialists

Even though Lisa is the head of the department, Alan is considered the go-to person for information within this informal network. He plays the role of central connector. Meanwhile, Paul operates on the perimeter of the network, offering expertise to members of the group as it's needed, but not necessarily connecting with many other colleagues frequently. Paul plays the role of peripheral specialist.

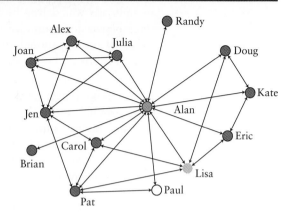

Source: Cross, R., & Prusak, L. (2002). "People Who Make Organizations Go—or Stop," *Harvard Business Review.* Retrieved June 25, 2012, from http://hbr.org/product/the-people-who-make-organizations-go-or-stop/an/R0206G-PDF-ENG.

---

created a challenge for managers because with them, more formal structures have decreased influence. The change has created an opportunity, however, for savvy managers and leaders, since these informal relationships or communication networks can be developed systematically.

There are four common role-players whose performance is critical to the productivity of any organization. These four role-players have huge influence within an organization:

- **Central connectors** link most people in an informal network with one another. These central connectors are the "go-to" people for information in a group. These people do not necessarily have to be leaders of a group. Sometimes the central connectors may be bottlenecks, for example, using their roles for gains, not responding fast enough, or struggling to keep up with their own work while fulfilling the central connector role. The solution is to map informal network flow so as to identify central connectors and reassign some duties, if appropriate. (See Figure 9-1 for an example of a network map.)

- **Boundary spanners** connect an informal network with another information network, for example, other parts of the company or similar networks in other organizations. One problem that might arise with boundary spanners is that they may be networking with the wrong person in another network. In this case, senior management can step in and help shape spanners' network contacts.

- **Information brokers** keep the different subgroups in an informal network together. They are like boundary spanners, but they only operate within the network. They may not be the central connector, but they wield the same power. They are characterized by a wealth of indirect connections. However, heavy reliance on information brokers can have a negative impact when they leave the firm. To solve this problem, central connectors should develop more connections with subgroups so that they may take on the role of information broker if needed.

- **Peripheral specialists** are those in informal networks that others rely on for specialized expertise. Giving them more responsibilities, such as attending more meetings or traveling, may reduce their time, which they need to stay ahead in their field.[49]

central connectors
Link most people in an informal network with one another.

boundary spanners
Connect an informal network with another information network.

information brokers
Keep the different subgroups in an informal network together.

peripheral specialists
Those in informal networks that others rely on for specialized expertise.

Social network analysis is a technique that lets users identify and map informal networks of people. It identifies the functions or activities where connectivity is most needed to improve productivity and then maps the corresponding networks. It is a method to collect information from people that can then be used to map sets of relationships within priority areas or an organization or department. One of the most effective ways to collect information is to create and conduct a survey. The information collected from the survey can then be used to create network maps that illustrate the relationships between the members of a group.

Through social network analysis, people can identify where they need to build more or better relationships. Focusing on the four dimensions discussed here can help managers and leaders improve their connections and better manage informal communication within an organizational context.

Communicating Change

Organizations are constantly changing, but perhaps there is nothing more challenging to an organization than communicating change to employees and successfully influencing them to accept that change without enormous resistance. The success of any change program is heavily reliant on the quality of communication about that change. Successfully implementing change within an organization involves communication on all organizational levels and in all forms: group discussion, one-on-one conversations, formal meetings, and in writing.

Typically, change arises from one of two sources within an organization. The traditional source of change is management, which is assumed to be in a better position to recognize the need for change and know how to implement it. However, this approach to change may fail or meet resistance if the need for such change is not effectively communicated to employees, the benefits of such change to them is not clearly understood, and a clear system of implementing the change is not provided.

Employees are a second source of change. This approach is beneficial because participation in decision making assumedly makes the resulting change more likely to be accepted and implemented. A strategic opportunity lies in this second source of change for the aspiring leader.

In general, however, change is resisted, particularly if it is significant. People resist change for a number of reasons:

- **Disruption of social relationships.** Changes that disrupt social relationships can create discomfort and cause anxiety.
- **Threat to roles.** Changes in organizational structure and individual roles may threaten a person's position, recognition, power, and sense of self-worth. If individuals perceive the change will result in a loss of esteem or recognition, they will resist. Even increased responsibilities may result in resistance if individuals lack confidence in their ability to perform the new duties.
- **Economic loss.** Employees may resist organizational or departmental changes that may be read as a signal for lower pay, less opportunity for advancement, or job loss.[50]

Successful strategic change depends on *backing* from those who authorize change, *accessibility* in the sense that managers and leaders understand what they are working toward, *specificity* in terms of the detailed planning, and *cultural receptivity* or the receptiveness of those affected by the change.[51]

A strategic process for implementing change applies the strategic elements examined earlier in this text:

1. Performing an analysis of the context and the audience
2. Designing a communication strategy
3. Developing tactics for strategy implementation

The questions provided in Table 9-4 should be asked during each of these phases.

Chapters 4 and 5 of this text have already examined processes for analyzing the context and the audience. Many of these considerations are also applied in developing the strategic design for a program to communicate change. It is important to emphasize that persuasion is often a process, as was discussed in Chapter 3. Therefore, when developing a structure for achieving the goals of a change campaign, a number of channels and media of communication may have to be used over a period of time. The change message may have to be introduced in phases by first informing employees of the change, then persuading them of the need for the change, and finally, providing them the specifics of how the change will be implemented.

Table 9-4 Analysis for Communicating Change.

PLANNING LEVEL	QUESTIONS
Contextual Analysis	1. Have employees readily assimilated other changes?
	2. Is the change congruent with the culture?
	3. Is the change seen as noncomplex and manageable?
	4. Is the change seen as advantageous over past practices?
	5. Are the benefits readily observable?
	6. Will key relationships be adversely affected?
Audience Analysis	1. Who are the major groups of employees that will be affected?
	2. How will each group be affected?
	3. What are the most likely points of resistance of each group?
	4. What are the communication preferences of each group?
	5. Who are the key opinion leaders of each group?
Strategic Design	1. What are the tentative communication goals for each audience?
	2. What are the common goals for the general audience?
	3. What is a unifying theme that energizes and motivates employees?
	4. How should communication resources be allocated?
	5. What is a general structure (phases) for achieving the goals and communicating the theme?
Tactical Analysis	1. What channels should be used?
	2. What are the key messages?
	3. What should be the timing of the various messages?
	4. Who should communicate the messages?
	5. How can employees voice their concerns?
	6. How should the process be monitored?

Source: Adapted from Clampitt, P. G. (2001). *Communicating for Managerial Effectiveness*, 2nd ed. (Thousand Oaks, CA: Sage).

Table 9-5 Leadership Practices for Organizational Change.

LEADERSHIP QUALITIES	DELIVERY TACTICS	CULTURAL ADAPTATIONS
Articulate the plan	**Be honest and open**	**Give them what they want**
Be passionate about the change	Tell the truth	Tailor rewards
Make a compelling case	Make communication a priority	Use money when feasible
Focus on results	Communicate face-to-face	Provide public recognition
Measure outcomes	Talk the talk	Encourage pride in work
		Improve the quality of life
Work the plan	**Cut to the chase**	
Drive change deeply	Build a shared understanding	**Overcome resistance**
Understand the work involved	Be clear	Replace personnel
Solicit feedback	Be consistent	Persevere
Walk the walk	Repeat yourself	Demonstrate the benefits
	Be concrete	Appeal to self-interest
Be a genuine team player	Use data persuasively	Encourage rule breaking
Trust and support your people	Be transparent	
Mold consensus	Be prompt	**Be resourceful**
Share credit		Engage leadership
Be visible	**Adapt your message**	Engage employees
Heed communications experts	Focus on internal messaging	Give ownership
	Communicate to all levels	Work from the bottom up
Face bad news	Know your audience	Provide training
Deal with the reality	Ask, "What's in it for me?"	Use outside expertise
Use urgency as a motivator		
Support problem solving		**Accept change as a way of life**
		Be patient
		Celebrate and repeat successes

Source: Adapted from King, C. L., Brooks, D., & Hartge, T. D. (2007). *Effective Communication Practices During Organizational Transformation: A Benchmarking Study of the U.S. Automobile Industry and U.S. Naval Aviation Enterprise.* Center for Defense Management Reform Sponsored Report Series. Retrieved November 7, 2009, from http://www.defensereform.org/_files/FY2007/NPS-CDMR-GM-07-001.pdf.

Table 9-5 identifies a number of communication practices that leaders might implement when communicating change.

The following section discusses qualities that leaders should try to communicate and practice to influence change. Following that is a discussion on delivery tactics for effectively delivering change messages. The last section on cultural adaptation identifies key areas of culture and system changes necessary to align the organization with the changes being proposed.

Leadership Qualities

In any change effort, it is critical that the organization have leaders that manage and shepherd the transformation through the organization. Current change research suggests that defining the change focus, guiding the change effort, and facilitating organizational participation are all important leader activities.[52] More specifically, the following key leadership elements in any change effort must be emphasized:

- **Articulate the plan.** What this means is that leaders must have the ability to articulate a plan for moving forward. Successful articulation means that leaders demonstrate passion for the idea, make their case in a compelling way, understand the need to focus on results, and insist on measuring outcomes.

- **Work the plan.** Good leaders must be capable of fully executing the plan and permeating the whole organization. What this often means is that leaders must be willing to drive change throughout the organization, take the time to understand what they're asking the organization to do, solicit feedback along the way, make minor adjustments without changing course, and embody the changes in their own behaviors. Soliciting feedback might take a variety of forms, such as inviting and responding to employee emails, interviewing employees on a regular basis, inviting employees to short meetings with executives, and sharing lunch with employees periodically.

- **Be a genuine team player.** Being a team player must move beyond platitudes: Leaders need to build trust and mold consensus, share credit, become visible throughout their organization, and strongly engage with communications experts.

- **Face bad news.** Part of being a leader is the willingness to deal with bad news, understand the urgencies that result, use those urgencies to motivate the organization, and commit to solving problems as they come up.

Delivery Tactics

At the heart of any change effort is the effectiveness of the message. A variety of message delivery tactics can be used to support organizational change efforts:

- **Be honest and open.** In communicating change efforts, it's important for organizations to tell the truth, even the bad news, about the current situation. However, there are good and bad ways to be honest. To have the best impact on people, it's important to pay attention to how you communicate, to recognize the importance of face-to-face interactions, and to make sure what is communicated has integrity. The benefits of face-to-face communication include the potential for more in-depth discussion, being more informative, grabbing the listener's attention, being more persuasive, being clearer, getting feedback, and establishing a better personal connection.

- **Cut to the chase.** Messages need to be highly accessible to audiences, particularly when communicating changes. It is critical to build understanding and persuade others by providing and repeating simple, concise, and consistent messages that use concrete, transparent data. Additionally, messages need to be delivered promptly.

- **Adapt your message.** Knowing whom to target and how to target them is a constant challenge in communicating change messages. Leaders have to pay close attention to internal audiences, communicate through all levels, know the specific needs of particular audiences, listen to feedback, and understand the impact the changes will have on their audiences.[53]

Cultural Adaptations

When priorities change, the culture needs to change with it. That means that systems and norms need to reflect the new goals of the organization. There are several key requirements in creating a change culture:

- **Give them what they want.** Causes and effects drive people, and it's important that a reward system be aligned with what the organization is trying to accomplish. There are numerous ways to creative incentives for employees; among them are money, public recognition, pride in work, and quality of life issues.
- **Overcome resistance.** Change and resistance go hand in hand, and leaders may need to draw on all their resources at some point to overcome them. At times, leaders may need to fire people. However, they often need to stick to the plan, demonstrate the benefits to employees, appeal to their self-interests, and sometimes encourage people to break the rules.
- **Be resourceful.** There are numerous resources within an organization, and a robust change culture avails itself of all of them. Those that are most critical include fully engaging leadership and employees, encouraging employee ownership of their areas of responsibility, recognizing the power of bottom-up inspiration, providing necessary training, and using outside expertise when necessary.
- **Accept change as a way of life.** The ultimate lesson in change management is in understanding that change never ends. This requires leaders to be patient, celebrate and repeat successes, and to learn from success and failure.[54]

Summary

Interpersonal communication involves mutual influence, usually for the purpose of managing relationships. As such, it is an important aspect of communication within an organization. Broadly speaking, there are three aspects of interpersonal communication: verbal communication, nonverbal communication, and listening.

Verbal communication can be characterized as one of three types of interpersonal style: assertive, avoiding, or aggressive. Aggressive communication is characterized by a focus on one's own needs with little to no regard for the other. Assertiveness, on the other hand, involves both—taking care of one's own needs as well as those of the other. Ideally, conversations in the workplace would involve genuine dialogue rather than debating with others to prove who is right and who is wrong.

Nonverbal communication comprises most of the information that is exchanged in a face-to-face communication situation. In nonverbal communication, communication channels are multiple and simultaneous. These channels include information that we receive from another person's facial expressions and eyes; body posture, movement, and appearance; the use of space; the use of time; touching; vocal cues; and clothing and other artifacts.

Listening is a much-needed skill in the workplace—most of our time in communication situations involves listening—unfortunately, it is the skill that is most cited for improvement by managers. Listening is different from hearing. Listening requires time, energy, and focus, whereas hearing is the ability to discern sounds. There are three types of listening: active, empathic, and critical. Active listening is "listening with a purpose." Empathic listening is a form of active listening with the goal of understanding the other person. Critical listening is used to evaluate the accuracy, meaningfulness, and usefulness of a message.

Additional tasks for organizational leaders are to motivate and to communicate change to employees. These are related issues because motivation may involve change in employees' behaviors and attitudes in relation to their work; however, change in management typically involves organizational changes that originate at the top of the organization. The success of any change program is heavily reliant on the quality of communication about that change. Successfully implementing organizational change involves communication on all organizational levels and in all forms: group discussion, one-on-one conversations, formal meetings, and in writing.

Key Terms

interpersonal communication, 251

trust, 251

avoidance, 252

aggressiveness, 252

assertiveness, 252

strategic alignment, 254

nonverbal communication, 254

kinesics, 254

somatotype, 255

proxemics, 256

territoriality, 256

personal space, 256

intimate distance, 256

personal distance, 256

social distance, 256

public distance, 256

chronemics, 257

polychronic time (P-time), 257

monochronic time (M-time), 257

haptics, 257

active listening, 260

feedback, 261

empathic listening, 261

critical listening, 261

need, 264

drive, 264

goal, 264

motive, 264

central connectors, 266

boundary spanners, 266

information brokers, 266

peripheral specialists, 266

Discussion Questions

1. What is your interpersonal style of communication? How might you become more assertive and better ensure that genuine dialogue is taking place?
2. What are the seven channels of nonverbal communication? Provide some examples of how nonverbal messages might be interpreted differently by people of differing cultures.
3. What are some of the barriers to effective listening that you commonly encounter? What are some strategies for overcoming each of these barriers?
4. What are the communication dispositions Redding identified that were found in leaders able to effectively motivate employees?
5. What are some communication practices or behaviors that leaders might use to help employees adapt to and accept organizational change?

Applications

1. Take the listening quiz on page 260 of this chapter, and then write a memo in which you identify listening skills that might be improved and set specific goals for their improvement.
2. Choose a country other than the one of your birth, and conduct research on common nonverbal behaviors and their meanings. Write a report that informs someone from the United States how to prepare for a visit to this country and better anticipate and interpret the meanings of nonverbal communication there.
3. Write an assessment of your interpersonal communication skills by identifying your interpersonal style, nonverbal communication, and listening style. It may be helpful to ask colleagues or peers questions about each of these interpersonal elements to get a clearer picture of how others see you. Be sure to choose people who will be honest in their answers. After assessing your interpersonal skills in each of these areas, create a plan to improve your interpersonal skills that identifies specific actions and outcomes within a specified time period.
4. Create an informal communication network map of a group in which you are involved. After identifying the four network roles, assess whether changes need to be made to make the persons who play those roles more effective. Write up your assessment and your recommendations.
5. Identify a change that you would like to see happen in an organization or group of which you are a part. Create a plan to implement that change through communication strategy and practice. What risks need to be identified and accounted for? Who would you need to communicate the plan to and what messages would need to be articulated?

CASE ANALYSIS

HAYWARD HEALTHCARE SYSTEMS, INC.

Bob Jackson is the new operations manager of the distribution center for Hayward Healthcare Systems, Inc., a mid-size, non-union company located in California. The distribution center is an $80-million-dollar-a-year operation that has fifty employees, including fifteen minorities and eighteen females in the workforce.

Jackson was transferred from another operations position in the company to fill this position because of some serious performance problems in the distribution center that had resisted all attempts at improvement. The center had experienced a very high level of defects (400 per month) and an unacceptable rate of errors in the orders taken from client hospitals. Jackson accepted the assignment knowing that top management would expect him to improve the performance of the distribution center in a relatively short period of time.

Jackson's first few weeks on the job were revealing, to say the least. He discovered that the five supervisors that his predecessor had selected to lead the center's workforce had little credibility with the employees. They had each been selected on the basis of their job seniority or their friendship with the previous manager.

The workforce was organized into three categories. *Pickers* identify supplies by code numbers in the storage area, remove packaged items from the shelves, and sort them into baskets. *Drivers* operate forklifts and electric trucks, moving baskets and boxes of supplies to different locations within the distribution center. *Loaders* transfer supplies onto and off of the forklifts and delivery trucks.

The Situation Mr. Jackson Encountered

Jackson found that his employees were either demoralized or had tough, belligerent attitudes toward management and other employees. Part of the problem, he soon learned, was a lax approach to background checks and prior job references. Seven employees were convicted felons who had been imprisoned for violent assaults on their victims. The previous manager had made all of the hiring decisions by himself without bothering to check on the applicants' references or backgrounds.

Jackson soon discovered that it was not unusual for employees to settle their differences with their fists or to use verbally abusive language to berate people who had offended them. His predecessor had unintentionally encouraged these disruptive activities by staying in his office and not being available to the other workers. He had relied largely on his discredited supervisors to handle their own disciplinary problems. Before long, the center employees felt they could handle their own affairs in any way they wanted, without any interference from management.

The Loading Dock Incident

While sitting in his office, planning to make several policy changes to improve the efficiency of the distribution center, one of Jackson's supervisors entered and reported that two of the loaders had just gotten into a heated dispute, and the situation on the loading dock was tense.

The dispute was between Ed Williams, an African-American, male employee, and Buddy Jones, a white, male employee, and focused on which radio station to play on the loading dock sound system. Williams is the only black employee who works on the loading dock. The company's policy permits employees to listen to music while they work and, in recent years, workers have considered listening to music to be a benefit that improves their working conditions.

Williams insisted that he couldn't stand to listen to the country music that Jones preferred to play. For his part, Jones claimed that Williams's choice of rap and hip-hop music was offensive to him and made working conditions difficult. An emotional and angry argument developed between the two men over their choices in music, and each yelled racial slurs at the other. Neither the company nor the division have a policy governing the choice of music permitted in the workplace. Apparently, whoever gets to work first chooses the music for the day.

Both Jones and Williams were known as tough employees who had previous disciplinary problems at Hayward Healthcare Systems. Jones had been incarcerated for eighteen months prior to being hired by the company. Jackson knew that he should take immediate action to resolve this problem and to avoid a potentially volatile escalation of the conflict. His supervisors told Jackson that, in the past, the previous manager would simply have hollered at the two antagonists in the conflict and then departed with no further action.

Jackson's objectives in resolving the conflict included the establishment of his own control in the workplace. He knew that he would have to change "business as usual" in the distribution center so that employees would respect his authority and would refrain from any further unprofessional conduct.

Discussion Questions

In determining the most appropriate solution to the dispute between Jackson's employees, you should consider the following questions:

1. What seems to be the cause of the conflict?
2. What style of conflict management are the distribution center's employees using?
3. What style of conflict management have these managers used in the past?
4. What should Mr. Jackson do to settle the conflict? Should either or both of the employees be punished for their behavior?

5. What can Mr. Jackson do over the long term to ensure that incidents such as the one described in this case are less likely to occur?

6. What can Mr. Jackson do to develop a group of supervisors who can provide the support he requires and who can properly direct the work of the employees in the distribution center?

7. How important is communication in this case? What should Mr. Jackson do to improve the quality of communication in the distribution center?

Writing Assignment

This assignment requires two documents: a professional business memo and a professional business letter. Please assume the role of Mr. Jackson, the distribution center operations manager. Cast your reply to the issues in this case in the form of a proposal memo to the distribution center director.

At a *minimum*, in your response, please identify the business and management issues, the legal issues, and the cultural issues present in this case. Please consider two additional questions:

- What must I do *right now* to solve the problem? What actions do I take immediately?
- What advice would I offer to senior management about this matter? Have any company policies (or lack of policies) contributed to the events described above?

Please address your business letter to all employees in the distribution center, explaining what's happened and what you and the company's leadership have decided to do about it.

This case was prepared by Ms. Kay Wigton with the assistance of James S. O'Rourke, Concurrent Professor of Management, as the basis for class discussion rather than to illustrate either effective or ineffective handling of an administrative situation. Personal and corporate identities have been disguised.

Endnotes

1. Beebe, S. A., Beebe, S. J., & Redmond, M. V. (2005). *Interpersonal communication: Relating to others* (4th ed.). Boston: Pearson.

2. Lencioni, P. M. (2002). *The five dysfunctions of a team*. San Francisco: Jossey-Bass.

3. Robbins, S. P. (2001). *Organizational behavior* (9th ed.). Upper Saddle River, NJ: Prentice Hall.

4. Eisenberg, E. M., & Goodall, H. L., Jr. (1993). *Organizational communication: Balancing creativity and constraint*. New York: St. Martin's Press, p. 252.

5. Eisenberg & Goodall, 1993, p. 252.

6. Pearson, J. C., Nelson, P. E., Titsworth, S., & Harter, L. (2003). *Human communication*. New York: McGraw-Hill, p. 214.

7. Eisenberg & Goodall, 1993, p. 252.

8. Orbe, M. P. (1996). Laying the foundation for co-cultural communication theory: An inductive approach to studying "nondominant" communication strategies and the factors that influence them. *Communication Studies*, 47, 157–176, p. 170.

9. Infante, D., Trebling, J., Sheperd, P., & Seeds, D. (1984). The relationship of argumentativeness to verbal aggression. *Southern Speech Communication Journal*, 50, 67–77.

10. Orbe, 1996, p. 170.

11. Yankelovich, D. (1999). *The magic of dialogue: Transforming conflict into cooperation*. New York: Simon & Schuster.

12. Eisenberg & Goodall, 1993, p. 252.

13. Burgoon, J. K., & Saine, T. (1978). *The unspoken dialogue: An introduction to nonverbal communication*. Boston: Houghton Mifflin.

14. Chaney, L. H., & Martin, J. S. (2011). *Intercultural business communication* (5th ed.). Boston: Prentice Hall.

15. Chaney & Martin, 2011.

16. Ibid.

17. Ibid.

18. Hensley, W. (1992). Why does the best looking person in the room always seem to be surrounded by admirers? *Psychological Reports*, 70, 457–469; Knapp, M. L., &

Hall, J. A. (1992). *Nonverbal communication in human interaction* (3rd ed.). Fort Worth: Harcourt Brace Jovanovich.

19. Brody, J. E. (1994, March 21). Notions of beauty transcend culture, new study suggests. *The New York Times*, A14.

20. Knapp & Hall, 1992; Widgery, R. N. (1974). Sex of receiver and physical attractiveness of source as determinants of initial credibility perception. *Western Speech, 38,* 13–17.

21. Knapp & Hall, 1992.

22. Kaplan, R. M. (1978). Is beauty talent? Sex interaction in the attractiveness halo effect. *Sex Roles, 4,* 195–204.

23. Gudykunst, W. B., & Ting-Toomey, S. (1988). *Culture and interpersonal communication.* Thousand Oaks, CA: Sage Publications.

24. Chaney & Martin, 2011.

25. Ibid.

26. Ibid.

27. Fisher, J. D., Rytting, M., & Heslin, R. (1976). Hands touching hands: Affective and evaluative effects of interpersonal touch. *Sociometry, 3,* 416–421; Jourard, S. M., & Rubin, J. E. (1968). Self-disclosure and touching: A study of two modes of interpersonal encounter and their inter-relation. *Journal of Humanistic Psychology, 8,* 39–48; and Henley, N. (1973–1974). Power, sex, and nonverbal communication. *Berkeley Journal of Sociology, 18,* 10–11.

28. Chaney & Martin, 2011.

29. Axtell, R. E. (1998). *Gestures.* New York: John Wiley & Sons, Inc.

30. Fisher, P. (1975). The future's past. *New Literary History, 6,* 587–606.

31. Taylor, L. C., & Compton, N. H. (1968). Personality correlates of dress conformity. *Journal of Home Economics, 60,* 653–656.

32. Henricks, S. H., Kelley, E. A., & Eicher, J. B. (1968). Senior girls' appearance and social acceptance. *Journal of Home Economics, 60,* 167–172.

33. Douty, H. I. (1963). Influence of clothing on perception of persons. *Journal of Home Economics, 55,* 197–202.

34. Gray, J., Jr. (1993). *The winning image.* New York: AMACOM.

35. Molloy, J. T. (1996). *New woman's dress for success.* New York: Warner.

36. Weinrauch, J., & Swanda, J. (1975). Examining the significance of listening: An exploratory study of contemporary management. *Journal of Business Communication, 13,* 25–32.

37. Nichols, R., & Stevens, L. (1983). Are you listening? *Language Arts, 60*(2), 163–165.

38. Salopek, J. (1999). Is anyone listening? Listening skills in the corporate setting. *Training and Development, 53,* 58–59.

39. Burley-Allen, M. (2001). Listen up. *HR Magazine, 46*(11), 115–119.

40. Burley-Allen, 2001.

41. Ibid.

42. Ibid.

43. Ibid.

44. Barker, L. L. (1971). *Listening behavior.* Englewood Cliffs, NJ: Prentice-Hall.

45. Kotter, J. P. (2001). What leaders really so. *Harvard Business Review 79*(11), 85–96.

46. Redding, W. C. (1972). *Communication within the organization: An interpretive review of theory and research.* New York: Industrial Communication Council.

47. Ray, E. B., & Miller, K. I. (1991). The influence of communication structure and social support on job stress and burnout. *Management Communication Quarterly, 4*(4), 506–527.

48. Herzberg, F. (1966). *Work and the nature of man.* New York: Collins.

49. Cross, R., & Prusak, L. (2002, June) The people who make organizations go—or stop. *Harvard Business Review, 80*(6), 105–112.

50. Rasberry, R. W., & Lemoine, L. F. (1986). *Effective managerial communication.* Boston: Kent Publishing Co.

51. Miller, S. (1997). Implementing strategic decisions: Four key success factors. *Organizational Studies*, *18*, 577–602.

52. King, C. L., Brooks, D., & Hartge, T. D. (2007). Effective communication practices during organizational transformation: A benchmarking study of the U.S. automobile industry and U.S. Naval Aviation Enterprise. Center for Defense Management Reform Sponsored Report Series. Retrieved November 7, 2009, from http://www.defensereform.org/_files/FY2007/NPS-CDMR-GM-07-001.pdf.

53. King et al., 2007.

54. Ibid.

Martin Barraud/OJO Images/Getty Images

Communicating in and Leading Teams

After reading this chapter, you will be able to

▸ Identify why groups form and understand the group formation process.

▸ Understand the roles team members take in groups and which are productive and which are not.

▸ Identify the causes of group cohesiveness and understand when high group cohesiveness might lead to low performance.

▸ Understand the types of influence exercised in groups and characteristics that lead to higher performance in a group.

▸ Understand the group decision-making process and how intercultural influences may affect it.

▸ Identify the types of conflict that arise in groups and the differing responses to conflict.

▸ Understand the elements of effective team leadership.

▸ Implement practices to effectively communicate in and lead virtual teams.

Case Questions:

1. What are some of the typical problems of working in a team or a group?
2. What additional challenges are faced by those working in a virtual team?
3. How might intercultural differences affect team functioning?
4. How might these challenges—for face-to-face groups and virtual teams—be successfully addressed?

The Case of the Virtual Marketing Team

"Hey, Jerry," Malcolm said as he entered Jerry's office. "I thought I would stop by and check in to see how the sales plan for the global rollout of the new e-reader was going."

"Seems like everything is A-OK," Jerry responded to his boss. "The team has been submitting ideas to target the product to each of our markets and it looks like there will be plenty of information to create a thorough plan."

Malcolm hesitated a moment. He knew that employees tended to tell their supervisors what they thought they wanted to hear. "Was this a case of that phenomenon?" he wondered at Jerry's response.

"Great to hear that everyone is involved and producing suggestions," Malcolm said. "But there is a downside, of course. Do you think all of this information can easily be formulated into a coherent plan by our deadline for rollout? Do you think that is even the right approach? Or do you think that we should create ad hoc committees to work on regional marketing plans?"

"Good questions," Jerry said. "But we haven't gotten that far, since we are currently in the 'gathering information' phase. That's probably the next step in the process. Trying to determine whether there are similarities by region or country in terms of the marketing approach and maybe then dividing up the marketing plan along those lines sounds like a good direction in which to go."

"Look, Jerry," Malcolm said. "This is an important product for us in terms of our revenue expectations. You're the team leader on this thing. You need to be thinking ahead to try to identify bottlenecks in the process, and then try to eliminate or streamline some the work that needs to be done. We need to be ready to go when the product is."

"I know, I know," Jerry said. "I'm not making excuses here, but leading a virtual team is a lot different than leading a typical project team. I've never met some of these people and don't know what to expect from them or how far I can push them without getting resistance or worse. I've got twenty-three salespeople scattered all over the world and I feel more like I'm trying to herd cats than run a marketing program sometimes."

During the 1980s, an explosion occurred in the use of teams in organizations. One of the goals of using teams was to do "more with less" in an era of shrinking resources and increased competition. Companies that have traditional, centralized, hierarchical structures are less efficient and responsive to rapidly changing market conditions. As the use of technology has expanded rapidly in organizations, virtual teams have become more common, bringing both benefits and new challenges to be addressed and solved.

Despite the widespread enthusiasm for teams, the definition of what constitutes a team remains ambiguous. However, there are two types of teams in organizations: project teams and work teams. *Project teams* are standing groups that help coordinate the successful completion of a particular project, product, or service. One type of project team is comprised of people working to design and develop a new product. Members of such a team may include engineers, manufacturing experts, marketing specialists, and quality assessment personnel, among others. In such teams, each member is an expert in one aspect of the project necessary for its success.

Work teams are intact groups of employees who are responsible for a "whole" work process or segment that delivers a product or service to an internal or external customer. For example, an eight-member work team at a Southern California aerospace firm is responsible for metallizing all components in the company. The team is housed together, has mapped its internal work flow, and is continually improving its work process. Work teams are characterized by their degree of empowerment or ability to self-direct or self-manage their work processes. However, true self-directed work teams are rare in the United States because of our history of use of the classical, hierarchical organizational structure. In other words, such teams would require a radical reframing of the power relationships in organizations, which few members of management are genuinely prepared to examine.[1]

A third type of team that is becoming more and more common because of the global transformation of business is the *virtual team*. IBM, for example, has more than 4,500 teams worldwide who do their work in shared digital space.

The success of such digital collaboration depends not only on the technology but also on people's ability to adopt a new way of working. What is important is the process that is used to help people make the required behavior changes. (More on communicating in virtual teams can be found later in this chapter.)

Regardless of whether an organization uses teams, group communication skills are necessary in any organization, because the group is the fundamental unit of social organization. Yet, achieving effective group communication is generally a challenge not only because of issues of empowerment and self-direction but also because of our cultural legacy. "This [increased use of groups] is perhaps the most difficult principle to adapt to Western, particularly U.S., organizations. Our romantic obsession with rugged individualism, our cultural preoccupation with individual initiative, achievement, and reward, and our philosophical and moral belief in the value of the individual all mitigate against our willing participation in groups."[2]

Christopher M. Avery, author of *Teamwork Is an Individual Skill*, agrees with this sentiment. "It's a social design problem. Teams are not unnatural, but we've made it difficult by the way we've socialized and organized ourselves [in our culture]."

However, according to Patrick M. Lencioni, author of *The Five Dysfunctions of a Team*, the challenges of creating effective groups can be overcome. The following are Lencioni's five dysfunctions of a team:

- **Absence of trust.** Without the willingness to be vulnerable to one another—to admit weaknesses, to acknowledge failures, to ask for help, to genuinely apologize from time to time—team members will suspect one another of being disingenuous and protective, Lencioni says.

- **Fear of conflict.** Team members who don't trust one another can't engage in meaningful debate. Although some conflict is destructive, other types of conflict lead to improved processes, products, and services.

- **Lack of commitment.** Commitment, according to Lencioni, is a function of two things: clarity about the task and buy-in to goals.

- **Avoidance of accountability.** Without commitment, team members often struggle to hold one another accountable for problems and to call attention to counterproductive behavior. Communicating expectations of team members is critical at the beginning of a relationship.

- **Inattention to results.** Without accountability, team members tend to put their own needs (such as ego, career development, and recognition) before those of the team. When this occurs, achievement of the team's goals may obviously suffer.

By anticipating these dysfunctional tendencies and taking steps to avoid them, effective teams can be put into place in the workplace. In this chapter, the issues that help contribute to effective group communication will be discussed. These include group structure and development, cohesiveness, influence, performance, decision making, and conflict. The chapter concludes with a discussion of leadership in groups and communicating in virtual teams.

Forming Groups

Groups form for a variety of reasons, including the need to collaborate to achieve particular tasks and because of interpersonal attraction. In organizational settings, the first of these reasons is typically the reason we work in groups; however, the interpersonal attractiveness of group members can contribute to successful group formation.

Collective Endeavors

Groups are the means to achieve goals that would be beyond the reach of a single individual. In a workplace setting, individuals often form groups because they can only accomplish some goals when several individuals pool their unique talents in a coordinated effort. Other tasks can be accomplished by an individual, but a group may be more efficient.

Interpersonal Attraction

A number of factors increase attraction between individuals and can contribute to group formation. These include the following:

Proximity. Proximity increases the opportunity for interaction and the likelihood a group will form. For example, students sitting in adjacent seats in a classroom often form cliques. Similarly, in a workplace situation, teams ideally would be arranged in adjacent offices or cubicles to increase communication and to help develop relationships built on trust. However, in virtual team situations, this is obviously not possible.

The similarity principle. We like people who are similar to us in some way. This occurs for several reasons. First, people who adopt the same values and attitudes that we do reassure us that our beliefs are accurate.[3] Second, similarity serves as a signal to suggest that future interactions will be free of conflict.[4] Third, once we discover that we are similar to another person, we tend to immediately feel a sense of unity with that person.[5] Fourth, disliking a person who seems similar may prove to be psychologically distressing.[6] The preference for similarity may have a negative effect on intercultural teams for these reasons: dissimilarity may suggest more conflict and more difficulty because of differences in values, attitudes, and communication preferences. Similarly, many workplace teams are not founded on member similarity—although, commonalities will likely exist. Instead, workplace teams typically are formed based on how members' skills complement each other.

The complementary principle. According to this principle, we are attracted to people who possess characteristics that complement our own personal characteristics.[7] For example, if you enjoy leading groups, you will tend not to be attracted to other individuals who strive for control of a group. Instead, you will probably respond more positively to those who accept your guidance. Perhaps you are an expert in marketing but also need expertise related to product manufacturing in order to create useful delivery schedules to distributors. Working in a team with experts from manufacturing can complement your skills to enable you to do your job more effectively.

The reciprocity principle. Liking tends to be met with liking in return. When we discover that somebody accepts and approves of us, we usually respond by liking them in return. Negative reciprocity also occurs in groups: We dislike those who seem to reject us. In terms of the purposes of business communication, the ability to convey goodwill by establishing positive and productive relationships with others might improve the process of group formation.

The minimax principle. People will join groups and remain in groups that provide them with the maximum number of valued rewards while incurring the fewest number of possible costs.[8] Rewards include acceptance by others, camaraderie, assistance in reaching personal goals, social support, exposure to new ideas, and opportunities to interact with people who are interesting and attractive. Although membership in a work team may not be voluntary, considering the minimax principle may help leaders ensure that teamwork goes more smoothly. As with the reciprocity principle, the ability to convey goodwill by establishing positive relationships with others may help in group formation.

In addition to the potential rewards of belonging to a team, people are usually attracted to groups whose members possess positively valued qualities, and they avoid groups of people with objectionable qualities. We prefer to associate with people who are generous, enthusiastic, punctual, dependable, helpful, strong, truthful, and intelligent.[9] We tend to dislike and reject people who possess socially unattractive

Niklas Savander, executive vice president and general manager of the Services and Software Division at Nokia, understands the world functions through personal relationships.

qualities—people who seem pushy, rude, or self-centered.[10] Boring people are particularly unappealing. Such people tend to be passive, but when they do interact, they speak slowly, pause before making a point, and drag out meetings. Those perceived as boring may also sidetrack the group unnecessarily, show little enthusiasm, and seem too serious and preoccupied with themselves. Therefore, the makeup of the group in terms of personal characteristics can also affect its success and members' morale.

Still, most of us do not join just any group that promises a favorable reward (cost ratio). Our decision to join a group is based on two factors: our **comparison level** and our **comparison level for alternatives**.[11] Comparison level (CL) is the standard by which individuals evaluate the desirability of group membership; CL is strongly influenced by previous relationships. If previous group memberships have been positive, a person's CL should be high compared to someone whose previous experience with groups has been one of higher costs and lower rewards. However, comparison level only predicts when we will be satisfied with membership in a group. Therefore, team leaders may also consider member's attitudes about groups before assigning them to a team to ensure best results.

To predict when people will join and leave groups, we must also consider the value of other, alternative groups. Comparison level for alternatives (CL$_{alt}$) can be defined as the lowest level of outcomes a member will accept in light of available alternative opportunities. CL$_{alt}$ largely determines whether members enter and exit groups whereas CL determines the satisfaction with membership.

Commitment to a group is in many cases determined by the availability of alternative groups. Members who feel that they have no alternative to remaining in the group are often the most committed. Members also become more committed to a group the more they put into it. Although members in workplace situations may not voluntarily be placed on a team, seeing more productive, coherent teams may affect them negatively in the sense that members may resent being placed on a less attractive team and may affect the group dynamic negatively.

Group Roles

Roles in groups structure behavior by dictating the "part" that members take as they interact. Once cast in a role, such as leader, outcast, or questioner, a group member tends to perform certain actions and interact with group members in a particular way. Sometimes groups deliberately create roles; this is called a formal group structure. However, even without a deliberate attempt to create a formal structure, the group will probably develop an informal group structure.

Broadly, there are three types of group roles: task roles, socioemotional or social maintenance roles, and individualistic roles. People who fulfill task roles focus on the group's goals, its task, and members' attempts to support one another as they work.

A group may need to accomplish its tasks, but it must also ensure that the interpersonal and emotional needs of the members are met. Such roles as "supporter,"

comparison level (CL)
The standard by which individuals evaluate the desirability of group membership; CL is strongly influenced by previous relationships.

comparison level for alternatives (CL$_{alt}$)
The lowest level of outcomes a member will accept in light of available alternative opportunities.

Bob Strong/Reuters/Landov

"clown," and even "critic" help satisfy the emotional needs of the group members. For a group to survive, it must both accomplish its tasks and maintain the relationships among its members.

A third set of roles, individualistic roles, are taken up by people who emphasize their own needs over those of the group. Members who adopt individualistic roles may do little work and demand that others take care of them. Typically, people in individualistic roles do not contribute to the proper functioning of a group. Group roles and their functions are listed in Table 10-1.

Table 10-1 Roles in Groups.

ROLE	FUNCTION
Task Roles	
Initiator/contributor	Recommends novel ideas about the problem at hand, new ways to approach the problem, or solutions not yet considered
Information seeker	Emphasizes getting the facts by calling for background information from others
Opinion seeker	Asks for more qualitative types of data, such as attitudes, values, and feelings
Information giver	Provides opinions, values, and feelings
Elaborator	Gives additional information—examples, rephrasings, implications—about points others make
Coordinator	Shows the relevance of each idea and its relationship to the overall problem
Orienter	Refocuses discussion on the topic whenever necessary
Evaluator/critic	Appraises the quality of the group's methods, logic, and results
Energizer	Stimulates the group to continue working when discussion flags
Procedural technician	Cares for operational details, such as the materials and machinery
Recorder	Takes notes and maintains records
Socioemotional Roles	
Encourager	Rewards others through agreement, warmth, and praise
Harmonizer	Mediates conflict among group members
Compromiser	Shifts his or her position on an issue to reduce group conflict
Gatekeeper/expediter	Smoothes communication by setting up procedures and ensuring equal participation from members
Standard setter	Expresses, or calls for discussion of, standards for evaluating the quality of the group process
Group observer/ commentator	Points out the positive and negative aspects of the group's dynamics and calls for change if necessary
Follower	Accepts the ideas others offer and serves as an audience for the group
Individualistic Roles	
Aggressor	Expresses disapproval of acts, ideas, feelings of others; attacks the group
Blocker	Resists the group's influence; opposes the group unnecessarily
Dominator	Asserts authority or superiority; is manipulative
Evader/self-confessor	Expresses personal interests, feelings, or opinions unrelated to group goals
Help seeker	Expresses insecurity, confusion, or self-deprecation
Recognition seeker	Calls attention to him or herself; is self-aggrandizing
Playboy/girl	Is uninvolved in the group, cynical, and nonchalant
Special-interest pleader	Remains apart from the group by acting as a representative of another social group or category

CriticalThinking

What group roles do you tend to play? What roles would you like to introduce into your repertoire? What roles should the competent communicator avoid?

Group Member Relations

Intermember relations also affect group structure. Intermember relations or the relations of the group members to one another are determined by patterns of status, attraction, and communication.

Status Hierarchies

Variations in dominance, prestige, and control among members reflect the group's status relations. Status patterns are often hierarchical and centralized. Status differences in groups violate our expectations of "equal treatment for all," but in the microsociety of a group, equality is the exception and inequality the rule. Initially, group members may start off on equal footing, but over time, status differentiation takes place. Who rises to the top of the heap and who remains on the bottom is partly determined by the individual and partly by the group. Individuals must communicate their claim to higher status, and the other group members must accept it. Individuals who deserve status are not always afforded status by their groups. Individuals who speak rapidly without hesitation, advise others what to do, and confirm others' statements are often more influential than individuals who signal submissiveness.

Attraction Relations

Just as members of the group can be ranked from low to high in terms of status, so, too, can the members be ordered from least liked to most liked.[12] Popular individuals are the most liked, rejected members are the least liked, neglected members are nominated neither as most nor least liked, and average members are liked by several others in the group.[13] Cliques also form in groups; these subgroups usually display homophily. In other words, members of cliques are often more similar to one another than they are to the members of the total group.

Individuals are generally considered more attractive if they possess socially attractive qualities, such as cooperativeness and physical appeal, but social standing also depends on the degree to which the individual's attributes match the qualities the group values. This match is referred to as person-group fit.

Communication Networks

intermember relations
The relations of the group members to one another, which are determined by patterns of status, attraction, and communication.

People of higher status and attraction often stay in close communication, whereas those on the bottom may be cut off from communication. The most important feature of a communication network is its degree of centralization. Networks can be centralized (one person controls the flow of information) or decentralized (all members can communicate with one another). The amount and type of information to

FIGURE 10-1 Common Communication Networks

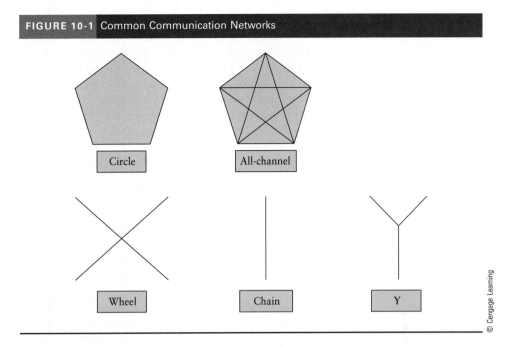

be delivered, or what is called "information saturation," determines the best communication network for any task. If the information is simple, centralized networks work best; if the information to be transmitted is complex, decentralized networks are more efficient.[14]

A person's position in a communication network can also have effects. As discussed in Chapter 9, those who are more peripheral in a communication network are usually those who are least satisfied, whereas those in central positions are most satisfied. Because the overall number of peripheral positions in a centralized network exceeds the number of central positions, the overall satisfaction in a centralized group is lower than the level of satisfaction in a decentralized group.

Research on communication networks commonly employs five different networks, illustrated in Figure 10-1. Leavitt found that the central person in a network such as the wheel usually becomes the leader and enjoys the position more than those on the periphery, where communication is more restricted.[15] Both the chain and the Y networks have characteristics similar to the wheel. The circle and the all-channel patterns are much less centralized, on the other hand, and are sometimes leaderless or have distributed leadership.

In summary, relations among group members can be affected by three things: a member's status within the group, a member's popularity within the group, and the type of network used within the group to disseminate information and a person's position in that network.

Stages of Group Development

Group cohesion, or unity, develops over time. It is the result of group development. There are five stages of group development: forming, storming, norming, performing, and adjourning.[16]

In the major processes in the *forming stage*, members become familiar with one another and the group; as well, members deal with issues of dependency and inclusion, the acceptance of a leader, and the development of group consensus. The characteristics of this stage include tentative, polite communications; concern over ambiguity and group goals; and an active leader and compliant members.

In the *storming or conflict stage*, the major processes include disagreement over procedures, expression of dissatisfaction, tension among members, and antagonism toward the leader. The characteristics of this stage include criticism of ideas, poor attendance, hostility, polarization, and coalition formation.

In the *norming stage*, major processes include the growth of cohesion; establishment of roles, standards, and relationships; and increased trust and communication. This stage is characterized by agreement on procedures, reduction in role ambiguity, and increased "we-ness."

In the *performing stage*, the major processes include goal achievement, high task achievement, and emphasis on performance and production. This stage is characterized by decision making, problem solving, and mutual cooperation.

In the *adjourning phase*, the major processes include termination of roles, completion of tasks, and reduction of dependency. This stage is characterized by disintegration and withdrawal, increased independence and emotionality, and regret.

Groups do not always develop in this order. Some groups manage to avoid particular stages, others move through the stages in a unique order, and still others develop in ways that cannot be described by this five-stage model. In addition, the demarcation between stages is often not clear-cut.

From a leadership or management perspective, it is valuable to recognize the stages of group formation and to intervene as appropriate. For example, in the norming stage, communication and other behaviors that began to appear in earlier stages is formalized into group or team norms. This process often occurs outside of members' consciousness and because of this, ineffective or undesirable norms may develop, such as an unstated norm that allows members to miss meetings or deadlines without any negative repercussions. To avoid these kinds of occurrences, team leaders can be prepared to intervene if negative norms appear within a team or can more proactively engage the team in creating norms that will help it to work effectively and efficiently.

CriticalThinking

Where do group norms come from? Why do we tend to conform to group norms? Is tension in a group desirable?

The Effects of Group Cohesion

Members are usually more satisfied with their team when it is cohesive rather than noncohesive. A cohesive group creates a healthier workplace, at least at the psychological level. Because people in cohesive groups respond to one another in a more positive fashion than the members of noncohesive groups, people experience less anxiety and tension.[17] Members of cohesive teams more readily accept the group's goals, decisions, and norms.

Membership in a cohesive team can prove problematic for members, however, if they become too dependent on the group. Furthermore, pressure to conform is also greater in cohesive groups, which also can potentially create problems. Evidence suggests that members of cohesive groups sometimes react very negatively and take harsh actions to bring dissenters into line when a group member goes against group consensus.[18] Cohesion can also increase negative group processes.[19] Cohesive groups vent their frustrations through interpersonal aggression: overt hostility, joking hostility, scapegoating, and domination of subordinate group members. In contrast, noncohesive groups tend to form coalitions among members.

Generally speaking, though, groups that succeed tend to be more cohesive, and groups that fail tend to be less cohesive. The cohesion-performance relation is strongest when group cohesion is based on commitment to the task rather than attraction or group pride.[20] This finding is important for team leaders who want to ensure that a team is successful. Success is more likely if members are committed to the goals of the group or the team objectives. Cohesion also counts more when the group's task requires high levels of interaction and interdependence.[21]

These findings explain why some groups, even though they are cohesive, are not productive: The members are not committed to the group's performance goals. Surveys indicate that fairly low standards of performance can develop within highly cohesive groups. As long as group norms encourage high productivity, cohesiveness and productivity are positively related.

Sources of Influence within a Group

Three types of influence can be exercised in group situations. Through **informational influence**, the group provides members with information that can be used to make decisions and form opinions. When **normative influence** occurs, members tailor their actions to fit the group's standards and conventions. **Interpersonal influence**, in contrast, occurs when the group uses verbal and nonverbal influence tactics to induce change.

Informational influence is not immune to the effects of social influence. In other words, we may discover new information by observing others' responses. Social comparison theory assumes that group members treat other people's responses as data when formulating opinions and making decisions. In some cases, teams actively gather information about members' opinions, but generally individuals gather information about others' views through routine discussion.[22] Unfortunately, this intuitive approach tends to be biased. Members of the majority, for example, tend to underestimate the size of their group, whereas minority members tend to overestimate the degree to which others agree with them.

People who consistently violate their group's norms are often reminded of their duty and are told to change their ways. They are often disliked, assigned lower-status jobs, and are dismissed from the group in some cases.[23] Normative influence explains why certain people, such as those with a high need for social approval and those who tend to be more authoritarian, conform more than others.[24] Nonconformists tend to be more self-confident, whereas counterconformists actively resist majority influence.

Interpersonal influence tactics include complaining, demanding, threatening, pleading, negotiating, pressuring, manipulating, and rejecting. The occurrence of rejection is more pronounced in more cohesive groups. In extreme cases, group members will eventually stop communicating with "disliked deviants," at least in cases where cohesive groups are working on relevant tasks.[25]

informational influence
When the group provides members with information that they can use to make decisions and form opinions.

normative influence
When group members tailor their actions to fit the group's standards and conventions.

interpersonal influence
When the group uses verbal and nonverbal influence tactics to induce change.

How does communication influence how a team performs? Please provide examples that illustrate your point from your own work or group experiences.

Group Performance

First of all, to perform well, groups must have the resources they need. They must have the skills, talents, and energy needed to successfully complete tasks. Secondly, the group must combine its resources effectively. Even if members have the resources required for a task, the group may fail if it does not marshal these resources successfully. Performance depends on the group's resources and the methods used to combine these resources to meet the demands of the group's task.

A group's performance also depends, in part, on its members' knowledge, skills, and abilities. On the task side, groups whose members are more skilled at the work to be done outperform groups comprised of less skilled workers. On the interpersonal side, members must be able to work well with others on joint tasks. Communication skills, leadership abilities, and a talent for managing conflicts are some of the qualities possessed by members of successful work teams. Some groups fail because they simply do not include members with the qualities and characteristics needed to complete their task.

Diversity can also help a group's performance. Diverse groups have an advantage when members are all highly skilled but these skills do not overlap. Diverse groups may be better at coping with changing work conditions because their wider range of talents and traits enhances flexibility. Diversity can also help groups to seek alternative solutions to problems and enhance creativity and innovation.

Diversity can also create problems in groups, though. Diverse groups may lack cohesion because of perceived dissimilarities. In addition, diversity in skill level—some members are competent but others are incompetent—does not appear to boost productivity.[26]

Groups that bring together people with similar personalities tend to outperform groups whose members have dissimilar personalities.[27] Classroom groups performed best when they were composed of individuals whose personality characteristics were similar and focused on goal attainment.[28]

Another negative effect on performance is **process losses**, or reductions in performance effectiveness or efficiency caused by faulty group processes, including motivational and coordination problems. Although a group obviously produces more than an individual, groups usually do not work at maximum efficiency. As more members are added to a group, it becomes increasingly less efficient. Secondly, people may not work as hard when they are in groups. This reduction of effort by individuals working in groups is called **social loafing**.[29] Social loafing occurs when individual input is not identifiable. When individual contributions are clearly known, evaluation apprehension sets in as we worry about how others will evaluate us. However, when we are anonymous and our contributions are unidentified, the presence of others reduces evaluation apprehension and social loafing

process losses
Reductions in performance effectiveness or efficiency caused by faulty group processes, including motivational and coordination problems.

social loafing
The reduction of effort by individuals working in groups.

becomes more likely.[30] Therefore, team leaders should ensure that members are assigned clearly measurable tasks that are evaluated with established outcomes.

Another cause of social loafing is the fact that group work often causes social dilemmas. Members may want to do their share to help the group reach its goals, but they are simultaneously tempted to concentrate on their own personal goals. So they engage in **free-riding**. People are most likely to free-ride when their contributions are combined in a single product and no one is monitoring the size of each person's contribution. Free-riding also increases when group members worry that their coworkers are holding back.

A third reason for social loafing is what is called the illusion of group productivity. Members of groups working on collective tasks generally think that their group is more productive than most.[31] Group members also generally do not feel that they are doing less than their fair share.

Groups can improve productivity in several ways:

1. Personal stake in the group's outcome should be increased. When individuals feel that a poor group performance will affect them personally, they do not loaf.[32]
2. Groups that set clear, attainable goals outperform groups whose members have lost sight of their objectives.[33]
3. Groups that set high goals tend to outproduce those with lower levels of aspiration.
4. Groups with realistic expectations about their chances of success also perform better. Unrealistic goals can undermine motivation, though.[34]
5. Increased unity can improve performance. However, increased cohesiveness improves performance only if group norms emphasize productivity.

Groups can take steps to discourage social loafing, such as the following:

1. **Establish a group responsibility norm.** From the beginning, group members should state the expectations for individual responsibility in the group and the importance of equal contribution by members to group tasks.
2. **Note the critical importance of each member's efforts.** The group leader should communicate the importance and essentialness of each individual's effort and contribution to completing the group task.
3. **Identify and evaluate individual contributions.** Each member should be provided specific and identifiable tasks, and the group should set aside time to evaluate each member's contribution to the project.
4. **Talk to the problem individual privately.** This step calls for the leader or a designated member to ask the member why his or her contribution is less than expected. Asking the problem individual to suggest ways that he or she might improve his or her performance may help in achieving buy-in to the group task.
5. **Confront the individual who is loafing as a group.** Group members should identify and describe the problem behavior in detail. The individual who is loafing should be asked how the problem might be solved. This step is effective only if group members avoid name-calling or personality attacks on the offender.
6. **Consult someone with more power.** When all these steps fail, the group should consult a teacher, supervisor, or someone with greater authority than the group members for advice or help. The authority figure may need to discuss the problem with the individual who is loafing.

free-riding
When group members do not work as hard when they believe others will compensate for this lack of effort.

7. **Fire the individual who is slacking.** This step should be taken only when all other attempts to obtain the cooperation of the individual who is loafing have failed.

8. **Sidestep the individual who is loafing.** The group may decide to reconfigure the individual responsibilities and tasks so that, even if the individual who is loafing does not contribute, the group can still accomplish its task. In the workplace, this step might result in a demotion or reassignment to another job or department.[35]

Group Decision Making

Groups can be useful in making decisions because more people potentially bring more information to the task. In addition, groups tend to process the information they have more thoroughly through discussion. For effective decision making, groups should ensure that the process they use is a productive one. Although groups can be useful for decision making, they also face some challenges.

Stages of Group Decision Making

Many groups consistently process information in four or more stages or steps. The following are some of these steps as practiced in the United States:

1. **Orientation.** The group identifies the problem to be solved and plans the process to use in reaching the decisions. Criteria that an optimal solution must meet should be identified as a way to weigh each option. Cultural differences can affect the approach that is best for the first stage of the process. Rather than immediately focusing on task accomplishment as is generally the case in the United States and Finland, some cultures prefer small talk to establish rapport. These include Australia and Sweden.

2. **Discussion.** The group gathers information about the situation, identifies and weighs options, and tests its assumptions.

3. **Decision.** Ideally, the criteria that were listed to identify the optimal solution can be used to select the best option. Groups also rely on an implicit or explicit social decision scheme to combine individual preferences into a collective decision. Common schemes include delegating, voting with various proportions needed for a decision, and consensus.

4. **Implementation.** The group carries out the decision and assesses its impact. Members are more likely to implement decisions when they are actively involved in the decision-making process.

The Challenges of Group Decision Making

Although group decision making can have productive outcomes, members should be aware of some of the challenges and limitations of such a process. One problem is the tendency for groups to spend too much of their discussion time examining shared information—details that two or more of the members know in common—rather than unshared information.[36] This tendency is called **oversampling**. Oversampling of shared information leads to poorer decisions when useful data might be revealed by considering the unshared information more closely. Oversampling of shared information increases when tasks have no demonstrably correct solution and when group leaders do not actively draw out unshared information.

oversampling
The tendency for groups to spend too much of their discussion time examining shared information—details that two or more of the group members know in common—rather than unshared information.

In addition, the usefulness of group discussion is limited, in part, by members' inability to express themselves clearly and by their limited listening skills. Not all group members have the interpersonal skills a discussion demands. When researchers asked 569 full-time employees what happened during a meeting to limit its effectiveness, they received 2,500 answers, which are provided in the Table 10-2.[37]

Sometimes, groups use discussion to avoid making decisions. In addition, judgment errors that cause people to overlook important information and overutilize unimportant information are often exacerbated in groups. These errors occur more frequently when group members are cognitively busy (that is, they are trying to work on too many tasks at once).

Common sense suggests that groups are more cautious than individuals, but early studies found that group discussion generates a shift in the direction of the more risky alternative. When researchers later found evidence of cautious shifts as well as risky ones, they concluded that the responses of groups tend to be more extreme than individual members' responses (the group polarization hypothesis).[38] Polarization is sustained by the desire to evaluate one's own opinions by comparing them to others' (social comparison theory), by exposure to other members' pro-risk and pro-caution arguments (persuasive arguments theory), and by groups' implicit reliance on a "risk-supported wins" social decision scheme.[39] Groups whose members are initially more risk-prone than cautious adopt this approach. In such groups, if one person supports a risky alternative, the group will not adopt it. But if two people support it, the group often accepts the risky recommendation.[40]

Cultural differences in negotiation styles and strategies can also affect the decision-making process. For example, Russian negotiating tactics include a need for authority, a need to avoid risk, and a need to control.[41] Considering two key negotiation styles help to illustrate how cultural differences may affect decision making. The competitive approach is common in the United States; it is more

Table 10-2 Group Decision-Making Challenges.

Problem (Frequency)	Description
Poor communication skills (10 percent)	Poor listening skills, ineffective voice, poor nonverbal skills, lack of effective visual aids, misunderstood or unclearly identified topic, repetition, use of jargon
Egocentric behavior (8 percent)	Domination of conversation and group, behaviors that are loud and overbearing, one-upmanship, show of power, manipulation, intimidation, filibustering, talking to hear self talk
Nonparticipation (7 percent)	Lack of full participation, speaking up, volunteering, active inclusion, and discussion
Sidetracked (6.5 percent)	Leaving main topic
Interruptions (6 percent)	Members interrupting speaker, talking over others, socializing, and allowing phone calls or messages from customers/clients
Negative leader behavior (6 percent)	Lack of organization, focus, preparation, control, decision making; being late, getting sidetracked
Attitudes and emotions (5 percent)	Poor attitude: defensive or evasive, argumentative, personal accusations, no courtesy or respect, complaining or griping, lack of control of emotions

Table 10-3 A Comparison of Negotiation Styles of Different Cultures.

ELEMENT	U.S. AMERICANS	JAPANESE	ARABS	MEXICANS
Group composition	Marketing-oriented	Function-oriented	Committee of specialists	Friendship-oriented
Number involved	2–3	4–7	4–6	2–3
Space orientation	Confrontational, competitive	Display harmonious relationship	Status	Close, friendly
Establishing rapport	Short period; direct to task	Longer period, until harmony	Long period, until trusted	Longer period, discuss family
Exchange of information	Documented, step by step, multimedia	Extensive, concentrate on receiving side	Less emphasis on technology, more on relationship	Less emphasis on technology, more on relationship
Persuasion tools	Time pressure, saving/making money	Maintain relationship, intergroup connections	Go-between, hospitality	Emphasis on family and social concerns, goodwill measured in generations
Use of language	Open/direct, sense of urgency	Indirect, appreciative, cooperative	Flattery, emotional, religious	Respectful, gracious
Decision-making process	Top management team	Collective	Team makes recommendation	Senior manager and secretary
Decision maker	Top management team	Middle line with team consensus	Senior manager	Senior manager
Risk taking	Calculated, personal responsibility	Low group responsibility	Religion-based	Personally responsible

Sources: Elashmawi, F., & Harris, P. (1998). *Multicultural management 2000.* (Houston: Butterworth-Heinemann); Ruch, W. V. (1989). *International handbook of corporate communication.* (Jefferson, NC: McFarland).

individualistic and persuasion-oriented. This approach looks for a solution that is best for the negotiator's side versus the win-win style that characterizes Chinese negotiations. A second-approach, problem solving, is generally considered better for intercultural situations since it identifies the need to adapt to national cultural differences as well as organizational ones. A brief comparison of the negotiation styles of different cultures is shown in Table 10-3.

Group decision making can be challenging because it requires the ability to consider and accommodate multiple interpretative frameworks—multiple versions of reality—and to emerge with a single recommendation or course of action.[42] This means that we must be willing to accept the inevitability of differences and to make a commitment to dialogue. Groups also can be more effective at decision making if they pay more attention to the procedure that they use to solve problems.[43]

Sources of Group Conflict

There are three types of group conflict: personal conflict, substantive conflict, and procedural conflict. Conflict can also be increased by other factors, such as competition within a group and the social dilemmas that groups can create for their members. Just as there are various types of conflict, group members can use several approaches to resolve it.

Personal Conflict

Personal conflict is rooted in individuals' dislike of other group members. For example, group members who treat others unfairly or impolitely create more conflict than those who are polite.[44]

The relationship between dislike and conflict explains why groups with greater diversity sometimes display more conflict than homogeneous groups. Just as similarity between members increases interpersonal attraction, dissimilarity tends to increase dislike and conflict.[45] Groups whose members have dissimilar personalities (for example, differences in authoritarianism, cognitive complexity, and temperament) generally do not get along as well as groups composed of people whose personalities are similar.[46] Groups whose members vary in terms of ability, experience, opinions, values, race, personality, ethnicity, and so on can capitalize on their members' wider range of resources and viewpoints, but these groups often suffer high levels of conflict.[47]

Substantive Conflict

When people discuss their problems and plans, they sometimes disagree with one another's analyses. These substantive conflicts, however, are integrally related to the group's work. Substantive conflict does not stem from personal disagreements between individuals but from disagreements about issues that are relevant to the group's real goals and outcomes. In other words, of the three types of conflict, substantive conflict has the potential to provide the most positive outcomes, such as making plans, increasing creativity, solving problems, deciding issues, and resolving conflicts of viewpoints.[48] Substantive conflict, in fact, is one of the reasons that groups are used to complete tasks.

Even though substantive conflicts help groups reach their goals, these impersonal conflicts can turn into personal ones. Members who disagree with the group, even when their position is a reasonable one, often provoke considerable animosity within the group. The dissenter who refuses to accept others' views is less liked. Group members who slow down the process of reaching consensus are often responded to negatively. Such pressures to conform can lead to what is called **groupthink**. To avoid this aspect of groupthink, groups should encourage members to take on the role of devil's advocate.

groupthink
Conformity-seeking behavior of cohesive groups that interferes with effective decision making.

Procedural Conflict

Although substantive conflicts occur when ideas, opinions, and interpretations clash, procedural conflicts occur when strategies, policies, and methods collide. Many groups can minimize procedural conflict by adopting formal rules that specify goals, decisional processes, and responsibilities.[49] Rules, however, can be overly formalized, which can hinder openness, creativity, and adaptability to change.

CriticalThinking

Of the three types of group conflict—personal, substantive, and procedural—which is the easiest to avoid? How might you use these strategies to avoid conflict in your groups? Your workplace?

Conflict and Competition

Conflict is more likely when group members compete against each other for such resources as money, power, time, prestige, or materials, instead of working with one another to reach common goals. When people compete, they must look out for their own interests instead of the group's interests or their comembers' interests. Because competing members can succeed only when others fail, they may even sabotage others' work, criticize it, and withhold information and resources that others might need.[50]

In contrast, members of cooperative groups enhance their outcomes by helping other members achieve success. Work units with high levels of cooperation have fewer latent tensions, personality conflicts, and verbal confrontations.[51]

Few situations involve pure cooperation or pure competition; the motive to compete is often mixed with the motive to cooperate. Furthermore, as the *norm of reciprocity* suggests, cooperation begets cooperation, whereas competition begets competition.

People's personalities contribute to conflict. Some people seem to be natural competitors, whereas others are more cooperative or individualistic.[52] **Competitors** view group disagreements as win–lose situations and find satisfaction in forcing their ideas on others.

Individuals with competitive value orientations are more likely to find themselves in conflicts. Furthermore, competitors rarely modify their behavior in response to the complaints of others because they are relatively unconcerned with maintaining smooth interpersonal relations. Two other value orientations in groups are those of cooperator and individualist. **Cooperators** value accommodative interpersonal strategies, whereas **individualists** are concerned only with their own outcomes. Individualists make decisions based on what they personally will achieve, with no concern for others' outcomes. They neither interfere with nor assist others' attempts to reach their goals. It should be noted that this definition of individualist differs from the conception of individualistic roles in groups in that the individualistic inclination in a group situation can negatively affect others. In the schema discussed here, competitive behavior is more akin to the individualistic roles that can arise in groups.

Social values vary across cultures. As was discussed in Chapter 4, Western societies such as the United States tend to value competition, whereas more cooperative and peaceful societies devalue individual achievement and avoid any kind of competitive games.[53] Group-oriented cultures value reaching consensus on all decisions and individuals avoid making individual decisions. These cultures include those of Japan, China, Brazil, and Africa, as well as Polynesians and Native Americans. In individual-oriented cultures, one person will probably control the discussion and make the final decisions. The United States is probably the most individualistic culture in the world, while Latin America, Great Britain, Australia, and Canada are also individualistic.[54]

Social Dilemmas

Groups create social dilemmas for their members. The members, as individuals, are motivated to maximize their own rewards and minimize their costs. Conflicts arise when individualistic motives trump group-oriented motives and the collective intervenes to redress the imbalance.

As mentioned earlier, one cause of conflict is the division of resources. When group members feel they are receiving too little for what they are giving, they

competitors
People who view group disagreements as win–lose situations and find satisfaction in forcing their views on others.

cooperators
Individuals who value accommodative interpersonal strategies in groups.

individualists
Individuals who are concerned only with their own outcomes in group situations.

ResponsibleCommunication

A new phenomenon that is gaining attention in a hyper-competitive global economy is workplace bullying. Bullies not only stifle productivity and innovation throughout the organization, they most often target an organization's best employees, because it is precisely those employees who are the most threatening to bullies.[55]

Recent commentators have used different ways to describe bullying behavior, but they agree that a bully is only interested in maintaining his or her power and control. Because bullies are cowards and are driven by deep-seated insecurities and fears of inadequacy, they intentionally wage a covert war against an organization's best employees—those who are highly skilled, intelligent, creative, ethical, able to work well with others, and independent (who refuse to be subservient or controlled by others).[56] Bullies can act alone or in groups, and bullying behavior can exist at

any level of an organization. Bullies can be superiors, subordinates, coworkers, and colleagues.

The problem with workplace bullying is that many bullies are hard to identify because they operate surreptitiously under the guise of being civil and cooperative. Although workplace bullying is being discussed more than ever before, and there may eventually be specific legislation outlawing such behavior, organizations cannot afford to wait for new laws to eradicate the bullies in their midst. Organizations must root out workplace bullying before it squelches their employees' creativity and productivity, or even drives out their best employees, thus fatally impacting an organization's ability to compete.[57]

Eradicating bullying behavior from an organization starts at the top because it is the head of any organization that sets the tone for whether bullying

behavior will be accepted, they say. An organization reflects the values, attitudes, and actions of its leadership. Leaders who ignore, or otherwise allow, these destructive behavior patterns to occur are eroding the health of their organizations and opening the door for some of their best talent to escape from this upsetting and counterproductive environment.[58]

Questions for Discussion

1. Have you witnessed or been the victim of a bully, workplace or otherwise? Do you agree with the assertion that allowing workplace bullying to occur can fatally impact an organization's ability to be competitive?

2. Do you agree with Richardson and McCord's assertion that eradicating bullying in the workplace is the responsibility of management? Do other employees have a role?

---

sometimes withdraw from the group, reduce their effort, and turn in work of lower quality. Group members who feel that they are receiving too much for what they are giving sometimes increase their efforts.

As conflicts escalate, group members often become more committed to their positions instead of more understanding of the positions taken by others. Conflict is exacerbated by members' tendencies to misperceive others and to assume that the other party's behavior is caused by personal rather than situational factors. This tendency is called the **fundamental attribution error**. As conflict worsens, group members will shift from weak to strong influence tactics, such as threats, punishment, and bullying.

fundamental attribution error Conflict that is exacerbated by members' tendencies to misperceive others and to assume that the other party's behavior is caused by personal rather than situational factors.

Conflict Resolution

In group and team work situations, the first dysfunction that occurs is a lack of trust. Trust is defined as the confidence among group members that their peers' intentions are good. In other words, we must believe that those with whom we

FIGURE 10-2 Styles of Conflict Resolution

Concern for self

High
aggressiveness

Competition

Collaboration

Compromise

Low
aggressiveness

Avoidance

Accommodation

Low cooperation

High cooperation

Concern for others

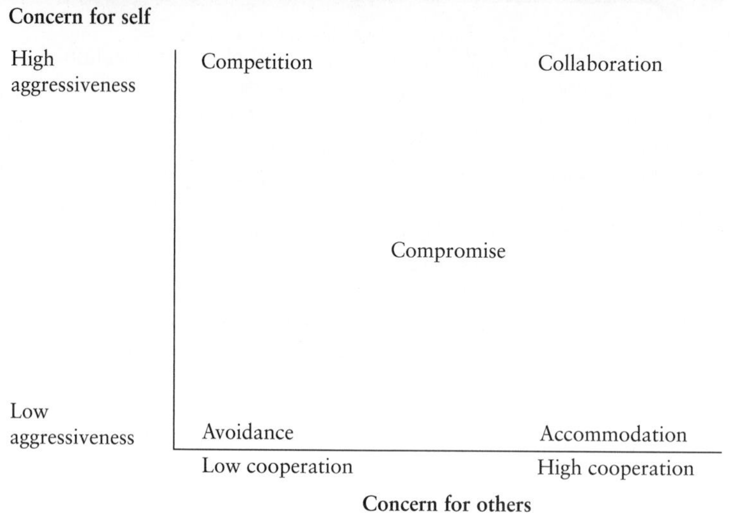

© Cengage Learning

work will not act opportunistically or take advantage of us and others to narrowly pursue their own self-interests.[59] Without trust, individuals are unable to use what is generally considered the most effective approach to conflict resolution: collaboration. Collaboration is built on trust. Collaboration is one of the five styles of conflict resolution illustrated in Figure 10-2.[60]

As Figure 10-2 indicates, the styles of conflict resolution can be understood by comparing how each relates in the areas of concern for others and concern for self, as well as by the level of aggressiveness and cooperation. The following is an explanation of the styles of conflict resolution:

- **Competition.** This style is characterized by high aggressiveness and low cooperation. Some people see conflict as a win–lose situation and use competitive and aggressive tactics to intimidate others. Fighting can take many forms, including authoritative mandates, challenges, arguing, insults, accusations, complaining, vengeance, and even physical violence.[61] An individual who uses a competing style exhibits a high concern for self and low concern for others.

- **Collaboration.** An individual who exhibits this style shows a high concern for others and for self. Because of this orientation, this style is characterized by assertive communication and high levels of cooperation. As such, it is considered a "win–win" approach, because a solution should be found that satisfies both parties.

- **Compromise.** This style is a middle ground. The emphasis is on achieving workable but not necessarily optimal solutions. Some consider this a "lose–lose" approach to conflict resolution.

- **Avoidance.** Individuals who practice this style show little concern for relationships or for task accomplishment. By avoiding conflict, they hope it will disappear. When students in small groups talked about their disagreements, they often said they adopted a "wait-and-see" attitude, hoping the problem would eventually go away.[62] Sometimes, however, avoiding is appropriate if you are a low-power person and the consequences of confrontation may be risky and harmful.

- **Accommodation.** This style is characterized by a high concern for relationships but a low concern for task accomplishment. Like avoiding, this can be a useful approach in groups that have shown a high degree of conflict. Accommodating others in this situation provides for an opportunity for tempers to cool and to move toward resolution. It can also be appropriate if the risk of yielding is low. For example, a group of your friends may disagree about where to eat dinner. The choice may be between two of your favorite restaurants; however, the one that most of your friends prefer is your second choice. Even so, because you like that restaurant, too, you have little to lose by yielding.

Of these five basic ways of resolving conflict, collaborating is more likely to promote group unity.

CriticalThinking

Describe a recent conflict you had with someone where you believe that poor communication on one or both parts was the culprit. What can be done to make sure this conflict does not occur again?

Our dislike of conflict and the need to promote cohesiveness can lead to an additional danger: groupthink. As mentioned earlier, groupthink occurs when group members dominate interaction, are intimidated by others, or care more about social acceptability than reaching the best solution. Groupthink occurs at the highest levels and can have serious consequences. It has been cited as causing the Bay of Pigs fiasco in the 1960s, the *Challenger* disaster in the 1980s, and the lack of effective preparation and response by the U.S. government to terrorism in the twenty-first century.

To avoid groupthink, teams should consider the following suggestions:

1. The leader should encourage participants to voice objections and critically evaluate ideas.
2. Members should take an impartial stance and not get wrapped up in ego and emotions, affording a more objective view of the decision.
3. More than one group can work on a problem, which may lead to radically different recommendations.
4. Each member can be encouraged to discuss the group's deliberations with people outside the group and get their feedback.
5. The group can invite outside experts in for their input and feedback.
6. The group can appoint a member to be devil's advocate to assure that the group explores all sides of each issue.
7. The group can be divided into subgroups, each of which works the problem separately and then reports back.

8. The group can hold a "second chance" meeting after reaching preliminary consensus, to allow members to express doubts and concerns that may have come up.[63]

In summary, it is useful to understand the benefits and potential problem areas of group work, because we will all work in groups throughout our lives. The issues surrounding such concerns as group structure and development, cohesiveness, influence, conflict, performance, and decision making should be understood and considered when working in groups or deciding whether a group approach is appropriate for a task.

Team Leadership

Leadership in work teams has become one of the most popular areas of leadership theory and research. It is critical to understand the role of leadership within teams to ensure their success. "Indeed, we would argue that effective leadership processes represent perhaps the most critical factor in the success of organizational teams."[64] By the same token, ineffective leadership is often seen as the primary reason teams fail.[65]

Team leadership may be performed by a formal team leader and/or shared by team members, a situation called **distributed leadership**.

A good leader needs to be flexible and have a broad repertoire of actions or skills to meet the team's diverse needs. The leader's role is to function in a manner that will help the group achieve effectiveness. The leader's goal is to solve team problems by analyzing the internal and external situation and selecting and implementing the appropriate behaviors to ensure team effectiveness.[66] The model of team leadership pictured in Figure 10-3 begins with the decisions that a leader must make; the next step is to take action and, hopefully, these actions will result in team effectiveness.

Leadership Decisions

The first decision a leader must make is whether it is appropriate to continue observing the team or to intervene and take action. The second decision is to determine the general task or relational function of the intervention that is needed. The final decision is whether to intervene at the internal level, or within the team itself, or at the external level.

- **Continue to monitor or take action?** The leader must monitor both the internal and external environment of the team to determine the next step. The leader may gather information from team members, from those outside the group, or from evaluating group outcomes. After gathering and interpreting information, leaders must take the right action based upon this information.
- **Intervene to meet task or relational goals?** The two critical functions of a group, task and socioemotional or relational goals, were discussed earlier in this chapter. This decision involves determining whether the team needs help with relational or task issues.
- **Intervene internally or externally?** The third strategic decision is the level of team process that needs attention: internal task or relational goals or external environmental factors. Internal issues might be group conflict or unclear goals whereas external issues might be lack of organizational support for the team.

distributed leadership
A situation in which team members share team leadership.

FIGURE 10-3 Hill's Model for Team Leadership

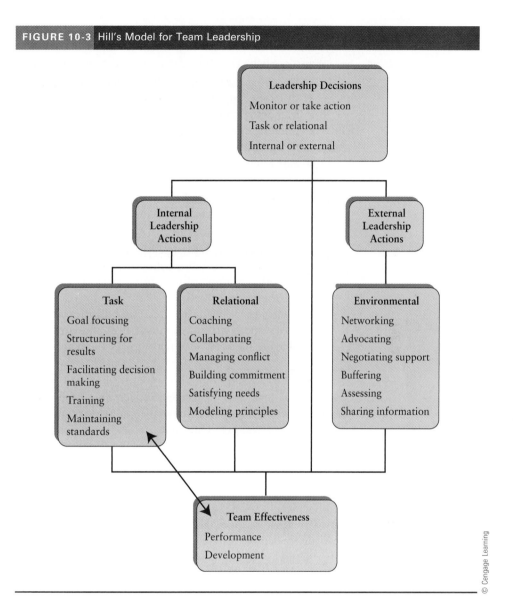

© Cengage Learning

Leadership Actions

As stated in the previous section, leadership actions may be internal or external; internal actions may focus on the task or the relational goals of the team.

- **Internal task actions.** Many of the task actions a leader might take are accomplished through communication. These include the following:
  - Goal focusing (clarifying, gaining agreement)
  - Structuring for results (planning, visioning, organization, clarifying roles, delegating)
  - Facilitating decision making (informing, coordinating, mediating, synthesizing, issue focusing)
  - Training members in task skills
  - Maintaining standards of excellence (assessing performance and addressing inadequate performance)

- **Internal relational actions.** The second set of leadership actions includes those that the leader might implement to improve team relationships. Many of these also are achieved through communication. They include the following:
  - Coaching team members in interpersonal skills
  - Collaborating (including, involving)
  - Managing conflict and power issues
  - Building commitment and team spirit (socializing, rewarding, innovating, recognizing)
  - Satisfying individual member needs (trusting, supporting, advocating)
  - Modeling ethical and principled practices (fair, consistent)
- **External environmental actions.** Again, many of these actions to improve the environmental interface with the team involve communication. Such actions include the following:
  - Networking and forming alliances (gathering information, increasing influence)
  - Advocating and representing the team
  - Negotiating upward to secure needed resources, support, and recognition for the team
  - Buffering the team from external distractions
  - Assessing environmental indicators of team effectiveness
  - Sharing relevant information with the team

Team Effectiveness

Two critical functions of team effectiveness are performance or task accomplishment and development or maintenance of the team. Team performance is the "quality of decision making, the ability to implement decisions, the outcomes of team work in terms of problems solved and work completed, and finally the quality of institutional leadership provided by the team."[67] Team development is the cohesiveness of the team and the ability of group members to satisfy their own needs while working effectively with other team members.

Effective groups have a clear, engaging direction; an enabling situation that contains structure, support, and coaching; and adequate resources.[68] Successful teams consistently demonstrate eight characteristics:

- **A clear elevating goal.** Teams often fail because they are given a vague task and then are asked to work out the details. Teams also fail because they let personal agendas or power issues replace their goal.
- **Results-driven structure.** Different types of teams have different types of structures. An effective team must use the appropriate structure; members need clear roles, a good communication system, methods for assessing individual performance, and an emphasis on fact-based judgments.
- **Competent team members.** Team members need not only sufficient information, education, and training, but also interpersonal and teamwork skills, and ideally certain personal characteristics, such as openness, supportiveness, action orientation, and a positive attitude.
- **Unified commitment.** A common occurrence is to call a group a team and then treat it as a collection of individuals. Teams don't just happen; they must be developed.
- **Collaborative climate.** A collaborative climate is one in which members can stay problem-focused, listen to and understand one another, feel free to take risks, and be willing to compensate for one another. To build a collaborative climate, trusting relationships need to be developed based on openness,

honesty, consistency, and respect. Effective team leaders ensure a collaborative climate by making communication safe, demanding and rewarding collaborative behavior, guiding the team's problem-solving efforts, and managing their own control needs.

- **Standards of excellence.** The organization or the team must set standards of excellence so that team members will feel pressure to perform at their highest levels. A leader can facilitate this process by requiring results, making expectations clear, reviewing results, providing feedback to resolve performance issues, and rewarding results.

- **External support.** A common mistake is to give teams challenging assignments but no organizational support to accomplish them. Organizations also often ask employees to work on difficult assignments but then do not reward them with raises or bonuses. Teams that are given the resources needed to do their jobs are recognized for their accomplishments and rewarded for team rather than individual performance and can achieve excellence.

- **Principled leadership.** Effective leaders are committed to the team's goals and give members autonomy to achieve those goals. Leaders can reduce team effectiveness by being unwilling to confront inadequate performance, having too many priorities, and overestimating the positive aspects of team performance.[69]

The model for team leadership is based on the assumption that the leader's job is to monitor the team and to take whatever action is deemed necessary to ensure team effectiveness. The model attempts to provide specific actions that leaders can perform to improve team functioning and effectiveness. In addition, team leaders need a wide repertoire of communication skills to monitor the team and take appropriate action.

Communicating in Virtual Teams

A 2010 study of 30,000 employees of multinational companies found that virtual teams face many of the same challenges that all teams do, but language difficulties, time-and-distance challenges, the absence of face-to-face contact, and, above all, the barriers posed by cultural differences and personal communication styles make virtual work far more complex.[70]

According to the survey, respondents indicated that virtual teams differed from and were more challenging than face-to-face teams in the following tasks:

- Managing conflict (73%)
- Making decisions (69%)
- Expressing opinions (64%) (This issue was particularly problematic in indirect cultures.)

Some of the recommendations of the study emphasized the need for virtual teams to establish specific work rules (such as those outlining rules for respectful interaction) that are often assumed in co-located teams. It also recommended that virtual teams need to pay greater attention to team structure than co-located teams do. In addition, virtual teams must carefully monitor and adhere to the work rules they have created. Finally, they need to be aware of the influence of culture on work styles and to develop procedures to assure intercultural effectiveness.[71]

The success of digital collaboration depends largely upon team members' abilities to adopt new ways of working. The previously cited study indicated that the most important characteristics of virtual team members were

- A willingness to share information (18%)
- Being proactively engaged (17%)

- Being collaborative (17%)
- Being organized (14%)
- Having good social skills (13%)
- Providing useful feedback (11%)
- Offering assistance to teammates (10%)[72]

It should be obvious that most of these characteristics are part of a repertoire of effective communication skills.

To help virtual team members adapt to the differences of teamwork, proper training is required. IBM, for example, has developed a process that can take as long as two months and that begins with one-on-one coaching of the team leader. Then, in a two-day, face-to-face meeting, a facilitator helps the team do the following:

- Align its mission.
- Clarify each member's role.
- Understand members' differing communication and work styles.
- Decide how the team will make decisions in its virtual workspace.
- Document and agree on team norms[73]

What IBM has found is that teams that invest in basic teamwork skills and team leadership succeed in working electronically. Teams that concentrate only on the enabling technology fail. This conclusion is supported by research that stresses the importance of building team relationships before focusing on task problems. "Virtual team leaders must be able to 'read' all the personal and contextual nuances in a world of electronic communications. They must be able to understand the possible causes of silence, misunderstanding, and slights without any of the usual signs to guide them. Leaders must be sensitive to the 'flow' of team processes, paying attention to the smallest matters to head off potential problems that could derail the team's task."[74]

The benefits of properly trained virtual teams include the following:

- When team members receive the same information at the same time and quickly, the conflict that comes from selective or secret information flow is avoided. Departmental politics are minimized.
- Accountability of team members to each other and to the work increases significantly. Participation and individual contributions by members are evident to everyone on the team.
- Even though members may be remote, decisions can be made with the knowledge and participation of the entire team.
- Because team members have the most current information, they can make high-quality decisions quickly.
- The digital space serves as a record. This has two benefits: (1) A record of any decision stays in the shared digital space, ensuring it will stick; and (2) relevant documents reside in that space and can be easily accessed. This ability also eliminates any ambiguity about which version is current.
- Important information stays with the team through changes in membership. New team members can become contributors faster because the team's history and intellectual capital reside in the shared space.[75]

As with many aspects of communication, the success of virtual teams often depends on adequate planning and preparation.

Summary

One channel of communication that has received a lot of attention in recent years in both the workplace and academic settings is group communication. Although the purposes of business communication and the importance of audience analysis apply to group communication just as they do to other channels of communication, the complex dynamics that arise from group situations require additional knowledge for strategy formulation. Much of the research about and many of the practices involved in interpersonal communication are applicable to group communication situations. Paying attention to group formation and group processes can help ensure that groups are productive. Special attention may need to be paid to decision-making processes and conflict resolution to ensure that the potential benefits of groups are achieved.

A good team leader needs to be flexible and have a broad repertoire of actions or skills to meet the team's diverse needs. The leader's role is to function in a manner that will help the group achieve effectiveness. The leader's goal is to solve team problems by analyzing the internal and external situation and selecting and implementing the appropriate behaviors to ensure team effectiveness. The model of team leadership begins with the decisions that a leader must make; the next step is to take action and, hopefully, these actions will result in team effectiveness.

As with other communication contexts, the success of virtual teams largely depends on adequate planning and preparation. An effective virtual team must align its mission, clarify each member's role, understand members' differing communication and work styles, decide how the team will make decisions in its virtual workspace, and document and agree on team norms.

Key Terms

comparison level (CL), 282
comparison level for alternatives (CL_{alt}), 282
intermember relations, 284
informational influence, 287
normative influence, 287
interpersonal influence, 287
process losses, 288
social loafing, 288

free-riding, 289
oversampling, 290
groupthink, 293
competitors, 294
cooperators, 294
individualists, 294
fundamental attribution error, 295
distributed leadership, 298

Discussion Questions

1. What are group norms, and how do they structure interactions within a group?
2. What are group roles and which roles occur most frequently in groups? Which roles are productive and why? Which roles are destructive and why?
3. What are the sources of conflict in groups? How can conflict be managed effectively?
4. Describe Hill's team leadership model. What communication skills are required to enhance team effectiveness in task accomplishment? Effectiveness of team relationships? Team effectiveness in terms of its relationship with its environment?
5. What is the critical aspect in the success of virtual teams? How might this aspect be ensured?

Applications

1. **Observe a group meeting.** Attempt to identify the stage of group formation for the team. Identify the roles that the respective members of the group play. If conflict occurs, what type is it? What types of conflict resolution behaviors are used to deal with the conflict?

After completing your observation, write a report to the team summarizing your findings and providing recommendations for how they might improve their team processes.

2. **Write a group contract.** One way to ensure that a group has the discussion that is necessary to begin on the path of performing is to create a group contract. Creating a group contract ensures that you have discussed your expectations of one another, assigned task responsibilities, created deadlines, and talked about group member roles. In addition, a group contract details the procedure for dealing with the failure to meet these agreed-upon expectations. To complete a group contract, review the following steps:

a. You and your group members should discuss and identify your expectations of one another regarding the completion of a team project. These expectations generally include concerns about participation, the meeting of deadlines, attendance at in-class group meetings and at other group meetings, and the revision of individual sections of your presentation or paper to meet group standards. Group standards regarding the quality of work expected or the grade desired are also often useful. In addition, you may want to agree upon deadlines for the various components of the project as well as assign group roles and responsibilities.

b. You and your group members should discuss and identify the consequences for not fulfilling these expectations. Specifying consequences is important for two reasons: (1) It provides an opportunity to empower group members; and (2) it mitigates against the enabling of free-riding and social loafing. An example of a consequence includes reducing the percentage of an individual's group grade if deadlines are not met or if revisions are not made to individual assignments as expected by the team. Another example of a consequence might be the termination of an individual's membership in the group if a certain number of contract transgressions occur.

c. Each group should write a contract that specifies its expectations of individual members as well as the consequences for not

fulfilling these expectations. You should be as specific as possible. For example, you should specify what constitutes poor attendance, inadequate participation, and low-quality work. Consequences for not fulfilling expectations should be as specific as your group's expectations. As discussed previously, your contract might also include a schedule as well as the assignment of group members' responsibilities.

3. **Team member evaluations.** Use the following template to generate an internal team review. Please rank team members according to their value to the team. Additionally, provide each team member with a short paragraph outlining this individual's strengths, and an additional paragraph outlining an area where this individual needs to improve.

To begin this process, record each team member's name and score his or her performance on a scale of 1 to 5 (1 being lowest and 5 being highest) for each of the team-related activities, using the following template.

Team Member:

Establishing decision-making policies	
Setting meeting agendas	
Setting timelines and meeting deadlines	
Identifying team needs	
Defining project goals	
Planning strategies to meet group goals	
Facilitating problem solving	
Developing conflict resolution rules	
Organizing collaborative sessions	
Assigning task responsibility	
Remaining flexible and accommodating the group	
Recommending action	

4. Conduct research and develop a plan to improve teamwork at your workplace. Write an informal proposal to your manager outlining your plan and explaining its benefits.

5. Conduct research on the benefits of virtual teams. Prepare a proposal for your manager, outlining the benefits and proposing a shift to virtual teams at your workplace.

CASE ANALYSIS

LAJOLLA SOFTWARE, INC.

Todd Batey returned from lunch with high hopes for a productive afternoon. Two large, long-term projects had just been completed and this would be his opportunity to dig through that stack of unopened mail, deferred memos, file folders, journals, and magazines he simply hadn't had found time to read.

Among the larger, more important projects Batey had worked on during the past several months was a new product launch in the company's enterprise software division. At the same time, he had been working with LaJolla Software's senior team on a highly confidential and potentially profitable strategic alliance: LaJolla executives were targeting several Japanese firms for a joint venture that would permit the company to distribute its famous "S-4" supply chain management software in Japan and, perhaps, throughout much of Asia.

Company Background

LaJolla Software, Inc. is a small but rapidly growing firm located in San Diego County in Southern California. This quirky back-bedroom start-up had grown from $8 in capital with no revenues just five years ago to a $150 million, publicly held firm that specialized in enterprise software, customized applications, and innovative thinking in systems integration and supply chain management. Chad Lucas and his college roommate, Joshua Flynn, had converted an interest in management information systems into a successful business long before most of their classmates had paid off their college loans.

Virtually all of their efforts had been internal, however. Lucas and Flynn hired half a dozen of the smartest young programmers and systems engineers in Southern California and began developing a product line. Perhaps their brightest move was to hire Todd Batey, a recent Santa Clara grad who specialized in marketing. Piece by piece, the team of Lucas and Flynn had put together a very strong business, but now things were beginning to move much more quickly. If they were to take advantage of the window of opportunity now open in the Far East, they would need more than bright programmers and a young marketing director. They would need a business partner who knows the territory.

Opportunity Knocks

As Batey tossed his soft drink cup in the recycling bin, one of the interns stuck her head in Todd's cubicle. "Chad and Josh need to see you."

"What's up?" he asked.

"No clue," she replied. "I just know something's happening and you're next on the agenda."

Batey grabbed his iPhone and headed down the hallway. With just seventy-five employees, LaJolla Software didn't take up much space: two floors of a modern office building where Torrey Pines Road meets the I-5. On a nice day (and they were almost all nice) you could see Pacific Beach from the windows in Batey's cubicle. Not much privacy, but a great view.

Batey walked into Chad Lucas's office without knocking. Formality was about as common around LaJolla Software as neckties. "You need to see me?" he asked.

"Hey, Todd," came the reply, "have a seat."

"We just got a fax from Masahiro," said Lucas. "Our endless series of trips to Tokyo has finally paid off." The fax in question was from Masahiro Fudaba, a senior vice president with Ichi Ban Heavy Industries of Japan.

"Really?" asked Batey.

"Finally," said Flynn. "We're going into partnership with Ichi Ban to form a joint venture. Their shareholders, business partners, bankers, and keiretsu executives have finally bought off on the deal." He paused for a just a moment. "Looks like the LaJolla team is going to Japan."

"First, though, we're going to have some Japanese visitors," said Lucas. "The word from Masahiro is that Kazushi Yakura and a team of eight Japanese managers will be here next week to begin the process of organizing our new, jointly owned company. Apparently Mr. Yakura will be here for just a few days. The transition team, however, is planning to stay until we have all the details worked out."

"How can I help?" asked Batey.

"Well," said Flynn, "we're engineers. You're the marketing guy, so we figured you would be the logical person to help make these folks feel welcome."

"More to the point," said Lucas, "we need to help the people on Ichi Ban's transition team understand a bit more about us. They know our business, our market, and our industry, but I'm not sure how much these guys know about the U.S., about California, or about doing business with Americans. According to Masahiro," he added, "only Mr. Yakura has been to the United States. Most of the others have never been out of Japan."

"Interesting," said Batey. "What else do we know about them?"

"Here's a list of people they've identified for the visit," said Lucas. "We have ages, job titles, and a little bit of background, including education and prior work experience, but not much else."

"What do you want them to know?" asked Batey.

"It's clear to me that we have to reduce their anxieties, eliminate their fears, and raise the level of mutual trust," said Flynn. "I know that you understand something about intercultural communication, so we'll leave the details up to you." He paused for a moment, then said, "Let's make it more than a Padres' game and a day at the zoo."

"No problem," said Batey. "I'll have a preliminary plan worked up for you by the close of business tomorrow."

Lucas and Flynn thanked the young marketing manager and expressed complete confidence in his ability to make the Japanese managers' visit productive and successful. Todd left Lucas's office and, heading down the hallway, thought to himself. "No problem? Maybe there is a problem here. What are we gonna do with these guys?"

Discussion Questions

1. Assume that your cubicle is near Todd Batey's and he has asked you for some advice on this subject. What would you say to him?

2. What objectives or measurable outcomes should Batey specify for his immersion into American culture for these visitors?

3. What American concepts can you safely assume these managers know and understand? What concepts do you think they *absolutely must* understand in order for the joint venture to succeed?

4. How would you go about showing them what the United States is all about? Where would you take them? What would you show them?

5. How can you be sure what your visitors will understand when they're ready to go home?

6. What sort of budget would you need for this program?

7. How much do you suppose other LaJolla Software employees understand about Japan and Japanese culture? Should any of them be involved in your effort to introduce North America to your new Asian business partners?

Writing Assignment

Please respond in writing to the issues presented in this case by preparing two documents: a communication strategy memo and a professional business letter.

In preparing these documents, you may assume one of two roles: You may identify yourself as an external management consultant who has been asked to provide advice to the officers of LaJolla Software, or you may assume the role of Todd Batey.

Either way, you must prepare a strategy memo addressed to Chad Lucas and Joshua Flynn that summarizes the details of the case, rank orders critical issues, discusses their implications (what they mean and why they matter), offers specific recommendations for action (assigning ownership and suspense dates for each), and shows how to communicate the solution to all who are affected by the recommendations.

You must also prepare a professional business letter for Mr. Lucas's signature. That document may be addressed to Kazushi Yakura, addressing his concerns in the case. Or, if you wish, you may address a letter from Mr. Lucas to all LaJolla Software employees, responding to their concerns and explaining what the company is doing to address the situation at hand. If you have questions about either of these documents, please consult your instructor.

This case was prepared by James S. O'Rourke, Concurrent Associate Professor of Management, as the basis for class discussion rather than to illustrate either effective or ineffective handling of an administrative situation.

Endnotes

1. Eisenberg, E. M., & Goodall, H. L., Jr. (1993). *Organizational communication: Balancing creativity and constraint*. New York: St. Martin's Press, p. 286.
2. Eisenberg & Goodall, 1993, p. 187.
3. Festinger, L. (1954). A theory of social comparison processes. *Human Relations, 7,* 117–140.
4. Insko, C. A., & Schopler, J. (1972). *Experimental social psychology*. New York: Academic Press.
5. Arkin, R. M., & Burger, J. M. (1980). Effects of unit relation tendencies on interpersonal attraction. *Social Psychology Quarterly, 43,* 380–391.
6. Festinger, L. (1957). *A theory of cognitive dissonance*. Stanford, CA: Stanford University Press; Heider, F. (1958). *The psychology of interpersonal relations*. New York: Wiley.
7. Kerckhoff, A. C., & Davis, K. E. (1962). Value consensus and need complementarity in mate selection. *American Sociological Review, 27,* 295–303; Levinger, G., Senn, D. J., & Jorgensen, B. W. (1970). Progress toward permanence in courtship: A test of the Kerckhoff-Davis hypothesis. *Sociometry, 33,* 427–433; Meyer, J. P., & Pepper, S. (1977). Need compatibility and marital adjustment in young married couples. *Journal of Personality and Social Psychology, 35,* 331–342.
8. Kelley, H. H., & Thibaut, J. W. (1978). *Interpersonal relations: A theory of interdependence*. New York: Wiley; Moreland, R. L., & Levine, J. M. (1982). Socialization in small groups: Temporal changes in individual-group relations. *Advances in Experimental Social Psychology, 15,* 137–192; Thibaut, J. W., & Kelley, H. H. (1959). *The social psychology of groups*. New York: Wiley.
9. Bonney, M. E. (1947). Popular and unpopular children: A sociometric study. *Sociometry Monographs,* No. 99, A80; Thibaut & Kelley, 1959.
10. Gilchrist, J. C. (1952). The formation of social groups under conditions of success and failure. *Journal of Abnormal and Social Psychology, 47,* 174–187; Iverson, M. A. (1964). Personality impressions of punitive stimulus persons of differential status. *Journal of Abnormal and Social Psychology, 68,* 617–626.
11. Thibaut & Kelley, 1959.
12. Maassen, G. H., Akkermans, W., & Van der Linden, J. L. (1996). Two-dimensional sociometric status determination with rating scales. *Small Group Research, 27,* 56–78.
13. Coie, J. D., Dodge, K. A., & Kupersmidt, J. B. (1990). Peer group behavior and social status. In S. R. Asher & J. D. Coie (Eds.), *Peer rejection in childhood* (pp. 17–59). New York: Cambridge University Press; Newcomb, A. E., Bukowski, W. M., & Pattee, L. (1993). Children's peer relations: A meta-analytic review of popular, rejected, neglected, controversial, and average sociometric status. *Psychological Bulletin, 113,* 99–128.
14. Shaw, M. E. (1964). Communication networks. *Advances in Experimental Social Psychology, 1,* 111–147.
15. Leavitt, H. (1951). Some effects of certain communication patterns on group performance. *Journal of Abnormal and Social Psychology, 51,* 38–50.
16. Tuckman, B. W. (1965). Developmental sequences in small groups. *Psychological*

Bulletin, 63, 384–399; and Tuckman, B. W., & Jensen, M. A. C. (1977). Stages of small group development revisited. *Group and Organizational Studies, 2,* 419–427.

17. Myers, A. E. (1962). Team competition, success, and the adjustment of group members. *Journal of Abnormal and Social Psychology, 65,* 325–332; Shaw, M. E., & Shaw, L. M. (1962). Some effects of sociometric grouping upon learning in a second grade classroom. *Journal of Social Psychology, 57,* 453–458.

18. Schachter, S. (1951). Deviation, rejection, and communication. *Journal of Abnormal and Social Psychology, 46,* 190–207.

19. French, J. R. P., Jr. (1941). The disruption and cohesion of groups. *Journal of Abnormal and Social Psychology, 36,* 361–377; Pepitone, A., & Reichling, G. (1955). Group cohesiveness and the expression of hostility. *Human Relations, 8,* 327–337.

20. Mullen, B., & Copper, C. (1994). The relation between group cohesiveness and performance: An integration. *British Journal of Social Psychology, 27,* 333–356.

21. Gully, S. M., Devine, D. J., & Whitney, D. J. (1995). A meta-analysis of cohesion and performance: Effects of levels of analysis and task interdependence. *Small Group Research, 26,* 497–520.

22. Gerard, H. B., & Orive, R. (1987). The dynamics of opinion formation. *Advances in Experimental Social Psychology, 20,* 171–202; Orive, R. (1988a). Group consensus, action immediacy, and opinion confidence. *Personality and Social Psychology Bulletin, 14,* 573–577; and Orive, R. (1988b). Social projection and social comparison of opinions. *Journal of Personality and Social Psychology, 54,* 943–964.

23. Schachter, 1951.

24. Bornstein, R. F. (1992). The dependent personality: Developmental, social, and clinical perspectives. *Psychological Bulletin, 112,* 3–23.

25. Schachter, 1951.

26. Tziner, A., & Eden, D. (1985). Effects of crew composition on crew performance: Does the whole equal the sum of its parts? *Journal of Applied Psychology, 70,* 85–93.

27. Shaw, M. E. (1981). *Group dynamics: The psychology of small group behavior* (3rd ed.). New York: McGraw-Hill.

28. Bond, M. H., & Shiu, W. Y. (1997). The relationship between a group's personality resources and the two dimensions of its group process. *Small Group Research, 28,* 194–217.

29. Williams, K. D., Harkins, S., & Latane, B. (1981). Identifiability as a deterrent to social loafing: Two cheering experiments. *Journal of Personality and Social Psychology, 40,* 303–311.

30. Harkins, S. G., & Jackson, J. M. (1985). The role of evaluation in eliminating social loafing. *Personality and Social Psychology Bulletin, 11,* 457–465; Harkins, S. G., & Szymanski, K. (1987). Social loafing and facilitation: New wine in old bottles. *Review of Personality and Social Psychology, 9,* 167–188; Harkins, S. G., & Szymanski, K. (1988). Social loafing and self-evaluation with an objective standard. *Journal of Experimental Social Psychology, 24,* 354–365; Jackson, J. M., & Latane, B. (1981). All alone in front of all those people: Stage fright as a function of number and type of co-performances and audience. *Journal of Personality and Social Psychology, 40,* 73–85; Szymanski, K., & Harkins, S. G. (1987). Social loafing and self-evaluation with a social standard. *Journal of Personality and Social Psychology, 53,* 891–897; Williams, Harkins, & Latane, 1981.

31. Polzer, J. T., Kramer, R. M., & Neale, M. A. (1997). Positive illusions about oneself and one's group. *Small Group Research, 28,* 243–266.

32. Brickner, M. A., Harkins, S. G., & Ostrom, T. M. (1986). Effects of personal involvement: Thought-provoking implications for social loafing. *Journal of Personality and Social Psychology, 51,* 763–770.

33. Weldon, E., & Weingart, L. R. (1993). Group goals and group performance. *British Journal of Social Psychology, 32,* 307–334.

34. Hinsz, V. B. (1995). Goal setting by groups performing an additive task: A comparison with individual goal setting. *Journal of Applied Social Psychology, 25,* 965–990.

35. Rothwell, J. D. (1998). *In mixed company: Small group communication* (3rd ed.). Fort Worth, TX: Harcourt Brace College Publishers, pp. 84–85.

36. Stasser, G. (1992). Pooling of unshared information during group discussions. In S. Worchel, W. Wood, & J. A. Simpson (Eds.), *Group process and productivity* (pp. 48–67). Newbury Park, CA: Sage; Stasser, G., Taylor, L. A., & Hanna, C. (1989). Information sampling in structured and unstructured discussions of three- and six-person groups. *Journal of Personality and Social Psychology, 57,* 67–78; and Wittenbaum, G. M., & Stasser, G. (1996). Management of information in small groups. In J. L. Nye & A. M. Brower (Eds.), *What's social about social cognition? Research on socially shared cognitions in small groups* (pp. 3–28). Thousand Oaks, CA: Sage.

37. Di Salvo, V. S., Nikkel, E., & Monroe, C. (1989). Theory and practice: A field investigation and identification of group members' perceptions of problems facing natural work groups. *Small Group Behavior, 20,* 551–567.

38. Myers, D. G., & Lamm, H. (1976). The group polarization phenomenon. *Psychological Bulletin, 83,* 602–627.

39. Clark, K. B. (1971). The pathos of power. *American Psychologist, 26,* 1047–57; Myers, D. G., & Lamm, H. (1975). The polarizing effect of group discussion. *American Scientist, 63,* 297–303; Myers & Lamm, 1976; Goethals, G. R., & Zanna, M. P. (1979). The role of social comparison in choice shifts. *Journal of Personality and Social Psychology, 37,* 1469–76; Myers, D. G. (1978). The polarizing effects of social comparison. *Journal of Experimental Social Psychology, 14,* 554–63; and Sanders, G. S., & Baron, R. S. (1977). Is social comparison irrelevant for producing choice shifts? *Journal of Experimental Social Psychology, 13,* 303–14.

40. Davis, J. H., Kameda, T., & Stasson, M. (1992). Group risk taking: Selected topics. In J. F. Yates (Ed.), *Risk-taking behavior* (pp. 63–199). Chichester: Wiley; Laughlin, P. R., & Earley, P. C. (1982). Social combination models, persuasive arguments theory, social comparison theory, and choice shift. *Journal of Personality and Social Psychology, 42,* 273–80; and Zuber, J. A., Crott, J. W., & Werner, J. (1992). Choice shift and group polarization: An analysis of the status of arguments and social decision schemes. *Journal of Personality and Social Psychology, 62,* 50–61.

41. Chaney, L. H., & Martin, J. S. (2011). *Intercultural business communication* (5th ed.). Boston: Prentice Hall.

42. Eisenberg & Goodall, 1993.

43. Hirokawa, R., & Rost, K. (1992). Effective group decision making in organizations. *Management Communication Quarterly, 5,* 267–388.

44. Ohbuchi, K., Chiba, S., & Fukushima, O. (1996). Mitigation of interpersonal conflicts: Politeness and time pressure. *Personality and Social Psychology Bulletin, 22,* 1035–42.

45. Rosenbaum, M. E. (1986). The repulsion hypothesis: On the nondevelopment of relationships. *Personality and Social Psychology, 51,* 1156–66.

46. Haythorn, W., Couch, A. S., Haefner, D., Langham, P., & Carter, L. F. (1956). The effects of varying combinations of authoritarian and equalitarian leaders and followers. *Journal of Abnormal and Social Psychology, 53,* 210–19; Shaw, 1981.

47. Moreland, R. L., Levine, J. M., & Wingert, M. L. (1996). Creating the ideal group: Composition effects at work. In E. Witte & J. Davis (Eds.), *Understanding group behavior: Small group processes and interpersonal relations* (vol. 2, pp. 11–35). Mahwah, NJ: Erlbaum.

48. McGrath, J. E. (1984). Small group research, that once and future field: An interpretation of the past with an eye to the future. *Group Dynamics: Theory, Research, and Practice, 1,* 7–27.

49. Houle, C. O. (1989). *Governing boards: Their nature and nurture*. San Francisco: Jossey-Bass.

50. Franken, R. E., & Brown, D. J. (1995). Why do people like competition? The motivation for winning, putting forth effort, improving one's performance, performing well, being instrumental, and expressing forceful/aggressive behavior. *Personality and Individual Differences*, *19*, 175–84; Franken, R. E., & Prpich, W. (1996). Dislike of competition and the need to win: Self-image concerns, performance concerns, and the distraction of attention. *Journal of Social Behavior and Personality*, *11*, 695–712; Steers, R. M., & Porter, L. W. (1991). *Motivation and work behavior* (4th ed.). New York: McGraw-Hill; and Tjosvold, D. (1995). Cooperation theory, constructive controversy, and effectiveness: Learning from crisis. In R. A. Guzzo, E. Salas, & Associates, *Team effectiveness and decision making in organizations* (pp. 79–112). San Francisco: Jossey-Bass.

51. Tjosvold, 1995.

52. Kelley, H. H. (1997). Expanding the analysis of social orientations by reference to the sequential-temporal structures of situations. *European Journal of Social Psychology*, *27*, 373–404; McClintock, C. G., Messick, D. M., Kuhlman, D. M., & Campos, F. T. (1973). Motivational bases of choice in three-choice decomposed games. *Journal of Experimental Psychology*, *9*, 572–90; Swap, W. C., & Rubin, J. Z. (1983). Measurement of interpersonal orientation. *Journal of Personality and Social Psychology*, *44*, 208–19.

53. Bonta, B. D. (1997). Cooperation and competition in peaceful societies. *Pyschological Bulletin*, *121*, 299–320; Fry, D. P., & Bjorkqvist, K. (Eds.). (1997). *Cultural variations in conflict resolution: Alternatives to violence*. Mahwah, NJ: Erlbaum; Van Lange, P. A. M., De Bruin, E. M. N., Otten, W., & Joireman, J. A. (1997). Development of prosocial, individualistic, and competitive orientations: Theory and preliminary evidence. *Journal of Personality and Social Psychology*, *37*, 858–64.

54. Hofstede, G., & Hofstede, G. J. (2005). *Cultures and organizations* (2nd ed.). New York: McGraw-Hill.

55. McCord, L. B., & Richardson, J. (2001), Are workplace bullies sabotaging your ability to compete? Retrieved September 4, 2005, from http://gbr.pepperdine.edu/014/bullies.html#10#10.

56. McCord & Richardson, 2001.

57. Ibid.

58. Ibid.

59. Lencioni, P. M. (2002). *The five dysfunctions of a team*. San Francisco: Jossey-Bass.

60. Blake, R., & Mouton, J. (1964). *The managerial grid*. Houston: Gulf Publishing; Kilmann, R., & Thomas, K. (1977). Developing a force-choice measure of conflict-handling behavior: The "MODE" instrument. *Educational and Psychological Measurement*, *37*, 309–25.

61. Morrill, C. (1995). *The executive way*. Chicago: University of Chicago Press.

62. Wall, V. D., Jr., & Nolan, L. L. (1987). Small group conflict: A look at equity, satisfaction, and styles of conflict management. *Small Group Behavior*, *18*, 188–211.

63. Gibson, J., & Hodgetts, R. (1986). *Organizational communication: A managerial approach*. New York: Academic Press.

64. Zaccaro, S. J., Rittman, A. L., & Marks, M. A. (2001). Team leadership. *Leadership Quarterly*, *12*, 451–483.

65. Stewart, G. L., & Manz, C. C. (1995). Leadership for self-managing work teams: A typology and integrative model. *Human Relations*, *48*(7), 747–70.

66. Fleishman, E. A., Mumford, M. D., Zaccaro, S. J., Levin, K. Y., Korotkin, A. L., & Hein, M. B. (1991). Taxonomic efforts in the description of leader behavior: A synthesis and functional interpretation. *Leadership Quarterly*, *2*(4), 245–87.

67. Nadler, D. A. (1998). Executive team effectiveness: Teamwork at the top. In D. A. Nadler & J. L. Spencer (Eds.), *Executive teams* (pp. 21–39). San Francisco, CA: Jossey-Bass, p. 24.

68. Hackman, J. R., & Walton, R. E. (1986). Leading groups in organizations. In P. S. Goodman & Associates (Eds.), *Designing effective work groups* (pp. 72–119). San Francisco, CA: Jossey-Bass.

69. Hackman, J. R., & Walton, R. E., 1986; LaFasto, F. M. J., & Larson, C. E. (2001). *When teams work best: 6000 team members and leaders tell what it takes to succeed.* Thousand Oaks, CA: Sage; and Larson, C. E., & LaFasto, F. M. J. (1989). *Teamwork: What must go right/what can go wrong.* Newbury Park, CA: Sage.

70. The Challenges of Working in Virtual Teams. (2010). *The challenges of working in virtual teams: Virtual teams survey report 2010.* New York: RW³ Culture Wizard. Retrieved February 4, 2013, from http://rw-3.com/VTSReportv7.pdf.

71. The Challenges of Working in Virtual Teams, 2010.

72. Ibid.

73. Dorsett, L. (2001, January) A week in a digital collaboration space: Fast electronic work groups. *Training & Development.* Retrieved February 20, 2005, from http://www.findarticles.com/p/articles/mi_m4467/is_1_55/ai_69414464/.

74. Pauleen, D. J. (2004). An inductively derived model of leader-initiated relationship building with virtual team members. *Journal of Management Information Systems,* 20(3), 227–256, p. 229.

75. Dorsett, 2001.

11

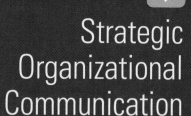

Strategic Organizational Communication

After reading this chapter, you will be able to

▶ Identify the three basic models for strategic organizational communication.

▶ Understand the value of creating a strategic communication plan for your organization.

▶ Conduct a communication audit to assess the current state of internal communication and identify areas for improvement.

▶ Develop an internal communication plan and assess its effectiveness.

▶ Consider and identify ways to improve interdepartmental communication.

▶ Understand the components of an external relations program.

▶ Understand the key functions of many external relations programs, which include
  - Public relations and image building
  - Investor relations
  - Issues management
  - Risk and crisis communication

▶ Deal successfully with the media, including performing interviews and handling crisis situations.

Case Questions:

1. How important is the role of managing an organization's reputation in its goal to remain a profitable institution?

The Case of the Exploding Muffler

"Did you see the news this morning?" Dolores Kaiser asked. She slapped the newspaper she was carrying down on the desk in front of her.

"Now what?" was the reply from Kevin LaPlace, North American president of Kerckhoff Motors, as he picked it up to review the front page.

"Another exploding muffler," Kaiser replied. "Fortunately, this time, though, the car didn't catch fire."

"Well, that's a relief—no one was injured or killed, I assume," said LaPlace.

"No, but we need to do something to stop this insanity. Our reputation is taking a huge hit here in the States. Is there any evidence that Germany is going to budge on our request for a recall?" Kaiser asked.

"I guess I'm going to have to fly to Frankfurt to make a case for how serious this is in terms of the effects on sales," LaPlace remarked. "You'd think the numbers I've been sending would be enough to persuade the management team over there that a recall is in order."

"I still can't believe that you as the North American president don't have the power to make these kinds of decisions," Kaiser said as she turned to the door. "Do you want me to ask Mark to bring you some coffee on my way out?"

"How about a double-shot espresso?" LaPlace said with a weak laugh. "This is going to be one of those days."

2. How important is it for organizations to have effective internal communication plans to manage routine information flow and to support timely decision making across departmental and international office boundaries?
3. How should an organization proactively plan for dealing with crisis situations to effectively manage public perception and to maintain the company's image and reputation?

linear model
Strategy consists of integrated decisions, actions or plans that will set and achieve viable organizational goals.

adaptive model
Strategy is focused on the continuous adjustment of the relationship between the organization and its environment.

co-alignment
Matching up opportunities and risks in the environment with the capabilities and resources of the organization.

interpretive model
Strategy is concerned with the management of meaning and with symbol construction aimed at legitimizing the organization by providing orienting metaphors and frames of reference that allow the organization and its environment to be understood by organizational stakeholders.

Models of Strategic Organizational Communication

Chaffee identified the three basic models of strategic communication at the organizational level as

- Linear
- Adaptive
- Interpretive[1]

In the **linear model**, "strategy consists of integrated decisions, actions or plans that will set and achieve viable organizational goals."[2] Using this model, managers identify goals, generate alternatives for achieving those goals, weigh the likelihood of success for each alternative, and then decide which to implement. This model is concerned with presenting managerial plans to stakeholders and with stakeholders' acceptance of those plans.

The **adaptive model** shifts the focus of strategy from sequential planning and implementation to continuous adjustment of the relationship between the organization and its environment. In the adaptive model, the organization is an open system in a dynamic environment where the "goal" is represented by co-alignment of the organization with its environment. **Co-alignment** refers to matching up opportunities and risks in the environment with the capabilities and resources of the organization. This model is less centralized than the linear model, but it still places strategy in the domain of management. It involves more than just messages aimed at informing and influencing stakeholders; it includes all of the communication processes involved in adapting to the organizational environment. These include information exchange and feedback processes within the organization and between the organization and its environment. (The adaptive model is based on systems theory.)

The **interpretive model** is concerned with the social construction of reality, which was discussed in Chapter 1. This model is based on a social contract view that "portrays the organization as a collection of cooperative agreements entered into by individuals with free will."[3] In this model, strategy is concerned with the management of meaning and with symbol construction aimed at legitimizing the organization by providing "orienting metaphors and frames of reference that allow the organization and its environment to be understood by organizational stakeholders."[4] Strategic communication is about negotiating and shaping stakeholders' understandings of what the organization is and what it does.

Even though these three models appear to be distinct, Chaffee argued that they are interrelated and interdependent and that more than one may be operating at the same time within an organization.

The relevant audiences for strategic communication at the organizational level are organizational stakeholders.[5] Organizational stakeholders include shareholders or owners, employees, customers or clients, or any important constituency that can be affected or can affect the organization.[6] These might include the government, media, activist groups, special interest coalitions, and communities.

Messages intended for strategic communication in organizations often are originated and produced by organizational subsystems composed of many individuals. Strategic communication can be a complex process in which a number of organizational units and individuals contribute to the design and dissemination of messages.

Strategic Internal Communication

Internal strategic communication or employee communication is management's efforts to provide information to and exert influence with the organizational membership. Internal communication should be an important feature of any management plan and considered a key contributor to organizational effectiveness and productivity.

Research by Gallup and others shows that engaged employees are more productive. They are more profitable, more customer-focused, safer, and more likely to withstand temptations to leave. The best-performing companies know that an employee engagement improvement strategy linked to the achievement of corporate goals will help them win in the marketplace.

However, there is evidence that many companies "do not apply the same analytical rigor to employee communications" as they do to financial and operational components of management strategy.[7] According to Gallup's research, in average organizations, the ratio of engaged to actively disengaged employees is 1.5:1. Actively disengaged employees erode an organization's bottom line while breaking the spirits of colleagues in the process. Within the U.S. workforce, Gallup estimates this cost to be more than $300 billion in lost productivity alone. Specifically, the costs to an organization from poor employee communication include

- Increased employee turnover
- Increased absenteeism
- Dissatisfied customers from poor customer service
- Higher product defect rates
- Lack of focus on business objectives
- Stifled innovation

Some of the common reasons for a lack of an internal communication program include the following attitudes of management:

1. **If I know it, then everyone must know it.** Management often assumes that because its members are aware of some piece of information, then everyone else is, too. Typically, employees aren't aware unless management makes a deliberate attempt to carefully convey information.

2. **Communication just happens.** Another frequent problem is that management does not really value communications or assumes that it just happens.

3. **We hate bureaucracy—we're "lean and mean."** When organizations are just getting started, their leaders can often pride themselves on not being burdened with what seems like bureaucratic overhead, such as extensive written policies and procedures. As the organization grows, it needs more communication and feedback to remain healthy, but the organization doesn't adjust to the growth and provide the appropriate communication plan. As a result, increasing confusion ensues—unless management matures and realizes the need for increased communication.

4. **Did you hear what I meant for you to hear?** As discussed earlier in this text, with today's increasingly diverse workforce, it's easy to believe you've conveyed information, but you may not be aware that they interpreted it differently than you intended.

5. **We need a solution now!** Particularly when personnel are tired or under stress, it's easy to do what's urgent rather than what's important.

internal strategic communication
Management's efforts to provide information to and exert influence with the organizational membership.

ResponsibleCommunication

The Gallup Organization created a feedback system for employers that would identify and measure elements of worker engagement most tied to the bottom line. After hundreds of focus groups and thousands of interviews with employees in a variety of industries, Gallup came up with the Q12, a twelve-question survey that identifies strong feelings of employee engagement. Results from the survey show a strong correlation between high scores and superior job performance. Here are those twelve questions:

- Do you know what is expected of you at work?
- Do you have the materials and equipment you need to do your work right?

- At work, do you have the opportunity to do what you do best every day?
- In the last seven days, have you received recognition or praise for doing good work?
- Does your supervisor, or someone at work, seem to care about you as a person?
- Is there someone at work who encourages your development?
- At work, do your opinions seem to count?
- Does the mission/purpose of your company make you feel your job is important?
- Are your associates (fellow employees) committed to doing quality work?

- Do you have a best friend at work?
- In the last six months, has someone at work talked to you about your progress?
- In the last year, have you had opportunities at work to learn and grow?

Questions for Discussion

1. What are the benefits to an organization of assessing employee engagement?
2. What are concrete steps that an organization might take to ensure high levels of employee engagement?
3. As a leader, what steps might you take to better ensure employee engagement?

Source: The Gallup Organization (Princeton, NJ, 2008).

6. **So what's to talk about?** Communications problems can arise when inexperienced management interprets its job to be solving problems and assumes that if there aren't any problems/crises, then there's nothing that needs to be communicated.
7. **If I need your opinion, I'll tell it to you.** Communications problems can arise when management simply sees no value whatsoever in communicating with subordinates, believing subordinates should shut up and do their jobs.[8]

It is important that management comprehends and fully supports the premise that organizations must have high degrees of communication. Too often, management learns the need for communication by having to respond to the lack of it.

One way to think about an organization's activities is to group them by functional area. Four common functional areas are orientation and indoctrination of employees, morale and satisfaction, compensation and benefits, and organizational change and development.[9]

- **Orientation and indoctrination.** Many organizations provide formal training sessions for new employees to orient them to the organization and their new position. Many organizations also have programs to socialize organizational members by reinforcing corporate values, beliefs, and practices.
- **Morale and satisfaction.** Special events, newsletters, and company magazines are instances of media that are often intended to improve employee's self-concepts, interpersonal relationships, and attitudes toward the organization.

- **Compensation and benefits.** The Employee Retirement Income Security Act (ERISA) requires organizations to make full and understandable disclosure of employee benefit programs.
- **Organizational change and development.** Change is a stressful process and as such, organizations should attempt to help employees deal with change. Employees may need a great deal of new information to understand the purposes and effects of major change and to cope with it. Common types of change in an organizational setting include mergers, new ventures, restructuring, and downsizing.

Most of these functions are housed in the human resources department; however, responsibility for newsletters, company magazines, special events, and activities of this nature are generally handled by corporate communication departments. It is thus important that activities managed by different departments be well coordinated. One way to manage this process is to create an internal communication plan.

CriticalThinking

Does your organizational have an internal or employee communication plan? If so, what are its elements? What works and what might be improved? If not, what kind of communication policies need to be developed and why?

Strategic External Communication

As a form of public or external communication, strategic organizational communication can require a substantial commitment of resources, including the purchase of advertising space in print and electronic media; time, space, and materials for special events; production facilities for Web sites, newsletters, company magazines, and video programs; and salaries and benefits for those who write, edit, and create the messages. **Public communication** is described as the process of one communicating with many.[10] This definition, however, oversimplifies the idea of a "source" for strategic communication activities and fails to recognize the transactional and dialogic nature of communication.

External strategic communication includes public relations and issues management efforts designed to influence consumers, communities, special-interest groups, voters, regulators, legislators, and others outside the organization.

External communication occurs in at least three major forms: (1) advertising and promoting products and services, (2) creating and maintaining a desirable public image for the organization, and (3) shaping public opinion on issues important to the organization. Traditionally, communication concerned with image building has been the responsibility of public relations practitioners. This area has expanded to include investor relations programs to market the company's stock to individuals and institutional investors and programs to manage and communicate about risk and crises situations.

In addition, many organizations have expanded external communication to include a new function—identifying and tracking public issues that concern the organization. An organization might try to change to respond to public criticism

public communication
The process of one communicating with many.

external strategic communication
Management's public relations and issues management efforts designed to influence consumers, communities, special-interest groups, voters, regulators, legislators, and others outside the organization.

or try to influence public opinion on important issues by advocating its own position in the public arena.[11]

Creating an Internal Communication Plan

Employees need to know the direction of the organization—how they can engage and participate—and they need feedback. To ensure that employees receive this information in an effective manner, an internal communication plan should be developed.

Five aspects of successful internal communication programs are:

- Management is supportive. Top and middle managers are involved in and responsible for communication.
- Professional communication staff is close to the issues and included in strategic planning. Communication is part of the business plan.
- Communication reinforces strategic objectives to all employees. Messages are adapted to their audience and consistent.
- Communication uses all appropriate media, but face-to-face is best.
- The communication program is formally and frequently assessed for effectiveness.

Before starting to develop any form of strategy for improvement, it is important to know where the organization currently stands in terms of the quality of communication with employees. The use of organizational diagnostics in the form of an audit is a useful place to start. This audit should be company-wide and differentiate divisions and levels, since identifying barriers to communication is important. The audit should help answer a number of important questions, including

- Are employees receiving accurate information?
- How are employees receiving regular information?
- Are messages consistent across the company?
- Do employees understand both the goals and the results of communications?[12]

Table 11-1 identifies sixteen essential strategic communications practices within organizations. They are grouped into three categories: (1) strategy, (2) implementation, and (3) support and alignment.

- **Strategy.** Includes the core tasks of communications planning and strategy development.
- **Implementation.** Includes practices most common to an organization with an *active* communications function.
- **Support and alignment.** Includes noncommunications-specific practices within the organization that help to ensure the communications function is successful.[13]

The table also offers quality standards or criteria for each practice. They describe in brief what the practices should look like. This list can be of value in the audit process. It can be used as a checklist to help determine if an organization is performing each strategic communications practice. But more importantly, the audit process can reveal if quality criteria are being met, and if not, where improvements can be made in how the practice is performed.

Conducting a Communication Audit

A communication audit collects data about current communication practices and uses that data to make assessments about organizational performance and capacity.

Table 11-1 Strategic Communications Practices.

	STRATEGIC COMMUNICATIONS PRACTICES	QUALITY CRITERIA/STANDARDS
Strategy	Identify the vision	The communications vision is aligned with, but distinct from, the organization's overall mission.
	Choose goals and outcomes	Goals and outcomes are well defined, measurable, and help guide a defined plan of action.
	Select target audiences	Audiences are specific and include key decision makers or individuals with influence on the issue.
	Develop messages	Messages are specific, clear, persuasive, reflect audience values, and include a solution or course of action.
	Identify credible messengers	Messengers are seen as credible by the target audiences and can be recruited and available to the cause.
	Choose communications channels and media	Channels and media are chosen for their access and availability to target audiences.
	Scan the context and competition	Risks and contextual variables that can affect communications success are identified and factored into planning when possible.
Implementation	Develop effective materials	Materials are developed in attractive, accessible, and varied formats for maximum exposure and visibility.
	Build valuable partnerships	Linkages exist with internal and external stakeholders who can help align with and carry the message.
	Train messengers	Internal messengers are trained in key messages and are consistent in their delivery.
	Conduct steady outreach	Outreach and dissemination to audiences through multiple outlets is regular and sustained.
	Monitor and evaluate	Activities and outcomes are regularly monitored and evaluated for purposes of accountability and continuous improvement.
Support and integration	Support communications at the leadership level	Management understands and supports communications as an integral part of organizational viability and success.
	Earmark sufficient resources	Fundraising regularly includes dedicated resources for communications practice.
	Integrate communications throughout the organization	Communications is seen as an integral part of every organizational project or strategy.
	Involve staff at all levels	Communications is not seen as an isolated function; most if not all staff members have some knowledge and/or participation in communications efforts.

Source: Adapted from Coffman, J. (2004). *Strategic Communications Audits.* Working paper prepared for Communications Consortium Media Center. Retrieved November 1, 2009, from http://www.mediaevaluationproject.org/WorkingPaper1.pdf.

When planning to conduct a communication audit, it is important to first determine if assessments about organizational practices will be made internally or by outside experts. The advantages of doing it internally are that direct costs are likely to be lower and the process may become an engaging organizational exercise that builds communications capacity in and of itself. The advantages to using outside experts are their objectivity, time and availability, the knowledge they bring from other organizations for comparison purposes, and the credibility that may accompany their credentials and expertise.

Regardless of whether the audit is done internally or externally, a common set of methods can be used to gather data needed to make assessments about practices. Common methods for gathering data include

- **Participant observation.** The individual conducting the audit participates in organizational activities involving communications in order to see how and when practices are performed.
- **Document review.** Communications documents (e.g., publications, campaign materials, press releases, etc.) are reviewed to assess the development and targeting of materials as a communications practice.
- **Focus groups.** Groups of five to fifteen people meet together in a moderated discussion and respond to open-ended questions about communications practices and organizational capacity. Their main advantage is the group interaction that takes place as participants react to and build on one another's responses.
- **Interviews.** Probably the most common audit method, interviews allow the person conducting the audit to better understand communications-related work processes. Interviews allow respondents to provide a rich qualitative sense of how practices are performed and how the organization treats communications. Interviews can also be conducted with the organization's external stakeholders or target audiences.
- **Surveys.** Surveys or questionnaires are the second most common audit method. They can be administered cheaply to all organizational staff within a short time frame, and they allow for standardization and comparison of responses.
- **Critical incident analysis.** Staff is asked to describe, through an interview or questionnaire, specific effective and ineffective experiences with communications. The purpose is to collect examples of experiences that staff find memorable in order to "see" how communications practices are performed within situational contexts.

Table 11-2 compares these methods on the basis of time, cost, and information yielded. While the use of one or more of these methods is recommended, it is also

Table 11-2 Comparison of Audit Methods.

METHOD	TIME	COST	INFORMATION YIELD
Interviews	30–60 minutes each	Moderately expensive (time to conduct, analyze)	Qualitative, in-depth data
Surveys	20–30 minutes each	Moderately expensive	Standardized data
Critical incident analysis	20–30 minutes each	Inexpensive	Specific examples of practice/process flow
Network analysis	20–30 minutes each	Expensive (analysis, software)	Process flow/interaction and integration
Participant observation	Variable	Expensive (time)	Process flow
Document review	20-60 minutes each	Expensive (time)	Material, message evaluation
Focus groups	1–2 hours	Moderately expensive (depends on number)	Qualitative in-depth data; specific

Source: Coffman, J. (2004). *Strategic Communications Audits.* Working paper prepared for Communications Consortium Media Center. Retrieved November 1, 2009, from http://www.mediaevaluationproject.org/WorkingPaper1.pdf.

possible to conduct the strategic communications audit informally by, for example, asking each staff member to give his or her own independent and subjective assessments based on existing knowledge and experience, or convening staff to make collective assessments.

Once the assessments are completed, the next step is to identify areas in which the organization can improve. The assessment of where the organization should be must be based on an accounting of the organization's realistic capabilities with respect to communications.

The strategic communications audit should result in more than just an identification of areas or practices that need to be improved. To maximize the chances that audit findings will be used and actual practice improved as a result, the audit should

- Demonstrate through data how communications problems are causing problems *in the present* (as opposed to speculating about their future impact). At the same time, the audit should reinforce practices that are current organizational strengths.
- Generate specific recommendations for *how* actual communication practice can be enhanced. Data need to be linked to concrete actions.
- Make transparent the organizational benefits of adopting those actions in addition to the weaknesses they are designed to address.
- Prioritize recommendations so organizations are not immobilized by the prospect of implementing them.[14]

Formal communications audits should be conducted about every five years. Informal audits on which organizations internally revisit their strategic communication capacity and performance levels may be done more frequently. Audits should also be considered after an organization experiences a critical incident that might affect communications, such as when the organization changes mission, changes leadership, or experiences a crisis.

CriticalThinking

Of data-gathering techniques discussed for conducting a communication audit, which would collect the best information and why? Which techniques might present problems and how might these be overcome or compensated for?

Developing the Internal Communication Plan

Once the organization has assessed its current communication practices and identified areas for improvement, an internal strategic communication plan can be developed. An effective approach in the development of the communications strategy is to answer the following:

- What are the organization's goals, ambitions, and strategic aspirations for the future?
- What do the people in the organization need to think, feel, and do in order to make those goals a reality?
- Where are employees now and what needs to change in their current perceptions, attitudes, or access to basic information?

- What is the role of the internal communication function in helping close the gap of what management wants for the future and what exists today?
- What are the roles and responsibilities of leaders, managers, employees, and communication professionals?
- What are the communication activities the organization is going to need—and who will be responsible for those activities?
- What are the resource levels needed?[15]

Twelve essential elements of a successful internal communications strategy are:

1. **Effective employee-directed communications must be led from the top.** Effective communications require the active commitment and endorsement of senior managers. It is not enough simply to develop a vision statement or formulate in general terms the values by which the company lives. Behavior is what counts. Managers must be seen to behave in a manner that is consistent with the ethos they are promoting.

2. **The essence of good communications is consistency.** If management tries to improve communications and fails because messages are inconsistent or are "good news only," the organization probably will not quietly settle back into the way they used to be.

3. **Successful employee communications owe as much to consistency, careful planning, and attention to detail as they do to charisma or natural gifts.** We might not all be another Zig Ziglar, Tony Robbins, or Bill Clinton, but with planning and attention to detail, successful communication plans can be implemented.

4. **Communication via the line manager is most effective.** Line manager-to-employee communication is an opportunity for people to ask questions and check that they have understood the issues correctly. However, be aware that business urgency and reality may dictate the need, on many occasions, to inform employees directly rather than relying entirely on communication down through the organizational hierarchy.

5. **Employee communications are not optional; they are part of business as usual and should be planned and budgeted for as such.** An employee communications plan—key themes, targets, objectives, and resources—provides a context in which to deliver initiatives that arise at short notice.

6. **There must be integration between internal and external communications.** There must be a fit between what management is telling people and what is being told to customers, shareholders, and the public. (By the same token, there must be a fit between what management is telling people, and what the external media is telling them.)

7. **Timing is critical.** However clearly expressed and well presented your message may be, if it arrives at the wrong time you might as well not have bothered. Old news is often worse than no news. Consequently, it is important to ensure that the channels you use can really deliver at the time you need them to.

8. **Tone is important.** Expressing overly gushing enthusiasm about a technical change of little real significance to employees or the public at large may detract from your own and the message's credibility.

9. **State your message from your audience's point of view.** Never lose sight of the "what's in it for your audience?" factor. People are more likely to listen if it is clear how the message affects them.

10. **Communication is a two-way process.** Employee communications are NOT a one-way information dump. Capturing feedback is of critical importance, and if management is not perceived as listening and acting on what it has been told, it risks no longer being able to solicit information.

11. **A single key theme or a couple of key themes is a means of giving coherence to a range of diverse employee communication initiatives.** In recent years, the overriding theme of many corporate employee communications has been the impact on the business of competition, regulation, and economic forces. Many messages and initiatives can therefore be evaluated according to the light they shed on one or more of these key themes.

12. **Set standards and stick to them.** Determine which channels of communication and media should be mandatory and which should be optional; establish quality standards for all channels and media and review these at least annually.[16]

The following sections provide two approaches to internal communication plans; one is an example of a plan developed by communication medium while the second focuses on upward and downward communication flow. (Upward and downward flow of communication was discussed in Chapter 5.)

An Internal Communication Plan Focused on Medium

Examples of employee communication media include the Intranet, Web sites, newsletters, memos, notice boards, the press, company magazines, blogs, and employee forums. Table 11-3, based on an actual example, illustrates how an organization might manage its internal communications with a focus on communication medium. The table also identifies the purpose for each media, its intended result, the communication department's role, and the frequency of the message.

An Internal Communication Plan Focused on Flow

As was discussed in Chapter 5, communication flows typically in three directions in an organization: upward, downward, and horizontally. One way to think about an effective internal communication program is to consider the flow of communication between management and employees—upward and downward—and create a plan to ensure that this flow is optimal. The following steps may be followed to create an internal communication plan designed around the flow of communication.[17]

Downward Communication   To ensure the effective downward flow of communication, an internal communication plan should

- Ensure every employee receives a copy of the strategic plan, which includes the organization's mission, vision, values statement, strategic goals, and strategies about how those goals will be reached.
- Ensure every employee receives an employee handbook that contains all up-to-date personnel policies.
- Develop a basic set of procedures for how routine tasks are conducted and include them in a standard operating manual.
- Ensure every employee has a copy of their job description and the organization chart.
- Regularly hold management meetings (at least every two weeks), even if there's nothing pressing to report. If meetings are held only when there's something to report, then communications will occur only when management has something

Table 11-3 Example of an Internal Communication Plan Organized by Medium.

MEDIUM	PURPOSE	INTENDED RESULT	COMMUNICATIONS DEPARTMENT ROLE	FREQUENCY
Emails				
Information bulletins ■ Director messages ■ Other organizational information	Inform, engage	Employees understand our purpose, progress, and how they connect	Consult, develop, publish	Weekly and as necessary
Activity reports	Inform	Employees understand what the rest of the organization is doing	Collect and publish	Monthly
Meetings				
Coffee with director	Inform, clarify, exchange	Employees connected with organization	Attend, notes if required	Twice a month
Brown bag lunch/ info sessions	Inform, clarify, exchange	Employees connected with organization	Plan, announce	Varies
Leadership team staff meeting (open to employees)	Model open organization, inform	Establish public record	Take notes	Weekly
All-manager meetings	Inform, clarify	Employees connected with organization	Note taking	Monthly
All-employee meetings	Inform, clarify	Employees connected with organization	Planning, logistics	Twice a year
Wednesday stand-up	Public forum to surface issues	Leadership visibility over problems, employee questions answered	Facilitate, record, track status	Weekly
Staff meetings	Inform, clarify		None	Various
Team meetings	Daily work		None	Various
Hallway conversations	Various		None	Various
Café conversations	Understanding		Facilitate	Various
Web pages				
Monthly news e-zine	Connect people to colleagues, to organization, to job	Employees connected and informed	Develop, publish	Monthly
Director staff meeting notes	Connect people to organization, document organization history	Employees connected and informed	Develop, publish	Weekly
Organization calendar	Provide visibility over organization activities		Maintain	As necessary
Stand-up meeting actions	Provide organization accountability	Employees connected and informed	Develop, publish	Weekly
Decision log	Document organizational decisions	Organization has record of decisions	Develop, publish	As necessary
Field guide to organization	Connections to organization	Employees understand how organization fits together	Develop, publish	As necessary

Source: Adapted from Coyote Enterprises. (2002). Retrieved October 31, 2009, from http://www.coyotecom.biz/commun/intcomplan.htm.

to say. The result is that communication will be one-way and the organization will suffer. Have meetings anyway, if only to establish that nothing significant has changed and there are no immediate problems.

- Hold full staff meetings every month to report how the organization is doing, major accomplishments, concerns, announcements about staff, and so on.
- Leaders and managers should have face-to-face contact with employees at least once a week. Even if the organization has more than twenty employees, management should stroll by once in a while.
- Regularly hold meetings to celebrate major accomplishments. This helps employees perceive what's important, gives them a sense of direction and fulfillment, and lets them know that leadership is on top of things.
- Ensure all employees receive yearly performance reviews, including their goals for the year, updated job descriptions, accomplishments, needs for improvement, and plans to help the employee accomplish the improvements.

Upward Communication To ensure the effective upward flow of communication, an internal communication plan should

- Ensure all employees give regular status reports to their supervisors. Include a section for what they did last week, will do next week, and any actions/issues to address.
- Ensure all supervisors meet one-on-one at least once a month with their employees to discuss how they are doing and hear about any current concerns. Even if the meeting is chitchat, it cultivates an important relationship between supervisor and employee.
- Use management and staff meetings to solicit feedback. Ask how it's going. Do a round table approach to hear from each person.
- Act on feedback from others. Write it down. Get back to it—if only to say you can't do anything about the reported problem or suggestion.
- Respect the "grapevine." It's probably one of the most prevalent and reliable forms of communications. Major "movements" in the organization usually first appear when employees feel it safe to share their feelings or opinions with peers.

Effective internal communication is a means to an end, not an end in itself. For employees to be fully engaged in their work and the organization, it needs to be demonstrated how an effective communication plan is linked to the solution of business problems.

External Communication Issues

Strategic external communication includes public relations and issues management efforts designed to influence consumers, communities, special-interest groups, voters, regulators, legislators, and others outside the organization, as mentioned previously. This section discusses these issues as well as investor, risk and crisis communication. From an individual communication perspective, it also explains how to handle the news media, a discussion that is particularly useful for dealing with crisis situations.

Public Relations and Image Building

Image building is defined as the process of creating the identity an organization wants its relevant publics to perceive.[18] **Identity** is the visual manifestation of the image of the organization as conveyed through its logo, products, services, buildings, stationery, uniforms, and other tangible items created by the organization to communicate with a variety of constituencies.[19]

image building
The process of creating the identity an organization wants its relevant public to perceive.

identity
The visual manifestation of the image of the organization as conveyed through its logo, products, services, buildings, stationery, uniforms, and other tangible items created by the organization to communicate with a variety of constituencies.

Image building has typically been associated with the field of public relations. Public relations may involve other activities, such as media relations, marketing publicity, and internal relations. **Public relations** is "the management function which evaluates public attitudes, identifies the policies and procedures of an individual or an organization with the public interest, and executes a program of action to earn public understanding and acceptance."[20]

Managing the Organization's Identity

One common process for managing an organization's identity is detailed below.

1. **Conduct an identity audit.** Similar in function to an internal communications audit, an external audit is intended to discover how the public currently views the organization, what its symbols represent to different constituencies, and whether the identity is up to date. It may involve interviews with top managers and other relevant constituencies, and a review of company literature, advertising, products, services, and facilities.
2. **Set identity objectives.** These goals should be set by top management and should explain how each constituency should react to specific identity proposals.
3. **Develop designs and names.** Once the audit is complete and objectives are in place, new designs for the company logo or product labeling and names of the company or products are developed to communicate these objectives.
4. **Develop prototypes.** Once the final designs are approved, prototypes are developed to identify reactions from the relevant publics.
5. **Launch and communicate.** This step typically involves public relations and advertising campaigns.
6. **Implement the program.** This step might take some time but usually is best approached by developing identity standards to ensure consistency across all uses of the new identity materials.

CriticalThinking

Can you identify an organization that has managed its identity successfully? What were the elements of that program? Can you identify an organization that has not been so successful at identity management? How might it improve its image?

public relations
The management function that evaluates public attitudes, identifies the policies and procedures of an individual or an organization with the public interest, and executes a program of action to earn public understanding and acceptance.

Creating a Web Presence

The Internet is a key component for corporate communication because of its speed, international access, and affordability. Creating a company Web site enables organizations to accomplish a number of activities, including

- Updating employees and customers about organizational changes.
- Selling products and services.
- Advertising employment opportunities.
- Creating a first point of contact for customers through order entry, customer service systems, and online call centers.

However, an effective Web presence may extend beyond the creation of an effective Web page. It will likely also include maintaining a blog that can help the Web site stand out and help consumers better understand the business. For one, it shows that you know what you're talking about. It helps you identify yourself as an expert or unique. Secondly, a blog is constantly updated. It gives readers a reason to come back to your site. The more contact you have with your consumers, the more likely they are to buy from you.

A third element of an effective Web presence is to develop an electronic newsletter that automatically updates customers on company, product, and services developments and offers them specials. Email marketing is one of the most effective ways to generate sales. Getting consumers to sign up for the email list means organizations no longer have to wait for them to come to it.

Another option for capturing leads is through the use of social media. Microblogs and social networks such as Facebook and Twitter can help organizations connect with and contact those within their core community. For this strategy to work, the company blog should serve as a central hub that sends consumers to the organization's respective social media profiles to build the connection.

Businesses with a Facebook Fan Page can include a Fan Box on the site to make it an easy process to fan the business page. If the organization has an active Twitter account, it should consider adding the "Follow Me on Twitter" button. These two elements can help turn a one-time reader into a connected consumer.

When you're building an online presence, the most important aspect is the company Web site. It's the hub for communication and makes a first impression of the company for visitors. It should include the right elements to maximize its effectiveness.

CriticalThinking

What makes a Web site useful and memorable in your opinion? Based upon your own Web site use, what should organizations avoid when designing Web pages?

Gaining Publicity

A major purpose of many public relations programs is to provide information to the media in the hope that it will be published or broadcast. The resulting coverage is called *publicity*. To be an effective publicist, one must be familiar with journalistic news values and know how to identify a news angle that will be interesting to journalists and the public.

Table 11-4 lists ways to create news for an organization. In general, aspects of news include the following:

- **Timeliness.** One way to makes news timely is to announce something when it happens. Another way is to offer information linked to events or holidays already of interest to the public. A third approach is to link announcements to current issues that are already in the news.
- **Prominence.** Prominence relates to the importance of the person or company involved in the announcement. Celebrities are more likely to get news attention, just as are influential business leaders and organizations.

Table 11-4 Ways to Create News for Your Organization.

Tie in with news events of the day.	Tie in with a holiday.
Cooperate with another organization on a joint project.	Make a trip.
Conduct a poll or a survey.	Make an award.
Tie in with a newspaper or broadcast station on a mutual project.	Hold a contest.
Issue a report.	Pass a resolution.
Arrange an interview with a celebrity.	Appear before public bodies.
Take part in a controversy.	Stage a special event.
Arrange for a testimonial.	Write a letter.
Make an analysis or a prediction.	Release a letter you received (with permission).
Form and announce names for a committee.	Adapt national reports and surveys for local use.
Hold an election.	Stage a debate.
Announce an appointment.	Tie in to a well-known week or day.
Celebrate an anniversary.	Honor an institution.
Issue a summary of facts.	Organize a tour.
	Inspect a project.
	Issue a commendation.
	Issue a protest.

Source: Wilcox, D. L., Ault, P. H., & Agee, W. K. (1995). *Public Relations Strategies and Tactics*, 4th ed. (New York: HarperCollins).

- **Proximity.** News that has a local angle is more likely to get published or broadcast, so it is important to "localize" information to the media outlets being targeted.
- **Significance.** Any event that affects a large number of people is more likely to get publicized by the media.
- **Unusualness.** Events or announcements that are out of the ordinary make them more attractive to the media.
- **Human interest.** Stories about other people are more interesting to the public, so it can be helpful to "humanize" announcements by connecting them to real people and telling the story through their eyes.
- **Conflict.** Controversial issues are more likely to get coverage in the news media.
- **Newness.** Information about new products or services is more likely to get publicized.

Investor Relations

Over the past forty years, investor relations has become an important part of corporate communication's function. Broadly speaking, those involved in investor relations are responsible for marketing the stock of public companies to investors either directly or through securities analysts. They provide information that analysts need to recommend the company's stock and that investors need to buy it.

Investor relations manages relations with both individual shareholders and institutional investors, such as pension and mutual funds, banks, and insurance companies. Individuals hold about 55 percent of all equities in the United States while institutional investors hold the remaining 45 percent. The financial community is typically targeted through "buy-side" and "sell-side" analysts. The buy-side represents individuals, fund and portfolio managers, and institutional analysts, while the sell-side represents individual and institutional brokers as well as investment banks.

Those working in investor relations reach institutions often through face-to-face meetings and the telephone. In addition, CEOs may address industry conferences or analyst or broker societies. Companies also host meetings in major financial centers and invite investors who own or may want to buy company stock.

To reach individuals, investor relations professionals may use direct mail to contact current shareholders, customers, or suppliers or try to generate visibility in the media.

Companies reach both types of investors through annual and quarterly reports, proxy statements, press releases, and annual meetings.

In order to develop a formal investor relations program, companies must answer four critical questions:

- **What is the current perception of the company in the investment community?** This question is best answered by surveying the financial community to determine what it needs from the company and how the company is viewed.
- **Where does investor relations fit within the company?** Investor relations is in a sensitive position both legally and ethically in terms of what can and cannot be shared with the public, investors, and the media. The person or persons given the job must be able to use judgment as well as to maintain good relations with those inside and outside the company.
- **What are the objectives of the investor relations program?** An effective investor relations program must provide a proactive marketing function that ensures the company's stock price is appropriate for the earnings outlook and the economy, limits stock price volatility, and understands the shareholder base as well as what is common in the industry. With this knowledge, the program should build the shareholder base and provide feedback to management regarding investor concerns.
- **What activities are necessary to achieve these objectives?** In order to achieve these objectives, the company must develop a message that includes management's philosophy, current conditions in the industry, and earnings potential.[21]

This and other information needs to be communicated to analysts and institutional investors in a timely manner. That is the role of investor relations.

Issues Management

In the past few decades, large organizations have moved beyond traditional image-building functions of public relations to deal more effectively with social and political issues that affect organizations and their relationships with various publics.[22] **Issues management** is "the organized activity of identifying emerging trends, concerns, or issues likely to affect an organization in the next few years and

issues management
The organized activity of identifying emerging trends, concerns, or issues likely to affect an organization in the next few years, and developing a wider and more positive range of organizational responses.

developing a wider and more positive range of organizational responses."[23] Issues management is related to risk and crisis management, two additional concepts related to organizational strategic communication that will be discussed later in this chapter.

Many of these attempts to influence the development of public policy decisions arise from conflicts among industries, which often involve legal regulation. Traditionally, many heavily regulated industries have relied upon lobbyists to influence the regulatory process. But many public issues do not become objects of legislative action until the issue has become highly politicized, and many organizations have used lobbying in ways that are almost exclusively self-serving. These approaches can be criticized as reactive as well as insensitive to the importance of public interest and response to such issues.

Issues management has become a concern because executives and managers tend to avoid dealing with public issues. "The most significant explanation of the failure of business to gain respect for its positions on public issues is that corporate leadership either does not recognize or ignores, the discernible trends which always precede issues."[24]

One model developed to explain how such failures occur characterizes organizational responses by two factors (1) the organization's stake in maintaining the status quo and (2) the perceived legitimacy of the public's complaints against the status quo.[25] According to the model, organizations will avoid a public issue if the stakes and perceived legitimacy are low. If the stakes are high and perceived legitimacy is low, organizations will tend to "stonewall" with cover-ups, distortions, and other methods. When stakes are low and perceived legitimacy is high, the organization attempts to accommodate critics through some sort of change. If both the stakes and the perceived legitimacy are high, the organization attempts to collaborate with critics.

The problem that this model identifies is that executive's perceptions of legitimacy may have little to do with the actual impact that a public issue may have on an organization. Because of this problem, organizations should develop some means of tracking and monitoring issues as they develop. Several techniques that organizations can use to track and predict the development of such issues include

- **Trend extrapolation.** A factor or variable is measured over time and statistical forecasting techniques are used to project a trend from these measurements.
- **Trend impact analysis.** After a trend is extrapolated, future events are identified that would affect the extrapolation and the trend is modified in light of these possible events.
- **Scanning.** Issues that might affect an organization are identified and monitored by use of volunteers who regularly scan print and electronic media for information.
- **Monitoring.** Monitoring tracks issues that have been identified through scanning using a systematic analysis of data. Monitoring may include public opinion polling, focus groups, and other forms of social science research.
- **Scenario writing.** Some organizations hire writers to develop and write scenarios that address the question, "What would happen if X came to pass?"[26]

These tools help organizations gather information about emerging public issues. But issues management doesn't stop here. The information that has been gathered can be used to affect decision making. This action typically takes one of two forms: organizational change or issue advocacy.

CriticalThinking

What public issues are you aware of that might have a negative effect on organizations? What industries would potentially be most affected by certain outcomes of these public concerns? What could organizations do to affect these outcomes?

Organizational Change and Issues Management

Issues management may be used to address potential regulatory challenges, but some managers use the information to create social responsibility programs. Such efforts are grounded in Chaffee's adaptive model of strategy that assumes an interdependency between the organization and its environment.

Starbucks Corp. is one example of a company that has created a social responsibility program. One aspect of Starbucks's program is its commitment to ethically sourcing and roasting its coffee. In fiscal 2007, 65 percent of Starbucks's coffee was purchased from C.A.F.E. (Coffee and Farmer Equity) Practices, which are approved suppliers who have integrated the company's standards for sustainability throughout the coffee supply chain. C.A.F.E. Practices suppliers—and other entities within Starbucks's supply network—must have certain practices in place that ensure safe, fair, and humane working conditions; the protection of workers' rights; and adequate living conditions. The minimum wage requirements and addressing child labor/forced labor/discrimination indicators are mandatory. In addition, in the growing and/or processing of coffee, measures must be in place to manage waste, protect water quality, conserve water and energy use, preserve biodiversity, and reduce agrochemical use. Starbucks's goal is to be purchasing 80 percent of its coffee through C.A.F.E. Practices by 2013, and extending the program's reach to areas in Africa and Asia. Starbucks uses such programs to differentiate itself as a leader in the coffee industry.

Issues Advocacy

Another form of action is advocacy of the organization's position on the issues. Public communication programs based on issues advocacy are different from typical image-building activities. Traditional image building is "usually rather general in scope and bland in character," whereas issues advocacy "addresses itself to specific controversial issues, presenting facts and arguments that project the sponsor's viewpoint ... to try to influence political decisions by molding public opinion."[27]

ExxonMobil, for example, engages in issues advocacy on a range of issues, including climate change, energy policy, and energy pricing. A recent ExxonMobil advocacy campaign on global warming acknowledged that it exists but tries to undermine the belief that it was caused by human activity. ExxonMobil's issues advocacy is carefully crafted to serve its strategic goals.

ResponsibleCommunication

Corporate social responsibility (CSR) is a concept whereby companies integrate social and environmental concerns into their business operations and in their interaction with their stakeholders (employees, customers, shareholders, investors, local communities, government) on a voluntary basis.

CSR is closely linked with the principles of sustainability, which argues that enterprises should make decisions based not only on financial factors, such as profits or dividends, but also based on the immediate and long-term social and environmental consequences of their activities.

CSR has become prominent in the language and strategy of business and by the growth of dedicated CSR organizations globally. Governments and international governmental organizations are increasingly encouraging CSR and forming CSR partnerships.

CSR is rapidly becoming a major part of all business management courses and a key global issue.

CSR provides a number of potential benefits to both the community and business, including

- Reduced costs
- Increased business leads
- Increased reputation
- Increased staff morale and skills development
- Improved relationships with the local community, partners, and clients
- Innovation in processes, products, and services
- Managing the risks a company faces

There are critics of CSR, however, who argue that it distracts from the fundamental economic role of businesses, while others say it may be used cynically and superficially as a public relations campaign in an attempt to preempt the role of governments as a watchdog over multinational corporations.

Questions for Discussion

1. What are some examples of CSR efforts that you have seen or with which you have been involved? Were these true attempts at more responsible business practices or more superficial in the sense that they were being used to simply affect an organization's image?
2. How were these CSR efforts communicated to the public and other stakeholders? Were these messages effective in terms of the medium chosen to communicate the message and the content of the message? Were they appropriately targeted to their intended audience or audiences?

Risk Communication and Crisis Communication

risk
The chance of loss (or gain).

risk communication
The process of communicating responsibly and effectively about the risk factors associated with industrial technologies, natural hazards, and human activities.

Risk and crisis communication are closely related but separate activities. **Risk** is "the chance of loss (or gain)."[28] In contrast, a crisis is more urgent and immediate and is commonly associated with a potential negative outcome. Crisis is thus an event or episode that is caused by risk.

Risk Communication

Risk management is concerned with identifying an organization's exposure to potential losses, preventing or reducing the likelihood of their occurrence, and mitigating potential loss. Risk management may include risk of theft, fraud, and workplace accidents, to larger catastrophic events, such as terrorist attacks and natural disasters. **Risk communication** is "the process of communicating responsibly and effectively about the risk factors associated with industrial technologies, natural hazards, and human activities."[29]

The basic responsibility of risk communication practitioners is promotion of "reasoned dialogue among stakeholders on the nature of the relevant risk factors and on acceptable risk management strategies."[30] Practitioners thus must understand how risks are perceived by relevant publics, be able to present expert risk assessments in ways nonexperts can understand, and help interested parties reach a shared understanding of risk.

Risk communication as an area of practice and scholarly attention has experienced rapid growth. A number of university centers exist to study risk communication, consulting firms offer risk communication services, degree programs in risk communication have been started, and hundreds of scholarly articles have been published on the subject in the past twenty years.

Crisis Communication

Crisis communication is an often overlooked aspect of an organization's management strategy. A 2004 study found that only between 5 and 25 percent of the Fortune 500 companies were prepared to manage an unfamiliar crisis.[31]

Crisis communication requires management in situations that affect an organization's relationships with its stakeholders, particularly those that draw media attention. Much of the crisis communication literature is concerned with this issue. For example, Benoit's theory of image restoration is concerned with crisis situations in which relevant audiences believe an organization is responsible for an offensive act. For Benoit, the important point is not whether the organization is actually responsible, but whether the public believes it is responsible. According to Benoit's theory, organizations can respond to crisis situations in five ways: They can deny responsibility, evade responsibility, reduce offensiveness of the act, take corrective action, or apologize.[32]

Discussions of crisis management typically focus on three issues: (1) planning and preparing for crisis events, (2) behavior of the organization during a crisis, and (3) communicating with important publics during the crisis.[33] Although this model separates communicating about the crisis from the planning and behavior stages, both of these latter issues are relevant to what is communicated and how.

Five steps in the planning process are to

1. Identify the potential crises.
2. Evaluate the impact of a crisis, not only in terms of the actual event but the public response to it.
3. Assign responsibility for execution of the crisis management program.
4. Put the plan in writing.
5. Rehearse the actions outlined in the plan.[34]

The types of disasters that an organization might face have been categorized as natural disasters, normal accidents, and abnormal or intentional accidents. Natural disasters include fires, earthquakes, or hurricanes.[35] Normal accidents is a term coined to describe industrial disasters such as those that occurred at Three Mile Island, Chernobyl, Bhopal, and Alaska due to the Exxon Valdez spill. Abnormal accidents occur because of deliberate action, such as bombings, kidnappings, cyberattacks, and other types of sabotage.[36]

One tool for accomplishing the first two steps in the planning process is to apply the "worst case scenario" technique.[37] The third step should be accomplished by limiting the number of people involved. "If you manage crisis by committee, you are doomed to failure.... There needs to be a chain of command and agreement on who's going to do the speaking."[38]

The communication objective in any crisis management strategy should depend upon the stage of the crisis.[39] In cases when communication programs can begin before a crisis occurs, messages should provide internalizing information to build a positive public opinion toward the organization. When it appears a crisis is imminent, the strategy should shift from internalizing messages to instructing messages that tell the public how to respond to the crisis. During the breakout stage of the crisis, instructing communication should intensify so that the affected publics know what to do. As the crisis subsides, communication may shift to adjusting messages intended to help people cope with the effects of the crisis. When the crisis is over, the organization can shift back to an internalizing message strategy.

Any crisis communication plan should provide training for dealing with the media regarding crisis management; identify communication lines with local communities and intervening agencies, such as the police; and provide a strategy for communicating with employees.

During a crisis, an organization should follow the steps outlined below:

1. **Get control of the situation.** This involves defining the problem and setting measurable communication objectives. In addition, it is important to communicate to employees how and where to get information.

2. **Gather information about the situation.** It is important that an organization has a means to stay up to date with the situation as it is happening so that it can respond quickly and appropriately. One way to accomplish this task is to create a crisis center that creates crisis response plans, monitors potential crises, and develops crisis response capabilities.

3. **Communicate early and often.** It will benefit the organization's credibility to be prepared and to explain what is happening and what the company is doing about it, and to provide information about resources available to affected parties to deal with the situation.

4. **Communicate directly with affected parties.** It is important to be prepared to communicate with the media and to do so promptly; it is also important to communicate directly with others who are affected, such as employees, customers, shareholders, and communities.

Handling the News Media

An organization should not wait for a crisis to develop relationships with members of the media if it wants to take advantage of the media's image-building capabilities. It is important that someone in the organization takes time to cultivate these relationships. Building relationships with the media is generally considered a better method than sending out mass-produced public releases, which may average a response rate of only 2 percent.[40]

An alternative is for corporate communication professionals to target their audience by doing research on the publications and writers who cover their industry or company. Ideally, someone in the company would keep a record of all articles published on the firm to make this job easier. Not only is it important to know who is covering the organization but also the angle the writer often takes.

In addition to identifying writers who cover your industry and targeting stories to them specifically, it is important that communication professionals within the organization are responsive to calls from the media. This means that those taking the calls need to be informed about the writer and need to gather information about the specifics of the call so that they can best identify the proper person within the company to address the issue. All of this needs to be done in a timely manner because of the constant deadline that most news organizations are under.

Preparing for a News Interview

Once an interview is scheduled, it is important for the person who is being interviewed to properly prepare. As with most other communication situations, preparation is the key to success in handling interviews with the media.

1. **Develop a strategy.** As with other messages, you should identify the purposes that you hope to achieve during the interview. You should also have a clear idea of who the intended audience is. Knowledge about these two issues should help you to determine the general content of your message and whether visuals or photos would be appropriate and, if so, what kind.

   Additional questions to consider involve those that your audience, the media, will be concerned about. These include what makes your story different from others or what makes it newsworthy.

2. **Refine and rehearse the message.** As with presentations and employment interviews, you should be clear about your central theme or message and develop examples, illustrations, and anecdotes that support the message. Your message should also be phrased in terms of the public's interests, not the company's.

3. **Confirm the details and ground rules.** Confirm the time, day, date, and location of the interview. If the interview is not at your office, make sure that you know how to get to the location and the time it will take to get there. For telephone or face-to-face interviews, find out whether the interview is being recorded and consider whether it is necessary for you to record the conversation as well. You must notify the party if you are recording a conversation.

4. **Make sure that you are up on the news.** You don't want to be taken by surprise, so it is important to be abreast of what is happening in the news that might affect your company or your industry.

5. **Prepare a note card with important details.** If you have trouble remembering numbers, put these on a small note card that you can refer to discreetly. Be judicious in your use of the card, since reading from it can detract from your ability to maintain a confident, credible image.

Performing the News Interview

Make sure that you arrive on time for the interview and that you look professional. It might be helpful to take a page from presidential candidates and consider whether loosening your tie or taking off your jacket will help you to better establish common ground with an audience who doesn't wear a suit to work. During the interview, practice the following points:

- **Lead with your main point.** Since you have a limited amount of time, make sure that you get your key message in early. Don't wait for the reporter to ask you a question that allows you to communicate your main message—he or she may not.
- **Express your key points from the public's point of view.** Telling the audience how the company's actions will contribute to better health or preserve jobs in the community may help it to better appreciate your points.

- **Use plain language.** Avoid language with which only those in your industry, company, or professional specialization are familiar.
- **Maintain control.** Focus on your goals for the interview and offer responses aimed at achieving those goals.
- **Be honest.** Tell the truth. If there is a problem, then focus the bulk of your discussion on the steps you are taking to avoid the problem in the future. Don't guess at the answer. If you don't know something, say so.
- **Take responsibility.** Again, unless the corporate attorney has advised otherwise, take responsibility for problems rather than blaming others.
- **Remain calm and avoid arguments.** Becoming emotional can undermine your credibility and make you look as if you have lost control and composure.
- **Rephrase the question.** You don't need to accept a reporter's premise. If a reporter uses words you wouldn't, don't repeat them. Correct them, if necessary.
- **Try to be friendly, helpful, and patient.** Shake hands with reporters and call them by name. Be enthusiastic about your company and your job, if appropriate for the occasion. Avoid becoming impatient with reporters or acting as if they or their questions are stupid.

The important thing is that you maintain your composure and appear to be likeable. Be honest, humble, and use humor when appropriate.

CriticalThinking

As you reflect upon interviews with organizational representatives that you have seen or heard in the media, what are the characteristics or abilities of an effective interviewee? What sort of statements should company representatives avoid during interview situations? What kinds of difficult questions might you anticipate in an interview with a media representative, and how might these questions be effectively answered?

Communicating during a Crisis

Many of the steps discussed above for handling the news media apply to communicating with the press during a crisis situation. Additional guidelines for dealing with the media during a crisis include:

- Anticipate questions and determine who will answer them. Ideally, question-and-answer sheets should be prepared for management personnel who may be asked questions by the news media. Anticipate which questions might be asked during a briefing and who should best respond.
- Prepare and deliver a brief statement. After introducing yourself and others representing your company, deliver a brief statement (less than two minutes in length) that focuses only on the facts that can be confirmed at that time.
- Outline your organization's current response effort and action plan.
- Limit the question-and-answer session to no more than ten minutes.
- Don't speculate or make predictions.
- Don't make any remarks "off the record." Such comments might lead reporters to believe there is more to the story that they can pursue.

As with many other types of professional communication situations, adequate preparation is often the key to a successful crisis briefing.

Summary

The three basic models of strategic communication at the organizational level are linear, adaptive, and interpretive. In the linear model, managers identify goals, generate alternatives for achieving those goals, weigh the likelihood of success for each alternative, and then decide which to implement. The adaptive model shifts the focus of strategy from sequential planning and implementation to continuous adjustment of the relationship between the organization and its environment. The interpretive model is concerned with the social construction of reality. In this model, strategic communication is about negotiating and shaping stakeholders' understandings of what the organization is and what it does. Even though these three models appear to be distinct, they are interrelated and interdependent and more than one may be operating at the same time within an organization.

The relevant audiences for strategic communication at the organizational level are organizational stakeholders. Organizational stakeholders include shareholders or owners, employees, customers or clients, or any important constituency that can be affected or can affect the organization. These might include the government, media, activist groups, special interest coalitions, and communities.

The first step in creating an internal communication plan is to assess the current communication situation. This is commonly done by performing a communication audit, which not only assesses the current state of internal communication but also identifies areas for improvement. Once the assessment is complete, an internal communication plan can be developed. It is important to periodically assess the plan for its effectiveness and make changes as needed to ensure effective communication throughout the organization.

Additional tasks for organizational leaders are to motivate and to communicate change to employees. These are related issues since motivation may involve change in employees' behaviors and attitudes in relation to their work; however, change management typically involves organizational changes that originate at the top of the organization. The success of any change program is heavily reliant on the quality of communication about that change. Successfully implementing organizational change involves communication on all organizational levels and in all forms: group discussion, one-on-one conversations, formal meetings, and in writing.

As a form of public communication, strategic external communication can require a substantial commitment of resources, including the purchase of advertising space in print and electronic media; time, space, and materials for special events; production facilities for Web sites, newsletters, company magazines, and video programs; and salaries and benefits for those who write, edit, and create the messages. Strategic external communication can be a complex process in which a number of organizational units and individuals contribute to the design and dissemination of messages. External strategic communication includes public relations and issues management efforts designed to influence consumers, communities, special-interest groups, voters, regulators, legislators, and others outside the organization. It may also include investor relations, which is intended to manage relationships with the investment community.

Other external strategic communication issues are risk and crisis communication, which are closely related but separate activities. Risk management is concerned with identifying an organization's exposure to potential losses, preventing or reducing the likelihood of their occurrence, and mitigating potential loss. Risk communication is the process of communicating responsibly and effectively about the risk factors associated with industrial technologies, natural hazards, and human activities. Crisis communication requires management in situations that affect an organization's relationships with its stakeholders, particularly those that draw media attention.

Key Terms

linear model, 313
adaptive model, 313

co-alignment, 313
interpretive model, 313

Discussion Questions

1. What are the three models of organizational strategy proposed by Chaffee? What are the characteristics of each?
2. What are some of the costs to an organization of poor employee communication? What are some of the common reasons that are cited for a lack of an employee communication plan?
3. What are the elements of a successful employee communication program?
4. What are some of the barriers to effective interdepartmental communication? What are some of the steps that can be taken to improve interdepartmental communication?
5. What are the steps involved in developing a strategic external relations program? What challenges might you anticipate in developing such a program and how might they be addressed?

Applications

1. Use participant observation to conduct a "mini" communication audit of an organization of which you are a part. Participant observation involves participating in organizational activities involving communication and assessing how and when communication is performed. Summarize the results of your observations in an informal report you address to the leader of the group.
2. Collect a variety of documents created by an organization. These might include publications, campaign materials, press releases, a Web site, and so on. Review the documents to assess their effectiveness in terms of strategic communication issues. That is, identify the audiences for the message, their purposes, and the channel and media used, and assess how well the documents meet these strategic goals. Write an informal report to the leader of the organization that summarizes your findings.
3. Select an organization to which you have access. Prepare a list of open-ended questions intended to elicit responses from employees or members of the organization about its communication practices. Conduct interviews with five persons who are members of the organization. Write an informal report to the leader of the organization that summarizes your findings.
4. Select an organization that has a Web presence. Then prepare an informal report in which you identify and analyze the effectiveness of the organization's logo, slogans, letterhead, product designs, and promotional materials in terms of how well you think they reinforce the themes identified in the company mission statement. In performing your analysis, take into consideration how they might be perceived by the major audiences or stakeholders for the materials.
5. Identify a recent crisis that an organization has faced. Conduct research on that crisis and write an informal report in which you (a) summarize the facts of the crisis situation, (b) prepare a two-minute statement that could be delivered to the press, and (c) identify potential questions you might receive from the press and provide your responses to them.

CASE ANALYSIS

SONY CORPORATION: THE PLAYSTATION NETWORK CRASH (A)

The Crash

On April 28, 2011, Sony Corporation shares had just fallen by more than 5 percent on the Tokyo Stock Exchange.[41] The company was suffering through a chaotic time period in its gaming division. Hackers had invaded the PlayStation Network roughly two weeks earlier during the period between April 17, 2011, and April 19, 2011.[42] In the words of Max Parker, writer for the *Pittsburgh Post-Gazette*, "To say the hackers did damage to Sony would be the understatement of the year. They crippled the network, knocking it out of commission for a little over a week, and the hackers had access to about 77 million users' personal information, including credit card data."[43]

The organization did not figure out the source of the intrusion until a week after the initial discovery and did not disclose information about the breach until that time. The general public questioned Sony's slow response and seemingly inadequate internal security systems.[44] The company was in the process of bringing the network back online and could not confirm how much of the accessed information would be used illegally by hackers.[45] The blogs were buzzing about how the company would respond in the coming days to this dreadful incident.

Company Background

Sony Corporation began in 1946 as the Tokyo Telecommunications Engineering Corporation named "Totsuko." Engineer Masaru Ibuka and physicist Akio Morita created the company to build and repair electrical equipment. Radios from the war were some of the organization's first products on the market.[46]

During the early post–World War II years, Japanese people wanted to hear about news around the world as well as rebuild their war-torn nation. Sony responded by creating a market for consumer electronics that included items such as radios, tape recorders, and electric rice cookers. The founders began thinking about entering the United States in the early 1950s but discovered that Americans had a difficult time pronouncing Japanese names including the words Morita and Totsuko.[47]

Ibuka-san and Morita-san believed that the company must come up with a new name to cater to the English-speaking market in North America. "Sony" was chosen in 1955 as a cross between the Latin word "Sonus" and the American phrase "Sonny boy." The founders wanted to instill a sense of youth and excitement in the organization while still staying true to its identity of sound equipment.[48] Over the years the company has expanded to cover various aspects of the electronics and multimedia industry with recognizable divisions in Sony Pictures, Sony Music, Sony Electronics, Sony Ericsson, and Sony Computer Entertainment. Despite its international presence, Sony Corporation has kept its main headquarters in Tokyo, Japan.[49]

Gaming

The company made its splash into computer entertainment by introducing the PlayStation console. The move initially began with a CD-ROM development venture in the 1980s with Philips. Sony gained the ability to approach home computers through the successes of this joint partnership. It approached Nintendo, a long-time developer with the idea of integrating CD technology with traditional cartridges in 1988. Disagreements and legal battles eventually disintegrated this relationship, and Sony decided to come up with its own console that would use solely CD-ROMs. The company had the ability to produce the hardware, but it bought a small European company called Psygnosis to meet software needs. In December 1994, after years of development, Sony introduced the PlayStation gaming console in Japan.[50]

Sony Corporation has developed the PlayStation console over the years with upgrades and new product introductions using the latest technology. It created a separate division called Sony Computer Entertainment in 1995 and placed it in Sunnyvale, California. Since the console's inception, there have been several modifications and three official generations. The latest generation is the PlayStation 3, or PS3 for short. The PS3 runs the latest disc technology called "Blu-Ray," which stores much more data than its predecessors the CD and the DVD. The console also contains a wireless card to access the Internet where networks are available, an internal hard drive to store additional data, digital audio and video outputs, applications for audio and video playback, and a general navigation screen. This latest installment of the PlayStation console is meant to provide more than just gaming and is expected to act as an all-in-one entertainment system.[51]

The PlayStation Network

Sony released the PlayStation Network with Qriocity services as part of the PlayStation 3 console introduction at the Business Briefing Meeting in 2006. Consumers could register and access the PSN for free via a PS3 console, a portable PSP console, or a personal computer. Numerous services are included on the network:[52]

- System updates
- Multiplayer gaming
- Internet browsing
- Chat functions with other users
- Downloads and streaming of music, movies, and games

Some of the listed services, including streaming and downloading of particular media, are offered only on a premium basis and require electronic transactions. Sony originally developed retail tickets available to consumers for online funds. However, recent improvements have replaced tickets with prepaid and online credit card transactions.[53] By April 30, 2011, the network had 77 million registered users with 12 million profiles containing credit card information.[54]

Timeline

The following list outlines activities surrounding the crash during a two-week period leading up to the weekend of April 30, 2011:

- *April 19, 2011:* Illegal activity was detected in the network servers.[55]
- *April 20, 2011:* Engineers discovered evidence of intrusion and shut down the network to prevent potential further damage.[56]
- *April 21, 2011:* Sony hired an external security consulting firm to further analyze problems.[57]

- *April 22, 2011:* The company provided the Federal Bureau of Investigation information about the breach and made a public comment on the sponsored blog suggesting PlayStation Network and Qriocity services were shut down due to an attack.[58]
- *April 23, 2011:* Forensic teams confirmed a sophisticated attack where intruders gained unauthorized privileges and hid their presence from administrators.[59]
- *April 24, 2011:* Sony did not update the public on progress but retained additional security consulting to help determine problems within the server.[60]
- *April 25, 2011:* Teams confirmed that account information including name, address, country, email, birth date, PlayStation Network/Qriocity password, login, handle, and network ID were stolen. However, research cannot confirm status of credit card information stored on the servers.[61]
- *April 26, 2011:* Kaz Hirai, head of Sony gaming, appeared at a Tokyo news conference to promote the release of new tablet personal computers. He was originally not scheduled to take questions during the event and left without discussing the network status.[62] The company alerts the public via email of the intrusion and begins notifying regulatory authorities in various states and nations.[63]
- *April 27, 2011:* Company continued to inform the proper authorities, and Sony shares fell by 2 percent on the Tokyo Stock Exchange with the news of potential data loss surfacing.[64] The first lawsuit against Sony due to the crash was filed by Kristopher Johns in California.[65]
- *April 28, 2011:* Stocks fell an additional 4.5 percent in Japan amidst the reactions before the long holiday weekend.[66]
- *April 29, 2011:* Sony refuted claims of 2.2 million credit card numbers stolen and being sold in online forums.[67]

Reactions: Consumers

On April 21, 2011, one day after Sony took down the PlayStation Network, Patrick Seybold, senior director for corporate communications and marketing, released a message to Sony's customers on the official *PlayStation.Blog*:

> *While we are investigating the cause of the Network outage, we wanted to alert you that it may be a full day or two before we're able to get the service completely back up and running. Thank you very much for your patience while we work to resolve this matter. Please stay tuned to this space for more details, and we'll update you again as soon as we can.*[68]

Consumers provided varying opinions, and gamers gave their thoughts about the inability to play games or watch movies and television shows. In comments posted to numerous Web sites including the *PlayStation.Blog* and the *Huffington Post*, users speculated reasons for the outage as well as expressed frustration over their inability to play the games that they were desperately waiting for.[69,70]

Over the next few days, Sony and its representatives kept the gaming community updated as details became clear. On April 21 and 22, messages were posted to the *PlayStation.Blog* notifying users that they believed that the outage was a result of an "external intrusion"[71] and that they were "working around the clock to bring them both (PlayStation Network and Qriocity) back online. "Our efforts to resolve this matter involve rebuilding our system to further strengthen our network infrastructure. Though this task is time-consuming, we decided it was worth the time necessary to provide the system with additional security."[72]

At this point, the overall mood went from frustration over the outage to support of Sony being a victim of hackers. Many in the gaming community turned their anger to Anonymous, a "global hacker collective."[73] This attitude existed until April 26, 2011, when emails from Sony executives and a message from Patrick Seybold notified PlayStation Network's users that their personal data, including credit card information, may have been stolen. In the message, Sony recommended that users "be especially aware of e-mail, telephone, and postal mail scams that ask for personal or sensitive information."[74] The company also made available the contact information for the three primary U.S. credit bureaus.[75]

The goodwill from the community evaporated in a matter of minutes. Even though a number of people remained supportive of Sony, a large portion of users reacted angrily to what they felt was a betrayal by Sony for not notifying them initially that their credit card information had potentially been stolen. (Please see Appendix A for additional comments.)

Reactions: Developers

During the first few days of the outage, developers maintained a fairly positive outlook. Outages had happened before, but gamers typically came back. Q-Games Developer Dylan Cuthbert was quoted saying:

> *PSN being out definitely affects our bottom line … but as long as the people who were going to be playing Shooter 2 and other PixelJunk titles will get right back in there playing them when it comes back up, we'll be happy and hopefully income won't be dented too much.*[76]

As the days continued to pass and news of the stolen credit card data was released, some developers retained their belief that the situation would be resolved without significant damage. Stewart Gilray of Just Add Water said, "Our belief is that whilst this is terrible news … it won't affect the user base too much."[77]

Other developers believed that the network outage caused anxiety over lost revenues as well as missed released dates. Ubisoft was scheduled to release a highly anticipated game *Outland* on April 27, 2011, but missed the release on the PSN while meeting its release date on Sony's competitor network Microsoft's Xbox Live Arcade.[78]

Smaller developers had much more to lose and worry about. Lol Scragg, founder of Cohort Studios, said, "We have our first self-funded, self-published PSN game Me Monster: Hear Me Roar, coming out next week, so from our point of view, the fact that the network isn't available is a big concern."[79]

Others, such as Ste Curran, creative director at games studio Zoe Mode, looked beyond the current discussion to speak of how the PlayStation Network hack would affect the future of digital media and online transaction. "From my perspective, the bigger issue is not about PSN, but confidence in digital distribution."[80]

Reactions: Partners

PlayStation Network partners with a number of services outside of gaming, such as Netflix, Hulu Plus, Qore, VUDU, and Music Unlimited in the United States. In addition, Sony offers various services globally including Vidzone (Europe), RTE (Republic of Ireland), now TV (Hong Kong), and many more services.

On April 27, 2011, management at Hulu offered their Hulu Plus members a "1-week credit toward your Hulu Plus subscription."[81] The credit was valued at "$2 off of this month's bill."[82]

Reactions: U.S. Government

U.S. senator Rick Blumenthal (D-Connecticut) sent a letter to Sony Computer Entertainment America's CEO Jack Tretton after the announcement of data loss on April 26, 2011, demanding answers for what Sony would do to both compensate and protect its users. In addition he chastised Sony for their failure to inform and protect users of the breach. (Please see full text in Appendix B.)

> *I am concerned that PlayStation Network users' personal and financial information may have been inappropriately accessed by a third party. Compounding this concern is the troubling lack of notification from Sony about the nature of the data breach. Although the breach occurred nearly a week ago, Sony has not notified customers of the intrusion, or provided information that is vital to allowing individuals to protect themselves from identity theft, such as informing users whether their personal or financial information may have been compromised. Nor has Sony specified how it intends to protect these consumers.[83]*

In response, Patrick Seybold commented on April 26, 2011:

> *I wanted to take this opportunity to clarify a point and answer one of the most frequently asked questions today.*
>
> *There's a difference in timing between when we identified there was an intrusion and when we learned of consumers' data being compromised. We learned there was an intrusion April 19th and subsequently shut the services down. We then brought in outside experts to help us learn how the*

> *intrusion occurred and to conduct an investigation to determine the nature and scope of the incident. It was necessary to conduct several days of forensic analysis, and it took our experts until yesterday to understand the scope of the breach. We then shared that information with our consumers and announced it publicly this afternoon.[84]*

Mr. Seybold accurately pointed out that the length of the delay was much shorter than the week that Senator Blumenthal spoke of, yet the reaction from the public was that any delay in notification was unacceptable. (Please see examples of responses in Appendix C.)

States have begun chiming in as well. Lawmakers as well as "attorneys general of several U.S. states are starting to rumble, starting with Connecticut's George Jepson, who said he is launching an investigation, while his counterparts in Missouri and Iowa are making the kind of public statements that are often precursor to investigations of their own."[85]

Reactions: Worldwide Governments

Government officials from across the world reacted as well to the PlayStation breach.

United Kingdom

Christopher Graham, information minister for the United Kingdom, made a statement saying that "We are contacting Sony and will be making further enquiries to establish the precise nature of the incident before deciding what action, if any, needs to be taken by this office."[86] His office is able to fine companies up to £500,000 for serious data breaches.

Canada

A spokesperson for Canada's Privacy Commissioner released a statement on April 28, 2011, stating that they were "currently looking into this matter and are seeking information from Sony."[87] In Canada's case, the investigation is likely to result in fairly limited legal repercussions, as their most relevant law, the Personal Information Protection and Electronic Documents Act, "does not state that notification is required in events of this nature."[88]

Lawsuits

Kristopher Johns of Alabama filed what is considered to be the first class-action lawsuit regarding the

PlayStation Network hacking. The plaintiff made complaints that Sony had failed to take "reasonable care to protect, encrypt, and secure the private and sensitive data of its users."[89] In addition, with the delay in notification Sony failed to allow members "to make an informed decision as to whether to change credit card numbers, close exposed accounts, check their credit reports or take risk mitigating actions."[90]

On the same day, Rebecca Mitchell filed a similar suit against Sony. A firm representing Ms. Mitchell said that the suit was filed because "Sony's responsibility is not only to provide services to its customers, but also to protect their personal and financial information. This breach of personal and financial data has exposed millions of Sony's customers to financial harm and jeopardized the security of their personal information. Sony broke its contract and violated its customers' trust."[91]

Legal Considerations

Laws are fairly convoluted on the issue of data security. In the United States, the federal government has many rules and requirements for federal agencies on how they maintain private information and notify parties of a breach. However, no federal laws pertain in the private sector outside of the healthcare industry and patient records.[92] This situation can be seen on the international stage where most other countries have only recently begun reviewing the necessity of codifying laws to address both data security as well as breach notification.

Data Security

The credit card industry has stepped in with rules and standards of its own where federal law fails to cover how the private sector protects data. The PCI Security Standards Council was created to develop security standards for the Payment Card Industry as the result of efforts by five of the world's largest credit card companies: American Express, Discover Financial Services, JCB International, MasterCard Worldwide, and Visa, Inc.[93]

The PCI Security Standards Council established the Payment Card Industry Data Security Standards, which listed out the minimum requirements that businesses handling credit card information would have to follow. Requirements include: "Install and maintain a firewall . . .," "Protect stored cardholder data," and "Restrict physical access to cardholder data."[94] Members of the PCI Security Standards Council are able to either fine or assess greater fees on those using their services for breaches of PCI Data Security Standards.

Breach Notification

State laws have been established to set requirements on how and when notification must be given to customers who have potentially fallen victim to a data security breach. California has one of the more detailed and strict set of requirements.

In California: "Requires notice to consumers of breach in the security, confidentiality, or integrity of unencrypted, computerized personal information held by a business or a government agency. Disclosure shall be made if the information was, or is reasonably believed to have been accessed by an unauthorized person. The disclosure shall be made in the most expedient time possible and without unreasonable delay, consistent with the legitimate needs of law enforcement or any measures necessary to determine the scope of the breach and restore the procedures consistent with timing requirements and provides notice in accordance with its policies or if the person or business abides by state or federal law, or provides greater protection and disclosure, then it is deemed in compliance."[95]

Similar Situations
Xbox LIVE Thirteen-Day Outage

In a similar network outage situation, on December 22, 2007, at the start of the Christmas holidays, Microsoft Xbox LIVE users awoke to find themselves unable to sign on to the Xbox LIVE network. Due to an unexpected number of new members to the service, Microsoft's Xbox LIVE servers crashed. Through thirteen days of intermittent service, Microsoft suffered through thousands of blogs, emails, messages, and news articles haranguing them for the outage. In way of apology, Microsoft offered its members a free downloadable arcade game that was valued at $10.[96] Given that they had recently announced during their five-year anniversary that they had "more than eight million members now actively engaged,"[97] this could have meant a potential loss of over $80 million in revenue.

Three Texans filed a class-action suit against Microsoft on January 4, 2008, alleging that because of the outage Microsoft had "failed to provide adequate access and service to Xbox Live and its subscribers."[98] Since Xbox LIVE was a paid service, they felt that Microsoft had failed to live up to its commitment.

How did all this affect Xbox LIVE membership? In an article in *Variety* magazine in 2009, authors said that Xbox LIVE had "17 million (users)"[99] as of February 25, 2009. They had more than doubled their total users in a little over a year.

Epsilon Data Management Hack

Epsilon Data Management, "the world's largest permission-based e-mail marketer"[100] suffered a breach of their network only a few weeks before the PlayStation Network hack. On March 30, 2011, engineers at Epsilon discovered that they had suffered the breach. Within forty-eight hours, Epsilon notified their clients and released a press release notifying the media and the public. The company was still the target of a number of investigations by the government at the time of the PSN hack.

Appendix A

+ *jonabbey on April 26th, 2011 at 1:01 pm said:*

> It's rather incredible that this is the first meaningful communication you have given us. Many of us who are savvy enough to be reading your blog are technical enough to be running our own Internet services, and you really can't go wrong by over-communicating, here.
>
> I hope you will be telling us more about how this happened.

+ *sid4peeps on April 26th, 2011 at 12:58 pm said:*

> YAWN...
>
> This update is about 6 days LATE. I think it is time to move to the other network, no regard for customers here.
>
> Toodles Sony.

+ *Korbei83 on April 26th, 2011 at 1:01 pm said:*

> If you have compromised my credit information, you will never receive it again.
>
> The fact that you've waited this long to divulge this information to your customers is deplorable. Shame on you.
>
> Excuse me while I go change my password.. oh wait. I can't.

+ *VisionaryLight on April 26th, 2011 at 1:03 pm said:*

> You really should have told us this last week. This is completely unacceptable.

+ *xxnike629xx on April 26th, 2011 at 1:07 pm said:*

> Talk about a massive wall of text..
>
> Dear PlayStation,
>
> Thank you for finally posting something.... but again a lot of nothing, but this time in the form of a massive wall of text.
>
> Thank you for compromising our personal information & credit cards.
>
> : sarcasm ::

+ *adolson on April 26th, 2011 at 1:09 pm said:*

> I should have known better than to trust Sony with my credit card info.

Appendix B

April 26, 2011

Mr. Jack Tretton
President and CEO
Sony Computer Entertainment America
919 East Hillsdale Boulevard
Foster City, CA USA 94404

Dear Mr. Tretton:

I am writing regarding a recent data breach of Sony's PlayStation Network service. I am troubled by the failure of Sony to immediately notify affected customers of the breach and to extend adequate financial data security protections.

It has been reported that on April 20, 2011, Sony's PlayStation Network suffered an "external intrusion" and was subsequently disabled. News reports estimate that 50 million to 75 million consumers—many of them children—access the PlayStation Network for video and entertainment. I understand that the PlayStation Network allows users to store credit card information online to facilitate the purchasing of content such as games and movies through the PlayStation Network. A breach of such a widely used service immediately raises concerns of data privacy, identity theft, and other misuse of sensitive personal and financial data, such as names, email addresses, and credit and debit card information.

When a data breach occurs, it is essential that customers be immediately notified about whether and to what extent their personal and financial information has been compromised. Additionally, PlayStation Network users should be provided with financial data security services, including free access to credit reporting services, for two years, the costs of which should be borne by Sony. Affected individuals should also be provided with sufficient insurance to protect them from the possible financial consequences of identity theft.

I am concerned that PlayStation Network users' personal and financial information may have been inappropriately accessed by a third party. Compounding this concern is the troubling lack of notification from Sony about the nature of the data breach. Although the breach occurred nearly a week ago, Sony has not notified customers of the intrusion, or provided information that is vital to allowing individuals to protect themselves from identity theft, such as informing users whether their personal or financial information may have been compromised. Nor has Sony specified how it intends to protect these consumers. PlayStation Network users deserve more complete information on the data breach, as well as the assurance that their personal and financial information will be securely maintained. I appreciate your prompt response on this important issue.

Sincerely,
Richard Blumenthal
United States Senate

Appendix C

+ *hoi1ma on April 26th, 2011 at 7:15 pm said:*

an intrusion would warrant a possible data compromise. could have warned us of this possibility whether it occur or not.

+ *yazter on April 26th, 2011 at 7:16 pm said:*

It's not the PSN downtime, it's your lack of update that left us in the dark.
I already bought an Xbox 360 (GT: Saturated Leaf) after spending a lot on a service that ignores us. Hope you resolve this. I'm sure it's a PR night mare now.

+ *Ratchet426 on April 26th, 2011 at 7:18 pm said:*

Five days to come to the conclusion that CC data might have been compromised seems about 4 days too long. If there was enough of a perceived breach to shut the entire PSN service down on the 19th I can't imagine that CC data breach wasn't also considered on the 19th.
Don't the recently enacted Red Flags regulations require companies to inform users of a POTENTIAL exposure of personal information/CC data within 24 hours?
By the way I am encouraged that the "veil of silence" has at least partially been lifted and we are hearing some actual useful information coming from Sony

+ *Smert_ on April 26th, 2011 at 7:20 pm said:*

Thanks guys, I know you're working hard. I appreciate the daily updates and clarifications.

+ *Bark-n-lice on April 26th, 2011 at 7:22 pm said:*

You found out yesterday. And you didn't go hey we better warn our customers ASAP. Moreover, if you had the slightest insight that our personal information was compromised we should of been told IMMEDIATELY. WHY DON'T YOU UNDERSTAND THAT!!!

+ *AJBS0NIC on April 26th, 2011 at 7:44 pm said:*

Doesn't any kind of breach warrant the possibility of personal info being compromised? Even if this wasn't confirmed you obviously must have had a hunch that this kind of thing could happen, otherwise you wouldn't have looked into it. An essential aspect of crisis PR is making sure all bases are covered. I'm not saying go into a panic any time there is a breach, but at the very *least* let your "valued customers" know that personal info being compromised is a possibility *from the start* so we could at least have a shot at taking care of ourselves. Not a week later when the damage has already been done. Seriously people, anything we do now is pretty much futile. Sorry guy, but I don't buy it.

Discussion Questions

1. What are the critical issues in this case? Who are the stakeholders?
2. What can Sony learn from other similar scenarios?

3. How will Sony compensate PSN consumers for this malfunction?
4. How can Sony not lose consumer confidence in products?
5. How should Sony handle the regulatory environment surrounding data theft protection?
6. What communications should Sony make and to whom?

This case was prepared by Research Assistants Shawn Chuong Do and Xiao-Feng (John) Hsu under the direction of James S. O'Rourke, Teaching Professor of Management, as the basis for class discussion rather than to illustrate either effective or ineffective handling of an administrative situation. Information was gathered from corporate as well as public sources.

SONY CORPORATION: THE PLAYSTATION NETWORK CRASH (B)

Response Overview

On April 30, 2011, Kaz Hirai, executive deputy president for Sony Corporation, and other members of the executive team apologized publicly at a news conference for the PlayStation Network hack and subsequent outage. He offered a timeline of events and gave an overview of what Sony was doing to strengthen the network and compensate its customers. He then drew attention to the growing threat of cyber-attack. "This criminal act against our network had a significant impact not only on our consumers, but our entire industry. These illegal attacks obviously highlight the widespread problem with cyber-security. We take the security of our consumers' information very seriously and are committed to helping our consumers protect their personal data."[101] He then spent the remainder of the one hour and forty-two minute press conference answering questions from reporters.

On the same day, Patrick Seybold, senior director of communications and marketing, issued an official press release on the *PlayStation.Blog*. The press release detailed the efforts Sony had made to repair and update the network, protect its consumers, and compensate the 77 million PlayStation Network users. (Please see Appendix A for full text.)

Restoration of Services

To the relief of gamers worldwide, Sony announced that they would proceed with a "phased rollout by region of (the) services shortly."[102]

Rebuilding and Enhancing

Sony outlined their efforts to rebuild the network and increase their security. They added an additional level of accountability by creating the position of chief information security officer. They also moved their network system to a new location and planned to implement a "forced system update" requiring users to change their passwords. Additionally, they implemented on their servers:

- "Added automated software monitoring and configuration management to help defend against new attacks;
- Enhanced levels of data protection and encryption;
- Enhanced ability to detect software intrusions within the network, unauthorized access and unusual activity patterns;
- Implementation of additional firewalls."[103]

Consumer Compensation

Kaz Hirai was quoted on the *PlayStation.Blog* as saying "Our Global audience of PlayStation Network and Qriocity consumers was disrupted. We have learned lessons along the way about the valued relationship with our consumers, and to that end, we will be launching a customer appreciation program for registered consumers as a way of expressing our gratitude for their loyalty during this network downtime, as we work even harder to restore and regain their trust in us and our services."[104] The blog went on to briefly outline the plans for its program, including free downloadable content, thirty-day free membership to PlayStation Plus, and thirty days of free Music Unlimited Services for subscribers to Sony's Qriocity service.

Reactions

Initial reaction from users commenting on the *PlayStation.Blog* was fairly positive. Many comments focused on the fact that they would again be able to use the PlayStation Network services rather than any of the other issues.[105]

However, not everyone was happy with the news; Chris Matyszczyk, contributor to CNET's Blog Network, posted a scathing entry in reaction to Kazuo Hirai's apology. He acknowledged that an apology had been made but, looking to the *PlayStation.Blog*, "wonder(s) just how many gamers—who now wonder every day whether their credit cards will be used to buy PSP Players—might just wish they could see a big headline that says 'We're Sorry.'"[106]

In addition, even though many consumers seemed satisfied to just move on, Dean Takahashi, writer for Venturebeat.com, wrote on April 30, 2011, "Gamers are slow to forgive. Many own a PlayStation 3 today because they were angry at Microsoft for letting them down when the Xbox 360 suffered from a huge number of breakdowns ..."[107] Hopefully, for Sony's sake, people will be more forgiving than Mr. Takahashi suggests.

Appendix A

Press Release: Some PlayStation Network and Qriocity Services to Be Available This Week

+ Posted by Patrick Seybold // Sr. Director, Corporate Communications & Social Media

SOME PLAYSTATION®NETWORK AND QRIOCITY™ SERVICES TO BE AVAILABLE THIS WEEK Phased Global Rollout of Services to Begin Regionally; System Security Enhanced to Provide Greater Protection of Personal Information

Tokyo, May 1, 2011 – Sony Computer Entertainment (SCE) and Sony Network Entertainment International (SNEI, the company) announced they will shortly begin a phased restoration by region of PlayStation®Network and Qriocity™ services, beginning with gaming, music and video services to be turned on. The company also announced both a series of immediate steps to enhance security across the network and a new customer appreciation program to thank its customers for their patience and loyalty.

Following a criminal cyber-attack on the company's data-center located in San Diego, California, U.S.A., SNEI quickly turned off the PlayStation Network and Qriocity services, engaged multiple expert information security firms over the course of several days and conducted an extensive audit of the system. Since then, the company has implemented a variety of new security measures to provide greater protection of personal information. SNEI and its third-party experts have conducted extensive tests to verify the security strength of the PlayStation Network and Qriocity services. With these measures in place, SCE and SNEI plan to start a phased rollout by region of the services shortly. The initial phase of the rollout will include, but is not limited to, the following:

- Restoration of Online game-play across the PlayStation®3 (PS3) and PSP® (PlayStation®-Portable) systems—This includes titles requiring online verification and downloaded games
- Access to Music Unlimited powered by Qriocity for PS3/PSP for existing subscribers
- Access to account management and password reset
- Access to download un-expired Movie Rentals on PS3, PSP and MediaGo
- PlayStation®Home
- Friends List
- Chat Functionality

Working closely with several outside security firms, the company has implemented significant security measures to further detect unauthorized activity and provide consumers with greater protection of their personal information. The company is also creating the position of Chief Information Security Officer, directly reporting to Shinji Hasejima, Chief Information Officer of Sony Corporation, to add a new position of expertise in and accountability for customer data protection and supplement existing information security personnel. The new security measures implemented include, but are not limited to, the following:

- Added automated software monitoring and configuration management to help defend against new attacks
- Enhanced levels of data protection and encryption
- Enhanced ability to detect software intrusions within the network, unauthorized access and unusual activity patterns
- Implementation of additional firewalls

The company also expedited an already planned move of the system to a new data center in a different location that has been under construction and development for several months. In addition, PS3 will have a forced system software update that will require all registered PlayStation Network users to change their account passwords before being able to sign into the service. As an added layer of security, that password can only be changed on the same PS3 in which that account was activated, or through validated email confirmation, a critical step to help further protect customer data.

The company is conducting a thorough and ongoing investigation and working with law enforcement to track down and prosecute those responsible for the illegal intrusion.

"This criminal act against our network had a significant impact not only on our consumers, but our entire industry. These illegal attacks obviously highlight the widespread problem with cyber-security. We take the security of our consumers' information very seriously and are committed to helping our consumers protect their personal data. In addition, the organization has worked around the clock to bring these services back online, and are doing so only after we had verified increased levels of security across our networks," said Kazuo Hirai, Executive Deputy President, Sony Corporation. "Our global audience of PlayStation Network and Qriocity consumers was disrupted. We have learned lessons along the way about the valued relationship with our consumers, and to that end, we will be launching a customer appreciation program for registered consumers as a way of expressing our gratitude for their loyalty during this network downtime, as we work even harder to restore and regain their trust in us and our services."

Complimentary Offering and "Welcome Back" Appreciation Program

While there is no evidence at this time that credit card data was taken, the company is committed to helping its customers protect their personal data and will provide a complimentary offering to assist users in enrolling in identity theft protection services and/or similar programs. The implementation will be at a local level and further details will be made available shortly in each region.

The company will also rollout the PlayStation Network and Qriocity "Welcome Back" program, to be offered worldwide, which will be tailored to specific markets to provide our consumers with a selection of service options and premium content as an expression of the company's appreciation for their patience, support and continued loyalty.

Central components of the "Welcome Back" program will include:

- Each territory will be offering selected PlayStation entertainment content for free download. Specific details of this content will be announced in each region soon.
- All existing PlayStation Network customers will be provided with 30 days free membership in the PlayStation Plus premium service. Current members of PlayStation Plus will receive 30 days free service.
- Music Unlimited powered by Qriocity subscribers (in countries where the service is available) will receive 30 days free service.

Additional "Welcome Back" entertainment and service offerings will be rolled out over the coming weeks as the company returns the PlayStation Network and Qriocity services to the quality standard users have grown to enjoy and strive to exceed those exceptions.

SNEI will continue to reinforce and verify security for transactions before resuming the PlayStation®-Store and other Qriocity operations, scheduled for this month.

For more information about the PlayStation Network and Qriocity services intrusion and restoration, please visit http://blog.us.playstation.com or http://blog.eu.playstation.com/

About Sony Corporation

Sony Corporation is a leading manufacturer of audio, video, game, communications, key device and information technology products for the consumer and professional markets. With its music, pictures, computer entertainment and on-line businesses, Sony is uniquely positioned to be the leading electronics and entertainment company in the world. Sony recorded consolidated annual sales of approximately $78 billion for the fiscal year ended March 31, 2010. Sony Global Web Site: http://www.sony.net/

About Sony Computer Entertainment Inc.

Recognized as the global leader and company responsible for the progression of consumer-based computer entertainment, Sony Computer Entertainment Inc. (SCEI) manufactures, distributes and markets the PlayStation® game console, the PlayStation®2 computer entertainment system, the PSP® (PlayStation® Portable) handheld entertainment system and the PlayStation®3 (PS3®) system. PlayStation has revolutionized home entertainment by introducing advanced 3D graphic processing, and PlayStation 2 further enhances the PlayStation legacy as the core of home networked entertainment. PSP is a handheld entertainment system that allows users to enjoy 3D games, with high-quality full-motion video, and high-fidelity stereo audio. PS3 is an advanced computer system, incorporating the state-of-the-art Cell processor with super computer like power. SCEI, along with its subsidiary divisions Sony Computer Entertainment America Inc., Sony Computer Entertainment Europe Ltd., and Sony Computer Entertainment Korea Inc. develops, publishes, markets and distributes software, and manages the third party licensing programs for these platforms in the respective markets worldwide. Headquartered in Tokyo, Japan, SCEI is an independent business unit of the Sony Group.

Discussion Questions

1. What can Sony do to regain the trust of its most valued consumers?
2. What are the long-term effects of the PSN hack likely to be for Sony?
3. Do you think that Sony could have responded in any other way to the discovery that they had been hacked?

This case was prepared by Research Assistants Shawn Chuong Do and Xiao-Feng (John) Hsu under the direction of James S. O'Rourke, Teaching Professor of Management, as the basis for class discussion rather than to illustrate either effective or ineffective handling of an administrative situation. Information was gathered from corporate as well as public sources.

Endnotes

1. Chaffee, E. E. (1985). Three models of strategy. *The Academy of Management Review* 10(1), 89–98,

2. Chaffee, 1985, p. 90.

3. Ibid., 1985, p. 93.

4. Ibid., 1985, p. 93.

5. Ibid., 1985.

6. Lim, G., Ahn, H., & Lee, H. (2005). Formulating strategy for stakeholder management: A case-based reasoning approach. *Expert Systems with Applications, 28*, 831–40.

7. Barrett, D. J. (2002). Change communication: Using strategic employee communication to facilitate major change. *Corporate Communication: An International Journal, 7*(4), 219–231, p. 219.

8. McNamara, C. (2008). Basics in internal organizational communications. Adapted from the *Field Guide to Leadership and Supervision*. Retrieved October 31, 2009 from http://managementhelp.org/mrktng/org_cmm.htm

9. Papa, M. J., Daniels, D. D., & Spiker, B. K. (2008). *Organizational communication: Perspectives and trends*. Los Angeles, CA: Sage Publications.

10. Wiseman, G., and Barker, L. (1967). *Speech—Interpersonal communication*. Chicago, IL: Chandler.

11. Sethi, S. P. (1982). *Up against the corporate wall: Modern corporations and social issues of the eighties* (4th ed.). Englewood Cliffs, NJ: Prentice Hall.

12. Morrison, M. (2008). How to write an internal communications plan and strategy. http://rapidbi.com/created/howtowritean internalcommunicationsplanandstrategy.html

13. Barrett, D. J. (2002). Change communication: Using strategic employee communication to facilitate major change. *Corporate Communication: An International Journal, 7*(4), 219–231.

14. Coffman, J. (2004). Strategic communications audits. Prepared for the Communications Consortium Media Center. Retrieved October 12, 2005, from http://www.media evaluationproject.org/WorkingPaper1.pdf

15. Morrison, M. (2008). How to write an internal communications plan and strategy. http://rapidbi.com/created/howtowriteaninternal communicationsplanandstrategy.html

16. Hopkins, L. (2009). Internal Communication: 12 Essential Elements. Retrieved October 31, 2009 from http://ezinearticles.com/?Internal -Communication:-12-Essential-Elements&id= 12286

17. Morrison, 2008.

18. Goldhaber, G. M. (1993). *Organizational communication* (6th ed.). Dubuque, IA: Brown & Benchmark.

19. Argenti, P. (1998). *Corporate communication* (2nd ed.). Boston, MA: Irwin/McGraw-Hill.

20. Cutlip, S. M., & Center, A. H. (1964). *Effective public relations* (3rd ed.). Englewood Cliffs, NJ: Prentice Hall, p. 4.

21. Argenti, P. (1998). *Corporate communication* (2nd ed.). Boston, MA: Irwin/McGraw-Hill.

22. Gaunt, P., & Ollenburger, J. (1995). Issues management revisited: A tool that deserves another look. *Public Relations Review, 21* (3), 199–210.

23. Coates, J., Coates, V., Jarratt, J., & Heinz, L. (1986). *Issues management: How you can plan, organize, and manage for the future.* Mt. Airy, MD: Lomond, p. ix.

24. Jones, B. L., & Chase, W. H. (1979). Managing public policy issues. *Public Relations Review, 5,* 3–23, p. 3.

25. Post, J. E. (1978). Corporate response models and public affairs management. *Public Relations Quarterly, 24,* 27–32.

26. Ewing, R. P. (1979, Winter). The uses of futurist techniques in issues management. *Public Relations Quarterly,* 15–18.

27. Sethi, 1982, p. 162.

28. Leiss, W. (2004). Effective risk communication practice. *Toxicology Letters, 149,* 399–404, p. 399.

29. Leiss, 2004, p. 401.

30. Ibid., 2004, p. 402.

31. Mitroff, I. I., & Alpasian, M. C. (2004, Spring). A toolkit for managing crises and preparing for the unthinkable. *The Mitroff Report, 1,* 81–88.

32. Benoit, W. L., (1997). Image repair discourse and crisis communication. *Public Relations Review, 23*(2), 177–186 and Benoit, W. L. (1995). *Apologies, excuses, and accounts: A theory of image restoration strategies.* Albany, NY: State University of New York Press.

33. Sturges, D. L. (1994). Communicating through crisis: A strategy for organizational survival. *Management Communication Quarterly, 7,* 297–316.

34. Englehart, B. (1995). Crisis communication: Communicating under fire. *The Journal of Management Advocacy Communication, 1,* 23–28, p. 28.

35. Mitroff. & Alpasian, 2004, Spring.

36. Perrow, C. (1984). *Normal Accidents: Living with High-Risk Technologies.* New York: Basic Books.

37. Barton, L. (1993). *Crisis in organizations: Managing and communicating in the heat of crisis.* Cincinnati, OH: SouthWestern.

38. Englehart, 1995, p. 28.

39. Sturges, 1994.

40. Argenti, 1998.

41. Layne, N. (2011). Update 2 – Sony shares fall 5 pct as PlayStation woes threaten outlook. *Reuters,* April 28, http://in.reuters.com/article /2011/04/28/idINIndia-56623820110428.

42. Gaudin, S. (2011). Sony warns users of data loss from PlayStation network hack. *Computerworld,* April 26, http://www.computerworld .com/s/article/9216191/Sony_warns_users_of _data_loss_from_PlayStation_network_hack.

43. Parker, M. (2011). Was Sony ready to welcome back the PSN? – Update. *Community Voices of the Pittsburgh Post-Gazette,* May 2, http:// communityvoices.sites.post-gazette.com/index .php/arts-entertainment-living/the-game-guy /28611-was-sony-ready-to-welcome-the-psn -back.

44. Gaudin. Sony warns users of data loss from PlayStation network hack.

45. Ibid.

46. About Sony: Sony corporate history. Accessed September 18, 2011, http://www .sony-europe.com/article/id/1178278971500.

47. Sony Corp. info: Sony history. Accessed September 18, 2011, http://www.sony.net /SonyInfo/CorporateInfo/History/SonyHistory.

48. About Sony: Sony corporate history.

49. Sony Corp. info: Sony history.

50. IGN Staff. (1998). History of the PlayStation. *IGN,* August 27, http://psx.ign.com/articles /060/060188p1.html.

51. Costa, D. (2006). Sony PlayStation 3 (Fall 2006). *PCMAG.COM,* November 16, http:// www.pcmag.com/article2/0,2817,2055092,00 .asp.

52. PlayStation 3 Features. PlayStation Network. Accessed September 18, 2011, http://us.playstation.com/ps3/features/ps3features network.html.

53. PS3 PlayStation Network. Facebook. Accessed September 27, 2011, http://www.facebook.com/OfficialPlaystationNetwork?sk=info.

54. Chip. (2011). Sony admits all 77 million PSN and Qriocity accounts have been compromised in a response to the US Congress. GSMArena.com Geeks at large [Web log comment], May 5, 2011, http://blog.gsmarena.com/sony-admits-all-77-million-psn-and-qriocity-accounts-have-been-compromised-in-a-response-to-the-us-congress.

55. Hirai, K. (Chairman of the board of directors for Sony Computer Entertainment of America). Eight-page letter to Congress, May 3, 2011, as cited in Johnson, J. (2011). They knew for six days: The PlayStation Network hack timeline. *Kotaku*, May 4, http://kotaku.com/5798510/the-playstation-network-hack-timeline.

56. Ibid.

57. Ibid.

58. Ibid.

59. Ibid.

60. Martyn, W. (2011). PlayStation Network hack timeline. *PCWorld*, May 1, http://www.pcworld.com/article/226802/playstation_network_hack_timeline.html.

61. Hirai. Eight-page letter to Congress.

62. Martyn. PlayStation Network hack timeline.

63. Hirai. Eight-page letter to Congress.

64. Martyn. PlayStation Network hack timeline.

65. *Kristopher Johns V. Sony Computer Entertainment America LLC & Sony Network Entertainment International LLC. 11-2063U.S. (2011)*, as cited in Pereira, C. First lawsuit filed against Sony over PSN data leak. 1up.com, April 27, 2011, http://www.1up.com/news/first-lawsuit-filed-against-sony-psn-data-leak.

66. Martyn. PlayStation Network hack timeline.

67. Ibid.

68. Seybold, P. (2011). Latest update on PSN outage. *PlayStation.Blog* [Web log comment], April 21, http://blog.us.playstation.com/2011/04/21/latest-update-on-psn-outage.

69. Ibid.

70. Praetorius, D. (2011). PlayStation 3 problems: PlayStation Network could be down for days. *Huffington Post*, April 21, http://www.huffingtonpost.com/2011/04/21/playstation-3-network-down_n_852106.html.

71. Seybold, P. (2011). Update on PlayStation Network/Qriocity services. *PlayStation.Blog* [Web log comment], April 22, http://blog.us.playstation.com/2011/04/22/update-on-playstation-network-qriocity-services.

72. Seybold, P. (2011). Latest update for PSN/Qriocity Services. *PlayStation.Blog* [Web log comment], April 23, http://blog.us.playstation.com/2011/04/23/latest-update-for-psnqriocity-services.

73. Fantz, A. (2011). Anonymous vows to take leaking to the next level. *CNNWorld*, February 23, http://articles.cnn.com/2011-02-23/world/wikileaks.anonymous_1_wikileaks-world-s-most-dangerous-website-daniel-domscheit-berg/2?_s=PM:WORLD.

74. Seybold, P. (2011). Update on PlayStation Network and Qriocity. *PlayStation.Blog* [Web log comment], April 26, http://blog.us.playstation.com/2011/04/26/update-on-playstation-network-and-qriocity.

75. Ibid.

76. Ransom-Wiley, J. (2011). PSN devs offer mixed reactions to cost of outage. *Joystiq*, April 27, http://www.joystiq.com/2011/04/27/psn-devs-offer-mixed-reactions-to-cost-of-outage.

77. Ibid.

78. Ibid.

79. Stuart, K. (2011). PlayStation Network hack: Industry reactions and theories. *Game Blog*, April 29, http://www.guardian.co.uk/technology/gamesblog/2011/apr/29/psn-hack-industry-reactions.

80. Ibid.

81. Lawler, R. (2011). Hulu Plus credits users for PlayStation Network downtime. *Engadget*, April 27, http://hd.engadget.com/2011/04/27/hulu-plus-credits-users-for-playstation-network-related-downtime.

82. Ibid.

83. Senator Blumenthal demands answers from Sony over data breach. *PS3 Blog.net*

[Web log comments], April 26, 2011, http://www.ps3blog.net/2011/04/26/senator-richard-blumenthal-demands-answers-from-sony-over-playstation-data-breach.

84. Seybold, P. (2011). Clarifying a few PSN points. *PlayStation.Blog* [Web log comments], April 26, http://blog.us.playstation.com/2011/04/26/clarifying-a-few-psn-points.

85. Hesseldahl, A. (2011). After the Playstation Hack, a legal pile-on against Sony. *All Things D*, April 28, http://allthingsd.com/20110428/after-the-playstation-hack-a-legal-pile-on-against-sony.

86. Williams, C. (2011). PlayStation Hack: Sony faces watchdog's questions. *The Telegraph*, April 27, http://www.telegraph.co.uk/technology/sony/8476441/PlayStation-hack-Sony-faces-watchdogs-questions.html.

87. Raspe, M. (2011). Canada's Privacy Commissioner to look into PSN privacy breach. *PSU PlayStation Universe*, April 28, http://www.psu.com/Canadas-Privacy-Commissioner-to-look-into-PSN-privacy-breach—a011487-p0.php.

88. Ibid.

89. Ogg, E. (2011). Sony sued for PlayStation Network data breach. *C|net News*, April 27, http://news.cnet.com/8301-31021_3-20057921-260.html.

90. Ibid.

91. Gamers sue Sony over PlayStation Network breach. Zimmerman Reed Attorneys, April 27, 2011, http://www.zimmreed.com/Sony-PlayStation-PR/57992.

92. Stevens, G. (2010). Federal information security and data breach notification laws. Congressional Research Service, January 28, http://www.fas.org/sgp/crs/secrecy/RL34120.pdf.

93. About the PCI Security Standards Council. PCI Security Standards Council, September 18, 2011, https://www.pcisecuritystandards.org/organization_info/index.php.

94. Ibid.

95. Notice of security breach laws. Consumers Union, July 11, 2011, http://www.defendyourdollars.org/2005/02/states_with_not.html.

96. Kohler, C. (2008). XBLA *Undertow*, free for your Live troubles. *Game|Life*, January 18, http://www.wired.com/gamelife/2008/01/xbla-undertow-f.

97. Yam, M. (2007). Xbox Live collects eight million users in five years. *Daily Tech* [Web log comment], November 14, http://www.dailytech.com/Xbox+Live+Collects+Eight+Million+Users+in+Five+Years/article9665.htm.

98. Romano, B. (2008). Xbox Live holiday outages prompts class action lawsuit. *The Seattle Times*, January 4, http://weblogs.variety.com/the_cut_scene/2009/02/comparing-playstation-network-and-xbox-live-revenue-is-what-matters.html.

99. Comparing Playstation Network and Xbox LIVE revenues is what matters. *Variety* [Web log comment], February 25, 2009, http://weblogs.variety.com/the_cut_scene/2009/02/comparing-playstation-network-and-xbox-live-revenue-is-what-matters.html.

100. Newman, J. (2011). Epsilon email hack: What you need to know. *PCWorld*, April 4, http://www.pcworld.com/article/224213/epsilon_email_hack_what_you_need_to_know.html.

101. Narcisse, E. (2011). Sony PlayStation president apologizes for PSN outage, promises service back this week. *TIME Techland*, May 2, http://techland.time.com/2011/05/02/sony-playstation-president-apologizes-for-psn-outage-promises-service-back-this-week.

102. Seybold, P. (2011). Press Release: Some PlayStation Network and Qriocity service to be available this week. *PlayStation.Blog* [Web log comments], April 30, http://blog.us.playstation.com/2011/04/30/press-release-some-playstation-network-and-qriocity-services-to-be-available-this-week.

103. Ibid.

104. Ibid.

105. Ibid.

106. Matyszczyk, C. (2011). Sony apologizes: A little late? *CNet News* [Web log comments], May 1, http://news.cnet.com/8301-17852_3-20058743-71.html.

107. Takahashi, D. (2011). What Sony does next is critical for its future in games. *GamesBeat*, April 30, http://venturebeat.com/2011/04/30/what-sony-does-next-is-critical-to-its-future-in-games.

Appendix A

Model Documents

This appendix opens with a discussion of some key elements of message formatting and design and then provides examples of a variety of business message formats, including memos, emails, letters, employment messages, short reports and proposals, and press releases. In addition to formatting examples, you will also find examples of messages intended for different purposes: routine claims, bad news, direct requests, and persuasive messages.

Design Elements

There are several aspects of visual impression to consider when designing a written message. These include the following:

- Format
- Use of space
- Font selection

Format

The *format* of the document should use the conventions of business writing. Most business audiences know what a memo should look like, just as they know the conventional format for a letter. Reports also have conventional formats with which most business audiences are familiar. If you do not follow these formats, you indicate to your reader that you are not familiar with those conventions and thus are undereducated in this regard or are not a professional, since you aren't aware of professional expectations and practices. This perception, of course, can affect your credibility.

The proper format to use depends upon your audience and purpose. If you are writing a hard-copy message to an audience that is *internal* to your organization, you should use a memo format. If you are writing a hard-copy message to an audience that is *external* to your organization, you should use a letter format. Email messages to both internal and external audiences use a combination of features from both letters and memos. Similarly, reports and proposals can be prepared for both internal and external audiences. These formats are typically used to deliver longer, more complex messages than those conveyed in a memo, letter, or email message. Another common business format is that of the résumé. Examples of each of these common business formats can be found later in this appendix.

Use of Space

Use of *space* on the page involves decisions about various design elements, including the width of the margins, the space between paragraphs, and the use of lists, headings, and graphics. Using space appropriately can make a document more pleasing and inviting to read. Use of space can have subtle effects upon the reader and can also send messages about you as the writer.

Typically, the margin width of business documents is one inch at the top, sides, and bottom of the page. Margins should not be too wide, since that sends the message that you are attempting to make your document look longer or more complete. They should not be too narrow, since that sends the message that you need to edit your document to make it fit the space provided, and that you may have failed to do so.

The conventional spacing of business documents, regardless of the format, is single spacing within paragraphs and double spacing between paragraphs. Because of this visual cue—a blank space between paragraphs—indenting the beginning of each paragraph is not necessary. Use of too much space between paragraphs can also make your document look as if it is not substantial in content or that you are stretching your information to make it look more substantial than it is.

Paragraphs in business documents should be seven to eight lines in length. Creating paragraphs that are shorter in length is called *chunking*. Chunking has a psychological effect on the reader that makes a document look easier to skim; provides more white space, which makes it more pleasing in appearance; and makes a document look easier to read overall. Readers may be discouraged from reading a document that contains one large paragraph or a few large paragraphs, because the document looks too difficult to skim or too time-consuming to read.

Font Choice

Font choice can affect the readability of a document as well as subtly set a tone for the document. There are two types of font: serif and sans serif. Examples of serif type include Times New Roman, Courier, and Bookman. Examples of sans serif type are Arial, Univers, and Verdana. Serif is typically used for large blocks of text, because it provides more information for the eye and is thus considered easier to read. However, serif type also gives a document a more conservative visual impression. It can therefore be used as a design element to create a particular image for your company.

Sans serif type, because of its cleaner appearance, gives a document a more modern look. If you wish your documents to look more modern, yet still be highly readable for your audiences, you might use sans serif type for headings and other design elements and serif for large blocks of text.

Another consideration when selecting a font is its size. Typically, a 12-point font size for written messages is considered large enough to be easily read by most audiences.

Message Formats

This section provides examples of a variety of messages, including memos, emails, letters, employment messages, reports and proposals, and press releases.

Memo Format

Much of the difficulty of properly formatting business messages has been eliminated by word processing and other types of software that provide document templates. An example of a memo format is provided in the figure below.

FIGURE A-1 Example of a Memo Format

Memorandum

To: All employees
From: Jane Doe, HR supervisor
Date: May 15, 2014
Subject: Memorial Day holiday observance

As you may know, the Memorial Day holiday falls on Monday, May 31, this year. That means that we will be closing our offices on Monday, May 31, to honor the holiday. Our offices will reopen on Tuesday, June 1.

We in the Human Resources department wish you all a happy and safe Memorial Day holiday.

A memorandum is an internal message that is characterized by its header, as shown in the example above. An important feature of the header is the Subject line. The Subject line should contain a specific, informative phrase intended to capture your audience's attention.

Like most business messages, memos are typically single-spaced, with double spaces between paragraphs. Typically, memos are not signed by the sender. However, if you wish to personalize a memo, signing your initials by your name is a common practice.

Letter Formats

As stated earlier, letters rather than memos are used to communicate more formally with audiences external to an organization. You may choose from several types of letter formats. The two most common are the block and the modified block format. An example of a block format for a letter is provided in Figure A-2.

As shown in Figure A-2, all text in a block format letter is left justified, or lined up with the left margin. This format is probably the most commonly used

FIGURE A-2 Example of a Block Format Letter

Salestek, Inc.
128 Main Street
Middletown, IA 73220

December 3, 2014

Melanie Smith
ABC Products Co.
346 Center Avenue
Berg, PA 23009

Dear Ms. Smith:

Your order of November 20, 2014 has been received and processed by our company. You should be receiving the shipment in five to seven business days.

Your business is appreciated, so please let us know how we might continue to provide you the best service possible. If you have any questions about the products you receive, please call me toll free at 1-800-644-9900.

Sincerely,

Todd Jones

Todd Jones
Shipping Manager

because the left justification makes it easier and faster to create.

An example of the second common type of letter format, modified block, is provided in Figure A-3.

In the modified block format letter, you will notice that the address of the sender, the date, and the signature block are aligned on the right side of the page.

Email Format

Formatting email messages is fairly simple, since the computer program you are using prompts you for the elements of the header. These elements are similar to those used in a memo: To, From, and Subject. Typically, the program you are using will automatically insert the information for the sender (yourself), while you need to type in the receiver's email address and the subject line. As in a memo, you should insert a specific, informative phrase intended to capture your audience's attention.

An email message also incorporates elements from a letter format. Both letters and email messages, for example, typically include a salutation at the beginning and a signature at the end. Most

---

FIGURE A-3 Example of a Modified Block Format Letter

Salestek, Inc.
128 Main Street
Middletown, IA 73220

December 3, 2014

Melanie Smith
ABC Products Co.
346 Center Avenue
Berg, PA 23009

Dear Ms. Smith:

Your order of November 20, 2014 has been received and processed by our company. You should be receiving the shipment in five to seven business days.

Your business is appreciated, so please let us know how we might continue to provide you the best service possible. If you have any questions about the products you receive, please call me toll free at 1-800-644-9900.

Sincerely,

Todd Jones

Todd Jones
Shipping Manager

© Cengage Learning

email programs enable you to create a signature file that will automatically be added to the end of each message when it is sent. A signature file includes the name, title, organization, and contact information of the sender.

Finally, it is important for an email message to be as grammatically correct as any other type of written message and to use correct punctuation and spelling, since errors can negatively affect the clarity of the message as well as the credibility of the sender. You should avoid using all capital letters when writing email messages, because it can appear as if you are shouting at the receiver. The use of all capital letters in an email can thus negatively affect the tone of the message.

Attention to tone is particularly important in email messages, since they can be written so quickly

and sent. You should never write an email message when you are experiencing negative emotions, such as frustration, impatience, or anger, since the emotions will undoubtedly come through in your message and may negatively affect your credibility and relationship with your audience. An example of an email message is provided in Figure A-4.

Résumé Formats

Another conventional format used in business situations is the résumé. The contents of a résumé should be narrowly targeted to show that you are well qualified for a particular position. Information is typically provided in three areas: work experience, education, and leadership or organization membership. Under each of these categories, information is typically provided in the form of bullet lists. Using

---

FIGURE A-4 Example of an Email Message

To:	Linda Roberts, Loan Officer
From:	Juan Alvarez, Director of Loan Compliance
Subject:	New Policies Affect Loans to Real-Estate Investors

Linda,

Please be aware of the new policies regarding mortgages to real-estate investors.

Loans can no longer be made to mortgage applicants who already have four or more outstanding mortgages. Because of the problems caused by the sub-prime lending situation, we are required to limit our exposure to mortgage debt. Applicants who have four or more active mortgages are now considered too risky because of a potential lack of liquidity in their current asset portfolio.

You will find this latest policy change attached to this message. Please come by my office if you have additional questions after reading the attached policy statement.

Regards,
Juan

© Cengage Learning

complete sentences and paragraphs should be avoided in a résumé, since they require your reader to spend more time retrieving the information he or she is looking for.

Several formats for résumés exist, but the most common and often most favored is the chronological résumé, in which you present your qualifications chronologically. In other words, your most recent experiences should appear at the top of each category, followed in descending order by those that are your least recent in time. An example of a chronological résumé is provided in Figure A-5.

An element that you might consider adding to a chronological résumé is an "objective" statement at its beginning. Experts disagree about the inclusion of an objective statement. Some say it is a necessary

FIGURE A-5 Example of a Chronological Résumé

Joan Donne
348 Elm Street
Middletown, MO 73301
203-667-3211

Work Experience

May 2012 to present — Staff Accountant, EST International
Jonestown, MO
- Prepared accounting reports for wholesale importer ($1 million annual sales)
- Handled budgeting, billing, and credit-processing functions
- Audited financial transactions with suppliers in three Asian countries

May 2012– Aug. 2010 — Accounting Intern, Outerwear Sports
St. Louis, MO
- Assisted in billing and credit-processing functions of retail business ($500,000 annual sales)
- Assisted in launching an online computer system to automate all accounting functions

Education

Bachelor's degree, Accounting, University of Missouri, 2007–2010
Dean's List 2008, 2009, 2010

Volunteer and Professional Experience
- Volunteer for Habitat for Humanity
- Secretary of Accounting Association of America

© Cengage Learning

element, while others say that the objective statement often adds little to a résumé. All agree that excellent objective statements are difficult to write. An excellent objective statement should identify the unique contributions that you can make to a particular employer. Reading the job description carefully can give you some idea of the specific skills, abilities, and personal characteristics that a particular employer is looking for.

Increasingly, résumés are being submitted electronically to Web job banks. Résumés submitted to job banks are reviewed by a search engine that is programmed to search for keywords that correspond to the qualifications for which the employer is looking. For this reason, it is important to list the qualifications for the job in a keywords section of the résumé. Of course, it is important that you do in fact have these

qualifications, since eventually a human being will read your résumé carefully and discover whether you are indeed qualified for the job.

As you may note, electronic résumés often do not contain some of the design elements of paper résumés because these may not appear as they do in a word processing program. An example of an electronic résumé is provided in Figure A-6.

Additional Employment Messages

Additional types of employment messages include application letters, follow-up or thank-you letters, job refusal and job acceptance letters, and resignation letters.

An application letter is often sent as a cover message for a résumé, while a follow-up letter is sent to

---

FIGURE A-6 Example of an Electronic Résumé

JOSEPH PRIESTLEY
89 Lincoln Street
Santa Fe, NM 78285-9063
512555-9823
jpriestley@hotmail.com

Professional Profile
- Technical proficiency in ERP systems, ACL, database, and spreadsheet software.
- Hands-on experience in accounting gained through internship with well-regarded local firm.
- Excellent interpersonal communication and teamwork skills developed through course projects and active involvement in student organizations.
- Ability to manage time effectively, excellent work ethic, and dedication to high-quality work as demonstrated by 3.87 GPA and part-time work to finance my education.

Keywords
Bachelor's degree in accounting. Entry-level accounting experience. Knowledge of basic accounting principles and practices. Excellent communication skills. Personal characteristics, including good work ethic, ability to manage time efficiently, and dedicated to producing quality work.

FIGURE A-6 Example of an Electronic Résumé, *continued*

Education

B.B.A., Accounting, University of New Mexico, May 2013, GPA 3.87
- Dean's List, 2010–2013
- Deanna D. Darling Academic Scholarship

Technical Skills

Proficient in Microsoft Office Suite, database and spreadsheet software, ERP systems, and ACL.

Related Employment

Intern, Gerald and Associates, CPAs, Santa Fe, NM June–August, 2012
- Shadowed auditor and helped to write numerous auditing reports for corporate clients.
- Created and maintained spreadsheets and databases, containing client audit information.
- Worked with audit teams to hone communication skills and developed phone skills necessary to effectively interact with professional clientele.

Other Employment
- Server, Bubba's BBQ, Sante Fe, NM 2011–2013
- Stockperson, University of New Mexico Bookstore, Santa Fe, NM 2010–2011

Leadership Activities

Beta Alpha Psi, honorary accounting society, 2011–2013, chapter president, 2012–2013 Chess Team, 2010–2013, president, 2012–2013

An attractive and fully formatted hard copy version of this document is available upon request.

thank the interviewer for an interview. A well-written application letter would focus on the audience's or employer's needs and concerns and show how the applicant will meet these needs and benefit the employer. Furthermore, a well-written application letter would provide concrete evidence to illustrate that the potential employee has the skills and abilities for which the employer is looking. It should be noted that an application letter differs from a résumé in that the information in a résumé is more general: it could be sent to any company or organization with a similar job opening. A letter, on the other hand, should be more specific to the needs of a particular organization.

Figure A-7 provides an example of an application letter that is audience-centered and that provides the information for which an employer is looking. The letter is in response to the following job advertisement:

A job advertisement is often the best source for identifying what an employer is looking for in an applicant. A well-written application letter will use

Example of a job advertisement

Entry-Level Accounting Position

XYZ Accounting Consultants is an international company that provides accounting services to large corporate clients. XYZ Accounting Consultants is currently looking for applicants for its entry-level accounting position. The qualified applicant should have the following:

- A bachelor's degree in accounting.
- Entry-level accounting experience.
- Knowledge of basic accounting principles and practices.
- Excellent communication skills.
- Such personal characteristics as being hardworking, able to manage time efficiently, and dedicated to producing quality work.

Please send letters of application and résumés to the manager of our Los Angeles office, 345 Figueroa Street, Los Angeles, CA 90001.

---

the same language as the advertisement to refer to the applicant's skills. Using the same language makes it easier for the employer to read the message, since he or she is looking for that information; it also shows that the applicant is knowledgeable about those qualifications and addresses them specifically.

It is often acceptable nowadays to send application letters via email. Figure A-8 provides a sample message to accompany an electronic submission of employment materials.

Another type of employment message is the follow-up letter or thank-you note. These messages should be sent after an interview to thank the interviewer for taking the time to speak with you and to emphasize your key selling points. The message also might be used to provide information that may be relevant to the position but which was not covered during the interview. A follow-up letter can be helpful in establishing goodwill and distinguishing you from other candidates who do not attend to the importance of goodwill in business relationships. An example of a follow-up letter is provided in Figure A-9.

Once you have been offered a job, it may be a good idea to formally accept the offer by sending a job acceptance message. An example of a job acceptance message sent via email is provided in Figure A-10.

You may receive job offers that you choose not to accept. In this case, you may wish to send a job refusal message. An example of a job refusal message sent via email is provided in Figure A-11.

On the other end of the career spectrum, there may come a time when you want to quit a job to take another or to take a break from employment. Figure A-12 provides an example of a message sent to resign from an employment situation using email.

Components of Reports and Proposals

Reports and proposals can be either informal or formal in design, style, and content. Informal reports and proposals typically use memo formats. The components that are often included in a formal report are listed below:

- Title page
- Table of contents
- Executive summary
- Introduction
- Background
- Discussion of the problem

FIGURE A-7 Example of an Audience-Focused Application

JoAnn Dunn
123 Sepulveda Street
Los Angeles, CA 90001
(213) 741-4567
jdunn@midtown.edu

February 1, 2014
Maria Munoz, Manager
XYZ Accounting Consultants
345 Figueroa Street
Los Angeles, CA 90001

Dear Ms. Munoz:

I am responding to your ad for an entry-level accountant that was posted on JOBSTAR. I have all the attributes your company is looking for in a new employee; I am knowledgeable of accounting principles and practices, I have recent accounting experience, and I am a hard worker with excellent time management skills.

As a student at Midtown University, I have taken many accounting courses to help me prepare for a career in accounting. These courses include Financial Accounting, Tax Accounting, and Accounting and the Law. I did very well in these courses, earning an "A" grade for my work in each. This knowledge prepares me well to begin contributing to your company's goals immediately as an entry-level accountant.

I have had the additional opportunity to put this knowledge into practice during my internship last summer at Deloitte and Touche. I assisted an account executive to audit and prepare reports for three Fortune 500 companies. This experience also enabled me to practice and improve my writing and speaking skills, which will benefit you by enabling me to represent your company as a well-spoken and credible professional.

I also work hard and have excellent time management skills. Not only was I able to attend college full-time and maintain a 3.5 GPA, but I also worked full-time as a sales associate at Office Max to fund my education. These characteristics will enable me to be an efficient employee who doesn't stop until I get the job done while still maintaining quality work.

I would like to schedule an interview with you to discuss my qualifications further. I will call you next week to set up an appointment at your earliest convenience.

Sincerely,

JoAnn Dunn

JoAnn Dunn

FIGURE A-8 Example of a Job Application Message Sent Electronically

To:	mthomas@axumpharma.com
From:	mmarvel@unj.edu
Subject:	Career Fair Follow-up: Résumé for Mary Anne Marvel

October 15, 2014

Monte Thomas
Human Resources Manager
Axum Pharmaceuticals, Inc.
1208 West 34th Street
New York, NY 23140-1000

Dear Mr. Thomas:

It was a pleasure meeting you at the career fair this morning. The opportunities offered in pharmaceutical sales identify your company as a leader in today's global marketplace.

My education and related work experience in sales enable me to be a valuable asset to your company.

- A degree in communication with a minor in marketing from the University of New Jersey.
- Knowledge of the medical field gained as an administrative assistant at Dr. Joan Petti's internal medicine practice.
- Customer service skills gained as a sales associate at North Street Drug and Pharmacy.
- Excellent communication skills gained through numerous group projects in an academic setting and through three years' experience working with colleagues and customers in fast-paced retail and healthcare environments.

Please review the attached résumé that you requested for additional information about my education and work experience. Please contact me so we can discuss my joining Axum Pharmaceuticals.

Sincerely,
MaryAnne Marvel

Alma Rosario
42 Doe Court
Miramar, CA 92145

September 19, 2014

William Wagner
Human Resource Director
Carson Fine Foods
301 Torrey Pines Road
La Jolla, CA 92037

Dear Mr. Wagner:

Thank you for taking the time to meet with me today to discuss the position of Financial Planning Analyst with Carson Fine Foods. During our discussion, you stated that you're looking for an organized and outgoing candidate to join your team. Through my previous work and life experience, I gained organizational and customer development skills and learned how to meet goals through teamwork. In my position with Biotech Inc., I communicated with internal and external customers and assisted in efficiency and customer relations for the Fraud Detection program. I am confident that my skills and background will make me an asset as a Financial Planning Analyst with Carson Fine Foods.

I am eager to discuss this opportunity with you further. Please let me know what additional information I can provide you and your colleagues in order to secure this position and begin working for your organization.

Sincerely,

Alma Rosario
Alma Rosario

FIGURE A-10   Example of a Job Acceptance Message

To: llouis@kmart.com

From: tturner@pmi.edu

Subject: Job Offer Follow-Up: I Accept

Leonard,

I accept your employment offer as a management trainee. Thank you for responding so quickly after our discussion on Tuesday.

As you requested, I have signed the agreement outlining the specific details of my employment. You should receive my fax of the signed agreement, and I have kept a copy for my records.

If you should need to speak with me before I report to work on June 15, please call me at 999-4321.

Best regards,
Tony

© Cengage Learning

- Conclusions
- Recommendations
- Appendixes, if appropriate

Figure A-13 provides a sample of an informal report delivered to an external audience using a letter format.

Proposals are sales documents that are intended to recommend changes or purchases within a company, or to show how your organization can meet the needs of another, if intended for an external audience. A formal proposal may include the following components:

- Proposed idea and purpose, or what is often called the "project description"
- Scope, or what you propose to do
- Methods or procedures to be used
- Materials and equipment needed
- Qualifications of personnel who will be working on the project
- Follow-up and/or evaluation of the project

- Budget or costs of the project
- Summary of proposal
- Appendixes, if appropriate

An example of a short proposal is provided in Figure A-14.

Press Releases

An example of a press release is provided in Figure A-15.

Messages for Differing Purposes

This section provides examples of messages for a variety of purposes: routine claims (Figure A-16), confirming order receipt (Figure A-17), extending credit (Figure A-18), bad news (claim denial) (Figure A-19), and a sales message for promoting a service (Figure A-20).

FIGURE A-11 Example of a Job Refusal Message

To: tmilburn@sunfashions.com

From: rosborne@smu.edu

Subject: Job Offer Decision

Tony,

I appreciate your spending time with me discussing the sales associate position.

Your feedback regarding my fit for your organization and the opportunities available to me were particularly valuable. Having received offers in both sales and marketing, I feel that a career in the latter field better suits my personality and long-term career goals. Today, I am accepting an entry-level marketing position with Fashion Trends Inc.

Thank you for your confidence demonstrated by the job offer. When I hear about Sun Fashion's continued success, I will think of the dedicated people who work for the company.

Sincerely,
Renee

FIGURE A-12 Example of a Resignation Message

To: bromans@firstnational.com

From: mromirez@firstnational.com

Subject: Pleasure of Serving First National Bank

Betsy,

My job as a customer service associate at First National Bank the past year has been a rewarding experience. It has taught me a great deal about the banking industry and providing excellent customer service.

Learning about the business of banking has been particularly exciting. From the time I declared a major in finance, I have wanted to work with investment products. Before I accepted my current position, that goal was discussed. Now, that goal is becoming a reality, as I have accepted a job as a sales trainee in the investment division of WideWorld beginning one month from today. If satisfactory with you, I would like June 1 to be my last day here.

Thank you for the confidence you placed in me, your support of customer service associates, and your feedback to help me continue growing as a valued employee. As I continue my career in investment banking, I will take with me many pleasant memories of my time with First National.

Best regards,
Maria

FIGURE A-13 Example of an Informal Report Using a Letter Format

April 3, 2014

Linda Ruiz
President, Massive Corp.
660 Western Avenue
Atlanta, GA 30360-1660

Dear Ms. Ruiz:

RECOMMENDATIONS FOR IMPLEMENTING INTERNAL COMMUNICATION PLAN
AT MASSIVE

Thank you for allowing us to assist you in the recent communication audit of
your organization. Studies have shown that improved communication practices
can minimize costly mistakes, improve morale, and improve customer relations,
all of which can add to the corporate bottom line.

Procedures

In preparing this report, data was gathered using a variety of methods. Interviews
were conducted with all management personnel regarding the flow and channels
of communication used in the organization as well their perceptions of communication effectiveness. Focus groups composed of employees from each of
the company's departments were also used to gather similar information and
perceptions from the rank and file. To double-check the validity of these methods
and the responses that we received to our questions, an online survey was
disseminated to all employees. The responses from these methods of data
gathering along with our proven knowledge of corporate communication policies
and practices led to the recommendations in this report.

Findings

Research revealed useful information concerning Massive's current communication process and practices.

Results of Interviews with Management Personnel

Across the board, management stated that it did not see any problems with the
communication flow and channels currently used at Massive. However, when

1

Internal Communication Plan, Page 2

specific questions were asked about productivity, efficiency, morale, and losses from mistakes and misunderstandings, a different picture emerged. Eighty percent of management personnel answered affirmatively to the following questions:

- Have you witnessed or heard about mistakes being made by employees because the information or instructions provided to them was interpreted incorrectly?
- Have you ever had an employee express frustration to you because he or she believed that management did not know what was occurring in his or her department or at lower levels of the organization?
- Do you think that the current communication process used by your organization could be streamlined to help make task completion by employees faster?

From our interviews with management personnel, two pictures emerged; on the surface, they believe communication practices and processes at Massive are sufficient, but when pressed about particular issues, the majority believed improvements could be made.

Results of Focus Groups with Employees

Nine focus groups were conducted with employees from each of Massive's departments. Focus group size ranged from eight to twelve persons. Unlike the responses we initially received from management, employees generally believed there were numerous areas of improvement in Massive's communication practices.

All participants said that management did not listen to employees at lower levels and did not solicit suggestions from them. The results, according to employees, was that management did not value employees, did not have the information it needed to make good decisions, and was reactive when dealing with problems rather than proactive.

Furthermore, employees said that they did not feel that management clearly communicated organizational goals, activities, and events. The result was that employees often felt disconnected and devalued because they were not seen as a source for solutions. Employees said that Massive did not have a team culture. In the words of one employee, Massive is "a collection of individuals, all going their own separate way."

FIGURE A-13 Example of an Informal Report Using a Letter Format, *continued*

Results of Company-Wide Questionnaire

Of the 405 questionnaires sent out via email, we received responses from 349 employees. The responses to the questionnaire closely followed the responses we received from employee focus groups. The results from the survey are summarized below. The questionnaire can be found in the Appendix.

Question	Always	Sometimes	Never
1	5 percent	34 percent	61 percent
2	10 percent	50 percent	40 percent
3			
4	16 percent	60 percent	24 percent
5	6 percent	42 percent	51 percent
6	20 percent	62 percent	15 percent
7	11 percent	34 percent	55 percent
8	19 percent	48 percent	31 percent

Recommendations

The primary recommendations for Massive are

1. Improve the upward flow of communication from employees to management. Not only does this recommendation require changes in the company's communication practices but also its organizational culture. Management needs to become more open to others' ideas and more informal with its interactions with employees. It also needs to become much more active in and present at daily operations throughout the company. More formally, departments need to have regular meetings to gather ideas from employees and this information needs to be spread throughout the company with additional meetings with management throughout the organization. Management should encourage employees to send them suggestions through all channels of communication.
2. Improved downward flow of communication from employees to management. Management needs to actively share corporate goals, strategies, activities, and events that affect the company and its employees. This can be done through a variety of channels, including regular email messages, weekly or monthly company meetings, and a monthly company newsletter posted on the company web site.
3. Improved horizontal flow of communication. This issue has been addressed in Step 1. Regular meetings between all department heads that share departmental activities and concerns as well as those of employees can lead to better decision making through better coordination of solutions.

FIGURE A-13 Example of an Informal Report Using a Letter Format, *continued*

Internal Communication Plan, Page 4

Advantages of Implementing Recommendations

Organizational studies have shown that implementing such a communication plan may result in a number of advantages:

- **Improved attitudes.** People who feel valued for their ideas and appreciated by management and colleagues generally have higher morale.
- **Increased productivity.** Enhanced, systematic communication plans can lead to higher-quality work, greater professional commitment, and increased company loyalty.
- **Better decision making.** Communication practices that enable companies to gather more information from knowledgeable parties often lead to better, more effective solutions.
- **Greater profitability.** Higher morale, increased productivity and more effective solutions lead to greater profitability.

Thank you for the opportunity to audit Massive's internal communication practices and to provide our results and recommendations for improvement. Please let us know how we can assist you further with the implementation of our proposed plan and the monitoring of its effectiveness.

Sincerely,

Hasan Hassoud

Hasan Hassoud, Consultant

ksm

Enclosure: Appendix

PROPOSAL FOR IMPLEMENTATION

OF INTERNAL COMMUNICATION PLAN

for Massive Corp.

by Hasan Hassoun, Communications Consultant

May 1, 2014

Purpose

After careful study, the management of Massive Corp. has decided to implement the internal communication plan that was recommended last month. The internal communication plan is designed to improve communication at every level of Massive Corp.

Proposed Plan Implementation

The implementation of the internal communication plan will be directed by myself, Hasan Hassoun. Three additional consultants, Jana Lowry, Teresa Warner, and Ted Mitchell, will complete the team involved with plan implementation.

Implementation Process

The implementation process will begin with a two-day retreat for all management personnel. This retreat will provide a number of sessions, including "Bringing about Corporate Culture Change," "Creating and Sharing Corporate Visions," "Leading Effective Meetings," and "Managing by Walking Around." The retreat will conclude with the creation of a schedule for regular meetings to be held at all levels of the organization. These meetings are intended to impart the new cultural values to employees and to provide for the transmission of information from employees to management and vice versa.

The next step in the process will take place at the scheduled meetings. Our consultants will attend the first of each of these departmental meetings. Consultants will then meet with each manager to provide feedback and coaching (if necessary) to support him or her in effective transmission of the corporate message as well as the gathering of information from employees.

1

Internal Communication Plan, Page 2

After the initial visit to each department meeting as well as those at the management and company-wide level, our consultants will visit a second meeting to observe how well managers are implementing their new skills and provide any needed feedback. If certain managers need additional support, this can be arranged. Subsequent meeting visits will be provided monthly for a period of six months.

Plan Assessment

At the end of the six-month period, our consultants will assess how well the plan has been implemented and whether employees believe it has been successful. This assessment will be performed using two methods: two focus groups composed of a random selection of employees and a second online questionnaire disseminated to all employees. The findings from this assessment will be communicated to Massive's corporate team.

Length of Plan Implementation

As outlined above, implementation of the plan will be performed over a six-month period, beginning with a two-day retreat and consisting of seven additional visits to all departmental, management, and company-wide meetings. If desired, an assessment of the plan implementation will be conducted at the end of six months. This assessment will consist of two one-hour focus groups and the dissemination of an online questionnaire to all employees.

Number of Participants

The plan will serve all Massive employees, which is reportedly 405.

Cost

Exact cost figures are as follows:

Professional fees for retreat workshop	$ 2,400.00
Rental of retreat site and meals for 20 persons	3,500.00
Professional fees for meeting visits and coaching	10,000.00
Plan assessment	2,000.00
Total	$17,900.00

Marine Industrial Corporation Acquires Renowned Process Improvement TechKron Inc.

Date: October 12, 2014

CONTACT INFORMATION:
Belinda Morales
Director OEM Sales
Tel: 502-210-1652
Email: bmorales@marineindustrial.com

TechKron Inc. Joins Marine Industrial Corporation
(EMAILWIRE.COM, October 12, 2014) San Diego, CA - Marine Industrial Corporation (QIS) acquires TechKron Inc. Known as an industry leader in quality assurance, Marine Industrial brings in TechKron, an ISO/IEC 17025:2005 accredited company with engineering capabilities, Advanced Product Quality Planning, Six Sigma, and Coordinate Measuring Machine Services to take its business to new heights in the automotive manufacturing processes.

The acquisition will improve Marine Industrial's Quality Engineering Department, add 100 employees to its workforce, and increase its market share and geographic footprint to Saginaw, MI, Baltimore, MD, Indianapolis, IN, and Spartanburg, SC.

Belinda Morales, director of Business Development, said, "The addition of TechKron's specialty services and expanded geographic footprint will allow Marine Industrial to provide a broader range of capabilities to our customers. In today's competitive manufacturing market, many organizations are faced with the never-ending challenge of continual cost reductions. Outsourcing of noncritical production services is becoming a more prevalent approach to such savings. Marine Industrial can facilitate this need by now offering even more cost-effective solutions with a greater diversity of services."

Leo Cragmoor, COO of TechKron states, "The acquisition of TechKron by Marine Industrial will provide a major benefit to our existing and future customers. They bring a level of expertise and experience that will compliment and enhance our core services. I am confident that the acquisition will allow us to further improve our quality of service and dramatically expand our market share."

Marine Industrial Corporation is an ISO-certified Quality Assurance Service provider that specializes in a diverse line of services targeted at reducing automotive manufacturing costs while increasing quality, productivity, and efficiency.

1

QIS Acquires TechKron, Page 2

Marine Industrial's core competencies include Engineering, Inspection, Sorting, Containment, Rework, Light Assembly, CMM, Training, Kitting, and Packaging. Marine Industrial is one of the largest such suppliers in the nation with 23 U.S. locations, six Mexico locations, and one Canadian location. Marine Industrial is an approved vendor for most major OEMs and has more than 2,500 active customers to date. By providing skilled and trained employees to our customers, Marine Industrial has become an integral part of the supply chain in every aspect of automotive production.

FIGURE A-16 Example of a Routine Claim

To: Tom Bowls <tbowls@computersolutions.com>

From: Jennifer Reagan <jreagan@lauder.com>

Subject: Laptop Repair or Replacement Needed

Mr. Bowls,

Please repair or send us a replacement for the laptop computer listed on the attached sales agreement. It has a faulty cooling fan. You should receive the computer tomorrow via overnight freight.

The computer was purchased six months ago under our agreement with your company to provide our salespeople with laptops. The computers are covered by a twelve-month warranty for faulty parts replacement. I spoke with your sales manager, Tom Wilkins, this morning and he instructed me to contact you for extradited service.

Our salesperson Maria Rodriguez eagerly awaits the return of her laptop. Our salespeople are highly dependent on their computers because they spend so much time on the road.

Thanks,
Jennifer Reagan

Purchasing Manager

FIGURE A-17 Example of an Online Order Confirmation

To: Dillon McCrea <dmcrea@pmail.com>

From: Maggie Fielding <mfielding@firstline.com>

Subject: Firstline welcomes Dillon as valued customer

Dillon,

Welcome to Firstline Insurance! I'm excited to see that you have enrolled as a new customer.

You will be contacted soon by your personal customer service representative, Lucille Burns. Lucille has been with the company for ten years and is well versed in our product line and receives top rankings in customer service.

Lucille will make sure that you have the right financial products that suit you and your family's needs. She will keep in touch regarding your family's changing needs and will inform you about beneficial changes to your financial planning.

I have complete confidence in the care you will receive from Lucille, but if for any reason you aren't completely satisfied or have other concerns, please let me know right away.

You can reach me at 213-561-8300, extension 201, or you can email me at mfielding@firstline.com.

Thank you for trusting in us for your insurance needs.

Best regards,

Maggie Fielding
Customer Service Manager
Firstline Insurance Corp.

P.S. Be sure to watch your mailbox for our Welcome to Firstline package sent to new customers. You will receive coupons for discounts at several retail and restaurant outlets in your area as a sign of our appreciation for your business.

FIGURE A-18 Example of Letter Extending Credit

January 24, 2014

Frances Ford
Purchasing Department
Pots and Pantries, Inc.
123 Colville Avenue
Spokane, WA 89001

Dear Ms. Ford:

Welcome to the most unique designs in glassware available in the U.S. Our expert buyers tour every region of the world to find the most innovative creations in kitchen and dining glassware.

Because of your current favorable credit rating, we are pleased to provide you with a $15,000 credit line subject to our standard 2/10, n/30 terms. By paying your invoice within ten days, you can save 2 percent on your glassware purchases.

You can use our convenient online ordering system to search our extensive line of glassware products and to place your orders. If you need additional assistance, please call our 24-hour service line, where you will be assisted by our number one-rated customer service personnel.

The most innovative glassware designs are now available to you and your customers, so please take some time to familiarize yourself with our extensive line.

Sincerely,

Luther Crosby

Luther Crosby
Credit Manager

June 14, 2014

Snowcap Limited
Attention: Lindsey Tucker
1905 Southhaven Street
Santa Fe, NM 87501-7313

Ladies and Gentlemen:

Restocking of Returned Merchandise

The HighFly skis you stocked this past season are skillfully crafted and made from the most innovative materials available. Maintaining a wide selection of quality skiing products is an excellent strategy for developing customer loyalty and maximizing your sales.

Our refund policies provide you the opportunity to keep a fully stocked inventory at the lowest possible cost. You receive full refunds for merchandise returned within 10 days of receipt. For unsold merchandise returned after the primary selling season, a modest 15 percent restocking fee is charged to cover our costs of holding this merchandise until next season. The credit applied to your account for $2,069.75 covers merchandise you returned at the end of February.

While relaxing from another great skiing season, take a look at our new HighFly skis and other items available in the enclosed catalog for the 2015 season. You can save 10 percent by ordering premium ski products before May 10.

Sincerely,

Galen Fondren
Credit Manager

Enclosure: Catalog

FIGURE A-20 Example of a Sales Message Promoting a Service

April 1, 2014

Louisa Fox, Marketing Manager
Learner Consumer Products Group
2304 Pike Market Street
Seattle, WA 90322

Dear Ms. Fox:

Are you looking for help developing your organization's social media platform? . . . improving your retail marketing? . . . planning your external communication program? . . . enhancing your mass advertising strategy? Then you need the services of the full-service brand engagement firm Souther and Associates to develop an integrated media plan that ensures your company's continued success.

With Souther and Associates' full-service capabilities, you will receive support in all of the following areas:

- Social media. Leverage the millions of conversations taking place through the use of social media by taking advantage of our four-step approach, which tracks conversations and dialogue; extracts insights from consumer conversations; interacts with key influences, brand advocates, and detractors; and measures consumer sentiment, advocacy, and engagement.

- Retail marketing. Engage consumers away from the noise and competing advertising, and reach them on an intimate, meaningful, and locally relevant level that will help you to drive trial, traffic, and sales.

- Communication planning. Build preference for your brand by translating emotional insights into high-impact brand strategy and innovation. Our experts bypass consumers' rational thinking with tools and techniques that are reactive and observational. Then, we integrate these emotional insights with your brand's functional benefits to create the foundation for lasting behavior change.

- Influence marketing. Mass advertising still plays an important role in branding, but these days, credibility is especially important, and who is more credible than a trusted professional? We identify professionals to give your products that powerful endorsement.

Visit www.souther.com today and check out the list of consulting services we provide and read real-life stories from past clients about how we increased brand awareness for them. If you contact us before May 15, you will also receive a free assessment of your current marketing program from our proprietary MarketLab analysis tool. Our team is ready to assist you in improving the impact of your marketing programs today. Please call me at 509-788-1302 to make an appointment with a consultant.

Sincerely,

Frank Forester

Frank Forester
Engagement Director

Enclosure

Appendix B

Punctuation, Sentence Structure, and Usage

This appendix contains the rules for common problems that occur in writing regarding punctuation, sentence structure, and grammar usage.

Punctuation

This section contains the rules for punctuation. These include the use of apostrophes, colons, commas, dashes, ellipses, hyphens, and semicolons.

Apostrophes

An apostrophe indicates possession. In addition, it is used to prevent misreading of confusing words.

1. Use an apostrophe to show possession.
   a. To form the possessive case of most singular nouns, add an apostrophe and an **-s,** such as "the **child's** backpack."
   b. When singular nouns end in **-s** or **-es,** add an apostrophe and an **-s** to the end of the word, such as "the **boss's** office."
   c. Add an apostrophe and an **-s** to show the possessive case of plural nouns that do not end in **-s** or **-es,** such as "the **children's** party."
   d. To show the possessive case of plural nouns ending in **-s** or **-es,** add only an apostrophe, such as "the **boys'** clubhouse."
   e. Add an apostrophe to show the possessive form of amounts, time, and the word "sake," such as in "one week's pay" or "for Pete's sake."
2. Use an apostrophe to replace missing letters or numbers, such as in can't (cannot) or class of '09 (class of 2009). In measurement, an apostrophe is used as a symbol for feet, such as in $3' \times 11''$.
3. Use an apostrophe in words, letters, or abbreviations if it is confusing without the use of an apostrophe, such as in "crossing the i's and dotting the t's" or "polka-dotted pj's."

Colons

A colon (:) is primarily a mark of introduction of something that follows in a sentence. Use a colon only after a complete sentence.

1. Use a colon to introduce a series or list after a complete sentence:

   I needed to get several things at the grocery store: breakfast cereal, milk, bread, cheese, and fruit.

2. Use a colon to introduce an element that explains the previous sentence:

   The instructor concluded with an important thought: The early bird gets the worm.

3. Use a colon to form an appositive (a word that further explains a noun or pronoun):

   We will learn presentation skills from the best of the best: Tony Robbins.

4. Use a colon in special situations:

   a. A salutation in a business letter—Dear Ms. Hershell:
   b. Figures giving time—11:30 p.m. or 6:00 a.m.
   c. Subtitles of books or magazines—*Eating like a King: Three Weeks in France's Wine Country.*
   d. Biblical references to clarify between the chapter and verse—Luke 17:21.

Commas

A comma is used to define the relationships of various elements of a sentence and to clarify meaning for the reader.

1. Use a comma before a coordinating conjunction (*and, but, so, yet, for, nor*) between two main clauses:

   Interest rates are low, but people still aren't buying houses.

2. Use a comma to set off nonessential elements from the rest of the sentence:

The company, which is headquartered in St. Louis, is planning to close ten regional offices.

3. Use a comma between items in a series of three or more:

   We had fried chicken, cole slaw, and apple cobbler at Uncle Bob's birthday party.

4. Use a comma to set off introductory elements at the beginning of a sentence:

   When her children went off to college, Carol started her own business.

5. Use a comma between two or more adjectives that equally modify the same word (these are called coordinate adjectives because each adjective describes the noun independently):

   The winding, gravel road led up to Martin's fishing cabin.

6. Use a comma to separate adjectives following a noun:

   Rudolpho, tanned and rested, returned to work ready for anything.

7. Use a comma in dates with at least three parts: day, month, year (place comma after the day):

   Jennifer's birthday is March 4, 1993.

8. Use a comma to separate the city from the state and the state from the rest of the sentence:

   Tucson, Arizona, is the best place to be in the winter.

9. Use a comma in numbers larger than three digits:

   The number of migrating birds returning this winter is estimated to be more than 240,000.

10. Use a comma to set off an appositive (a word that further explains a noun or pronoun).

    Theda, George's first wife, lives across town.

11. Use a comma after the name of a person being addressed in the beginning of a sentence:

    Leo, please drop off the mail on your way to school.

12. Use a comma before *such as*, *including*, and *especially* when the information that follows is not essential to the meaning of the sentence:

We use a variety of communication media in the office, including email, telephone, and fax.

13. Use a comma to separate transitional words from the rest of the sentence:

    Cecilia, however, will not be joining us for dinner.

14. Use a comma after a conjunctive adverb (*however, consequently, furthermore, therefore, otherwise*) that separates two complete sentences. (A semicolon must also be used before the conjunctive adverb.)

    I should go to bed early tonight; otherwise, I will be very tired for tomorrow's exam.

15. Use a comma inside quotation marks: "Man the lifeboats," the captain yelled.

Dashes

Dashes (—) are used to provide emphasis or clarity. Create a dash with two hyphens, and do not space before or after the dash.

1. Use a dash to create emphasis:

   The team leader—if you can call her that—missed our last meeting.

2. Use a dash to create greater clarity when other punctuation is used in a sentence:

   Some of the things needed to remodel the living room—paint, a ladder, and drop cloths—still need to be purchased.

3. Use a dash to separate elements in the sentence that abruptly interrupt the meaning:

   The children need 10,000 points—more or less—to qualify for the prize.

4. Use a dash to introduce items in a series when you want to create greater emphasis than a colon:

   We ate everything on the buffet—roast beef, barbecued chicken, poached salmon, grilled pork chops, and three kinds of dessert.

Ellipsis Points

Ellipsis points consist of three dots with spaces in between each dot (...). Ellipsis points are used to indicate missing words in a direct quotation. Ellipsis points can also be used at the end of a sentence when it seems to fade out before completing the thought.

1. Use ellipsis points to indicate missing words in a direct quotation:

   The minister said, "We must learn to love our neighbor … as we love ourselves."

2. Use ellipsis points to indicate the sentence fades out before completing the thought:

   Lisa yawned and said, "I'm just SO tired … When are we going to get there?"

Hyphens

A hyphen is used to connect two or more words in a sentence. Hyphenated words can act as modifiers or as compound words that can stand alone.

1. Use a hyphen with a compound modifier (two words used together to modify another word) when it comes before a noun:

   There is nothing like an old-fashioned root-beer float in the summer.

2. Use a hyphen with numbers between twenty-one and ninety-nine that are written out:

   Twenty-four children attended the birthday party.

3. Use a hyphen with some prefixes and suffixes (the prefixes *pre*, *post*, *self*, *pro*, and *ex* always require a hyphen, and the suffix *elect* always requires a hyphen):

   The leader of the group was a self-proclaimed minister.

4. Use a hyphen with short fractions:

   One-half of the men had graduated from college.

5. Use a hyphen with some computer terms that contain *e*:

   She downloaded a new book on her e-reader.

6. Use a hyphen between numbers to indicate a sequence of numbers:

   Seats are still available in rows 5–10.

Semicolons

A semicolon is stronger than a comma but weaker than a period because it does not indicate the end of

a complete thought. Use a semicolon only when two sentences are closely related. Use a semicolon to separate the following elements:

1. Two complete sentences that are closely related when no conjunction (*and*, *but*, *or*, *nor*, *for*, *yet*, *so*) is between them:

   It rained for eight hours straight; the main roads were flooded.

2. Items in a series when one or more of the main elements already contains commas:

   The concert is scheduled for Chicago, Illinois; Boston, Massachusetts; and St. Louis, Missouri.

3. Two complete sentences joined by a transitional expression that functions as a conjunctive adverb (*however*, *moreover*, *consequently*, etc.):

   We had three weeks' vacation; however, we were unable to leave home because our car had broken down.

4. Elements in a sentence that would become confusing with the addition of another comma:

   When you sell the house, leave the stove; but take the refrigerator.

Sentence Structure

This section discusses common problems related to correct sentence structure. The topics are subject–verb agreement, pronoun–antecedent agreement, fragments, run-on sentences, comma splices, and clauses.

Subject–Verb Agreement

In grammatically correct sentences, the subject should agree with the verb. To determine if the subject and verb agree in a sentence, first locate the subject. Second, decide whether the subject is singular or plural. Finally, write the appropriate form of the verb. Using the following rules will help you to write sentences free from subject–verb agreement errors.

1. Use a singular verb with a singular subject and a plural verb with a plural subject:

   Singular: Bill [singular subject] drives [singular verb] to work on Tuesdays and Thursdays.

Plural: The girls [plural subject] fly [plural verb] whenever they get the opportunity.

2. Use a plural verb with two or more subjects joined by *and*. This is known as a compound subject:

A policeman [subject 1] and a fireman [subject 2] were [plural verb] injured in the explosion.

3. Use a singular verb with two or more singular subjects joined by *or* or *nor*:

Lisa [subject 1] or Connie [subject 2] is going [singular verb] to work the night shift.

4. Use a verb that agrees with the closer subject when a singular subject and a plural subject are joined by *or* or *nor*:

Todd [singular subject] or the children [plural subject] walk [plural verb] the dog to the park every day.

5. Use a singular verb with a collective noun that names a group of people acting as a single unit:

The staff [collective noun] has had [singular verb] a pay freeze for the past year.

6. Use a plural verb with a collective noun that names a group of people acting independently of one another (club, family, class, team, platoon, faculty, jury, staff, board, audience, committee, etc.):

The team [collective noun] are beginning [plural verb indicates the collective noun was acting independently] their own projects to ensure that the company's financial goals are met.

7. Use a singular verb with a title even though the title might be plural:

The Little Foxes [plural title] is [singular verb] a popular play.

8. Use a singular verb with the name of one company even though it might contain a compound noun:

Dewie, Jones, and Cheatham [company] is [singular verb] the best accounting firm in the city.

9. Use a singular verb with an amount (money, distance, time) when it is expressed as a single unit:

Fifteen hundred dollars [amount expressed as a single unit] is [singular verb] the advertised price of the mountain bike.

10. Use a verb that agrees with the antecedent of the pronoun with *who*, *which*, and *that*:

John wants the dogs [antecedent of who] who run [plural verb] the neighborhood secured.

11. Use the appropriate singular or plural verb form with an indefinite pronoun, depending on whether the indefinite pronoun is singular or plural:

Singular: Each [singular indefinite pronoun] of the teams has [singular verb] an equal chance of winning.

Plural: Both [plural indefinite pronoun] of the teams have [plural verb] an equal chance of winning.

Pronoun–Antecedent Agreement

The function of pronouns—*I, me, you, he, him, she, her, it, we, us, they, them*—is to replace nouns or other pronouns in a sentence. The antecedent is the word to which the pronoun refers. Be certain that a pronoun agrees with its antecedent.

1. The basic idea behind pronoun–antecedent agreement is for the singular or plural construction to remain parallel.

Singular: The *boy* sent a present to *his* sick friend, Joshua.

Plural: The *boys* sent a present to *their* sick friend, Joshua.

2. When using pronouns to refer to collective nouns, remember such nouns are always considered singular because they are taken as a single entity.

Incorrect: Goldman Sachs sent quarterly reports to their shareholders.

Correct: Goldman Sachs sent quarterly reports to its shareholders.

3. Pronouns should clearly reference a particular word. Avoid using vague pronouns alone. Common vague pronouns include *it, that, these, they, this, those, which.*

Vague: *They* are always handing in their assignments late.

(To whom does the word *they* refer?)

Fragments

A sentence fragment is a group of words that does not express a complete thought. Sentence fragments can be turned into complete sentences by adding words that will complete the thought. Remember— a sentence must contain a subject (noun) and a verb. The following are reasons that fragments occur:

1. The fragment contains no subject.

   Fragment: Splashing water on his face and wiping it with a towel.

   Sentence with subject: Splashing water on his face and wiping it with a towel, Luther tried to clear his head.

2. The fragment contains no verb.

   Fragment: Fuchsias, daisies, hollyhocks, roses, and marigolds.

   Sentence with verb: Fuchsias, daisies, hollyhocks, roses, and marigolds ringed the restored Victorian home.

3. The fragment results from using a dependent clause.

   Dependent clause: Although Terry said he would return it to the store.

   Complete sentence: Although Terry said he would return it to the store, the defective toaster still sat on the kitchen counter.

Run-on Sentences

A run-on sentence is two complete sentences (main clauses) that are run together without correct punctuation. The following rules are for correcting run-on sentences:

1. Place an end punctuation mark (period, question mark, exclamation mark) between the two sentences:

   Lisa wanted a cup of coffee. She hoped it would help wake her up.

2. Use a comma and a coordinating conjunction (*and, but, or, nor, for, so, yet*) to link the two sentences:

   Lisa wanted a cup of coffee, but she wasn't sure it would help wake her up.

3. Use a semicolon to separate and connect the two closely related ideas:

   Lisa wanted a cup of coffee; she hoped it would help wake her up.

4. Form a simple sentence by adding a word to subordinate one sentence to the other:

   Lisa wanted a cup of coffee because she hoped it would help wake her up.

Comma Splices

A comma splice occurs when two main clauses are separated by a comma without a coordinating conjunction (*and, but, or, nor, for, so, yet*). The following rules are ways to correct a comma splice.

1. Place an end mark (period, question mark, exclamation mark) between the two clauses to form two sentences.

   Comma splice: The house was enormous, it was four stories tall.

   Correction with end mark: The house was enormous. It was four stories tall.

2. Leave the comma and add a coordinating conjunction (*and, but, or, nor, for, so, yet*) to link the sentences.

   Comma splice: The house was enormous, it was four stories tall.

   Correction with coordinating conjunction: The house was enormous, and it was four stories tall.

3. Use a semicolon to separate and connect the two closely related ideas.

   Comma splice: The house was enormous, it was four stories tall.

   Correction with semicolon: The house was enormous; it was four stories tall.

Clauses

A clause contains a subject, verb, and modifiers— but is not necessarily a complete sentence. The following are some types of clauses that should help you ensure that you write clear, concise sentences:

1. **Independent clause:** An independent clause is a group of words that can stand alone as a complete sentence. While independent and dependent clauses can have a subject and a verb, only an independent clause can stand

alone. Another name for an independent clause is main clause.

The cat [subject] is [verb] waiting at the door.

2. **Compound sentence:** Two independent clauses can be joined together to make a compound sentence by either adding a comma and a coordinating conjunction or a semicolon between the two clauses.

    The cat is waiting at the door [independent clause 1], and the dog is lying on the couch [independent clause 2].

3. **Dependent clause:** A dependent clause is a group of words containing a subject and a verb that cannot stand alone. Dependent clauses are introduced by subordinating conjunctions and followed by a comma. The following example could be added to the independent clause example to form a complex sentence; however, the phrase is not a complete sentence on its own.

    But [subordinating conjunction] it [subject] is [verb] wet from the rain [modifier].

4. **Relative clause:** A relative clause is the clause introduced by a relative pronoun. Relative pronouns are *who*, *whom*, *which*, and *that*.

    The cat that is waiting at the door [that is waiting at the door = relative clause] is wet from the rain.

5. **Nonrestrictive clause:** A nonrestrictive clause adds information about the antecedent but does not limit the antecedent. Remember, an antecedent is the word being referred to.

    The cat [antecedent], which is wet from the rain, [which is wet from the rain = nonrestrictive clause] is waiting at the door.

6. **Restrictive clause:** A restrictive clause limits the antecedent and is necessary to the meaning of the sentence.

    Everyone [antecedent] who has seasonal flu [who has seasonal flu = restrictive clause] is required to stay home during the fever stage.

    (The clause, "who has seasonal flu," restricts the antecedent, "everyone," because it further defines who "everyone" is in the sentence.)

Usage

This section discusses common problems involving the use of adjectives and adverbs, capitalization, and *who* and *whom*.

Adjectives and Adverbs

Adjectives and adverbs are modifiers or words that further explain or restrict another word in a sentence.

Adjectives

An adjective modifies a noun or pronoun by describing what it is. Adjectives are placed before a noun or pronoun.

> *Correct:* The red [adjective = describes the color of the apple] apple [noun] sat on the teacher's desk.
>
> *Incorrect:* The apple [noun] red [adjective] sat on the teacher's desk.

Adverbs

An adverb modifies a verb to describe how something is done or an adjective to further describe a noun or pronoun's state of being.

1. Adverbs are often formed by adding –ly to an adjective, and an adverb can go after *or before* the verb.

    > *Correct:* He paints [verb] beautifully [adverb = describes how he paints].
    >
    > *Correct:* She quickly [adverb = describes how she moved] threw [verb] the hot pan in the sink.

2. An adverb can describe an adjective. When using an adverb to describe an adjective, place the adverb before the adjective.

    > *Correct:* Tim's extremely [adverb = describes how fast Tim's motorcycle is] fast [adjective = describes Tim's motorcycle] motorcycle is going to be ridden in this weekend's race.
    >
    > *Incorrect:* Tim's fast [adjective] extremely [adverb] motorcycle is going to be ridden in this weekend's race.

3. An adverb that describes frequency (*always, never, sometimes, often,* etc.) usually comes

before the main verb or phrase it is describing.

Correct: Melinda is often [adverb that describes how late Melinda is for work] late for work [adjective clause that describes the subject *Melinda*].

Incorrect: Melinda is late for work [adjective] often [adverb].

Capitalization

Capitalization is used to begin a sentence and indicate proper nouns in a sentence to make reading easier.

1. Capitalize the first word to begin a sentence, direct quotation, each line in a list, or the first word after a colon when a complete sentence follows the colon:

   - Katie crossed the street.
   - The teacher will discuss
     - Writing email messages
     - Preparing for the mid-term exam
     - Completing the team assignments
   - This is my favorite saying: A bird in hand is worth two in the bush.

2. Capitalize a proper noun (a name that specifies a specific person, place, or thing):

   - *Someone's name:* Lisa Rogers was elected class president.
   - *Geographical names:* The group visited China during spring break.
   - *Nouns followed by numbers or letters:* Our airplane is Flight 1203 to Los Angeles.
   - *Titles before a person's name:* Chief Running Bull spoke to the crowd.
   - *Titles of high distinction:* The President will appear on television tonight.
   - *Course titles:* All students are required to take Business Communication 105.
   - *A specific degree:* Lisa is studying to earn a master's degree in Political Science.
   - *Organizations and departments within organizations:* The Boys and Girls Clubs of America organized its annual fund-raiser.
   - *Brand names and trademarks:* John ordered a Pepsi with his hamburger.

   - *Government groups and laws:* Congress passed a bill to support the First Amendment.
   - *Historical events and time periods:* We are studying the Middle Ages now, but I am really looking forward to reading about the Renaissance later in the term.
   - *Days of the week, months, and holidays:* My favorite holiday is Christmas.
   - *Religious references:* The Methodist minister will read from the Bible on Sunday.
   - *Races, languages, and nationalities:* While many Americans are Caucasian or of African descent, a growing proportion are Hispanic.
   - *Computer terminology:* The teacher instructed us to use the Internet for our research.
   - *Celestial bodies:* The Earth revolves around the Sun.

3. Capitalize the pronoun *I.*

Who versus Whom

Who and *whom* are pronouns. The following charts identify (1) the correct pronoun case for *who* and *whom* and (2) how to use *who* and *whom*, depending upon their case in a sentence.

	Subjective Case	**Objective Case**	**Possessive Case**
Singular	Who	Whom	Whose
	Whoever	Whomever	Whosever
Plural	Who	Whom	Whose
	Whoever	Whomever	Whosever

Using Who and Whom		
Case	**Pronoun**	**Use in a Sentence**
Subjective	Who	Subject of a verb or a complement
	Whoever	
Objective	Whom	Direct object, indirect object, object of a preposition
	Whomever	
Possessive	Whose	Indicates ownership
	Whosever	

Who or Whoever

1. Use *who* or *whoever* when the pronoun is the subject of a verb:

   Who wants to eat at Wendy's?

2. Use *who* or *whoever* when the pronoun is a subject complement:

   The man who was hospitalized was who?

3. Use *who* or *whoever* when the pronoun is the subject of a subordinate clause:

   I wonder who threw the rock through the store window?

Whom or Whomever

1. Use *whom* or *whomever* when the pronoun is the direct object of a verb:

   Whom did he finally ask to take him home?

2. Use *whom* or *whomever* when the pronoun is the object of a preposition:

   With whom were you planning to spend the weekend?

3. Use *whom* or *whomever* when the pronoun is the object of a verb in a subordinate clause:

   I wonder whom the teacher will select to play the Tin Man in the school play.

Glossary

active listening Listening with a purpose, which involves paraphrasing, asking questions for clarification, and providing feedback.

adaptive capacity The ability to change one's style and approach to fit the culture, context, or condition of an organization.

adaptive model Strategy is focused on the continuous adjustment of the relationship between the organization and its environment.

aggressiveness Asserting one's rights and needs at the expense of others through hurtful expression, self-promotion, attempts to control others, and argumentativeness.

AIDA approach A popular model for organizing persuasive messages; AIDA is the acronym for *attention*, *interest*, *desire*, and *action*.

anticipatory socialization The process we use to develop a set of expectations and beliefs about how people communicate in various formal and informal work settings.

appropriate feedback Feedback that is honest, reflects the communicator's true understanding and judgment, and is appropriate for the subject, audience, and occasion or context.

articulate To pronounce all words clearly and fluently.

assertiveness Self-enhancing, expressive communication that takes into account both the communicator's and others' needs.

attribution The assignment of meaning to other people's behavior.

audience-centered communication Communication that considers the needs, concerns, and expectations of the audience.

avoidance A conscious attempt to avoid engaging with people in the dominant group.

boundary spanners Connect an informal network with another information network.

call to action A conclusion to a persuasive message that is intended to convince the reader to fully consider the writer's or speaker's proposal and, ideally, commit to a decision or take the next step.

central connectors Link most people in an informal network with one another.

chronemics Values related to time, which refer to the way that people organize and use time and the messages that are created because of our organization and use of time.

claim Often a general or abstract idea presented as fact.

co-alignment Matching up opportunities and risks in the environment with the capabilities and resources of the organization.

coherence The logical flow of ideas throughout a paragraph.

collectivist culture A culture in which cooperation rather than competition is encouraged and in which individual goals are sacrificed for the good of the group.

common ground The interests, goals, and commonalities of belief that the communicator shares with the audience.

comparison level (CL) The standard by which individuals evaluate the desirability of group membership; CL is strongly influenced by previous relationships.

comparison level for alternatives (CL$_{alt}$) The lowest level of outcomes a member will accept in light of available alternative opportunities.

competitors People who view group disagreements as win–lose situations and find satisfaction in forcing their views on others.

compliance-gaining Attempts made by a communicator to influence another person to do something that the person otherwise might not do.

compliance-resisting The refusal to comply with another person's attempts at influence.

confirmation bias A tendency to distort information that contradicts the beliefs and attitudes we currently hold.

context The situation or setting in which communication occurs.

contextual intelligence The awareness of and ability to adapt to the context.

cooperators Individuals who value accommodative interpersonal strategies in groups.

corporate identity The visual manifestation of the image of the organization as conveyed through its logo, products, services, buildings, stationery, uniforms, and other tangible items created by the organization to communicate with a variety of constituencies.

correlation A consistent relationship between two or more variables.

critical listening Listening used to evaluate the accuracy, meaningfulness, and usefulness of a message.

critical thinking The intellectually disciplined process of actively and skillfully conceptualizing, applying, analyzing, synthesizing, and/or evaluating information gathered from, or generated by, observation, experience, reflection, reasoning, or communication as a guide to belief and action.

culture The learned beliefs, values, rules, norms, symbols, and traditions that are common to a group of people.

defensive communication climate An organizational climate in which individuals feel threatened.

demographics The statistical data about a particular population, including its age, income, education level, and so on.

diagram A two-dimensional drawing that shows the important parts of objects.

dialogic model of communication This model of communication takes other people's points of view into account, acknowledging that the speaker and the listener may have different perspectives.

dialogue A conversation among two or more persons. From the dialogic perspective, that dialogue would be characterized by such attributes as trust, lack of pretense, sincerity, humility, respect, directness, open-mindedness, honesty, concern for others, empathy, non-manipulative intent, equality, and acceptance of others as individuals with intrinsic worth, regardless of differences of opinion or belief.

distributed leadership A situation in which team members share team leadership.

drive The state of an individual associated with the need, such as hunger or thirst.

egocentric Concerned with the self rather than others or society.

emotional intelligence The assortment of non-cognitive skills that influence our ability to cope with the pressures and demands of the environment.

empathic listening A form of active listening with the goal of understanding the other person.

ethnocentrism The belief that your own cultural background—including its ways of analyzing problems, values, beliefs, language, and verbal and nonverbal communication—is correct and that other cultures are somehow inferior.

ethos An ethical appeal that refers to information that provides credibility to ourselves or our position.

evidence More specific statement of fact that supports a statement.

extemporaneous speaking Public speaking that is delivered spontaneously rather than being read or memorized in advance.

external strategic communication Management's public relations and issues management efforts designed to influence consumers, communities, special-interest groups, voters, regulators, legislators, and others outside the organization.

face The public image of individuals, or groups, that their society sees and evaluates based on cultural norms and values.

false dichotomy A dichotomy that is not jointly exhaustive (i.e., there are other alternatives) or that is not mutually exclusive (i.e., the alternatives overlap). A false dichotomy may be the product of either–or thinking.

feedback The listener's verbal and nonverbal responses to the speaker and his or her message.

forecasting Elements of a text or oral presentation that tell the audience what the reader or speaker will cover next.

free-riding When group members do not work as hard when they believe others will compensate for this lack of effort.

fundamental attribution error Conflict that is exacerbated by members' tendencies to misperceive others and to assume that the other party's behavior is caused by personal rather than situational factors.

goal The outcome that the person perceives will eliminate a need.

goodwill In the business communication context, the ability to create and maintain positive, productive relationships with others.

graph A visual element used to compare the values of several items; sometimes called *charts*.

groupthink Conformity-seeking behavior of cohesive groups that interferes with effective decision making.

haptics Communicating through the use of bodily contact or touch.

high self-monitors People who are highly aware of their impression-management behavior and efforts.

image building The process of creating the identity an organization wants its relevant public to perceive.

impression formation The process of integrating a variety of observations about a person into a coherent impression of that person.

impression management The attempt to control the impression of ourselves that we present to others in any communication situation.

individualistic culture A culture with an "I" focus in which competition, not cooperation, is encouraged and individual initiative and achievement are highly valued.

individualists Individuals who are concerned only with their own outcomes in group situations.

inference A conclusion about the unknown based upon the known.

influence The power to affect the thoughts or actions of others.

information brokers Keep the different subgroups in an informal network together.

informational influence When the group provides members with information that they can use to make decisions and form opinions.

intercultural communication The exchange of information among people of different cultural backgrounds.

intermember relations The relations of the group members to one another, which are determined by patterns of status, attraction, and communication.

internal strategic communication Management's efforts to provide information to and exert influence with the organizational membership.

interpersonal communication Communication involving mutual influence, usually for the purpose of managing relationships.

interpersonal dominance The relational, behavioral, and interactional state that reflects the actual achievement—by means of communication—of influence or control over another person.

interpersonal influence When the group uses verbal and nonverbal influence tactics to induce change.

interpersonal intelligence The ability to understand others.

interpretive model Strategy is concerned with the management of meaning and with symbol construction aimed at legitimizing the organization by providing orienting metaphors and frames of reference that allow the organization and its environment to be understood by organizational stakeholders.

intimate distance This distance is used to communicate affection, give comfort, and to protect. It is used in private rather than public situations and extends to about 18 inches.

intrapersonal communication One's communication with oneself, including memories, experiences, feelings, ideas, and attitudes.

intrapersonal intelligence The ability to form an accurate model of oneself and to use this model effectively.

issues management The organized activity of identifying emerging trends, concerns, or issues likely to affect an organization in the next few years, and developing a wider and more positive range of organizational responses.

kinesics The study of posture, movement, gestures, and facial expression as channels of communication.

leadership Influence of people within an organizational setting through the orchestration of relationships.

linear model Strategy consists of integrated decisions, actions or plans that will set and achieve viable organizational goals.

logos Consists of information such as facts or statistics; also known as *logical appeal*.

low self-monitors People who have little awareness about how others perceive them and little knowledge about how to interact appropriately with others.

management The coordination and organization of activities within an organization.

monochronic time (M-time) A cultural orientation to time in which people do one thing at a time and are more task-oriented than relationship-oriented.

monologue Talking to oneself. From a dialogic perspective, a?monologue is characterized by such qualities as deception, superiority, exploitation, dogmatism, domination, insincerity, pretense, personal self-display, self-aggrandizement, judgmentalism that stifles free expression, coercion, possessiveness, condescension, self-defensiveness, and viewing others as objects to be manipulated.

motive The learned state that affects behavior by moving an individual toward a perceived goal.

need A lack or imbalance that creates dissatisfaction in an individual.

networking Establishing and maintaining relationships with others.

nonverbal communication The attributes or actions of humans, other than the use of words themselves, which have socially shared meaning, are intentionally sent or interpreted as intentional, are consciously sent or consciously received, and have the potential for feedback from the receiver.

normative influence When group members tailor their actions to fit the group's standards and conventions.

organizational culture The system of shared meanings and practices within an organization that distinguish it from other organizations.

outgroup homogeneity effect The tendency to think members of other groups are all the same.

oversampling The tendency for groups to spend too much of their discussion time examining shared information—details that two or more of the group members know in common—rather than unshared information.

pathos An emotional appeal; an attempt to win over the audience by appealing to its emotions, often by telling a story or evoking a picture with which the audience can empathize.

pauses Temporary breaks in speech used to emphasize important points and enhance the meanings of words and phrases.

perception Awareness of the elements of the environment made possible through our senses.

perceptual mind-set Our cognitive and psychological predispositions to see the world in a certain way.

performance appraisal A structured formal interaction between a subordinate and supervisor that usually takes the form of a periodic interview in which the work performance of the subordinate is examined and discussed, with a view to identifying weaknesses and strengths as well as opportunities for improvement and skills development.

peripheral specialists Those in informal networks that others rely on for specialized expertise.

personal distance The distance, ranging from 18 inches to 4 feet, that is used by those in the United States for conversation and nonintimate exchanges.

personal space The physical distance between yourself and others with which you feel comfortable.

pitch The sound quality of the speaker's voice, ranging from low and deep to high and squeaky.

plurality The recognition that there are multiple different interpretations of any situation and that no one communicator can control all these interpretations.

polychronic time (P-time) A cultural orientation to time in which people are well adapted to doing several things at once and do not mind interruptions.

power bases The differing sources or bases of power within an organization.

process losses Reductions in performance effectiveness or efficiency caused by faulty group processes, including motivational and coordination problems.

projected cognitive similarity The tendency to assume others have the same norms and values as your own cultural group.

proxemics The study of human space, which revolves around two concepts: territoriality and personal space.

public communication The process of one communicating with many.

public distance This distance exceeds 12 feet and is used most often for public speaking.

public relations The management function that evaluates public attitudes, identifies the policies and procedures of an individual or an organization with the public interest, and executes a program of action to earn public understanding and acceptance.

rate of delivery The speed at which one speaks.

rational explanation Explanation that includes some sort of formal presentation, analysis, or proposal and usually involves the presentation of evidence.

reasoned skepticism The process of actively searching for meaning, analyzing and synthesizing information, and judging the worth of that information.

reflexivity The capacity for reflection.

risk The chance of loss (or gain).

risk communication The process of communicating responsibly and effectively about the risk factors associated with industrial technologies, natural hazards, and human activities.

self-awareness An understanding of the self, including one's attitudes, values, beliefs, strengths, and weaknesses.

self-centered communication Communication that fails to consider the needs, concerns, or interests of its audience.

self-concept How we think about ourselves and describe ourselves to others.

self-esteem How we like and value ourselves and how we feel about ourselves.

self-fulfilling prophecy The idea that we see ourselves in ways that are consistent with how others see us.

social construction or social construct Any phenomenon "invented" or "constructed" by participants in a particular culture or society and existing because people agree to behave as if it exists or to follow certain conventional rules.

social distance This distance ranges from 4 to 8 feet and is used for professional communication.

social loafing The reduction of effort by individuals working in groups.

somatotype Body type, which is a combination of height, weight, and muscularity.

stereotyping A standardized mental picture that is held in common by members of a group and that represents an oversimplified opinion, prejudiced attitude, or uncritical judgment.

strategic alignment The degree to which your nonverbal messages match your oral ones.

strategy Plan for obtaining a specific goal or result that involves big-picture analysis.

style The level of formality in written communications.

supportive communication climate An organizational climate in which individuals do not feel threatened.

table A visual element used to present data in words, numbers, or both, in columns and rows.

tactics Concrete actions taken to implement a strategy.

territoriality Our need to establish and maintain certain spaces as our own.

tone The implied attitude of the communicator toward his or her audience.

transitions Elements that assist the audience in moving from one topic to another through words and phrases that link the ideas being developed by the writer or speaker.

trust The confidence that our peers' intentions are good.

vocal distractions or disfluencies Speaking "errors" such as stammers, stutters, double starts, and excessive use of filler words such as *um* and *uh*.

vocal variety The varying use of the vocal aspects of volume, rate, and pitch.

volume The relative sound level of speech; it must be loud enough to be heard, but not so loud as to be overwhelming.

Index

Note: Boxes are indicated by b; Photos are indicated by p; Tables are indicated by t.